Contemporary Calculus III

For the
students

A free, color PDF version is available online at
http://scidiv.bellevuecollege.edu/dh/Calculus_all/Calculus_all.html

Dale Hoffman
Bellevue College
Author web page: http://scidiv.bellevuecollege.edu/dh/

This text is licensed under a Creative Commons Attribution-Share Alike 3.0 United States License.

You are **free**:
  to Share – to copy, distribute, display and perform the work
  to Remix – to make derivative works

Under the following conditions:
  Attribution: You must attribute the work in the manner specified by the author
    (but not in any way that suggests that they endorse you or your work)
  Share Alike: If you alter, transform or build upon this work, you must distribute
    the resulting work only under the same, similar or compatible license.

Copyright © 2011 Dale Hoffman   6/26/2012

WELCOME to CALCULUS III

Calculus III is a continuation of Calculus I and II and consists of three major topics.

Chapter 9 contains a brief review of polar equations and parametric equations and shows how we can apply the ideas and techniques of derivatives and integrals in these settings.

Chapter 10 presents infinite series, one of the basic building blocks at the beginning of the development of calculus. The main goal of this chapter is to be able to represent functions as power series. Power series are important in later mathematics courses such as differential equations and are used in many areas of applications.

Chapter 11 is an introduction to vectors in two and three dimensions, operations on these vectors, and then the use of vectors to determine equations for lines and planes in 3D. Vectors will be a major tool for the ideas and techniques in our later examination of curves and surfaces in 3D and for our application of calculus to these curves and surfaces.

So welcome back for more calculus.

WELCOME to CALCULUS

Calculus is the mathematics of CHANGE and almost everything in our world is changing.

Calculus is among the most important and useful developments of human thought, and, even though it is over 300 years old, it is still considered the beginning and cornerstone of modern mathematics. It is a wonderful and beautiful and useful set of ideas and techniques

You will see the fundamental ideas of this course over and over again in future courses in mathematics, the sciences (physical, biological and social) as well as in economics, engineering and others.

But calculus is an intellectual step up from your previous mathematics courses. Many of the ideas are more carefully defined, and they have both a functional and a graphical meaning Some of the algorithms are more complicated, and in many cases you will need to decide on the appropriate algorithm to use. And there is a huge variety of applications, too many to be able to discuss each one in class in detail.

What this means for you, the student.

Probably more than in your previous mathematics classes you need
* to think about the concepts as well as the techniques,
* to think about the patterns as well as the individual steps,
* to think about the meaning of the concepts and techniques in the context of particular applications,
* to think about how the ideas and techniques apply to functions given by graphs and tables as well as by formulas, and
* to spend enough time (1 to 2 hours each day) doing problems to sort out the concepts and to master the techniques and to get better and more efficient with the algebra skills that are vital to success.

Sometimes all this mental stretching can seem overwhelming, but stick with it (and do lots of problems). It can even become fun.

So welcome to calculus.

CONTEMPORARY CALCULUS III: Contents

How to Succeed in Beginning Calculus
Calculus takes time. Do not get behind. Use the textbook intelligently.
Working the problems. Work together. Study with a friend.
Work in small groups.

Chapter 9: Polar Coordinates, Parametric Equations & Conic Sections

9.1 Polar Coordinates

9.2 Calculus with Polar Coordinates

9.3 Parametric Equations

9.4 Calculus with Parametric Equations

9.4.5 Bezier Curves

9.5 Conic Sections

9.6 Properties of the Conic Sections

Odd numbered solutions for Chapter 9

Chapter 10: Infinite Series & Power Series

10.0 Introduction to Sequences & Series

10.1 Sequences

10.2 Infinite Series

10.3 Geometric and Harmonic Series

10.3.5 An Interlude and Introduction

10.4 Positive Term Series: Integral & P-Tests

10.5 Positive Term Series: Comparison Tests

10.6 Alternating Sign Series

10.7 Absolute Convergence and the Ratio Test

10.8 Power Series

10.9 Representing Functions with Power Series

10.10 Taylor and Maclaurin Series

10.11 Approximation Using Taylor Series

10.12 Fourier Series

Odd numbered solutions for Chapter 10

Chapter 11: Vectors, Lines and Planes in 3D

11.0 Moving Beyond Two Dimensions

11.1 Vectors in the Plane

11.2 Rectangular Coordinates in Three Dimensions

11.3 Vectors in Three Dimensions

11.4 Dot Product

11.5 Cross Product

11.6 Lines and Planes in Three Dimensions

11.7 Vector Reflections

Appendix – Sketching in 3D

Odd numbered solutions for Chapter 11

Appendix A; Trigonometry Reference Facts

Appendix B: Derivative and Integral Reference Facts

How to Succeed in Beginning Calculus

The following comments are based on over thirty years of watching students succeed and fail in calculus courses at universities, colleges and community colleges and of listening to their comments as they went through their study of calculus. This is the best advice we can give to help you succeed.

Calculus takes time. Almost no one fails calculus because they lack sufficient "mental horsepower". Most people who do not succeed are unwilling (or unable) to devote the necessary time to the course. The "necessary time" depends on how smart you are, what grade you want to earn and on how competitive the calculus course is. Most calculus teachers and successful calculus students agree that 2 (or 3) hours every weeknight and 6 or 7 hours each weekend is a good way to begin if you seriously expect to earn an A or B grade. If you are only willing to devote 5 or 10 hours a week to calculus outside of class, you should consider postponing your study of calculus.

Do NOT get behind. The brisk pace of the calculus course is based on the idea that "if you are in calculus, then you are relatively smart, you have succeeded in previous mathematics courses, and you are willing to work hard to do well." It is terribly hard to **catch up** and **keep up** at the same time. A much safer approach is to work very hard for the first month and then evaluate your situation. If you do get behind, spend a part of your study time catching up, but spend most of it trying to follow and understand what is going on in class.

Go to class, every single class. We hope your calculus teacher makes every idea crystal clear, makes every technique obvious and easy, is enthusiastic about calculus, cares about you as a person, and even makes you laugh sometimes. If not, you still need to attend class. You need to hear the vocabulary of calculus spoken and to see how mathematical ideas are strung together to reach conclusions. You need to see how an expert problem solver approaches problems. You need to hear the announcements about homework and tests. And you need to get to know some of the other students in the class. Unfortunately, when students get a bit behind or confused, they are most likely to miss a class or two (or five). That is absolutely the worst time to miss classes. Come to class anyway. Ask where you can get some outside tutoring or counseling. Ask a classmate to help you for an hour after class. If you must miss a class, ask a classmate what material was covered and skim those sections before the next class. Even if you did not read the material, come back to class as soon as possible.

Work together. Study with a friend. Work in small groups. It is much more fun and is very effective for doing well in calculus. Recent studies, and our personal observations, show that students who **regularly** work together in small groups are less likely to drop the course and are more likely to get A's or B's. You need lots of time to work on the material alone, but study groups of 3–5 students, working together 2 or 3 times a week for a couple hours, seem to help everyone in the group. Study groups offer you a way to get and give help on the material and they can provide an occasional psychological boost ("misery loves company?"). They are a place to use the mathematical language of the course, to trade mathematical tips, and to "cram" for the next day's test. Students in study groups are less likely to miss important points in the course, and they get to know some very nice people, their classmates.

Use the textbook effectively. There are a number of ways of using a mathematics textbook:

    i.   to gain an overview of the concepts and techniques,
    ii.   to gain an understanding of the material,
    iii.   to master the techniques, and
    iv.   to review the material and see how it connects with the rest of the course.

The first time you read a section, just try to see what problems are being discussed. Skip around, look at the pictures, and read some of the problems and the definitions. If something looks complicated, skip it. If an example looks interesting, read it and try to follow the explanation. This is an exploratory phase. Don't highlight or underline at this stage — you don't know what is important yet and what is just a minor detail.

The next time through the section, proceed in a more organized fashion, reading each introduction, example, explanation, theorem and proof. This is the beginning of the "mastery" stage. If you don't understand the explanation of an example, put a question mark (in pencil) in the margin and go on. Read and try to understand each step in the proofs and ask yourself why that step is valid. If you don't see what justified moving from one step to another in the proof, pencil in question marks in the margin. This second phase will go more slowly than the first, but if you don't understand some details just keep going. Don't get bogged down yet.

Finally, worry about the details. Go quickly over the parts you already understand, but slow down and try to figure out the parts marked with question marks. Try to solve the example problems before you refer to the explanations. If you now understand parts that were giving you trouble, cross out the question marks. If you still don't understand something, put in another question mark and **write down** your question to ask your teacher, tutor, or classmate.

Finally it is time to try the problems at the end of the section. Many of them are similar to examples in the section, but now you need to solve them. Some of the problems are more complicated than the examples, but they still require the same basic techniques. Some of the problems will require that you use concepts and facts from earlier in the course, a combination of old and new concepts and techniques. Working lots of problems is the "secret" of success in calculus.

Working the Problems: Many students read a problem, work it out and check the answer in the back of the book. If their answer is correct, they go on to the next problem. If their answer is wrong, they manipulate (finagle, fudge, massage) their work until their new answer is correct, and then they go on to the next problem. **Do not try the next problem yet!** Before going on, spend a short time, just half a minute, thinking about what you have just done in solving the problem. Ask yourself, "What was the point of this problem?" , "What big steps did I have to take to solve this problem?" , "What was the **process**?" Do not simply review every single step of the solution process. Instead, look at the outline of the solution, the **process**. If your first answer was wrong, ask yourself, "What about this problem should have suggested the right process the first time?" As much learning and retention can take place in the 30 seconds you spend reviewing the **process** as took place in the 10 minutes you took to solve the problem. A correct answer is important, but a **correct process, carefully used, will get you many correct answers**.

There is one more step which too many students omit. **Go back and quickly look over the section one more time.** Don't worry about the details, just try to understand the overall logic and layout of the section. Ask yourself, "What was I expected to learn in this section?" Typically this last step, a review and overview, goes quickly, but it is very valuable. It can help you see and retain the important ideas and connections.

Good luck. Work hard. Have Fun.
Calculus is beautiful and powerful.

9.1 POLAR COORDINATES

The rectangular coordinate system is immensely useful, but it is not the only way to assign an address to a point in the plane and sometimes it is not the most useful. In many experimental situations, our location is fixed and we or our instruments, such as radar, take readings in different directions (Fig. 1); this information can be graphed using rectangular coordinates (e.g., with the angle on the horizontal axis and the measurement on the vertical axis). Sometimes, however, it is more useful to plot the information in a way similar to the way in which it was collected, as magnitudes along radial lines (Fig. 2). This system is called the Polar Coordinate System.

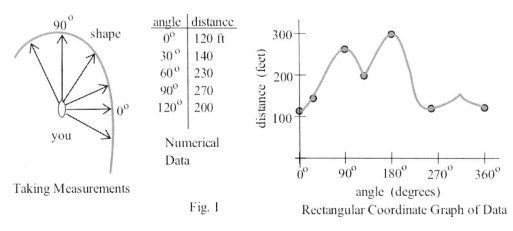

In this section we introduce polar coordinates and examine some of their uses. We start with graphing points and functions in polar coordinates, consider how to change back and forth between the rectangular and polar coordinate systems, and see how to find the slopes of lines tangent to polar graphs. Our primary reasons for considering polar coordinates, however, are that they appear in applications, and that they provide a "natural" and easy way to represent some kinds of information.

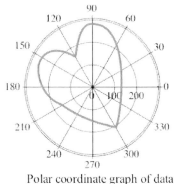

Polar coordinate graph of data
Fig. 2

Example 1: SOS! You've just received a distress signal from a ship located at A on your radar screen (Fig. 3). Describe its location to your captain so your vessel can speed to the rescue.

Solution: You could convert the relative location of the other ship to rectangular coordinates and then tell your captain to go due east for 7.5 miles and north for 13 miles,

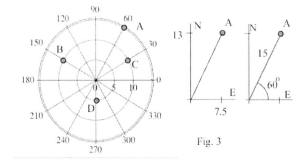

Fig. 3

but that certainly is not the quickest way to reach the other ship. It is better to tell the captain to sail for 15 miles in the direction of 60°. If the distressed ship was at B on the radar screen, your vessel should sail for 10 miles in the direction 150°. (Real radar screens have 0° at the top of the screen, but the convention in mathematics is to put 0° in the direction of the positive x–axis and to measure positive angles counterclockwise from there. And a real sailor speaks of "bearing" and "range" instead of direction and magnitude.)

Practice 1: Describe the locations of the ships at C and D in Fig. 3 by giving a distance and a direction to those ships from your current position at the center of the radar screen.

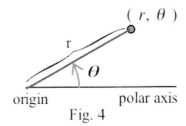

Fig. 4

Points in Polar Coordinates

To construct a polar coordinate system we need a starting point (called the **origin** or **pole**) for the magnitude measurements and a starting direction (called the **polar axis**) for the angle measurements (Fig. 4).

A polar coordinate pair for a point P in the plane is an ordered pair (r,θ) where r is the directed distance along a radial line from O to P, and θ is the angle formed by the polar axis and the segment OP (Fig. 4).

The angle θ is positive when the angle of the radial line OP is measured counterclockwise from the polar axis, and θ is negative when measured clockwise.

Degree or Radian Measure for θ? Either degree or radian measure can be used for the angle in the polar coordinate system, but when we differentiate and integrate trigonometric functions of θ we will want all of the angles to be given in radian measure. From now on, we will primarily use radian measure. You should assume that all angles are given in radian measure unless the units " ° " ("degrees") are shown.

Example 2: Plot the points with the given polar coordinates: A(2, 30°), B(3, $\pi/2$), C(–2, $\pi/6$), and D(–3, 270°).

Solution: To find the location of A, we look along the ray that makes an angle of 30° with the polar axis, and then take two steps in that direction (assuming 1 step = 1 unit). The locations of A and B are shown in Fig. 5.

To find the location of C, we look along the ray which makes an angle of $\pi/6$ with the polar axis, and then we take two steps backwards since r = –2 is negative. Fig. 6 shows the locations of C and D.

Notice that the points B and D have different addresses, (3, $\pi/2$) and (–3, 270°), but the same location.

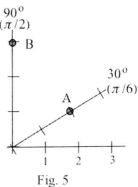

Fig. 5

Practice 2: Plot the points with the given polar coordinates: A(2, π/2), B(2, −120°), C(−2, π/3), D(−2, −135°), and E(2, 135°). Which two points coincide?

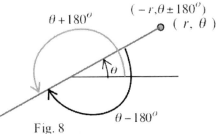

Fig. 6

Each polar coordinate pair (r, θ) gives the location of one point, but each location has lots of different addresses in the polar coordinate system: the polar coordinates of a point are not unique. This nonuniqueness of addresses comes about in two ways. First, the angles θ, θ ± 360°, θ ± 2·360°, . . . all describe the same radial line (Fig. 7), so the polar coordinates (r, θ), (r, θ ± 360°), (r, θ ± 2·360°), . . . all locate the same point.

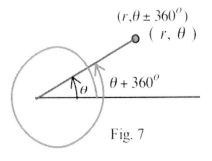

Fig. 7

Secondly, the angle θ ± 180° describes the radial line pointing in exactly the opposite direction from the radial line described by the angle θ (Fig. 8), so the polar coordinates (r, θ) and (−r, θ ± 180°) locate the same point. A polar coordinate pair gives the location of exactly one point, but the location of one point is described by many (an infinite number) different polar coordinate pairs.

Fig. 8

Note: In the rectangular coordinate system we use (x, y) and y = f(x): first variable independent and second variable dependent. In the polar coordinate system we use (r, θ) and r = f(θ): first variable dependent and second variable independent, a reversal from the rectangular coordinate usage.

Practice 3: Table 1 contains measurements to the edge of a plateau taken by a remote sensor which crashed on the plateau. Fig. 9 shows the data plotted in rectangular coordinates. Plot the data in polar coordinates and determine the shape of the top of the plateau.

angle	distance	angle	distance
0°	28 feet	150°	22 feet
20°	30	180°	18
40°	36	210°	21
60°	27	230°	13
80°	24	270°	10
100°	24	330°	18
130°	30	340°	30

Table 1

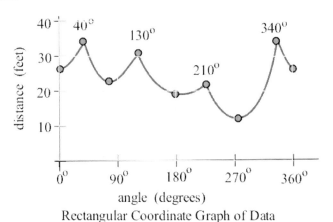

Rectangular Coordinate Graph of Data

Fig. 9

Graphing Functions in the Polar Coordinate System

In the rectangular coordinate system, we have worked with functions given by tables of data, by graphs, and by formulas. Functions can be represented in the same ways in polar coordinates.

- If a function is given by a table of data, we can graph the function in polar coordinates by plotting individual points in a polar coordinate system and connecting the plotted points to see the shape of the graph. By hand, this is a tedious process; by calculator or computer, it is quick and easy.

- If the function is given by a rectangular coordinate graph of magnitude as a function of angle, we can read coordinates of points on the rectangular graph and replot them in polar coodinates. In essence, as we go from the rectangular coordinate graph to the polar coordinate graph we "wrap" the rectangular graph around the "pole" at the origin of the polar coordinate system. (Fig. 10)

(a) rectangular coordinates   (b) polar

Fig. 10

- If the function is given by a formula, we (or our calculator) can graph the function to help us obtain information about its behavior. Typically, a graph is created by evaluating the function at a lot of points and then plotting the points in the polar coordinate system. Some of the following examples illustrate that functions given by simple formulas may have rather exotic graphs in the polar coordinate system.

If a function is already given by a polar coordinate graph, we can use the graph to answer questions about the behavior of the function. It is usually easy to locate the maximum value(s) of r on a polar coordinate graph, and, by moving counterclockwise around the graph, we can observe where r is increasing, constant, or decreasing.

Example 3: Graph $r = 2$ and $r = \pi - \theta$ in the polar coordinate system for $0 \leq \theta \leq 2\pi$.

Solution: $r = 2$: In every direction θ, we simply move 2 units along the radial line and plot a point. The resulting polar graph (Fig. 11b) is a circle centered at the origin with a radius of 2. In the rectangular coordinate system, the graph of a constant $y = k$ is a horizontal line. In the polar coordinate system, the graph of a constant $r = k$ is a circle with radius $|k|$.

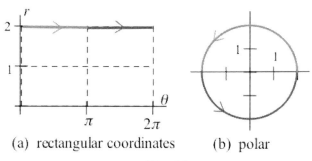

(a) rectangular coordinates   (b) polar

Fig. 11

$r = \pi - \theta$: The rectangular coordinate graph of $r = \pi - \theta$ is shown in Fig. 12a. If we read the values of r and θ from the rectangular coordinate graph and plot them in polar coordinates, the result is the shape in Fig. 12b. The different line thicknesses are used in the figures to help you see which values from the rectangular graph became which parts of the loop in the polar graph.

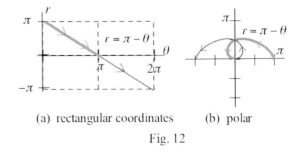
(a) rectangular coordinates   (b) polar
Fig. 12

Practice 4: Graph $r = -2$ and $r = \cos(\theta)$ in the polar coordinate system.

Example 4: Graph $r = \theta$ and $r = 1 + \sin(\theta)$ in the polar coordinate system.

Solution: $r = \theta$: The rectangular coordinate graph of $r = \theta$ is a straight line (Fig. 13a). If we read the values of r and θ from the rectangular coordinate graph and plot them in polar coordinates, the result is the spiral, called an Archimedean spiral, in Fig. 13b.

(a) rectangular coordinates   (b) polar
Fig. 13

$r = 1 + \sin(\theta)$: The rectangular coordinate graph of $r = 1 + \sin(\theta)$ is shown in Fig. 14a, and it is the graph of the sine curve shifted up 1 unit. In polar coordinates, the result of adding 1 to sine is much less obvious and is shown in Fig. 14b.

(a) rectangular coordinates   (b) polar
Fig. 14

Practice 5: Plot the points in Table 2 in the polar coordinate system and connect them with a smooth curve. Describe the shape of the graph in words.

angle (radians)	distance (meters)
0	3.0
π/6	1.9
π/4	1.7
π/3	1.6
π/2	2.0

Table 2

Fig. 15 shows the effects of adding various constants to the rectangular and polar graphs of r = sin(θ). In rectangular coordinates the result is a graph shifted up or down by k units. In polar coordinates, the result **may** be a graph with an entirely different shape (Fig. 16).

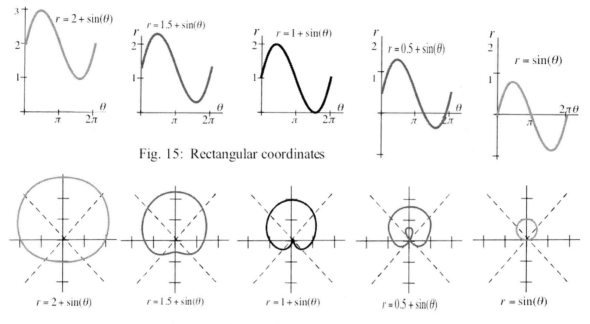

Fig. 15: Rectangular coordinates

Fig. 16: Polar coordinates

Fig. 17 shows the effects of adding a constant to the independent variable in rectangular coordinates, and the result is a horizontal shift of the original graph. In polar coordinates, Fig. 18, the result is a rotation of the original graph. Generally it is difficult to find formulas for rotated figures in rectangular coordinates, but rotations are easy in polar coordinates.

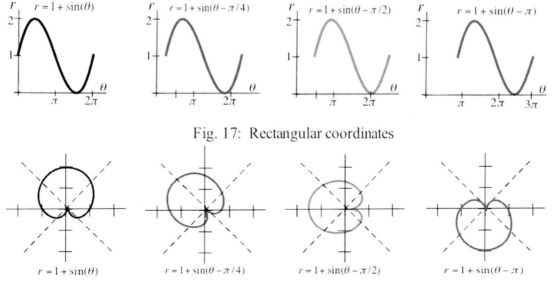

Fig. 17: Rectangular coordinates

Fig. 18: Polar coordinates

The formulas and names of several functions with exotic shapes in polar coordinates are given in the problems. Many of them are difficult to graph "by hand," but by using a graphing calculator or computer you can enjoy the shapes and easily examine the effects of changing some of the constants in their formulas.

Converting Between Coordinate Systems

Sometimes both rectangular and polar coordinates are needed in the same application, and it is necessary to change back and forth between the systems. In such a case we typically place the two origins together and align the polar axis with the positive x–axis. Then the conversions are straightforward exercises using trigonometry and right triangles (Fig. 19).

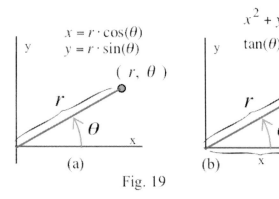

Fig. 19

Polar to Rectangular (Fig. 19a)

$x = r \cdot \cos(\theta)$

$y = r \cdot \sin(\theta)$

Rectangular to Polar (Fig. 19b)

$r^2 = x^2 + y^2$

$\tan(\theta) = \frac{y}{x}$ (if $x \neq 0$)

Example 5: Convert (a) the polar coordinate point $P(7, 0.4)$ to rectangular coordinates, and (b) the rectangular coordinate point $R(12, 5)$ to polar coordinates.

Solution: (a) $r = 7$ and $\theta = 0.4$ (Fig. 20) so $x = r \cdot \cos(\theta) = 7 \cdot \cos(0.4) \approx 7(0.921) = 6.447$ and
$y = 7 \cdot \sin(0.4) \approx 7(0.389) = 2.723$.

(b) $x = 12$ and $y = 5$ so $r^2 = x^2 + y^2 = 144 + 25 = 169$ and
$\tan(\theta) = y/x = 5/12$ so we can take $r = 13$ and
$\theta = \arctan(5/12) \approx 0.395$. The polar coordinate addresses
$(13, 0.395 \pm n \cdot 2\pi)$ and $(-13, 0.395 \pm (2n+1) \cdot \pi)$ give the location
of the same point.

Fig. 20

The conversion formulas can also be used to convert function equations from one system to the other.

Example 6: Convert the rectangular coordinate linear equation $y = 3x + 5$ (Fig. 21) to a polar coordinate equation.

Solution: This simply requires that we replace x with r·cos(θ) and y with r·sin(θ). Then

y = 3x + 5 becomes r·sin(θ) = 3r·cos(θ) + 5

so r·(sin(θ) − 3cos(θ)) = 5 and r = 5/(sin(θ) − 3cos(θ)). This final representation is valid only for θ such that sin(θ) − 3cos(θ) ≠ 0.

Fig. 21

Practice 6: Convert the polar coordinate equation $r^2 = 4r \cdot \sin(\theta)$ to a rectangular coordinate equation.

Example 7: **Robotic Arm**: A robotic arm has a hand at the end of a 12 inch long forearm which is connected to an 18 inch long upper arm (Fig. 22). Determine the position of the hand, relative to the shoulder, when θ = 45° (π/4) and φ = 30° (π/6).

Fig. 22: Robot arm

Solution: The hand is 12·cos(π/4 + π/6) ≈ 3.1 inches to the right of the elbow (Fig. 23) and 12sin(π/4 + π/6) ≈ 11.6 inches above the elbow. Similarly, the elbow is 18·cos(π/4) ≈ 12.7 inches to the right of the shoulder and 18·sin(π/4) ≈ 12.7 inches above the shoulder. Finally, the hand is approximately 3.1 + 12.7 = 15.8 inches to the right of the shoulder and approximately 11.6 + 12.7 = 24.3 inches above the shoulder. In polar coordinates, the hand is approximately 29 inches from the shoulder, at an angle of about 57° (about 0.994 radians) above the horizontal.

Fig. 23

Practice 7: Determine the position of the hand, relative to the shoulder, when θ = 30° and φ = 45°.

Graphing Functions in Polar Coordinates on a Calculator or Computer

Some calculators and computers are programmed to graph polar functions simply by keying in the formula for r, either as a function of θ or of t, but others are only designed to display rectangular coordinate graphs. However, we can graph polar functions on most of them as well by using the rectangular to polar conversion formulas, selecting the parametric mode (and the radian mode) on the calculator, and then graphing the resulting parametric equations in the rectangular coordinate system:

To graph r = r(θ) for θ between 0 and 3π,

define x(t) = r(t)·cos(t) and y(t) = r(t)·sin(t)

and graph the parametric equations x(t), y(t) for t taking values from 0 to 9.43.

Which Coordinate System Should You Use?

There are no rigid rules. Use whichever coordinate system is easier or more "natural" for the problem or data you have. Sometimes it is not clear which system to use until you have graphed the data both ways, and some problems are easier if you switch back and forth between the systems.

Generally, the polar coordinate system is easier if

- the data consists of measurements in various directions (radar)
- your problem involves locations in relatively featureless locations (deserts, oceans, sky)
- rotations are involved.

Typically, the rectangular coordinate system is easier if

- the data consists of measurements given as functions of time or location (temperature, height)
- your problem involves locations in situations with an established grid (a city, a chess board)
- translations are involved.

PROBLEMS

1. Give the locations in polar coordinates (using radian measure) of the points labeled A, B, and C in Fig. 24.

2. Give the locations in polar coordinates (using radian measure) of the points labeled D, E, and F in Fig. 24.

3. Give the locations in polar coordinates (using radian measure) of the points labeled A, B, and C in Fig. 25.

4. Give the locations in polar coordinates (using radian measure) of the points labeled D, E, and F in Fig. 25.

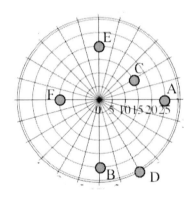

Fig. 24

In problems 5–8, plot the points A – D in polar coordinates, connect the dots by line segments in order (A to B to C to D to A), and name the approximate shape of the resulting figure.

5. A(3, 0°), B(2, 120°), C(2, 200°), and D(2.8, 315°).

6. A(3, 30°), B(2, 130°), C(3, 150°), and D(2, 280°).

7. A(2, 0.175), B(3, 2.269), C(2, 2.618), and D(3, 4.887).

8. A(3, 0.524), B(2, 2.269), C(3, 2.618), and D(2, 4.887).

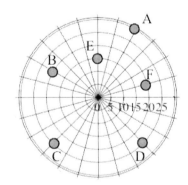

Fig. 25

In problems 9–14, the rectangular coordinate graph of a function $r = r(\theta)$ is shown. Sketch the polar coordinate graph of $r = r(\theta)$.

9. The graph in Fig. 26.   10. The graph in Fig. 27.   11. The graph in Fig. 28.

Fig. 26

Fig. 27

Fig. 28

12. The graph in Fig. 29.   13. The graph in Fig. 30.   14. The graph in Fig. 31.

Fig. 29

Fig. 30

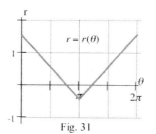
Fig. 31

15. The rectangular coordinate graph of $r = f(\theta)$ is shown in Fig. 32.
    (a) Sketch the rectangular coordinate graphs of $r = 1 + f(\theta)$, $r = 2 + f(\theta)$, and $r = -1 + f(\theta)$.
    (b) Sketch the polar coordinate graphs of $r = f(\theta)$, $r = 1 + f(\theta)$, $r = 2 + f(\theta)$, and $r = -1 + f(\theta)$.

Fig. 32

16. The rectangular coordinate graph of $r = g(\theta)$ is shown in Fig. 33.
    (a) Sketch the rectangular coordinate graphs of $r = 1 + g(\theta)$, $r = 2 + g(\theta)$, and $r = -1 + g(\theta)$.
    (b) Sketch the polar coordinate graphs of $r = g(\theta)$, $r = 1 + g(\theta)$, $r = 2 + g(\theta)$, and $r = -1 + g(\theta)$.

Fig. 33

17. The rectangular coordinate graph of $r = f(\theta)$ is shown in Fig. 34.
    (a) Sketch the rectangular coordinate graphs of $r = 1 + f(\theta)$, $r = 2 + f(\theta)$, and $r = -1 + f(\theta)$.
    (b) Sketch the polar coordinate graphs of $r = f(\theta)$, $r = 1 + f(\theta)$, $r = 2 + f(\theta)$, and $r = -1 + f(\theta)$.

Fig. 34

18. The rectangular coordinate graph of $r = g(\theta)$ is shown in Fig. 35.

    (a) Sketch the rectangular coordinate graphs of $r = 1 + g(\theta)$, $r = 2 + g(\theta)$, and $r = -1 + g(\theta)$.

    (b) Sketch the polar coordinate graphs of $r = g(\theta)$, $r = 1 + g(\theta)$, $r = 2 + g(\theta)$, and $r = -1 + g(\theta)$.

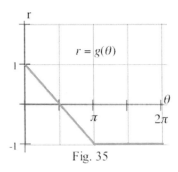

Fig. 35

19. Suppose the rectangular coordinate graph of $r = f(\theta)$ has the horizontal asymptote $r = 3$ as θ grows arbitrarily large. What does that tell us about the polar coordinate graph of $r = f(\theta)$ for large values of θ?

20. Suppose the rectangular coordinate graph of $r = f(\theta)$ has the vertical asymptote $\theta = \pi/6$: $\lim_{\theta \to \pi/6} f(\theta) = +\infty$. What does that tell us about the polar coordinate graph of $r = f(\theta)$ for values of θ near $\pi/6$?

A computer or graphing calculator is recommended for the problems marked with a * .

In problems 21–40, graph the functions in polar coordinates for $0 \le \theta \le 2\pi$.

21. $r = -3$
22. $r = 5$
23. $\theta = \pi/6$
24. $\theta = 5\pi/3$

25. $r = 4 \cdot \sin(\theta)$
26. $r = -2 \cdot \cos(\theta)$
27. $r = 2 + \sin(\theta)$
28. $r = -2 + \sin(\theta)$

29. $r = 2 + 3 \cdot \sin(\theta)$
30. $r = \sin(2\theta)$
*31. $r = \tan(\theta)$
*32. $r = 1 + \tan(\theta)$

*33. $r = \dfrac{3}{\cos(\theta)}$
*34. $r = \dfrac{2}{\sin(\theta)}$
*35. $r = \dfrac{1}{\sin(\theta) + \cos(\theta)}$
36. $r = \dfrac{\theta}{2}$

37. $r = 2 \cdot \theta$
38. $r = \theta^2$
39. $r = \dfrac{1}{\theta}$
40. $r = \sin(2\theta) \cdot \cos(3\theta)$

*41. $r = \sin(m\theta) \cdot \cos(n\theta)$ produces lovely graphs for various small integer values of m and n. Go exploring with a graphic calculator to find values of m and n which result in shapes you like.

*42. Graph $r = \dfrac{1}{1 + 0.5 \cdot \cos(\theta + a)}$, $0 \le \theta \le 2\pi$, for $a = 0, \pi/6, \pi/4$, and $\pi/2$. How are the graphs related?

*43. Graph $r = \dfrac{1}{1 + 0.5 \cdot \cos(\theta - a)}$, $0 \le \theta \le 2\pi$, for $a = 0, \pi/6, \pi/4$, and $\pi/2$. How are the graphs related?

*44. Graph $r = \sin(n\theta)$, $0 \le \theta \le 2\pi$, for $n = 1, 2, 3$, and 4 and count the number of "petals" on each graph. Predict the number of "petals" for the graphs of $r = \sin(n\theta)$ for $n = 5, 6$, and 7, and then test your prediction by creating those graphs.

*45. Repeat the steps in problem 44 but using $r = \cos(n\theta)$.

In problems 46–49, convert the rectangular coordinate locations to polar coordinates.

46. $(0, 3), (5, 0),$ and $(1, 2)$
47. $(-2, 3), (2, -3),$ and $(0, -4)$.
48. $(0, -2), (4, 4),$ and $(3, -3)$
49. $(3, 4), (-1, -3),$ and $(-7, 12)$.

In problems 50–53, convert the polar coordinate locations to rectangular coordinates.

50. $(3, 0), (5, 90°),$ and $(1, \pi)$
51. $(-2, 3), (2, -3),$ and $(0, -4)$.
52. $(0, 3), (5, 0),$ and $(1, 2)$
53. $(2, 3), (-2, -3),$ and $(0, 4)$.

Problems 54–60 refer to the robotic arm in Fig. 36.

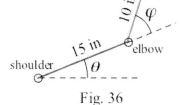

Fig. 36

54. Determine the position of the hand, realtive to the shoulder, when $\theta = 60°$ and $\phi = -45°$.

55. Determine the position of the hand, relative to the shoulder, when $\theta = -30°$ and $\phi = 30°$.

56. Determine the position of the hand, relative to the shoulder, when $\theta = 0.6$ and $\phi = 1.2$.

57. Determine the position of the hand, relative to the shoulder, when $\theta = -0.9$ and $\phi = 0.4$.

58. Suppose the robot's shoulder can pivot so that $-\pi/2 \leq \theta \leq \pi/2$, but the elbow is broken and ϕ is always $0°$. Sketch the points the hand can reach.

59. Suppose the robot's shoulder can pivot so that $-\pi/2 \leq \theta \leq \pi/2$, and the elbow can pivot so that $-\pi/2 \leq \phi \leq \pi/2$. Sketch the points the hand can reach.

60. Suppose the robot's shoulder can pivot so that $-\pi/2 \leq \theta \leq \pi/2$, and the elbow can pivot completely so $-\pi \leq \phi \leq \pi$. Sketch the points the hand can reach.

*61. Graph $r = \dfrac{1}{1 + a \cdot \cos(\theta)}$ for $0 \leq \theta \leq 2\pi$ and $a = 0.5, 0.8, 1, 1.5,$ and 2. What shapes do the various values of a produce?

*62. Repeat problem 61 with $r = \dfrac{1}{1 + a \cdot \sin(\theta)}$.

Some Exotic Curves (and Names)

Many of the following curves were discovered and named even before polar coordinates were invented. In most cases the path of a point moving on or around some object is described. You may enjoy using your calculator to graph some of these curves or you can invent your own exotic shapes. (An inexpensive source for these shapes and names is <u>A Catalog Of Special Plane Curves</u> by J. Dennis Lawrence, Dover Publications, 1972, and the page references below are to that book)

Some Classics:

Cissoid ("like ivy") of Diocles (about 200 B.C.):	$r = a \sin(\theta) \cdot \tan(\theta)$	p. 98
Right Strophoid ("twisting") of Barrow (1670):	$r = a(\sec(\theta) - 2\cos(\theta))$	p. 101
Trisectrix of Maclaurin (1742):	$r = a \sec(\theta) - 4a \cos(\theta)$	p. 105
Lemniscate ("ribbon") of Bernoulli (1694):	$r^2 = a^2 \cos(2\theta)$	p. 122
Conchoid ("shell") of Nicomedes (225 B.C.):	$r = a + b \cdot \sec(\theta)$	p. 137
Hippopede ("horse fetter") of Proclus (about 75 B.C.):	$r^2 = 4b(a - b\sin^2(\theta))$	p. 144 b = 3, a = 1, 2, 3, 4
Devil's Curve of Cramer (1750):	$r^2(\sin^2(\theta) - \cos^2(\theta)) = a^2 \sin^2(\theta) - b^2 \cos^2(\theta)$	p. 151 a = 2, b = 3
Nephroid ("kidney") of Freeth:	$r = a \cdot (1 + 2\sin(\frac{\theta}{2}))$	p. 175 a = 3

Some of our own: (Based on their names, what shapes do you expect for the following curves?)

Piscatoid of Pat (1992): $r = \frac{1}{\cos(\theta)} - 3\cos(\theta)$ for $-1.1 \leq \theta \leq 1.1$ Window x: (–2, 1) and y: (–1, 1)

Kermitoid of Kelcey (1992) :
  $r = 2.5 \cdot \sin(2\theta) \cdot (\theta - 4.71) \cdot \text{INT}(\theta/\pi) + \{ 5 \cdot \sin^3(\theta) - 3 \cdot \sin^9(\theta)\} \cdot \{ 1 - \text{INT}(\theta/\pi) \}$ for $0 \leq \theta \leq 2\pi$
    Window x: (–3, 3) and y: (–1, 4)

Bovine Oculoid: $r = 1 + \text{INT}(\theta/(2\pi))$ for $0 \leq \theta \leq 6\pi$ (≈ 18.85) Window x: (–5, 5) and y: (–4, 4)

A Few Reference Facts

The polar form of the linear equation $Ax + By + C = 0$ is $r \cdot (A \cdot \cos(\theta) + B \cdot \sin(\theta)) + C = 0$

The equation of the line through the polar coordinate points (r_1, θ_1) and (r_2, θ_2) is
$$r \cdot \{ r_1 \cdot \sin(\theta - \theta_1) + r_2 \cdot \sin(\theta_2 - \theta) \} = r_1 \cdot r_2 \cdot \sin(\theta_2 - \theta_1)$$

The graph of $r = a \cdot \sin(\theta) + b \cdot \cos(\theta)$ is a circle through the origin with center (b/2, a/2) and radius $\frac{1}{2}\sqrt{a^2 + b^2}$. (Hint: multiply each side by r, and then convert to rectangular coordinates.)

The equations $r = \frac{1}{1 \pm a \cdot \cos(\theta)}$ and $r = \frac{1}{1 \pm a \cdot \sin(\theta)}$ are conic sections with one focus at the origin.

  If $a < 1$, the denominator is **never** 0 for $0 \leq \theta < 2\pi$ and the graph is an **ellipse**.

  If $a = 1$, the denominator is 0 for **one** value of θ, $0 \leq \theta < 2\pi$, and the graph is a **parabola**.

  If $a > 1$, the denominator is 0 for **two** values of θ, $0 \leq \theta < 2\pi$, and the graph is a **hyperbola**.

Section 9.1 PRACTICE Answers

Practice 1: Point C is at a distance of 10 miles in the direction 30°. D is 5 miles at 270°.

Practice 2: The points are plotted in Fig. 37.

Practice 3: See Fig. 38.

The top of the plateau is roughly rectangular.

Practice 4: The graphs are shown in Figs. 39 and 40.

Note that the graph of $r = \cos(\theta)$ traces out a circle **twice**; once as θ goes from 0 to π, and a second time as θ goes from π to 2π.

Fig. 37

Fig. 38

(a) rectangular coordinates

(b) polar coordinates

Fig. 39

(a) rectangular coordinates

 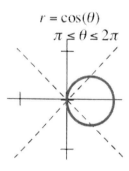

(b) polar coordinates

Fig. 40

Practice 5: The points are plotted in Fig. 41.

The points (almost) lie on a straight line.

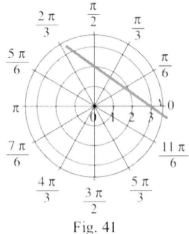

Fig. 41

Practice 6: $r^2 = x^2 + y^2$ and $r \cdot \sin(\theta) = y$ so $r^2 = 4r \cdot \sin(\theta)$ becomes $x^2 + y^2 = 4y$.

Putting this last equation into the standard form for a circle (by completing the square) we have $x^2 + (y - 2)^2 = 4$, the equation of a circle with center at $(0, 2)$ and radius 2.

Practice 7: See Fig. 42.

For point A, the "elbow," relative to O, the "shoulder:"

$$x = 18 \cdot \cos(30^\circ) \approx 15.6 \text{ inches and } y = 18 \cdot \sin(30^\circ) = 9 \text{ inches.}$$

For point B, the "hand," relative to A:

$$x = 12 \cdot \cos(75^\circ) \approx 3.1 \text{ inches and } y = 12 \cdot \sin(75^\circ) \approx 11.6 \text{ inches.}$$

Then the retangular coordinate location of the B relative to O is

$$x \approx 15.6 + 3.1 = 18.7 \text{ inches and } y \approx 9 + 11.6 = 20.6 \text{ inches.}$$

The polar coordinate location of B relative to O is

$$r = \sqrt{x^2 + y^2} \approx 27.8 \text{ inches and } \theta \approx 47.7^\circ \text{ (or 0.83 radians)}$$

Fig. 42

9.2 CALCULUS IN THE POLAR COORDINATE SYSTEM

The previous section introduced the polar coordinate system and discussed how to plot points, how to create graphs of functions (from data, a rectangular graph, or a formula), and how to convert back and forth between the polar and rectangular coordinate systems. This section examines calculus in polar coordinates: rates of changes, slopes of tangent lines, areas, and lengths of curves. The results we obtain may look different, but they all follow from the approaches used in the rectangular coordinate system.

Polar Coordinates and Derivatives

In the rectangular coordinate system, the derivative dy/dx measured both the rate of change of y with respect to x and the slope of the tangent line. In the polar coordinate system two different derivatives commonly appear, and it is important to distinguish between them.

$\dfrac{dr}{d\theta}$ measures the **rate of change** of r with respect to θ.

The sign of $\dfrac{dr}{d\theta}$ tells us whether r is increasing or decreasing as θ increases.

$\dfrac{dy}{dx}$ measures the **slope** $\dfrac{\Delta y}{\Delta x}$ **of the tangent line** to the polar graph of r.

We can use our usual rules for derivatives to calculate the derivative of a polar coordinate equation r with respect to θ, and dr/dθ tells us how r is changing with respect to (increasing) θ. For example, if dr/dθ > 0 then the directed distance r is increasing as θ increases (Fig. 1). However, dr/dθ is **NOT** the slope of the line tangent to the polar graph of r. For the simple spiral r = θ (Fig. 2), $\dfrac{dr}{d\theta}$ = 1 > 0 for all values of θ; but the slope of the tangent line, $\dfrac{dy}{dx}$, may be positive (at A and C) or negative (at B and D).

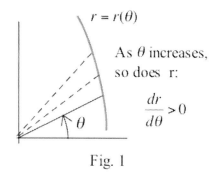
Fig. 1

Similarly, $\dfrac{dx}{d\theta}$ is the rate of change of the x-coordinate of the graph with respect to (increasing) θ, and $\dfrac{dy}{d\theta}$ is the rate of change of the y-coordinate of the graph with respect to (increasing) θ. The values of the derivatives dy/dθ and dx/dθ depend on the location on the graph. They will also be used to calculate the slope $\dfrac{dy}{dx}$ of the tangent line, and also to express the formula for arc length in polar coordinates.

Fig. 2

Example 1: State whether the values of $dr/d\theta$, $dx/d\theta$, $dy/d\theta$, and dy/dx are + (positive), – (negative), 0 (zero), or U (undefined) at the points A and B on the graph in Fig. 3.

Solution: The values of the derivatives at A and B are given in Table 1.

Practice 1: Fill in the rest of Table 1 for points labeled C and D.

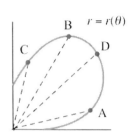

Fig. 3

When r is given by a formula we can calculate dy/dx, the slope of the tangent line, by using the polar–rectangular conversion formulas and the Chain Rule. By the Chain Rule $\frac{dy}{d\theta} = \frac{dy}{dx}\frac{dx}{d\theta}$, so we can solve for $\frac{dy}{dx}$ by dividing each side of the equation by $\frac{dx}{d\theta}$.

Point	$\frac{dx}{d\theta}$	$\frac{dy}{d\theta}$	$\frac{dr}{d\theta}$	$\frac{dy}{dx}$
A	+	+	+	+
B	–	0	–	0
C				
D				

Table 1

Then the slope $\frac{dy}{dx}$ of the line tangent to the polar coordinate graph of $r(\theta)$ is

(1) $\quad \dfrac{dy}{dx} = \dfrac{\frac{dy}{d\theta}}{\frac{dx}{d\theta}} = \dfrac{\frac{d(r\cdot\sin(\theta))}{d\theta}}{\frac{d(r\cdot\cos(\theta))}{d\theta}}$.

Since r is a function of θ, $r = r(\theta)$, we may use the product rule and the Chain Rule for derivatives to calculate each derivative and to obtain

(2) $\quad \dfrac{dy}{dx} = \dfrac{r\cdot\cos(\theta) + r'\cdot\sin(\theta)}{-r\cdot\sin(\theta) + r'\cdot\cos(\theta)}$ (with $r' = dr/d\theta$) .

The result in (2) is difficult to remember, but the starting point (1) and derivation are straightforward.

Example 2: Find the slopes of the lines tangent to the spiral $r = \theta$ (shown in Fig. 2) at the points $P(\pi/2, \pi/2)$ and $Q(\pi, \pi)$.

Solution: $y = r\cdot\sin(\theta) = \theta\cdot\sin(\theta)$ and $x = r\cdot\cos(\theta) = \theta\cdot\cos(\theta)$ so

$$\frac{dy}{dx} = \frac{\frac{d(r\cdot\sin(\theta))}{d\theta}}{\frac{d(r\cdot\cos(\theta))}{d\theta}} = \frac{\frac{d(\theta\cdot\sin(\theta))}{d\theta}}{\frac{d(\theta\cdot\cos(\theta))}{d\theta}} = \frac{\theta\cdot\cos(\theta) + 1\cdot\sin(\theta)}{-\theta\cdot\sin(\theta) + 1\cdot\cos(\theta)} .$$

At the point P, $\theta = \pi/2$ and $r = \pi/2$ so $\dfrac{dy}{dx} = \dfrac{\frac{\pi}{2}\cdot 0 + 1\cdot(1)}{-\frac{\pi}{2}\cdot(1) + 1\cdot(0)} = -\dfrac{2}{\pi} \approx -0.637$.

At the point Q, $\theta = \pi$ and $r = \pi$ so $\dfrac{dy}{dx} = \dfrac{\pi\cdot(-1) + 1\cdot(0)}{-\pi\cdot(0) + 1\cdot(-1)} = \dfrac{-\pi}{-1} = \pi \approx 3.142$.

The function $r = \theta$ is steadily increasing, but the slope of the line tangent to the polar graph can negative or positive or zero or even undefined (where?).

Practice 2:   Find the slopes of the lines tangent to the cardioid
r = 1 – sin(θ) (Fig. 4) when θ = 0, π/4, and π/2.

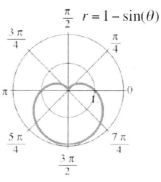

Areas in Polar Coordinates

The patterns for calculating areas in rectangular and polar coordinates look different, but they are derived in the same way: partition the area into pieces, calculate areas of the pieces, add the small areas together to get a Riemann sum, and take the limit of the Riemann sum to get a definite integral. The major difference is the shape of the pieces: we use thin rectangular pieces in the rectangular system and thin sectors (pieces of pie) in the polar system. The formula we need for the area of a sector can be found by using proportions (Fig. 5):

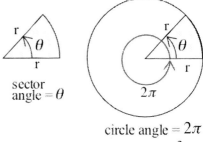

Fig. 5

$$\frac{\text{area of sector}}{\text{area of whole circle}} = \frac{\text{sector angle}}{\text{angle of whole circle}} = \frac{\theta}{2\pi}$$

so (area of sector) = $\frac{\theta}{2\pi}$ (area of whole circle) = $\frac{\theta}{2\pi}(\pi r^2) = \frac{1}{2} r^2 \theta$.

Figures 6 and 7 refer to the area discussion after the figures.

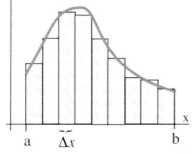

Fig. 6 Area with rectangular
coordinates

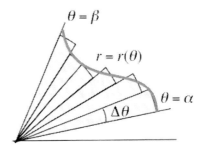

Fig. 7: Area with polar
coordinates

Area in Rectangular Coordinates (Fig. 6)	**Area in Polar Coordinates** (Fig. 7)
Partition the domain x of the rectangular coordinate function into small pieces of width Δx.	Partition the domain θ of the polar coordinate function into small pieces of angular width $\Delta\theta$.
Build rectangles on each piece of the domain.	Build "nice" shapes (pieces of pie shaped sectors) along each piece of the domain.
Calculate the area of each piece (rectangle): $$\text{area}_i = (\text{base}_i)\cdot(\text{height}_i) = f(x_i)\cdot\Delta x_i .$$	Calculate the area of each piece (sector): $$\text{area}_i = \frac{1}{2}(\text{radius}_i)^2(\text{angle}_i) = \frac{1}{2}r_i^2\,\Delta\theta_i .$$
Approximate the total area by adding the small areas together, a Riemann sum: $$\text{total area} \approx \sum \text{area}_i = \sum f(x_i)\cdot\Delta x_i .$$	Approximate the total area by adding the small areas together, a Riemann sum: $$\text{total area} \approx \sum \text{area}_i = \sum \frac{1}{2}r_i^2\,\Delta\theta_i .$$
The limit of the Riemann sum is a definite integral: $$\text{Area} = \int_{x=a}^{b} f(x)\,dx .$$	The limit of the Riemann sum is a definite integral: $$\text{Area} = \int_{\theta=\alpha}^{\beta} \tfrac{1}{2}r^2(\theta)\,d\theta .$$

If r is a continuous function of θ, then the limit of the Riemann sums is a finite number, and we have a formula for the area of a region in polar coordinates.

Area In Polar Coordinates

The area of the region bounded by a continuous function $r(\theta)$ and radial lines at angles $\theta = \alpha$ and $\theta = \beta$ is

$$\text{area} = \int_{\theta=\alpha}^{\beta} \tfrac{1}{2}r^2(\theta)\,d\theta .$$

Example 3: Find the area inside the cardioid $r = 1 + \cos(\theta)$. (Fig. 8)

Solution: This is a straightforward application of the area formula.

$$\text{Area} = \int_{\theta=0}^{2\pi} \frac{1}{2}(1 + \cos(\theta))^2 \, d\theta = \frac{1}{2} \int_{\theta=0}^{2\pi} \{1 + 2\cos(\theta) + \cos^2(\theta)\} \, d\theta$$

$$= \frac{1}{2} \left\{ \theta + 2\sin(\theta) + \frac{1}{2}\left[\theta + \frac{1}{2}\sin(2\theta)\right] \right\} \Bigg|_0^{2\pi}$$

$$= \frac{1}{2} \left\{ [2\pi + 0 + \frac{1}{2}(2\pi + 0)] - [0 + 0 + 0] \right\} = \frac{3}{2}\pi.$$

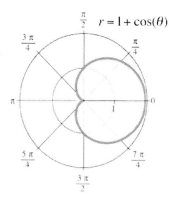

Fig. 8

We could also have used the symmetry of the region and determined this area by integrating from 0 to π (Fig. 9) and multiplying the result by 2.

Practice 3: Find the area inside one "petal" of the rose $r = \sin(3\theta)$. (Fig. 10)

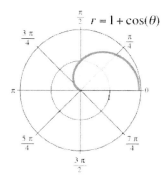

Fig. 9

We can also calculate the area between curves in polar coordinates.

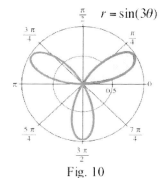

Fig. 10

The area of the region (Fig. 11) between the continuous curves $r_1(\theta) \le r_2(\theta)$ for $\alpha \le \theta \le \beta$ is

$$\int_{\theta=\alpha}^{\beta} \frac{1}{2} r_2^2(\theta) \, d\theta - \int_{\theta=\alpha}^{\beta} \frac{1}{2} r_1^2(\theta) \, d\theta$$

$$= \int_{\theta=\alpha}^{\beta} \frac{1}{2} \{r_2^2(\theta) - r_1^2(\theta)\} \, d\theta.$$

It is a good idea to sketch the graphs of the curves to help determine the endpoints of integration.

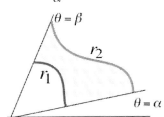

Fig. 11

Example 4: Find the area of the shaded region in Fig. 12.

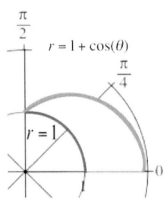

Solution: A_1 = area between the circle and the origin = $\int_{\theta=0}^{\pi/2} \frac{1}{2} 1^2 \, d\theta$

$= \frac{1}{2} \theta \Big|_0^{\pi/2} = \frac{\pi}{4} \approx 0.785$.

A_2 = area between the cardioid and the origin = $\int_{\theta=0}^{\pi/2} \frac{1}{2}(1 + \cos(\theta))^2 \, d\theta$

Fig. 12

$= \frac{3}{4}\theta + \sin(\theta) + \frac{1}{8}\sin(2\theta) \Big|_0^{\pi/2} = \{ \frac{3\pi}{8} + 1 + 0 \} - \{ 0 + 0 + 0 \} \approx 2.178$.

The area we want is $A_2 - A_1 = 1 + \frac{3\pi}{8} - \frac{\pi}{4} = 1 + \frac{\pi}{8} \approx 1.393$.

Practice 4: Find the area of the region outside the cardioid $1 + \cos(\theta)$ and inside the circle $r = 2$. (Fig. 13)

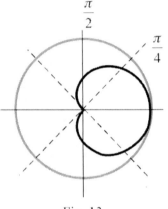

Fig. 13

Arc Length in Polar Coordinates

The patterns for calculating the lengths of curves in rectangular and polar coordinates look different, but they are derived from the Pythagorean Theorem and the same sum we used in Section 5.2 (Fig. 14):

$$\text{length} \approx \sum \sqrt{(\Delta x)^2 + (\Delta y)^2} = \sum \sqrt{(\tfrac{\Delta x}{\Delta \theta})^2 + (\tfrac{\Delta y}{\Delta \theta})^2} \, \Delta \theta.$$

If x and y are differentiable functions of θ, then as $\Delta\theta$ approaches 0, $\Delta x/\Delta\theta$ approaches $dx/d\theta$, $\Delta y/\Delta\theta$ approaches $dy/d\theta$, and the Riemann sum approaches the definite integral

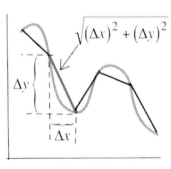

$$\text{length} = \int_{\theta=\alpha}^{\beta} \sqrt{(\tfrac{dx}{d\theta})^2 + (\tfrac{dy}{d\theta})^2} \, d\theta.$$

Fig. 14

Replacing x with $r \cdot \cos(\theta)$ and y with $r \cdot \sin(\theta)$, we have $dx/d\theta = -r \sin(\theta) + r' \cos(\theta)$ and $dy/d\theta = r \cos(\theta) + r' \sin(\theta)$. Then $(dx/d\theta)^2 + (dy/d\theta)^2$ inside the square root simplifies to $r^2 + (r')^2$ and we have a more useful form of the integral for arc length in polar coordinates.

Arc Length

If r is a differentiable function of θ for $\alpha \leq \theta \leq \beta$, then the length of the graph of r is

$$\text{Length} = \int_{\theta=\alpha}^{\beta} \sqrt{(r)^2 + \left(\frac{dr}{d\theta}\right)^2}\, d\theta.$$

Problems

Derivatives

In problems 1–4, fill in the table for each graph with + (positive), – (negative), 0 (zero), or U (undefined) for each derivative at each labeled point.

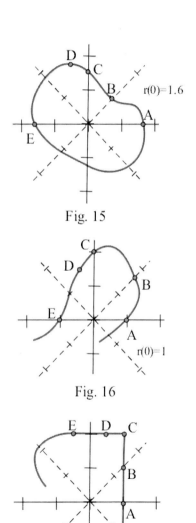

Fig. 15

1. Use Fig. 15.

Point	$\frac{dr}{d\theta}$	$\frac{dx}{d\theta}$	$\frac{dy}{d\theta}$	$\frac{dy}{dx}$
A				
B				
C				
D				
E				

2. Use Fig. 16.

Point	$\frac{dr}{d\theta}$	$\frac{dx}{d\theta}$	$\frac{dy}{d\theta}$	$\frac{dy}{dx}$
A				
B				
C				
D				
E				

3. Use Fig. 17.

Point	$\frac{dr}{d\theta}$	$\frac{dx}{d\theta}$	$\frac{dy}{d\theta}$	$\frac{dy}{dx}$
A				
B				
C				
D				
E				

4. Use Fig. 18.

Point	$\frac{dr}{d\theta}$	$\frac{dx}{d\theta}$	$\frac{dy}{d\theta}$	$\frac{dy}{dx}$
A				
B				
C				
D				
E				

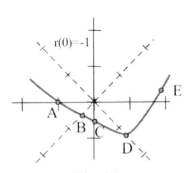

Fig. 18

In problems 5–8, sketch the graph of the polar coordinate function $r = r(\theta)$ for $0 \le \theta \le 2\pi$, label the points with the given polar coordinates on the graph, and calculate the values of $\frac{dr}{d\theta}$ and $\frac{dy}{dx}$ at the points with the given polar coordinates.

5. $r = 5$ at $A(5, \pi/4)$, $B(5, \pi/2)$, and $C(5, \pi)$.

6. $r = 2 + \cos(\theta)$ at $A(2 + \frac{\sqrt{2}}{2}, \pi/4)$, $B(2, \pi/2)$, and $C(1, \pi)$.

7. $r = 1 + \cos^2(\theta)$ at $A(2, 0)$, $B(3/2, \pi/4)$, and $C(1, \pi/2)$.

8. $r = \frac{6}{2 + \cos(\theta)}$ at $A(2, 0)$, $B(3, \pi/2)$, and $C(\frac{24 - 6\sqrt{2}}{7}, \pi/4) \approx (2.216, \pi/4)$.

9. Graph $r = 1 + 2 \cdot \cos(\theta)$ for $0 \le \theta \le 2\pi$, and show that the graph goes through the origin when $\theta = 2\pi/3$ and $\theta = 4\pi/3$. Calculate dy/dx when $\theta = 2\pi/3$ and $\theta = 4\pi/3$. How can a curve have two different tangent lines (and slopes) when it goes through the origin?

10. Graph the cardiod $r = 1 + \sin(\theta)$ for $0 \le \theta \le 2\pi$.
    (a) At what points on the cardioid does $dx/d\theta = 0$? (b) At what points on the cardiod does $dy/d\theta = 0$?
    (c) At what points on the cardioid does $dr/d\theta = 0$? (d) At what points on the cardiod does $dy/dx = 0$?

11. Show that if a polar coordinate graph goes through the origin when the angle is θ_0 (and if $dr/d\theta$ exists and does not equal 0 there), then the slope of the tangent line at the origin is $\tan(\theta_0)$. (Suggestion: Evaluate formula (2) for dy/dx at the point $(0, \theta_0)$.)

Areas

In problems 12–20, represent each area as a definite integral. Then evaluate the integral exactly or using Simpson's rule (with n = 100).

12. The area of the shaded region in Fig. 19.

13. The area of the shaded region in Fig. 20.

14. The area of the shaded region in Fig. 21.

15. The area in the first quadrant outside the circle $r = 1$ and inside the cardiod $r = 1 + \cos(\theta)$.

16. The region in the second quadrant bounded by $r = \theta$ and $r = \theta^2$.

17. The area inside one "petal" of the graph of (a) $r = \sin(3\theta)$ and (b) $r = \sin(5\theta)$.

18. The area (a) inside the "peanut" $r = 1.5 + \cos(2\theta)$ and (b) inside $r = a + \cos(2\theta)$ (a > 1).

19. The area inside the circle $r = 4 \cdot \sin(\theta)$.

20. The area of the shaded region in Fig. 22.

21. Goat and Square Silo: (This problem does not require calculus.)

    One end of a 40 foot long rope is attached to the middle of a wall of a 20 foot square silo, and the other end is tied to a goat (Fig. 23).

    (a) Sketch the region that the goat can reach.

    (b) Find the area of the region that the goat can reach.

    (c) Can the goat reach more area if the rope is tied to the corner of the silo?

Fig. 19

Fig. 20

Fig. 21

Fig. 22

Fig. 23

22. **Goat and Round Silo:** One end of a 10π foot long rope is attached to the wall of a round silo that has a radius of 10 feet, and the other end is tied to a goat (Fig. 24).

   (a) Sketch the region the goat can reach.

   (b) Justify that the area of the region in Fig. 25 as the goat goes around the silo from having θ feet of rope taut against the silo to having $\theta + \Delta\theta$ feet taut against the silo is approximately
   $$\frac{1}{2}(10\pi - 10\cdot\theta)^2 \Delta\theta.$$

   (c) Use the result from part (b) to help calculate the area of the region that the goat can reach.

Fig. 24

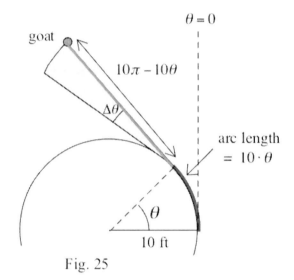

Fig. 25

Arc Lengths

In problems 23–29, represent the length of each curve as a definite integral. Then evaluate the integral exactly or using your calculator.

23. The length of the spiral $r = \theta$ from $\theta = 0$ to $\theta = 2\pi$.

24. The length of the spiral $r = \theta$ from $\theta = 2\pi$ to $\theta = 4\pi$.

25. The length of the cardiod $r = 1 + \cos(\theta)$.

26. The length of $r = 4\cdot\sin(\theta)$ from $\theta = 0$ to $\theta = \pi$.

27. The length of the circle $r = 5$ from $\theta = 0$ to $\theta = 2\pi$.

28. The length of the "peanut" $r = 1.2 + \cos(2\theta)$.

29. The length (a) of one "petal" of the graph of $r = \sin(3\theta)$ and (b) of one "petal" of $r = \sin(5\theta)$.

30. Assume that r is a differentiable function of θ. Verify that $\{\frac{dx}{d\theta}\}^2 + \{\frac{dy}{d\theta}\}^2 = \{r\}^2 + \{\frac{dr}{d\theta}\}^2$ by replacing x with $r\cdot\cos(\theta)$ and y with $r\cdot\sin(\theta)$ in the left side of the equation, differentiating, and then simplifying the result to obtain the right side of the equation.

Section 9.2   PRACTICE Answers

Practice 1: The values are shown in Fig. 26.

Point	$\dfrac{dx}{d\theta}$	$\dfrac{dy}{d\theta}$	$\dfrac{dr}{d\theta}$	$\dfrac{dy}{dx}$
A	+	+	+	+
B	−	0	−	0
C	−	−	−	+
D	−	+	+	−

Fig. 26

Practice 2: $r = 1 - \sin(\theta)$ and $r' = -\cos(\theta)$.

$$\frac{dy}{dx} = \frac{\frac{dy}{d\theta}}{\frac{dx}{d\theta}} = \frac{r\cdot\cos(\theta) + r'\cdot\sin(\theta)}{-r\cdot\sin(\theta) + r'\cdot\cos(\theta)}$$

$$= \frac{(1-\sin(\theta))\cdot\cos(\theta) + (-\cos(\theta))\cdot\sin(\theta)}{-(1-\sin(\theta))\cdot\sin(\theta) + (-\cos(\theta))\cdot\cos(\theta)} = \frac{\cos(\theta) - 2\sin(\theta)\cdot\cos(\theta)}{-\sin(\theta) + \sin^2(\theta) - \cos^2(\theta)}.$$

When $\theta = 0$, $\dfrac{dy}{dx} = \dfrac{1-0}{-0+0-1} = -1$.

When $\theta = \dfrac{\pi}{4}$, $\dfrac{dy}{dx} = \dfrac{(1/\sqrt{2}) - 2(1/\sqrt{2})(1/\sqrt{2})}{-(1/\sqrt{2}) + (1/\sqrt{2})^2 - (1/\sqrt{2})^2} = \dfrac{1/\sqrt{2} - 1}{-1/\sqrt{2} + \frac{1}{2} - \frac{1}{2}} = \sqrt{2} - 1 \approx 0.414$.

When $\theta = \dfrac{\pi}{2}$, $\dfrac{dy}{dx} = \dfrac{0-0}{-1+1-0}$ which is undefined. Why does this result make sense in terms of the graph of the cardioid $r = 1 - \sin(\theta)$?

Practice 3: One "petal" of the rose $r = \sin(3\theta)$ is swept out as θ goes from 0 to $\pi/3$ (see Fig. 10) so the endpoints of the area integral are 0 and $\pi/3$.

$$\text{area} = \int_{\theta=\alpha}^{\beta} \frac{1}{2} r^2(\theta)\, d\theta = \int_{\theta=0}^{\pi/3} \frac{1}{2} \{\sin(3\theta)\}^2\, d\theta \qquad \text{(then using integral table entry \#13)}$$

$$= \frac{1}{2}\left\{ \frac{1}{2}\theta - \frac{1}{4(3)}\sin(2\cdot 3\theta) \right\}\Big|_{0}^{\pi/3} = \frac{1}{2}\left\{ \left[\frac{\pi}{6} - \frac{1}{12}(0)\right] - [0-0] \right\} = \frac{\pi}{12} \approx 0.262.$$

Practice 4: The area we want in Fig. 13 is

$$\{\text{area of circle}\} - \{\text{area of cardioid from Example 3}\} = \pi(2)^2 - \frac{3}{2}\pi = \frac{5}{2}\pi \approx 7.85.$$

9.3 PARAMETRIC EQUATIONS

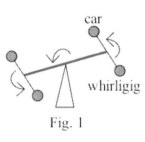

Fig. 1

Some motions and paths are inconvenient, difficult or impossible for us to describe by a single function or formula of the form $y = f(x)$.

- A rider on the "whirligig" (Fig. 1) at the carnival goes in circles at the end of a rotating bar.
- A robot delivering supplies in a factory (Fig. 2) needs to avoid obstacles.
- A fly buzzing around the room (Fig. 3) and a molecule in a solution follow erratic paths.
- A stone caught in the tread of a rolling wheel has a smooth path with some sharp corners (Fig. 4).

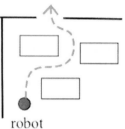

Fig. 2

Parametric equations provide a way to describe all of these motions and paths. And parametric equations generalize easily to describe paths and motions in 3 dimensions.

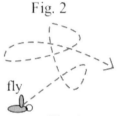

Fig. 3

Parametric equations were used briefly in earlier sections (2.5: Applications of the Chain Rule and 5.2: Arc Length). In those sections the equations were always given. In this section we look at functions given parametrically by data, graphs, and formulas and examine how to build formulas to describe some motions parametrically. The last curve in this section is the cycloid, one of the most famous curves in mathematics. The next section considers calculus with parametric equations: slopes of tangent lines, arc lengths, and areas.

Fig. 4

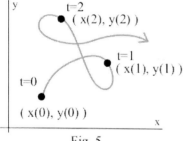

Fig. 5

Parametric equations describe the location of a point (x,y) on a graph or path as a function of a single independent variable t, a "parameter" often representing time. In 2 dimensions, the coordinates x and y are functions of the variable t: $x = x(t)$ and $y = y(t)$ (Fig. 5). In 3 dimensions, the z coordinate is also a function of t: $z = z(t)$. With parametric equations we can also analyze the forces acting on an object separately in each coordinate direction and then combine the results to see the overall behavior of the object. Parametric equations often provide an easier way to understand and build equations for complicated motions.

Graphing Parametric Equations

The data for creating a parametric equation graph can be given as a table of values, as graphs of $(t, x(t))$ and $(t, y(t))$, or as formulas for x and y as functions of t.

Example 1: Table 1 is a record of the location of a roller coaster car relative to its starting location. Use the data to sketch a graph of the car's path for the first 7 seconds.

t	x(t)	y(t)	t	x(t)	y(t)
0	0	70	7	90	55
1	30	20	8	105	85
2	70	50	9	125	100
3	60	75	10	130	80
4	30	70	11	150	65
5	32	35	12	180	75
6	60	15	13	200	30

Table 1

Solution: Figure 6 is a plot of the (x, y) locations of the car for t = 0 to 7 seconds. The points are connected by a smooth curve to show a possible path of the car.

Fig. 6: Roller coaster for 0≤t≤7 seconds

Practice 1: Use the data in Table 1 to sketch the path of the roller coaster for the next 6 seconds.

Note: Clearly the graph in Fig. 6 is not the graph of a function y = f(x). But every y = f(x) function has an easy parametric representation by setting x(t) = t and y(t) = f(t).

Sometimes a parametric graph can show patterns that are not clearly visible in individual graphs.

Example 2: Figures 7a and 7b are graphs of the populations of rabbits and foxes on an island. Use these graphs to sketch a parametric graph of rabbits (x–axis) versus foxes (y–axis) for $0 \le t \le 10$ years.

Solution: The separate rabbit and fox population graphs give us information about each population separately, but the parametric graph helps us see the effects of the interaction between the rabbits and the foxes more clearly.

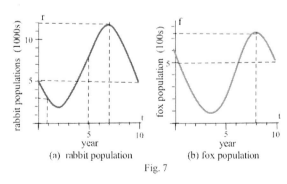

Fig. 7

For each time t we can read the rabbit and fox populations from the separate graphs (e.g., when t = 1, there are approximately 3000 rabbits and 400 foxes so x ≈ 3000 and y ≈ 400) and then combine this information to plot a single point on the parametric graph. If we repeat this process for a large number of values of t, we get a graph (Fig. 8) of the "motion" of the rabbit and fox populations over a period of time, and we can ask questions about why the populations might show this behavior.

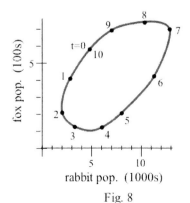

Fig. 8

The type of graph in Fig. 8 is very common for "predator–prey" interactions. Some two–species populations tend to approach a "steady state" or "fixed point" (Fig. 9). However, many two–species population graphs tend to cycle over a period of time as in Fig. 9.

Fig. 9

Fig. 10

Practice 2: What would it mean if the rabbit–fox parametric equation graph hit the horizontal axis as in Fig. 10?

Example 3: Graph the pair of parametric equations $x(t) = 2t - 2$ and $y(t) = 3t + 1$.

Solution: Table 2 shows the values of x and y for several values of t. These points are plotted in Fig. 11, and the graph appears to be a straight line.

t	x(t)	y(t)
0	–2	1
1	0	4
2	2	7
–1	–4	–2

Table 2

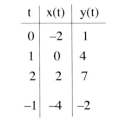

$x(t) = 2t - 2$
$y(t) = 3t + 1$

Fig. 11

Usually it is not possible to write y as a simple function of x, but in this case we can do so. By solving $x = 2t - 2$ for $t = \frac{1}{2} x + 1$ and then replacing the t in the equation $y = 3t + 1$,

we get $y = 3t + 1 = 3\{ \frac{1}{2} x + 1 \} + 1 = \frac{3}{2} x + 4$, a linear function of x.

Practice 3: Graph the pair of parametric equations $x(t) = 3 - t$ and $y(t) = t^2 + 1$. Write y as a function of x alone and identify the shape of the graph.

Example 4: Graph the pair of parametric equations $x(t) = 3 \cdot \cos(t)$ and $y(t) = 2 \cdot \sin(t)$ for $0 \leq t \leq 2\pi$, and show that these equations satisfy the relation $\frac{x^2}{9} + \frac{y^2}{4} = 1$ for all values of t.

Solution: The graph, an ellipse, is shown in Fig. 12.

$$\frac{x^2}{9} + \frac{y^2}{4} = \frac{3^2 \cdot \cos^2(t)}{9} + \frac{2^2 \cdot \sin^2(t)}{4} = \cos^2(t) + \sin^2(t) = 1.$$

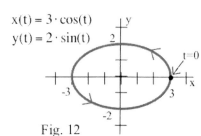

Practice 4: Graph the pair of parametric equations $x(t) = \sin(t)$ and $y(t) = 5 \cdot \cos(t)$ for $0 \leq t \leq 2\pi$, and show that these equations satisfy the relation $\frac{x^2}{1} + \frac{y^2}{25} = 1$ for all values of t.

Fig. 12

9.3 Parametric Equations   Contemporary Calculus   4

Example 5: Describe the motion of a point whose position is
x(t) = –R·sin(t) and y(t) = –R·cos(t).

Solution: The point starts at x(0) = –R·sin(0) = 0 and y(0) = –R·cos(0) = –R. By plotting x(t) and y(t) for several other values of t (Fig. 13), we can see that the point is rotating clockwise around the origin. Since $x^2(t) + y^2(t) = R^2 \sin^2(t) + R^2 \cos^2(t) = R^2$, we know the point is always on the circle of radius R which is centered at the origin.

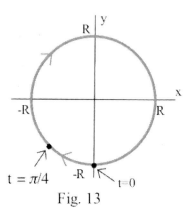

Fig. 13

Practice 5: The path of each parametric equation given below is a circle with radius 1 and center at the origin. If an object is located at the point (x, y) at time t seconds:
(a) Where is the object at t = 0? (b) Is the object traveling clockwise or counterclockwise around the circle? (c) How long does it take the object to make 1 revolution?

A: x = cos(2t), y = sin(2t)   B: x = –cos(3t), y = sin(3t)   C: x = sin(4t), y = –cos(4t)

Putting Motions Together

If we know how an object moves horizontally and how it moves vertically, then we can put these motions together to see how it moves in the plane.

If an object is thrown straight upward with an initial velocity of A feet per second, then its height after t seconds is $y(t) = A \cdot t - \frac{1}{2} g \cdot t^2$ feet where g = 32 feet/second^2 is the downward acceleration of gravity (Fig. 14a). If an object is thrown horizontally with an initial velocity of B feet per second, then its horizontal distance from the starting place after t seconds is x(t) = B·t feet (Fig. 14b).

Fig. 14

Example 6: Write an equation for the position at time t (Fig. 14c) of an object thrown at an angle of 30° with the ground (horizontal) with an initial velocity 100 feet per second.

Solution: If the object travels 100 feet along a line at an angle of 30° to the horizontal ground (Fig. 15), then it travels $100 \cdot \sin(30°) = 50$ feet upward and $100 \cdot \cos(30°) \approx 86.6$ feet sideways, so $A = 50$ and $B = 86.6$. The position of the object at time t is

$$y(t) = 50 \cdot t - \frac{1}{2} g t^2 \text{ and } x(t) = 86.6 \cdot t .$$

Fig. 15

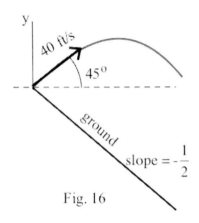

Fig. 16

Practice 6: A ball is thrown upward at an angle of 45° (Fig. 16) with an initial velocity of 40 ft/sec.

(a) Write the parametric equations for the position of the ball as a function of time.

(b) Use the parametric equations to find when and then where the ball will hit the sloped ground. (Suggestion: set $y(t) = -0.5 x(t)$ from part (a) and solve for t. Then use that value of t to evaluate x(t) and y(t).)

Sometimes the location or motion of an object is measured by an instrument which is in motion itself (e.g., tracking a pod of migrating whales from a moving ship), and we want to determine the path of the object independent of the location of the instrument. In that case, the "absolute" location of the object with respect to the origin is the sum of the relative location of the object (pod of whales) with respect to the instrument (ship) and the location of the instrument (ship) with respect to the origin. The same approach works for describing the motion of linked objects such as connected gears.

Example 7: **Carnival Ride** The car (Fig. 17) makes one counterclockwise revolution (r = 8 feet) about the pivot point A every 2 seconds and the long arm (R = 20 feet) makes one counterclockwise revolution about its pivot point (the origin) every 5 seconds. Assume that the ride begins with the two arms along the positive x–axis and sketch the path you think the car will follow. Find a pair of parametric equations to describe the position of the car at time t.

Solution: The position of the car relative to its pivot point A is $x_c(t) = 8 \cdot \cos(\frac{2\pi}{2} t)$ and $y_c(t) = 8 \cdot \sin(\frac{2\pi}{2} t)$.

The position of the pivot point A relative to the origin is $x_p(t) = 20 \cdot \cos(\frac{2\pi}{5} t)$ and $y_p(t) = 20 \cdot \sin(\frac{2\pi}{5} t)$, so the location of the car, relative to the origin, is

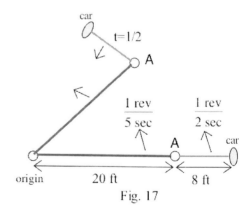

Fig. 17

$$x(t) = x_p(t) + x_c(t) = 20 \cdot \cos(\tfrac{2\pi}{5} t) + 8 \cdot \cos(\tfrac{2\pi}{2} t) \text{ and}$$

$$y(t) = y_p(t) + y_c(t) = 20 \cdot \sin(\tfrac{2\pi}{5} t) + 8 \cdot \sin(\tfrac{2\pi}{2} t).$$

Use a graphing calculator to graph the path of the car for 5 seconds.

Example 8: **Cycloid** A light is attached to the edge of a wheel of radius R which is rolling along a level road (Fig. 18). Find parametric equations to describe the location of the light.

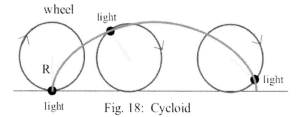

Fig. 18: Cycloid

Solution: We can describe the location of the axle of the wheel, the location of the light relative to the axle, and then put the results together to get the location of the light.

The axle of the wheel is always R inches off the ground, so the y coordinate of the axle is $y_a(t) = R$ (Fig. 19). When the wheel has rotated t radians about its axle, the wheel has rolled a distance of $R \cdot t$ along the road, and the x coordinate of the axle is $x_a(t) = R \cdot t$.

Fig. 19

The position of the light relative to the axle is $x_l(t) = -R \cdot \sin(t)$ and $y_l(t) = -R \cdot \cos(t)$ (see Example 3) so the position of the light is

$$x(t) = x_a(t) + x_l(t) = R \cdot t - R \cdot \sin(t) = R \cdot \{ t - \sin(t) \} \text{ and}$$

$$y(t) = y_a(t) + y_l(t) = R - R \cdot \cos(t) = R \cdot \{ 1 - \cos(t) \}.$$

This curve is called a **cycloid**, and it is one of the most famous and interesting curves in mathematics. Many great mathematicians and physicists (Mersenne, Galileo, Newton, Bernoulli, Huygens, and others) examined the cycloid, determined its properties, and used it in physical applications.

Practice 7: A light is attached r units from the axle of an R inch radius wheel (r < R) that is rolling along a level road (Fig. 20). Use the approach of the solution to Example 8 to find parametric equations to describe the location of the light. The resulting curve is called an curate cycloid.

Fig. 20

The cycloid, the path of a point on a rolling circle, was studied in the early 1600's by Mersenne (1588–1648) who thought the path might be part of an ellipse (it isn't). In 1634 Roberval determined the parametric form of the cycloid and found the area under the cycloid as did Descartes and Fermat. This was done before Newton (1642–1727) was even born; they used various specialized geometric approaches to solve the area problem. About the same time Galileo determined the area experimentally by cutting a cycloid region from a sheet of lead and balancing it against a number of circular regions (with the same radius as the circle which generated the cycloid) cut from the same material. How many circles do you think balanced the cycloid region's area (Fig. 21)?

Fig. 21

However, the most amazing properties of the cycloid involve motion along a cycloid–shaped path, and their discovery had to wait for Newton and the calculus. These calculus–based properties are discussed at the end of the next section.

PROBLEMS

For problems 1–4, use the data in each table to create three graphs:
(a) $(t, x(t))$, (b) $(t, y(t))$, and (c) the parametric graph $(x(t), y(t))$.
(Connect the points with straight line segments to create the graph.)

1. Use Table 3.
2. Use Table 4.
3. Use Table 5.
4. Use Table 6.

t	x(t)	y(t)
0	2	1
1	2	0
2	−1	0
3	1	−1

Table 3

t	x(t)	y(t)
0	0	1
1	1	1
2	1	−1
3	2	0

Table 4

t	x(t)	y(t)
0	1	2
1	−1	−1
2	1	2
3	0	2

Table 5

t	x(t)	y(t)
0	0	1
1	−1	0
2	0	−2
3	3	1

Table 6

For problems 5–8, use the data in the given graphs of (t, x(t)) and (t, y(t)) to sketch the parametric graph (x(t), y(t)).

5. Use x and y from Fig. 22.
6. Use x and y from Fig. 23.
7. Use x and y from Fig. 24.
8. Use x and y from Fig. 25.

9. Graph $x(t) = 3t - 2$, $y(t) = 1 - 2t$. What shape is this graph?

10. Graph $x(t) = 2 - 3t$, $y(t) = 3 + 2t$. What shape is this graph?

Fig. 22

Fig. 23

11. Calculate the slope of the line through the points $P = (x(0), y(0))$ and $Q = (x(1), y(1))$ for $x(t) = at + b$ and $y(t) = ct + d$.

12. Graph $x(t) = 3 + 2 \cdot \cos(t)$, $y(t) = -1 + 3 \cdot \sin(t)$ for $0 \le t \le 2\pi$. Describe the shape of the graph.

13. $x(t) = -2 + 3 \cdot \cos(t)$, $y(t) = 1 - 4 \cdot \sin(t)$ for $0 \le t \le 2\pi$. Describe the shape of the graph.

Fig. 24

Fig. 25

14. Graph (a) $x(t) = t^2$, $y(t) = t$, (b) $x(t) = \sin^2(t)$, $y(t) = \sin(t)$, and (c) $x(t) = t, y(t) = \sqrt{t}$. Describe the similarities and the differences among these graphs.

15. Graph (a) $x(t) = t$, $y(t) = t$, (b) $x(t) = \sin(t)$, $y(t) = \sin(t)$, and (c) $x(t) = t^2, y(t) = t^2$. Describe the similarities and the differences among these graphs.

16. Graph $x(t) = (4 - \frac{1}{t})\cos(t)$, $y(t) = (4 - \frac{1}{t})\sin(t)$ for $t \ge 1$. Describe the behavior of the graph.

17. Graph $x(t) = \frac{1}{t} \cdot \cos(t)$, $y(t) = \frac{1}{t} \cdot \sin(t)$ for $t \ge \pi/4$. Describe the behavior of the graph.

18. Graph $x(t) = t + \sin(t)$, $y(t) = t^2 + \cos(t)$ for $0 \le t \le 2\pi$. Describe the behavior of the graph.

Problems 19–22 refer to the rabbit–fox population graph shown in Fig. 26 which shows several different population cycles depending on the various numbers of rabbits and foxes. Wildlife biologists sometimes try to control animal populations by "harvesting" some of the animals, but it needs to be done with care. The thick dot on the graph is the fixed point for this two–species population.

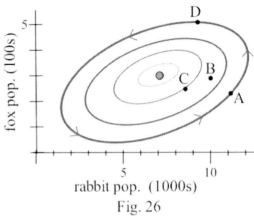

Fig. 26

19. Suppose there are currently 11,000 rabbits and 200 foxes (point A on the graph), and 1,000 rabbits are "harvested" (removed from the population). Does the harvest shift the populations onto a cycle closer to or farther from the fixed point?

20. Suppose there are currently 10,000 rabbits and 300 foxes (point B on the graph), and 100 foxes are "harvested." Does the harvest shift the populations onto a cycle closer to or farther from the fixed point?

21. Suppose there are currently 8,000 rabbits and 250 foxes (point C on the graph), and 1,000 rabbits die during a hard winter. Does the wildlife biologist need to take action to maintain the population balance? Justify your response.

22. Suppose there are currently 9,000 rabbits and 500 foxes (point D on the graph), and 2,000 rabbits die during a hard winter. Does the wildlife biologists need to take action to maintain the population balance? Justify your response.

23. Suppose x and y are functions of the form $x(t) = a \cdot t + b$ and $y(t) = c \cdot t + d$ with $a \neq 0$ and $c \neq 0$. Write y as a function of x alone and show that the parametric graph (x, y) is a straight line. What is the slope of the resulting line?

24. The parametric equations given in (a) – (e) all satisfy $x^2 + y^2 = 1$, and, for $0 \leq t \leq 2\pi$, the path of each object is a circle with radius 1 and center at the origin. Explain how the motions of the objects **differ**.
    (a) $x(t) = \cos(t), y(t) = \sin(t)$,   (b) $x(t) = \cos(-t), y(t) = \sin(-t)$,   (c) $x(t) = \cos(2t), y(t) = \sin(2t)$,
    (d) $x(t) = \sin(t), y(t) = \cos(t)$, and   (e) $x(t) = \cos(t + \pi/2), y(t) = \sin(t + \pi/2)$

25. From a tall building you observe a person is walking along a straight path while twirling a light (parallel to the ground) at the end of a string. (a) If the person is walking slowly, sketch the path of the light. (b) How would the graph change if the person was running? (c) Sketch the path for a person walking (running) along a parabolic path.

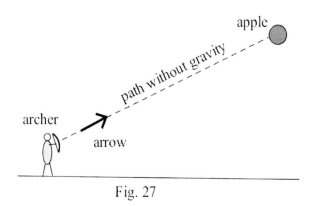

Fig. 27

26. **William Tell and the Falling Apple:** William Tell is aiming directly at an apple, and releases the arrow at exactly the same instant that the apple stem breaks. In a world without gravity (or air resistance), the apple remains in place after the stem breaks, and the arrow flies in a straight line to hit the apple (Fig. 27). Sketch the path of the apple and the arrow in a world with gravity (but still no air). Does the arrow still hit the apple? Why or why not?

27. Find the radius R of a circle which generates a cycloid starting at the point (0,0) and

    (a) passing through the point $(10\pi, 0)$ on its first complete revolution $(0 \le t \le 2\pi)$..

    (b) passing through the point (5, 2) on its first complete revolution. (A calculator is helpful here.)

    (c) passing through the point (2, 3) on its first complete revolution. (A calculator is helpful here.)

    (d) passing through the point $(4\pi, 8)$ on its first complete revolution.

The Ferris Wheel and the Apple (problems 28 – 30).

28. Your friends are on the Ferris wheel illustrated in Fig. 28, and at time t seconds, their location is given parametrically as
    $(-20 \sin(\frac{2\pi}{15} t) , 30 - 20 \cos(\frac{2\pi}{15} t))$.

    (a) Is the Ferris wheel turning clockwise of counterclockwise?

    (b) How many seconds does it take the Ferris wheel to make a revolution?

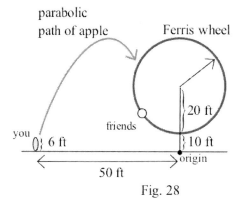

Fig. 28

29. You are 50 feet to the left of the Ferris wheel in problem 28, and you toss an apple from a height of 6 feet above the ground at an angle of 45°. Write parametric equations for the location of the apple (relative to the origin in Fig. 29) at time t if

    (a) its initial velocity is 30 feet per second, and (b) its initial velocity is V feet per second.

30. Help — the Ferris wheel won't stop! To keep your friends on the Ferris wheel in problem 28 from getting too hungry, you toss an apple to them (at time t = 0). Write an equation for the distance between the apple and your friends at time t. Somehow, find a value for the initial velocity V of the apple so that it comes close enough for your friend to catch it, within 2 feet. (Note: A calculator or computer is probably required for this problem.)

Section 9.3 — PRACTICE Answers

Practice 1: A possible path for the car is shown in Fig. 29.

Practice 2: If the (rabbit, fox) parametric graph touches the horizontal axis, then there are 0 foxes: the foxes are extinct.

Practice 3: $x = 3 - t$ and $y = t^2 + 1$.
Then $t = 3 - x$ and $y = (3-x)^2 + 1 = x^2 - 6x + 10$.
The graph in Fig. 30 is parabola, opening upward, with vertex at $(3,1)$.

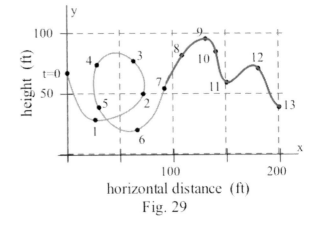

Fig. 29

Practice 4: The parametric graph of $x(t) = \sin(t)$ and $y(t) = 5\cos(t)$ is shown in Fig. 31. For all t,

$$\frac{x^2}{1} + \frac{y^2}{25} = \frac{\sin^2(t)}{1} + \frac{25\cos^2(t)}{25} = \sin^2(t) + \cos^2(t) = 1.$$

Practice 5: A: Starts at $(1,0)$, travels counterclockwise, and takes $2\pi/2 = \pi$ seconds to make one revolution.

B: Starts at $(-1,0)$, travels clockwise, and takes $2\pi/3$ seconds to make one revolution.

C: Starts at $(0,-1)$, travels counterclockwise, and takes $2\pi/4 = \pi/2$ seconds to make one revolution.

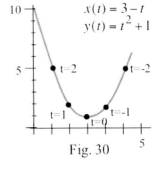

Fig. 30

Fig. 31

Practice 6: (a) $x(t) = 40\cdot\cos(45°)\cdot t$, $y(t) = 40\cdot\sin(45°)\cdot t - 16t^2$.

(b) Let $A = 40\cdot\sin(45°) = 40\cdot\cos(45°) \approx 28.284$.
Then the ball is at $x(t) = At$ and $y(t) = At - 16t^2$.

Along the ground line, $y = -\frac{1}{2}x$ so the ball intersects the ground when $y(t) = -\frac{1}{2}x(t)$: $At - 16t^2 = -\frac{1}{2}At$.

When $t \neq 0$, we can solve $At - 16t^2 = -\frac{1}{2}At$ for $t = \frac{3}{32}A$.

Putting $t = \frac{3}{32}A$ into the equations for the location of the ball, we have

$$x(\tfrac{3}{32}A) = A\cdot(\tfrac{3}{32}A) = \tfrac{3}{32}A^2 \text{ and } y(\tfrac{3}{32}A) = A\cdot(\tfrac{3}{32}A) - 16(\tfrac{3}{32}A)^2 = -\tfrac{3}{64}A^2.$$

The ball hits the ground after $t = \frac{3}{32}A = \frac{3}{32}\cdot 40\cdot\sin(45°) \approx \mathbf{2.652}$ **seconds**.

The ball hits the ground at the location $x = \frac{3}{32}A^2 = \mathbf{75}$ **feet** and $y = -\frac{3}{64}A^2 = \mathbf{-37.5}$ **feet**.

Practice 7: Axle: $x_a = R\cdot t$ and $y_a = R$. Light relative to the axle: $x_l = -r\cdot\sin(t)$ and $y_l = -r\cdot\cos(t)$.
Then $x(t) = x_a + x_l = R\cdot t - r\cdot\sin(t)$ and $y(t) = y_a + y_l = R - r\cdot\cos(t)$.

9.4 CALCULUS AND PARAMETRIC EQUATIONS

The previous section discussed parametric equations, their graphs, and some of their uses for visualizing and analyzing information. This section examines some of the ideas and techniques of calculus as they apply to parametric equations: slope of a tangent line, speed, arc length, and area. Slope, speed, and arc length were considered earlier (in optional parts of sections 2.5 and 5.2), and the presentation here is brief. The material on area is new and is a variation on the Riemann sum development of the integral. This section ends with a presentation of some of the properties of the cycloid.

Slope (also see section 2.5)

If $x(t)$ and $y(t)$ are differentiable functions of t, then the derivatives dx/dt and dy/dt measure the rates of change of x and y with respect to t: dx/dt and dy/dt tell how fast each variable is changing. The derivative dy/dx measures the slope of the line tangent to the parametric graph $(x(t), y(t))$. To calculate dy/dx we need to use the Chain Rule:

$$\frac{dy}{dt} = \frac{dy}{dx} \cdot \frac{dx}{dt} .$$

Dividing each side of the Chain Rule by $\frac{dx}{dt}$, we have $\frac{dy}{dx} = \frac{dy/dt}{dx/dt}$.

Slope with Parametric Equations

If $x(t)$ and $y(t)$ are differentiable functions of t and $\frac{dx}{dt} \neq 0$,

then the **slope** of the line tangent to the parametric graph is $\frac{dy}{dx} = \frac{dy/dt}{dx/dt}$.

Example 1: The location of an object is given by the parametric equations $x(t) = t^3 + 1$ feet and $y(t) = t^2 + t$ feet at time t seconds.

(a) Evaluate $x(t)$ and $y(t)$ at $t = -2, -1, 0, 1,$ and 2, and then graph the path of the object for $-2 \leq t \leq 2$.

(b) Evaluate dy/dx for $t = -2, -1, 0, 1,$ and 2. Do your calculated values for dy/dx agree with the shape of your graph in part (a)?

t	x	y	dy/dx
–2	–7	2	–3/12= –1/4
–1	0	0	–1/3
0	1	0	undefined
1	2	2	3/3 = 1
2	9	6	5/12

Table 1

Solution: (a) When $t = -2$,
$x = (-2)^3 + 1 = -7$ and
$y = (-2)^2 + (-2) = 2$. The other values for x and y are given in Table 1.
The graph of (x, y) is shown in Fig. 1.

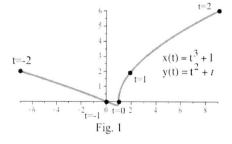

Fig. 1

(b) $dy/dt = 2t + 1$ and $dx/dt = 3t^2$ so $\frac{dy}{dx} = \frac{2t+1}{3t^2}$. When $t = -2$, $\frac{dy}{dx} = \frac{-3}{12}$. The other values for dy/dx are given in Table 1.

Practice 1: Find the equation of the line tangent to the graph of the parametric equations in Example 1 when $t = 3$.

An object can "visit" the same location more than once, and a parametric graph can go through the same point more than once.

Example 2: Fig. 2 shows the x and y coordinates of an object at time t.

Fig. 2

(a) Sketch the parametric graph $(x(t), y(t))$, the position of the object at time t.
(b) Give the coordinates of the object when $t = 1$ and $t = 3$.
(c) Find the slopes of the tangent lines to the parametric graph when $t = 1$ and $t = 3$.

Solution: (a) By reading the x and y values on the graphs in Fig. 2, we can plot points on the parametric graph. The parametric graph is shown in Fig. 3.

(b) When $t = 1$, $x = 2$ and $y = 2$ so the parametric graph goes through the point (2,2). When $t = 3$, the parametric graph goes through the same point (2,2).

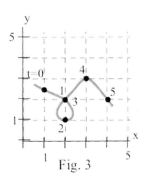

Fig. 3

(c) When $t = 1$, $dy/dt \approx -1$ and $dx/dt \approx +1$ so $\frac{dy}{dx} = \frac{dy/dt}{dx/dt} \approx \frac{-1}{+1} = -1$.
When $t = 3$, $dy/dt \approx +1$ and $dx/dt \approx +1$ so $\frac{dy}{dx} \approx \frac{+1}{+1} = +1$.
These values agree with the appearance of the parametric graph in Fig. 3.

The object goes through the point (2,2) twice (when t=1 and t=3), but it is traveling in a different direction each time.

Practice 2: (a) Estimate the slopes of the lines tangent to the parametric graph when $t = 2$ and $t = 5$.
(b) When does $y'(t) = 0$ in Fig. 2?
(c) When does the parametric graph in Fig. 3 have a maximum? A minimum?
(d) How are the maximum and minimum points on a parametric graph related to the derivatives of $x(t)$ and $y(t)$?

Speed

If we know how fast an object is moving in the x direction (dx/dt) and how fast in the y direction (dy/dt), it is straightforward to determine the speed of the object, how fast it is moving in the xy–plane.

If, during a short interval of time Δt, the object's position changes Δx in the x direction and Δy in the y direction (Fig. 4), then the object has moved $\sqrt{(\Delta x)^2 + (\Delta y)^2}$ in Δt time. Then

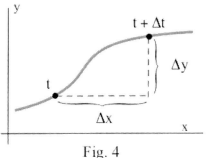

Fig. 4

$$\text{average speed} = \frac{\text{distance moved}}{\text{time change}} = \frac{\sqrt{(\Delta x)^2 + (\Delta y)^2}}{\Delta t}$$

$$= \sqrt{\left(\frac{\Delta x}{\Delta t}\right)^2 + \left(\frac{\Delta y}{\Delta t}\right)^2} \ .$$

If x(t) and y(t) are differentiable functions of t, and if we take the limit of the average speed as Δt approaches 0, then

$$\text{speed} = \lim_{\Delta t \to 0} \{\text{average speed}\} = \lim_{\Delta t \to 0} \sqrt{\left(\frac{\Delta x}{\Delta t}\right)^2 + \left(\frac{\Delta y}{\Delta t}\right)^2} = \sqrt{\left(\frac{dx}{dt}\right)^2 + \left(\frac{dy}{dt}\right)^2} \ .$$

Speed with Parametric Equations

If   an object is located at (x(t), y(t)) at time t, and x(t) and y(t) are differentiable functions of t ,

then   the **speed** of the object is $\sqrt{\left(\frac{dx}{dt}\right)^2 + \left(\frac{dy}{dt}\right)^2}$.

Example 3: At time t seconds an object is located at (cos(t) feet, sin(t) feet) in the plane. Sketch the path of the object and show that it is travelling at a constant speed.

Solution: The object is moving in a circular path (Fig. 5). dx/dt = –sin(t) feet/second and dy/dt = cos(t) feet/second so at all times the speed of the object is

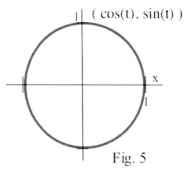

Fig. 5

$$\sqrt{\left(\frac{dx}{dt}\right)^2 + \left(\frac{dy}{dt}\right)^2} = \sqrt{(-\sin(t))^2 + (\cos(t))^2}$$

$$= \sqrt{\sin^2(t) + \cos^2(t)} = \sqrt{1} = 1 \text{ foot per second.}$$

Practice 3: Is the object in Example 2 traveling faster when $t = 1$ or when $t = 3$? When $t = 1$ or when $t = 2$?

Arc Length (also see section 5.2)

In section 5.2 we approximated the total length L of a curve by partitioning the curve into small pieces (Fig. 6), approximating the length of each piece using the distance formula, and then adding the lengths of the pieces together to get

$$L \approx \sum \sqrt{(\Delta x)^2 + (\Delta y)^2}$$

$$= \sum \sqrt{\left(\frac{\Delta x}{\Delta x}\right)^2 + \left(\frac{\Delta y}{\Delta x}\right)^2} \, \Delta x \text{ , a Riemann sum.}$$

As Δx approaches 0, the Riemann sum approaches the definite integral

$$L = \int_{x=a}^{b} \sqrt{1 + \left(\frac{dy}{dx}\right)^2} \, dx.$$

A similar approach also works for parametric equations, but in this case we factor out a Δt from the original summation:

$$L \approx \sum \sqrt{(\Delta x)^2 + (\Delta y)^2} = \sum \sqrt{\left(\frac{\Delta x}{\Delta t}\right)^2 + \left(\frac{\Delta y}{\Delta t}\right)^2} \, \Delta t \text{ (a Riemann sum)}$$

$$\longrightarrow \int_{t=a}^{b} \sqrt{\left(\frac{dx}{dt}\right)^2 + \left(\frac{dy}{dt}\right)^2} \, dt \text{ as } \Delta t \to 0.$$

Arc Length with Parametric Equations

If $x(t)$ and $y(t)$ are differentiable functions of t

then the length of the parametric graph from $(x(a), y(a))$ to $(x(b), y(b))$ is

$$L = \int_{t=a}^{t=b} \sqrt{\left(\frac{dx}{dt}\right)^2 + \left(\frac{dy}{dt}\right)^2} \, dt$$

Fig. 6

Example 4: Find the length of the cycloid

$x = R(t - \sin(t))$ $y = R(1 - \cos(t))$

for $0 \le t \le 2\pi$. (Fig. 7)

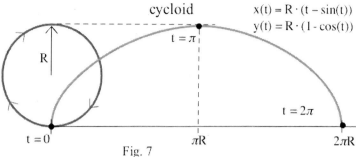

Fig. 7

Solution: Since $dx/dt = R(1 - \cos(t))$ and $dy/dt = R \cdot \sin(t)$,

$$L = \int_{t=a}^{b} \sqrt{\left(\frac{dx}{dt}\right)^2 + \left(\frac{dy}{dt}\right)^2} \, dt =$$

$$\int_{t=0}^{2\pi} \sqrt{(R(1-\cos(t)))^2 + (R\cdot\sin(t))^2} \, dt$$

$$= R \int_{t=0}^{2\pi} \sqrt{1 - 2\cos(t) + \cos^2(t) + \sin^2(t)} \, dt = R \int_{t=0}^{2\pi} \sqrt{2 - 2\cdot\cos(t)} \, dt.$$

By replacing θ with $t/2$ in the formula $\sin^2(\theta) = \frac{1 - \cos(2\theta)}{2}$ we have $\sin^2(t/2) = \frac{1 - \cos(t)}{2}$

so $2 - 2\cdot\cos(t) = 4\cdot\sin^2(t/2)$, and the integral becomes

$$L = R \int_{t=0}^{2\pi} 2\cdot\sin(t/2) \, dt = 2R\{-2\cdot\cos(t/2)\}\Big|_0^{2\pi} = 2R\{-2\cdot\cos(\pi) + 2\cdot\cos(0)\} = \mathbf{8R}.$$

The length of a cycloid arch is 8 times the radius of the rolling circle that generated the cycloid.

Practice 4: Represent the length of the ellipse $x = 3\cdot\cos(t)$

$y = 2\cdot\sin(t)$ for for $0 \le t \le 2\pi$ (Fig. 8). as a definite

integral. Use Simpson's rule with n = 20 to approximate

the value of the integral.

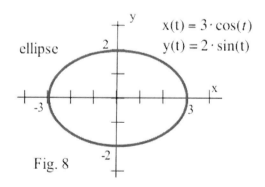

Fig. 8

Area

When we first discussed area and developed the definite integral, we approximated the area of a positive function y (Fig. 9) by partitioning the domain $a \leq x \leq b$ into pieces of length Δx, finding the areas of the thin rectangles, and approximating the total area by adding the little areas together:

$$A \approx \sum y \, \Delta x \quad \text{(a Riemann sum)}.$$

As Δx approached 0, the Riemann sum approached the definite integral $\int_{x=a}^{x=b} y \, dx$.

Fig. 9

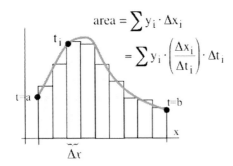

For parametric equations, the independent variable is t and the domain is an interval [a, b].

If x is an increasing function of t, then a partition of the t–interval [a, b] into pieces of length Δt induces a partition along the x–axis (Fig. 10), and we can use the induced partition of the x–axis to approximate the total area by

$$A \approx \sum y \, \Delta x = \sum y \, \frac{\Delta x}{\Delta t} \, \Delta t \quad \text{which approaches the definite}$$

integral $A = \int_{t=a}^{t=b} y \cdot \left(\frac{dx}{dt}\right) dt$ as Δt approaches 0.

Fig. 10

Area with Parametric Equations

If y and dx/dt do not change sign for $a \leq t \leq b$,

then the **area** between the graph (x, y) and the x–axis is $A = \left| \int_{t=a}^{t=b} y \cdot \left(\frac{dx}{dt}\right) dt \right|$.

The requirement that y not change sign for $a \le t \le b$ is to prevent the parametric graph from being above the x–axis sometimes and below the x–axis sometimes. The requirement that dx/dt not change sign for $a \le t \le b$ is to prevent the graph from "turning around" (Fig. 11). If either of those situations occurs, some of the area is evaluated as positive and some of the area is evaluated as negative.

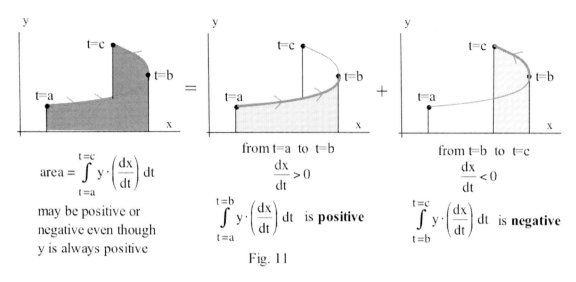

$$\text{area} = \int_{t=a}^{t=c} y \cdot \left(\frac{dx}{dt}\right) dt$$

may be positive or negative even though y is always positive

from t=a to t=b
$$\frac{dx}{dt} > 0$$
$$\int_{t=a}^{t=b} y \cdot \left(\frac{dx}{dt}\right) dt \text{ is \textbf{positive}}$$

from t=b to t=c
$$\frac{dx}{dt} < 0$$
$$\int_{t=b}^{t=c} y \cdot \left(\frac{dx}{dt}\right) dt \text{ is \textbf{negative}}$$

Fig. 11

Example 5: Find the area of the ellipse $x = a \cdot \cos(t), y = b \cdot \sin(t)$ (a,b > 0) in the first quadrant (Fig. 12).

Solution: The derivative $dx/dt = -a \cdot \sin(t)$, and in the first quadrant $0 \le t \le \pi/2$. Then the

$$\text{area of the ellipse in first quadrant} = \left| \int_{t=a}^{b} y \cdot \left(\frac{dx}{dt}\right) dt \right|$$

$$= \left| \int_{t=0}^{\pi/2} \{ b \cdot \sin(t) \} \cdot (-a \cdot \sin(t)) \, dt \right|$$

$$= \left| -ab \int_{t=0}^{\pi/2} \sin^2(t) \, dt \right| = ab \int_{t=0}^{\pi/2} \sin^2(t) \, dt \quad (\text{replace } \sin^2(t) \text{ with } \frac{1-\cos(2t)}{2})$$

$$= \frac{1}{2} ab \int_{t=0}^{\pi/2} 1 - \cos(2t) \, dt = \frac{1}{2} ab \left\{ t - \frac{1}{2} \cdot \sin(2t) \right\} \Big|_0^{\pi/2} = \frac{1}{4} ab\pi .$$

The area of the whole ellipse is $4\{ \frac{1}{4} ab\pi \} = \boldsymbol{\pi ab}$.

If $a = b$, the ellipse is a circle with radius $r = a = b$, and its area is πr^2 as expected.

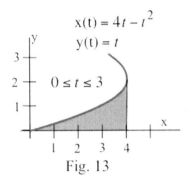

Practice 5: Let $x(t) = 4t - t^2$ and $y(t) = t$ (Fig. 13).

(a) Represent the shaded area in Fig. 13 as an integral and evaluate the integral.

(b) Evaluate $\int_{t=0}^{t=3} t \cdot (4 - 2t)\, dt$. Does this value represent an area?

Area under a Cycloid: (Fig. 7) For all $t \geq 0$, $x = R(t - \sin(t)) \geq 0$, $y = R(1 - \cos(t)) \geq 0$, and $dx/dt = R(1 - \cos(t)) \geq 0$ so we can use the area formula. Then

$$\text{area} = \left| \int_{t=a}^{b} y \cdot \left(\frac{dx}{dt}\right) dt \right| = \left| \int_{t=0}^{2\pi} \{R(1 - \cos(t))\} \cdot (R(1 - \cos(t)))\, dt \right|$$

$$= R^2 \int_{t=0}^{2\pi} 1 - 2\cos(t) + \cos^2(t)\, dt \quad (\text{replace } \cos^2(t) \text{ with } \frac{1 + \cos(2t)}{2} \text{ and integrate})$$

$$= R^2 \{ t - 2\sin(t) + \frac{1}{2} t + \frac{1}{4} \sin(2t) \} \Big|_0^{2\pi} = R^2 \{ 2\pi + \pi \} = 3\pi R^2.$$

The area under one arch of a cycloid is 3 times the area of the circle that generates the cycloid.

Properties of the Cycloid

Suppose you and a friend decide to have a contest to see who can build a slide that gets a person from point A to point B (Fig. 14) in the shortest time. What shape should you make your slide — a straight line, part of a circle, or something else? Assuming that the slide is frictionless and that the only acceleration is due to gravity, John Bernoulli showed that the **shortest time** ("brachistochrone" for "brachi" = short and "chrone" = time) path is a cycloid that starts at A that also goes through the point B. Fig. 15 shows the cycloid paths for A and B as well as the cycloid paths for two other "finish" points, C and D.

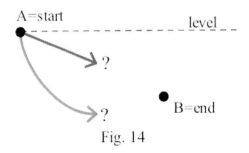

Fig. 14

Even before Bernoulli solved the brachistochrone problem, the astronomer (physicist, mathematician) Huygens was trying to design an accurate pendulum clock. On a standard pendulum clock (Fig. 16), the path of the bob is part of a circle, and the period of the swing depends on the displacement angle of the bob. As friction slows the bob, the displacement angle gets smaller and the clock slows down.

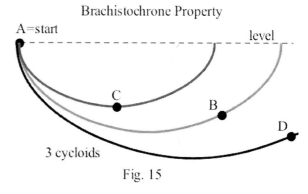

Huygens designed a clock (Fig. 17) whose bob swung in a curve so that the period of the swing did not depend on the displacement angle. The curve Huygens found to solve the **same time** ("tautochrone" for "tauto" = same and "chrone" = time) problem was the cycloid. Beads strung on a wire in the shape of a cycloid (Fig. 18) reach the bottom in the same amount of time, no matter where along the wire (except the bottom point) they are released.

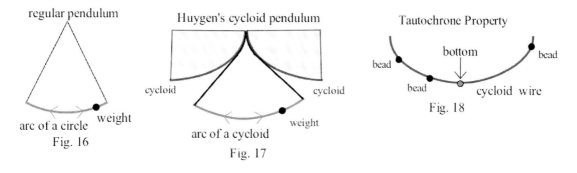

The brachistochane and tautochrone problems are examples from a field of mathematics called the Calculus of Variations. Typical optimization problems in calculus involve finding a point or number that maximizes or minimizes some quantity. Typical optimization problems in the Calculus of Variations involve finding the curve or function that maximizes or minimizes some quantity. For example, what curve or shape with a given length encloses the greatest area? (Answer: a circle) Modern applications of Calculus of Variations include finding routes for airliners and ships to minimize travel time or fuel consumption depending on prevailing winds or currents.

PROBLEMS

Slope

For problems 1–8, (a) sketch the parametric graph (x,y),

(b) find the slope of the line tangent to the parametric graph at the given values of t, and

(c) find the points (x,y) at which dy/dx is either 0 or undefined.

1. $x(t) = t - t^2$, $y(t) = 2t + 1$ at $t = 0, 1,$ and 2.

2. $x(t) = t^3 + t$, $y(t) = t^2$ at $t = 0, 1,$ and 2.

3. $x(t) = 1 + \cos(t)$, $y(t) = 2 + \sin(t)$ at $t = 0, \pi/4,$ and $\pi/2$.

4. $x(t) = 1 + 3 \cdot \cos(t)$, $y(t) = 2 + 2 \cdot \sin(t)$ at $t = 0, \pi/4, \pi/2,$ and π.

5. $x(t) = \sin(t)$, $y(t) = \cos(t)$ at $t = 0, \pi/4, \pi/2,$ and 17.3.

6. $x(t) = 3 + \sin(t)$, $y(t) = 2 + \sin(t)$ at $t = 0, \pi/4, \pi/2,$ and 17.3.

7. $x(t) = \ln(t)$, $y(t) = 1 - t^2$ at $t = 1, 2,$ and e.

8. $x(t) = \arctan(t)$, $y(t) = e^t$ at $t = 0, 1,$ and 2.

In problems 9–12, the graphs of x(t) and y(t) are given.

Use this graphical information to estimate

(a) the slope of the line tangent to the parametric graph at $t = 0, 1, 2,$ and 3, and

(b) the points (x,y) at which dy/dx is either 0 or undefined.

9. x(t) and y(t) in Fig. 19.

10. x(t) and y(t) in Fig. 20.

11. x(t) and y(t) in Fig. 21.

12. x(t) and y(t) in Fig. 22.

Fig. 19

Fig. 20

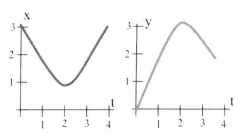

Fig. 21

Speed

For problems 13–20, the locations x(t) and y(t) (in feet) of an object are given at time t seconds. Find the speed of the object at the given times.

13. $x(t) = t - t^2$, $y(t) = 2t + 1$ at $t = 0, 1,$ and 2.

14. $x(t) = t^3 + t$, $y(t) = t^2$ at $t = 0, 1,$ and 2.

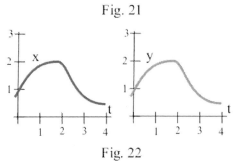

Fig. 22

15. $x(t) = 1 + \cos(t)$, $y(t) = 2 + \sin(t)$ at $t = 0, \pi/4, \pi/2$, and π.

16. $x(t) = 1 + 3 \cdot \cos(t)$, $y(t) = 2 + 2 \cdot \sin(t)$ at $t = 0, \pi/4, \pi/2$, and π.

17. x and y in Fig. 19 at $t = 0, 1, 2, 3$, and 4.

18. x and y in Fig. 20 at $t = 0, 1, 2$, and 3.

19. x and y in Fig. 21 at $t = 0, 1, 2$, and 3.

20. x and y in Fig. 22 at $t = 0, 1, 2$, and 3.

21. At time t seconds an object is located at the point $x(t) = R \cdot (t - \sin(t))$, $y(t) = R \cdot (1 - \cos(t))$ (in feet).
    (a) Find the speed of the object at time t. (b) At what time is the object traveling fastest?
    (c) Where is the object on the cycloid when it is traveling fastest?

22. At time t seconds an object is located at the point $x(t) = 5 \cdot \cos(t)$, $y(t) = 2 \cdot \sin(t)$ (in feet).
    (a) Find the speed of the object at time t. (b) At what time is the object traveling fastest?
    (c) Where is the object on the ellipse when it is traveling fastest?

Arc Length

For problems 23–28, (a) represent the arc length of each parametric function as a definite integral, and
(b) evaluate the integral (if necessary, use your calculator's **fnInt()** feature to evaluate the integral).

23. $x(t) = t - t^2$, $y(t) = 2t + 1$ for $t = 0$ to 2.

24. $x(t) = t^3 + t$, $y(t) = t^2$ for $t = 0$ to 2.

25. $x(t) = 1 + \cos(t)$, $y(t) = 2 + \sin(t)$ for $t = 0$ to π.

26. $x(t) = 1 + 3 \cdot \cos(t)$, $y(t) = 2 + 2 \cdot \sin(t)$ for $t = 0$ to π.

27. x and y in Fig. 23 for $t = 1$ to 3.

28. x and y in Fig. 22 for $t = 0$ to 2.

Fig. 23

Area

For problems 29–34, (a) represent the area of each region as a definite integral, and
(b) evaluate the integral (if necessary, use your calculator's **fnInt()** feature to evaluate the integral).

29. $x(t) = t^2$, $y(t) = 4t^2 - t^4$ for $0 \le t \le 2$.

30. $x(t) = 1 + \sin(t)$, $y(t) = 2 + \sin(t)$ for $0 \le t \le \pi$.

31. $x(t) = t^2$, $y(t) = 1 + \cos(t)$ for $0 \le t \le 2$.

32. $x(t) = \cos(t)$, $y(t) = 2 - \sin(t)$ for $0 \le t \le \pi/2$.

33. "Cycloid" with a square wheel: Find the area under one "arch" of the path of a point on the corner of a "rolling" square that has sides of length R. (This problem does not require calculus.)

34. The region bounded between the x–axis and the curate cycloid $x(t) = R \cdot t - r \cdot \sin(t)$, $y(t) = R - r \cdot \cos(t)$ for $0 \le t \le 2\pi$.

Section 9.4   **PRACTICE Answers**

Practice 1: $\frac{dy}{dt} = 2t + 1$, so when $t = 3$, $\frac{dy}{dt} = 7$. $\frac{dx}{dt} = 3t^2$, so when $t = 3$, $\frac{dx}{dt} = 27$.

Finally, $\frac{dy}{dx} = \frac{dy/dt}{dx/dt}$ so when $t = 3$, $\frac{dy}{dx} = \frac{7}{27}$.

When $t = 3$, $x = 28$ and $y = 12$ so the equation of the tangent line is $y - 12 = \frac{7}{27}(x - 28)$.

Practice 2: (a) When $t = 2$, $dy/dx \approx 0$. When $t = 5$, $dy/dx \approx -1$.

(b) In Fig. 2, $\frac{dy}{dt} = 0$ when $t \approx 2$ and $t \approx 4$.

(c) In Fig. 3, a minimum occurs when $t \approx 2$ and a maximum when $t \approx 4$.

(d) If the parametric graph has a maximum or minimum at $t = t^*$, then dy/dt is either 0 or undefined when $t = t^*$.

Practice 3: When $t = 1$, speed $= \sqrt{(dx/dt)^2 + (dy/dt)^2} \approx \sqrt{(1)^2 + (-1)^2} = \sqrt{2} \approx 1.4$ ft/sec.
When $t = 2$, speed $= \sqrt{(dx/dt)^2 + (dy/dt)^2} \approx \sqrt{(-1)^2 + (0)^2} = \sqrt{1} = 1$ ft/sec.
When $t = 3$, speed $= \sqrt{(dx/dt)^2 + (dy/dt)^2} \approx \sqrt{(1)^2 + (1)^2} = \sqrt{2} \approx 1.4$ ft/sec.

Practice 4: Length $= \int_{t=0}^{2\pi} \sqrt{(-3\sin(t))^2 + (2\cos(t))^2}\ dt$

≈ 15.87 (using my calculator's **fnInt()** feature)

Practice 5: (a) $A = \int_{t=0}^{2} t \cdot (4 - 2t)\ dt = 2 \cdot t^2 - \frac{2}{3} t^3 \Big|_0^2 = \{ 8 - \frac{16}{3} \} - \{ 0 - 0 \} = \frac{8}{3}$.

(b) $\int_{t=0}^{3} t \cdot (4 - 2t)\ dt = 2 \cdot t^2 - \frac{2}{3} t^3 \Big|_0^3 = \{ 18 - 18 \} - \{ 0 - 0 \} = 0$.

This integral represents {shaded area in Fig. 13} – { area from $t = 2$ to $t = 3$ }.

9.4½ BEZIER CURVES — Getting the shape you want

Historically, parametric equations were often used to model the motion of objects, and that is the approach we have seen so far. But more recently, as computers became more common in design work and manufacturing, a need arose to efficiently find formulas for shapes such as airplane wings and automobile bodies and even letters of the alphabet that designers or artists had created.

One simple but inefficient method for describing and storing the shape of a curve is to measure the location and save the coordinates of hundreds or thousands of points along the curve. This result is called a "bitmap" of the shape. However, bitmaps typically require a large amount of computer memory, and when the bitmap is reconverted from stored coordinates back into a graphic image, originally smooth curves often appear jagged (Fig. 1). Also, when these bitmapped shapes are stretched or rotated, the new location of every one of the points must be calculated, a relatively slow process.

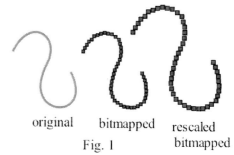
original   bitmapped   rescaled bitmapped
Fig. 1

A second method, still simple but more efficient than bitmaps, is to store fewer points along the curve, but to automatically connect consecutive points with line segments (Fig. 2). Less computer memory is required since fewer coordinates are stored, and stretches and rotations are calculated more quickly since the new locations of fewer points are needed. This method is commonly used in computer graphics to store and redraw surfaces (Fig. 3). Sometimes instead of saving the coordinates of each point, a "vector" is used to describe how to get to the next point from the previous point, and the result is a "vector map" of the curve. The major drawback of this method is that the stored and redrawn curve consists of straight segments and corners even though the original curve may have been smooth.

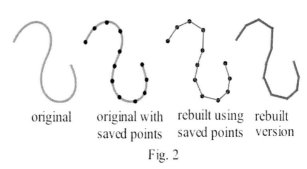
original   original with saved points   rebuilt using saved points   rebuilt version
Fig. 2

original surface   surface rebuilt using points and line segments

Fig. 3

The primary building block for curves and surfaces represented as line segments is the line segment given by parametric equations.

Example 1: Show that the parametric equations
$$x(t) = (1 - t) \cdot x_0 + t \cdot x_1 \text{ and}$$
$$y(t) = (1 - t) \cdot y_0 + t \cdot y_1$$
for $0 \leq t \leq 1$ go through the points $P_0 = (x_0, y_0)$ and $P_1 = (x_1, y_1)$ (Fig. 4) and that the slope is
$$\frac{dy}{dx} = \frac{y_1 - y_0}{x_1 - x_0}$$
for all values of t between 0 and 1.

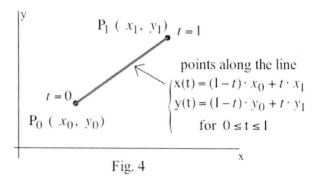

Fig. 4

We typically abbreviate the pair of parametric equations as $P(t) = (1 - t) \cdot P_0 + t \cdot P_1$.

Solution: $x(0) = (1 - 0) \cdot x_0 + 0 \cdot x_1 = x_0$ and $y(0) = (1 - 0) \cdot y_0 + 0 \cdot y_1 = y_0$ so $P(0) = P_0$.

$x(1) = (1 - 1) \cdot x_0 + 1 \cdot x_1 = x_1$ and $y(1) = (1 - 1) \cdot y_0 + 1 \cdot y_1 = y_1$ so $P(1) = P_1$.

$$\frac{dy(t)}{dt} = -y_0 + y_1 \text{ and } \frac{dx(t)}{dt} = -x_0 + x_1$$

so $\frac{dy}{dx} = \frac{dy/dt}{dx/dt} = \frac{y_1 - y_0}{x_1 - x_0}$, the slope of the line segment from P_0 to P_1.

Practice 1: Use the pattern of Example 1 to write parametric equations for the line segments that
(a) connect (1,2) to (5,4), (b) connect (5,4) to (1,2), and (c) connect (6,–2) to (3,1).

Bezier Curves

One solution to the problem of efficiently saving and redrawing a smooth curve was independently developed in the 1960s by two French automobile engineers, Pierre Bezier (pronounced "bez–ee–ay") who worked for Renault automobile company and P. de Casteljau who worked for Citroen. Originally, the solutions were considered industrial secrets, but Bezier's work was eventually published first. The curves that result using Bezier's method are called Bezier curves. The method of Bezier curves allow us to efficiently store information about smooth (and not–so–smooth) shapes and to quickly stretch, rotate and distort these shapes. Bezier curves are now commonly used in computer–aided design work and in most computer drawing programs. They are also used to specify the shapes of letters of the alphabet in different fonts. By using this method, a computer and a laser printer can have many different fonts in many different sizes available without using a large amount of memory. (Bezier curves were used to produce most of the graphs in this book.)

Here we define Bezier curves and examine some of their properties. At the end of this section some optional material describes the mathematical construction of Bezier curves.

Definition: Bezier Curve

The Bezier curve $B(t)$ defined for the four points $P_0, P_1, P_2,$ and P_3 (Fig. 5) is

$$B(t) = (1-t)^3 \cdot P_0 + 3(1-t)^2 \cdot t \cdot P_1 + 3(1-t) \cdot t^2 \cdot P_2 + t^3 \cdot P_3$$

for $0 \leq t \leq 1$:

$x(t) = (1-t)^3 \cdot x_0 + 3(1-t)^2 \cdot t \cdot x_1 + 3(1-t) \cdot t^2 \cdot x_2 + t^3 \cdot x_3$ and
$y(t) = (1-t)^3 \cdot y_0 + 3(1-t)^2 \cdot t \cdot y_1 + 3(1-t) \cdot t^2 \cdot y_2 + t^3 \cdot y_3$.

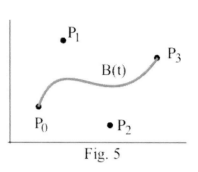
Fig. 5

The four points $P_0, P_1, P_2,$ and P_3 are called **control points** for the Bezier curve. Fig. 6 shows Bezier curves for several sets of control points. The dotted lines connecting the control points in Fig. 6 are shown to help illustrate the relationship between the graph of $B(t)$ and the control points.

Example 2: Plot the points $P_0 = (0,3)$, $P_1 = (1,5)$, $P_2 = (3,-1)$, and $P_3 = (4,0)$, and determine the equation of the Bezier curve for these control points. Then graph the Bezier curve.

Solution:

$x(t) = (1-t)^3 \cdot 0 + 3(1-t)^2 \cdot t \cdot 1 + 3(1-t) \cdot t^2 \cdot 3 + t^3 \cdot 4 = -2t^3 + 3t^2 + 3t$.
$y(t) = (1-t)^3 \cdot 3 + 3(1-t)^2 \cdot t \cdot 5 + 3(1-t) \cdot t^2 \cdot (-1) + t^3 \cdot 0$
$= 15t^3 - 24t^2 + 6t + 3$.

The control points and the graph of $B(t) = (x(t), y(t))$ are shown in Fig. 7.

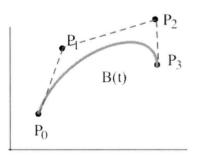

Practice 2: Plot the points $P_0 = (0, 4)$, $P_1 = (1, 2)$, $P_2 = (4, 2)$, and $P_3 = (4, 4)$, and determine the equation of the Bezier curve for these control points. Then graph the Bezier curve.

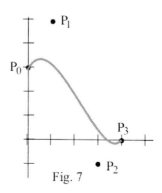
Fig. 7

Fig. 6: Several Bezier curves as P_2 is moved

Properties of Bezier Curves

Bezier curves have a number of properties that make them particularly useful for design work, and some of them are stated below. These properties are verified at the end of this section.

(1) $B(0) = P_0$ and $B(1) = P_3$ so the Bezier curve goes through the points P_0 and P_3.

This property guarantees that $B(t)$ goes through specified points. If we want two Bezier curves to fit together, it is important that the value at the end of one curve matches the starting value of the next curve. This property guarantees that we can control the values of the Bezier curves at their endpoints by choosing appropriate values for the control points P_0 and P_3.

(2) $B(t)$ is a cubic polynomial.

This is an important property because it guarantees that $B(t)$ is continuous and differentiable at each point so its graph is connected and smooth at each point. It also guarantees that the graph of $B(t)$ does not "wiggle" too much between control points.

(3) $B'(0)$ = slope of the line segment from P_0 to P_1; $B'(1)$ = slope of the line segment from P_2 to P_3.

This is an important property because it means we can match the ending slope of one curve with the starting slope of the next curve to result in a smooth connection. We can see in Fig. 6 that the dotted line from P_0 to P_1 is tangent to the graph of $B(t)$ at the point P_0.

(4) For $0 \leq t \leq 1$, the graph of $B(t)$ is in the region whose corners are the control points.

Visually, property (4) means that if we put a rubber band around the four control points $P_0, P_1, P_2,$ and P_3 (Fig. 8), then the graph of $B(t)$ will be inside the rubber banded region. This is an important property of Bezier curves because it guarantees that the graph of $B(t)$ does not get too far from the four control points.

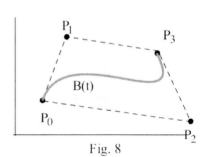

Fig. 8

Example 3: Find a formula for a Bezier curve that goes through the points $(1, 1)$ and $(0,0)$ and is shaped like an "S."

Solution: Since we want the curve to begin at the point $(1,1)$ and end at $(0,0)$ we can put $P_0 = (1,1)$ and $P_3 = (0,0)$. A little experimentation with values for P_1 and P_2 indicates that $P_1 = (-1, 2)$ and $P_2 = (2, -1)$ gives a mediocre "S" shape (Fig. 9). Then the formula for $B(t)$ is

$$B(t) = (1-t)^3 \cdot P_0 + 3(1-t)^2 \cdot t \cdot P_1 + 3(1-t) \cdot t^2 \cdot P_2 + t^3 \cdot P_3$$

for $0 \leq t \leq 1$, and

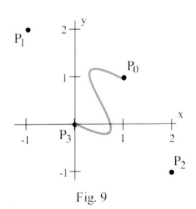

Fig. 9

$$x(t) = (1-t)^3 \cdot x_0 + 3(1-t)^2 \cdot t \cdot x_1 + 3(1-t) \cdot t^2 \cdot x_2 + t^3 \cdot x_3 = (1-t)^3 \cdot 1 + 3(1-t)^2 \cdot t \cdot (-1) + 3(1-t) \cdot t^2 \cdot 2 + t^3 \cdot 0$$

and

$$y(t) = (1-t)^3 \cdot y_0 + 3(1-t)^2 \cdot t \cdot y_1 + 3(1-t) \cdot t^2 \cdot y_2 + t^3 \cdot y_3 = (1-t)^3 \cdot 1 + 3(1-t)^2 \cdot t \cdot 2 + 3(1-t) \cdot t^2 \cdot (-1) + t^3 \cdot 0$$

Certainly other values of P_1 and P_2 can give similar shapes.

Practice 3: Find a formula for a Bezier curve that goes through the points $(0, 0)$ and $(0,1)$ and is shaped like a "C."

Example 4: Find a formula for a Bezier curve that goes through the point $(0, 5)$ with a slope of 2 and through the point $(6, 1)$ with a slope of 3.

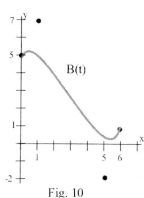

Fig. 10

Solution: Since we want to curve to begin at $(0,5)$ and end at $(6,1)$, we put $P_0 = (0,5)$ and $P_3 = (6,1)$. To get the slopes we need to pick P_1 so the slope of the line segment from P_0 to P_1 is 2: going "over 1 and up 2" to get $P_1 = (1,7)$ works fine as do several other points. Similarly, to get the right slope at P_3 we can go "back 1 and down 3" to get $P_2 = (5, -2)$. The Bezier curve for $P_0 = (0,5), P_1 = (1,7), P_2 = (5,-2)$, and $P_3 = (6,1)$ is

$$x(t) = (1-t)^3 \cdot 0 + 3(1-t)^2 \cdot t \cdot 1 + 3(1-t) \cdot t^2 \cdot 5 + t^3 \cdot 6 = -6t^3 + 9t^2 + 3t \text{ and}$$
$$y(t) = (1-t)^3 \cdot 5 + 3(1-t)^2 \cdot t \cdot 7 + 3(1-t) \cdot t^2 \cdot (-2) + t^3 \cdot 1 = 23t^3 - 33t^2 + 6t + 5.$$

The graph of this B(t) is shown in Fig. 10.

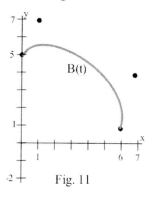

Fig. 11

Keeping the previous values of P_0, P_1 and P_3, we could pick P_2 by going "over 1 and up 3" to $P_2 = (7,4)$, and the graph of the B(t) for this choice of P_2 is shown in Fig. 11. The graph for B(t) when $P_1 = (2,9)$ and $P_2 = (5.5, -0.5)$ is shown in Fig. 12. These, and other choices of P_1 and P_2 satisfy the conditions specified in the problem: the choice of which one you use depends on the other properties of the shape that you want the curve to have.

Practice 4: Find a formula for a Bezier curve that goes through the point $(1, 3)$ with a slope of -2 and through the point $(5, 3)$ with a slope of -1.

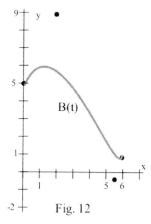

Fig. 12

Example 5: Find formulas for a pair of Bezier curves so that the first starts at the point $A = (0,3)$ with slope 2, the second ends at the point $C = (7,2)$ with slope 1, and the curves connect at the point $B = (4,6)$ with slope 0.

Solution: For the first Bezier curve B(t) take $P_0 = A = (0,3), P_1 = (1,5)$ (to get the slope 2),

$P_3 = B = (4,6)$, and $P_2 = (3,6)$ (to get the slope 0 at the connecting point). Then,

for $0 \le t \le 1$, $x(t) = (1-t)^3 \cdot 0 + 3(1-t)^2 \cdot t \cdot 1 + 3(1-t) \cdot t^2 \cdot 3 + t^3 \cdot 4$ and

$y(t) = (1-t)^3 \cdot 3 + 3(1-t)^2 \cdot t \cdot 5 + 3(1-t) \cdot t^2 \cdot 6 + t^3 \cdot 6$.

For the second Bezier curve $C(t)$ take $P_0 = B = (4,6)$, $P_1 = (5,6)$ (to get the slope 0 at the connecting point), $P_3 = C = (7,2)$, and $P_2 = (6,1)$ (to get the slope 1). Then,

for $0 \le t \le 1$, $x(t) = (1-t)^3 \cdot 4 + 3(1-t)^2 \cdot t \cdot 5 + 3(1-t) \cdot t^2 \cdot 6 + t^3 \cdot 7$ and

$y(t) = (1-t)^3 \cdot 6 + 3(1-t)^2 \cdot t \cdot 6 + 3(1-t) \cdot t^2 \cdot 1 + t^3 \cdot 2$.

Fig. 13 shows the graphs of $B(t)$ and $C(t)$ and illustrates how they connect, continuously and smoothly, at the common point $(4, 6)$.

Fig. 13

Using Bezier Curves

In practice, Bezier curves are usually used in computer design or manufacturing programs, and the user of Bezier curves does not have to know the mathematics behind them. But the program creator does!

Typically a designer sketches a crude shape for an object and then moves certain points to locations specified by the plans. Sometimes the designer adds additional points along the curve to "fix" the location of the curve. These "fixed" points along the curve become the endpoints P_0 and P_3 for each of the sections of the curve that will be described by a Bezier formula. Then, for each section of the curve, the designer visually experiments with different locations of the interior control points P_1 and P_2 to get the shape "just right."

Meanwhile, the computer program adjusts the formulas for the Bezier curves based on the current locations of the control points for each section, and, when the design is complete, saves the locations of the control points.

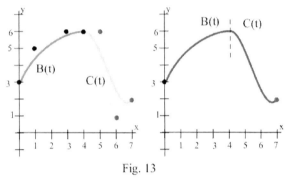

Fig. 14

You may never need to calculate the formulas for Bezier curves (outside of a mathematics class), but if you do any computer–aided design work you will certainly be using these curves. And the ideas and formulas for Bezier curves in two dimensions extend very easily and naturally to describe paths in three dimensions such as the route of a highway exit ramp (Fig. 14) or the path of a hydraulic hose for the landing gear of an airplane.

Mathematical Construction of Bezier Curves & Verifications of Their Properties

In order to use and program Bezier curves we don't need to know where the formulas came from, but their construction is a beautiful piecing–together of simple geometric ideas.

The first idea is the parametric representation of a line segment from point
P_A to P_B as $L(t) = (1-t) \cdot P_A + t \cdot P_B$ for $0 \le t \le 1$.

This parametric pattern for a line is used in the construction of a Bezier curve.

When $t = 0$, the point is $L(0) = P_A$. When $t = 1$, $L(1) = P_B$. When $t = 0.5$, $L(0.5)$ is the midpoint of the line from P_A to P_B (Fig. 15). When $t = 0.2$, $L(0.2)$ is 20% of the way along the line L from P_A to P_B.

Fig. 15

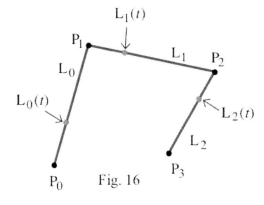

Fig. 16

To construct the Bezier curve for the four control points $P_0, P_1, P_2,$ and P_3 we start by fixing a value of t between 0 and 1. Then we find the point $L_0(t)$ along the parametric line from P_0 to P_1, the point $L_1(t)$ along the parametric line from P_1 to P_2, and the point $L_2(t)$ along the parametric line from P_2 to P_3 (Fig. 16):

$$L_0(t) = (1-t) \cdot P_0 + t \cdot P_1,$$
$$L_1(t) = (1-t) \cdot P_1 + t \cdot P_2,$$
$$L_2(t) = (1-t) \cdot P_2 + t \cdot P_3.$$

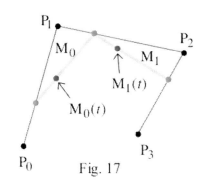

Fig. 17

For the fixed value of t, we then find the point $M_0(t)$ along the parametric line from the point $L_0(t)$ to the point $L_1(t)$, and the point $M_1(t)$ along the parametric line from the point $L_1(t)$ to the point $L_2(t)$ (Fig. 17):

$$M_0(t) = (1-t) \cdot L_0(t) + t \cdot L_1(t)$$
$$M_1(t) = (1-t) \cdot L_1(t) + t \cdot L_2(t).$$

For the same fixed value of t, we finally find the point $B(t)$ along the parametric line from the point $M_0(t)$ to the point $M_1(t)$ (Fig. 18):

$$B(t) = (1-t) \cdot M_0(t) + t \cdot M_1(t).$$

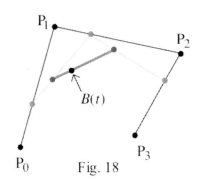

Fig. 18

As the variable t takes on different values between 0 and 1, the points $L_0(t), L_1(t),$ and $L_2(t)$ move along the lines connecting $P_0, P_1, P_2,$ and P_3. Similarly, the points $M_0(t)$ and $M_1(t)$ move along the lines connecting $L_0(t), L_1(t),$ and $L_2(t)$, and the point $B(t)$ moves along the line connecting $M_0(t)$ and $M_1(t)$. It is all quite dynamic.

Fig. 19 shows these points and lines for several values of t between 0 and 1.

We can use the previous geometric construction to obtain the formula for B(t) given in the definition of Bezier curves by working backwards from $B(t) = (1 - t) \cdot M_0(t) + t \cdot M_1(t)$:

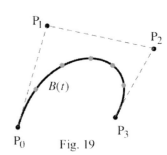

Fig. 19

$$\begin{aligned}
B(t) &= (1-t) \cdot M_0 + t \cdot M_1 \\
&= (1-t) \cdot \{(1-t) \cdot L_0 + t \cdot L_1\} + t \cdot \{(1-t) \cdot L_1 + t \cdot L_2\} \quad \text{replacing } M_0 \text{ and } M_1 \text{ in terms of } L_0, L_1 \text{ and } L_2 \\
&= (1-t)^2 \cdot L_0 + 2(1-t) \cdot t \cdot L_1 + t^2 \cdot L_2 \quad \text{simplifying} \\
&= (1-t)^2 \cdot \{(1-t) \cdot P_0 + t \cdot P_1\} + 2(1-t) \cdot t \cdot \{(1-t) \cdot P_1 + t \cdot P_2\} + t^2 \cdot \{(1-t) \cdot P_2 + t \cdot P_3\} \\
&\quad \text{replacing } L_0, L_1 \text{ and } L_2 \text{ in terms of } P_0, P_1, P_2 \text{ and } P_3 \\
&= (1-t)^3 \cdot P_0 + 3(1-t)^2 \cdot t \cdot P_1 + 3(1-t) \cdot t^2 \cdot P_2 + t^3 \cdot P_3 \quad \text{simplifying}
\end{aligned}$$

Verifications of Properties (1) – (4)

Property (1) is easy to verify by evaluating B(0) and B(1):

$B(0) = (1-0)^3 \cdot P_0 + 3(1-0)^2 \cdot 0 \cdot P_1 + 3(1-0) \cdot t^2 \cdot P_2 + 0^3 \cdot P_3 = P_0$. Similarly,

$B(1) = (1-1)^3 \cdot P_0 + 3(1-1)^2 \cdot 1 \cdot P_1 + 3(1-1) \cdot 1^2 \cdot P_2 + 1^3 \cdot P_3 = P_3$.

Property (2) is clear from the defining formula for B(t), or we can expand the powers of $1 - t$ and t and collect the similar terms to rewrite B(t) as

$B(t) = (-P_0 + 3P_1 - 3P_2 + P_3) \cdot t^3 + (3P_0 - 6P_1 + 3P_2) \cdot t^2 + (-3P_0 + 3P_1) \cdot t + (P_0)$.

Property (3) can be verified using the rewritten form from Property 2,

$x(t) = (-x_0 + 3x_1 - 3x_2 + x_3) \cdot t^3 + (3x_0 - 6x_1 + 3x_2) \cdot t^2 + (-3x_0 + 3x_1) \cdot t + (x_0)$ and

$y(t) = (-y_0 + 3y_1 - 3y_2 + y_3) \cdot t^3 + (3y_0 - 6y_1 + 3y_2) \cdot t^2 + (-3y_0 + 3y_1) \cdot t + (y_0)$.

Then $\dfrac{d\,x(t)}{d\,t} = 3(-x_0 + 3x_1 - 3x_2 + x_3) \cdot t^2 + 2(3x_0 - 6x_1 + 3x_2) \cdot t + (-3x_0 + 3x_1)$ and

$\dfrac{d\,y(t)}{d\,t} = 3(-y_0 + 3y_1 - 3y_2 + y_3) \cdot t^2 + 2(3y_0 - 6y_1 + 3y_2) \cdot t + (-3y_0 + 3y_1)$.

When $t = 0$, $\dfrac{d\,x(t)}{d\,t} = -3x_0 + 3x_1 = -3(x_1 - x_0)$ and $\dfrac{d\,x(t)}{d\,t} = -3(y_1 - y_0)$ so

$\dfrac{d\,B(t)}{d\,t} = \dfrac{d\,y(t)/dt}{d\,x(t)/dt} = \dfrac{-3(y_1 - y_0)}{-3(x_1 - x_0)} = \dfrac{y_1 - y_0}{x_1 - x_0}$ = slope of the line from P_0 to P_1.

The verification that B '(1) equals the slope of the line segment from P_2 to P_3 is similar: evaluate $x'(1), y'(1)$ and $B'(1) = \dfrac{y'(1)}{x'(1)}$.

We will not verify Property (4) here, but it follows from the fact that each point on the Bezier curve is a "weighted average" of the four control points. For $0 \le t \le 1$, each of the coefficients $(1-t)^3$, $3(1-t)^2 \cdot t$, $3(1-t) \cdot t^2$ and t^3 is between (or equal to) 0 and 1, and they always add up to 1 (just expand the powers and add them to check this statement).

Problems

In problems 1 – 6, pairs of points, P_A and P_B, are given. In each problem (a) sketch the line segment L from P_A and P_B, and (b) plot the locations of the points $L(0.2), L(0.5),$ and $L(0.9)$ on the line segment in part (a). Finally, (c) determine the equation of the line segment $L(t)$ from P_A and P_B and graph it.

1. P_A and P_B are given in Fig. 20. 2. P_A and P_B are given in Fig. 21.

3. P_A and P_B are given in Fig. 22. 4. P_A and P_B are given in Fig. 23.

Fig. 20

Fig. 21

Fig. 22

Fig. 23

5. $P_A = (1, 4)$ and $P_B = (5, 1)$. 6. $P_A = (8, 5)$ and $P_B = (4, 3)$.

7. Show that the parametric equations for the line segment given in Example 1,
$$x(t) = (1 - t) \cdot x_0 + t \cdot x_1 \text{ and } y(t) = (1 - t) \cdot y_0 + t \cdot y_1 \text{ for } 0 \le t \le 1,$$
is equivalent to the parametric equations
$$x(t) = x_0 + t \cdot \Delta x \text{ and } y(t) = y_0 + t \cdot \Delta y \text{ for } 0 \le t \le 1 \text{ where } \Delta x = x_1 - x_0 \text{ and } \Delta y = y_1 - y_0.$$

In problems 8 – 13, find the parametric equations for a Bezier curve with the given control points or the given properties.

8. $P_0 = (1, 0), P_1 = (2, 3), P_2 = (5, 2), P_3 = (6, 3)$ 9. $P_0 = (0, 5), P_1 = (2, 3), P_2 = (1, 4), P_3 = (4, 2)$

10. $P_0 = (5, 1), P_1 = (3, 3), P_2 = (3, 5), P_3 = (2, 1)$ 11. $P_0 = (6, 5), P_1 = (6, 3), P_2 = (2, 5), P_3 = (2, 0)$

12. $P_0 = (0, 1), P_3 = (4, 1)$ and $B'(0) = 1, B'(1) = -3$ 13. $P_0 = (5, 1), P_3 = (1, 3)$ and $B'(0) = 2, B'(1) = 3$

In problems 14 – 17, sets of control points P_0, P_1, P_2, and P_3 are shown. Sketch a reasonable Bezier curve for the given control points.

14. P_0, P_1, P_2, and P_3 are given in Fig. 24.

15. P_0, P_1, P_2, and P_3 are given in Fig. 25.

16. P_0, P_1, P_2, and P_3 are given in Fig. 26.

17. P_0, P_1, P_2, and P_3 are given in Fig. 27.

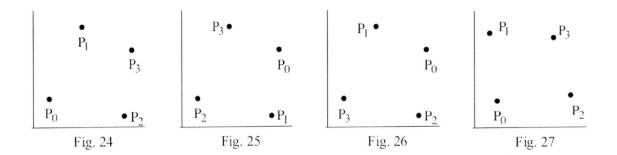

Fig. 24   Fig. 25   Fig. 26   Fig. 27

In problems 18 – 21, sets of control points P_0, P_1, P_2, and P_3 are shown as well as a curve C(t). For each problem explain why we can be certain that C(t) is NOT the Bezier curve for the given control points (state which property or properties of Bezier curves C(t) does not have).

18. P_0, P_1, P_2, and P_3 are given in Fig. 28.

19. P_0, P_1, P_2, and P_3 are given in Fig. 29.

20. P_0, P_1, P_2, and P_3 are given in Fig. 30.

21. P_0, P_1, P_2, and P_3 are given in Fig. 31.

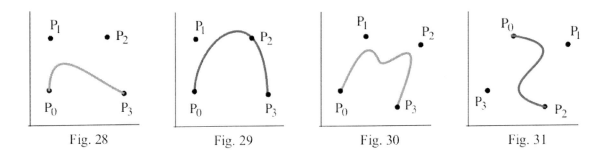

Fig. 28   Fig. 29   Fig. 30   Fig. 31

In problems 22 – 23, find a pair of Bezier curves that satisfy the given conditions.

22. B(0) = (0, 5), B '(0) = 2, B(1) = C(0) = (3, 1), B '(1) = C '(0) = 2, C(1) = (6, 2), and C '(1) = 4.

23. B(0) = (0, 5), B '(0) = 2, B(1) = C(0) = (3, 1), B '(1) = C '(0) = 2, C(1) = (6, 2), and C '(1) = 4

Some Applications of Bezier Curves

The following Applications illustrate just a few of the wide variety of design applications of Bezier curves. This combination of differentiation and algebra is very powerful.

Applications

For each of the following applications, write the equation of a Bezier curve B(t) that satisfies the requirements of the application, and then use your calculator/computer to graph B(t).
(Typically in these applications, the starting and ending points, P_0 and P_3, are specified, but several choices of the control points P_1 and P_2 meet the requirements of the application. Select P_1 and P_2 so the resulting graph of B(t) satisfies the requirements of the application and is also "visually pleasing.")

1. You have been hired to design an escalator for a shopping mall, and the design requirements are that the entrance and exit of the escalator must be horizontal (Fig. 32), the total rise is 20 feet, and the total run is 30 feet.

   (a) Find the equation of a Bezier curve B(t) that meets these design requirements and graph it.
   (Suggestion: Place the origin at the lower left end of the escalator.)

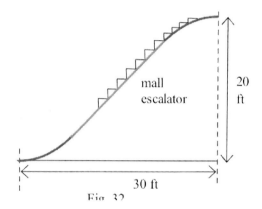
Fig. 32

   (b) In practice, the middle section of an escalator is straight, and each end consists of a curved section (a Bezier curve) that smoothly converts our horizontal motion to motion along the straight section and then to horizontal motion again for our exit. Find the equation of a Bezier curve that models the curve at the entrance to the up escalator (Fig. 33), and the equation of the straight line section.

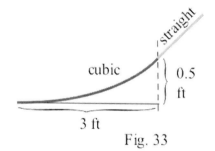
Fig. 33

2. To design the exit ramp on a highway (Fig. 34), you need to find the equation of a Bezier curve so that at the beginning of the exit the elevation is 20 feet with a slope of –0.05 (about 3°), and 600 feet later, measured horizontally, the elevation is 0 feet and the ramp is horizontal.

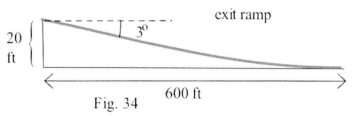
Fig. 34

3. Find a Bezier curve that describes the final 60 feet of the ski jump shown in Fig. 35.

4. Find a Bezier curve that describes the left half of the arch shown in Fig. 36.

5. Find two Bezier curves B(t) and C(t) that describe the pieces of the curve for the top half of the hull of the Concordia Yawl that is 40 feet long, has a beam of 10 feet, and a transom width of 2 feet (Fig. 37).

Fig. 35

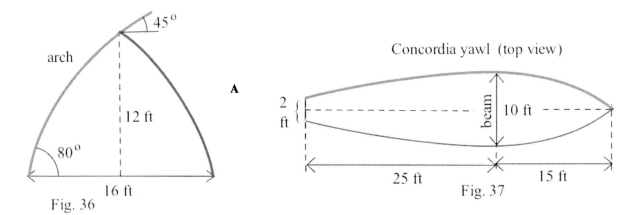

Fig. 36

Fig. 37

Final Note: The examples and applications given here have consisted of only one or two Bezier curves, and they are intended only as an introduction to the ideas and techniques of fitting Bezier curves to particular situations. But these ideas extend very nicely to curves that require pieces of several different Bezier curves for a good fit (Fig. 38) and even to curves and surfaces in three dimensions. Unfortunately, the systems of equations tend to grow very large for these extended applications.

Fig. 38

Practice Answers

Practice 1: (a) $x(t) = (1-t) \cdot x_0 + t \cdot x_1 = (1-t) \cdot 1 + t \cdot 5 = 1 + 4t$,

$y(t) = (1-t) \cdot y_0 + t \cdot y_1 = (1-t) \cdot 2 + t \cdot 4 = 2 + 2t$.

(b) $x(t) = 5 - 4t$, $y(t) = 4 - 2t$

(c) $x(t) = 6 - 3t$, $y(t) = -2 + 3t$

Practice 2: $P_0 = (0,4)$, $P_1 = (1,2)$, $P_2 = (4,2)$, and $P_3 = (4,4)$. Then

$x(t) = (1-t)^3 \cdot 0 + 3(1-t)^2 \cdot t \cdot 1 + 3(1-t) \cdot t^2 \cdot 4 + t^3 \cdot 4 = -5t^3 + 6t^2 + 3t$.

$y(t) = (1-t)^3 \cdot 4 + 3(1-t)^2 \cdot t \cdot 2 + 3(1-t) \cdot t^2 \cdot 2 + t^3 \cdot 4 = 6t^2 - 6t + 4$.

The control points and the graph of $B(t) = (x(t), y(t))$ are shown in Fig. 39.

Practice 3: Take $P_0 = (0,0)$ and $P_3 = (0,1)$ to get the correct endpoints.

Take $P_1 = (-1,-1)$ and $P_2 = (-1,2)$ to get a "C" shape. Then

$x(t) = (1-t)^3 \cdot 0 + 3(1-t)^2 \cdot t \cdot (-1) + 3(1-t) \cdot t^2 \cdot (-1) + t^3 \cdot 0$

$y(t) = (1-t)^3 \cdot 0 + 3(1-t)^2 \cdot t \cdot (-1) + 3(1-t) \cdot t^2 \cdot 2 + t^3 \cdot 1$.

The control points and the graph of $B(t) = (x(t), y(t))$ are shown in Fig. 40.

Practice 4: Take $P_0 = (1,3)$ and $P_3 = (5,3)$ to get the correct endpoints.

Take $P_1 = (2,1)$ and $P_2 = (4,4)$ to get the correct slopes. Then

$x(t) = (1-t)^3 \cdot 1 + 3(1-t)^2 \cdot t \cdot 2 + 3(1-t) \cdot t^2 \cdot 4 + t^3 \cdot 5$

$y(t) = (1-t)^3 \cdot 3 + 3(1-t)^2 \cdot t \cdot 1 + 3(1-t) \cdot t^2 \cdot 4 + t^3 \cdot 3$.

The control points and the graph of
$B(t) = (x(t), y(t))$ are shown in Fig. 41.

Other choices for P_1 and P_2 can also yield correct slopes, and then we

have different formulas for $x(t)$ and $y(t)$

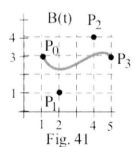

Fig. 41

9.5 CONIC SECTIONS

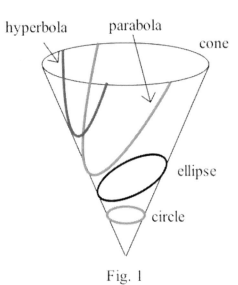

Fig. 1

The conic sections are the curves obtained when a cone is cut by a plane (Fig. 1). They have attracted the interest of mathematicians since the time of Plato, and they are still used by scientists and engineers. The early Greeks were interested in these shapes because of their beauty and their representations by sets of points that met certain distance definitions (e.g., the circle is the set of points at a fixed distance from a given point). Mathematicians and scientists since the 1600s have been interested in the conic sections because the planets, moons, and other celestial objects follow paths that are (approximately) conic sections, and the reflective properties of the conic sections are useful for designing telescopes and other instruments. Finally, the conic sections give the **complete** answer to the question, "what is the shape of the graph of the general quadratic equation $Ax^2 + Bxy + Cy^2 + Dx + Ey + F = 0$?"

This section discusses the "cut cone" and distance definitions of the conic sections and shows their standard equations in rectangular coordinate form. The section ends with a discussion of the discriminant, an easy way to determine the shape of the graph of any standard quadratic equation $Ax^2 + Bxy + Cy^2 + Dx + Ey + F = 0$. Section 9.6 examines the polar coordinate definitions of the conic sections, some of the reflective properties of the conic sections, and some of their applications.

Cutting A Cone

When a (right circular double) cone is cut by a plane, only a few shapes are possible, and these are called the conic sections (Fig. 1). If the plane makes an angle of θ with the horizontal, and $\theta < \alpha$, then the set of points is an ellipse (Fig. 2). When $\theta = 0 < \alpha$, we have a circle, a special case of an ellipse (Fig. 3). If $\theta = \alpha$, a parabola is formed (Fig. 4), and if $\theta > \alpha$, a hyperbola is formed (Fig. 5). When the plane goes through the vertex of the cone, degenerate conics are formed: the degenerate ellipse ($\theta < \alpha$) is a point, the degenerate parabola ($\theta = \alpha$) is a line, and a degenerate hyperbola ($\theta > \alpha$) is a pair of intersecting lines.

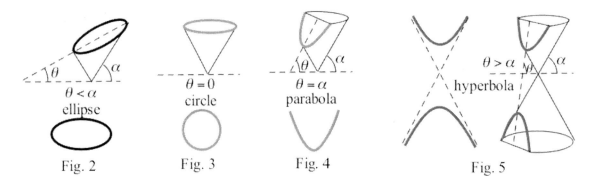

Fig. 2   Fig. 3   Fig. 4   Fig. 5

The conic sections are lovely to look at, but we will not use the conic sections as pieces of a cone because the "cut cone" definition of these shapes does not easily lead to formulas for them. To determine formulas for the conic sections it is easier to use alternate definitions of these shapes in terms of distances of points from fixed points and lines. Then we can use the formula for distance between two points and some algebra to derive formulas for the conic sections.

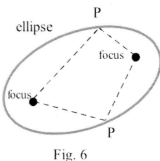

Fig. 6

The Ellipse

Ellipse: An ellipse is the set of all points P for which the **sum** of the distances from P to two fixed points (called foci) **is a constant**: dist(P, one focus) + dist(P, other focus) = constant. (Fig. 6)

Example 1: Find the set of points whose distances from the foci $F_1 = (4,0)$ and $F_2 = (-4, 0)$ add up to 10.

Solution: If the point $P = (x, y)$ is on the ellipse, then the distances $PF_1 = \sqrt{(x-4)^2 + y^2}$ and $PF_2 = \sqrt{(x+4)^2 + y^2}$ must total 10 so we have the equation

$$PF_1 + PF_2 = \sqrt{(x-4)^2 + y^2} + \sqrt{(x+4)^2 + y^2} = 10 \text{ (Fig. 7)}$$

Moving the second radical to the right side of the equation, squaring both sides, and simplifying, we get

$$4x + 25 = 5\sqrt{(x+4)^2 + y^2} \ .$$

Squaring each side again and simplifying, we have $225 = 9x^2 + 25y^2$ so, after dividing each side by 225,

$$\frac{x^2}{25} + \frac{y^2}{9} = 1 \ .$$

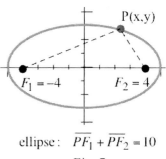

ellipse: $\overline{PF_1} + \overline{PF_2} = 10$

Fig. 7

Practice 1: Find the set of points whose distances from the foci $F_1 = (3,0)$ and $F_2 = (-3, 0)$ add up to 10.

Using the same algebraic steps as in Example 1, it can be shown (see the Appendix at the end of the problems) that the set of points $P = (x,y)$ whose distances from the foci $F_1 = (c,0)$ and $F_2 = (-c, 0)$ add up to 2a (a > c) is described by the formula

$$\frac{x^2}{a^2} + \frac{y^2}{b^2} = 1 \text{ where } b^2 = a^2 - c^2 \ .$$

(a) $a > b$

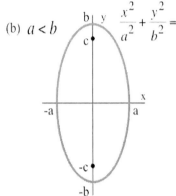

(b) $a < b$

Fig. 8

Ellipse

The standard formula for an ellipse is $\dfrac{x^2}{a^2} + \dfrac{y^2}{b^2} = 1$.

a = b: The ellipse is a circle.

a > b: (Fig. 8a)   The vertices are at ($\pm a, 0$) on the x–axis,
the foci are at ($\pm c, 0$) with $c = \sqrt{a^2 - b^2}$, and
for any point P on the ellipse,
dist(P, one focus) + dist(P, other focus) = 2a.
The length of the semimajor axis is a.

a < b: (Fig. 8b)   The vertices are at ($0, \pm b$) on the y–axis,
the foci are at ($0, \pm c$) with $c = \sqrt{b^2 - a^2}$, and
for any point P on the ellipse,
dist(P, one focus) + dist(P, other focus) = 2b.
The length of the semimajor axis is b.

Practice 2: Use the information in the box to determine the vertices, foci, and length of the semimajor axis of the ellipse $\dfrac{x^2}{169} + \dfrac{y^2}{25} = 1$.

The Parabola

Parabola: A parabola is the set of all points P for which the distance from P to a fixed point (focus) **is equal to** the distance from P to a fixed line (directrix): dist(P, focus) = dist(P, directrix). (Fig. 9)

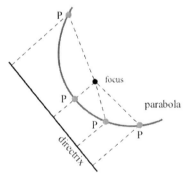

dist(P, focus) = dist(P, directrix)
Fig. 9

Example 2: Find the set of points P = (x,y) whose distance from the focus F = (4,0) equals the distance from the directrix x = –1.

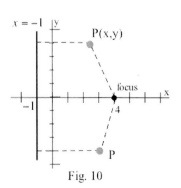

Fig. 10

Solution: The distance $PF = \sqrt{(x-4)^2 + y^2}$, and the distance from P to to the directrix (Fig. 10) is x+1. If these two distances are equal then we have the equation $\sqrt{(x-4)^2 + y^2} = x + 1$.

Squaring each side,
$$(x-4)^2 + y^2 = (x+1)^2$$
so $x^2 - 8x + 16 + y^2 = x^2 + 2x + 1$.

This simplifies to $x = \frac{1}{10} y^2 + \frac{3}{2}$, the equation of a parabola opening to the right (Fig. 11).

Practice 3: Find the set of points $P = (x,y)$ whose distance from the focus $F = (0,2)$ equals the distance from the directrix $y = -2$.

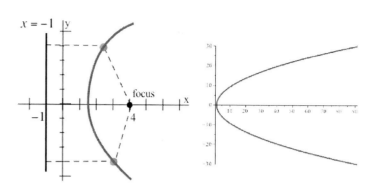

parabola: $x = \frac{3}{2} + \frac{1}{10} y^2$ (two scales)

Fig. 11

(a) $y = ax^2$ $(a > 0)$

(b) $x = ay^2$ $(a > 0)$

Fig. 12

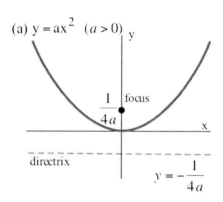

Parabola

The standard parabola $y = ax^2$ opens around the y–axis (Fig. 12a) with vertex = (0,0), focus = $(0, \frac{1}{4a})$, and directrix $y = -\frac{1}{4a}$.

The standard parabola $x = ay^2$ opens around the x–axis (Fig. 12b) with vertex = (0,0), focus = $(\frac{1}{4a}, 0)$, and directrix $x = -\frac{1}{4a}$.

Proof for the case $y = ax^2$:

The set of points $p = (x,y)$ that are equally distant from the focus $F = (0, \frac{1}{4a})$ and the directrix $y = -\frac{1}{4a}$ satisfy the distance equation

PF = PD so

$$\sqrt{x^2 + (y - \frac{1}{4a})^2} = (y + \frac{1}{4a})\ .$$ Squaring each side, we have

$x^2 + (y - \frac{1}{4a})^2 = (y + \frac{1}{4a})^2$ and $x^2 + y^2 - \frac{2}{4a} y + \frac{1}{16a^2} = y^2 + \frac{2}{4a} y + \frac{1}{16a^2}$.

Then $x^2 = \frac{2}{4a} y + \frac{2}{4a} y = \frac{1}{a} y$ and, finally, $y = ax^2$.

Practice 4: Prove that the set of points P=(x,y) that are equally distant from the focus F = ($\frac{1}{4a}$, 0), and directrix $x = -\frac{1}{4a}$ satisfy the equation $x = ay^2$.

Hyperbola

Hyperbola: A hyperbola is the set of all points P for which the **difference** of the distances from P to two fixed points (foci) **is a constant**:

dist(P, one focus) − dist(P, other focus) = constant. (Fig. 13)

Example 3: Find the set of points for which the **difference** of the distances from the points to the foci $F_1 = (5,0)$ and $F_2 = (-5, 0)$ is always 8.

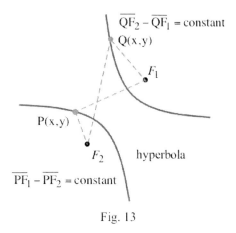

Fig. 13

Solution: If the point P = (x, y) is on the hyperbola, then the difference of the distances $PF_1 = \sqrt{(x-5)^2 + y^2}$ and $PF_2 = \sqrt{(x+5)^2 + y^2}$ is 8 so we have the equation

$$PF_1 - PF_2 = \sqrt{(x-5)^2 + y^2} - \sqrt{(x+5)^2 + y^2} = 8 \quad \text{(Fig. 14)}.$$

Moving the second radical to the right side of the equation, squaring both sides, and simplifying, we get

$$5x + 16 = -4\sqrt{(x+5)^2 + y^2}.$$

Squaring each side again and simplifying, we have $9x^2 - 16y^2 = 144$.

After dividing each side by 144, $\frac{x^2}{16} - \frac{y^2}{9} = 1$.

If we start with the difference $PF_2 - PF_1 = 8$, we have the equation

$$\sqrt{(x+5)^2 + y^2} - \sqrt{(x-5)^2 + y^2} = 8.$$

Solving this equation, we again get $9x^2 - 16y^2 = 144$ and

$$\frac{x^2}{16} - \frac{y^2}{9} = 1.$$

Fig. 14

Using the same algebraic steps as in the Example 3, it can be shown (see the Appendix at the end of the problems) that the set of points P = (x,y) whose distances from the foci $F_1 = (c,0)$ and $F_2 = (-c, 0)$ differ by 2a (a < c) is described by the formula

$$\frac{x^2}{a^2} - \frac{y^2}{b^2} = 1 \quad \text{where} \quad b^2 = c^2 - a^2.$$

(a) hyperbola $\frac{x^2}{a^2} - \frac{y^2}{b^2} = 1$

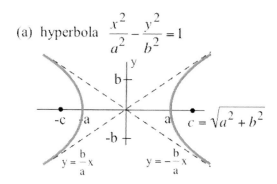

(b) hyperbola $\frac{y^2}{b^2} - \frac{x^2}{a^2} = 1$

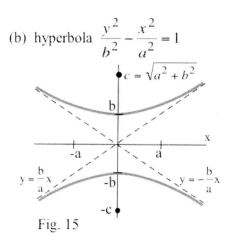

Fig. 15

Hyperbola

The standard hyperbola $\frac{x^2}{a^2} - \frac{y^2}{b^2} = 1$

opens around the x–axis (Fig. 15a)

with vertices at ($\pm a, 0$), foci at ($\pm\sqrt{a^2 + b^2}$, 0),

and linear asymptotes $y = \pm \frac{b}{a} x$.

The standard hyperbola $\frac{y^2}{b^2} - \frac{x^2}{a^2} = 1$

opens around the y–axis (Fig. 15b)

with vertices at ($0, \pm b$), foci at ($0, \pm\sqrt{a^2 + b^2}$),

and linear asymptotes $y = \pm \frac{b}{a} x$.

Practice 5: Graph the hyperbolas $\frac{x^2}{25} - \frac{y^2}{16} = 1$ and $\frac{y^2}{25} - \frac{x^2}{16} = 1$ and find the linear asymptotes for each hyperbola.

Visually distinguishing the conic sections

If you only observe a small part of the graph of a conic section, it may be impossible to determine which conic section it is, and you may need to look at more of its graph. Near a vertex or in small pieces, all of the conic sections can be quite similar in appearance, but on a larger graph the ellipse is easy to distinguish from the other two. On a large graph, the hyperbola and parabola can be distinguished by noting that the hyperbola has two linear asymptotes and the parabola has no linear asymptotes.

The General Quadratic Equation and the Discriminant

Every equation that is quadratic in the variables x or y or both can be written in the form

$$Ax^2 + Bxy + Cy^2 + Dx + Ey + F = 0 \text{ where A through F are constants.}$$

The form $Ax^2 + Bxy + Cy^2 + Dx + Ey + F = 0$ is called the **general quadratic equation**.

In particular, each of the conic sections can be written in the form of a general quadratic equation by clearing all fractions and collecting all of the terms on one side of the equation. What is perhaps surprising is that the graph of a general quadratic equation is always a conic section or a degenerate form of a conic section. Usually the graph of a general quadratic equation is not centered at the origin and is not symmetric about either axis, but the shape is always an ellipse, parabola, hyperbola, or degenerate form of one of these.

Even more surprising, a quick and easy calculation using just the coefficients A, B, and C of the general quadratic equation tells us the shape of its graph: ellipse, parabola, or hyperbola. The value obtained by this simple calculation is called the discriminant of the general quadratic equation.

Discriminant

The **discriminant** of the the general quadratic form $Ax^2 + Bxy + Cy^2 + Dx + Ey + F = 0$

is the value $\mathbf{B^2 - 4AC}$.

Example 4: Write each of the following in its general quadratic form and calculate its discriminant.

(a) $\dfrac{x^2}{25} + \dfrac{y^2}{9} = 1$ (b) $3y + 7 = 2x^2 + 5x + 1$ (c) $5x^2 + 3 = 7y^2 - 2xy + 4y + 8$

Solution: (a) $9x^2 + 25y^2 - 225 = 0$ so $A = 9, C = 25, F = -225$, and $B = D = E = 0$. $B^2 - 4AC = -900$.

(b) $2x^2 + 5x - 3y - 6 = 0$ so $A = 2, D = 5, E = -3, F = -6$, and $B = C = 0$. $B^2 - 4AC = 0$.

(c) $5x^2 + 2xy - 7y^2 - 4y - 5 = 0$ so $A = 5, B = 2, C = -7, D = 0, E = -4$ and $F = -5$.
$B^2 - 4AC = 4 - 4(5)(-7) = 144$.

Practice 6: Write each of the following in its general quadratic form and calculate its discriminant.

(a) $1 = \dfrac{x^2}{36} - \dfrac{y^2}{9}$ (b) $x = 3y^2 - 5$ (c) $\dfrac{x^2}{16} + \dfrac{(y-2)^2}{25} = 1$

One very important property of the discriminant is that it is invariant under translations and rotations, its value does not change even if the graph is rigidly translated around the plane and rotated. When a graph is shifted or rotated or both, its general quadratic equation changes, but the discriminant of the new quadratic equation is the same value as the discriminant of the original quadratic equation. And we can determine the shape of the graph simply from the sign of the discriminant.

Quadratic Shape Theorem

The graph of the general quadratic equation $Ax^2 + Bxy + Cy^2 + Dx + Ey + F = 0$ is

an ellipse if	$B^2 - 4AC < 0$	(degenerate forms: one point or no points)
a parabola if	$B^2 - 4AC = 0$	(degenerate forms: two lines, one line, or no points)
a hyperbola if	$B^2 - 4AC > 0$	(degenerate form: pair of intersecting lines).

The proofs of this result and of the invariance of the discriminant under translations and rotations are "elementary" and just require a knowledge of algebra and trigonometry, but they are rather long and are very computational. A proof of the invariance of the discriminant under translations and rotations and of the Quadratic Shape Theorem is given in the Appendix after the problem set.

Example 5: Use the discriminant to determine the shapes of the graphs of the following equations.

(a) $x^2 + 3xy + 3y^2 = -7y - 4$ (b) $4x^2 + 4xy + y^2 = 3x - 1$ (c) $y^2 - 4x^2 = 0$.

Solution: (a) $B^2 - 4AC = 3^2 - 4(1)(3) = -3 < 0$. The graph is an ellipse.

(b) $B^2 - 4AC = 4^2 - 4(4)(1) = 0$. The graph is a parabola.

(c) $B^2 - 4AC = 0^2 - 4(-4)(1) = 16 > 0$. The graph is a hyperbola — actually a degenerate hyperbola. The graph of $0 = y^2 - 4x^2 = (y + 2x)(y - 2x)$ consists of the two lines $y = -2x$ and $y = 2x$.

Practice 7: Use the discriminant to determine the shapes of the graphs of the following equations.

(a) $x^2 + 2xy = 2y^2 + 4x + 3$ (b) $y^2 + 2x^2 = xy - 3y + 7$ (c) $2x^2 - 4xy = 3 + 5y - 2y^2$.

Sketching Standard Ellipses and Hyperbolas

The graphs of general ellipses and hyperbolas require plotting lots of points (a computer or calculator can help), but it is easy to sketch good graphs of the standard ellipses and hyperbolas. The steps for doing so are given below.

Graphing the Standard Ellipse $\dfrac{x^2}{a^2} + \dfrac{y^2}{b^2} = 1$

1. Sketch short vertical line segments at the points $(\pm a, 0)$ on the x–axis and short horizontal line segments at the points $(0, \pm b)$ on the y–axis (Fig. 16a). Draw a rectangle whose sides are formed by extending the line segments.

2. Use the tangent line segments in step 1 as guide to sketching the ellipse (Fig. 16b). The graph of the ellipse is always inside the rectangle except at the 4 points that touch it.

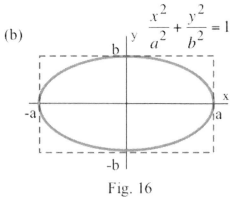

Fig. 16

Graphing the Standard Hyperbolas $\dfrac{x^2}{a^2} - \dfrac{y^2}{b^2} = 1$ and $\dfrac{y^2}{b^2} - \dfrac{x^2}{a^2} = 1$

1. Sketch the rectangle that intersects the x–axis at the points $(\pm a, 0)$ and the y–axis at the points $(0, \pm b)$. (Fig. 17a)

2. Draw the lines which go through the origin and the corners of the rectangle from step 1. (Fig. 17b) These lines are the asymptotes of the hyperbola.

3. For $\dfrac{x^2}{a^2} - \dfrac{y^2}{b^2} = 1$, plot the points $(\pm a, 0)$ on the hyperbola, and use the asymptotes from step 2 as a guide to sketching the rest of the hyperbola. (Fig. 17c)

3'. For $\dfrac{y^2}{b^2} - \dfrac{x^2}{a^2} = 1$, plot the points $(0, \pm b)$ on the hyperbola, and use the asymptotes from step 2 as a guide to sketching the rest of the hyperbola. (Fig. 17d)

The graph of the hyperbola is always outside the rectangle except at the 2 points which touch it.

(a)

(b)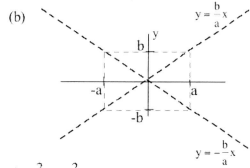

(c) $\dfrac{x^2}{a^2} - \dfrac{y^2}{b^2} = 1$

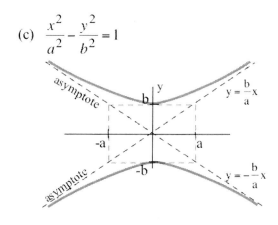

(d) $\dfrac{y^2}{b^2} - \dfrac{x^2}{a^2} = 1$

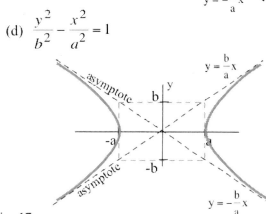

Fig. 17

Symmetry of the Conic Sections

Symmetry properties of the conic sections can simplify the task of graphing them. A parabola has one line of symmetry, so once we have graphed half of a parabola we can get the other half by folding along the line of symmetry. An ellipse and a hyperbola each have two lines of symmetry, so once we have graphed one fourth of an ellipse or hyperbola we can get the rest of the graph by folding along each line of symmetry.

Fig. 18

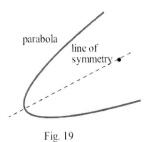

Fig. 19

- The parabola is symmetric about the line through the focus and the vertex (Fig. 18).
- The ellipse is symmetric about the line through the two foci. It is also symmetric about the perpendicular bisector of the line segment through the two foci (Fig. 19).
- The hyperbola is symmetric about the line through the two foci and about the perpendicular bisector of the line segment through the two foci (Fig. 20).

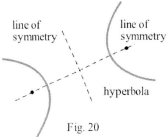

Fig. 20

The Conic Sections as "Shadows of Spheres"

There are a lot of different shapes at the beach on a sunny day, even conic sections. Suppose we have a sphere resting on a flat surface and a point radiating light.

- If the point of light is higher than the top of the sphere, then the shadow of the sphere is an ellipse (Fig. 21).
- If the point of light is exactly the same height as the top of the sphere, then the shadow of the sphere is a parabola (Fig. 22).
- If the point of light is lower than the top of the sphere, then the shadow of the sphere is one branch of a hyperbola (Fig. 23).

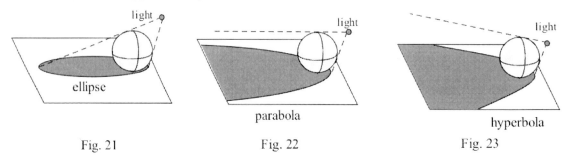

Fig. 21   Fig. 22   Fig. 23

PROBLEMS

1. What is the shape of the graph of the set of points whose distances from (6,0) and (−6,0) always add up to 20? Find an equation for the graph.

2. What is the shape of the graph of the set of points whose distances from (2,0) and (−2,0) always add up to 20? Find an equation for the graph.

3. What is the shape of the graph of the set of points whose distance from the point (0,5) is equal to the distance from the point to the line $y = -5$? Find an equation for the graph.

4. What is the shape of the graph of the set of points whose distance from the point (2,0) is equal to the distance from the point to the line $x = -4$? Find an equation for the graph.

5. Give the standard equation for the ellipse in Fig. 24.

6. Give the standard equation for the ellipse in Fig. 25.

Fig. 24

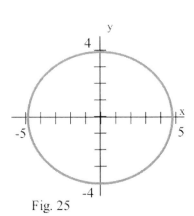

Fig. 25

7. What lines are linear asymptotes for the hyperbola $4x^2 - 9y^2 = 36$, and where are the foci?

8. What lines are linear asymptotes for the hyperbola $25x^2 - 4y^2 = 100$, and where are the foci?

9. What lines are linear asymptotes for the hyperbola $5y^2 - 3x^2 = 15$, and where are the foci?

10. What lines are linear asymptotes for the hyperbola $5y^2 - 3x^2 = 120$, and where are the foci?

In problems 11–16, rewrite each equation in the form of the general quadratic equation $Ax^2 + Bxy + Cy^2 + Dx + Ey + F = 0$ and then calculate the value of the discriminant. What is the shape of each graph?

11. (a) $\frac{x^2}{4} + \frac{y^2}{25} = 1$ (b) $\frac{x^2}{a^2} + \frac{y^2}{b^2} = 1$ 12. (a) $\frac{x^2}{4} - \frac{y^2}{25} = 1$ (b) $\frac{x^2}{a^2} - \frac{y^2}{b^2} = 1$

13. $x + 2y = 1 + \frac{3}{x-y}$

14. $y = \frac{5 + 2y - x^2}{4x + 5y}$

15. $x = \frac{7x - 3 - 2y^2}{2x + 4y}$

16. $x = \frac{2y^2 + 7x - 3}{2x + 5y}$

Problems 17–20 illustrate that a small change in the value of just **one** coefficient in the quadratic equation $Ax^2 + Bxy + Cy^2 + Dx + Ey + F = 0$ can have a dramatic effect on the shape of the graph. Determine the shape of the graph for each formula.

17. (a) $2x^2 + 3xy + 2y^2 +$ (*terms for x, y, and a constant*) = 0.
    (b) $2x^2 + 4xy + 2y^2 +$ (*terms for x, y, and a constant*) = 0.
    (c) $2x^2 + 5xy + 2y^2 +$ (*terms for x, y, and a constant*) = 0.
    (d) What are the shapes if the coefficients of the xy term are 3.99, 4, and 4.01?

18. (a) $1x^2 + 4xy + 2y^2 +$ (*terms for x, y, and a constant*) = 0.
    (b) $2x^2 + 4xy + 2y^2 +$ (*terms for x, y, and a constant*) = 0.
    (c) $3x^2 + 4xy + 2y^2 +$ (*terms for x, y, and a constant*) = 0.
    (d) What are the shapes if the coefficients of the x^2 term are 1.99, 2, and 2.01?

19. (a) $x^2 + 4xy + 3y^2 +$ (*terms for x, y, and a constant*) = 0.
    (b) $x^2 + 4xy + 4y^2 +$ (*terms for x, y, and a constant*) = 0.
    (c) $x^2 + 4xy + 5y^2 +$ (*terms for x, y, and a constant*) = 0.
    (d) What are the shapes if the coefficients of the y^2 term are 3.99, 4, and 4.01?

20. Just changing a single sign can also dramatically change the shape of the graph.

    (a) $x^2 + 2xy + y^2 + $ (*terms for x, y, and a constant*) $= 0$.

    (b) $x^2 + 2xy - y^2 + $ (*terms for x, y, and a constant*) $= 0$.

21. Find the volume obtained when the region enclosed by the ellipse $\dfrac{x^2}{2^2} + \dfrac{y^2}{5^2} = 1$ is rotated

    (a) about the x–axis, and (b) about the y–axis.

22. Find the volume obtained when the region enclosed by the ellipse $\dfrac{x^2}{a^2} + \dfrac{y^2}{b^2} = 1$ is rotated

    (a) about the x–axis, and (b) about the y–axis.

23. Find the volume obtained when the region enclosed by the hyperbola $\dfrac{x^2}{2^2} - \dfrac{y^2}{5^2} = 1$ and the vertical

    line $x = 10$ is rotated (a) about the x–axis, and (b) about the y–axis.

24. Find the volume obtained when the region enclosed by the
    hyperbola $\dfrac{x^2}{a^2} - \dfrac{y^2}{b^2} = 1$ and the vertical line $x = L$

    (Fig. 26) is rotated (a) about the x–axis, and (b) about
    the y–axis. (Assume $a < L$.)

25. Find the ratio of the area of the shaded parabolic region in
    Fig. 27 to the area of the rectangular region.

26. Find the ratio of the volumes obtained when the parabolic
    and rectangular regions in Fig. 27 are rotated about the y–
    axis.

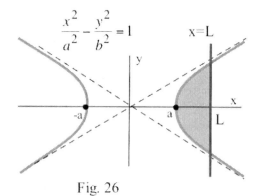

Fig. 26

Fig. 27

String Constructions of Ellipses, Parabolas, and Hyperbolas   (Optional)

All of the conic sections can be drawn with the help of some pins and string, and the directions and figures show how it can be done. For each conic section, you are asked to determine and describe why each construction produces the desired shape.

Ellipse: Pin the two ends of the string to a board so the string is not taut. Put the point of a pencil in the bend in the string (Fig. 28), and, keeping the string taut, draw a curve.

27. How is the distance between the vertices of the ellipse related to the length of the string?

28. Explain why this method produces an ellipse, a set of points whose distances from the two fixed points (foci) always sum to a constant. What is the constant?

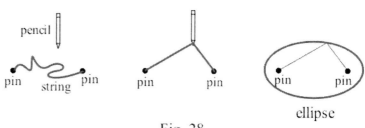

Fig. 28

29. What happens to the shape of the ellipse as the two foci are moved closer together (and the piece of string stays the same length)? Draw several ellipses using the same piece of string and different fixed points, and describe the results.

Parabola: Pin one end of the string to a board and the other end to the corner of a T–square bar that is the same length as the string. Put the point of a pencil in the bend in the string (Fig. 29) and keep the string taut. As the T–square is slid sideways, the pencil draws a curve.

30. Explain why this method produces a parabola, a set of points whose distance from a fixed point (one end of the string) is equal to the distance from a fixed line (the edge of the table).

31. What happens if the length of the string is slightly shorter than the length of the T–square bar? Draw several curves with several slightly shorter pieces of string and describe the results. What shapes are the curves?

32. Find a way to use pins, string and a pencil to sketch the graph of a hyperbola.

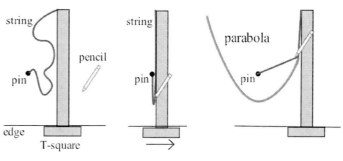

Fig. 29

Section 9.5 PRACTICE Answers

Practice 1: $F_1 = (3,0)$, $F_2 = (-3,0)$, and $P = (x,y)$. We want $\text{dist}(F_1, P) + \text{dist}(F_2, P) = 10$ so

$$\text{dist}((x,y),(3,0)) + \text{dist}((x,y),(-3,0)) = 10 \text{ and}$$

$$\sqrt{(x-3)^2 + y^2} + \sqrt{(x+3)^2 + y^2} = 10.$$

Moving the second radical to the right side and squaring, we get

$$(x-3)^2 + y^2 = 100 - 20\sqrt{(x+3)^2 + y^2} + (x+3)^2 + y^2 \text{ and}$$

$$x^2 - 6x + 9 + y^2 = 100 - 20\sqrt{(x+3)^2 + y^2} + x^2 + 6x + 9 + y^2 \text{ so}$$

$$-12x - 100 = -20\sqrt{(x+3)^2 + y^2}.$$

Dividing each side by -2 and then squaring, we have

$$36x^2 + 600x + 2500 = 100(x^2 + 6x + 9 + y^2) \text{ so}$$

$$1600 = 64x^2 + 100y^2 \text{ and}$$

$$1 = \frac{64x^2}{1600} + \frac{100y^2}{1600} = \frac{x^2}{25} + \frac{y^2}{16}.$$

Practice 2: $a = 13$ and $b = 5$ so the vertices of the ellipse are $(13, 0)$ and $(-13, 0)$. The value of c is $\sqrt{169 - 25} = 12$ so the foci are $(12, 0)$ and $(-12, 0)$. The length of the semimajor axis is 13.

Practice 3: $\text{dist}(P, \text{focus}) = \text{dist}(P, \text{directrix})$ so $\text{dist}((x,y),(0,2)) = \text{dist}((x,y), \text{line } y=-2)$:

$$\sqrt{(x-0)^2 + (y-2)^2} = y + 2.$$

Squaring, we get $x^2 + y^2 - 4y + 4 = y^2 + 4y + 4$ so $x^2 = 8y$ or $y = \frac{1}{8}x^2$.

Practice 4: This is similar to Practice 3: $\text{dist}(P, \text{focus}) = \text{dist}(P, \text{directrix})$ so

$$\text{dist}((x,y),(\tfrac{1}{4a}, 0)) = \text{dist}((x,y), \text{line } x = -\tfrac{1}{4a}). \text{ Then}$$

$$\sqrt{(x - \tfrac{1}{4a})^2 + (y - 0)^2} = x + \frac{1}{4a}. \text{ Squaring each side we get}$$

$$x^2 - 2x\frac{1}{4a} + \frac{1}{16a^2} + y^2 = x^2 + 2x\frac{1}{4a} + \frac{1}{16a^2} \text{ so } y^2 = \frac{1}{a}x \text{ and } x = ay^2.$$

Practice 5: The graphs are shown in Fig. 30. Both hyperbolas have the same linear asymptotes: $y = \frac{4}{5} x$ and $y = -\frac{4}{5} x$.

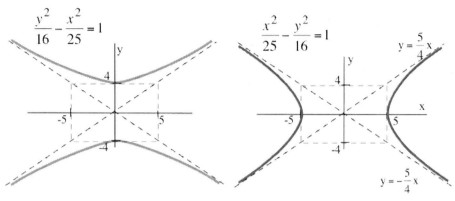

Fig. 30

Practice 6: (a) $324 = 9x^2 - 36y^2$ so $9x^2 - 36y^2 - 324 = 0$.

$A = 9, B = 0$, and $C = -36$ so $D = 0 - 4(9)(-36) = $ **576**.

(b) $0x^2 + 0xy + 3y^2 - x - 5 = 0$.

$A = 0, B = 0$, and $C = 3$ so $D = 0 - 4(0)(3) = $ **0**.

(c) $25x^2 + 16(y-2)^2 = 400$ so $25x^2 + 16y^2 - 64y + 48 - 400 = 0$.

$A = 25, B = 0$, and $C = 16$ so $D = 0 - 4(25)(16) = $ **–1600**.

Practice 7: (a) $x^2 + 2xy - 2y^2 - 4x - 3 = 0$.

$A = 1, B = 2, C = -2$ so $D = 4 - 4(1)(-2) = 12 > 0$: hyperbola.

(b) $2x^2 - 1xy + 1y^2 + 3y - 7 = 0$.

$A = 2, B = -1, C = 1$ so $D = 1 - 4(2)(1) = -7 < 0$: ellipse.

(c) $2x^2 - 4xy + 2y^2 - 5y - 3 = 0$.

$A = 2, B = -4$, and $C = 2$ so $D = 16 - 4(2)(2) = 0$: parabola.

Appendix for 9.5: Conic Sections

Deriving the Standard Forms from Distance Definitions of the Conic Sections

Ellipse

> Ellipse An ellipse is the set of all points P so the **sum** of the distances of P from two fixed points (called foci) **is a constant**.

If F_1 and F_2 are the foci (Fig. 40), then for every point P on the ellipse, the distance from P to F_1 PLUS the distance from P to F_2 is a constant: $PF_1 + PF_2 = $ constant. If the center of the ellipse is at the origin and the foci lie on the x–axis at $F_1 = (c, 0)$ and $F_2 = (-c, 0)$, we can translate the words into a formula:

$$PF_1 + PF_2 = \text{constant} \quad \text{becomes} \quad \sqrt{(x-c)^2 + y^2} + \sqrt{(x+c)^2 + y^2} = 2a.$$

(Calling the constant 2a simply makes some of the later algebra easier.)

By moving the second radical to the right side of the equation, squaring each side, and simplifying, we get

$$\sqrt{(x-c)^2 + y^2} = 2a - \sqrt{(x+c)^2 + y^2}$$

$$(x-c)^2 + y^2 = 4a^2 - 4a\sqrt{(x+c)^2 + y^2} + (x+c)^2 + y^2$$

$$\text{so} \quad x^2 - 2xc + c^2 + y^2 = 4a^2 - 4a\sqrt{(x+c)^2 + y^2} + x^2 + 2xc + c^2 + y^2$$

$$\text{and} \quad xc + a^2 = a\sqrt{(x+c)^2 + y^2}.$$

Squaring each side again and simplifying, we get

$$(xc + a^2)^2 = a^2\{(x+c)^2 + y^2\} \quad \text{so} \quad x^2c^2 + 2xca^2 + a^4 = a^2x^2 + 2xca^2 + a^2c^2 + a^2y^2$$

$$\text{and} \quad a^2(a^2 - c^2) = x^2(a^2 - c^2) + y^2 a^2.$$

Finally, dividing each side by $a^2(a^2 - c^2)$, we get $\dfrac{x^2}{a^2} + \dfrac{y^2}{a^2 - c^2} = 1$.

By setting $b^2 = a^2 - c^2$, we have $\dfrac{x^2}{a^2} + \dfrac{y^2}{b^2} = 1$, the standard form of the ellipse.

Hyperbola

Hyperbola: A hyperbola is the set of all points P so the **difference** of the distances of P from the two fixed points (foci) **is a constant**.

If F_1 and F_2 are the foci (Fig. 9), then for every point P on the hyperbola, the distance from P to F_1 MINUS the distance from P to F_2 is a constant: $PF_1 - PF_2 =$ constant (Fig. 42). If the center of the hyperbola is at the origin and the foci lie on the x–axis at $F_1 = (c, 0)$ and $F_2 = (-c, 0)$, we can translate the words into a formula:

$$PF_1 - PF_2 = \text{constant} \quad \text{becomes} \quad \sqrt{(x-c)^2 + y^2} - \sqrt{(x+c)^2 + y^2} = 2a.$$

(Calling the constant 2a simply makes some of the later algebra easier.)

The algebra which follows is very similar to that used for the ellipse.

Moving the second radical to the right side of the equation, squaring each side, and simplifying, we get

$$\sqrt{(x-c)^2 + y^2} = 2a + \sqrt{(x+c)^2 + y^2}$$

$$(x-c)^2 + y^2 = 4a^2 + 4a\sqrt{(x+c)^2 + y^2} + (x+c)^2 + y^2$$

$$\text{so} \quad x^2 - 2xc + c^2 + y^2 = 4a^2 + 4a\sqrt{(x+c)^2 + y^2} + x^2 + 2xc + c^2 + y^2$$

$$\text{and} \quad xc + a^2 = -a\sqrt{(x+c)^2 + y^2} \; .$$

Squaring each side again and simplifying, we get

$$(xc + a^2)^2 = a^2 \{ (x+c)^2 + y^2 \} \quad \text{so} \quad x^2c^2 + 2xca^2 + a^4 = a^2x^2 + 2xca^2 + a^2c^2 + a^2y^2$$

$$\text{and} \quad x^2(c^2 - a^2) - y^2a^2 = a^2(c^2 - a^2) \; .$$

Finally, dividing each side by $a^2(c^2 - a^2)$, we get $\dfrac{x^2}{a^2} + \dfrac{y^2}{c^2 - a^2} = 1$.

By setting $b^2 = c^2 - a^2$, we have $\dfrac{x^2}{a^2} - \dfrac{y^2}{b^2} = 1$, the standard form of the hyperbola.

Invariance Properties of the Discriminant

The **discriminant** of $Ax^2 + Bxy + Cy^2 + Dx + Ey + F = 0$ is $d = \mathbf{B^2 - 4AC}$.

The Discriminant $B^2 - 4AC$ is invariant under translations (shifts):

If a point (x, y) is shifted h units up and k units to the right, then the coordinates of the new point are $(x', y') = (x+h, y+k)$. To show that the discriminant of $Ax^2 + Bxy + Cy^2 + Dx + Ey + F = 0$ is invariant under translations, we need to show that the discriminant of $Ax^2 + Bxy + Cy^2 + Dx + Ey + F = 0$ and the discriminant of $A(x')^2 + B(x')(y') + C(y')^2 + Dx' + Ey' + F = 0$ are equal for $x' = x + h$ and $y' = y + k$.

The discriminant of $Ax^2 + Bxy + Cy^2 + Dx + Ey + F = 0$ is equal to $B^2 - 4AC$.
Replacing x' with $x+h$ and y' with $y+k$,

$$A(x')^2 + B(x')(y') + C(y')^2 + Dx' + Ey' + F$$
$$= A(x+h)^2 + B(x+h)(y+k) + C(y+k)^2 + D(x+h) + E(y+k) + F$$
$$= A(x^2 + 2xh + h^2) + B(xy + xk + yh + hk) + C(y^2 + 2yk + k^2) + D(x+h) + E(y+k) + F$$
$$= Ax^2 + Bxy + Cy^2 + (2Ah + Bk + D)x + (Bh + 2Ck + E)y + (Ah^2 + Bhk + Ck^2 + Dh + Ek + F).$$

The discriminant of this final formula is $B^2 - 4AC$, the same as the discriminant of $Ax^2 + Bxy + Cy^2 + Dx + Ey + F$. In fact, a translation does not change the values of the coefficients of x^2, xy, and y^2 (the values of A, B, and C) so the discriminant is unchanged.

The Discriminant $B^2 - 4AC$ is invariant under rotation by an angle θ:

If a point (x, y) is rotated about the origin by an angle of θ, then the coordinates of the new point are $(x', y') = (x \cdot \cos(\theta) - y \cdot \sin(\theta), x \cdot \sin(\theta) + y \cdot \cos(\theta))$. To show that the discriminant of $Ax^2 + Bxy + Cy^2 + Dx + Ey + F = 0$ is invariant under rotations, we need to show that the discriminant of $Ax^2 + Bxy + Cy^2 + Dx + Ey + F = 0$ and the discriminant of $A(x')^2 + B(x')(y') + C(y')^2 + Dx' + Ey' + F = 0$ are equal when $x' = x \cdot \cos(\theta) - y \cdot \sin(\theta)$ and $y' = x \cdot \sin(\theta) + y \cdot \cos(\theta)$.

The discriminant of $Ax^2 + Bxy + Cy^2 + Dx + Ey + F = 0$ is equal to $B^2 - 4AC$.
Replacing x' with $x \cdot \cos(\theta) - y \cdot \sin(\theta) = xc - ys$ and y' with $x \cdot \sin(\theta) + y \cdot \cos(\theta) = xs + yc$

$$A(x')^2 + B(x')(y') + C(y')^2 + Dx' + Ey' + F = 0$$
$$= A(xc - ys)^2 + B(xc - ys)(xs + yc) + C(xs + yc)^2 + \ldots \text{(terms without } x^2, xy, \text{ and } y^2)$$
$$= A(x^2c^2 - 2xysc + y^2s^2) + B(x^2sc - xys^2 + xyc^2 - y^2sc) + C(x^2s^2 + 2xysc + y^2c^2) + \ldots$$
$$= (Ac^2 + Bsc + Cs^2)x^2 + (-2Asc - Bs^2 + Bc^2 + 2Csc)xy + (As^2 + Bsc + Cc^2)y^2 + \ldots$$

Then $A' = Ac^2 + Bsc + Cs^2$, $B' = -2Asc - Bs^2 + Bc^2 + 2Csc$, and $C' = As^2 + Bsc + Cc^2$, so the new discriminant is

9.5 Conic Sections

$$(B')^2 - 4(A')(C')$$
$$= (-2Asc - Bs^2 + Bc^2 + 2Csc)^2 - 4(Ac^2 + Bsc + Cs^2)(As^2 + Bsc + Cc^2)$$
$$= \{ s^4(B^2) + s^3c(4AB - 4BC) + s^2c^2(4A^2 - 8AC - 2B^2 + 4C^2) + sc^3(-4AB + 4BC) + c^4(B^2) \}$$
$$\quad - 4\{ s^4(AC) + s^3c(AB - BC) + s^2c^2(A^2 - B^2 + C^2) + sc^3(-AB + BC) + c^4(AC) \}$$
$$= s^4(B^2 - 4AC) + s^2c^2(2B^2 - 8AC) + c^4(B^2 - 4AC)$$
$$= (B^2 - 4AC)(s^4 + 2s^2c^2 + c^4) = (B^2 - 4AC)(s^2 + c^2)(s^2 + c^2) = (B^2 - 4AC) \text{, the original discriminant.}$$

The invariance of the discriminant under translation and rotation shows that any conic section can be translated so its "center" is at the origin and rotated so its axis is the x–axis without changing the value of the discriminant: the value of the discriminant depends strictly on the shape of the curve, not on its location or orientation. When the axis of the conic section is the x–axis, the standard quadratic equation $Ax^2 + Bxy + Cy^2 + Dx + Ey + F = 0$
does not have an xy term (B=0) so we only need to investigate the reduced form
$Ax^2 + Cy^2 + Dx + Ey + F = 0$.

1) $A = C = 0$ (discriminant d=0). A straight line. (special case: no graph)

2) $A = C \neq 0$ (d<0).   A circle. (special cases: a point or no graph)

3) $A = 0, C \neq 0$ or $A \neq 0, C = 0$ (d=0):   A parabola. (special cases: 2 lines, 1 line, or no graph)

4) A and C both positive or both negative (d<0):   An Ellipse. (special cases: a point or no graph)

5) A and C have opposite signs (d>0):   A Hyperbola.   (special case: a pair of intersecting lines)

9.6 PROPERTIES OF THE CONIC SECTIONS

This section presents some of the interesting and important properties of the conic sections that can be proven using calculus. It begins with their reflection properties and considers a few ways these properties are used today. Then we derive the polar coordinate form of the conic sections and use that form to examine one of the reasons conic sections are still extensively used: the paths of planets, satellites, comets, baseballs, and even subatomic particles are often conic sections. The section ends with a specialized examination of elliptical orbits. To understand and describe the motions of the universe, at telescopic and microscopic levels, we need conic sections!

Reflections on the Conic Sections

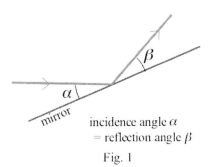

incidence angle α
= reflection angle β
Fig. 1

This discussion of reflection assumes that the angle of incidence of a light ray or billiard ball is equal to the angle of reflection of the ray or ball. The assumption is valid for light rays and mirrors (Fig. 1) but is not completely valid for balls: the spin of the ball before it hits the wall may make the reflection angle smaller than, greater than, or equal to the incidence angle.

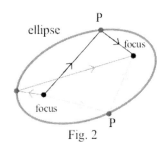

Fig. 2

Reflection Property of an Ellipse

An elliptical mirror reflects light from one focus to the other focus (Fig. 2) and all of the light rays take the same amount of time to be reflected to the other focus.

Outline of a proof: We can assume that the ellipse is oriented so its equation is

$$\frac{x^2}{a^2} + \frac{y^2}{b^2} = 1 \quad \text{(Fig. 3) and } a > b > 0.$$

Then the foci are at the points $F_1 = (-c, 0)$ and $F_2 = (c, 0)$ with $c = \sqrt{a^2 - b^2}$.

To show that the light rays from one focus are always reflected to the other focus, we need to show that angle α, the angle between the ray from F_1 and the tangent line to the ellipse, is equal to angle β, the angle between the tangent to the ellipse and the ray to F_2.

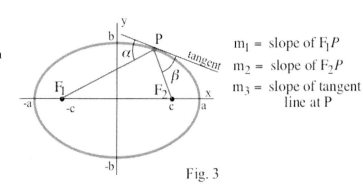

m_1 = slope of F_1P
m_2 = slope of F_2P
m_3 = slope of tangent line at P

Fig. 3

The most direct way to show that $\alpha = \beta$ is to start by calculating the slopes m_1 = slope of the line from F_1 to P, m_2 = the slope of the line from P to F_2, and m_3 = the slope of the tangent line:

$$m_1 = \frac{y}{x+c} \,, \quad m_2 = \frac{y}{x-c} \,, \text{ and, by implicit differentiation, } m_3 = \frac{-x}{y} \frac{b^2}{a^2} \,.$$

Then, from section 0.2, we know that $\tan(\alpha) = \dfrac{m_3 - m_1}{1 + m_1 m_3}$ and $\tan(\beta) = \dfrac{m_2 - m_3}{1 + m_2 m_3}$ so we just need to evaluate $\tan(\alpha)$ and $\tan(\beta)$ and show that they are equal. Since the process is algebraically tedious and not very enlightening, it has been relegated to an Appendix after the problem set.

Since straight paths from one focus to the ellipse and back to the other focus all have the same length (the definition of an ellipse), all of the light rays from the one focus take the same amount of time to reach the other focus. If a small stone is dropped into an elliptical pool at one focus (Fig. 4), then the waves radiate in all directions, reflect off the sides of the pool to the other focus and create a splash there because they all arrive at the same time. Similarly, if a room is in the shape of an (half) ellipsoid of revolution (Fig. 5), then the sound waves from a whisper at one focus will bounce off the walls and all arrive at the same time at the other focus where an eavesdropper can hear the conversation.

Fig. 4

elliptical pool table
Fig. 6

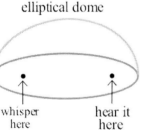

Fig. 5

Practice 1: What simple directions ensure that a ball shot from anywhere on an elliptical pool table (Fig. 6) will bounce off one wall and go into the single hole located at a focus of the ellipse?

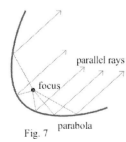

Fig. 7

Reflection Property of a Parabola

A parabolic mirror reflects light from the focus in a line parallel to the axis of the parabola (Fig. 7). In reverse, incoming light rays parallel to the axis are reflected to the focus.

Outline of a proof: If the parabolic mirror is given by $x = ay^2$ (Fig. 8), then its focus is at $F = (\frac{1}{4a}, 0)$ and the parabola is symmetric with respect to the x–axis. To prove the reflection property of the parabola, we need to show that $\alpha = \beta$ or, since α and β are both acute angles, that $\tan(\alpha) = \tan(\beta)$. From Fig. 8 we calculate that

$$m_1 = 0, \quad m_2 = \frac{y}{x - \frac{1}{4a}} = \frac{4ay}{4ax - 1} = \frac{4ay}{4a^2y^2 - 1}, \text{ and, by implicit}$$

differentiation, $m_3 = \frac{1}{2ay}$.

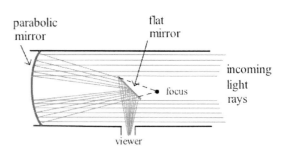

Fig. 8

Since $m_1 = 0$, we know that $\tan(\alpha) = \frac{m_3 - m_1}{1 + m_1 m_3} = m_3 = \frac{1}{2ay}$.

An elementary but tedious algebraic argument shows that $\tan(\beta) = \frac{m_2 - m_3}{1 + m_2 m_3}$ simplifies to the same value as $\tan(\alpha)$ so $\tan(\alpha) = \tan(\beta)$ and $\alpha = \beta$.

Because of this reflection property, the parabola is used in a variety of instruments and devices. Mirrors in reflecting telescopes are parabolic (Fig. 9) so that the dim incoming (parallel) light rays from distant stars are all reflected to an eyepiece at the mirror's focus for viewing. Similarly, radio telescopes use a parabolic surface to collect weak signals. A well known scientific supply company sells an 18 inch diameter parabolic reflector "ideal for a broad range of applications including solar furnaces, solar energy collectors, and parabolic and directional microphones." For outgoing light, flashlights and automobile headlights use (almost) parabolic mirrors so a light source set at the focus of the mirror creates a tight beam of light (Fig. 10).

Fig. 9: Reflecting telescope

Fig. 10

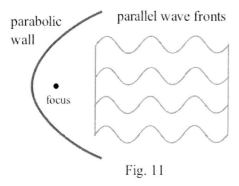

Fig. 11

Not only are incoming parallel rays reflected to the same point, but they reach that point at the same time. More precisely, if two objects start at the same distance from the y–axis and travel parallel to the x–axis, they both travel the same distance to reach the focus. If they are traveling at the same speed, they reach the focus together. An incoming linear wave front (Fig. 11) is reflected by a parabolic wall to create a splash at the focus. A small stone dropped into a wave tank at the focus of a parabola creates a linear outgoing wave. This "same distance" property of the reflection is something you can prove.

Practice 2: An object starts at the point (p,q), travels to the left until it encounters the parabola $x = ay^2$ (Fig. 12) and then goes straight to the focus at $(\frac{1}{4a}, 0)$. Show that the total distance traveled, L_1 plus L_2, equals $p + \frac{1}{4a}$ so the total distance is the same for all values of q. (Assume that $p > aq^2$ so the starting point is to the left of the parabola.)

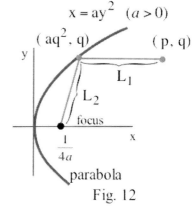

Fig. 12

The hyperbola also has a reflection property, but it is less useful than those for ellipses and parabolas.

Reflection Property of an Hyperbola

An hyperbolic mirror reflects light aimed at one focus to the other focus (Fig. 13).

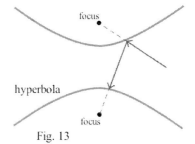

Fig. 13

Polar Coordinate Forms for the Conic Sections

In the rectangular coordinate system, the graph of the general quadratic equation $Ax^2 + Bxy + Cy^2 + Dx + Ey + F = 0$ is always a conic section, and the value of the discriminant $B^2 - 4AC$ tells us which type. In the polar coordinate system, an even simpler function describes all of the conic section shapes, and a single parameter in that function tells us the shape of the graph.

> For $e \geq 0$, the polar coordinate graphs of $r = \dfrac{k}{1 \pm e \cdot \cos(\theta)}$ and $r = \dfrac{k}{1 \pm e \cdot \sin(\theta)}$
>
> are conic sections with one focus at the origin.
>
> If $e < 1$, the graph is an ellipse. (If $e = 0$, the graph is a circle.)
>
> If $e = 1$, the graph is a parabola.
>
> If $e > 1$, the graph is an hyperbola.
>
> The number e is called the **eccentricity** of the conic section.

Fig. 14 shows graphs of $r = \dfrac{1}{1 + e \cdot \cos(\theta)}$ for several values of e.

Fig. 14

For an ellipse, the eccentricity = $\dfrac{\text{dist(center, focus)}}{\text{dist(center, vertex)}}$ (Fig. 15).

If the eccentricity of an ellipse is close to zero, then the ellipse is "almost" a circle. If the eccentricity of an ellipse is close to 1, the ellipse is rather "narrow."

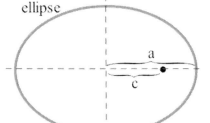

Fig. 15

For a hyperbola, the eccentricity = $\frac{\text{dist(center, focus)}}{\text{dist(center, vertex)}}$ (Fig. 16).
If the eccentricity of a hyperbola is close to 1, then the hyperbola is "narrow." If the eccentricity of a hyperbola is very large, the hyperbola "opens wide."

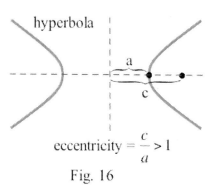

Fig. 16

Proof: The proof uses a strategy common in mathematics: move the problem into a system we know more about. In this case we move the problem from the polar coordinate system to the rectangular coordinate system, put the resulting equation into the form of a general quadratic equation, and then use the discriminant to determine the shape of the graph.

If $r = \dfrac{k}{1 + e \cdot \cos(\theta)}$, then $r + e \cdot r \cdot \cos(\theta) = k$. Replacing r with $\sqrt{x^2 + y^2}$ and $r \cdot \cos(\theta)$ with x, we get $\sqrt{x^2 + y^2} + e \cdot x = k$ and $\sqrt{x^2 + y^2} = k - e \cdot x$.

Squaring each side and collecting all of the terms on the right gives the equivalent general quadratic equation

$$(1 - e^2)x^2 + y^2 + 2kex - k = 0 \text{ so } A = 1 - e^2, B = 0, \text{ and } C = 1.$$

The discriminant of this general quadratic equation is $B^2 - 4AC = 0 - 4(1 - e^2)(1) = 4(e^2 - 1)$ so

if $e < 1$, then $B^2 - 4AC < 0$ and the graph is an ellipse,

if $e = 1$, then $B^2 - 4AC = 0$ and the graph is an parabola, and

if $e > 1$, then $B^2 - 4AC > 0$ and the graph is an hyperbola.

The graph of $r = \dfrac{k}{1 + e \cdot \cos(\theta)}$ is a conic section, and the value of the eccentricity tells which shape the graph has. We will not prove that one focus of the conic section is at the origin, but it's true.

Practice 3: Graph $r = \dfrac{k}{1 + (0.8) \cdot \cos(\theta)}$ for $k = 0.5, 1, 2,$ and 3. What effect does the value of k have on the graph?

Subtracting a constant α from θ rotates a polar coordinate graph counterclockwise about the origin by an angle of α, but does not change the shape of the graph, so the graphs of

$$r = \frac{k}{1 + e \cdot \cos(\theta - \alpha)}$$ are all conic sections whose shapes depend on the size of the parameter e.

In particular, the polar graphs of $r = \dfrac{1}{1 - e \cdot \cos(\theta)}$, $r = \dfrac{1}{1 + e \cdot \sin(\theta)}$, and $r = \dfrac{1}{1 - e \cdot \sin(\theta)}$

are conic sections, rotations about the origin of the graphs of $r = \dfrac{1}{1 + e \cdot \cos(\theta)}$, since

$-\cos(\theta) = \cos(\theta - \pi)$, $\sin(\theta) = \cos(\theta - \pi/2)$, and $-\sin(\theta) = \cos(\theta - -\pi/2)$. Fig. 17 shows several of these graphs for $e = 0.8$.

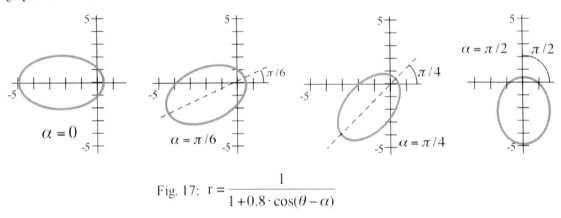

Fig. 17: $r = \dfrac{1}{1 + 0.8 \cdot \cos(\theta - \alpha)}$

The Path of Every Object in the Universe is a Conic Section (not really)

Rather than engage in endless philosophical discussion about how the planets ought to move, Tycho Brahe (1546–1601) had a better idea about how to find out how they actually do move — collect data! Even before the invention of the telescope, he built an observatory, and with the aid of devices like protractors he carefully cataloged the positions of the planets for 20 years. Just before his death, he passed this accumulated data to Johannes Kepler to edit and publish. From these remarkable data, Kepler deduced his three laws of planetary motion, the first of which says **each planet moves in an elliptical orbit with the sun at one focus** (Fig. 18). From Kepler's laws, Newton was able to deduce that a force, gravity, held the planets in orbits and that the force varied inversely as the square of the distance between the planet and the sun. From this "inverse square" fact it can be shown that the position of one object (e.g., a planet) with respect to another (e.g., the sun) is given by the polar coordinate formula

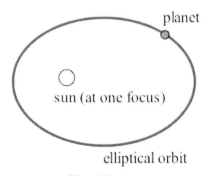

Fig. 18

$$r = \frac{h}{1 + (h-1)\cdot\cos(\theta)} \quad \text{where} \quad h = \frac{r_0 \cdot v_0^2}{GM}$$

r_0 = initial distance (m), v_0 = initial velocity (m/s)

G = universal gravitation constant ($6.7 \times 10^{-11} \frac{N\,m^2}{kg^2}$)

M = mass of the sun or "other object" (kg).

You should recognize the pattern of this formula as the pattern for the conic sections with eccentricity

$$e = |h - 1| = \left| \frac{r_0 \cdot v_0^2}{GM} - 1 \right|.$$

In a "two body" universe, all motion paths are conic sections, and the shape of the conic section is determined by the value of $r_0 \cdot v_0^2$. If the object is far away or moving very rapidly or both, then $r_0 \cdot v_0^2 > 2GM$, the eccentricity is greater than one, and the path is a hyperbola. If the objects are relatively close and/or moving slowly, then $r_0 \cdot v_0^2 < 2GM$ (the situation with each planet and the sun), the eccentricity is less than one and the path is an ellipse. If $r_0 \cdot v_0^2 = 2GM$, then the eccentricity is 1 and the path is a parabola. If $r_0 \cdot v_0^2 = GM$, then the eccentricity is 0 and the path is a circle. It is rare to encounter values of r_0 and v_0 so $r_0 \cdot v_0^2$ exactly equals GM or 2GM.

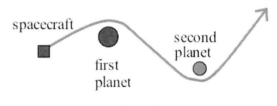

Fig. 19

The universe obviously contains more than two bodies and the paths of most objects are not conic sections, but there are still important situations in which the force on an object is due almost entirely to the gravitational attraction between it and one other body. For example, scientists and engineers use the position formula to determine the orbital position and velocity needed to put a satellite into an orbit with the desired eccentricity, and the position formula was used to help calculate how close Voyager 2 should come to Jupiter and Saturn so the gravity of those planets could be used to change the path of Voyager 2 to a hyperbola and send it on to other planets (Fig. 19). The conic sections even appear at less grand scales. In a vacuum, the path of a thrown baseball (or bat) is a parabola, unless it is thrown hard enough to achieve an elliptical orbit. And at the subatomic scale, Rutherford (1871 – 1937) discovered that alpha particles shot toward the nucleus of an atom are repelled away from the nucleus along hyperbolic paths (Fig. 20). Conic sections are everywhere.

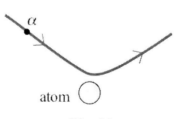

Fig. 20

Elliptical Orbits

When a planet orbits a sun, the orbit is an ellipse, and we can use information about ellipses to calculate information about these orbits.

The position of a planet in elliptical orbit around a sun is given by the polar equation

$$r = \frac{k}{1 + e \cdot \cos(\theta)}$$

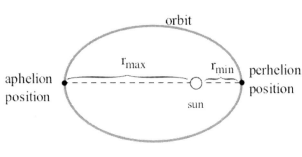

Fig. 21

for some value of the eccentricity $e < 1$ (Fig. 21). The planet is closest (at perhelion) to the sun when $\theta = 0$ and this minimum distance is $r_{min} = \frac{k}{1+e}$. The greatest distance (at aphelion) occurs when $\theta = \pi$ and that distance is $r_{max} = \frac{k}{1-e}$. If the width of the ellipse (technically, the length of the major axis) is 2a, then

$$2a = r_{min} + r_{max} = \frac{k}{1+e} + \frac{k}{1-e} = \frac{2k}{1-e^2}$$

so $k = a(1 - e^2)$ and the position of the planet is given by

$$r = \frac{a(1-e^2)}{1 + e \cdot \cos(\theta)} \quad \text{with} \quad r_{min} = \frac{a(1-e^2)}{1+e} = a(1-e) \quad \text{and} \quad r_{max} = \frac{a(1-e^2)}{1-e} = a(1+e).$$

Example 4: We want to put a satellite in an elliptical orbit around the earth (radius $\approx$ 6360 km) so the maximum height of the satellite is 20,000 km and the minimum height is 10,000 km (Fig. 22). Find the eccentricity of the orbit and give a polar formula for its position.

Solution: r_{max} = maximum height plus the radius of the earth = 26,360 km and r_{min} = minimum height plus the radius of the earth = 16,360 km so $a(1 + e) = 26,360$ and $a(1 - e) = 16,360$. Dividing these last two quantities, we have

$$\frac{r_{max}}{r_{min}} = \frac{26360}{16360} = \frac{a(1+e)}{a(1-e)} = \frac{1+e}{1-e} \quad \text{and} \quad e = \frac{10000}{42720} \approx \mathbf{0.234}$$

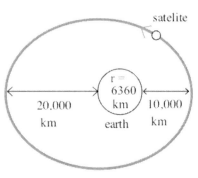

Fig. 22

Using $r_{min} = a(1 - e) = a(1 - 0.234) = 16360$ we have $a \approx 21358$.

Finally, $r = \dfrac{a(1-e^2)}{1 + e \cdot \cos(\theta)} = \dfrac{\mathbf{20189}}{\mathbf{1 + (0.234) \cdot \cos(\theta)}}$.

Practice 4: Pluto's orbit has an eccentricity of 0.2481 and its semimajor axis is 5,909 million kilometers. Find the minimum and maximum distance of Pluto from the sun during one orbit. The orbit of Neptune has an eccentricity of 0.0082 with a semimajor axis of 4,500 million kilometers. Is Neptune ever farther from the sun than Pluto?

PROBLEMS

Reflection properties

1. For the ellipse in Fig. 23, how far does a ball travel as it moves from one focus to any point on the ellipse and on to the other focus?

Fig. 23

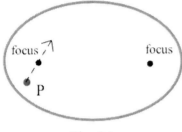

Fig. 24

2. In Fig. 24 a ball rolls from point P over the the focus at A and keeps rolling. Sketch the path of the ball for the first 5 bounces it makes off of the ellipse. What does the path of the ball look like after "a long time?"

3. In Fig. 25 a ball rolls from point P toward the the focus at A and bounces off of the hyperbola. Sketch the path of the ball for the first 5 bounces it makes off of the hyperbola. What does the path of the ball look like after "a long time?"

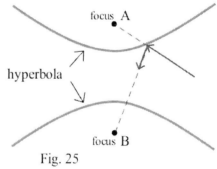

Fig. 25

4. An explosion is set off at one focus inside a very strong ellipsoidal shell. What might happen to a piece of graphite located at the other focus?

5. A straight wave front is approaching a parabolic jetty. Why wouldn't you want your boat to be at the focus of the parabola?

6. The members of a marching band are grouped near point A (Fig. 26), the focus of a parabola. At a signal from the director, the band members each march (at the same speed) in different directions toward the parabola, immediately turn and then march due west. What shape will the formation have after all of the marchers have made their turns?

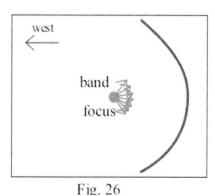

Fig. 26

7. A reflecting telescope is built with a parabolic mirror and a hyperbolic mirror (Fig. 27) so F_1 is the focus of the parabola and F_1 and F_2 are the foci of the hyperbola. Trace the paths of the incoming parallel light rays a, b, and c as they reflect off both mirrors. Why is the eyepiece located at F_2 ?

8. Make a slight design change in the telescope in Fig. 27 so the eyepiece can be located at the point off to the side of the parabolic mirror.

Fig. 27

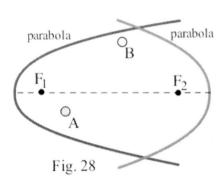

Fig. 28

9. The billiards table in Fig. 28 consists of parts of two parabolas: the right parabola has focus F_1 and the left parabola has focus F_2. (a) Determine a strategy for shooting the balls located at A and B to make a two–cushion (i.e., two bounce) shot into the hole located at F_2. (b) Are there any places on the table where your strategy in part (a) does not work? (Unfortunately for my ability to win at billiards, the angle of incidence does not necessarily equal the angle of reflection. But assume they are equal for these problems.)

10. The billiards table in Fig. 29 consists of parts of two ellipses: the short ellipse has foci F_1 and F_2 and the tall ellipse has foci F_2 and F_3.

   (a) Determine a strategy for shooting the balls located at A and B to make a two–cushion (i.e., two bounce) shot into the hole located at F_3.

   (b) Are there any places on the table where your strategy in part (a) does not work?

Fig. 29

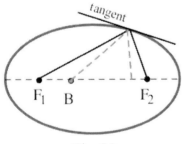

Fig. 30

11. Use Fig. 30 to help explain geometrically why a ball located on the major axis of an ellipse between the two foci is always reflected back to a point on the major axis between the two foci.

12. Is a rectangular reflection path (Fig. 31) possible for the ellipse

   (a) $\frac{x^2}{25} + \frac{y^2}{16} = 1$? (b) $\frac{x^2}{a^2} + \frac{y^2}{b^2} = 1$?

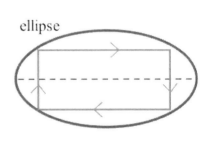

Fig. 31

Polar forms

In problems 13–18, determine the eccentricity of each conic section, identify the shape, and determine where it crosses the x and y axes.

13. $r = \dfrac{11}{3 + 5\cdot\cos(\theta)}$

14. $r = \dfrac{8}{7 + 3\cdot\sin(\theta + \pi/6)}$

15. $r = \dfrac{1}{2 + 2\cdot\sin(\theta - \pi/3)}$

16. $r = \dfrac{-4}{3 - 3\cdot\cos(\theta)}$

17. $r = \dfrac{17}{7 - 5\cdot\cos(\theta + 3\pi)}$

18. $r = \dfrac{3}{4 - 2\cdot\sin(\theta + \pi/11)}$

In problems 19–24, sketch each ellipse and determine the coordinates of the foci. (Reminder: In the standard polar coordinate form used here, one focus is always at the origin.)

19. $r = \dfrac{6}{2 + \cos(\theta)}$

20. $r = \dfrac{6}{2 + \sin(\theta)}$

21. $r = \dfrac{12}{3 - \sin(\theta)}$

22. $r = \dfrac{12}{3 - \cos(\theta)}$

23. $r = \dfrac{3}{2 + \sin(\theta - \pi/4)}$

24. $r = \dfrac{3}{2 + \cos(\theta + \pi/4)}$

In problems 25 and 26, represent the length and area of each ellipse as definite integrals and use Simpson's rule with n = 100 to approximate the values of the integrals.

25. $r = \dfrac{1}{1 + 0.5\cdot\cos(\theta)}$

26. $r = \dfrac{1}{1 + 0.9\cdot\cos(\theta)}$

Conic section paths:

Problems 27–30 refer to the two objects in Fig. 32. Determine the shape of the path of object B. (Object A has mass 10^{19} kg, r = 10^5 m)

27. v = 17.6 m/s

28. v = 115 m/s

29. v = 120 m/s

30. Determine a velocity for B so that the path is a parabola.

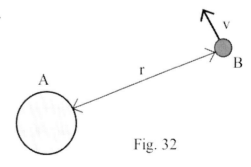

Fig. 32

31. An object at a distance r from the center of a planet of mass M (Fig. 33) has velocity v. Determine conditions on v as a function of r, M, and G so the resulting path is (a) circular, (b) elliptical, (c) parabolic, and (d) hyperbolic.

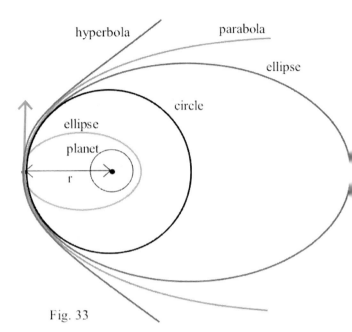

Fig. 33

Problems 32–34 refer to Earth and moon orbits: use
$G = 6.7 \times 10^{-11}$ N·m^2/kg^2,
$M_{Earth} = 5.98 \times 10^{24}$ kg,
$r_{Earth} = 6.360 \times 10^6$ m,
$M_{moon} = 7 \times 10^{22}$ kg, and
$r_{moon} = 1.738 \times 10^6$.

32. At the Earth's surface, determine a velocity so that the resulting path is circular. This is the minimum velocity needed to achieve "orbit," a very low orbit.

33. At the Earth's surface, determine a velocity so that the resulting path is parabolic. This is the minimum velocity needed to escape from orbit, and is called the "escape velocity".

34. At the moon's surface, determine the minimum orbital velocity and the (minimum) escape velocity.

Elliptical orbits

35. We want to put a satellite into orbit around Earth so the maximum altitude of the satellite is 1000 km and the minimum altitude is 800 km. Find the eccentricity of this orbit and give a polar coordinate formula for its position.

36. The Earth follows an elliptical orbit around the sun, and this ellipse has a semimajor axis of 149.6×10^6 km and an eccentricity of 0.017. (a) Determine the maximum and minimum distances of the Earth from the sun. (b) How far apart are the two foci of this ellipse?

37. Determine the altitude needed for an Earth satellite to make one orbit on a circular path every 24 hours ("geosyncronous"). (Since the orbit is circular and the satellite makes one orbit every 24 hours, you can determine the velocity v (in m/s) as a function of the distance r from the center of the Earth. Since the orbit is circular, $e = 0$ and $r \cdot v^2 = GM$.)

Section 9.6   PRACTICE Answers

Practice 1: "Shoot the ball toward the left focus." Since the table is an ellipse, the ball will roll over the focus, hit the wall, and be reflected into the hole at the other focus.

Practice 2: L_1 = distance from (p, q) to $(a \cdot q^2, q) = p - a \cdot q^2$.

L_2 = distance from $(a \cdot q^2, q)$ to $(\frac{1}{4a}, 0)$

$= \sqrt{(a \cdot q^2 - \frac{1}{4a})^2 + (q - 0)^2} = \sqrt{a^2 q^4 - 2aq^2(\frac{1}{4a}) + \frac{1}{16a^2} + q^2}$

$= \sqrt{a^2 q^4 - \frac{1}{2} q^2 + \frac{1}{16a^2} + q^2}$

$= \sqrt{a^2 q^4 + \frac{1}{2} q^2 + \frac{1}{16a^2}} = \sqrt{(aq^2 + \frac{1}{4a})^2} = aq^2 + \frac{1}{4a}$.

Therefore, $L_1 + L_2 = (p - a \cdot q^2) + (aq^2 + \frac{1}{4a}) = p + \frac{1}{4a}$.

Practice 3: The graphs of $r = \dfrac{k}{1 + (0.8) \cdot \cos(\theta)}$

for $k = 0.5, 1,$ and 2 are shown in Fig. 34. Each graph is an ellipse with eccentricity 0.8 and one focus at the origin. The value of k determines the size of the ellipse. The larger the magnitude of k, the larger the ellipse.

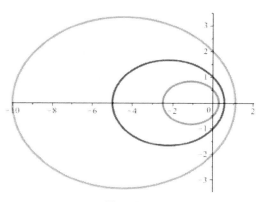

Fig. 34

Practice 4: For Pluto: $e = 0.2481$ and semimajor axis length = 5,909 km ($a = 5{,}909$ km).

$r_{min} = a(1 - e) = 5909(0.7519) \approx 4443$ km.

$r_{max} = a(1 + e) = 5909(1.2481) \approx 7375$ km.

For Neptune: $e = 0.0082$ and $a = 4{,}500$ km.

$r_{min} = a(1 - e) = 4500(0.9918) \approx 4463$ km, a distance closer than Pluto at its closest!

$r_{max} = a(1 + e) = 4500(1.0082) \approx 4537$ km.

In fact, Neptune is the farthest planet from the sun between January 1979 and March 1999. Now that Pluto has been reclassified as a "dwarf plane," Neptune is always the farthest planet from the sun. Poor Pluto.

Appendix: Reflection Property of the Ellipse

Let $P = (x,y)$ be on the ellipse $\dfrac{x^2}{a^2} + \dfrac{y^2}{b^2} = 1$ with foci at $(-c, 0)$ and $(c, 0)$ for $c = \sqrt{a^2 - b^2}$.

Then the slopes (Fig. 40) are m_1 = slope from P to $(-c,0)$ = $\dfrac{y}{x+c}$, m_2 = slope from P to $(c,0)$ = $\dfrac{y}{x-c}$,

and m_3 = slope of tangent line to ellipse at (x,y) = $\dfrac{-x}{y}\dfrac{b^2}{a^2}$ (by implicit differentiation).

We know that $\tan(\alpha) = \dfrac{m_3 - m_1}{1 + m_1 m_3}$ and $\tan(\beta) = \dfrac{m_2 - m_3}{1 + m_2 m_3}$, and we want to show that $\alpha = \beta$ or, equivalently, that $\tan(\alpha) = \tan(\beta)$.

$$\tan(\alpha) = \frac{m_3 - m_1}{1 + m_1 m_3} = \frac{\dfrac{-x}{y}\dfrac{b^2}{a^2} - \dfrac{y}{x+c}}{1 + \dfrac{y}{x+c}\dfrac{-x}{y}\dfrac{b^2}{a^2}} \qquad \text{multiply top \& bottom by } ya^2(x+c)$$

$$= \frac{-xb^2(x+c) - y^2 a^2}{ya^2(x+c) - xyb^2} = \frac{-x^2 b^2 - xb^2 c - y^2 a^2}{xya^2 + ya^2 c - xyb^2}$$

$$= \frac{-xb^2 c - (x^2 b^2 + y^2 a^2)}{xy(a^2 - b^2) + ya^2 c} \qquad x^2 b^2 + y^2 a^2 = a^2 b^2 \text{ and } a^2 - b^2 = c^2$$

$$= \frac{-xb^2 c - a^2 b^2}{xyc^2 + ya^2 c} = \frac{-b^2}{yc}\frac{xc + a^2}{xc + a^2} = \frac{-b^2}{yc}.$$

Similarly, $\tan(\beta) = \dfrac{m_2 - m_3}{1 + m_2 m_3} = \dfrac{\dfrac{y}{x-c} - \dfrac{-x}{y}\dfrac{b^2}{a^2}}{1 + \dfrac{y}{x-c}\dfrac{-x}{y}\dfrac{b^2}{a^2}}$ multiply top & bottom by $ya^2(x-c)$

$$= \frac{y^2 a^2 + xb^2(x-c)}{ya^2(x-c) - xyb^2} = \frac{x^2 b^2 - xb^2 c + y^2 a^2}{xya^2 - ya^2 c - xyb^2}$$

$$= \frac{-xb^2 c + (x^2 b^2 + y^2 a^2)}{xy(a^2 - b^2) - ya^2 c} \qquad (x^2 b^2 + y^2 a^2 = a^2 b^2 \text{ and } a^2 - b^2 = c^2)$$

$$= \frac{-xb^2 c + a^2 b^2}{xyc^2 - ya^2 c} = \frac{-b^2}{yc}\frac{xc - a^2}{xc - a^2} = \frac{-b^2}{yc} = \tan(\alpha). \text{ (Yes!)}$$

Reflection Property of the Parabola $x = ay^2$ with focus $(\frac{1}{4a}, 0)$

The slopes of the line segments in Fig. 41 are m_1 = slope of "incoming" ray = 0,

m_2 = slope from P to focus = $\dfrac{y}{x - \frac{1}{4a}}$ = $\dfrac{4ay}{4ax - 1}$ = $\dfrac{4ay}{4a^2y^2 - 1}$, and, by implicit differentiation,

m_3 = slope of the tangent line at (x,y) = $\dfrac{1}{2ay}$.

We know that $\tan(\alpha) = \dfrac{m_3 - m_1}{1 + m_1 m_3}$ and $\tan(\beta) = \dfrac{m_2 - m_3}{1 + m_2 m_3}$, and we want to show that $\alpha = \beta$ or, equivalently, that $\tan(\alpha) = \tan(\beta)$.

$\tan(\alpha) = \dfrac{m_3 - m_1}{1 + m_1 m_3} = m_3 = \dfrac{1}{2ay}$

$\tan(\beta) = \dfrac{m_2 - m_3}{1 + m_2 m_3} = \dfrac{\dfrac{4ay}{4a^2y^2 - 1} - \dfrac{1}{2ay}}{1 + \dfrac{4ay}{4a^2y^2 - 1} \cdot \dfrac{1}{2ay}}$ multiply top & bottom by $(4a^2y^2 - 1)(2ay)$

$= \dfrac{8a^2y^2 - 4a^2y^2 + 1}{(4a^2y^2 - 1)(2ay) + 4ay} = \dfrac{4a^2y^2 + 1}{8a^3y^3 - 2ay + 4ay}$

$= \dfrac{4a^2y^2 + 1}{8a^3y^3 + 2ay} = \dfrac{4a^2y^2 + 1}{2ay(4a^2y^2 + 1)} = \dfrac{1}{2ay} = \tan(\alpha)$. (Yes!)

There are other, more geometric ways to prove this result.

Chapter Nine

Section 9.1   Odd Answers

1. A: $(25, 0)$ B: $(25, 3\pi/2)$ C: $(15, \pi/6)$ 3. A: $(30, \pi/3)$ B: $(20, 5\pi/6)$ C: $(25, 5\pi/4)$

5. Graph is given. Shape is almost rectangular.

7. Graph is given.

9. Graph is given.

11. Graph is given.

13. Graph is given.

15. Graphs are given.

Prob. 5   Prob. 7

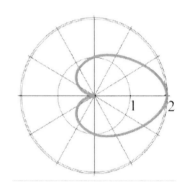

Prob. 9   Prob. 11   Prob. 13

Prob. 15

17. Graphs are given.

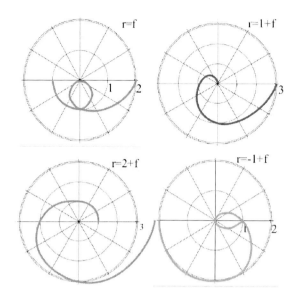

Prob. 17

19. The polar graph will approach (spiral in or out to) a circle of radius 3.

21. Circle centered at origin with radius 3.

23. Line through the origin making an angle of π/6 with the x–axis.

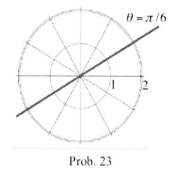

Prob. 21   Prob. 23

25. A circle sitting atop the x–axis, touching the origin.

27. Graph is given.

29. Graph is given.

31. Graph is given.

Prob. 25

Prob. 27

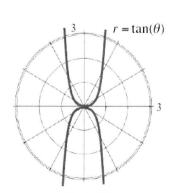

Prob. 29   Prob. 31

33. Graph is given. A vertical line through the rectangular coordinate point (3,0).

35. Graph is given. A line: in rectangular coordinates y = 1 − x.

37. Graph is given: a fast growing spiral.

39. Graph is given.

41. {m = 1, n = 2}, {m = 2, n = 4}, {m = 3, n = 3}, {m = 4, n = 4} all have pleasing shapes. Find some others for yourself.

43. The graphs are given. The graph for a = 0 is rotated π/6, π/4, and π/2 counterclockwise about the origin as a = π/6, π/4, and π/2 respectively.

45.
n	1	2	3	4	5	6	7	8
# petals	1	4	3	8	5	12	7	16

47. Rectangular (−2, 3) is polar ($\sqrt{13}$, 2.159).
Rect (2, −3) is polar ($\sqrt{13}$, 5.300) or (−$\sqrt{13}$, 2.159).
Rect (0, −4) is polar (−4, π/2) or (4, 3π/2).

49. Rectangular (3, 4) is polar (5, 0.927).
Rect (−1, −3) is polar ($\sqrt{10}$, 4.391).
Rect (−7, 12) is polar ($\sqrt{193}$, −1.043) or ($\sqrt{193}$, −1.043 + π) ≈ ($\sqrt{193}$, 2.099).

51. Polar (−2, 3) is rect. (1.98, −0.282).   Polar (2, −3) is rect. (−1.98, −0.282).   Polar (0, −4) is rect. (0, 0).

53. Polar (2, 3) is rect. (−1.98, 0.282).   Polar (−2, −3) is rect. (1.98, 0.282).   Polar (0, 4) is rect. (0, 0).

55. x = 15·cos(−30°) + 10·cos(0°) ≈ 22.99 inches to the right of the shoulder.
y = 15·sin(−30°) + 10·sin(0°) ≈ −7.5 inches or 7.5 inches **below** the shoulder.
Polar location of hand: (24.18, −18.07°) or (24.18, −0.32).

57. x = 15·cos(−0.9) + 10·cos(−0.5) ≈ 18.10 inches to the right of the shoulder.
y = 15·sin(−0.9) + 10·sin(−0.5) ≈ 16.54 inches **below** the shoulder.   Polar is (24.52, -0.74).

Prob. 33   Prob. 35

Prob. 37   Prob. 39

Prob. 43

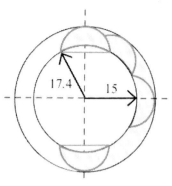

Prob. 59

59. Figure is given: $-\pi/2 \le \theta \le \pi/2$ and $-\pi/2 \le \phi \le \pi/2$. The robot's hand can reach the shaded region.

60. Figure is given: $-\pi/2 \le \theta \le \pi/2$ and $-\pi \le \phi \le \pi$. The robot's hand can reach the shaded region.

61. On your own.

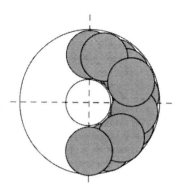

Prob. 60

Section 9.2   Odd Answers

1. | Point | dr/dθ | dx/dθ | dy/dθ | dy/dx |
    |---|---|---|---|---|
    | A | – | – | + | – |
    | B | 0 | – | + | – |
    | C | + | – | + | – |
    | D | + | – | 0 | 0 |
    | E | – | + | – | – |

2. | Point | dr/dθ | dx/dθ | dy/dθ | dy/dx |
    |---|---|---|---|---|
    | A | + | + | + | + |
    | B | + | – | + | – |
    | C | – | – | – | + |
    | D | – | – | – | + |
    | E | + | – | – | + |

3. | Point | dr/dθ | dx/dθ | dy/dθ | dy/dx |
    |---|---|---|---|---|
    | A | 0 | 0 | + | Und. |
    | B | + | 0 | + | Und. |
    | C | U | U | U | U |
    | D | – | – | 0 | 0 |
    | E | + | – | 0 | 0 |

4. | Point | dr/dθ | dx/dθ | dy/dθ | dy/dx |
    |---|---|---|---|---|
    | A | – | + | – | – |
    | B | – | + | – | – |
    | C | + | + | – | – |
    | D | + | + | 0 | 0 |
    | E | + | + | + | + |

5. The polar graph is a circle centered at the origin with radius 5.
   At A: $dr/d\theta = 0$, $dy/dx = -1$. At B: $dr/d\theta = 0$, $dy/dx = 0$.
   At C: $dr/d\theta = 0$, $dy/dx = $ Und.

7. The graph is given.
   At A: $dr/d\theta = 0$, $dy/dx = $ Und. At B: $dr/d\theta = -1$, $dy/dx = -1/5$.
   At C: $dr/d\theta = 0$, $dy/dx = 0$.

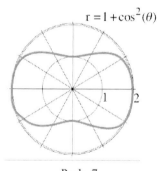

Prob. 7

9. When $\theta = 2\pi/3$, $dy/dx = -\sqrt{3}$. When $\theta = 4\pi/3$, $dy/dx = +\sqrt{3}$.

11. We have $\dfrac{dy}{dx} = \dfrac{r\cdot\cos(\theta) + \dfrac{dr}{d\theta}\cdot\sin(\theta)}{-r\cdot\sin(\theta) + \dfrac{dr}{d\theta}\cdot\cos(\theta)}$,

    so if $r(\theta) = 0$ (and $\dfrac{dr}{d\theta}$ exists and $\dfrac{dr}{d\theta} \ne 0$)

    then $\dfrac{dy}{dx} = \dfrac{\dfrac{dr}{d\theta}\cdot\sin(\theta)}{\dfrac{dr}{d\theta}\cdot\cos(\theta)} = \tan(\theta)$.

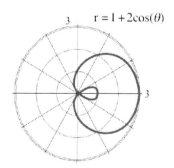

Prob. 9

13. $\frac{9}{16}\pi^2 \approx 5.552$

15. {area of cardioid in first quad.} – {area of circle in first quad.} = $\{1 + \frac{3\pi}{8}\} - \{\frac{\pi}{4}\} = 1 + \frac{\pi}{8} \approx 1.393$. This problem is worked out in Example 4.

17. 3-petal: $A = \frac{1}{2}\int_0^{\pi/3} \sin^2(3\theta)\,d\theta = \frac{\pi}{12} \approx 0.262$. 5-petal: $A = \frac{1}{2}\int_0^{\pi/5} \sin^2(5\theta)\,d\theta = \frac{\pi}{20} \approx 0.157$.

19. $A = \pi(2)^2 = 4\pi \approx 12.566$

21. (b) add several semicircular regions to get $\frac{1}{2}\pi(40)^2 + \frac{1}{2}\pi(30)^2 + \frac{1}{2}\pi(10)^2 = 1300\pi\ \text{ft}^2 \approx 4{,}084.1\ \text{ft}^2$

   (c) $\frac{3}{4}\pi(40)^2 + \frac{1}{2}\pi(20)^2 = 1400\pi\ \text{ft}^2 \approx 4{,}398.2\ \text{ft}^2 > 4{,}084.1\ \text{ft}^2$

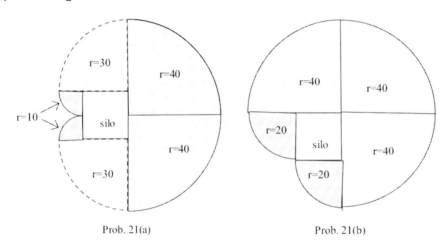

Prob. 21(a)   Prob. 21(b)

23. $r = \theta$, $dr/d\theta = 1$, $L = \int_0^{2\pi} \sqrt{\theta^2 + 1}\,d\theta \approx 21.256$ (using Simpson's rule with n = 20).

25. $r = 1 + \cos(\theta)$, $dr/d\theta = -\sin(\theta)$,

$$L = \int_0^{2\pi} \sqrt{\{1+\cos(\theta)\}^2 + \{-\sin(\theta)\}^2}\,d\theta = \int_0^{2\pi} \sqrt{2 + 2\cos(\theta)}\,d\theta = \int_0^{2\pi} \sqrt{4\cos^2(\theta/2)}\,d\theta$$

$$= 2\int_0^{2\pi} |\cos(\theta/2)|\,d\theta = 4\int_0^{\pi} \cos(\theta/2)\,d\theta = 8\sin(\theta/2)\Big|_0^{\pi} = 8.$$

(Simpson's rule with n = 20 gives the same result.)

27. 10π

29. $r = \sin(3\theta)$, $dr/d\theta = 3\cdot\cos(3\theta)$, $L = \int_0^{\pi/3} \sqrt{\sin^2(3\theta) + \{3\cdot\cos(3\theta)\}^2}\,d\theta \approx 2.227$ (Simpson, n = 20).

Section 9.3 Odd Answers

1. Graph is given.   3. Graph is given.

5. Graph is given.   7. Graph is given.

9. Graph is given: a straight line.

11. $(x(0), y(0)) = (b, d)$ and
    $(x(1), y(1)) = (a+b, c+d)$ so
    slope $= \dfrac{(c+d) - d}{(a+b) - b} = \dfrac{c}{a}$.

13. Graph is given.

15. Graphs are given.
    (a) is the entire line $y = x$.
    (b) is the "half–line" $y = x$ for $x \geq 0$.
    (c) is the line segment $y = x$ for
       $-1 \leq x \leq 1$: the location oscillates
       along the line between $(-1, -1)$ and $(1,1)$.
    All of these graphs satisfy the same realationship between x
    and y, $y = x$, but the graphs cover different parts of the
    graph of $y = x$ (different domains).

17. The graph is given. The graph begins
    at $\left(\dfrac{2\sqrt{2}}{\pi}, \dfrac{2\sqrt{2}}{\pi}\right)$ when $t = \pi/4$,
    and then it spirals counterclockwise
    around and in toward the origin.
    As t increases from $\pi/4$, the radial
    distance of a point on the graph
    decreases, approaching 0.

19. closer to

21. No. The new values give a point very close to the fixed point for these
    populations so the system will be in good balance.

Prob. 1

Prob. 3

Prob. 5   Prob. 7

Prob. 9

Prob. 13

Prob. 15

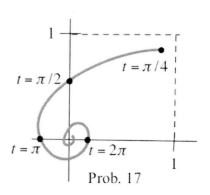
Prob. 17

23. Solve $x = at + b$ for t and substitute this value of t into the equation $y = cx + d$. Then $t = \dfrac{x-b}{a}$ and

$y = c\left(\dfrac{x-b}{t}\right) + d = \dfrac{c}{a}x + \left(d - \dfrac{b}{a}\right)$, the equation of a straight line with slope $\dfrac{c}{a}$. The slope $\dfrac{c}{a}$ of y as a function of x is the slope of y as a function of t divided by the slope of x as a function of t.

25. Sketches of some possible paths are given.

Prob. 25

27. (a) $x = R(t - \sin(t))$, $y = R(1 - \cos(t))$. If $t = 2\pi$, then $(x, y) = (2\pi R, 0) = (10\pi, 0)$ so $R = 5$.

(b) Set $x = R(t - \sin(t)) = 5$ and $y = R(1 - \cos(t)) = 2$, divide y by x to eliminate R, solve (graphically or using Newton's method or some other way) to get $t \approx 3.820$. Substitute this value into the equation for x or y and solve for $R \approx 1.124$.

(c) Set $x = R(t - \sin(t)) = 2$ and $y = R(1 - \cos(t)) = 3$, divide y by x to eliminate R, solve (graphically or using Newton's method or some other way) to get $t \approx 1.786$. Substitute this value into the equation for x or y and solve for $R \approx 2.472$.

(d) Set $x = R(t - \sin(t)) = 4\pi$ and $y = R(1 - \cos(t)) = 8$ and solve to get $t = \pi$ and $R = 4$.

29. (a) $x = -50 + 30\left(\dfrac{1}{\sqrt{2}}\right) \cdot t = -50 + (15\sqrt{2}) \cdot t$ feet and

$y = 6 + 30\left(\dfrac{1}{\sqrt{2}}\right) \cdot t - 16t^2 = 6 + (15\sqrt{2}) \cdot t - 16t^2$ feet.

(b) $x = -50 + V\left(\dfrac{\sqrt{2}}{2}\right) \cdot t$ feet and $y = 6 + V\left(\dfrac{\sqrt{2}}{2}\right) \cdot t - 16t^2$ feet.

Section 9.4 Odd Answers

1. (a) The graph is given.

(b) $dx/dt = 1 - 2t$, $dy/dt = 2$. When $t = 0$, $dy/dx = 2$. When $t = 1$, $dy/dx = -2$. When $t = 2$, $dy/dx = -2/3$.

(c) dy/dx is never 0. dy/dx is undefined when $t = 1/2$: at $(x, y) = (1/4, 2)$.

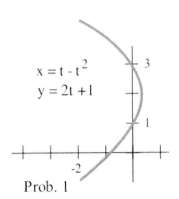

$x = t - t^2$
$y = 2t + 1$

Prob. 1

3. (a) The graph is given.

    (b) $dx/dt = -\sin(t)$, $dy/dt = \cos(t)$. When $t = 0$, dy/dx is undefined.
    When $t = \pi/4$, $dy/dx = -1$. When $t = \pi/2$, $dy/dx = 0$.

    (c) $dy/dx = 0$ whenever $t = (k+\frac{1}{2})\pi$ for k an integer. dy/dx is undefined whenever $t = k\pi$ for k an integer.

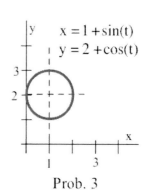
Prob. 3

5. (a) The graph is given.

    (b) $dx/dt = \cos(t)$, $dy/dt = -\sin(t)$. When $t = 0$, $dy/dx = 0$. When $t = \pi/4$, $dy/dx = -1$. When $t = \pi/2$, dy/dx is undefined.
    When $t = 17.3$, $dy/dx \approx 47.073$.

    (c) $dy/dx = 0$ whenever $t = k\pi$ for k an integer. dy/dx is undefined whenever $t = (k+\frac{1}{2})\pi$ for k an integer.

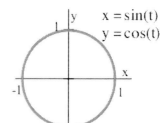

7. (a) The graph is given.

    (b) $dx/dt = 1/t$, $dy/dt = -2t$. When $t = 1$, $dy/dx = -2$.
    When $t = 2$, $dy/dx = -8$. When $t = e$, $dy/dx = -2e^2$.

    (c) The function is only defined for $t > 0$, and for all $t > 0$ the slope of the tangent line dy/dx is defined and is not equal to 0.

Prob. 5

Prob. 7

9. (a) $m_0 \approx \frac{-1}{1} = -1$. $m_1 \approx \frac{0}{1} = 0$. $m_2 \approx \frac{0}{1} = 0$. m_3 is undefined.

    (b) $dy/dx = 0$ when $t = 1$ and $t = 2$.

11. (a) $m_0 \approx \frac{2}{-1} = -2$. $m_1 \approx \frac{1}{-1} = -1$. m_2 is undefined. $m_3 = \frac{-1}{1} = -1$.

    (b) dy/dx is undefined when $t = 2$.

13. $dx/dt = 1 - 2t$, $dy/dt = 2$ so $v = \sqrt{(1-2t)^2 + (2)^2} = \sqrt{4t^2 - 4t + 5}$.
    $v_0 = \sqrt{5} \approx 2.24$ ft/s, $v_1 = \sqrt{5} \approx 2.24$ ft/s, $v_2 = \sqrt{13} \approx 3.61$ ft/s.

15. $dx/dt = -\sin(t)$, $dy/dt = \cos(t)$ so
    $v = \sqrt{(-\sin(t))^2 + (\cos(t))^2} = \sqrt{\sin^2(t) + \cos^2(t)} = 1$ ft/s for all values of t.
    $v_0 = v_{\pi/4} = v_{\pi/2} = v_\pi = 1$ ft/s.

17. $v_0 \approx \sqrt{(1)^2 + (-1)^2} = \sqrt{2} \approx 1.41$ ft/s. $\quad v_1 \approx \sqrt{(1)^2 + (0)^2} = 1$ ft/s.
    $v_2 \approx \sqrt{(1)^2 + (0)^2} = 1$ ft/s. $\quad v_3 \approx \sqrt{(0)^2 + (-1)^2} = 1$ ft/s.
    $v_4 \approx \sqrt{(-1)^2 + (-1)^2} = \sqrt{2} \approx 1.41$ ft/s.

19. $v_0 \approx \sqrt{(-1)^2 + (2)^2} = \sqrt{5} \approx 2.24$ ft/s. $v_1 \approx \sqrt{(-1)^2 + (1)^2} = \sqrt{2} \approx 1.41$ ft/s.

    $v_2 \approx \sqrt{(0)^2 + (0)^2} = 0$ ft/s. $v_3 \approx \sqrt{(1)^2 + (-1)^2} = \sqrt{2} \approx 1.41$ ft/s.

21. (a) $dx/dt = R(1 - \cos(t))$ and $dy/dt = R\sin(t)$ so
    $v = \sqrt{R^2(1-\cos(t))^2 + R^2(\sin(t))^2} = |R|\sqrt{2}\sqrt{1 - \cos(t)}$ ft/s.

    (b) v is maximum when $\cos(t) = -1$, when $t = (2k+1)\pi$ seconds for k an integer.

    (c) $v_{max} = 2R$ ft/s.

23. $L = \int_0^2 \sqrt{(1-2t)^2 + 2^2}\, dt \approx 4.939$ (using a calculator).

25. π (half the circumference of the circle).

27. $x = 3 - t, y = 1 + \frac{1}{2}t$. $L = \int_1^3 \sqrt{(-1)^2 + (1/2)^2}\, dt = 2 \cdot \frac{\sqrt{5}}{2} = \sqrt{5} \approx 2.24$.

    Alternately, the graph of (x, y) is a straight line, and we can calculate the distance from $(x(1), y(1)) = (2, 1.5)$ to the point $(x(3), y(3)) = (0, 2.5)$: distance $= \sqrt{2^2 + 1^2} = \sqrt{5}$.

29. $y = 4t^2 - t^4$, $dx/dt = 2t$. $A = \int_0^2 (4t^2 - t^4) \cdot 2t\, dt = 2t^4 - \frac{1}{3}t^6 \Big|_0^2 = 32 - \frac{64}{3} = \frac{32}{3}$.

31. $y = 1 + \cos(t)$, $dx/dt = 2t$. $A = \int_0^2 (1 + \cos(t)) \cdot 2t\, dt \approx 4.805$ (using a calculator).

33. See Fig. 24. $A = \frac{\pi R^2}{4} + \frac{R^2}{2} + \frac{\pi R^2}{2} + \frac{R^2}{2} + \frac{\pi R^2}{4} = \pi R^2 + R^2 = R^2(\pi + 1)$.

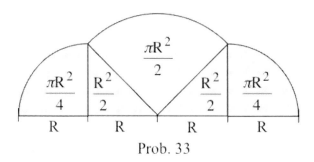

Prob. 33

Section 9.4.5 Odd Answers

1. $P_A = (0,4)$, $P_B = (5,2)$. $x(t) = 0 + 5t = (1-t) \cdot 0 + t \cdot 5$ and $y(t) = 4 + (-2)t = (1-t) \cdot 4 + t \cdot 2$.

3. $P_A = (4,3)$, $P_B = (1,2)$. $x(t) = 4 - 3t = (1-t) \cdot 4 + t \cdot 1$ and $y(t) = 3 - 1t = (1-t) \cdot 3 + t \cdot 2$.

5. $P_A = (1,4)$, $P_B = (5,1)$. $x(t) = 1 + 4t = (1-t) \cdot 1 + t \cdot 5$ and $y(t) = 4 + (-3)t = (1-t) \cdot 4 + t \cdot 1$

7. If we start with the equation $x(t) = x_0 + t \cdot \Delta x$ and replace Δx with $x_1 - x_0$ then
$x(t) = x_0 + t \cdot (x_1 - x_0) = x_0 + t \cdot x_1 - t \cdot x_0 = (1-t) \cdot x_0 + t \cdot x_1$ which is the pattern we wanted.
The algebra for y(t) is similar.

For problems 9-13 the Bezier pattern is
$$B(t) = (1-t)^3 \cdot P_0 + 3(1-t)^2 t \cdot P_1 + 3(1-t)t^2 \cdot P_2 + t^3 \cdot P_3$$

9. $x(t) = (1-t)^3 \cdot 0 + 3(1-t)^2 t \cdot 2 + 3(1-t)t^2 \cdot 1 + t^3 \cdot 4$
$y(t) = (1-t)^3 \cdot 5 + 3(1-t)^2 t \cdot 3 + 3(1-t)t^2 \cdot 4 + t^3 \cdot 2$

11. $x(t) = (1-t)^3 \cdot 6 + 3(1-t)^2 t \cdot 6 + 3(1-t)t^2 \cdot 2 + t^3 \cdot 2$
$y(t) = (1-t)^3 \cdot 5 + 3(1-t)^2 t \cdot 3 + 3(1-t)t^2 \cdot 5 + t^3 \cdot 0$

13. $P_0 = (5,1)$ and $B'(0) = 2$ tells us that P_1 could be (5+1, 1+2) or (5+2, 1+4) or (5+h, 1 + 2h)
We pick $P_1 = (6,3)$
$P_3 = (1,3)$ and $B'(1) = 3$ tells us P_2 could be (1+1,3+3) or (1+h, 3+3h).
We pick $P_2 = (2,6)$.
$x(t) = (1-t)^3 \cdot 5 + 3(1-t)^2 t \cdot 6 + 3(1-t)t^2 \cdot 2 + t^3 \cdot 1$
$y(t) = (1-t)^3 \cdot 1 + 3(1-t)^2 t \cdot 3 + 3(1-t)t^2 \cdot 6 + t^3 \cdot 3$

14. See Fig. 20.   15. See Fig. 21.
16. See Fig. 22.   17. See Fig. 23.

18. Violates Property (3): B'(1) does not equal the slope of the segment from P_2 to P_3

19. Violates Property (3) at B(1). Also violates Property (4) since the B(t) graph goes outside the "rubber band" around the 4 control points.

20. Violates Property (2). Since the graph of B(t) has 3 "turns" then B(t) is not a cubic polynomial (which can only have 2 turns).

21. Violates Property (1): B(1) = P_2 instead of P_3.

Fig. 20

Fig. 21

Fig. 22

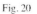
Fig. 23

Section 9.5   Odd Answers

1. An ellipse. Figure is given. Since $b^2 + 6^2 = 10^2$, $b = 8$. $c = \sqrt{a^2 - b^2}$ so $6 = \sqrt{a^2 - 64}$ and $a = 10$. The ellipse is given by $\dfrac{x^2}{10^2} + \dfrac{y^2}{8^2} = 1$.

Prob. 1

3. A parabola with focus at (0,5) and vertex at (0,0). The parabola has an equation of the form $y = ax^2$ with $\dfrac{1}{4a} = 5$ so $a = \dfrac{1}{20}$. The parabola is given by $y = \dfrac{1}{20} x^2$.

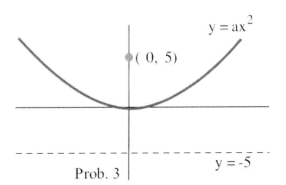
Prob. 3

5. $\dfrac{x^2}{4} + \dfrac{y^2}{9} = 1$.

7. Linear asymptotes: $y = \dfrac{2}{3} x$ and $y = -\dfrac{2}{3} x$. (Set $4x^2 - 9y^2 = 0$ and solve for y.) $c^2 = a^2 + b^2 = 4 + 9$ so $c = \sqrt{13}$: foci are at $(\sqrt{13}, 0)$ and $(-\sqrt{13}, 0)$.

9. Linear asymptotes: $y = \sqrt{\dfrac{3}{5}} x$ and $y = -\sqrt{\dfrac{3}{5}} x$. Foci: $(0, \sqrt{8})$ and $(0, -\sqrt{8})$.

11. (a) $25x^2 + 4y^2 + (-100) = 0$: discriminant $= (0)^2 - 4(25)(4) = -400 < 0$. The graph is an ellipse.
    (b) $b^2 x^2 + a^2 y^2 + (a^2 b^2) = 0$: discriminant $= (0)^2 - 4(a^2)(b^2) = -4a^2 b^2 < 0$. The graph is an ellipse.

13. $x^2 + xy - 2y^2 - x + y - 3 = 0$: discriminant $= (1)^2 - 4(1)(-2) = 9 > 0$. The graph is a hyperbola.

15. $2x^2 + 4xy + 2y^2 - 7x + 3 = 0$: discriminant $= (4)^2 - 4(2)(2) = 0$. The graph is a parabola.

17. (a) $B^2 - 4AC = 9 - 4(2)(2) < 0$: ellipse.
    (b) $B^2 - 4AC = 16 - 4(2)(2) = 0$: parabola.
    (c) $B^2 - 4AC = 25 - 4(2)(2) > 0$: hyperbola.
    (d) same answers as for parts (a), (b), and (c).

19. (a) $B^2 - 4AC = 16 - 4(1)(3) > 0$: hyperbola.
    (b) $B^2 - 4AC = 16 - 4(1)(4) = 0$: parabola.
    (c) $B^2 - 4AC = 16 - 4(1)(5) < 0$: ellipse.
    (d) same answers as for parts (a), (b), and (c).

21. Figure is shown.

(a) About the x–axis: $V = 2\int_0^2 \pi y^2\, dx = 2\pi \int_0^2 25(1 - \frac{x^2}{4})\, dx$

$= 50\pi \{x - \frac{x^3}{12}\}\Big|_0^2 = \frac{200\pi}{3}$.

(b) About the y–axis: $V = 2\int_0^5 \pi x^2\, dy$

$= 2\pi \int_0^5 4(1 - \frac{y^2}{25})\, dx = 8\pi\{y - \frac{y^3}{75}\}\Big|_0^5 = \frac{80\pi}{3}$.

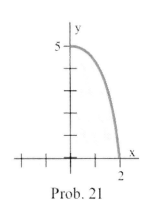
Prob. 21

23. Figure is shown.

(a) About the x–axis: $V = \int_2^{10} \pi y^2\, dx$

$= \pi \int_2^{10} 25(\frac{x^2}{4} - 1)\, dx = 25\pi \{\frac{x^3}{12} - x\}\Big|_2^{10}$

$= 25\pi\{(\frac{1000}{12} - 10) - (\frac{8}{12} - 2)\} = \frac{5600\pi}{3} \approx 5864.3$.

(b) About the y–axis: $V = 2\pi \int_0^{10\sqrt{6}} \{100 - 4(\frac{y^2}{25} + 1)\}\, dy = 2\pi\{96y - \frac{4y^3}{75}\}\Big|_0^{10\sqrt{6}}$

$= 20\sqrt{6}\,\pi\{96 - \frac{2400}{75}\} = \frac{3840\sqrt{6}\,\pi}{3} \approx 9850$.

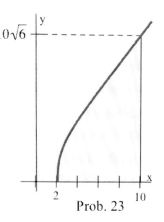
Prob. 23

25. $A_{parabolic} = \int_a^b ax^2\, dx = \frac{1}{3}ax^3\Big|_a^b = \frac{1}{3}ab^3$. $A_{rectangular} = ab^2 \cdot b = ab^3$. $\frac{A_{parabolic}}{A_{rectangular}} = \frac{1}{3}$.

27. The length of the string is the distance between the vertices.

29. When the pins (foci) are far apart, the ellipse tends to be long and narrow, cigar shaped. As the pins are moved closer together, the ellipse becomes more rounded and circular. In the limit, with the pins together, the ellipse is a cirle with diameter equal to the length of the string.

31. The curves are parabolas As the string is shortened, the vertex is moved up and the parabola narrows, approaching a vertical ray in the limit as the length of the string nears the vertical distance from the pin to the corner of the T–square where the string is attached.

Section 9.6   Odd Answers

1. 12 units, independent of where it bounces off of the ellipse.

3. After a "long time," the ball oscillates (almost) along a line between the vertices of the hyperbola.

5. All of the energy along the wave front is reflected to the focus of the parabolic jetty at the same time   The boat would be struck by a wave of considerable force.

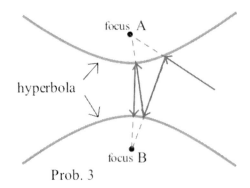
Prob. 3

7. The traced rays are shown. The eyepiece is located at F_2 because all of the incoming light is focused there.

9. (a) Roll the ball toward the focus F1 . The paths of A and B are shown.
   (b) The strategy in part (a) does not work for a ball in the shaded region. Why not?

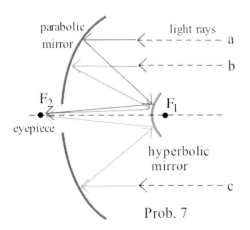
Prob. 7

11. At any point E on the ellipse, the angle of incidence equals the angle of reflection so the angles α and β are equal and the angle a and b are equal. Since {angle a} > {angle α} we have that {angle b} > {angle β} and the ball is reflected to a point C between the two foci.

13. $r = \dfrac{11/3}{1 + (5/3)\cos(\theta)}$ so e = 5/3 > 1 and the graph is a hyperbola. The hyperbola crosses the x–axis when $\theta = 0$ and π: at the points (11/8, 0) and (11/2, 0). It crosses the y–axis when $\theta = \pi/2$ and $3\pi/2$: at the points (0, 11/3) and (0, –11/3).

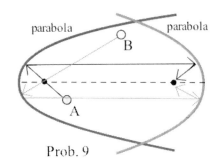
Prob. 9

15. $r = \dfrac{1/2}{1 + 1 \cdot \sin(\theta - \pi/3)}$ so e = 1 and the graph is a parabola.

The parabola crosses the x–axis when $\theta = 0$ and π: approximately at the points (3.73 , 0) and (–0.27 , 0). It crosses the y–axis when $\theta = \pi/2$ and $3\pi/2$: at the points (0, 1/3) and (0, –1).

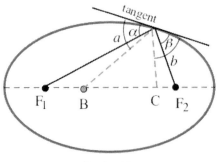
Prob. 11

17. $r = \dfrac{17/7}{1 - (5/7)\cdot \cos(\theta + 3\pi)}$ so $e = 5/7 \le 1$ and the graph is an ellipse.

The ellipse crosses the x–axis when $\theta = 0$ and π: approximately at the points $(1.42, 0)$ and $(-8.5, 0)$. It crosses the y–axis when $\theta = \pi/2$ and $3\pi/2$: at the points $(0, 2.43)$ and $(0, -2.43)$.

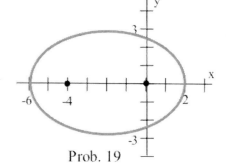
Prob. 19

19. One focus is at $(0,0)$ and, by symmetry, the other focus is at $(-4, 0)$.

21. One focus is at $(0,0)$ and, by symmetry, the other focus is at $(0, 3)$.

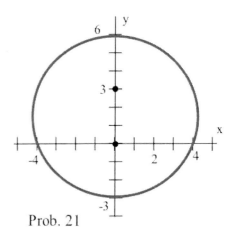
Prob. 21

23. See Fig. 41. This one is more difficult because the ellipse is tilted, but we can still use the symmetry of the ellipse and the fact that it is tilted at an angle of $\pi/4$ to the x–axis. One focus is at $(0,0)$ and the other focus is at $(1.41, -1.41)$.

25. $r = \dfrac{1}{1 + 0.5\cdot\cos(\theta)}$.

$\dfrac{dr}{d\theta} = -(1 + 0.5\cdot\cos(\theta))^{-2}\cdot\{-0.5\cdot\sin(\theta)\} = \dfrac{\sin(\theta)}{2 + \cos(\theta)}$.

Length $= \displaystyle\int_0^{2\pi} \sqrt{(r)^2 + (dr/d\theta)^2}\, d\theta \approx 7.659$

Area $= \displaystyle\int_0^{2\pi} \tfrac{1}{2} r^2(\theta)\, d \approx 4.8368$

Prob. 23

Both integrals were approximated using Simpson's rule with $n = 20$)

27. $h = \dfrac{r_o v_o^2}{GM} = \dfrac{10^5 (17.6)^2}{(6.7)(10^{-11})(10^{19})} = \dfrac{3.097 \times 10^7}{6.7 \times 10^8} \approx 4.62 \times 10^{-2}$ so $e = |h - 1| \approx 0.95 < 1$

and the path is an ellipse (but a long narrow ellipse such as a comet might have).

29. $h = \dfrac{r_o v_o^2}{GM} = \dfrac{10^5 (120)^2}{(6.7)(10^{-11})(10^{19})} = \dfrac{1.44 \times 10^9}{6.7 \times 10^8} \approx 2.149$ so $e = |h - 1| \approx 1.149 > 1$ and the path is a hyperbola.

31. $e = \dfrac{r \cdot v^2}{GM} - 1$.

   (a) The path is circular if $e = 0$, so $\dfrac{r \cdot v^2}{GM} - 1 = 0$ and $v = \sqrt{\dfrac{GM}{r}}$.

   (b) The path is elliptical if $e < 1$, so $\dfrac{r \cdot v^2}{GM} - 1 < 1$ and
   $v < \sqrt{\dfrac{2GM}{r}} = \sqrt{2}\sqrt{\dfrac{GM}{r}} = \sqrt{2} \cdot \{\text{circular velocity}\}$.

   (c) The path is parabolic if $e = 1$, so $v = \sqrt{\dfrac{2GM}{r}} = \sqrt{2}\sqrt{\dfrac{GM}{r}} = \sqrt{2} \cdot \{\text{circular velocity}\}$.

   (d) The path is hyperbolic if $e > 1$, so $v > \sqrt{\dfrac{2GM}{r}} = \sqrt{2}\sqrt{\dfrac{GM}{r}} = \sqrt{2} \cdot \{\text{circular velocity}\}$.

33. We want $v = \sqrt{\dfrac{2GM}{r}} = \sqrt{\dfrac{2(6.7 \times 10^{-11})(5.98 \times 10^{24})}{6.36 \times 10^6}} \approx \sqrt{1.26 \times 10^8} \approx 11{,}225$ m/s or

   approximately 25,110 miles per hour.

35. $r_{max} = 1000 + r_{earth} \approx 7.36 \times 10^6$. $r_{min} = 800 + r_{earth} \approx 7.16 \times 10^6$.
   $2a = r_{min} + r_{max} \approx 14.520 \times 10^6$ so $a \approx 7.26 \times 10^6$.
   Also, $r_{max} = a(1 + e)$ so $7.36 \times 10^6 = 7.26 \times 10^6 (1 + e)$ and $e \approx 0.01377$.
   Finally, $k = a(1 - e^2) \approx 7.26 \times 10^6 (1 - (0.01377)^2) \approx 7.2586 \times 10^6$ so
   $r = \dfrac{k}{1 + e \cdot \cos(\theta)} \approx \dfrac{7.2586 \times 10^6}{1 + (0.01377) \cdot \cos(\theta)}$.

37. On your own.

10.0 INTRODUCTION TO SEQUENCES AND SERIES

Chapter 10 is an introduction to two special topics in calculus, sequences and series. The main idea underlying this chapter is that **polynomials are easy**, and that even the hard functions such as sin(x) and log(x) can be represented as "big polynomials."

Polynomials are easy. It is easy to do arithmetic (evaluate, add, subtract, multiply, and even divide) with polynomials. It is easy to do calculus (differentiate and integrate) with polynomials. And, strangely enough, every polynomial is <u>completely</u> determined by its value and the values of all of its derivatives at x = 0: if we know the values of P(0), P'(0), P''(0), etc., we can determine a formula for P(x) that is valid for all x.

Unfortunately, many of the important functions we need for applications (sin, cos, exp, log) are not polynomials: sin and cos have too many wiggles; exp grows too fast; and log has an asymptote. However, even these "hard" functions are "almost" polynomials and share many properties with polynomials:

For some values of x (to be specified in later sections), many important functions can be represented as "big polynomials" called power series:

$$\sin(x) = x - \frac{x^3}{2 \cdot 3} + \frac{x^5}{2 \cdot 3 \cdot 4 \cdot 5} - \frac{x^7}{2 \cdot 3 \cdot 4 \cdot 5 \cdot 6 \cdot 7} + \ldots + (-1)^n \frac{x^{2n+1}}{(2n+1)!} + \ldots \quad \text{for } n = 0, 1, 2, \ldots$$

$$\cos(x) = 1 - \frac{x^2}{2} + \frac{x^4}{2 \cdot 3 \cdot 4} - \frac{x^6}{2 \cdot 3 \cdot 4 \cdot 5 \cdot 6} + \ldots + (-1)^n \frac{x^{2n}}{(2n)!} + \ldots$$

$$\exp(x) = 1 + x + \frac{x^2}{2} + \frac{x^3}{2 \cdot 3} + \frac{x^4}{2 \cdot 3 \cdot 4} + \ldots + \frac{x^n}{n!} + \ldots$$

$$\frac{1}{1-x} = 1 + x + x^2 + x^3 + x^4 + \ldots + x^n + \ldots$$

the " . . . " at the end means the pattern of the terms continues "forever"

In this chapter we examine
- what it means to sum an **infinite** number of terms,
- how to do algebra and calculus with series ("big polynomials"),
- how to represent functions as series ("big polynomials"), and
- how to use such series ("big polynomials") to calculate derivatives, integrals, and even solve differential equations.

First, however, we need to lay a foundation, and that foundation is the study of lists of numbers, their properties and behavior.

Section 10.1 focuses on this foundation material. It introduces lists of numbers, called sequences, and examines some specific sequences we will need later. It also introduces the idea of the convergence of a sequence and examines some ways we can determine whether or not a sequence converges.

Sections 10.2 to 10.7 focus on what it means to add up an infinite number of numbers, an infinite series, and on how we can determine whether the resulting sum is a finite number.

Sections 10.8 to 10.11 generalize the idea of an infinite series of numbers to infinite series that contain a variable. These series that contain powers of a variable are called power series. These sections discuss how we can represent and approximate functions such as $\sin(x)$ and e^x with power series, how accurate these approximations are for commonly needed functions, and how we can use them with derivatives and integrals.

PROBLEMS

These problems illustrate, at an elementary level, some of the problems and concepts we will examine more deeply in this chapter. They are intended to start you thinking in certain ways that are useful and necessary for Chapter 10.

Patterns in lists of numbers

For problems 1 – 6, the first four numbers $a_1, a_2, a_3,$ and a_4 in a list are given. (a) Write the next two numbers in the list, (b) write a formula for the 5th number a_5 in the list and (c) write a formula for the nth number a_n in the list.

1. 2, 4, 8, 16, ___ , ___
2. 3, 9, 27, 81, ___ , ___
3. –1, +1, –1, +1, ___ , ___
4. 1, 1/2, 1/3, 1/4, ___ , ___
5. 1, 2, 6, 24, ___ , ___
6. 1, 4, 9, 16, ___ , ___

For problems 7 – 11, evaluate each of the four given numbers and write the next two numbers in the list.

7. 1, 1 + 1/2, 1 + 1/2 + 1/3, 1 + 1/2 + 1/3 + 1/4, _____ , _____
8. 1, 1 + 1/2, 1 + 1/2 + 1/4, 1 + 1/2 + 1/4 + 1/6, _____ , _____
9. 1, 1 – 1/2, 1 – 1/2 + 1/4, 1 – 1/2 + 1/4 – 1/8, _____ , _____
10. 1, 1 + 2, 1 + 2 + 4, 1 + 2 + 4 + 8, _____ , _____
11. 1, 1 – 1, 1 – 1 + 1, 1 – 1 + 1 – 1, _____ , _____

Lists and graphs

For problems 12 – 15, (a) fill in the next two entries in the table and (b) graph the function for $x = 1, 2, \ldots 6$. These particular functions are defined only for integer values of x.

12.
x	f(x)
1	2
2	4
3	8
4	16
5	
6	

13.
x	g(x)
1	−1
2	+1
3	−1
4	+1
5	
6	

14.
x	s(x)
1	1 + 1/2
2	1 + 1/2 + 1/3
3	1 + 1/2 + 1/3 + 1/4
4	1 + 1/2 + 1/3 + 1/4 + 1/5
5	
6	

15.
x	t(x)
1	1 − 1/2
2	1 − 1/2 + 1/4
3	1 − 1/2 + 1/4 − 1/8
4	1 − 1/2 + 1/4 − 1/8 + 1/16
5	
6	

Polynomials and sine, cosine, and the exponential function

16. (a) Fill in the table for $P(x) = x - \dfrac{x^3}{2 \cdot 3}$ and $\sin(x)$.

    (b) Graph $y = P(x)$ and $y = \sin(x)$ for $-2 \leq x \leq 2$.

    (c) Repeat parts (a) and (b) for $P(x) = x - \dfrac{x^3}{2 \cdot 3} + \dfrac{x^5}{2 \cdot 3 \cdot 4 \cdot 5}$.

x	P(x)	sin(x)	| P(x) − sin(x) |
0			
0.1			
0.2			
0.3			
1.0			
2.0			

17. (a) Fill in the table for $P(x) = 1 - \dfrac{x^2}{2}$ and $\cos(x)$.

    (b) Graph $y = P(x)$ and $y = \cos(x)$ for $-2 \leq x \leq 2$.

    (c) Repeat parts (a) and (b) for $P(x) = 1 - \dfrac{x^2}{2} + \dfrac{x^4}{2 \cdot 3 \cdot 4}$.

x	P(x)	cos(x)	| P(x) − cos(x) |
0			
0.1			
0.2			
0.3			
1.0			
2.0			

18. (a) Fill in the table for $P(x) = 1 + x + \dfrac{x^2}{2}$ and e^x.

    (b) Graph $y = P(x)$ and $y = e^x$ for $-2 \leq x \leq 2$.

    (c) Repeat parts (a) and (b) for $P(x) = 1 + x + \dfrac{x^2}{2} + \dfrac{x^3}{3}$.

x	P(x)	e^x	| P(x) − e^x |
0			
0.1			
0.2			
0.3			
1.0			
2.0			

Polynomials and their values at x = 0

These problems illustrate how we can determine a formula for a polynomial when we know the values of the polynomial and its derivatives at $x = 0$.

In problems 19 – 24, $P(x) = Ax + B$ is a linear polynomial, and the values of $P(0)$ and $P\,'(0)$ are given. Find the values of A and B and write a formula for $P(x)$.

19. $P(0) = 5$, $P\,'(0) = 3$ 20. $P(0) = -2$, $P\,'(0) = 7$ 21. $P(0) = 4$, $P\,'(0) = -1$

22. $P(0) = 8$, $P\,'(0) = 5$ 23. $P(0) = 4$, $P\,'(0) = 0$ 24. $P(0) = -3$, $P\,'(0) = -2$

25. How are the values of A and B related to the values of $P(0)$ and $P\,'(0)$?

In problems 26 – 31, $P(x) = Ax^2 + Bx + C$ is a quadratic polynomial, and the values of $P(0)$, $P\,'(0)$, and $P\,''(0)$ are given. Find the values of A, B, and C and write a formula for $P(x)$.

26. $P(0) = 5$, $P\,'(0) = 3$, $P\,''(0) = 4$ 27. $P(0) = -2$, $P\,'(0) = 7$, $P\,''(0) = 6$

28. $P(0) = 4$, $P\,'(0) = -1$, $P\,''(0) = -2$ 29. $P(0) = 8$, $P\,'(0) = 5$, $P\,''(0) = 10$

30. $P(0) = 4$, $P\,'(0) = 0$, $P\,''(0) = -4$ 31. $P(0) = -3$, $P\,'(0) = -2$, $P\,''(0) = 4$

32. How are the values of A, B, and C related to the values of $P(0)$, $P\,'(0)$, and $P\,''(0)$?

In problems 33 – 38, $P(x) = Ax^3 + Bx^2 + Cx + D$ is a cubic polynomial, and the values of $P(0)$, $P\,'(0)$, $P\,''(0)$, and $P\,'''(0)$ are given. Find the values of A, B, C, and D and write a formula for $P(x)$.

33. $P(0) = 5$, $P\,'(0) = 3$, $P\,''(0) = 4$, $P\,'''(0) = 6$ 34. $P(0) = -2$, $P\,'(0) = 7$, $P\,''(0) = 6$, $P\,'''(0) = 18$

35. $P(0) = 4$, $P\,'(0) = -1$, $P\,''(0) = -2$, $P\,'''(0) = -12$ 36. $P(0) = 8$, $P\,'(0) = 5$, $P\,''(0) = 10$, $P\,'''(0) = 12$

37. $P(0) = 4$, $P\,'(0) = 0$, $P\,''(0) = -4$, $P\,'''(0) = 36$ 38. $P(0) = -3$, $P\,'(0) = -2$, $P\,''(0) = 4$, $P\,'''(0) = 36$

39. How are the values of A, B, C, and D related to the values of $P(0)$, $P\,'(0)$, $P\,''(0)$, and $P\,'''(0)$?

10.1 SEQUENCES

Sequences play important roles in several areas of theoretical and applied mathematics. As you study additional mathematics you will encounter them again. In this course, however, their role is primarily as a foundation for our study of series ("big polynomials"). In order to understand how and where it is valid to represent a function such as sine as a series, we need to examine what it means to add together an infinite number of values. And in order to understand this infinite addition we need to analyze lists of numbers (called sequences) and determine whether or not the numbers in the list are converging to a single value. This section examines sequences, how to represent sequences graphically, what it means for a sequence to converge, and several techniques to determine if a sequence converges.

Example 1: A person places $100 in an account that pays 8% interest at the end of each year. How much will be in the account at the end of 1 year, 2 years, 3 years, and n years?

Solution: After one year, the total is the principal plus the interest: $100 + (.08)100 = (1.08) \cdot 100 = \$108$.

At the end of the second year, the amount is 108% of the amount at the start of the second year:

$(1.08)\{ (1.08)100 \} = (1.08)^2 \cdot 100 = \$116.64$.

At the end of the third year, the amount is 108% of the amount at the start of the third year:

$(1.08)\{ (1.08)^2 \, 100 \} = (1.08)^3 \cdot 100 = \$125.97$.

These results are shown in Fig. 1. In general, at the end of the nth year, the amount in the account is $(1.08)^n \cdot 100$ dollars.

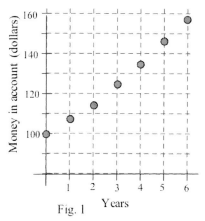

Fig. 1

Practice 1: A layer of protective film transmits two thirds of the light that reaches that layer. How much of the incoming light is transmitted through 1 layer, 2 layers, 3 layers, and n layers? (Fig. 2)

The Example and Practice each asked for a list of numbers in a definite order: a first number, then a second number, and so on. Such a list of numbers in a definite order is called a **sequence**. An infinite sequence is one that just keeps going and has no last number. Often the pattern of a sequence is clear from the first few numbers, but in order to precisely specify a sequence, a rule for finding the value of the nth term, a_n ("a sub n"), in the sequence is usually given.

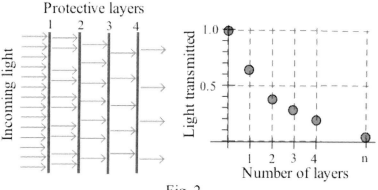

Fig. 2

Example 2: List the next two numbers in each sequence and give a rule for calculating the nth number, a_n:

(a) $1, 4, 9, 16, \ldots$ (b) $-1, 1, -1, 1, \ldots$ (c) $\frac{1}{2}, \frac{1}{4}, \frac{1}{8}, \frac{1}{16}, \ldots$

Solution: (a) $a_5 = 25, a_6 = 36,$ and $a_n = n^2$. (b) $a_5 = -1, a_6 = 1,$ and $a_n = (-1)^n$.

(c) $a_5 = \frac{1}{32}, a_6 = \frac{1}{64}$, and $a_n = (\frac{1}{2})^n = \frac{1}{2^n}$.

Practice 2: List the next two numbers in each sequence and give a rule for calculating the nth number, a_n:

(a) $1, \frac{1}{2}, \frac{1}{3}, \frac{1}{4}, \ldots$ (b) $\frac{-1}{2}, \frac{1}{4}, \frac{-1}{8}, \frac{1}{16}, \ldots$ (c) $2, 2, 2, 2, \ldots$

Definition and Notation

Since a sequence gives a single value for each integer n, a sequence is a function, but a function whose domain is restricted to the integers.

> **Definition**
>
> A **sequence** is a function whose domain is all integers greater than or equal to a starting integer.

Most of our sequences will have a starting integer of 1, but sometimes it is convenient to start with 0 or another integer value.

Notation: The symbol a_n represents a single number called the nth term.

The symbol $\{ a_n \}$ represents the entire sequence of numbers, the set of all terms.

The symbol $\{ rule \}$ represents the sequence generated by the rule.

The symbol $\{ a_n \}_{n=3}$ represents the sequence that starts with $n = 3$.

Because sequences are functions, we can add, subtract, multiply, and divide them, and we can combine them with other functions to form new sequences. We can also graph sequences, and their graphs can sometimes help us describe and understand their behavior.

Example 3: For the sequences given by $a_n = 3 - \frac{1}{n}$ and $b_n = \frac{1}{2^n}$, graph the points (n, a_n) and (n, b_n) for $n = 1$ to 5. Calculate the first 5 terms of $c_n = a_n + b_n$ and graph the points (n, c_n).

Solution: $c_1 = (3 - \frac{1}{1}) + (\frac{1}{2^1}) = 2.5, c_2 = 2.75, c_3 \approx 2.792$,

$c_4 = 2.8125, c_5 = 2.83125$. The graphs of $(n, a_n), (n, b_n),$ and (n, c_n) are shown in Fig. 3.

Practice 3: For a_n and b_n in the previous example, calculate the first 5 terms of $c_n = a_n - b_n$ and $d_n = (-1)^n b_n$ and graph the points (n, c_n) and (n, d_n).

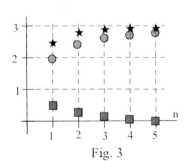

Fig. 3

Recursive Sequences

A recursive sequence is a sequence defined by a rule that gives each new term in the sequence as a combination of some of the previous terms. We already encountered a recursive sequence when we studied Newton's Method for approximating roots of a function (Section 2.7). Newton's method for finding the roots of a function generates a recursive sequence $\{x_1, x_2, x_3, x_4, ...\}$, as do successive iterations of a function and other operations.

Example 4: Let $f(x) = x^2 - 4$. Take $x_1 = 3$ and apply Newton's method (Section 2.7) to calculate x_2 and x_3. Give a rule for x_n.

Solution: $f(x) = x^2 - 4$ so $f'(x) = 2x$, and, by Newton's method,

$$x_2 = x_1 - \frac{f(x_1)}{f'(x_1)} = 3 - \frac{f(3)}{f'(3)} = 3 - \frac{5}{6} = \frac{13}{6} \approx 2.1667.$$

$$x_3 = x_2 - \frac{f(x_2)}{f'(x_2)} = \frac{13}{6} - \frac{f(13/6)}{f'(13/6)} = \frac{13}{6} - \frac{25}{156} = \frac{313}{156} \approx 2.0064.$$

In general, $x_n = x_{n-1} - \dfrac{f(x_{n-1})}{f'(x_{n-1})} = x_{n-1} - \dfrac{(x_{n-1})^2 - 4}{2x_{n-1}}$.

The terms $x_1, x_2, ...$ approach the value 2, one solution of $x^2 - 4 = 0$. The sequence $\{x_n\}$ is a recursive sequence since each term x_n is defined as a function of the previous term x_{n-1}.

Practice 4: Let $f(x) = 2x - 1$, and define $a_n = f(f(f(...f(a_0)...)))$ where the function is applied n times. Put $a_0 = 3$ and calculate $a_1, a_2,$ and a_3. Note that a_n can be defined recursively as $a_n = f(a_{n-1})$.

Example 5: Let $a_n = 1/2^n$, and define a second sequence $\{s_n\}$ by the rule that s_n is the **sum** of the first n terms of a_n. Calculate the values of s_n for n = 1 to 5.

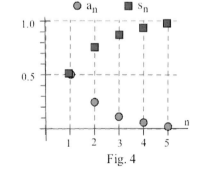

Solution: $s_1 = a_1 = 1/2,\qquad s_2 = a_1 + a_2 = 1/2 + 1/4 = 3/4$,
$s_3 = a_1 + a_2 + a_3 = 1/2 + 1/4 + 1/8 = 7/8$, $s_4 = 15/16$,
and $s_5 = 31/32$. (Fig. 4)

Fig. 4

You should notice two patterns in these sums.
First, it appears that $s_n = (2^n - 1)/2^n$.
Second, you can simplify the addition process: each term s_n is the sum of the previous term s_{n-1} and the a_n term: $s_n = s_{n-1} + a_n$. We will meet this second pattern again in the next section.

Practice 5: Let $b_0 = 0$ and, for n > 0, define $b_n = b_{n-1} + 1/3^n$. Calculate b_n for n = 1 to 4.

Limits of Sequences: Convergence

Since sequences are discrete functions defined only on integers, some calculus ideas for continuous functions are not applicable to sequences. One type of limit, however, is used: the limit as n approaches infinity. Do the values a_n eventually approach (or equal) some number?

We say that the limit of a sequence $\{ a_n \}$ is L if the terms a_n are arbitrarily close to L for sufficiently large values of n — the terms at the beginning of the sequence can be any values, but for large values of n, the a_n terms are all close to L. The following definition puts this idea more precisely.

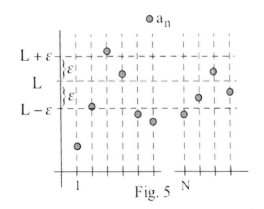

Definition

$\lim\limits_{n \to \infty} a_n = L$ if for any $\varepsilon > 0$ ("epsilon > 0")

there is an index N (typically depending on ε)

so that a_n is within ε of L whenever

n is larger than N :

$n > N$ implies $|a_n - L| < \varepsilon$ (Fig. 5)

If a sequence has a finite limit L, we say that the sequence "converges to L." If a sequence does not have a finite limit, we say the sequence "diverges." Typically a sequence diverges because its terms grow infinitely large (positively or negatively) or because the terms oscillate and do not approach a single number.

Example 7: For $a_n = 3 + 1/n^2$ show that $\lim\limits_{n \to \infty} a_n = 3$.

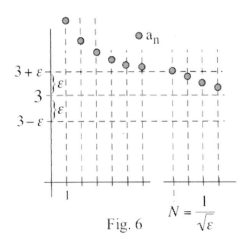

Fig. 6 $N = \dfrac{1}{\sqrt{\varepsilon}}$

Solution: We need to show that for any positive ε, there is a number N so that the distance from a_n to L, $|a_n - L|$, is less than ε whenever n is larger than N. For this particular sequence and limit we need to show that for any positive ε, there is a number N so that (Fig. 6)

$|(3 + 1/n^2) - 3| < \varepsilon$ whenever $n > N$.

To determine what N might be, we solve the inequality

$|(3 + 1/n^2) - 3| < \varepsilon$ for n in terms of ε:

$|1/n^2| < \varepsilon$ so $1/\varepsilon < n^2$ and $n > 1/\sqrt{\varepsilon}$.

So for **any** positive ε, we can take $N = 1/\sqrt{\varepsilon}$ (or the next larger integer). Then for $n > N$ we know that

$n > 1/\sqrt{\varepsilon}$ so $1/n^2 < \varepsilon$ and $|(3 + 1/n^2) - 3| < \varepsilon$.

Practice 6: For $a_n = (n+1)/n$ show that $\lim_{n \to \infty} a_n = 1$. (Fig. 7)

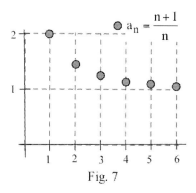

Fig. 7

The limit of a sequence, as n approaches infinity, depends only on the behavior of the terms of the sequence for large values of n (the "tail end") and not on the values of the first few (or few thousand) terms. As a consequence, we can insert or delete any **finite** number of terms without changing the convergence behavior of the sequence.

Sequences are functions, so limits of sequences share many properties with limits of other functions, and we state only a few of them.

Uniqueness Theorem

If a sequence converges to a limit, then the limit is unique.
A sequence can not converge to two different values.

A proof of the Uniqueness Theorem is given after the problem set.

Sometimes it is useful to replace a sequence $\{a_n\}$, a function whose domain is integers, with a function f whose domain is the real numbers so $a_n = f(n)$. If $f(x)$ has a limit as "$x \to \infty$," as x gets arbitrarily large, then $f(n)$ has the same limit as "$n \to \infty$" (Fig. 8). This replacement of "x" with "n" allows us to use earlier results about functions, particularly L'Hopital's Rule, to calculate limits of sequences.

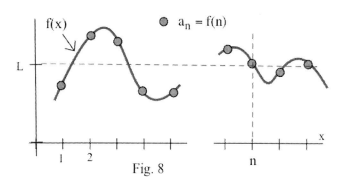

Fig. 8

Theorem: If $a_n = f(n)$ and $\lim_{x \to \infty} f(x) = L$

then $\{a_n\}$ converges to L: $\lim_{n \to \infty} a_n = L$

Example 8: Calculate $\lim_{n \to \infty} \left(1 + \frac{2}{n}\right)^n$.

Solution: The terms of the sequence are $a_n = \left(1 + \frac{2}{n}\right)^n$, so we can define $f(x) = \left(1 + \frac{2}{x}\right)^x$ by replacing the integer values n with real number values x. Then $a_n = f(n)$, and we can use

L'Hopital's rule to get $\lim\limits_{x \to \infty} \left(1 + \dfrac{2}{x}\right)^x = e^2$ (Section 3.7, Example 6). Finally, we can conclude that

$$\lim_{n \to \infty} \left(1 + \frac{2}{n}\right)^n = e^2 \approx 7.389 \quad \text{(Fig. 9)}.$$

Practice 7: Calculate $\lim\limits_{n \to \infty} \dfrac{\ln(n)}{n}$.

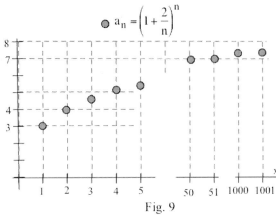

Fig. 9

A **subsequence** is an infinite set of terms from a sequence that occur in the same order as they appear in the original sequence. The sequence of even integers $\{2, 4, 6, \ldots\}$ is a subsequence of the sequence of all positive integers $\{1, 2, 3, 4, \ldots\}$. The sequence of reciprocals of primes $\{1/2, 1/3, 1/5, 1/7, \ldots\}$ is a subsequence of the sequence of the reciprocals of all positive integers $\{1, 1/2, 1/3, 1/4, 1/5, \ldots\}$. Subsequences inherit some properties from their original sequences.

Subsequence Theorem

Every subsequence of a convergent sequence converges to the same limit as the original sequence:

if $\quad \lim\limits_{n \to \infty} a_n = L$ and $\{b_n\}$ is a subsequence of $\{a_n\}$,

then $\quad \lim\limits_{n \to \infty} b_n = L$. (Fig. 10)

If the sequence $\{a_n\}$ does not converge, then the subsequence $\{b_n\}$ may or may not converge.

Corollary: If two subsequences of the same sequence converge to two different limits, then the original sequence diverges.

Example 9: Show that the sequence $\left\{ \dfrac{(-1)^n n}{n+1} \right\}$ diverges.

Solution: If n is even, then the even terms $a_n = \dfrac{(-1)^{\text{even}} n}{n+1} = \dfrac{n}{n+1}$ converge to +1 so the subsequence of even terms converges to 1.

If n is odd, then the odd terms $a_n = \dfrac{(-1)^{\text{odd}} n}{n+1} = \dfrac{-n}{n+1}$ converge to −1 so the subsequence of odd terms converges to −1. Finally, since the two subsequences converge to different values, we can conclude that the original sequence $\left\{ \dfrac{(-1)^n n}{n+1} \right\}$ diverges.

Fig. 10

Practice 8: Show that the sequence $\{\sin(n\pi/2)\}$ diverges.

Bounded and Monotonic Sequences

A sequence $\{a_n\}$ is **bounded above** if there is a value A so that $a_n \leq A$ for all values of n: A is called an **upper bound** of the sequence (Fig. 11). Similarly, $\{a_n\}$ is **bounded below** if there is a value B so that $B \leq a_n$ for all n: B is called a **lower bound** of the sequence. A sequence is **bounded** if it has an upper bound and a lower bound. All of the terms of a bounded sequence are between (or equal to) the upper and lower bounds (Fig. 12)

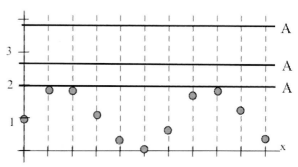

Fig. 11: Several upper bounds of the sequence $a_n = 1 + \sin(n)$

A **monotonically increasing** sequence is a sequence in which each term is greater than or equal to the previous term, $a_1 \leq a_2 \leq a_3 \leq \ldots$ (Fig. 13); a **monotonically decreasing** sequence is one in which each term is less than or equal to the previous term, $a_1 \geq a_2 \geq a_3 \geq \ldots$ (Fig. 14). A monotonic sequence does not oscillate: if one term is larger than a previous term and another term is smaller than a previous term, then the sequence is not monotonic increasing or decreasing.

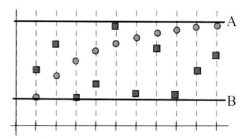

Fig. 12: Two bounded sequences

There are three basic ways to show that a sequence is monotonically increasing:

(i) by showing that $a_{n+1} \geq a_n$ for all n,

(ii) by showing that all the a_n are positive and $\dfrac{a_{n+1}}{a_n} \geq 1$ for all n, or

(iii) by showing that $a_n = f(n)$ for integer values n and $f'(x) \geq 0$ for all $x > 0$.

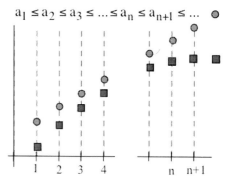

Two monotonic increasing sequences
Fig. 13

Practice 9: List three ways you can show that a sequence is monotonically decreasing.

Example 10: Show that the sequence $a_n = \dfrac{2^n}{n!}$ is monotonically decreasing by showing that $\dfrac{a_{n+1}}{a_n} \leq 1$ for all n.

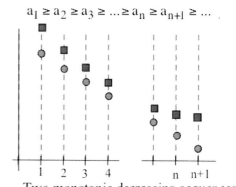

Two monotonic decreasing sequences
Fig. 14

Solution: $a_n = \dfrac{2^n}{n!} = \dfrac{2^n}{1 \cdot 2 \cdot 3 \cdot \ldots \cdot n}$ and $a_{n+1} = \dfrac{2^{n+1}}{(n+1)!} = \dfrac{2^n \cdot 2}{1 \cdot 2 \cdot 3 \cdot \ldots \cdot n \cdot (n+1)}$.

Then $\quad \dfrac{a_{n+1}}{a_n} = \dfrac{2^n \cdot 2}{1 \cdot 2 \cdot 3 \cdot \ldots \cdot n \cdot (n+1)} \cdot \dfrac{1 \cdot 2 \cdot 3 \cdot \ldots \cdot n}{2^n} \quad$ by inverting and multiplying

$\quad = \dfrac{2^n \cdot 2}{2^n} \cdot \dfrac{1 \cdot 2 \cdot 3 \cdot \ldots \cdot n}{1 \cdot 2 \cdot 3 \cdot \ldots \cdot n \cdot (n+1)} \quad$ by reorganizing the top and bottom

$\quad = \dfrac{2}{n+1} \leq 1$ for all positive integers n.

Practice 10: Show that $\left\{ \left(\dfrac{2}{3}\right)^n \right\}$ is monotonically decreasing.

Since the behavior of a monotonic sequence is so regular, it is usually easy to determine if a monotonic sequence has a finite limit: all we need to do is show that it is bounded.

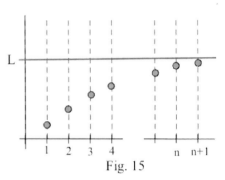

Fig. 15

Monotone Convergence Theorem

If a monotonic sequence is bounded,

then the sequence converges. (Fig. 15)

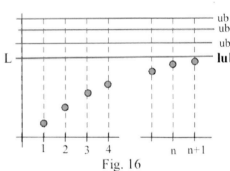

Fig. 16

Idea for a proof for a monotonically increasing sequence that is bounded above:

If the sequence $\{a_n\}$ is bounded above, then $\{a_n\}$ has an infinite number of upper bounds (Fig. 16), and each of these upper bounds is larger than every a_n. If L is the smallest of the upper bounds (the least upper bound) of $\{a_n\}$, then there is a value a_N as close as we want to L (otherwise there would be an upper bound smaller than L). Finally, if a_N is close to L, then the later values, a_n with $n \geq N$, are even closer to L because $\{a_n\}$ is monotonically increasing, so L is the limit of $\{a_n\}$.

Cauchy and other mathematicians accepted this theorem on intuitive and geometric grounds similar to the "idea for a proof" given above, but later mathematicians felt more rigor was needed. However, even the mathematician Dedekind who supplied much of that rigor recognized the usefulness of geometric intuition.

"Even now such resort to geometric intuition in a first presentation of differential calculus, I regard as exceedingly useful, from a didactic standpoint, and indeed indispensable if one does not wish to lose too much time." (Dedekind, Essays on the Theory of Numbers, 1901 (Dover, 1963), pp. 1–2)

10.1 Sequences

PROBLEMS In problems 1 – 6, find a rule which describes the given numbers in the sequence.

1. $1, 1/4, 1/9, 1/16, 1/25, \ldots$
2. $1, 1/8, 1/27, 1/64, 1/125, \ldots$
3. $0, 1/2, 2/3, 3/4, 4/5, \ldots$
4. $-1, 1/3, -1/9, 1/27, -1/81, \ldots$
5. $1/2, 2/4, 3/8, 4/16, 5/32, \ldots$
6. $7, 7, 7, 7, 7, \ldots$

(Bonus: O, T, T, F, F, S, S, E, ?, ?)

In problems 7 – 18, calculate the first 6 terms (starting with n = 1) of each sequence and graph these terms.

7. $\left\{ 1 - \dfrac{2}{n} \right\}$
8. $\left\{ 3 + \dfrac{1}{n^2} \right\}$
9. $\left\{ \dfrac{n}{2n-1} \right\}$
10. $\left\{ \dfrac{\ln(n)}{n} \right\}$

11. $\left\{ 3 + \dfrac{(-1)^n}{n} \right\}$
12. $\left\{ 4 + (-1)^n \right\}$
13. $\left\{ (-1)^n \dfrac{n-1}{n} \right\}$
14. $\left\{ \cos(n\pi/2) \right\}$

15. $\left\{ \dfrac{1}{n!} \right\}$
16. $\left\{ \dfrac{n+1}{n!} \right\}$
17. $\left\{ \dfrac{2^n}{n!} \right\}$
18. $\left\{ \left(1 + \dfrac{1}{n}\right)^n \right\}$

In problems 19 – 24, calculate the first 10 terms (starting with n = 1) of each sequence.

19. $a_1 = 2$ and $a_{n+1} = -a_n$
20. $b_1 = 3$ and $b_{n+1} = 1/b_n$

21. $\left\{ \sin\left(\dfrac{2\pi n}{3}\right) \right\}$
22. $a_1 = 2, a_2 = 3$, and, for $n \geq 3$, $a_n = a_{n-1} - a_{n-2}$

23. c_n = the sum of the first n positive integers

24. d_n = the sum of the first n prime numbers (2 is the first prime)

In problems 25 – 28, state whether each sequence appears to be converging or diverging. If you think the sequence is converging, mark its limit as a value on the vertical axis. (***Important Note:*** *The behavior of a sequence can change drastically after awhile, and the first terms have **no** influence on whether or not the sequence converges. However, sometimes the first few terms are the only values we have, and we need to reach a **tentative** conclusion based on those values.*)

25. Sequences A and B in Fig. 17.
26. Sequences C and D in Fig. 18.

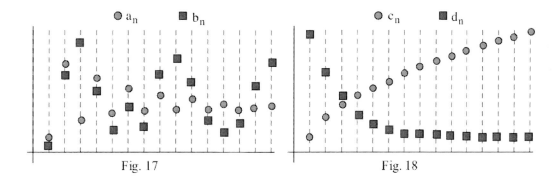

Fig. 17   Fig. 18

27. Sequences E and F in Fig. 19.   28. Sequences G and H in Fig. 20.

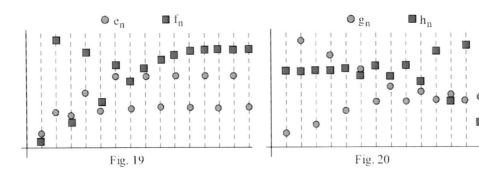

Fig. 19   Fig. 20

In problems 29 – 43, state whether each sequence converges or diverges. If the sequence converges, find its limit.

29. $\left\{ 1 - \dfrac{2}{n} \right\}$ 30. $\{ n^2 \}$ 31. $\left\{ \dfrac{n^2}{n+1} \right\}$ 32. $\left\{ 3 + \dfrac{1}{n^2} \right\}$

33. $\left\{ \dfrac{n}{2n-1} \right\}$ 34. $\left\{ \dfrac{\ln(n)}{n} \right\}$ 35. $\left\{ \ln\left(3 + \dfrac{7}{n}\right) \right\}$ 36. $\left\{ 3 + \dfrac{(-1)^{n+1}}{n} \right\}$

37. $\{ 4 + (-1)^n \}$ 38. $\left\{ (-1)^n \dfrac{n-1}{n} \right\}$ 39. $\left\{ \dfrac{1}{n!} \right\}$ 40. $\left\{ \left(1 + \dfrac{3}{n}\right)^n \right\}$

41. $\left\{ \left(1 - \dfrac{1}{n}\right)^n \right\}$ 42. $\left\{ \dfrac{\sqrt{n}-3}{\sqrt{n}+3} \right\}$ 43. $\left\{ \dfrac{(n+2)(n-5)}{n^2} \right\}$

In problems 44 – 47, prove that the sequence converges to the given limit by showing that for any $\varepsilon > 0$, you can find an N which satisfies the conditions of the definition of convergence.

44. $\lim\limits_{n \to \infty} 2 - \dfrac{3}{n} = 2$ 45. $\lim\limits_{n \to \infty} \dfrac{3}{n^2} = 0$

46. $\lim\limits_{n \to \infty} \dfrac{7}{n+1} = 0$ 47. $\lim\limits_{n \to \infty} \dfrac{3n-1}{n} = 3$

In problems 48 – 53, use subsequences to help determine whether the sequence converges or diverges. If the sequence converges, find its limit.

48. $\{ (-1)^n 3 \}$ 49. $\left\{ \dfrac{1}{n^{\text{th}} \text{ prime}} \right\}$ 50. $\left\{ (-1)^n \dfrac{n+1}{n} \right\}$

51. $\left\{ (-2)^n \left(\dfrac{1}{3}\right)^n \right\}$ 52. $\left\{ \left(1 + \dfrac{1}{3n}\right)^{3n} \right\}$ 53. $\left\{ \left(1 + \dfrac{5}{n^2}\right)^{(n^2)} \right\}$

In problems 54 – 58, calculate $a_{n+1} - a_n$ and use that value to determine whether $\{ a_n \}$ is monotonic increasing, monotonic decreasing, or neither.

54. $\left\{ \dfrac{3}{n} \right\}$ 55. $\left\{ 7 - \dfrac{2}{n} \right\}$ 56. $\left\{ \dfrac{n-1}{2n} \right\}$ 57. $\{ 2^n \}$ 58. $\left\{ 1 - \dfrac{1}{2^n} \right\}$

In problems 59 – 63, calculate a_{n+1}/a_n and use that value to determine whether each sequence is monotonic increasing, monotonic decreasing, or neither.

59. $\left\{\dfrac{n+1}{n!}\right\}$ 60. $\left\{\dfrac{n}{n+1}\right\}$ 61. $\left\{\left(\dfrac{5}{4}\right)^n\right\}$ 62. $\left\{\dfrac{n^2}{n!}\right\}$ 63. $\left\{\dfrac{n}{e^n}\right\}$

In problems 64 – 68, use derivatives to determine whether each sequence is monotonic increasing, monotonic decreasing, or neither.

64. $\left\{\dfrac{n+1}{n}\right\}$ 65. $\left\{5-\dfrac{3}{n}\right\}$ 66. $\left\{n\cdot e^{-n}\right\}$ 67. $\left\{\cos(1/n)\right\}$ 68. $\left\{\left(1+\dfrac{1}{n}\right)^3\right\}$

In problems 69 – 73, show that each sequence is monotonic.

69. $\left\{\dfrac{n+3}{n!}\right\}$ 70. $\left\{\dfrac{n}{n+1}\right\}$ 71. $\left\{1-\dfrac{1}{2^n}\right\}$ 72. $\left\{\sin(1/n)\right\}$ 73. $\left\{\dfrac{n+1}{e^n}\right\}$

74. The Fibonacci sequence (after Leonardo Fibonacci (1170–1250) who used it to model a population of rabbits) is obtained by setting the first two terms equal to 1 and then defining each new term as the sum of the two previous terms: $a_n = a_{n-1} + a_{n-2}$ for $n \geq 3$. (a) Write the first 7 terms of this sequence. (b) Calculate the successive ratios of the terms, a_n/a_{n-1}. (These ratios approach the "golden mean," approximately 1.618)

75. Heron's method for approximating roots: To approximate the square root of a positive number N, put $a_1 = N$ and let $a_{n+1} = \dfrac{1}{2}\left(a_n + \dfrac{N}{a_n}\right)$. Then $\{a_n\}$ converges to $\sqrt{N}$. Calculate a_1 through a_4 for $N = 4, 9,$ and 5. (Heron's method is equivalent to Newton's method applied to the function $f(x) = x^2 - N$.)

76. **Hailstone Sequence** For the initial or "seed" value h_0, define the hailstone sequence by the rule

$$h_n = \begin{cases} 3\cdot h_{n-1} + 1 & \text{if } h_{n-1} \text{ is odd} \\ \dfrac{1}{2}\cdot h_{n-1} & \text{if } h_{n-1} \text{ is even} \end{cases}$$

Define the **length** of the sequence to be the first value of n so that $h_n = 1$. If the seed value is $h_0 = 3$, then $h_1 = 3(3) + 1 = 10$, $h_2 = (10)/2 = 5$, $h_3 = 3(5) + 1 = 16$, $h_4 = 16/2 = 8$, $h_5 = 4$, $h_6 = 2$, and $h_7 = 1$ so the **length** of the hailstone sequence is 7 for the seed value $h_0 = 3$.

(a) Find the length of the hailstone sequence for each seed value from 2 to 10.
(b) Find the length of the hailstone sequence for a seed value $h_0 = 2^n$.
** (c) Open question (no one has been able to answer the this question): Is the length of the hailstone sequence finite for every seed value?

(This is called the hailstone sequence because for some seed values, the terms of the sequence rise and drop just like the path of a hailstone as it forms. This sequence is attributed to Lothar Collatz and (c) is also called Ulam's conjecture, Syracuse's problem, Kakutani's problem and Hasse's algorithm. "The 3n+1 sequence has probably consumed more CPU time than any other number theoretic conjecture," says Gaston Gonnett of Zurich.)

77. **Negative Eugenics:** Suppose that individuals with the gene combination "aa" do not reproduce and those with the combinations "aA" and "AA" do reproduce. When the initial proportion of individuals with "aa" is $a_0 = p$ (typically a small number), then the proportion of individuals with "aa" in the kth generation is $a_k = \dfrac{p}{kp + 1}$. Use this formula for a_k to answer the following questions.

    (a) If 2% of a population initially have the combination "aa" and these individuals do not reproduce, then how many generations will it take for the proportion of individuals with "aa" to drop to 1%?

    (b) In general, find the number of generations until the proportion of individuals with "aa" is half of the initial proportion.

    ("Negative eugenics" is a strategy in which individuals with an undesirable trait are prevented from reproducing. It is not an effective strategy for traits carried by recessive genes (the above example) which are uncommon (p small) in a species which reproduces slowly (people). Mathematics shows that the social strategy of sterilizing people with some undesirable trait, as proposed in the early 20th century, won't effectively reduce the trait in the population.)

78. The fractional part of a number is the number minus its integer part: $x - \text{INT}(x)$. The sequence of fractional parts of multiples of a number x is the sequence with terms $a_n = n \cdot x - \text{INT}(n \cdot x)$. The behavior of the sequence of fractional parts of the multiples of a number is one way in which rational numbers differ from irrational numbers.

    (a) Let $a_n = nx - \text{INT}(nx)$ be the fractional part of the nth multiple of x. Calculate a_1 through a_6 for $x = 1/3$. These are the fractional parts of the first 6 multiples of 1/3.

    (b) Calculate the fractional parts of the first 9 multiples of 3/4, and 2/5.

    (c) Calculate the fractional parts of the first 5 multiples of π.

*   (d) Let $a_n = n \cdot \pi - \text{INT}(n \cdot \pi)$ be the fractional part of the nth multiple of π. Is it possible for two different multiples of π to have the same fractional part? (Suggestion: Assume the answer is yes and derive a contradiction. Assume that $a_n = a_m$ for some $m \neq n$, and derive the contradiction that $\pi = \dfrac{\text{INT}(n\pi) - \text{INT}(m\pi)}{n-m}$. Why is this a contradiction?)

An Alternate Way to Visualize Sequences and Convergence

A sequence is a function, and we have graphed sequences in the xy plane in the same way we graphed other functions: since $a_n = f(n)$, we plotted the point (n, a_n). If the sequence $\{a_n\}$ converges to L, then the points (n, a_n) are eventually (for big values of n) close to or on the horizontal line $y = L$.

We can also graph a sequence $\{a_n\}$ in one dimension, on the x–axis. For each value of n, we plot the point $x = a_n$. Then the graph of $\{a_n\}$ consists of a collection of points on the x–axis. Fig. 21 shows the one dimensional graphs of $a_n = \frac{1}{n}$, $b_n = 2 + \frac{(-1)^n}{n}$, and $c_n = (-1)^n$.

Fig. 21

If $\{a_n\}$ converges to L, then the points $x = a_n$ are eventually (for big values of n) close to or on the point $x = L$. If we build a narrow box, with width $2\varepsilon > 0$, and center the box at the point $x = L$, then all of the points a_n will fall into the box once n is larger than some value N.

79. Suppose that the sequence $\{a_n\}$ converges to 3 and that you place a single grain of sand at each point $x = a_n$ on the x–axis. Describe the likely result (a) after a few grains have been placed and (b) after a lot (thousands or millions) of grains have been placed.

80. Suppose the sequence $\{a_n\}$ converges to 3, $\{b_n\}$ converges to 1, and that you place a single grain of sand at each point $(x, y) = (a_n, b_n)$ on the xy–plane. Describe the likely result (a) after a few grains have been placed and (b) after a lot (thousands or millions) of grains have been placed.

81. Suppose that $a_n = \sin(n)$ for positive integers n. If you place a single grain of sand at each point $x = a_n$ on the x–axis. Describe the likely result (a) after a few grains have been placed and (b) after a lot (thousands or millions) of grains have been placed. (c) Do two grains ever end up on the same point?

82. Suppose that $a_n = \cos(n)$, and $b_n = \sin(n)$ for positive integers n. If you place a single grain of sand at each point $(x, y) = (a_n, b_n)$ on the xy–plane. Describe the likely result (a) after a few grains have been placed and (b) after a lot (thousands or millions) of grains have been placed.

Practice Answers

Practice 1: One layer transmits 2/3 of the original light. Two layers transmit $(\frac{2}{3})(\frac{2}{3}) = (\frac{2}{3})^2$ of the original light. Three layers transmit $(\frac{2}{3})^3$, and, in general, n layers transmit $(\frac{2}{3})^n$ of the original light.

Practice 2:
(a) $1, 1/2, 1/3, 1/4, 1/5, 1/6, \ldots, 1/n, \ldots$
(b) $-1/2, 1/4, -1/8, 1/16, -1/32, 1/64, \ldots, (-1/2)^n$ or $(-1)^n (1/2)^n, \ldots$
(c) $2, 2, 2, 2, 2, \ldots, 2, \ldots$

Practice 3: $c_n = a_n - b_n$: $c_1 = (3 - \frac{1}{1}) - (\frac{1}{2}) = \frac{3}{2} = 1.5$, $c_2 = (3 - \frac{1}{2}) - (\frac{1}{2^2}) = \frac{9}{4} = 2.25$,

$c_3 = (3 - \frac{1}{3}) - (\frac{1}{2^3}) = \frac{61}{24} \approx 2.542$, $c_4 = (3 - \frac{1}{4}) - (\frac{1}{2^4}) = \frac{43}{16} \approx 2.687$,

$c_5 = (3 - \frac{1}{5}) - (\frac{1}{2^5}) = \frac{443}{160} \approx 2.769$

$d_n = (-1)^n b_n$: $d_1 = (-1)^1 (\frac{1}{2}) = -\frac{1}{2}$, $d_2 = (-1)^2 (\frac{1}{2^2}) = \frac{1}{4}$, $d_3 = (-1)^3 (\frac{1}{2^3}) = -\frac{1}{8}$,

$d_4 = \frac{1}{16}$, $d_2 - \frac{1}{32}$

Practice 4: $a_0 = 3$: $a_1 = f(a_0) = 2(3) - 1 = 5$, $a_2 = f(a_1) = 2(5) - 1 = 9$, $a_3 = f(a_2) = 2(9) - 1 = 17$

Practice 5: $b_1 = b_0 + \frac{1}{3} = 0 + \frac{1}{3} = \frac{1}{3}$, $b_2 = b_1 + \frac{1}{9} = \frac{4}{9}$, $b_3 = b_2 + \frac{1}{27} = \frac{13}{27}$, $b_4 = b_3 + \frac{1}{81} = \frac{40}{81}$

Practice 6: For $a_n = (n+1)/n$ show that $\lim_{n \to \infty} a_n = 1$:

We need to show that for any positive ε, there is a number N so that the distance from $a_n = \frac{n+1}{n}$ to L, $|a_n - L|$, is less than ε whenever n is larger than N.

For this particular $|a_n - L| = |\frac{n+1}{n} - 1| = |\frac{n}{n} + \frac{1}{n} - 1| = |\frac{1}{n}|$.

To determine what N might be, we solve the inequality

$|\frac{1}{n}| < \varepsilon$ for n in terms of ε: $|1/n| < \varepsilon$ so $1/\varepsilon < n$ and $n > 1/\varepsilon$.

So for **any** positive ε, we can take $N = 1/\varepsilon$ (or any larger number).

Then $n > N = 1/\varepsilon$ implies that $\varepsilon > \frac{1}{n} = |\frac{1}{n}| = |\frac{n+1}{n} - 1| = |a_n - L|$.

Practice 7: $\lim\limits_{n\to\infty} \dfrac{\ln(n)}{n}$: Since $\lim\limits_{n\to\infty} \ln(x) = \infty$ and $\lim\limits_{n\to\infty} x = \infty$, we can use L'Hopital's rule

(Section 3.7). $D(\ln(x)) = \dfrac{1}{x}$ and $D(x) = 1$, so $\lim\limits_{n\to\infty} \dfrac{\ln(n)}{n} = \lim\limits_{x\to\infty} \dfrac{1/x}{1} = 0$.

Then $\lim\limits_{x\to\infty} \dfrac{\ln(x)}{x} = 0$ and $\lim\limits_{n\to\infty} \dfrac{\ln(n)}{n} = 0$.

Practice 8: We can show that $a_n = \{ \sin(\dfrac{\pi n}{2}) \}$ diverges by finding two subsequences b_n and c_n of a_n so that the subsequences b_n and c_n converge to different limiting values.

Let $\{ b_n \}$ consist of the terms $\{ a_1, a_5, a_9, \ldots, a_{4n-3}, \ldots \} = \{ \sin(\pi/2), \sin(5\pi/2),$ $\sin(9\pi/2), \ldots, \sin(\dfrac{(4n-3)\pi}{2}), \ldots \} = \{ 1, 1, 1, \ldots, 1, \ldots \}$. Then $\lim\limits_{n\to\infty} b_n = 1$.

Let $\{ c_n \}$ consist of the terms $\{ a_2, a_4, a_6, \ldots, a_{2n}, \ldots \} = \{ \sin(2\pi/2), \sin(4\pi/2),$ $\sin(6\pi/2), \ldots, \sin(\dfrac{2n\pi}{2}), \ldots \} = \{ 0, 0, 0, \ldots, 0, \ldots \}$. Then $\lim\limits_{n\to\infty} c_n = 0$.

Since the subsequences $\{ b_n \}$ and $\{ c_n \}$ have different limits, we can conclude that the original sequence $\{ a_n \}$ diverges. (Note: Many other pairs of subsequences also work in place of the $\{ b_n \}$ and $\{ c_n \}$ that we used.)

Practice 9: (i) by showing that $a_{n+1} \leq a_n$ for all n,

(ii) by showing that all the a_n are positive and $\dfrac{a_{n+1}}{a_n} \leq 1$ for all n, or

(iii) by showing that $a_n = f(n)$ for integer values n and $f'(x) \leq 0$ for all $x \geq 1$.

Practice 10: Show that $\{ (\dfrac{2}{3})^n \}$ is monotonically decreasing.

Using method (i) of Practice 9: $(\dfrac{2}{3}) < 1$ so multiplying each side by $(\dfrac{2}{3})^n > 0$ we have $(\dfrac{2}{3})(\dfrac{2}{3})^n < 1(\dfrac{2}{3})^n$ and $(\dfrac{2}{3})^{n+1} < (\dfrac{2}{3})^n$ so $a_{n+1} < a_n$.

We could have used method (ii) of Practice 9 instead: $a_{n+1} = (\dfrac{2}{3})^{n+1}$ and $a_n = (\dfrac{2}{3})^n$ so $\dfrac{a_{n+1}}{a_n} = \dfrac{(2/3)^{n+1}}{(2/3)^n} = \dfrac{2}{3} < 1$ so $\{ (\dfrac{2}{3})^n \}$ is monotonically decreasing.

Appendix: Proof of the Uniqueness Theorem

The proof starts by assuming that the limit is not unique. Then we show that this assumption of nonuniqueness leads to a contradiction so the assumption is false and the limit is unique.

Suppose that a sequence $\{a_n\}$ converges to two different limits L_1 and L_2. Then the distance between L_1 and L_2 is $d = |L_1 - L_2| > 0$. Since $\{a_n\}$ converges to L_1, then for any $\varepsilon > 0$ there is an N_1 so that $n > N_1$ implies $|a_n - L_1| < \varepsilon$. Take $\varepsilon = d/3$. Then there is an N_1 so $n > N_1$ implies $|a_n - L_1| < \varepsilon = d/3$. Similarly, there is an N_2 so that $n > N_2$ implies $|a_n - L_2| < \varepsilon = d/3$. Finally, if n is larger than both N_1 and N_2, then both conditions are satisfied and

$$\begin{aligned}
d = |L_1 - L_2| &= |(a_n - L_2) - (a_n - L_1)| &&\text{by adding } 0 = a_n - a_n \text{ inside the absolute value} \\
&\leq |a_n - L_2| + |a_n - L_1| &&\text{by the Triangle Inequality} \\
&< d/3 + d/3 &&\text{since } |a_n - L_1| < \varepsilon = d/3 \text{ and } |a_n - L_2| < \varepsilon = d/3 \\
&= 2d/3.
\end{aligned}$$

We have found that $0 < d < \frac{2}{3} d$, a contradiction, and we can conclude the assumption, $L_1 \neq L_2$, is false. A sequence **can not** converge to two different values.

(Note: *We chose $\varepsilon = d/3$ because it "works" for our purpose by leading to a contradiction. Several other choices, any ε less than $d/2$, also lead to the contradiction. Since the definition says "for **any** $\varepsilon > 0$," we picked one we wanted.*)

10.2 INFINITE SERIES

Our goal in this section is to add together the numbers in a sequence. Since it would take a "very long time" to add together the infinite number of numbers, we first consider finite sums, look for patterns in these finite sums, and take limits as more and more numbers are included in the finite sums.

What does it mean to add together an infinite number of terms? We will define that concept carefully in this section. Secondly, is the sum of all the terms a finite number? In the next few sections we will examine a variety of techniques for determining whether an infinite sum is finite. Finally, if we know the sum is finite, can we determine the value of the sum? The difficulty of finding the exact value of the sum varies from very easy to very, very difficult.

Example 1: A golf ball is thrown 9 feet straight up into the air, and on each bounce it rebounds to two thirds of its previous height (Fig. 1). Find a sequence whose terms give the distances the ball travels during each successive bounce. Represent the **total** distance traveled by the ball as a sum.

Solution: The heights of the successive bounces are 9 feet, $(\frac{2}{3}) \cdot 9$ feet, $(\frac{2}{3}) \cdot [(\frac{2}{3}) \cdot 9]$ feet, $(\frac{2}{3})^3 \cdot 9$ feet, and so forth. On each bounce, the ball rises and falls so the distance traveled is twice the height of that bounce:

$$18 \text{ feet}, (\frac{2}{3}) \cdot 18 \text{ feet}, (\frac{2}{3}) \cdot (\frac{2}{3}) \cdot 18 \text{ feet}, (\frac{2}{3})^3 \cdot 18 \text{ feet}, (\frac{2}{3})^4 \cdot 18 \text{ feet}, \ldots .$$

The total distance traveled is the sum of the bounce–distances:

$$\text{total distance} = 18 + (\frac{2}{3}) \cdot 18 + (\frac{2}{3}) \cdot (\frac{2}{3}) \cdot 18 + (\frac{2}{3})^3 \cdot 18 + (\frac{2}{3})^4 \cdot 18 + \ldots$$

$$= 18 \left\{ 1 + \frac{2}{3} + (\frac{2}{3})^2 + (\frac{2}{3})^3 + (\frac{2}{3})^4 + \ldots \right\}$$

At the completion of the first bounce the ball has traveled 18 feet. After the second bounce, it has traveled 30 feet, a total of 38 feet after the third bounce, $43\frac{1}{3}$ feet after the fourth, and so on. With a calculator and some patience, we see that after the 20th bounce the ball has traveled a total of approximately 53.996 feet, after the 30th bounce approximately 53.99994 feet, and after the 40th bounce approximately 53.9999989 feet.

Practice 1: A tennis ball is thrown 10 feet straight up into the air, and on each bounce it rebounds to 40% of its previous height. Represent the total distance traveled by the ball as a sum, and find the total distance traveled by the ball after the completion of its third bounce. (Fig. 2)

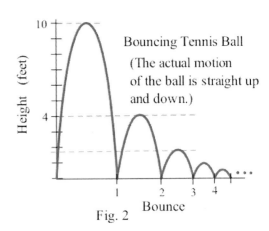

Fig. 2

Infinite Series

The infinite sums in the Example and Practice are called infinite series, and they are the objects we will start to examine in this section.

Definitions

An **infinite series** is an expression of the form

$$a_1 + a_2 + a_3 + a_4 + \ldots \quad \text{or} \quad \sum_{k=1}^{\infty} a_k .$$

The numbers $a_1, a_2, a_3, a_4, \ldots$ are called the **terms** of the series. (Fig. 3)

Example 2: Represent the following series using the sigma notation. (a) $1 + 1/3 + 1/9 + 1/27 + \ldots$,
(b) $-1 + 1/2 - 1/3 + 1/4 - 1/5 + \ldots$, (c) $18(2/3 + 4/9 + 8/27 + 16/81 + \ldots)$
(d) $0.777\ldots = 7/10 + 7/100 + 7/1000 + \ldots$, and (e) $0.222\ldots$

Solution: (a) $1 + 1/3 + 1/9 + 1/27 + \ldots = \sum_{k=0}^{\infty} (\frac{1}{3})^k$ or $\sum_{k=1}^{\infty} (\frac{1}{3})^{k-1}$

(b) $-1 + 1/2 - 1/3 + 1/4 - 1/5 + \ldots = \sum_{k=1}^{\infty} (-1)^k \frac{1}{k}$ (c) $18 \sum_{k=1}^{\infty} (\frac{2}{3})^k$

(d) $0.777\ldots = 7/10 + 7/100 + 7/1000 + \ldots = \sum_{k=1}^{\infty} \frac{7}{10^k}$ (e) $\sum_{k=1}^{\infty} \frac{2}{10^k}$

Practice 2: Represent the following series using the sigma notation. (a) $1 + 2 + 3 + 4 + \ldots$,
(b) $-1 + 1 - 1 + 1 - \ldots$ (c) $2 + 1 + 1/2 + 1/4 + \ldots$
(d) $1/2 + 1/4 + 1/6 + 1/8 + 1/10 + \ldots$ (e) $0.111\ldots$

In order to determine if the infinite series adds up to a finite value, we examine the sums as more and more terms are added.

Definition

The **partial sums** s_n of the infinite series $\sum_{k=1}^{\infty} a_k$ are the numbers

$s_1 = a_1$,

$s_2 = a_1 + a_2$,

$s_3 = a_1 + a_2 + a_3$,

. . .

In general, $s_n = a_1 + a_2 + a_3 + \ldots + a_n = \sum_{k=1}^{n} a_k$

or, recursively, as $s_n = s_{n-1} + a_n$.

The partial sums form the **sequence of partial sums** $\{ s_n \}$.

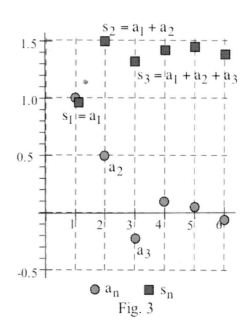

Fig. 3

Example 3: Calculate the first 4 partial sums for the following series.

(a) $1 + 1/2 + 1/4 + 1/8 + 1/16 + \ldots$, (b) $\sum_{k=1}^{\infty} (-1)^k$, and (c) $\sum_{n=1}^{\infty} \frac{1}{n}$.

Solution: (a) $s_1 = 1, s_2 = 1 + 1/2 = 3/2, s_3 = 1 + 1/2 + 1/4 = 7/4, s_4 = 1 + 1/2 + 1/4 + 1/8 = 15/8$

It is usually easier to use the recursive version of s_n:

$s_3 = s_2 + a_3 = 3/2 + 1/4 = 7/4$ and $s_4 = s_3 + a_4 = 7/4 + 1/8 = 15/8$.

(b) $s_1 = (-1)^1 = -1$, $s_2 = s_1 + a_2 = -1 + (-1)^2 = 0$, $s_3 = s_2 + a_3 = 0 + (-1)^3 = -1$, $s_4 = 0$.

(c) $s_1 = 1, s_2 = 3/2, s_3 = 11/6, s_4 = 25/12$.

Practice 3: Calculate the first 4 partial sums for the following series.

(a) $1 - 1/2 + 1/4 - 1/8 + 1/16 - \ldots$, (b) $\sum_{k=1}^{\infty} (\frac{1}{3})^k$, and (c) $\sum_{n=2}^{\infty} \frac{(-1)^n}{n}$.

If we know the values of the partial sums s_n, we can recover the values of the terms a_n used to build the s_n.

Example 4: Suppose $s_1 = 2.1$, $s_2 = 2.6$, $s_3 = 2.84$, and $s_4 = 2.87$ are the first partial sums of $\sum_{k=1}^{\infty} a_k$. Find the values of the first four terms of $\{ a_n \}$.

Solution: $s_1 = a_1$ so $a_1 = 2.1$. $s_2 = a_1 + a_2$ so $2.6 = 2.1 + a_2$ and $a_2 = 0.5$.

Similarly, $s_3 = a_1 + a_2 + a_3$ so $2.84 = 2.1 + 0.5 + a_3$ and $a_3 = 0.24$. Finally, $a_4 = 0.03$.

10.2 Infinite Series

An alternate solution method starts with $a_1 = s_1$ and then uses the fact that $s_n = s_{n-1} + a_n$ so $a_n = s_n - s_{n-1}$. Then

$$a_2 = s_2 - s_1 = 2.6 - 2.1 = 0.5.$$
$$a_3 = s_3 - s_2 = 2.84 - 2.6 = 0.24, \text{ and}$$
$$a_4 = s_4 - s_3 = 2.87 - 2.84 = 0.03.$$

Practice 4: Suppose $s_1 = 3.2$, $s_2 = 3.6$, $s_3 = 3.5$, $s_4 = 4$, $s_{99} = 7.3$, $s_{100} = 7.6$, and $s_{101} = 7.8$ are partial sums of $\sum_{k=1}^{\infty} a_k$. Find the values of a_1, a_2, a_3, a_4, and a_{100}.

Example 5: Graph the first five **terms** of the series $\sum_{k=1}^{\infty} (\frac{1}{2})^k$. Then graph the first five **partial sums**.

Solution: $a_1 = \left(\frac{1}{2}\right)^1 = \frac{1}{2}$, $a_2 = \left(\frac{1}{2}\right)^2 = \frac{1}{4}$, $a_3 = \left(\frac{1}{2}\right)^3 = \frac{1}{8}$, $a_4 = \frac{1}{16}$, $a_4 = \frac{1}{32}$

$s_1 = \frac{1}{2}$, $s_2 = \frac{1}{2} + \frac{1}{4} = \frac{3}{4}$, $s_3 = \frac{1}{2} + \frac{1}{4} + \frac{1}{8} = \frac{7}{8}$, $s_4 = \frac{15}{16}$, and $s_5 = \frac{31}{32}$.

These values are graphed in Fig. 4.

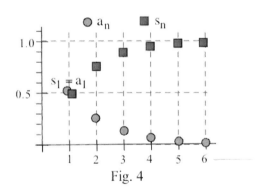

Fig. 4

Practice 5: Graph the first five terms of the series

$\sum_{k=1}^{\infty} (-\frac{1}{2})^k$. Then graph the first five partial sums.

Convergence of a Series

The convergence of a series is defined in terms of the behavior of the sequence of partial sums. If the partial sums, the sequence obtained by adding more and more of the terms of the series, approaches a finite number, we say the **series** converges to that finite number. If the sequence of partial sums diverges (does not approach a single finite number), we say that the **series** diverges.

Definitions

Let $\{s_n\}$ be the sequence of partial sums

of the series $\sum\limits_{k=1}^{\infty} a_k$: $s_n = \sum\limits_{k=1}^{n} a_k$

If $\{s_n\}$ is a convergent sequence, (Fig. 5)

we say the series $\sum\limits_{k=1}^{\infty} a_k$ **converges**.

If the sequence of partial sums $\{s_n\}$ converges to A,

we say the series $\sum\limits_{k=1}^{\infty} a_k$ **converges to A**

or **the sum of the series is A**,

and we write $\sum\limits_{k=1}^{\infty} a_k = A$.

If the sequence of partial sums $\{s_n\}$ diverges,

we say the series $\sum\limits_{k=1}^{\infty} a_k$ **diverges**.

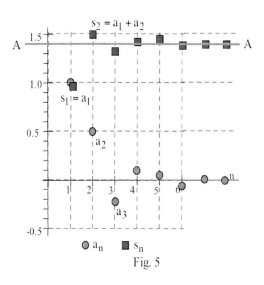

Fig. 5

Example 6: In the next section we present a method for determining that the nth partial sum

of $\sum\limits_{k=1}^{\infty} (\frac{1}{2})^k$ is $s_n = \dfrac{2^n - 1}{2^n} = 1 - \dfrac{1}{2^n}$. Use this result to evaluate the limit of $\{s_n\}$.

Does the series $\sum\limits_{k=1}^{\infty} (\frac{1}{2})^k$ converge? If so, to what value?

Solution: $\lim\limits_{n \to \infty} s_n = \lim\limits_{n \to \infty} 1 - \dfrac{1}{2^n} = 1$ (Fig. 6), so $\sum\limits_{k=1}^{\infty} (\frac{1}{2})^k$ converges to 1: $\sum\limits_{k=1}^{\infty} (\frac{1}{2})^k = 1$.

Practice 6: The nth partial sum of $\sum\limits_{k=1}^{\infty} (-\frac{1}{2})^k$ is $s_n = -\dfrac{1}{3} + \dfrac{1}{3} \cdot (-\dfrac{1}{2})^n$. Use this result to

evaluate the limit of $\{s_n\}$. Does the series $\sum\limits_{k=1}^{\infty} (-\frac{1}{2})^k$ converge? If so, to what value?

The next theorem says that if a series converges, then the terms of the series must approach 0. When a series is convergent then the partial sums s_n approach a finite limit (Fig. 3) so all of the s_n must be close to that limit when n is large. Then s_n and s_{n-1} must be close to each other (why?) and $a_n = s_n - s_{n-1}$ must be close to 0.

Theorem: If the series $\sum_{k=1}^{\infty} a_k$ converges, then $\lim_{k \to \infty} a_k = 0$.

We can NOT use this theorem to conclude that a series converges. If the terms of the series do approach 0, then the series may or may not converge — more information is needed to draw a conclusion. However, an alternate form of the theorem, called the nth Term Test for Divergence, is **very useful for quickly concluding that some series diverge.**

---

n^{th} Term Test for Divergence of a Series

If the terms a_n of a series do not approach 0 (as "$n \to \infty$")

then the series diverges:

if $\lim_{n \to \infty} a_n \neq 0$, then $\sum_{n=1}^{\infty} a_n$ diverges.

Example 7: Which of these series diverge **by the nth Term Test**?

(a) $\sum_{n=1}^{\infty} (-1)^n$ (b) $\sum_{n=1}^{\infty} (\frac{3}{4})^n$ (c) $\sum_{n=1}^{\infty} (1 + \frac{1}{n})^n$ (d) $\sum_{n=1}^{\infty} \frac{1}{n}$

Solution: (a) $a_n = (-1)^n$ oscillates between -1 and $+1$ and does not approach 0. $\sum_{n=1}^{\infty} (-1)^n$ **diverges**.

(b) $a_n = (\frac{3}{4})^n$ approaches 0 so $\sum_{n=1}^{\infty} (\frac{3}{4})^n$ **may or may not** converge.

(c) $a_n = (1 + \frac{1}{n})^n$ approaches $e \neq 0$, so $\sum_{n=1}^{\infty} (1 + \frac{1}{n})^n$ **diverges**.

(d) $a_n = \frac{1}{n}$ approaches 0 so $\sum_{n=1}^{\infty} \frac{1}{n}$ **may or may not** converge.

We can be certain that (a) and (c) diverge. We don't have enough information yet to decide about (b) and (d). (In the next section we show that (b) converges and (d) diverges.)

Practice 7: Which of these series diverge by the nth Term Test?

(a) $\sum_{n=1}^{\infty} (-0.9)^n$ (b) $\sum_{n=1}^{\infty} (1.1)^n$ (c) $\sum_{n=1}^{\infty} \sin(n\pi)$ (d) $\sum_{n=1}^{\infty} \frac{1}{\sqrt{n}}$

New Series From Old

If we know about the convergence of a series, then we also know about the convergence of several related series.

- Inserting or deleting a "few" terms, any **finite** number of terms, does not change the convergence or divergence of a series. The insertions or deletions typically change the sum (the limit of the partial sums), but they do not change whether or not the series converges. (Inserting or deleting an infinite number of terms can change the convergence or divergence.)

- Multiplying each term in a series by a nonzero constant does not change the convergence or divergence of a series:

    Suppose $c \neq 0$. $\sum_{n=1}^{\infty} a_n$ converges if and only if $\sum_{n=1}^{\infty} c \cdot a_n$ converges.

- Term–by–term addition and subtraction of the terms of two convergent series result in convergent series. (Term by term multiplication and division of series do not have such nice results.)

Theorem:

If $\sum_{n=1}^{\infty} a_n$ and $\sum_{n=1}^{\infty} b_n$ converge with $\sum_{n=1}^{\infty} a_n = A$ and $\sum_{n=1}^{\infty} b_n = B$,

then $\sum_{n=1}^{\infty} C \cdot a_n = C \cdot A$,

$\sum_{n=1}^{\infty} (a_n + b_n) = A + B$, and

$\sum_{n=1}^{\infty} (a_n - b_n) = A - B$.

The proofs of these statements follow directly from the definition of convergence of a series and from results about convergence of sequences (of partial sums).

PROBLEMS

In problems 1 – 6, rewrite each sum using sigma notation starting with k = 1.

1. $1 + \frac{1}{2} + \frac{1}{3} + \frac{1}{4} + \frac{1}{5} + ...$

2. $1 + \frac{1}{4} + \frac{1}{9} + \frac{1}{16} + \frac{1}{25} + ...$

3. $\frac{2}{3} + \frac{2}{6} + \frac{2}{9} + \frac{2}{12} + \frac{2}{15} + \frac{2}{18} + ...$

4. $\sin(1) + \sin(8) + \sin(27) + \sin(64) + \sin(125) + ...$

5. $(-\frac{1}{2}) + (\frac{1}{4}) + (-\frac{1}{8}) + (\frac{1}{16}) + (-\frac{1}{32}) + ...$

6. $(-\frac{1}{3}) + (\frac{1}{9}) + (-\frac{1}{27}) + (\frac{1}{81}) + (-\frac{1}{243}) + ...$

In problems 7 – 14, calculate and graph the first four partial sums s_1 to s_4 of the given series $\sum_{n=1}^{\infty} a_n$.

7. $\sum_{n=1}^{\infty} n^2$

8. $\sum_{n=1}^{\infty} (-1)^n$

9. $\sum_{n=1}^{\infty} \frac{1}{n+2}$

10. $\sum_{n=1}^{\infty} \{ \frac{1}{n} - \frac{1}{n+1} \}$

11. $\sum_{n=1}^{\infty} \frac{1}{2^n}$

12. $\sum_{n=1}^{\infty} (-\frac{1}{2})^n$

In problems 13 – 18, the first five partial sums s_1 to s_5 are given. Find the first four terms a_1 to a_4 of the series.

13. $s_1 = 3, s_2 = 2, s_3 = 4, s_4 = 5, s_5 = 3$

14. $s_1 = 3, s_2 = 5, s_3 = 4, s_4 = 6, s_5 = 5$

15. $s_1 = 4, s_2 = 4.5, s_3 = 4.3, s_4 = 4.8, s_5 = 5$

16. $s_1 = 4, s_2 = 3.7, s_3 = 3.9, s_4 = 4.1, s_5 = 4$

17. $s_1 = 1, s_2 = 1.1, s_3 = 1.11, s_4 = 1.111, s_5 = 1.1111$

18. $s_1 = 1, s_2 = 0.9, s_3 = 0.93, s_4 = 0.91, s_5 = 0.92$

In problems 19 – 28, represent each repeating decimal as a series using the sigma notation.

19. 0.888 ...
20. 0.333 ...
21. 0.555 ...
22. 0.111 ...
23. 0.aaa ...
24. 0.232323 ...
25. 0.171717 ...
26. 0.838383 ...
27. 0.070707 ...
28. 0.ababab ...

29. Find a pattern for a fraction representation of the repeating decimal 0.abcabcabc ... .

30. A golf ball is thrown 20 feet straight up into the air, and on each bounce it rebounds to 60% of its previous height. Represent the total distance traveled by the ball as a sum.

31. A "super ball" is thrown 15 feet straight up into the air, and on each bounce it rebounds to 80% of its previous height. Represent the total distance traveled by the ball as a sum.

32. Each special washing of a pair of overalls removes 80% of the radioactive particles attached to the overalls. Represent, as a sequence of numbers, the percent of the original radioactive particles that remain after each washing.

33. Each week, 20% of the argon gas in a container leaks out of the container. Represent, as a sequence of numbers, the percent of the original argon gas that remains in the container at the end of the $1^{st}, 2^{nd}, 3^{rd}$, and n^{th} weeks.

34. Eight people are going on an expedition by horseback through desolate country. The people and scientific equipment (fishing gear) require 12 horses, and additional horses are needed to carry food for the horses. Each horse can carry enough food to feed 2 horses for the trip. Represent the number of horses needed to carry food as a sum. (Start of a solution: The original 12 horses will require 6 new horses to carry their food. The 6 new horses require 3 additional horses to carry their food. The 3 additional horses require another 1.5 horses to carry food for them, etc.)

Which of the series in problems 35 – 43, definitely diverge by the nth Term Test? What can we conclude about the other series in these problems?

35. $\sum_{n=1}^{\infty} \left(\frac{1}{4}\right)^n$

36. $\sum_{n=1}^{\infty} \frac{7}{n}$

37. $\sum_{n=1}^{\infty} \left(\frac{4}{3}\right)^n$

38. $\sum_{n=1}^{\infty} \left(-\frac{7}{4}\right)^2$

39. $\sum_{n=1}^{\infty} \frac{\sin(n)}{n}$

40. $\sum_{n=1}^{\infty} \frac{\ln(n)}{n}$

41. $\sum_{n=1}^{\infty} \cos\left(\frac{1}{n}\right)$

42. $\sum_{n=1}^{\infty} \frac{n^2-20}{n^2+4}$

43. $\sum_{n=1}^{\infty} \frac{n^2-20}{n^5+4}$

Practice Answers

Practice 1: The heights of the bounces are $10, (0.4) \cdot 10, (0.4) \cdot (0.4) \cdot 10, (0.4)^3 \cdot 10, \ldots$ so the distances traveled (up and down) by the ball are $20, (0.4) \cdot 20, (0.4) \cdot (0.4) \cdot 20, (0.4)^3 \cdot 20, \ldots$
The total distance traveled is

$$20 + (0.4) \cdot 20 + (0.4)^2 \cdot 20 + (0.4)^3 \cdot 20 + \ldots = 20\{ 1 + 0.4 + (0.4)^2 + (0.4)^3 + \ldots \} = 20 \sum_{k=0}^{\infty} (0.4)^k$$

After 3 bounces the ball has traveled $20 + (0.4)(20) + (0.4)^2(20) = 20 + 8 + 3.2 = 31.2$ feet.

Practice 2: (a) $\sum_{k=1}^{\infty} k$ (b) $\sum_{k=1}^{\infty} (-1)^k$

(c) $2(1 + \frac{1}{2} + \frac{1}{4} + ...) = 2 \sum_{k=0}^{\infty} (\frac{1}{2})^k$ or $\sum_{k=0}^{\infty} (\frac{1}{2})^{k-1}$ or $\sum_{k=1}^{\infty} (\frac{1}{2})^{k-2}$

(d) $\sum_{k=1}^{\infty} \frac{1}{2k}$ (e) $\frac{1}{10} + \frac{1}{100} + \frac{1}{1000} + ... = \frac{1}{10} + \frac{1}{10^2} + \frac{1}{10^3} + ... = \sum_{k=1}^{\infty} (\frac{1}{10})^k$ or $\sum_{k=1}^{\infty} \frac{1}{10^k}$

Practice 3: (a) Partial sums: $1, 1/2, 3/4, 5/8$ (b) $\frac{1}{3} + \frac{1}{9} + \frac{1}{27} + ...$; partial sums: $\frac{1}{3}, \frac{4}{9}, \frac{13}{27}, \frac{40}{81}$

(c) $\frac{1}{2} - \frac{1}{3} + \frac{1}{4} - ...$; partial sums: $\frac{1}{2}, \frac{1}{6}, \frac{10}{24} = \frac{5}{12}, \frac{13}{60}$

Practice 4: $a_1 = s_1 = 3.2$, $a_2 = s_2 - s_1 = (3.6) - (3.2) = 0.4$, $a_3 = s_3 - s_2 = (3.5) - (3.6) = -0.1$,

$a_4 = s_4 - s_3 = (4) - (3.5) = 0.5$, $a_{100} = s_{100} - s_{99} = (7.6) - (7.3) = 0.3$

Practice 5: $a_1 = -1/2, a_2 = 1/4, a_3 = -1/8, a_4 = 1/16, a_5 = -1/32$

$s_1 = a_1 = -\frac{1}{2}$, $s_2 = a_1 + a_2 = -\frac{1}{2} + \frac{1}{4} = -\frac{1}{4}$,

$s_3 = s_2 + a_3 = -\frac{1}{4} - \frac{1}{8} = -\frac{3}{8} \approx -0.375$,

$s_4 = s_3 + a_4 = -\frac{3}{8} + \frac{1}{16} = -\frac{5}{16} \approx -0.3125$,

$s_5 = s_4 + a_5 = -\frac{5}{16} - \frac{1}{32} = -\frac{11}{32} \approx -0.34375$,

The graphs of a_n and s_n are shown in Fig. 6.

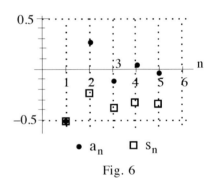

Fig. 6

Practice 6: $\lim_{n \to \infty} s_n = \lim_{n \to \infty} -\frac{1}{3} + \frac{1}{3} \cdot (-\frac{1}{2})^n = -\frac{1}{3} + \frac{1}{3} \cdot 0$

$= -\frac{1}{3}$.

The limit, as "$n \to \infty$", of s_n is a finite number, so $\sum_{k=1}^{\infty} (-\frac{1}{2})^k$ **converges to** $-\frac{1}{3}$.

Practice 7: (a) $\sum_{n=1}^{\infty} (-0.9)^n$: $a_n = (-0.9)^n$ approaches 0 so $\sum_{n=1}^{\infty} (-0.9)^n$ **may converge.**

(b) $\sum_{n=1}^{\infty} (1.1)^n$: $a_n = (1.1)^n$ "approaches infinity" so $\sum_{n=1}^{\infty} (1.1)^n$ **diverges.**

(c) $\sum_{n=1}^{\infty} \sin(n\pi) = 0 + 0 + 0 + ...$: $\sin(n\pi) = 0$ "approaches 0" so $\sum_{n=1}^{\infty} \sin(n\pi)$ **may converge.**

(d) $\sum_{n=1}^{\infty} \frac{1}{\sqrt{n}}$: $a_n = \frac{1}{\sqrt{n}}$ approaches 0 so $\sum_{n=1}^{\infty} \frac{1}{\sqrt{n}}$ **may converge.**

(Later in this chapter we will show that series (a) and (c) converge and series (d) diverges.)

Appendix: Programming Partial Sums of Numerical Series

MAPLE commands for $\sum_{n=1}^{100} \frac{1}{n}$, $\sum_{n=1}^{100} \frac{1}{n^2}$, $\sum_{n=1}^{100} \frac{1}{n!}$:

> sum(1/n , n=1..100) ;   (then press ENTER key)

> sum(1/n^2 , n=1..100) ;

> sum(1/(n!) , n=1..100) ;

TI–85 program for $\sum_{n=1}^{M} \frac{1}{n}$

    Prgm1:NUMSUM
    Disp "NUM TERMS ="
    Input M
    1 → A
    0 → N
    Lbl ONE
    N+1 → N
    1/N → A   (value of the new term)   1/N → A
    S + A → S   (add new term to partial sum)   S + A → S
    If N<M   (test if need next term)   If N<M
    Goto ONE
    Disp S
    Stop   Stop

For $\sum_{n=1}^{M} \frac{1}{n^2}$ change the bold line to **1/(N*N) → A**. For $\sum_{n=1}^{M} \frac{1}{n!}$ change the bold line to **A/N → A**.

10.3 GEOMETRIC AND HARMONIC SERIES

This section uses ideas from Section 10.2 about series and their convergence to investigate some special types of series. Geometric series are very important and appear in a variety of applications. Much of the early work in the 17th century with series focused on geometric series and generalized them. Many of the ideas used later in this chapter originated with geometric series. It is easy to determine whether a geometric series converges or diverges, and when one does converge, we can easily find its sum. The harmonic series is important as an example of a divergent series whose terms approach zero. A final type of series, called "telescoping," is discussed briefly. Telescoping series are relatively uncommon, but their partial sums exhibit a particularly nice pattern.

Geometric Series: $\sum_{k=0}^{\infty} C \cdot r^k = C + C \cdot r + C \cdot r^2 + C \cdot r^3 + \ldots$

Example 1: Bouncing Ball: A "super ball" is thrown 10 feet straight up into the air. On each bounce, it rebounds to four fifths of its previous height (Fig. 1) so the sequence of heights is 10 feet, 8 feet, 32/5 feet, 128/25 feet, etc.
(a) How far does the ball travel (up and down) during its nth bounce? (b) Use a sum to represent the total distance traveled by the ball.

Fig. 1

Solution: Since the ball travels up and down on each bounce, the distance traveled during each bounce is twice the height of the ball on that bounce so $d_1 = 2(10 \text{ feet}) = 20$ feet, $d_2 = 16$ feet, $d_3 = 64/5$ feet, and, in general, $d_n = \frac{4}{5} \cdot d_{n-1}$. Looking at these values in another way,

$d_1 = 20$, $d_2 = \frac{4}{5} \cdot (20)$, $d_3 = \frac{4}{5} d_2 = \frac{4}{5} \cdot \frac{4}{5} \cdot 20 = (\frac{4}{5})^2 (20)$, $d_4 = \frac{4}{5} \cdot d_3 = \frac{4}{5} \cdot ((\frac{4}{5})^2 (20)) = (\frac{4}{5})^3 \cdot (20)$,

and, in general, $d_n = (\frac{4}{5})^{n-1} \cdot (20)$.

In theory, the ball bounces up and down forever, and the total distance traveled by the ball is the sum of the distances traveled during each bounce (an up and down flight):

(first bounce) + (second bounce) + (third bounce) + (forth bounce) + . . .

$= 20 + \frac{4}{5}(20) + (\frac{4}{5})^2 (20) + (\frac{4}{5})^3 (20) + \ldots$

$= 20 \cdot (1 + \frac{4}{5} + (\frac{4}{5})^2 + (\frac{4}{5})^3 + \ldots) = 20 \cdot \sum_{k=0}^{\infty} (\frac{4}{5})^k$.

Practice 1: **Cake:** Three calculus students want to share a small square cake equally, but they go about it in a rather strange way. First they cut the cake into 4 equal square pieces, each person takes one square, and one square is left (Fig. 2). Then they cut the leftover piece into 4 equal square pieces, each person takes one square and one square is left. And they keep repeating this process. (a) What fraction of the total cake does each person "eventually" get? (b) Represent the amount of cake each person gets as a geometric series: (amount of first piece) + (amount of second piece) + . . .

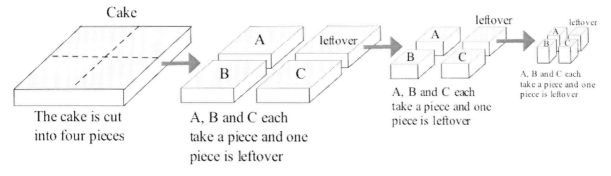

Fig. 2: Sharing a cake evenly among three students

Each series in the previous Example and Practice problems is a Geometric series, a series in which each term is a fixed multiple of the previous term. Geometric series have the form

$$\sum_{k=0}^{\infty} C \cdot r^k = C + C \cdot r + C \cdot r^2 + C \cdot r^3 + \ldots = C \cdot \sum_{k=0}^{\infty} r^k$$

with $C \neq 0$ and $r \neq 0$ representing fixed numbers. Each term in the series is r times the previous term. Geometric series are among the most common and easiest series we will encounter. A simple test determines whether a geometric series converges, and we can even determine the "sum" of the geometric series.

Geometric Series Theorem

The geometric series $\sum_{k=0}^{\infty} r^k = 1 + r + r^2 + r^3 + \ldots$ $\begin{cases} \text{converges to } \frac{1}{1-r} & \text{if } |r| < 1 \\ \text{diverges} & \text{if } |r| \geq 1 \end{cases}$

Proof: **If $|r| \geq 1$,** then $|r^k|$ approaches 1 or $+\infty$ as k becomes arbitrarily large, so the terms $a_k = r^k$ of the geometric series do not approach 0. Therefore, by the nth term test for divergence, the series diverges.

If $|r| < 1$, then the terms $a_k = r^k$ of the geometric series approach 0 so the series may or may not converge, and we need to examine the limit of the partial sums $s_n = 1 + r + r^2 + r^3 + \ldots + r^n$ of the series. For a geometric series, a clever insight allows us to calculate those partial sums:

$$(1-r) \cdot s_n = (1-r) \cdot (1 + r + r^2 + r^3 + \ldots + r^n)$$

$$= 1 \cdot (1 + r + r^2 + r^3 + \ldots + r^n) - r \cdot (1 + r + r^2 + r^3 + \ldots + r^n)$$

$$= (1 + r + r^2 + r^3 + \ldots + r^n) - (r + r^2 + r^3 + r^4 + \ldots + r^n + r^{n+1})$$

$$= 1 - r^{n+1}.$$

Since $|r| < 1$ we know $r \neq 1$ so we can divide the previous result by $1 - r$ to get

$$s_n = 1 + r + r^2 + r^3 + \ldots + r^n = \frac{1 - r^{n+1}}{1 - r} = \frac{1}{1-r} - \frac{r^{n+1}}{1-r}.$$

This formula for the nth partial sum of a geometric series is sometimes useful, but now we are interested in the limit of s_n as n approaches infinity. Since $|r| < 1$, r^{n+1} approaches 0 as n approaches infinity, so we can conclude that the partial sums $s_n = \frac{1}{1-r} - \frac{r^{n+1}}{1-r}$ approach $\frac{1}{1-r}$ (as "n → ∞").

The geometric series $\sum_{k=0}^{\infty} r^k$ converges to the value $\frac{1}{1-r}$ when $-1 < r < 1$.

Finally, $\sum_{k=0}^{\infty} C \cdot r^k = C \cdot \sum_{k=0}^{\infty} r^k$ so we can easily determine whether or not $\sum_{k=0}^{\infty} C \cdot r^k$ converges and to what number.

Example 2: How far did the ball in Example 1 travel?

Solution: The distance traveled, $20(1 + \frac{4}{5} + (\frac{4}{5})^2 + (\frac{4}{5})^3 + \ldots)$, is a geometric series with $C = 20$ and $r = 4/5$. Since $|r| < 1$, the series $1 + \frac{4}{5} + (\frac{4}{5})^2 + (\frac{4}{5})^3 + \ldots$ converges to $\frac{1}{1-r} = \frac{1}{1 - 4/5} = 5$, so the total distance traveled is

$$20(1 + \frac{4}{5} + (\frac{4}{5})^2 + (\frac{4}{5})^3 + \ldots) = 20(5) = \textbf{100 feet}.$$

Repeating decimal numbers are really geometric series in disguise, and we can use the Geometric Series Theorem to represent the exact value of the sum as a fraction.

Example 3: Represent the repeating decimals $0.\overline{4}$ and $0.\overline{13}$ as geometric series and find their sums.

Solution: $0.\overline{4} = 0.444\ldots = \frac{4}{10} + \frac{4}{100} + \frac{4}{1000} + \ldots = \frac{4}{10} \cdot (1 + \frac{1}{10} + (\frac{1}{10})^2 + (\frac{1}{10})^3 + \ldots)$

which is a geometric series with $a = 4/10$ and $r = 1/10$. Since $|r| < 1$, the geometric series converges to $\dfrac{1}{1-r} = \dfrac{1}{1-1/10} = \dfrac{10}{9}$, and $0.\overline{4} = \dfrac{4}{10}\left(\dfrac{10}{9}\right) = \dfrac{4}{9}$.

Similarly, $0.\overline{13} = 0.131313\ldots = \dfrac{13}{100} + \dfrac{13}{10000} + \dfrac{13}{1000000} + \ldots$

$= \dfrac{13}{100} \cdot \left(1 + \dfrac{1}{100} + \left(\dfrac{1}{100}\right)^2 + \left(\dfrac{1}{100}\right)^3 + \ldots\right)$

$= \dfrac{13}{100} \cdot \left(\dfrac{1}{1-1/100}\right) = \dfrac{13}{100}\left(\dfrac{100}{99}\right) = \dfrac{13}{99}$.

Practice 2: Represent the repeating decimals $0.\overline{3}$ and $0.\overline{432}$ as geometric series and find their sums.

One reason geometric series are important for us is that some series involving powers of x are geometric series.

Example 4: $\sum_{k=0}^{\infty} 3x^k = 3 + 3x + 3x^2 + \ldots$ and $\sum_{k=0}^{\infty}(2x-5)^k = 1 + (2x-5) + (2x-5)^2 + \ldots$

are geometric series with $r = x$ and $r = 2x - 5$, respectively. Find the values of x for each series so that the series converges.

Solution: A geometric series converges if and only if $|r| < 1$, so the first series converges if and only if $|x| < 1$, or, equivalently, $-1 < x < 1$. The sum of the first series is $\dfrac{3}{1-x}$.

In the second series $r = 2x - 5$ so the series converges if and only if $|2x - 5| < 1$. Removing the absolute value and solving for x, we get $-1 < 2x - 5 < 1$, and (adding 5 to each side and then dividing by 2) $2 < x < 3$. The second series converges if and only if $2 < x < 3$. The sum of the second series is $\dfrac{1}{1-(2x-5)}$ or $\dfrac{1}{6-2x}$.

Practice 3: The series $\sum_{k=0}^{\infty}(2x)^k$ and $\sum_{k=0}^{\infty}(3x-4)^k$ are geometric series. Find the ratio r for each series, and find all values of x for each series so that the series converges.

The series in the previous Example and Practice are called "power series" because they involve powers of the variable x. Later in this chapter we will investigate other power series which are not geometric series (e.g., $1 + x + x^2/2 + x^3/3 + \ldots$), and we will try to find values of x which guarantee that the series converge.

Harmonic Series: $\sum_{k=1}^{\infty} \frac{1}{k}$

The series $\sum_{k=1}^{\infty} \frac{1}{k}$ is one of the best known and most important **divergent** series. It is called the **harmonic series** because of its ties to music (Fig. 3).

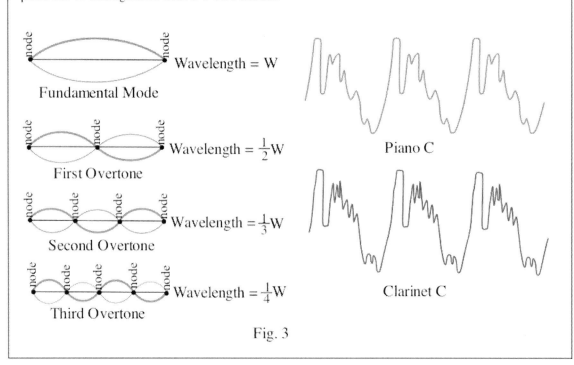

A taut piece of string such as a guitar string or a piano wire can only vibrate so that an integer number of waves are formed. The fundamental mode determines the note being played, and the number and intensity of the harmonics (overtones) present determine the characteristic quality of the sound. Because of these different characteristic qualities, a middle C (264 vibrations per second) played on a piano can be distinguished from a C on a clarinet.

Fig. 3

If we simply calculate partial sums of the harmonic series, it is not clear that the series diverges — the partial sums s_n grow, but as n becomes large, the values of s_n grow very, very slowly. Fig. 4 shows the values of n needed for the partial sums s_n to finally exceed the integer values 4, 5, 6, 8, 10, and 15. To examine the divergence of the harmonic series, brain power is much more effective than a lot of computing power.

n	s_n
31	4.0224519544
83	5.00206827268
227	6.00436670835
1,674	8.00048557200
12,367	10.00004300827
1,835,421	15.00000378267

Fig. 4

We can show that the harmonic series is divergent by showing that the terms of the harmonic series can be grouped into an infinite number of disjoint "chunks" each of which has a sum larger than 1/2. The series $\sum_{k=1}^{\infty} \frac{1}{2}$ is clearly divergent because the partial sums grow arbitrarily large: by adding enough of the terms together we can make the partial sums, $s_n > n/2$, larger than any predetermined number. Then we can conclude that the partial sums of the harmonic series also approach infinity so the harmonic series diverges.

> **Theorem:** The harmonic series $\sum_{k=1}^{\infty} \frac{1}{k} = 1 + \frac{1}{2} + \frac{1}{3} + \frac{1}{4} + \ldots$ **diverges**.

Proof: (This proof is essentially due to Oresme in 1630, twelve years before Newton was born. In 1821 Cauchy included Oresme's proof in a "Course in Analysis" and it became known as Cauchy's argument.)

Let S represent the sum of the harmonic series, $S = 1 + \frac{1}{2} + \frac{1}{3} + \frac{1}{4} + \ldots$, and group the terms of the series as indicated by the parentheses:

$$S = 1 + \frac{1}{2} + \left(\frac{1}{3} + \frac{1}{4}\right) + \left(\frac{1}{5} + \frac{1}{6} + \frac{1}{7} + \frac{1}{8}\right) + \left(\frac{1}{9} + \frac{1}{10} + \ldots + \frac{1}{16}\right) + \left(\frac{1}{17} + \ldots + \frac{1}{32}\right) + \ldots$$

    ↑   ↑   ↑   ↑

2 terms, each greater   4 terms, each greater   8 terms, each greater   16 terms, each greater
than or equal to 1/4   than or equal to 1/8   than or equal to 1/16   than or equal to 1/32

Each group in parentheses has a sum greater than 1/2, so

$$S > 1 + \frac{1}{2} + \left(\frac{1}{2}\right) + \left(\frac{1}{2}\right) + \left(\frac{1}{2}\right) + \ldots \text{ and}$$

the sequence of partial sums $\{s_n\}$ does not converge to a finite number. Therefore, the harmonic series diverges.

The harmonic series is an example of a **divergent** series whose terms, $a_k = 1/k$, approach 0. If the terms of a series approach 0, the series may or may not converge — we need to investigate further.

Telescoping Series

Sailors in the seventeenth and eighteenth centuries used telescopes (Fig. 5) which could be extended for viewing and collapsed for storing. Telescoping series get their name because they exhibit a similar "collapsing" property. Telescoping series are rather uncommon. But they are easy to analyze, and it can be useful to recognize them.

Sailor's telescope

Fig. 5

10.3 Geometric and Harmonic Series

Example 5: Determine a formula for the partial sum s_n of the series $\sum_{k=1}^{\infty} \left[\dfrac{1}{k} - \dfrac{1}{k+1} \right]$.

Then find $\lim_{n \to \infty} s_n$. (Suggestion: It is tempting to algebraically consolidate terms, but the pattern is clearer in this case if you first write out all of the terms.)

Solution: $s_1 = a_1 = 1 - \dfrac{1}{2}$. In later values of s_n, part of each term cancels part of the next term:

$$s_2 = a_1 + a_2 = \left(1 - \dfrac{1}{2}\right) + \left(\dfrac{1}{2} - \dfrac{1}{3}\right) = 1 - \dfrac{1}{3}$$

$$s_3 = a_1 + a_2 + a_3 = \left(1 - \dfrac{1}{2}\right) + \left(\dfrac{1}{2} - \dfrac{1}{3}\right) + \left(\dfrac{1}{3} - \dfrac{1}{4}\right) = 1 - \dfrac{1}{4}$$

In general, many of the pieces in each partial sum "collapse" and we are left with a simple form of s_n:

$$s_n = a_1 + a_2 + \ldots + a_{n-1} + a_n = \left(1 - \dfrac{1}{2}\right) + \left(\dfrac{1}{2} - \dfrac{1}{3}\right) + \ldots + \left(\dfrac{1}{n-1} - \dfrac{1}{n}\right) + \left(\dfrac{1}{n} - \dfrac{1}{n+1}\right) = 1 - \dfrac{1}{n+1}$$

Finally, $\lim_{n \to \infty} s_n = \lim_{n \to \infty} 1 - \dfrac{1}{n+1} = 1$ so the series converges to 1: $\sum_{k=1}^{\infty} \left[\dfrac{1}{k} - \dfrac{1}{k+1} \right] = 1$.

Practice 4: Find the sum of the series $\sum_{k=3}^{\infty} \left[\sin\left(\dfrac{1}{k}\right) - \sin\left(\dfrac{1}{k+1}\right) \right]$.

PROBLEMS

In problems 1 – 6, rewrite each geometric series using the sigma notation and calculate the value of the sum.

1. $1 + \dfrac{1}{3} + \dfrac{1}{9} + \dfrac{1}{27} + \ldots$

2. $1 + \dfrac{2}{3} + \dfrac{4}{9} + \dfrac{8}{27} + \ldots$

3. $\dfrac{1}{8} + \dfrac{1}{16} + \dfrac{1}{32} + \dfrac{1}{64} + \ldots$

4. $1 - \dfrac{1}{2} + \dfrac{1}{4} - \dfrac{1}{8} + \dfrac{1}{16} - \ldots$

5. $-\dfrac{2}{3} + \dfrac{4}{9} - \dfrac{8}{27} + \ldots$

6. $1 + \dfrac{1}{e} + \dfrac{1}{e^2} + \dfrac{1}{e^3} + \ldots$

7. Rewrite each series in the form of a sum of r^k, and then show that

   (a) $\dfrac{1}{2} + \dfrac{1}{4} + \dfrac{1}{8} + \ldots = 1$, $\dfrac{1}{3} + \dfrac{1}{9} + \dfrac{1}{27} + \ldots = \dfrac{1}{2}$, and (b) for $a > 1$, $\dfrac{1}{a} + \dfrac{1}{a^2} + \dfrac{1}{a^3} + \ldots = \dfrac{1}{a-1}$.

8. A ball is thrown 10 feet straight up into the air, and on each bounce, it rebounds to 60% of its previous height. (a) How far does the ball travel (up and down) during its nth bounce. (b) Use a sum to represent the total distance traveled by the ball. (c) Find the total distance traveled by the ball.

9. An old tennis ball is thrown 20 feet straight up into the air, and on each bounce, it rebounds to 40% of its previous height. (a) How far does the ball travel (up and down) during its nth bounce? (b) Use a sum to represent the total distance traveled by the ball. (c) Find the total distance traveled by the ball.

10. Eighty people are going on an expedition by horseback through desolate country. The people and gear require 90 horses, and additional horses are needed to carry food for the original 90 horses. Each additional horse can carry enough food to feed 3 horses for the trip. How many additional horses are needed? (The original 90 horses will require 30 extra horses to carry their food. The 30 extra horses require 10 more horses to carry their food. etc.)

11. The mathematical diet you are following says you can eat "half of whatever is on the plate," so first you bite off one half of the cake and put the other half back on the plate. Then you pick up the remaining half from the plate (it's "on the plate"), bite off half of that, and return the rest to the plate. And you continue this silly process of picking up the piece from the plate, biting off half, and returning the rest to the plate. (a) Represent the total amount you eat as a series. (b) How much of the cake is **left** after 1 bite, 2 bites, n bites? (c) "Eventually," how much of the cake do you eat?

12. Suppose in Fig. 6 we begin with a square with sides of length 1 (area = 1) and construct another square inside by connecting the midpoints of the sides. Then the new square has area 1/2. If we continue the process of constructing each new square by connecting the midpoints of the sides of the previous square, we get a sequence of squares each of which has 1/2 half the area of the previous square. Find the total area of all of the squares.

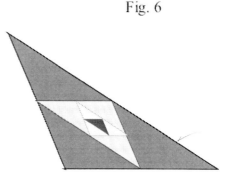

Fig. 6

13. Suppose in Fig. 7 we begin with a triangle with area 1 and construct another triangle inside by connecting the midpoints of the sides. Then the new triangle has area 1/4. Imagine that this construction process is continued and find the total area of all of the triangles.

Fig. 7

14. Suppose in Fig. 8 we begin with a circle of radius 1 and construct 2 more circles inside, each with radius 1/2. Continue the process of constructing two new circles inside each circle from the previous step and find the total area of the circles.

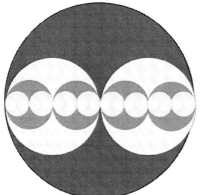

Fig. 8

10.3 Geometric and Harmonic Series   Contemporary Calculus   9

15. The construction of the Helga von Koch snowflake begins with an equilateral triangle of area 1 (Fig. 9). Then each edge is subdivided into three equal lengths, and three equilateral triangles, each with area 1/9, are built on these "middle thirds" adding a total of 3(1/9) to the original area. The process is repeated: at the next stage, 3·4 equilateral triangles, each with area 1/81, are built on the new "middle thirds" adding 3·4·(1/81) more area. (a) Find the total area that results when this process is repeated forever.

number of edges	# triangles added	area of each triangle	total area added
3	0	0	0
3·4	3	1/9	3/9
$3·4^2$	3·4	$1/9^2$	$3·4/9^2 = (3/9)(4/9)$
$3·4^3$	$3·4^2$	$1/9^3$	$3·4^2/9^3 = (3/9)(4^2/9^2)$
$3·4^4$	$3·4^3$	$1/9^4$	$3·4^3/9^4 = (3/9)(4^3/9^3)$

so the total added area of the snowflake is

$$1 + \frac{3}{9} + (\frac{3}{9})(\frac{4}{9}) + (\frac{3}{9})(\frac{4^2}{9^2}) + (\frac{3}{9})(\frac{4^3}{9^3}) + \ldots$$

(b) Express the perimeter of the Koch Snowflake as a geometric series and find its sum.
(The area is finite, but the perimeter is infinite.)

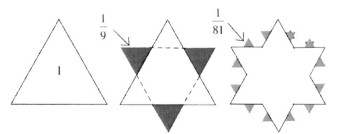

Fig. 9: Helga von Koch Snowflake

16. Harmonic Tower: The base of a tower is a cube whose edges are each one foot long. On top of it are cubes with edges of length 1/2, 1/3, 1/4, ... (Fig. 10).

   (a) Represent the total height of the tower as a series. Is the height finite?
   (b) Represent the total surface area of the cubes as a series.
   (c) Represent the total volume of the cubes as a series.
   (In the next section we will be able to determine if this surface area and volume are finite or infinite.)

17. The base of a tower is a sphere whose radius is each one foot long. On top of each sphere is another sphere with radius one half the radius of the sphere immediately beneath it (Fig 11). (a) Represent the total height of the tower as a series and find its sum. (b) Represent the total surface area of the spheres as a series and find its sum. (c) Represent the total volume of the spheres as a series and find its sum.

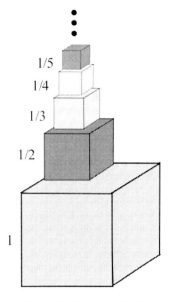

Fig. 10: Harmonic Tower

18. Represent the repeating decimals $0.\overline{6}$ and $0.\overline{63}$ as geometric series and find the value of each series as a simple fraction.

19. Represent the repeating decimals $0.\overline{8}$, $0.\overline{9}$, and $0.\overline{285714}$ as geometric series and find the value of each series as a simple fraction.

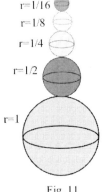

Fig. 11

20. Represent the repeating decimals $0.\bar{a}$, $0.\overline{ab}$, and $0.\overline{abc}$ as geometric series and find the value of each series as a simple fraction. What do you think the simple fraction representation is for $0.\overline{abcd}$?

In problems 21 – 32, find all values of x for which each geometric series converges.

21. $\sum_{k=1}^{\infty} (2x+1)^k$

22. $\sum_{k=1}^{\infty} (3-x)^k$

23. $\sum_{k=1}^{\infty} (1-2x)^k$

24. $\sum_{k=1}^{\infty} 5x^k$

25. $\sum_{k=1}^{\infty} (7x)^k$

26. $\sum_{k=1}^{\infty} (x/3)^k$

27. $1 + \frac{x}{2} + \frac{x^2}{4} + \frac{x^3}{8} + \ldots$

28. $1 + \frac{2}{x} + \frac{4}{x^2} + \frac{8}{x^3} + \ldots$

29. $1 + 2x + 4x^2 + 8x^3 + \ldots$

30. $\sum_{k=1}^{\infty} (2x/3)^k$

31. $\sum_{k=1}^{\infty} \sin^k(x)$

32. $\sum_{k=1}^{\infty} e^{kx} = \sum_{k=1}^{\infty} (e^x)^k$

33. One student thought the formula was $1 + x + x^2 + x^3 + \ldots = \frac{1}{1-x}$. The second student said "That can't be right. If we replace x with 2, then the formula says the sum of the positive numbers $1 + 2 + 4 + 8 + \ldots$ is a negative number $\frac{1}{1-2} = -1$." Who is right? Why?

34. **The Classic Board Problem:** If you have identical 1 foot long boards, they can be arranged to hang over the edge of a table. One board can extend 1/2 foot beyond the edge (Fig. 12), two boards can extend 1/2 + 1/4 feet, and, in general, n boards can extend $1/2 + 1/4 + 1/6 + \ldots + 1/(2n)$ feet beyond the edge.

    (a) How many boards are needed for an arrangement in which the entire top board is beyond the edge of the table?

    (b) How many boards are needed for an arrangement in which the entire top two boards are beyond the edge of the table?

    (c) How far can an arrangement extend beyond the edge of the table?

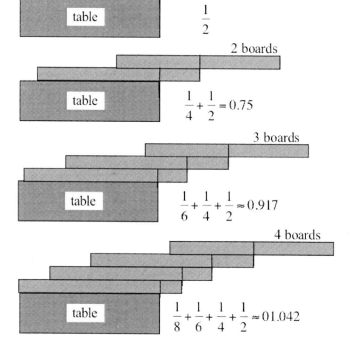

Fig. 12

In problems 35 – 40, calculate the value of the partial sum for $n = 4$ and $n = 5$ and find a formula for s_n. (The patterns may be more obvious if you do not simplify each term.)

35. $\sum_{k=3}^{\infty} \left[\frac{1}{k} - \frac{1}{k+1} \right]$

36. $\sum_{k=1}^{\infty} \left[\frac{1}{k} - \frac{1}{k+2} \right]$

37. $\sum_{k=1}^{\infty} [k^3 - (k+1)^3]$

38. $\sum_{k=1}^{\infty} \ln\left(\frac{k}{k+1}\right)$

39. $\sum_{k=3}^{\infty} [f(k) - f(k+1)]$

40. $\sum_{k=1}^{\infty} [g(k) - g(k+2)]$

In problems 41 – 44, calculate s_4 and s_5 for each series and find the limit of s_n as n approaches infinity. If the limit is a finite value, it represents the value of the infinite series.

41. $\sum_{k=1}^{\infty} \sin(\frac{1}{k}) - \sin(\frac{1}{k+1})$

42. $\sum_{k=2}^{\infty} \cos(\frac{1}{k}) - \cos(\frac{1}{k+1})$

43. $\sum_{k=2}^{\infty} \frac{1}{k^2} - \frac{1}{(k+1)^2}$

44. $\sum_{k=3}^{\infty} \ln(1 - \frac{1}{k^2})$ (Suggestion: Rewrite $1 - \frac{1}{k^2}$ as $\frac{1 - \frac{1}{k}}{1 - \frac{1}{k+1}}$)

Problems 45 and 46 are outlines of two "proofs by contradiction" that the harmonic series is divergent. Each proof starts with the assumption that the "sum" of the harmonic series is a finite number, and then an obviously false conclusion is derived from the assumption. Verify that each step follows from the assumption and previous steps, and explain why the conclusion is false.

45. Assume that $H = 1 + \frac{1}{2} + \frac{1}{3} + \frac{1}{4} + \frac{1}{5} + \frac{1}{6} + \frac{1}{7} + \ldots$ is a finite number, and let

$O = 1 + \frac{1}{3} + \frac{1}{5} + \frac{1}{7} + \ldots$ be the sum of the "odd reciprocals," and $E = \frac{1}{2} + \frac{1}{4} + \frac{1}{6} + \frac{1}{8} + \ldots$

be the sum of the "even reciprocals." Then

(i) $H = O + E$,   (ii)   each term of O is larger than the corresponding term of E so $O > E$,

and   (iii) $E = \frac{1}{2} + \frac{1}{4} + \frac{1}{6} + \frac{1}{8} + \ldots = \frac{1}{2} \{ 1 + \frac{1}{2} + \frac{1}{3} + \frac{1}{4} + \ldots \} = \frac{1}{2} H$.

Therefore $H = O + E > \frac{1}{2} H + \frac{1}{2} H = H$ (so "H is strictly bigger than H," a contradiction).

II. Assume that $H = 1 + \frac{1}{2} + \frac{1}{3} + \frac{1}{4} + \frac{1}{5} + \frac{1}{6} + \frac{1}{7} + \ldots$ is a finite number, and, starting with the second term, group the terms into groups of three. Then, using $\frac{1}{n-1} + \frac{1}{n} + \frac{1}{n+1} > 3 \cdot \frac{1}{n}$, we have

$H = 1 + (\frac{1}{2} + \frac{1}{3} + \frac{1}{4}) + (\frac{1}{5} + \frac{1}{6} + \frac{1}{7}) + (\frac{1}{8} + \frac{1}{9} + \frac{1}{10}) + \ldots$

$> 1 + (\quad 1 \quad) + (\quad \frac{1}{2} \quad) + (\quad \frac{1}{3} \quad) + \ldots$

$= 1 + (1 + \frac{1}{2} + \frac{1}{3} + \frac{1}{4} + \ldots) = 1 + H$. Therefore, $H > 1 + H$ (so "H is bigger than $1 + H$").

46. Jacob Bernoulli (1654–1705) was a master of understanding and manipulating series by breaking a difficult series into a sum of easier series. He used that technique to find the sum of the non–geometric series

$$\sum_{k=1}^{\infty} \frac{k}{2^k} = 1/2 + 2/4 + 3/8 + 4/16 + 5/32 + \ldots + k/2^k + \ldots$$ in his book <u>Ars Conjectandi</u>, 1713.

Show that $1/2 + 2/4 + 3/8 + 4/16 + 5/32 + \ldots + n/2^n + \ldots$ can be written as

$1/2 + 1/4 + 1/8 + 1/16 + 1/32 + \ldots + 1/2^n + \ldots$ (a)

plus $1/4 + 1/8 + 1/16 + 1/32 + \ldots + 1/2^n + \ldots$ (b)

plus $1/8 + 1/16 + 1/32 + \ldots + 1/2^n + \ldots$ (c)

plus . . . etc.

Find the values of the geometric series (a), (b), (c), etc. and then find the sum of these values (another geometric series).

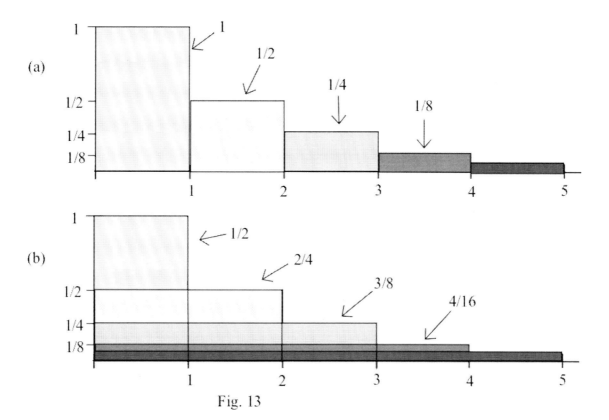

Fig. 13

47. Bernoulli's approach in problem 46 can also be interpreted as a geometric argument for representing the area in Fig. 13 in two different ways. (a) Represent the total area in Fig. 13a as a (geometric) sum of the areas of the side–by–side rectangles, and find the sum of the series. (b) Represent the total area of the stacked rectangles in Fig. 13b as a sum of the areas of the horizontal slices.

Since both series represent the same total area, the values of the series are equal.

48. Use the approach of problem 46 to find a formula for the sum of

   (a) the value of $\displaystyle\sum_{k=1}^{\infty}\frac{k}{3^k} = 1/3 + 2/9 + 3/27 + 4/81 + \ldots + k/3^k + \ldots$ and

   (b) a formula for the value of $\displaystyle\sum_{k=1}^{\infty}\frac{k}{c^k} = 1/c + 2/c^2 + 3/c^3 + 4/c^4 + \ldots + k/c^k + \ldots$ for $c > 1$.

   (answers: (a) 3/4, (b) $c/(c-1)^2$)

Practice Answers

Practice 1: (a) Since they each get equal shares, and the whole cake is distributed, they each get 1/3 of the cake. More precisely, after step 1, 1/4 of the cake remains and 3/4 was shared. After step 2, $(1/4)^2$ of the cake remains and $1 - (1/4)^2$ was shared. After step n, $(1/4)^n$ of the cake remains and $1 - (1/4)^n$ was shared. So after step n, each student has $(\frac{1}{3})(1 - (1/4)^n)$ of the cake. "Eventually," each student gets (almost) $\frac{1}{3}$ of the cake.

(b) $(\frac{1}{4}) + (\frac{1}{4})^2 + (\frac{1}{4})^3 + \ldots = (\frac{1}{4})\{ 1 + (\frac{1}{4}) + (\frac{1}{4})^2 + \ldots \}$

Practice 2: $0.\overline{3} = 0.333\ldots = \frac{3}{10} + \frac{3}{100} + \frac{3}{1000} + \ldots = \frac{3}{10} \cdot (1 + \frac{1}{10} + (\frac{1}{10})^2 + (\frac{1}{10})^3 + \ldots)$

which is a geometric series with $a = 3/10$ and $r = 1/10$. Since $|r| < 1$, the geometric series converges to $\frac{1}{1-r} = \frac{1}{1-1/10} = \frac{10}{9}$, and $0.\overline{3} = \frac{3}{10}(\frac{10}{9}) = \frac{3}{9} = \frac{1}{3}$.

Similarly, $0.\overline{432} = 0.432432432\ldots = \frac{432}{1000} + \frac{432}{1000000} + \frac{432}{1000000000} + \ldots$

$= \frac{432}{1000} \cdot (1 + \frac{1}{1000} + (\frac{1}{1000})^2 + (\frac{1}{100})^3 + \ldots)$

$= \frac{432}{1000} \cdot (\frac{1}{1 - 1/1000}) = \frac{432}{1000}(\frac{1000}{999}) = \frac{432}{999} = \frac{16}{37}$.

Practice 3: $r = 2x$: If $|2x| < 1$, then $-1 < 2x < 1$ so $-1/2 < x < 1/2$.

$\displaystyle\sum_{k=0}^{\infty}(2x)^k$ converges (to $\frac{1}{1-2x}$) when $-1/2 < x < 1/2$.

$r = 3x - 4$: If $|3x - 4| < 1$, then $-1 < 3x - 4 < 1$ so $3 < 3x < 5$ and $1 < x < 5/3$.

$\displaystyle\sum_{k=0}^{\infty}(3x - 4)^k$ converges (to $\frac{1}{1 - (3x-4)} = \frac{1}{5 - 3x}$) when $1 < x < 5/3$.

Practice 4: Let $s_n = \sum_{k=3}^{n} \sin(\frac{1}{k}) - \sin(\frac{1}{k+1})$

$= \{\sin(\frac{1}{3}) - \sin(\frac{1}{4})\} + \{\sin(\frac{1}{4}) - \sin(\frac{1}{5})\} + \{\sin(\frac{1}{5}) - \sin(\frac{1}{6})\} + ... + \{\sin(\frac{1}{n}) - \sin(\frac{1}{n+1})\}$

$= \sin(\frac{1}{3}) - \sin(\frac{1}{n+1})$.

Then $\lim_{n\to\infty} s_n = \lim_{n\to\infty} \{\sin(\frac{1}{3}) - \sin(\frac{1}{n+1})\} = \sin(\frac{1}{3})$ so the series converges to $\sin(\frac{1}{3})$:

$\sum_{k=1}^{\infty} \sin(\frac{1}{k}) - \sin(\frac{1}{k+1}) = \sin(\frac{1}{3}) \approx 0.327$.

Appendix: MAPLE and WolframAlpha for Partial Sums of Geometric Series

MAPLE command for

$\sum_{n=0}^{100} \frac{3}{2^n}$: sum(3*(1/2)^n , n=0..100) ;   (then press ENTER key)

$\sum_{n=0}^{\infty} \frac{3}{2^n}$: sum(3*(1/2)^n , n=0..infinity) ;   (then press ENTER key)

WolframAlpha   (free at   http://www.wolframalpha.com)

Asking   sum 3/2^k , k = 1 to infinity

gives the sum of the infinite series and a graph of the partial sums.

Asking   sum 3/2^k , k = 1 to 100

gives the sum as an exact fraction (strange) and as a decimal.

10.3.5 AN INTERLUDE

The previous three sections introduced the topics of sequences and series, discussed the meaning of convergence of series, and examined geometric series in some detail. The ideas, definitions, and results in those sections are fundamental for understanding and working with the material in the rest of this chapter and for later work in theoretical and applied mathematics.

The material in the next several sections is of a different sort — it is more technical and specialized. In order to work effectively with power series we need to know where (for which values of x) the power series converge. And to determine that convergence we need additional methods. In the next several sections we examine several methods for determining where particular series converge or diverge. These methods are called "convergence tests."

- The Integral Test in Section 10.4 says that a series converges if and only if a certain related improper integral is finite. This result lets us change a question about convergence of a series into a question about the convergence of an integral. Sometimes the related integral is easy to evaluate so it is easy to determine the convergence of the series. (Sometimes the related integral is very difficult to evaluate.) The integral test is then used to determine the convergence of P–series, the whole family of series of the form $\sum_{k=1}^{\infty} \frac{1}{k^p}$.

- Section 10.5 introduces some methods for determining the convergence of a new series by comparing the new series with some series which we already know converge or diverge. These comparison tests can be very powerful and useful, but their power and usefulness depends on already knowing about the convergence of some particular series to compare against the new series. Typically we will compare new series against two types of series, geometric series and P–series.

- In Section 10.6 we derive a result about the convergence of a series $\sum_{k=1}^{\infty} a_k$ by examining the ratios of successive terms of the series, a_{k+1}/a_k . If this ratio is small enough, then we will be able to conclude that the series converges. If the ratio is large enough, then we will be able to conclude that the series diverges. Unfortunately, sometimes the value of the ratio will not allow us to conclude anything.

- Section 10.7 examines series whose terms alternate in sign, such as the "alternating harmonic series," $1 - 1/2 + 1/3 - 1/4 + \ldots$, and discusses methods to determine whether these alternating series converge.

Each of these sections is rather short and focuses on one or two tests of convergence. As you study the material in each section by itself, you need to be able to use the method discussed in that section. When you finish all of the sections, you also need to be able to decide which convergence test to use.

PROBLEMS

These problems illustrate some of the reasoning that is used in sections 10.4 – 10.7, but they do not assume any information from those sections.

Integrals and sums

1. Which shaded region in Fig. 1 has the larger area, the sum or the integral?

2. Which shaded region in Fig. 2 has the larger area, the sum or the integral?

Fig. 1

3. Represent the area of the shaded region in Fig. 3 as an infinite series.

4. Represent the area of the shaded region in Fig. 4 as an infinite series.

Fig. 2

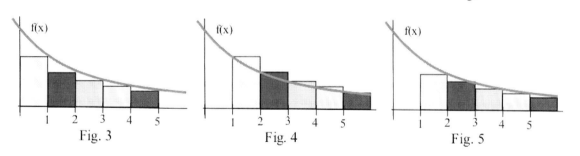

Fig. 3   Fig. 4   Fig. 5

5. Represent the area of the shaded region in Fig. 5 as an infinite series.

6. Which of the following represents the shaded area in Fig. 6?
   (a) $f(0) + f(1)$ (b) $f(1) + f(2)$
   (c) $f(2) + f(3)$ (d) $f(3) + f(4)$

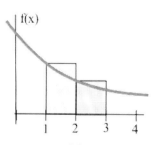

Fig. 6

7. Which of the following represents the shaded area in Fig. 7?

   (a) f(0) + f(1)   (b) f(1) + f(2)   (c) f(2) + f(3)   (d) f(3) + f(4)

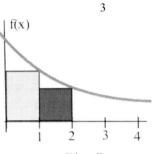

Fig. 7

8. Which of the following represents the shaded area in Fig. 8?

   (a)   f(0) + f(1)   (b) f(1) + f(2)   (c) f(2) + f(3)   (d) f(3) + f(4)

Fig. 8

9. Which of the following represents the shaded area in Fig. 9?

   (a) f(0) + f(1)   (b) f(1) + f(2)   (c) f(2) + f(3)   (d) f(3) + f(4)

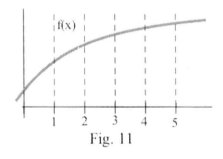

Fig. 9

10. Arrange the following four values in increasing order (Fig. 10):

    (a) $\int_1^3 f(x)\,dx$ (b) $\int_2^4 f(x)\,dx$ (c) f(1) + f(2)   (d) f(2) + f(3)

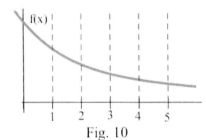

Fig. 10

11. Arrange the following four values in increasing order (Fig. 11):

    (a) $\int_1^4 f(x)\,dx$ (b) $\int_2^5 f(x)\,dx$

    (c) f(1) + f(2) + f(3)   (d) f(2) + f(3) + f(4)

Fig. 11

Comparisons

12. You want to get a summer job operating a type of heavy equipment, and you know there are certain height requirements in order for the operator to fit safely in the cab of the machine. You don't remember what the requirements are, but three of your friends applied. Tom was rejected as too tall. Sam was rejected as too short. Justin got a job. Should you apply for the job if

    (a) you are taller than Tom? Why?   (b) you are taller than Sam? Why?

    (c) you are shorter than Sam? Why?   (d) you are shorter than Justin? Why?

    (e) List the comparisons which indicate that you are the wrong height for the job.

    (f) List the comparisons which do not give you enough information about whether you are an acceptable height for the job.

13. You know Wendy did well on the Calculus test and Paula did poorly, but you haven't received your test back yet. If the instructor tells you the following, what can you conclude?
    (a) "You did better than Wendy." (b) "You did better than Paula."
    (c) "You did worse than Wendy." (d) "You did worse than Paula."

14. You have recently taken up mountain climbing and are considering a climb of Mt. Baker. You know that Mt. Index is too easy to be challenging, but that Mt. Liberty Bell is too difficult for you. Should you plan a climb of Mt. Baker if an experienced climber friend tells you that
    (a) "Baker is easier than Index." (b) "Baker is more difficult than Index."
    (c) "Baker is easier than Liberty Bell." (d) "Baker is more difficult than Liberty Bell."
    (e) Which comparisons indicate that Baker is appropriate: challenging but not too difficult?
    (f) Which comparisons indicate that Baker is not appropriate?

15. As a student you have had Professors Good and Bad for classes, and they each lived up to their names. Now you are considering taking a class from Prof. Unknown whom you don't know. What can you expect if
    (a) a classmate who had Good and Unknown says "Unknown was better than Good" ?
    (b) a classmate who had Good and Unknown says "Good was better than Unknown" ?
    (c) a classmate who had Bad and Unknown says "Unknown was better than Bad" ?
    (d) a classmate who had Bad and Unknown says "Bad was better than Unknown" ?

In problems 16 – 19, all of the series converge. In each pair, which series has the larger sum?

16. $\sum_{k=1}^{\infty} \frac{1}{k^2+1}$, $\sum_{k=1}^{\infty} \frac{1}{k^2}$

17. $\sum_{k=2}^{\infty} \frac{1}{k^3-5}$, $\sum_{k=2}^{\infty} \frac{1}{k^3}$

18. $\sum_{k=1}^{\infty} \frac{1}{k^2+3k-1}$, $\sum_{k=1}^{\infty} \frac{1}{k^2}$

19. $\sum_{k=3}^{\infty} \frac{1}{k^2+5k}$, $\sum_{k=3}^{\infty} \frac{1}{k^3+k-1}$

Ratios of successive terms

In problems 20 – 28, a formula is given for each term a_k of a sequence. For each sequence (a) write a formula for a_{k+1}, (b) write the ratio a_{k+1}/a_k, and (c) simplify the ratio a_{k+1}/a_k.

20. $a_k = 3k$

21. $a_k = k + 3$

22. $a_k = 2k + 5$

23. $a_k = 3/k$

24. $a_k = k^2$

25. $a_k = 2^k$

26. $a_k = (1/2)^k$

27. $a_k = x^k$

28. $a_k = (x-1)^k$

In problems 29–36, state whether the series converges or diverges and calculate the ratio a_{k+1}/a_k.

29. $\sum_{k=1}^{\infty} (\frac{1}{2})^k$

30. $\sum_{k=1}^{\infty} (\frac{1}{5})^k$

31. $\sum_{k=1}^{\infty} 2^k$

32. $\sum_{k=1}^{\infty} (-3)^k$

33. $\sum_{k=1}^{\infty} 4$

34. $\sum_{k=1}^{\infty} (-1)^k$

35. $\sum_{k=1}^{\infty} \frac{1}{k}$

36. $\sum_{k=1}^{\infty} \frac{7}{k}$

Alternating terms

For problems 37 – 40, s_n represents the nth partial sum of the series with terms a_k (e.g., $s_3 = a_1 + a_2 + a_3$).

In each problem, circle the appropriate symbol: "<" or "=" or ">."

37. If $a_5 > 0$, then $s_4 \;<\;=\;>\; s_5$.

38. If $a_5 = 0$, then $s_4 \;<\;=\;>\; s_5$.

39. If $a_5 < 0$, then $s_4 \;<\;=\;>\; s_5$.

40. If $a_{n+1} > 0$ for all n, then $s_n \;<\;=\;>\; s_{n+1}$ for all n.

41. If $a_{n+1} < 0$ for all n, then $s_n \;<\;=\;>\; s_{n+1}$ for all n.

42. If $a_4 > 0$ and $a_5 < 0$, then how do $s_3, s_4,$ and s_5 compare?

43. If $a_4 = 0.2$ and $a_5 = -0.1$ and $a_6 = 0.2$, then how do $s_3, s_4,$ and s_5 compare?

44. If $a_4 = -0.3$ and $a_5 = 0.2$ and $a_6 = -0.1$, then how do $s_3, s_4,$ and s_5 compare?

45. If $a_4 = -0.3$ and $a_5 = -0.2$ and $a_6 = 0.1$, then how do $s_3, s_4,$ and s_5 compare?

In problems 46 – 50, the first 8 terms $a_1, a_2, \ldots, a_8$ of a series are given. Calculate and graph the first 8 partial sums $s_1, s_2, \ldots, s_8$ of the series and describe the pattern of the graph of the partial sums.

46. $a_1 = 2, a_2 = -1, a_3 = 2, a_4 = -1, a_5 = 2, a_6 = -1, a_7 = 2, a_8 = -1$.

47. $a_1 = 2, a_2 = -1, a_3 = 0.9, a_4 = -0.8, a_5 = 0.7, a_6 = -0.6, a_7 = 0.5, a_8 = -0.4$.

48. $a_1 = 2, a_2 = -1, a_3 = 1, a_4 = -1, a_5 = 1, a_6 = -1, a_7 = 1, a_8 = -1$.

49. $a_1 = -2, a_2 = 1.5, a_3 = -0.8, a_4 = 0.6, a_5 = -0.4, a_6 = 0.2, a_7 = 2, a_8 = -0.1$.

50. $a_1 = 5, a_2 = 1, a_3 = -0.6, a_4 = -0.4, a_5 = 0.2, a_6 = 0.1, a_7 = 0.1, a_8 = -0.2$.

51. What condition on the terms a_k guarantees that the graph of the partial sums s_n follows an "up–down–up–down" pattern?

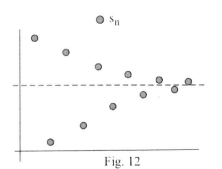

Fig. 12

52. What condition on the terms a_k guarantees that the graph of the partial sums s_n forms a "narrowing funnel" pattern in Fig. 12 ?

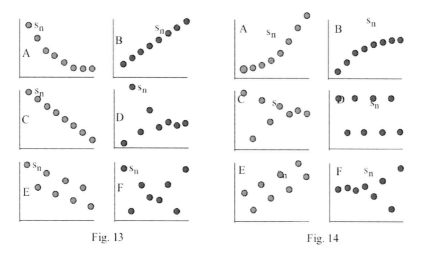

Fig. 13   Fig. 14

53. Fig. 13 shows the graphs of several partial sums s_n.
    (a) For which graphs do the terms a_k alternate in sign?
    (b) For which graphs do the $|a_k|$ decrease?
    (c) For which graphs do the terms a_k alternate in sign and decrease in absolute value?

54. Fig. 14 shows the graphs of several partial sums s_n.
    (a) For which graphs do the terms a_k alternate in sign?
    (b) For which graphs do the $|a_k|$ decrease?
    (c) For which graphs do the terms a_k alternate in sign and decrease in absolute value?

55. The geometric series $\sum_{k=0}^{\infty} (-\frac{1}{2})^k = 1 - \frac{1}{2} + \frac{1}{4} - \ldots$ converges to $\frac{1}{1-(-1/2)} = \frac{1}{3/2} = \frac{2}{3}$.

    Graph the horizontal line $y = \frac{2}{3}$ and then graph the partial sums $s_0, \ldots, s_8$ of $\sum_{k=0}^{\infty} (-\frac{1}{2})^k$.

56. The geometric series $\sum_{k=0}^{\infty} (-0.6)^k = 1 - 0.6 + 0.36 - \ldots$ converges to $\frac{1}{1-(-0.6)} = \frac{1}{1.6} = 0.625$.

    Graph the horizontal line $y = 0.625$ and then graph the partial sums $s_0, \ldots, s_8$ of $\sum_{k=0}^{\infty} (-0.6)^k$.

57. The geometric series $\sum_{k=0}^{\infty} (-2)^k = 1 - 2 + 4 - \ldots$ diverges ($|r| = |-2| = 2 > 1$). Graph the partial sums $s_0, \ldots, s_8$ of $\sum_{k=0}^{\infty} (-2)^k$.

10.4 POSITIVE TERM SERIES: INTEGRAL TEST & P–TEST

This section discusses two methods for determining whether some series are convergent. The first, the integral test, says that a given series converges if and only if a related improper integral converges. This lets us trade a question about the convergence of a series for a question about the convergence of an improper integral. The second convergence test, the P–test, says that the convergence of one particular type of series, the sum $\sum_{k=1}^{\infty} \frac{1}{k^p}$, depends only on the value of p. These tests only apply to series whose terms are positive. And, unfortunately, the tests only tell us if the series converge or diverge, but they do not tell us the actual sum of the series.

The Integral Test is the more fundamental and general of the two tests examined in this section, and it is used to prove the P–Test. The P–Test, however, is easier to apply and is likely to be the test you use more often.

Integral Test

A series can be thought of as a sum of areas of rectangles each having a base of one unit (Fig. 1). With this area interpretation of series there is a natural connection between series and integrals and between the convergence of a series and the convergence of an appropriate improper integral.

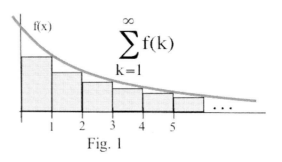

Fig. 1

Example 1: Suppose the shaded region in Fig. 2a can be painted using 3 gallons of paint. How much paint is needed for the shaded region in Fig. 2b?

Solution: We don't have enough information to determine the exact amount of paint needed for the region in Fig. 2b, but the total of the rectangular areas is smaller than the area in Fig. 2a so less than 3 gallons of paint are needed for the region in Fig. 2b.

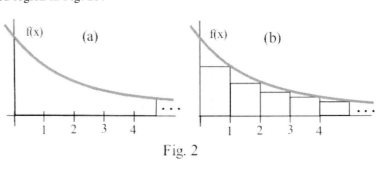

Fig. 2

Practice 1: Suppose the area of the shaded region in Fig. 3a is infinite. What can you say about the total area of the rectangular regions in Fig. 3b?

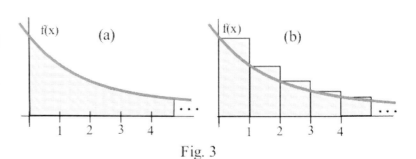

Fig. 3

The geometric reasoning used in Example 1 and Practice 1 can also be used to determine the convergence and divergence of some series.

Example 2: (a) Which is larger: $\sum_{k=2}^{\infty} \frac{1}{k^2}$ or $\int_{1}^{\infty} \frac{1}{x^2} dx$?

(b) Use the result of (a) to show that $\sum_{k=2}^{\infty} \frac{1}{k^2}$ is convergent.

Solution: Fig. 4 illustrates that the area of the rectangles, $\frac{1}{2^2} + \frac{1}{3^2} + \frac{1}{4^2} + \ldots + \frac{1}{n^2}$, is less than the area under the graph of the function $f(x) = \frac{1}{x^2}$ for $1 \leq x \leq n$:

$$\sum_{k=2}^{n} \frac{1}{k^2} < \int_{1}^{n} \frac{1}{x^2} dx \quad \text{so} \quad \sum_{k=2}^{n} \frac{1}{k^2} < \int_{1}^{\infty} \frac{1}{x^2} dx = 1 \text{ for every } n \geq 2.$$

Therefore, the partial sums of $\sum_{k=2}^{\infty} \frac{1}{k^2}$ are bounded. Also, each term $a_k = \frac{1}{k^2}$ is positive, so the partial sums of $\sum_{k=2}^{\infty} \frac{1}{k^2}$ are monotonically increasing. So, by the Monotonic Theorem of Section 10.1, the sequence of partial sums converges, so the series $\sum_{k=2}^{\infty} \frac{1}{k^2}$ is convergent.

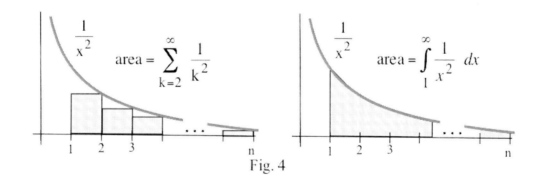

Fig. 4

The reasoning of Example 2 can be extended to the comparison of other series and the appropriate integrals.

Integral Test

Suppose f is a **continuous, positive, decreasing** function on $[1, \infty)$ and $a_k = f(k)$.

The series $\sum_{k=1}^{\infty} a_k$ converges **if and only if** the integral $\int_1^{\infty} f(x)\,dx$ converges.

Equivalently, (a) if $\int_1^{\infty} f(x)\,dx$ converges, then $\sum_{k=1}^{\infty} a_k$ converges,

and (b) if $\int_1^{\infty} f(x)\,dx$ diverges, then $\sum_{k=1}^{\infty} a_k$ diverges.

The proof is simply a careful use of the reasoning in the previous Examples.

Proof: Assume that f is a continuous, positive, decreasing function on $[1, \infty)$ and that $a_k = f(k)$.

Part (a): Assume that $\int_1^{\infty} f(x)\,dx$ converges: $\lim_{n \to \infty} \int_1^n f(x)\,dx$ is a finite number.

Since each $a_k > 0$, the sequence of partial sums s_n is increasing. If we arrange the rectangles under the graph of f as in Fig. 5, it is clear that

$$s_n = \sum_{k=1}^{n} a_k = a_1 + \sum_{k=2}^{n} a_k \leq a_1 + \int_1^n f(x)\,dx \leq a_1 + \int_1^{\infty} f(x)\,dx \ .$$

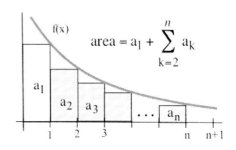

$\{s_n\}$ is a bounded, increasing sequence so, by the Monotone Convergence Theorem of Section 10.1, $\{s_n\}$ converges and $\sum_{k=1}^{\infty} a_k$ is convergent.

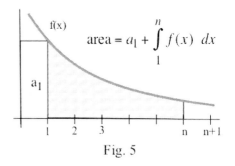

Fig. 5

Part (b): Assume that $\int_1^\infty f(x)\,dx$ diverges: $\lim_{n\to\infty} \int_1^n f(x)\,dx = \infty$.

If we arrange the rectangles under the graph of f as in Fig. 6, it is clear that

$$s_n = \sum_{k=1}^{n} a_k \geq \int_1^{n+1} f(x)\,dx \quad \text{for all } n,$$

so $\lim_{n\to\infty} s_n \geq \lim_{n\to\infty} \int_1^n f(x)\,dx = \infty$.

In other words, $\lim_{n\to\infty} s_n = \infty$ and $\sum_{k=1}^{\infty} a_k$ diverges.

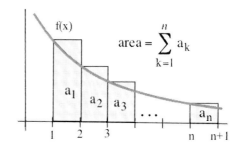

The inequalities in the proof relating the partial sums of the series to the values of integrals are sometimes used to approximate the values of the partial sums of a series:

$$\int_1^{n+1} f(x)\,dx \leq \sum_{k=1}^{n} a_k \leq a_1 + \int_1^{n} f(x)\,dx .$$

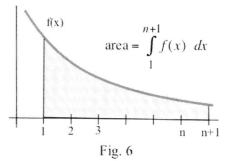

Fig. 6

We can use this last set of inequalities with $a_k = \frac{1}{k}$ and $n = 1,000$ to conclude that

$$\int_1^{10^3+1} \frac{1}{x}\,dx \leq \sum_{k=1}^{10^3} \frac{1}{k} \leq 1 + \int_1^{10^3} \frac{1}{x}\,dx \quad \text{so} \quad 7.48646986155 \leq \sum_{k=1}^{10^3} \frac{1}{k} \leq 8.48547086055 .$$

(If $n = 1,000,000$, then the same type of reasoning shows that the partial sum of $1/k$ from $k = 1$ to $k = 10^6$ is between 13.815511 and 14.815510 .)

If the series does not start with $k = 1$, a Corollary of the Integral Test can be used.

Corollary: If f satisfies the hypotheses of the Integral Test on $[N, \infty)$ and $a_k = f(k)$,

then $\sum_{k=N}^{\infty} a_k$ and $\int_N^{\infty} f(x)\,dx$ both converge or both diverge.

Example 3: Use the Integral Test to determine whether (a) $\sum_{k=1}^{\infty} \frac{1}{k^3}$ and (b) $\sum_{k=2}^{\infty} \frac{1}{k \cdot \ln(k)}$ converge.

Solution: (a) If $f(x) = \dfrac{1}{x^3}$, then $a_k = f(k)$ and f is continuous, positive and decreasing on $[1, \infty)$.

Then $\displaystyle\int_1^\infty \dfrac{1}{x^3}\,dx = \lim_{n\to\infty} \int_1^n \dfrac{1}{x^3}\,dx = \lim_{n\to\infty}\left(-\dfrac{1}{2x^2}\right)\Big|_1^n$

$$= \lim_{n\to\infty}\left(-\dfrac{1}{2n^2}\right) - \left(-\dfrac{1}{2\cdot 1^2}\right) = \dfrac{1}{2}.$$

The integral $\displaystyle\int_1^\infty \dfrac{1}{x^3}\,dx$ converges so the series $\displaystyle\sum_{k=1}^\infty \dfrac{1}{k^3}$ converges.

(b) If $f(x) = \dfrac{1}{x\cdot \ln(x)}$, then $a_k = f(k)$ and f is continuous, positive and decreasing on $[2, \infty)$.

Then $\displaystyle\int_2^\infty \dfrac{1}{x\cdot\ln(x)}\,dx = \lim_{n\to\infty}\int_2^n \dfrac{1}{x\cdot\ln(x)}\,dx = \lim_{n\to\infty} \ln(\ln(x))\Big|_2^n$

$$= \lim_{n\to\infty} \ln(\ln(n)) - \ln(\ln(2)) = \infty.$$

The integral $\displaystyle\int_2^\infty \dfrac{1}{x\cdot\ln(x)}\,dx$ diverges so the series $\displaystyle\sum_{k=2}^\infty \dfrac{1}{k\cdot\ln(k)}$ diverges.

Practice 2: Use the Integral Test to determine whether (a) $\displaystyle\sum_{k=4}^\infty \dfrac{1}{\sqrt{k}}$ and (b) $\displaystyle\sum_{k=1}^\infty e^{-k}$ converge.

Note: The Integral Test does not give the value of the sum, it only answers the question of whether the series converges or diverges. Typically the value of the improper integral is not equal to the sum of the series.

P–Test for Convergence of $\displaystyle\sum_{k=1}^\infty \dfrac{1}{k^p}$

The P–Test is very easy to use. And it answers the convergence question for a whole family of series.

P–Test

The series $\displaystyle\sum_{k=1}^\infty \dfrac{1}{k^p}$ $\begin{cases} \text{converges} & \text{if } p > 1 \\ \text{diverges} & \text{if } p \leq 1. \end{cases}$

Proof: If **p = 1**, then $\sum_{k=1}^{\infty} \frac{1}{k^p} = \sum_{k=1}^{\infty} \frac{1}{k}$, the harmonic series, which we already know diverges (by Section 10.3 or, using the Integral Test, since $\int_{1}^{\infty} \frac{1}{x} dx$ diverges to infinity.)

The proof for $p \neq 1$ is a straightforward application of the Integral Test on $f(x) = 1/x^p$.

If $p \neq 1$, then
$$\int_{1}^{\infty} \frac{1}{x^p} dx = \int_{1}^{\infty} x^{-p} dx = \lim_{A \to \infty} \int_{1}^{A} x^{-p} dx$$
$$= \lim_{A \to \infty} \left(\frac{1}{1-p}\right) \cdot x^{1-p} \Big|_{1}^{A}$$
$$= \lim_{A \to \infty} \left(\frac{1}{1-p}\right) \cdot A^{1-p} - \left(\frac{1}{1-p}\right) \cdot 1$$

As we examine the limit of A^{1-p}, there are two cases to consider: $p < 1$ and $p > 1$.

If **p < 1**, then $1 - p > 0$ so A^{1-p} approaches infinity as A approaches infinity. Then $\int_{1}^{\infty} \frac{1}{x^p} dx$ diverges, so, by the Integral Test, $\sum_{k=1}^{\infty} \frac{1}{k^p}$ diverges.

If **p > 1**, then $p - 1 > 0$ and $A^{1-p} = \frac{1}{A^{p-1}}$ approaches 0 as A approaches infinity. Then $\int_{1}^{\infty} \frac{1}{x^p} dx$ converges, so, by the Integral Test, $\sum_{k=1}^{\infty} \frac{1}{k^p}$ converges.

Example 3: Use the P–Test to determine whether (a) $\sum_{k=1}^{\infty} \frac{1}{k^2}$ and (b) $\sum_{k=4}^{\infty} \frac{1}{\sqrt{k}}$ converge.

Solution: The convergence of both series have already been determined using the Integral Test, but the P–Test is much easier to apply.

(a) $p = 2 > 1$ so $\sum_{k=1}^{\infty} \frac{1}{k^2}$ converges.   (b) $p = 1/2 < 1$ so $\sum_{k=4}^{\infty} \frac{1}{\sqrt{k}}$ diverges.

The P–Test is very easy to use (Is the exponent $p > 1$ or is $p \leq 1$?), and it is also very useful. In the next section we will compare new series with series whose convergence we already know, and most often this comparison is with some P–series whose convergence we know about from the P–Test.

Note: **The P–Test does not give the value of the sum, it only answers the question of whether the series converges of diverges.**

PROBLEMS

In problems 1 – 15 show that the function determined by the terms of the given series satisfies the hypotheses of the Integral Test, and then use the Integral Test to determine whether the series converges or diverges.

1. $\sum_{k=1}^{\infty} \dfrac{1}{2k+5}$

2. $\sum_{k=1}^{\infty} \dfrac{1}{(2k+5)^2}$

3. $\sum_{k=1}^{\infty} \dfrac{1}{(2k+5)^{3/2}}$

4. $\sum_{k=1}^{\infty} \dfrac{\ln(k)}{k}$

5. $\sum_{k=2}^{\infty} \dfrac{1}{k \cdot (\ln(k))^2}$

6. $\sum_{k=1}^{\infty} \dfrac{1}{k^2} \cdot \sin\left(\dfrac{1}{k}\right)$

7. $\sum_{k=1}^{\infty} \dfrac{1}{k^2+1}$

8. $\sum_{k=1}^{\infty} \dfrac{1}{k^2+100}$

9. $\sum_{k=1}^{\infty} \left\{ \dfrac{1}{k} - \dfrac{1}{k+3} \right\}$

10. $\sum_{k=1}^{\infty} \left\{ \dfrac{1}{k} - \dfrac{1}{k+1} \right\}$

11. $\sum_{k=1}^{\infty} \dfrac{1}{k(k+5)}$

12. $\sum_{k=2}^{\infty} \dfrac{1}{k^2-1}$

13. $\sum_{k=1}^{\infty} k \cdot e^{-(k^2)}$

14. $\sum_{k=1}^{\infty} k^2 \cdot e^{-(k^3)}$

15. $\sum_{k=1}^{\infty} \dfrac{1}{\sqrt{6k+10}}$

For problems 16 – 20, (a) use the P–Test to determine whether the given series converges, and then (b) use the Integral Test to verify your convergence conclusion of part (a).

16. $\sum_{k=1}^{\infty} \dfrac{1}{k^2}$

17. $\sum_{k=1}^{\infty} \dfrac{1}{k^3}$

18. $\sum_{k=2}^{\infty} \dfrac{1}{k}$

19. $\sum_{k=2}^{\infty} \dfrac{1}{\sqrt{k}}$

20. $\sum_{k=3}^{\infty} \dfrac{1}{k^{2/3}}$

21. $\sum_{k=3}^{\infty} \dfrac{1}{k^{3/2}}$

In the proof of the Integral Test, we derived an inequality bounding the values of the partial sums $s_n = \sum_{k=1}^{n} a_k$ between the values of two integrals: $\int_{1}^{n+1} f(x)\,dx \leq \sum_{k=1}^{n} a_k \leq a_1 + \int_{1}^{n} f(x)\,dx$. For problems 22 – 27, use this inequality to determine bounds on the values of $s_{10}, s_{100},$ and $s_{1,000,000}$ for the given series.

22. $\sum_{k=1}^{\infty} \dfrac{1}{k^2}$ (Note: The exact value of $\sum_{k=1}^{\infty} \dfrac{1}{k^2}$ is $\dfrac{\pi^2}{6}$ but it beyond our means to prove that in this course.)

23. $\sum_{k=1}^{\infty} \frac{1}{k^3}$ 24. $\sum_{k=1}^{\infty} \frac{1}{k}$ 25. $\sum_{k=1}^{\infty} \frac{1}{k+1000}$

26. $\sum_{k=1}^{\infty} \frac{1}{k^2+1}$ 27. $\sum_{k=1}^{\infty} \frac{1}{k^2+100}$

28. Euler's Constant: Define $g_1 = 1 - \ln(1) = 1$,

$g_2 = (1 + \frac{1}{2}) - \ln(2) \approx 0.806853$,

$g_3 = (1 + \frac{1}{2} + \frac{1}{3}) - \ln(3) \approx 0.734721$, and, in general,

$g_n = (1 + \frac{1}{2} + \frac{1}{3} + \frac{1}{4} + \ldots + \frac{1}{n}) - \ln(n)$.

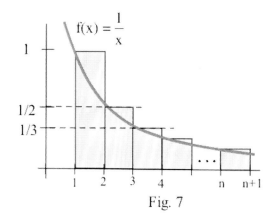

Fig. 7

(a) Make several copies of Fig. 7, and shade the regions represented by g_2, g_3, g_4, and g_n.

(b) Provide a geometric argument that $g_n > 0$ for all $n \geq 1$.

(c) Provide a geometric argument that $\{g_n\}$ is monotonically decreasing: $g_{n+1} < g_n$ for all $n \geq 1$.

(d) Conclude from parts (b) and (c) and the Monotone Convergence Theorem (Section 10.1) that $\{g_n\}$ converges.

(Note: The value to which $\{g_n\}$ converges is denoted by "γ," the lower case Greek letter gamma, and is called Euler's constant. It is not even known if γ is a rational number. $\gamma \approx 0.5772157 \cdots$.)

29. (a) Show that the integral $\int_{2}^{\infty} \frac{1}{x \cdot (\ln x)^q} dx$ converges for $q > 1$ and diverges for $q \leq 1$.

(b) Use the result of part (a) to state a "Q test" for $\sum_{k=2}^{\infty} \frac{1}{k \cdot (\ln k)^q}$.

In problems 30 – 33, use the result of Problem 29 to determine whether the given series converge.

30. $\sum_{k=2}^{\infty} \frac{1}{k \cdot \ln(k)}$ 31. $\sum_{k=2}^{\infty} \frac{1}{k \cdot (\ln k)^3}$ 32. $\sum_{k=2}^{\infty} \frac{1}{k \cdot \sqrt{\ln k}}$ 33. $\sum_{k=2}^{\infty} \frac{1}{k \cdot \ln(k^3)}$

Practice Answers

Practice 1: { total area of rectangular pieces } > { area under the curve in Fig. 3a } so if the shaded area in Fig. 3a is infinite, then the shaded area in Fig. 3b is also infinite.

Practice 2: (a) Let $f(x) = \frac{1}{\sqrt{x}}$. Then $a_k = f(k)$ and f is continuous, positive and decreasing on $[1, \infty)$.

Then $\int_4^\infty \frac{4}{\sqrt{x}} dx = \lim_{n \to \infty} \int_1^n \frac{1}{\sqrt{x}} dx = \lim_{n \to \infty} 2x^{1/2} \Big|_4^n$

$= \lim_{n \to \infty} 2\sqrt{n} - 2\sqrt{4} = \infty$.

The integral $\int_4^\infty \frac{1}{\sqrt{x}} dx$ diverges so the series $\sum_{k=4}^\infty \frac{1}{\sqrt{k}}$ diverges.

(Note: It will be easier to determine that this series diverges by using the P–Test which occurs right after this Practice problem in the text.)

(b) Let $f(x) = e^{-x}$. Then $e^{-k} = a_k = f(k)$ and f is continuous, positive and decreasing on $[1, \infty)$.

Then $\int_1^\infty e^{-x} dx = \lim_{n \to \infty} \int_1^n e^{-x} dx = \lim_{n \to \infty} -e^{-x} \Big|_1^n = \lim_{n \to \infty} \left(-e^{-n}\right) - \left(-e^{-1}\right)$

$= \lim_{n \to \infty} \left(-\frac{1}{e^n}\right) - \left(-\frac{1}{e}\right) = \frac{1}{e} \approx 0.368$.

The integral $\int_1^\infty e^{-x} dx$ converges so the series $\sum_{k=1}^\infty e^{-k}$ converges.

10.5 POSITIVE TERM SERIES: COMPARISON TESTS

This section discusses how to determine whether some series converge or diverge by comparing them with other series which we already know converge or diverge. In the basic Comparison Test we compare the two series term by term. In the more powerful Limit Comparison Test, we compare limits of ratios of the terms of the two series. Finally, we focus on the parts of the terms of a series that determine whether the series converges or diverges.

Comparison Test

Informally, if the individual terms of our series are smaller than the corresponding terms of a known convergent series, then our series converges. If our series is larger, term by term, than a known divergent series then our series diverges. If the individual terms of our series are larger than the corresponding terms of a convergent series or smaller than the corresponding terms of a divergent series, then our series may converge or diverge — the Comparison Test does not tell us.

Comparison Test

Suppose we want to determine whether $\sum_{k=1}^{\infty} a_k$ converges or diverges.

(a) If there is a convergent series $\sum_{k=1}^{\infty} c_k$ with $0 < a_k \leq c_k$ for all k, then $\sum_{k=1}^{\infty} a_k$ converges.

(b) If there is a divergent series $\sum_{k=1}^{\infty} d_k$ with $a_k \geq d_k > 0$ for all k, then $\sum_{k=1}^{\infty} a_k$ diverges.

Proof: Since all of the terms of the a_k, c_k, and d_k series are positive, their sequences of partial sums are all monotonic increasing. The proof compares the partial sums of the various series.

(a) Suppose that $0 < a_k \leq c_k$ for all k and that $\sum_{k=1}^{\infty} c_k$ converges. Since $\sum_{k=1}^{\infty} c_k$ converges,

then the partial sums $t_n = \sum_{k=1}^{n} c_k$ approach a finite limit: $\lim_{n \to \infty} t_n = L$.

For each n, $s_n \leq t_n$ (why?) so $\lim_{n \to \infty} s_n \leq \lim_{n \to \infty} t_n = L$, and the sequence $\{ s_n \}$ is bounded by L. Finally, by the Monotone Convergence Theorem, we can conclude that $\{s_n\}$ converges and that the series $\sum_{k=1}^{\infty} a_k$ converges.

(b) Suppose that $a_k \geq d_k > 0$ for all k and that $\sum_{k=1}^{\infty} d_k$ diverges. Since $\sum_{k=1}^{\infty} d_k$ diverges, then the partial sums $u_n = \sum_{k=1}^{n} d_k$ approach infinity: $\lim_{n \to \infty} u_n = \infty$. Then

$$\lim_{n \to \infty} s_n \geq \lim_{n \to \infty} u_n = \infty$$

so the sequence of partial sums $\{s_n\}$ diverges and the series $\sum_{k=1}^{\infty} a_k$ diverges.

The Comparison Test requires that we select and compare our series against a series whose convergence or divergence is known, and that choice requires that we know a collection of series that converge and some that diverge. Typically, we pick a p–series or a geometric series to compare with our series, but this choice requires some experience and practice.

Example 1: Use the Comparison Test to determine the convergence or divergence of

(a) $\sum_{k=1}^{\infty} \frac{1}{k^2 + 3}$ and (b) $\sum_{k=1}^{\infty} \frac{k+1}{k^2}$.

Solution: For these two series it is useful to compare with p–series for appropriate values of p.

(a) For all k, $\frac{1}{k^2 + 3} < \frac{1}{k^2}$, and $\sum_{k=1}^{\infty} \frac{1}{k^2}$ converges (P–Test, p = 2)

so $\sum_{k=1}^{\infty} \frac{1}{k^2 + 3}$ converges.

(b) For all k, $\frac{k+1}{k^2} = \frac{1}{k} + \frac{1}{k^2} > \frac{1}{k}$.

Since $\sum_{k=1}^{\infty} \frac{1}{k}$ diverges (P–Test, p = 1), we conclude that $\sum_{k=1}^{\infty} \frac{k+1}{k^2}$ diverges.

Practice 1: Use the Comparison Test to determine the convergence or divergence of

(a) $\sum_{k=3}^{\infty} \frac{1}{\sqrt{k-2}}$ and (b) $\sum_{k=1}^{\infty} \frac{1}{2^k + 7}$.

Example 2: A student has shown algebraically that $\frac{1}{k^2} < \frac{1}{k^2-1} < \frac{1}{k}$ for all $k \geq 2$. From this information and the Comparison Test, what can the student conclude about the convergence of the series $\sum_{k=2}^{\infty} \frac{1}{k^2-1}$?

Solution: Nothing. The Comparison Test only gives a definitive answer if our series is smaller than a convergent series or if our series is larger than a divergent series. In this example, our series is larger than a convergent series, $\sum \frac{1}{k^2}$, and is smaller than a divergent series, $\sum \frac{1}{k}$, so we can not conclude anything about the convergence of $\sum_{k=2}^{\infty} \frac{1}{k^2-1}$.

However, we can show that if $k \geq 2$ then $\frac{1}{k^2-1} < \frac{2}{k^2}$. Since $\sum_{k=2}^{\infty} \frac{2}{k^2}$ converges (P–Test), we can conclude that $\sum_{k=2}^{\infty} \frac{1}{k^2-1}$ converges. Next in this section we present a variation on the Comparison Test that allows us to quickly conclude that $\sum_{k=2}^{\infty} \frac{1}{k^2-1}$ converges.

Limit Comparison Test

The exact value of the sum of a series depends on every part of the terms of the series, but if we are only asking about convergence or divergence, some parts of the terms can be safely ignored. For example, the three series with terms $1/k^2$, $1/(k^2+1)$, and $1/(k^2-1)$ converge to different values,

$$\sum_{k=2}^{\infty} \frac{1}{k^2} \approx 0.645, \quad \sum_{k=2}^{\infty} \frac{1}{k^2+1} \approx 0.577, \quad \sum_{k=2}^{\infty} \frac{1}{k^2-1} = 0.750,$$

but they all do converge. The "+ 1" and "– 1" in the denominators affect the value of the final sum, but they do not affect whether that sum is finite or infinite. When k is a large number, the values of $1/(k^2+1)$ and $1/(k^2-1)$ are both very close to the value of $1/k^2$, and the convergence or divergence of the series $\sum_{k=2}^{\infty} \frac{1}{k^2+1}$ and $\sum_{k=2}^{\infty} \frac{1}{k^2-1}$ can be predicted from the convergence or divergence of the series $\sum_{k=2}^{\infty} \frac{1}{k^2}$.

The Limit Comparison Test states these ideas precisely.

10.5 Positive Term Series: Comparison Tests

> **Limit Comparison Test**
>
> Suppose $a_k > 0$ for all k, and we want to determine whether $\sum_{k=1}^{\infty} a_k$ converges or diverges.
>
> If there is a series $\sum_{k=1}^{\infty} b_k$ so that $\lim_{k \to \infty} \frac{a_k}{b_k} = L$, a **positive, finite** value,
>
> then $\sum_{k=1}^{\infty} a_k$ and $\sum_{k=1}^{\infty} b_k$ both converge or both diverge.

Idea for a proof: The key idea is that if $\lim_{k \to \infty} \frac{a_k}{b_k} = L$ is a **positive, finite** value, then, when n is very large, $\frac{a_k}{b_k} \approx L$ so $a_k \approx L \cdot b_k$ and $\sum_{k=N}^{\infty} a_k \approx L \cdot \sum_{k=N}^{\infty} b_k$. If one of these series converges, then so does the other. If one of these series diverges, then so does the other. When n is a relatively small number, the a_k and b_k values may not have a ratio close to L, but the first "few" values of a series do not affect the convergence or divergence of the series. A proof of the Limit Comparison Test is given in an Appendix after the Practice Answers.

Example 3: Put $a_k = \frac{1}{k^2}$, $b_k = \frac{1}{k^2 + 1}$, and $c_k = \frac{1}{k^2 - 1}$ and show that $\lim_{k \to \infty} \frac{a_k}{b_k} = 1$ and $\lim_{k \to \infty} \frac{a_k}{c_k} = 1$. Since $\sum_{k=2}^{\infty} \frac{1}{k^2}$ converges (P–Test, p = 2) we can conclude that $\sum_{k=2}^{\infty} \frac{1}{k^2 + 1}$ and $\sum_{k=2}^{\infty} \frac{1}{k^2 - 1}$ both converge too.

Solution: $\frac{a_k}{b_k} = \frac{1/k^2}{1/(k^2+1)} = \frac{k^2 + 1}{k^2} = 1 + \frac{1}{k^2} \longrightarrow 1$ so L = 1 is positive and finite.

Similarly, $\frac{a_k}{c_k} = \frac{1/k^2}{1/(k^2-1)} = \frac{k^2 - 1}{k^2} = 1 - \frac{1}{k^2} \longrightarrow 1$ so L = 1 is positive and finite.

Practice 2: (a) Find a p–series to "limit–compare" with $\sum_{k=2}^{\infty} \frac{k^2 + 5k}{k^3 + k^2 + 7}$.

(Suggestion: put $a_k = \frac{k^2 + 5k}{k^3 + k^2 + 7}$ and find a value of p so that $b_k = \frac{1}{k^p}$ and $\lim_{k \to \infty} \frac{a_k}{b_k} = L$, a positive, finite value.) Does $\sum_{k=2}^{\infty} \frac{k^2 + 5k}{k^3 + k^2 + 7}$ converge?

(b) Find a p–series to compare with $\sum_{k=3}^{\infty} \frac{5}{\sqrt{k^4 - 11}}$. Does $\sum_{k=3}^{\infty} \frac{5}{\sqrt{k^4 - 11}}$ converge?

The Limit Comparison Test is particularly useful because it allows us to ignore some parts of the terms that cause algebraic difficulties but that have no effect on the convergence of the series.

Using "Dominant Terms"

To use the Limit Comparison Test we need to pick a new series to compare with our given series. One effective way to pick the new series is to form the new series using the largest power of the variable (dominant term) from the numerator and the largest power of the variable (dominant term) from the denominator. The "dominant term" series consists of $\frac{\text{dominant term in the numerator}}{\text{dominant term in the denominator}}$. Then the Limit Comparison Test allows us to conclude that the original series converges if and only if the "dominant term" series converges.

Example 4: For each of the given series, form a new series consisting of the dominant terms from the numerator and the denominator. Does the series of dominant terms converge?

(a) $\sum_{k=3}^{\infty} \frac{5k^2 - 3k + 2}{17 + 2k^4}$ (b) $\sum_{k=1}^{\infty} \frac{1 + 4k}{\sqrt{k^3 + 5k}}$ (c) $\sum_{k=1}^{\infty} \frac{k^{23} + 1}{5k^{10} + k^{26} + 3}$.

Solution: (a) The dominant terms of the numerator and denominator are $5k^2$ and $2k^4$, respectively, so the "dominant term" series is $\sum_{k=3}^{\infty} \frac{5k^2}{2k^4} = \frac{5}{2} \sum_{k=3}^{\infty} \frac{1}{k^2}$ which converges (P–Test, p = 2).

(b) The dominant terms of the numerator and denominator are $4k$ and $k^{3/2}$, respectively, so the "dominant term" series is $\sum_{k=1}^{\infty} \frac{4k}{k^{3/2}} = 4 \sum_{k=3}^{\infty} \frac{1}{k^{1/2}}$ which diverges (P–Test, p = 1/2).

(c) The dominant terms of the numerator and denominator are k^{23} and k^{26}, respectively, so the "dominant term" series is $\sum_{k=1}^{\infty} \frac{k^{23}}{k^{26}} = \sum_{k=1}^{\infty} \frac{1}{k^3}$ which converges (P–Test, p = 3).

Using the Limit Comparison Test to compare the given series with the "dominant term" series, we can conclude that the given series (a) and (c) converge and that the given series (b) diverges.

Practice 3: For each of the given series, form a new series consisting of the dominant terms from the numerator and the denominator. Does the series of dominant terms converge? Do the given series converge?

(a) $\sum_{k=1}^{\infty} \frac{3k^4 - 5k + 2}{1 + 17k^2 + 9k^5}$ (b) $\sum_{k=1}^{\infty} \frac{\sqrt{1+9k}}{k^2 + 5k - 2}$ (c) $\sum_{k=1}^{\infty} \frac{k^{25} + 1}{5k^{10} + k^{26} + 3}$.

Experienced users of series commonly use "dominant terms" to make quick and accurate judgments about the convergence or divergence of a series. With practice, so can you.

PROBLEMS

In problems 1 – 12 use the Comparison Test to determine whether the given series converge or diverge.

1. $\sum_{k=1}^{\infty} \frac{\cos^2(k)}{k^2}$

2. $\sum_{k=1}^{\infty} \frac{3}{k^3 + 7}$

3. $\sum_{n=3}^{\infty} \frac{5}{n-1}$

4. $\sum_{n=1}^{\infty} \frac{2+\sin(n)}{n^3}$

5. $\sum_{j=1}^{\infty} \frac{3+\cos(j)}{j}$

6. $\sum_{j=1}^{\infty} \frac{\arctan(j)}{j^{3/2}}$

7. $\sum_{k=1}^{\infty} \frac{\ln(k)}{k}$

8. $\sum_{k=1}^{\infty} \frac{k-1}{k \cdot 1.5^k}$

9. $\sum_{k=1}^{\infty} \frac{k+9}{k \cdot 2^k}$

10. $\sum_{n=1}^{\infty} \frac{n^3 + 7}{n^4 - 1}$

11. $\sum_{n=1}^{\infty} \frac{1}{1+2+3+\ldots+(n-1)+n}$

12. $\sum_{k=1}^{\infty} \frac{1}{k!} = \sum_{k=1}^{\infty} \frac{1}{1 \cdot 2 \cdot 3 \cdot \ldots \cdot (k-1) \cdot k}$

In problems 13 – 21 use the Limit Comparison Test (or the Nth Term Test) to determine whether the given series converge or diverge.

13. $\sum_{k=3}^{\infty} \frac{k+1}{k^2 + 4}$

14. $\sum_{j=1}^{\infty} \frac{7}{\sqrt{j^3 + 3}}$

15. $\sum_{w=1}^{\infty} \frac{5}{w+1}$

16. $\sum_{n=1}^{\infty} \frac{7n^3 - 4n + 3}{3n^4 + 7n^3 + 9}$

17. $\sum_{k=1}^{\infty} \frac{k^3}{(1+k^2)^3}$

18. $\sum_{k=1}^{\infty} \left(\frac{\arctan(k)}{k} \right)^2$

19. $\sum_{n=1}^{\infty} \left(\frac{5 - \frac{1}{n}}{n} \right)^3$

20. $\sum_{w=1}^{\infty} \left(1 + \frac{1}{w}\right)^w$

21. $\sum_{j=1}^{\infty} \left(1 - \frac{1}{j}\right)^j$

10.5   Positive Term Series: Comparison Tests   Contemporary Calculus

In problems 22 – 30 use "dominant term" series to determine whether the given series converge or diverge.

22. $\sum_{n=3}^{\infty} \dfrac{n+100}{n^2-4}$

23. $\sum_{k=1}^{\infty} \dfrac{7k}{\sqrt{k^3+5}}$

24. $\sum_{k=1}^{\infty} \dfrac{5}{k+1}$

25. $\sum_{j=1}^{\infty} \dfrac{j^3-4j+3}{2j^4+7j^6+9}$

26. $\sum_{n=1}^{\infty} \dfrac{5n^3+7n^2+9}{(1+n^3)^2}$

27. $\sum_{n=1}^{\infty} \left(\dfrac{\arctan(3n)}{2n}\right)^2$

28. $\sum_{k=1}^{\infty} \left(\dfrac{3-\dfrac{1}{k}}{k}\right)^2$

29. $\sum_{j=1}^{\infty} \dfrac{\sqrt{j^3+4j^2}}{j^2+3j-2}$

30. $\sum_{k=1}^{\infty} \dfrac{k+9}{k \cdot 2^k}$

Putting it all together

In problems 31 – 51 use any of the methods from this or previous sections to determine whether the given series converge or diverge. Give reasons for your answers.

31. $\sum_{n=2}^{\infty} \dfrac{n^2+10}{n^3-2}$

32. $\sum_{k=1}^{\infty} \dfrac{3k}{\sqrt{k^5+7}}$

33. $\sum_{k=1}^{\infty} \dfrac{3}{2k+1}$

34. $\sum_{j=1}^{\infty} \dfrac{j^2-j+1}{3j^4+2j^2+1}$

35. $\sum_{n=1}^{\infty} \dfrac{2n^3+n^2+6}{(3+n^2)^2}$

36. $\sum_{n=1}^{\infty} \left(\dfrac{\arctan(2n)}{3n}\right)^3$

37. $\sum_{k=1}^{\infty} \left(\dfrac{1-\dfrac{2}{k}}{k}\right)^3$

38. $\sum_{j=1}^{\infty} \dfrac{\sqrt{j^2+4j}}{j^3-2}$

39. $\sum_{k=1}^{\infty} \dfrac{k+5}{k \cdot 3^k}$

40. $\sum_{n=1}^{\infty} \dfrac{1+\sin(n)}{n^2+4}$

41. $\sum_{k=1}^{\infty} \dfrac{k+2}{\sqrt{k^2+1}}$

42. $\sum_{k=1}^{\infty} \dfrac{\sin(k\pi)}{k+1}$

43. $\sum_{j=1}^{\infty} \dfrac{3}{e^j+j}$

44. $\sum_{n=1}^{\infty} \dfrac{(2+3n)^2+9}{(1+n^3)^2}$

45. $\sum_{n=1}^{\infty} \left(\dfrac{\tan(3)}{2+n}\right)^2$

46. $\sum_{n=1}^{\infty} \sin^2\left(\dfrac{1}{n}\right)$

47. $\sum_{n=1}^{\infty} \sin^3\left(\dfrac{1}{n}\right)$

48. $\sum_{n=1}^{\infty} \cos^2\left(\dfrac{1}{n}\right)$

49. $\sum_{j=1}^{\infty} \cos^3\left(\dfrac{1}{j}\right)$

50. $\sum_{n=1}^{\infty} \tan^2\left(\dfrac{1}{n}\right)$

51. $\sum_{n=1}^{\infty} \left(1-\dfrac{2}{n}\right)^n$

Review for Positive Term Series: Converge or Diverge

State whether the given series converge or diverge and give reasons for your answer. You may need any of the methods discussed so far as well as some ingenuity.

R1. $\sum_{n=3}^{\infty} \dfrac{5}{3^n}$

R2. $\sum_{j=3}^{\infty} \dfrac{5+\cos(j^3)}{j^2}$

R3. $\sum_{w=1}^{\infty} \dfrac{2}{3+\sin(w^3)}$

R4. $\sum_{n=1}^{\infty} \dfrac{5}{(1/3)^n}$

R5. $\sum_{k=1}^{\infty} e^{-k}$

R6. $\sum_{w=1}^{\infty} \sin^2\left(\dfrac{1}{w}\right)$ (Hint: for $0 \leq x \leq 1$, $\sin(x) \leq x$)

R7. $\sum_{k=1}^{\infty} \sin\left(\dfrac{1}{k^3}\right)$ (see the R6 hint)

R8. $\sum_{j=1}^{\infty} \cos^2\left(\dfrac{1}{j}\right)$

R9. $\sum_{n=3}^{\infty} \dfrac{5+\cos(n^2)}{n^3}$

R10. $\sum_{k=1}^{\infty} \dfrac{1}{k \cdot (3+\ln(k))}$

R11. $\sum_{j=1}^{\infty} \dfrac{1}{j \cdot (3+\ln(j))^2}$

R12. $\sum_{n=1}^{\infty} \dfrac{4}{n \cdot \arctan(n)}$

R13. $\sum_{n=3}^{\infty} \dfrac{4 \cdot \arctan(n)}{n}$

R14. $\sum_{k=1}^{\infty} \dfrac{\ln(k)}{k^3}$

R15. $\sum_{k=1}^{\infty} \dfrac{\ln(k)}{k^2}$

R16. $\sum_{j=1}^{\infty} \left(\dfrac{j}{2j+3}\right)^j$

R17. $\sum_{n=1}^{\infty} \dfrac{1+n}{1+n^2}$

R18. $\sum_{n=1}^{\infty} [\sin(n) - \sin(n+1)]$

R19. $\sum_{k=1}^{\infty} \sqrt{\dfrac{k^3+5}{k^5+3}}$

R20. $\sum_{k=1}^{\infty} \dfrac{1}{k^k}$

R21. $\sum_{n=1}^{\infty} n^{1/n}$

Practice Answers

Practice 1: (a) For $k > 3$, $0 < k-2 < k$ so $0 < \sqrt{k-2} < \sqrt{k}$ and $\dfrac{1}{\sqrt{k-2}} > \dfrac{1}{\sqrt{k}} = \dfrac{1}{k^{1/2}}$.

$\sum_{k=3}^{\infty} \dfrac{1}{k^{1/2}}$ diverges (P–test, p = 1/2) so $\sum_{k=3}^{\infty} \dfrac{1}{\sqrt{k-2}}$ diverges.

(b) For $k > 1$, $2^k + 7 > 2^k > 0$ so $\dfrac{1}{2^k+7} < \dfrac{1}{2^k}$.

$\sum_{k=3}^{\infty} \dfrac{1}{2^k} = \sum_{k=3}^{\infty} \left(\dfrac{1}{2}\right)^k$ which is a convergent geometric series (r = 1/2) so $\sum_{k=3}^{\infty} \dfrac{1}{2^k+7}$ converges.

Practice 2: (a) $a_k = \dfrac{k^2 + 5k}{k^3 + k^2 + 7}$. Put $b_k = \dfrac{1}{k^1}$. Then

$$\dfrac{a_k}{b_k} = \dfrac{\frac{k^2+5k}{k^3+k^2+7}}{\frac{1}{k^1}} = \left(\dfrac{k^1}{1}\right)\dfrac{k^2+5k}{k^3+k^2+7} = \dfrac{k^3+5k^2}{k^3+k^2+7} = \dfrac{k^3\left(1+\frac{5}{k}\right)}{k^3\left(1+\frac{1}{k}+\frac{7}{k^3}\right)} \longrightarrow 1$$

so $L = 1$ is positive and finite, and $\sum_{k=1}^{\infty} a_k$ and $\sum_{k=1}^{\infty} b_k$ both converge or both diverge.

Since we know $\sum_{k=1}^{\infty} b_k = \sum_{k=1}^{\infty} \dfrac{1}{k}$ diverges (P–test, p=1 or as the Harmonic series),

we can conclude that $\sum_{k=1}^{\infty} a_k = \sum_{k=1}^{\infty} \dfrac{k^2+5k}{k^3+k^2+7}$ diverges

(b) $a_k = \dfrac{5}{\sqrt{k^4 - 11}}$. Put $b_k = \dfrac{1}{\sqrt{k^4}} = \dfrac{1}{k^2}$. Then

$$\dfrac{a_k}{b_k} = \dfrac{\frac{5}{\sqrt{k^4-11}}}{\frac{1}{k^2}} = \dfrac{k^2}{1}\cdot\dfrac{5}{\sqrt{k^4-11}} = \dfrac{5}{1}\sqrt{\dfrac{k^4}{k^4-11}} \longrightarrow \dfrac{5}{1}\sqrt{1} = 5$$

so $L = 5$ is positive and finite, and $\sum_{k=1}^{\infty} a_k$ and $\sum_{k=1}^{\infty} b_k$ both converge or both diverge.

Since we know $\sum_{k=1}^{\infty} b_k = \sum_{k=1}^{\infty} \dfrac{1}{k^2}$ converges (P–test, p=2), we can conclude that

$$\sum_{k=1}^{\infty} a_k = \sum_{k=1}^{\infty} \dfrac{5}{\sqrt{k^4-11}} \text{ converges.}$$

Practice 3: (a) $\sum_{k=1}^{\infty} \dfrac{3k^4}{9k^5} = \dfrac{1}{3}\sum_{k=1}^{\infty} \dfrac{1}{k}$ which diverges (P–test, p = 1) so $\sum_{k=1}^{\infty} \dfrac{3k^4 - 5k + 2}{1+17k^2+9k^5}$ diverges.

(b) $\sum_{k=1}^{\infty} \dfrac{\sqrt{9k}}{k^2} = 3\sum_{k=1}^{\infty} \dfrac{k^{1/2}}{k^2} = 3\sum_{k=1}^{\infty} \dfrac{1}{k^{3/2}}$ which converges (P–test, p = 3/2)

so $\sum_{k=1}^{\infty} \dfrac{\sqrt{1+9k}}{k^2 + 5k - 2}$ converges.

(c) $\sum_{k=1}^{\infty} \frac{k^{25}}{k^{26}} = \sum_{k=1}^{\infty} \frac{1}{k}$ which diverges (P–test, p = 1) so $\sum_{k=1}^{\infty} \frac{k^{25}+1}{5k^{10}+k^{26}+3}$ diverges.

Appendix: Proof of the Limit Comparison Test

(a) Suppose $\sum_{k=1}^{\infty} b_k$ converges and that $\lim_{k \to \infty} \frac{a_k}{b_k} = L$, a **positive, finite** value.

Since $\lim_{k \to \infty} \frac{a_k}{b_k} = L$, there is a value N so that $\frac{a_k}{b_k} < L+1$ when $k \geq N$. Then

$a_k < b_k \cdot (L+1)$ when $k \geq N$, and $\sum_{k=N}^{\infty} a_k < (L+1) \cdot \sum_{k=N}^{\infty} b_k$. Since $\sum_{k=N}^{\infty} b_k$

converges, we can conclude that $\sum_{k=N}^{\infty} a_k$ converges so $\sum_{k=1}^{\infty} a_k$ also converges.

(b) Suppose $\sum_{k=1}^{\infty} b_k$ diverges and that $\lim_{k \to \infty} \frac{a_k}{b_k} = L$, a **positive, finite** value.

Since $\lim_{k \to \infty} \frac{a_k}{b_k} = L$, there is a value N so that $\frac{a_k}{b_k} > L/2 > 0$ when $k \geq N$. Then

$a_k > \frac{L}{2} \cdot b_k$ when $k \geq N$, and $\sum_{k=N}^{\infty} a_k \geq \frac{L}{2} \cdot \sum_{k=N}^{\infty} b_k$. Since $\sum_{k=N}^{\infty} b_k$ diverges, we

can conclude that $\sum_{k=N}^{\infty} a_k$ diverges so $\sum_{k=1}^{\infty} a_k$ also diverges.

10.6 ALTERNATING SERIES

In the last two sections we considered tests for the convergence of series whose terms were all positive. In this section we examine series whose terms change signs in a special way: they alternate between positive and negative. And we present a very easy-to-use test to determine if these alternating series converge.

An **alternating series** is a series whose terms alternate between positive and negative. For example, the following are alternating series:

(1) $\quad 1 - \frac{1}{2} + \frac{1}{3} - \frac{1}{4} + \frac{1}{5} - \ldots + (-1)^{k+1} \frac{1}{k} + \ldots = \sum_{k=1}^{\infty} (-1)^{k+1} \frac{1}{k} \quad$ (alternating harmonic series)

(2) $\quad -\frac{1}{3} + \frac{2}{4} - \frac{3}{5} + \frac{4}{6} - \frac{5}{7} + \ldots + (-1)^{k} \frac{k}{k+2} + \ldots = \sum_{k=1}^{\infty} (-1)^{k} \frac{k}{k+2}$

(3) $\quad -\frac{1}{\sqrt{3}} + \frac{1}{\sqrt{5}} - \frac{1}{\sqrt{7}} + \frac{1}{\sqrt{9}} + \frac{1}{\sqrt{11}} - \ldots + (-1)^{k} \frac{1}{\sqrt{2k+1}} + \ldots = \sum_{k=1}^{\infty} (-1)^{k} \frac{1}{\sqrt{2k+1}}$.

Figures 1, 2 and 3 show graphs and tables of values of several partial sums s_n for each of these series. As we move from left to right in each graph (as n increases), the partial sums alternately get larger and smaller, a common pattern for the partial sums of alternating series. The same pattern appears in the tables.

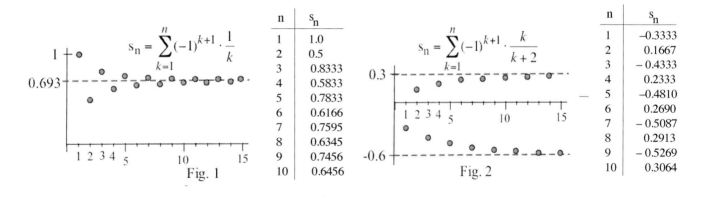

Fig. 1

Fig. 2

Fig. 3

Alternating Series Test

The following result provides a very easy way to determine that some alternating series converge. It says that if the absolute values of the terms decrease monotonically to 0 then the series converges. This is the main result for alternating series.

Alternating Series Test

If the numbers a_n satisfy the three conditions

(i) $a_n > 0$ for all n (each a_n is positive)

(ii) $a_n > a_{n+1}$ (the terms a_n are monotonically decreasing)

(iii) $\lim\limits_{n \to \infty} a_n = 0$

then the **alternating series** $\sum\limits_{n=1}^{\infty} (-1)^{n+1} a_n$ converges.

Proof: In order to show that the alternating series converges, we need to show that the sequence of partial sums approaches a finite limit, and we do so in this case by showing that the sequence of even partial sums $\{s_2, s_4, s_6, \ldots\}$ and the sequence of odd partial sums $\{s_1, s_3, s_5, \ldots\}$ each approach the same value.

Even partial sums:

$s_2 = a_1 - a_2 > 0$ since $a_1 > a_2$

$s_4 = a_1 - a_2 + a_3 - a_4 = s_2 + (a_3 - a_4) > s_2$ since $a_3 > a_4$

$s_6 = a_1 - a_2 + a_3 - a_4 + a_5 - a_6 = s_4 + (a_5 - a_6) > s_4$ since $a_5 > a_6$.

In general, the sequence of even partial sums is positive and increasing

$s_{2n+2} = s_{2n} + (a_{2n+1} - a_{2n+2}) > s_{2n} > 0$ since $a_{2n+1} > a_{2n+2}$.

Also,

$s_{2n} = a_1 - a_2 + a_3 - a_4 + a_5 - \ldots - a_{2n-2} + a_{2n-1} - a_{2n}$

$= a_1 - (a_2 - a_3) - (a_4 - a_5) \ldots - (a_{2n-2} - a_{2n-1}) - a_{2n} < a_1$.

so the sequence of even partial sums is bounded above by a_1.

Since the sequence $\{s_2, s_4, s_6, \ldots\}$ of even partial sums is increasing and bounded, the Monotone Convergence Theorem of Section 10.1 tells us that sequence of even partial sums converges to some finite limit: $\lim\limits_{n \to \infty} s_{2n} = L$.

Odd partial sums:

$$s_{2n+1} = s_{2n} + a_{2n+1} \text{ so } \lim_{n \to \infty} s_{2n+1} = \lim_{n \to \infty} s_{2n} + \lim_{n \to \infty} a_{2n+1} = L + 0 = L.$$

Since the sequence of even partial sums and the sequence of odd partial sums both approach the same limit L, we can conclude that the limit of the sequence of partial sums is L and that the series $\sum_{n=1}^{\infty} (-1)^{n+1} a_n$ converges to L: $\sum_{n=1}^{\infty} (-1)^{n+1} a_n = L.$

Example 1: Show that each of the three alternating series satisfies the three conditions in the hypothesis of the Alternating Series Test. Then we can conclude that each of them converges.

(a) $\quad 1 - \frac{1}{2} + \frac{1}{3} - \frac{1}{4} + \ldots = \sum_{n=1}^{\infty} (-1)^{n+1} \frac{1}{n}$

(b) $\quad \frac{3}{1} - \frac{3}{\sqrt{2}} + \frac{3}{\sqrt{3}} - \frac{3}{\sqrt{4}} + \ldots = \sum_{n=1}^{\infty} (-1)^{n+1} \frac{3}{\sqrt{n}}$

(c) $\quad \frac{7}{2 \cdot \ln(2)} - \frac{7}{3 \cdot \ln(3)} + \frac{7}{4 \cdot \ln(4)} - \ldots = \sum_{n=2}^{\infty} (-1)^{n} \frac{7}{n \cdot \ln(n)}.$

Solution: (a) This series is called the **alternating harmonic series**. (i) $a_n = \frac{1}{n} > 0$ for all positive n. (ii) Since $n < n+1$, then $\frac{1}{n} > \frac{1}{n+1}$ and $a_n > a_{n+1}$.

(iii) $\lim_{n \to \infty} a_n = \lim_{n \to \infty} \frac{1}{n} = 0$. Therefore, the alternating harmonic series converges.

Fig. 1 shows some partial sums for the alternating harmonic series.

(b) $a_n = \frac{3}{\sqrt{n}} > 0$. Since $n < n+1$, we have $\sqrt{n} < \sqrt{n+1}$ and $\frac{3}{\sqrt{n}} > \frac{3}{\sqrt{n+1}}$.

$\lim_{n \to \infty} a_n = \lim_{n \to \infty} \frac{3}{\sqrt{n}} = 0$. The series $\frac{3}{1} + \frac{3}{\sqrt{2}} + \frac{3}{\sqrt{3}} + \frac{3}{\sqrt{4}} + \ldots$ converges.

(c) $a_n = \frac{7}{n \cdot \ln(n)} > 0$ for $n \geq 2$. Since $n < n+1$ and $\ln(n) < \ln(n+1)$, we have

$n \cdot \ln(n) < (n+1) \cdot \ln(n+1)$ and $\frac{7}{n \cdot \ln(n)} > \frac{7}{(n+1) \cdot \ln(n+1)}$.

$\lim_{n \to \infty} a_n = \lim_{n \to \infty} \frac{7}{n \cdot \ln(n)} = 0$. The series $\sum_{n=2}^{\infty} (-1)^n \frac{7}{n \cdot \ln(n)}$ converges.

Practice 1: Show that these two alternating series satisfy the three conditions in the hypothesis of the Alternating Series Test. Then we can conclude that each of them converges.

(a) $1 - \frac{1}{4} + \frac{1}{9} - \frac{1}{16} + \ldots = \sum_{n=1}^{\infty} (-1)^{n+1} \frac{1}{n^2}$

(b) $\frac{3}{\ln(2)} - \frac{3}{\ln(3)} + \frac{3}{\ln(4)} - \frac{3}{\ln(5)} + \ldots = \sum_{n=2}^{\infty} (-1)^n \frac{3}{\ln(n)}$

Example 2: Does $\sum_{n=1}^{\infty} (-1)^{n+1} \frac{n}{n+2}$ converge?

Solution: $a_n = \frac{n}{n+2} > 0$, but $\lim_{n \to \infty} a_n = \lim_{n \to \infty} \frac{n}{n+2} = 1 \neq 0$. Since the terms do not approach 0, we can conclude from the Nth Term Test For Divergence (Section 10.2) that the series diverges.

Fig. 2 shows some of the partial sums for this series. You should notice that the even and the odd partial sums in Fig. 2 are approaching two different values.

Practice 2: (a) Does $\sum_{n=1}^{\infty} (-1)^{n+1} n$ converge? (b) Does $\sum_{n=1}^{\infty} (-1)^{n+1} \frac{1}{\sqrt{2n+1}}$ converge?

Example Of A Divergent Alternating Series

If the terms of a series, any series, do not approach 0, then the series must diverge (N^{th} Term Test For Divergence). If the terms do approach 0 the series may converge or may diverge. There are divergent alternating series whose terms approach 0 (but the approach to 0 is not monotonic). For example, $\frac{3}{2} - \frac{1}{2} + \frac{3}{4} - \frac{1}{4} + \frac{3}{6} - \frac{1}{6} + \frac{3}{8} - \frac{1}{8} + \ldots$ is an alternating series whose terms approach 0, but the series diverges.

The even partial sums of our new series are

$s_2 = \frac{3}{2} - \frac{1}{2} = 1$,

$s_4 = \frac{3}{2} - \frac{1}{2} + \frac{3}{4} - \frac{1}{4} = (\frac{3}{2} - \frac{1}{2}) + (\frac{3}{4} - \frac{1}{4}) = 1 + \frac{1}{2}$,

$s_6 = \frac{3}{2} - \frac{1}{2} + \frac{3}{4} - \frac{1}{4} + \frac{3}{6} - \frac{1}{6} = (\frac{3}{2} - \frac{1}{2}) + (\frac{3}{4} - \frac{1}{4}) + (\frac{3}{6} - \frac{1}{6}) = 1 + \frac{1}{2} + \frac{1}{3}$,

and $s_{2n} = 1 + \frac{1}{2} + \frac{1}{3} + \ldots + \frac{1}{n}$.

You should recognize that these partial sums are the partial sums of the harmonic series, a divergent series, so the partial sums of our new series diverge and our new series is divergent. If the terms of an alternating series approach 0, but not monotonically, then the Alternating Series Test does not apply, and the series may converge or it may diverge.

Approximating the Sum of an Alternating Series

If we know that a series converges and if we add the first "many" terms together, then we expect that the resulting partial sum is close to the value S obtained by adding all of the terms together. Generally, however, we do not know how close the partial sum is to S. The situation with many alternating series is much nicer. The next result says that for some alternating series (those that satisfy the three conditions in the next box), the difference between S and the nth partial sum of the alternating series, $|S - s_n|$, is less than the magnitude of the next term in the series, a_{n+1}.

Estimation Bound for Alternating Series

If $\quad$ S is the sum of an alternating series $\sum_{n=1}^{\infty} (-1)^{n+1} a_n$

that satisfies the three conditions

(i) $\quad a_n > 0$ for all n $\quad$ (each a_n is positive),

(ii) $\quad a_n > a_{n+1}$ $\quad$ (the terms are monotonically decreasing),

and (iii) $\quad \lim_{n \to \infty} a_n = 0$ $\quad$ (the terms approach 0),

then the nth partial sum s_n is within a_{n+1} of the sum S: $\quad s_n - a_{n+1} < S < s_n + a_{n+1}$

and $|\text{ approximation "error" using } s_n \text{ as an estimate of S}| = |S - s_n| < a_{n+1}$.

Note: This Estimation Bound only applies to alternating series. It is tempting, but wrong, to use it with other types of series.

Geometric idea behind the Estimation Bound:

If we have an alternating series that satisfies the hypothesis of the Estimation Bound, then the graph of the sequence $\{s_n\}$ of partial sums is "trumpet–shaped" or "funnel–shaped" (Fig. 4). The partial sums are alternately above and below the value S, and they "squeeze" in on the value S. Since the distance from s_n to S is less than the distance between the successive terms s_n and s_{n+1} (Fig. 5), then

$|S - s_n| < |s_n - s_{n+1}| = a_{n+1}$.

Proof of the Estimation Bound for Alternating Series:

Fig. 4

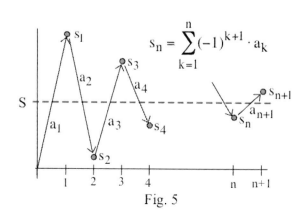

Fig. 5

$$S - s_n = (a_1 - a_2 + a_3 - a_4 + \ldots + (-1)^{n+1}a_n + (-1)^{n+2}a_{n+1} \ldots) - (a_1 - a_2 + a_3 - a_4 + \ldots + (-1)^{n+1}a_n)$$

$$= (-1)^{n+2}a_{n+1} + (-1)^{n+3}a_{n+2} + (-1)^{n+4}a_{n+3} + \ldots$$

$$= (-1)^{n+2}(a_{n+1} - a_{n+2} + a_{n+3} - \ldots).$$

Then $0 \leq |S - s_n|$
$$= |(-1)^{n+2}(a_{n+1} - a_{n+2} + a_{n+3} - a_{n+4} + a_{n+5} \ldots)|$$

$$= a_{n+1} - a_{n+2} + a_{n+3} - a_{n+4} + a_{n+5} \ldots \quad \text{since } |(-1)^{n+2}| = 1 \text{ and the rest is positive}$$

$$= a_{n+1} - (a_{n+2} - a_{n+3}) - (a_{n+4} - a_{n+5}) - \ldots < a_{n+1}.$$

The Estimation Bound is typically used in two different ways. Sometimes we know the value of n, and we want to know how close s_n is to S. Sometimes we know how close we want s_n to be to S, and we want to find a value of n to ensure that level of closeness. The next two Examples illustrate these two different uses of the Estimation Bound.

Example 3: How close is $\sum_{n=1}^{4} (-1)^{n+1} \frac{1}{n^2} = 1 - \frac{1}{4} + \frac{1}{9} - \frac{1}{16} \approx 0.79861$ to the sum $\sum_{n=1}^{\infty} (-1)^{n+1} \frac{1}{n^2}$?

Solution: $a_n = \frac{1}{n^2}$ and $s_4 = \sum_{n=1}^{4} (-1)^{n+1} \frac{1}{n^2} = 1 - \frac{1}{4} + \frac{1}{9} - \frac{1}{16} \approx 0.79861$ so, by the Estimation Bound, we can conclude that $|S - s_4| < a_5 = \frac{1}{25} = 0.04$: 0.79861 is within 0.04 of the exact value S. Then $0.79861 - 0.04 < S < 0.79861 + 0.04$ and $0.75861 < S < 0.83861$.

Similarly, $s_9 = 1 - \frac{1}{4} + \frac{1}{9} - \frac{1}{16} + \ldots + \frac{1}{81} \approx 0.82796$ is within $a_{10} = \frac{1}{100} = 0.01$ of the exact value of S, and $s_{99} \approx 0.822517$ is within $a_{100} = \frac{1}{100^2} = 0.0001$ of the exact value of S. Then $0.822517 - 0.0001 < S < 0.822517 + 0.0001$ and $0.822417 < S < 0.822617$.

Practice 3: Evaluate s_4 and s_9 for the alternating series $\sum_{n=1}^{\infty} (-1)^{n+1} \frac{1}{n^3}$ and determine bounds for $|S - s_4|$ and $|S - s_9|$.

Example 4: Find the number of terms needed so that s_n is within 0.001 of the exact value of $\sum_{n=1}^{\infty} (-1)^{n+1} \frac{1}{n!}$ and evaluate s_n.

Solution: We know $|S - s_n| < a_{n+1}$ so we want to find n so that $a_{n+1} \leq 0.001 = \frac{1}{1000}$. With a little numerical experimentation on a calculator, we see that $6! = 720$ and $1/720$ is not small enough, but

$7! = 5{,}040 > 1{,}000$ so $\frac{1}{7!} = \frac{1}{5040} \approx 0.000198 < 0.001$. Since $n+1 = 7$, $s_6 \approx 0.631944$ is the first partial sum guaranteed to be within 0.001 of S. In fact, s_6 is within $\frac{1}{5040} \approx 0.000198$ of S, so $0.631746 < S < 0.632142$.

Practice 4: Find the number of terms needed so s_n is within 0.001 of the value of $\sum_{n=1}^{\infty} (-1)^{n+1} \frac{1}{n^3 + 5}$ and evaluate s_n.

The Estimation Bound guarantees that s_n is **within** a_{n+1} of S. In fact, s_n is often much closer than a_{n+1} to S. The value a_{n+1} is an **upper bound** on how far s_n can be from S.

Note 1: The first **finite** number of terms do not affect the convergence or divergence of a series (they do effect the sum S) so we can use the Alternating Series Test and the Estimation Bound if the terms of a series "eventually" satisfy the conditions of the hypotheses of these results. By "eventually" we mean there is a value M so that for $n > M$ the series is an alternating series.

Note 2: If a series has some positive terms and some negative terms and if those terms do NOT "eventually" alternate signs, then we can NOT use the Alternating Series Test – it simply does not apply to such series.

PROBLEMS

In problems 1 – 6 you are given the values of the first four **terms** of a series. (a) Calculate and graph the first four partial sums for each series. (b) Which of the series are not alternating series?

1. $1, -0.8, 0.6, -0.4$
2. $-1, 1.5, -0.7, 1$
3. $-1, 2, -3, 4$
4. $2, -1, -0.5, 0.3$
5. $-1, -0.6, 0.4, 0.2$
6. $2, -1, 0.5, -0.3$

In problems 7 – 12 you are given the values of the first five **partial sums** of a series. Which of the series are not alternating series? Why?

7. $2, 1, 3, 2, 4$
8. $2, 1, 1.8, 1.4, 1.6$
9. $2, 3, 2.1, 2.9, 2.8$
10. $-3, -1, -2.5, -1.5, -2$
11. $-1, 1, -0.8, -0.6, -0.4$
12. $-2.3, -1.6, -1.4, -1.8, -1.7$

13. Fig. 6 shows the graphs of the partial sums of three series. Which is/are not the partial sums of alternating series? Why?

14. Fig. 7 shows the graphs of the partial sums of three series. Which is/are not the partial sums of alternating series? Why?

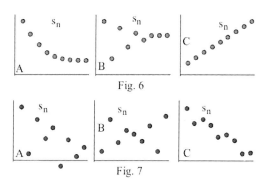

Fig. 6

Fig. 7

15. Fig. 8 shows the graphs of the partial sums of three series. Which is/are not the partial sums of alternating series? Why?

Fig. 8

Fig. 9

16. Fig. 9 shows the graphs of the partial sums of three series. Which is/are not the partial sums of alternating series? Why?

In problems 17 – 31 determine whether the given series converge or diverge.

17. $\sum_{n=1}^{\infty} (-1)^{n+1} \frac{1}{n+5}$

18. $\sum_{n=2}^{\infty} (-1)^{n} \frac{1}{\ln(n)}$

19. $\sum_{n=1}^{\infty} (-1)^{n+1} \frac{n}{n^2+3}$

20. $\sum_{n=5}^{\infty} (-0.99)^{n+1}$

21. $\sum_{n=1}^{\infty} (-1)^{n} \frac{|n+3|}{|n+7|}$

22. $\sum_{n=1}^{\infty} (-1)^{n+1} \sin(\frac{1}{n})$

23. $\sum_{n=4}^{\infty} \frac{\cos(n\pi)}{n}$

24. $\sum_{n=3}^{\infty} \frac{\sin(n\pi)}{n}$

25. $\sum_{n=1}^{\infty} (-1)^{n+1} \frac{\ln(n)}{n}$

26. $\sum_{n=3}^{\infty} (-1)^{n+1} \frac{\ln(n)}{\ln(n^3)}$

27. $\sum_{n=2}^{\infty} (-1)^{n+1} \frac{\ln(n^3)}{\ln(n^{10})}$

28. $\sum_{n=1}^{\infty} (-1)^{n+1} \frac{5}{\sqrt{n+7}}$

29. $\sum_{n=1}^{\infty} \frac{(-2)^{n+1}}{1+(-3)^n}$

30. $\sum_{n=3}^{\infty} (-1)^{n+1} \frac{(-2)^{n+1}}{1+3^n}$

31. $\sum_{n=1}^{\infty} \cos(n\pi) \cdot \sin(\pi/n)$

In problems 32 – 40, (a) calculate s_4 for each series and determine an upper bound for how far s_4 is from the exact value S of the infinite series. Then (b) use s_4 find lower and upper bounds on the value of S so that {lower bound} < S < {upper bound}.

32. $\sum_{n=1}^{\infty} (-1)^{n+1} \frac{1}{n+6}$

33. $\sum_{n=1}^{\infty} (-1)^{n} \frac{1}{\ln(n+1)}$

34. $\sum_{n=1}^{\infty} (-1)^{n+1} \frac{2}{\sqrt{n+21}}$

35. $\sum_{n=1}^{\infty} (-0.8)^{n+1}$

36. $\sum_{n=1}^{\infty} (-\frac{1}{3})^{n}$

37. $\sum_{n=1}^{\infty} (-1)^{n+1} \sin(\frac{1}{n})$

38. $\sum_{n=1}^{\infty} (-1)^{n+1} \frac{1}{n^2}$

39. $\sum_{n=1}^{\infty} (-1)^{n} \frac{1}{n^3}$

40. $\sum_{n=1}^{\infty} \frac{\cos(n\pi)}{n+\ln(n)}$

10.6 Alternating Series   Contemporary Calculus

In problems 41 – 50 find the number of terms needed to guarantee that s_n is within the specified distance D of the exact value S of the sum of the given series.

41. $\sum_{n=1}^{\infty} \frac{(-1)^{n+1}}{n+6}$, D = 0.01

42. $\sum_{n=1}^{\infty} \frac{(-1)^n}{\ln(n+1)}$, D = 0.01

43. $\sum_{n=1}^{\infty} \frac{(-1)^n}{\sqrt{n}}$, D = 0.01

44. $\sum_{n=1}^{\infty} (-0.8)^{n+1}$, D = 0.003

45. $\sum_{n=1}^{\infty} (-\frac{1}{3})^n$, D = 0.002

46. $\sum_{n=1}^{\infty} (-1)^{n+1} \sin(\frac{1}{n})$, D = 0.06

47. $\sum_{n=1}^{\infty} (-1)^{n+1} \frac{1}{n^2}$, D = 0.001

48. $\sum_{n=1}^{\infty} (-1)^n \frac{1}{n^3}$, D = 0.0001

49. $\sum_{n=1}^{\infty} \frac{\cos(n\pi)}{n + \ln(n)}$, D = 0.04

Problems 50 – 60 ask you to use the series $S(x)$, $C(x)$, and $E(x)$ given below. For each problem,
(a) substitute the given value for x in the series, (b) evaluate s_3, the sum of the first three terms of the series, (c) determine an upper bound on the error | actual sum − s_3 | = | S − s_3 |.
(The partial sums of $S(x)$, $C(x)$, and $E(x)$ approximate $\sin(x)$, $\cos(x)$, and e^x, respectively.)

$$S(x) = x - \frac{x^3}{2\cdot 3} + \frac{x^5}{2\cdot 3\cdot 4\cdot 5} - \frac{x^7}{2\cdot 3\cdot 4\cdot 5\cdot 6\cdot 7} + \ldots + (-1)^n \frac{x^{2n+1}}{(2n+1)!} + \ldots$$

$$C(x) = 1 - \frac{x^2}{2} + \frac{x^4}{2\cdot 3\cdot 4} - \frac{x^6}{2\cdot 3\cdot 4\cdot 5\cdot 6} + \ldots + (-1)^n \frac{x^{2n}}{(2n)!} + \ldots$$

$$E(x) = 1 + x + \frac{x^2}{2} + \frac{x^3}{2\cdot 3} + \frac{x^4}{2\cdot 3\cdot 4} + \ldots + \frac{x^n}{n!} + \ldots$$

50. $x = 0.5$ in $S(x)$

51. $x = 0.3$ in $S(x)$

52. $x = 1$ in $S(x)$

53. $x = 0.1$ in $S(x)$

54. $x = -0.3$ in $S(x)$

55. $x = 1$ in $C(x)$

56. $x = 0.5$ in $C(x)$

57. $x = -0.2$ in $C(x)$

58. $x = -0.3$ in $C(x)$

59. $x = -1$ in $E(x)$

60. $x = -0.5$ in $E(x)$

61. $x = -0.2$ in $E(x)$

Practice Answers

Practice 1: (a) (i) $a_n = \frac{1}{n^2} > 0$ for all n. (ii) $n^2 < (n+1)^2$ so $\frac{1}{n^2} > \frac{1}{(n+1)^2}$ and $a_n > a_{n+1}$.

(iii) $\lim_{n\to\infty} a_n = \lim_{n\to\infty} \frac{1}{n^2} = 0$. The series $\sum_{n=1}^{\infty} (-1)^{n+1} \frac{1}{n^2}$ converges.

(b) (i) $a_n = \frac{3}{\ln(n)} > 0$ for all n≥2. (ii) $\ln(n) < \ln(n+1)$ so $\frac{3}{\ln(n)} > \frac{3}{\ln(n+1)}$ and $a_n > a_{n+1}$.

(iii) $\lim_{n\to\infty} a_n = \lim_{n\to\infty} \frac{3}{\ln(n)} = 0$. The series $\sum_{n=1}^{\infty} (-1)^n \frac{3}{\ln(n)}$ converges.

Practice 2: (a) $|(-1)^{n+1} n| = |n| \longrightarrow \infty \neq 0$ so the terms $(-1)^{n+1} n$ do NOT approach 0, and the **series diverges** by the nth Term Test for Divergence (Section 10.2).

(b) (i) $a_n = \dfrac{1}{\sqrt{2n+1}} > 0$ for all $n \geq 1$.

(ii) $2n+1 < 2(n+1) + 1$ so $\sqrt{2n+1} < \sqrt{2(n+1)+1}$ and $\dfrac{1}{\sqrt{2n+1}} > \dfrac{1}{\sqrt{2(n+1)+1}}$ so $a_n > a_{n+1}$.

(iii) $\lim\limits_{n \to \infty} a_n = \lim\limits_{n \to \infty} \dfrac{1}{\sqrt{2n+1}} = 0$. Therefore, by the Alternating Series Test,

the series $\sum\limits_{n=1}^{\infty} (-1)^{n+1} \dfrac{1}{\sqrt{2n+1}}$ converges.

Practice 3: $\sum\limits_{n=1}^{\infty} (-1)^{n+1} \dfrac{1}{n^3}$: $s_4 = 1 - \dfrac{1}{8} + \dfrac{1}{27} - \dfrac{1}{64} \approx 0.896412$.

$|S - s_4| < |a_5| = |(-1)^6 \dfrac{1}{5^3}| = \dfrac{1}{125} = 0.008$ so $s_4 - 0.008 < S < s_4 + 0.008$

and $0.888412 < S < 0.904412$.

$s_9 \approx 0.9021164$. $|S - s_9| < |a_{10}| = |(-1)^{11} \dfrac{1}{10^3}| = \dfrac{1}{1000} = 0.001$ so

$s_9 - 0.001 < S < s_9 + 0.001$ and $0.90\mathbf{1}116 < S < 0.90\mathbf{3}116$.

Practice 4: We need to find a value for n so $|a_{n+1}| < 0.001$.

$|a_{n+1}| = \left|(-1)^{n+2} \dfrac{1}{(n+1)^3 + 5}\right| = \dfrac{1}{(n+1)^3 + 5}$

n	$|a_{n+1}|$
1	$\dfrac{1}{2^3+5} = \dfrac{1}{13} \approx 0.0769$
2	$\dfrac{1}{3^3+5} = \dfrac{1}{32} \approx 0.03125$
8	$\dfrac{1}{9^3+5} = \dfrac{1}{734} \approx 0.00136$
9	$\dfrac{1}{10^3+5} = \dfrac{1}{1005} \approx 0.000995 < 0.001$

Since $|a_{10}| < 0.001$ we can be sure that s_9 is within 0.001 of S.

$s_9 = \sum\limits_{n=1}^{9} (-1)^{n+1} \dfrac{1}{n^3+5} = \dfrac{1}{6} - \dfrac{1}{13} + \dfrac{1}{32} - \ldots + \dfrac{1}{1005} \approx 0.112156571145$ so

$0.11\mathbf{1}156571145 < S < 0.11\mathbf{3}156571145$.

10.7 ABSOLUTE CONVERGENCE and the RATIO TEST

The series we examined in the previous sections all behaved very regularly with regard to the signs of the terms: the signs of the terms were either all the same or they alternated between + and −. However, there are series whose signs do not behave in such regular ways, and in this section we examine some techniques for determining whether those series converge or diverge.

Two Examples

Suppose we have the two series whose terms have magnitudes $\frac{1}{n}$ and $\frac{1}{n^2}$, but we don't know whether each term is positive or negative:

(a) $\sum_{n=1}^{\infty} * \frac{1}{n} = (*1) + (*\frac{1}{2}) + (*\frac{1}{3}) + (*\frac{1}{4}) + \ldots + (*\frac{1}{n}) + \ldots$ where each $*$ is either $+$ or $-$.

(b) $\sum_{n=1}^{\infty} * \frac{1}{n^2} = (*1) + (*\frac{1}{4}) + (*\frac{1}{9}) + (*\frac{1}{16}) + \ldots + (*\frac{1}{n^2}) + \ldots$ where each $*$ is either $+$ or $-$.

These two series behave very differently depending on how we replace the each "$*$" with $+$ or $-$ signs.

Series (a): $\sum_{n=1}^{\infty} * \frac{1}{n}$

If we **always** replace "$*$" with a $+$, then we have the harmonic series which diverges.

If we **always** replace "$*$" with a $-$, then we have the -1 times the harmonic series which diverges.

If we **alternate** replacing "$*$" with $+$ and $-$, then we have the alternating harmonic series which converges.

The answer we have to give to the question "Does series (a) converge?" is "It depends on how the signs of the terms are chosen."

Series (b): $\sum_{n=1}^{\infty} * \frac{1}{n^2}$

If we always replace "$*$" with a $+$, then we have a series which converges (by the P–Test with

p = 2). This is the largest value series (b) can have.

If we always replace "$*$" with a $-$, then we have -1 times a convergent series so the series

converges. This is the smallest value series (b) can have.

If we replace the "$*$" with $+$ or $-$ in some other way, then the result is some number between the largest and smallest possible values (both of which are finite numbers), and the result must be some finite number.

The answer to the question "Does series (b) converge?" is "Yes, no matter how the $*$ are replaced with $+$ or $-$." The value of the sum is affected by how the signs are chosen, but the series does converge.

Series (a) and (b) illustrate the distinction we want to examine in this section. Series (a) is an example of a **conditionally convergent** series since the convergence depends on how the "*" are replaced. Series (b) is an example of an **absolutely convergent** series since it does not matter how the "*" are replaced. Series (b) is convergent even when we are adding all positive terms or all negative terms.

The following definitions make the distinctions precise.

Definitions

> **Definition:** A series $\sum_{n=1}^{\infty} a_n$ is **absolutely convergent** if $\sum_{n=1}^{\infty} |a_n|$ converges.

Series (b) is absolutely convergent.

> **Definition:** A series $\sum_{n=1}^{\infty} a_n$ is **conditionally convergent** if it is convergent but not absolutely convergent (i.e., if $\sum_{n=1}^{\infty} a_n$ converges, but $\sum_{n=1}^{\infty} |a_n|$ diverges).

The alternating harmonic series $\sum_{n=1}^{\infty} (-1)^{n+1} \frac{1}{n}$ is conditionally convergent because

$\sum_{n=1}^{\infty} (-1)^{n+1} \frac{1}{n}$ converges but $\sum_{n=1}^{\infty} \left| (-1)^{n+1} \frac{1}{n} \right| = \sum_{n=1}^{\infty} \frac{1}{n}$ diverges.

Example 1: Determine whether these series are absolutely convergent, conditionally convergent, or divergent.

(a) $\sum_{n=1}^{\infty} (-1)^{n+1} \frac{1}{\sqrt{n}}$ (b) $\sum_{k=1}^{\infty} \frac{\sin(k)}{k^2}$ (c) $\sum_{j=1}^{\infty} (-1)^{j+1} \frac{j^2}{j+1}$

Solution: (a) $\sum_{n=1}^{\infty} \left| (-1)^{n+1} \frac{1}{\sqrt{n}} \right| = \sum_{n=1}^{\infty} \frac{1}{\sqrt{n}}$ which diverges by the P–Test with $p = 1/2 < 1$

so the series is not absolutely convergent. $\frac{1}{\sqrt{n}} \longrightarrow 0$ monotonically so the

alternating series $\sum_{n=1}^{\infty} (-1)^{n+1} \frac{1}{\sqrt{n}}$ converges by the Alternating Series Test.

The series $\sum_{n=1}^{\infty} (-1)^{n+1} \frac{1}{\sqrt{n}}$ is conditionally convergent.

(b) $\sum_{k=1}^{\infty} \left| \frac{\sin(k)}{k^2} \right| \leq \sum_{k=1}^{\infty} \frac{1}{k^2}$ which converges by the P–Test,

so $\sum_{k=1}^{\infty} \frac{\sin(k)}{k^2}$ is absolutely convergent.

(c) $\left| (-1)^{j+1} \frac{j^2}{j+1} \right| = j - 1 + \frac{1}{j+1} \longrightarrow \infty \neq 0$ so $\sum_{j=1}^{\infty} (-1)^{j+1} \frac{j^2}{j+1}$ diverges.

Practice 1: Determine whether these series are absolutely convergent, conditionally convergent, or divergent.

(a) $\sum_{n=2}^{\infty} (-1)^n \frac{5}{\ln(n)}$ (b) $\sum_{k=1}^{\infty} \frac{\cos(\pi k)}{k^2}$

An important result about absolutely convergent series is that they are also convergent.

Absolute Convergence Theorem

Every absolutely convergent series is convergent: if $\sum_{n=1}^{\infty} |a_n|$ converges, then $\sum_{n=1}^{\infty} a_n$ converges.

Since the series $\sum_{n=1}^{\infty} \left| * \frac{1}{n^2} \right| = \sum_{n=1}^{\infty} \frac{1}{n^2}$ is absolutely convergent, the series $\sum_{n=1}^{\infty} * \frac{1}{n^2}$ converges no matter how the "$*$" is replaced with $+$ and $-$ signs.

Proof of the Absolute Convergence Theorem:

If $a_n \geq 0$ then $a_n = |a_n|$, and if $a_n < 0$ then $a_n = -|a_n|$. In either case we have $-|a_n| \leq a_n \leq |a_n|$.

Adding $|a_n|$ to each piece of $-|a_n| \leq a_n \leq |a_n|$, we have $0 \leq |a_n| + a_n \leq 2|a_n|$ for all n.

Let $b_n = |a_n| + a_n \geq 0$ for all n.

Since $b_n \geq 0$ and $b_n \leq 2|a_n|$, the terms of a convergent series, then, by the Comparison Test we know that $\sum_{n=1}^{\infty} b_n$ converges.

Finally, $a_n = (|a_n| + a_n) - |a_n| = b_n - |a_n|$ so the series $\sum_{n=1}^{\infty} a_n = \sum_{n=1}^{\infty} b_n - \sum_{n=1}^{\infty} |a_n|$

is the difference of two convergent series, and we can conclude that the series $\sum_{n=1}^{\infty} a_n$ converges.

The following corollary (the contrapositive form of the Absolute Convergence Theorem) is sometimes useful for showing that a series is not absolutely convergent.

Corollary:

If a series is not convergent, then it is not absolutely convergent:

$$\text{if } \sum_{n=1}^{\infty} a_n \text{ diverges, then } \sum_{n=1}^{\infty} |a_n| \text{ diverges.}$$

The Ratio Test

The following test is useful for determining whether a given series is absolutely convergent, and it will be used often in Section 10.8 when we want to determine where a power series converges. It says that we can be certain that a given series is absolutely convergent, if the limit of the ratios of successive terms has a value less than 1. The Ratio Test is very important and will be used very often in the next sections on power series.

The Ratio Test

Suppose $\lim_{n \to \infty} \left| \dfrac{a_{n+1}}{a_n} \right| = L$.

(a) If $L < 1$, then the series $\sum_{n=1}^{\infty} a_n$ is absolutely convergent (and also convergent).

(b) If $L > 1$, then the series $\sum_{n=1}^{\infty} a_n$ is divergent.

(c) If $L = 1$, then the series $\sum_{n=1}^{\infty} a_n$ may converge or may diverge (the Ratio Test does not help).

A proof of the Ratio Test is rather long and is included in an Appendix after the Practice Answers for this section. Part (a) is proved by showing that if $L < 1$, then the series is, term–by–term, less than a convergent geometric series. Part (b) is proved by showing that if $L > 1$, then the terms of the series do not approach 0 so the series diverges. Part (c) is proved by giving two series, one convergent and one divergent, that both have $L = 1$.

One powerful aspect of the Ratio Test is that it is very "mechanical" — we simply calculate a particular limit and then we (often) have a conclusion about the convergence or divergence of the series.

Example 2: Use the Ratio Test to determine if these series are absolutely convergent:

(a) $\sum_{n=1}^{\infty} \dfrac{2^n n}{5^n}$

(b) $\sum_{n=1}^{\infty} \dfrac{n^2}{n!}$.

Solution: (a) $a_n = \dfrac{2^n n}{5^n}$ so $a_{n+1} = \dfrac{2^{n+1}(n+1)}{5^{n+1}}$. Then

$$\left|\dfrac{a_{n+1}}{a_n}\right| = \left|\dfrac{\dfrac{2^{n+1}(n+1)}{5^{n+1}}}{\dfrac{2^n n}{5^n}}\right| = \left|\dfrac{2^{n+1}}{2^n}\dfrac{5^n}{5^{n+1}}\dfrac{n+1}{n}\right| = \left|\dfrac{2}{5}\dfrac{n+1}{n}\right| \longrightarrow \dfrac{2}{5} < 1$$

so $\sum_{n=1}^{\infty} \dfrac{2^n n}{5^n}$ is absolutely convergent.

(b) $a_n = \dfrac{n^2}{n!}$ so $a_{n+1} = \dfrac{(n+1)^2}{(n+1)!}$. Then

$$\left|\dfrac{a_{n+1}}{a_n}\right| = \left|\dfrac{\dfrac{(n+1)^2}{(n+1)!}}{\dfrac{n^2}{n!}}\right| = \left|\dfrac{n!}{(n+1)!}\dfrac{(n+1)^2}{n^2}\right| = \left|\dfrac{1}{n+1}\left(\dfrac{n+1}{n}\right)^2\right| \longrightarrow 0 < 1$$

so $\sum_{n=1}^{\infty} \dfrac{n^2}{n!}$ is absolutely convergent.

Practice 2: Use the Ratio Test to determine if these series are absolutely convergent:

(a) $\sum_{n=1}^{\infty} (-1)^{n+1} \dfrac{e^n}{n!}$ (b) $\sum_{n=1}^{\infty} \dfrac{n^5}{3^n}$.

The Ratio Test is very useful for determining values of a variable which guarantee the absolute convergence (and convergence) of a series. This is a method we will use often in the rest of this chapter.

Example 3: For which values of x is the series $\sum_{n=1}^{\infty} \dfrac{(x-3)^n}{n}$ absolutely convergent?

Solution: $a_n = \dfrac{(x-3)^n}{n}$ so $a_{n+1} = \dfrac{(x-3)^{n+1}}{n+1}$. Then

$$\left|\dfrac{a_{n+1}}{a_n}\right| = \left|\dfrac{\dfrac{(x-3)^{n+1}}{n+1}}{\dfrac{(x-3)^n}{n}}\right| = \left|\dfrac{(x-3)^{n+1}}{(x-3)^n}\dfrac{n}{n+1}\right| \to |x-3| = L.$$

Now we simply need to solve the inequality $|x-3| < 1$ (L < 1) for x.

If $|x-3| < 1$, then $-1 < x - 3 < 1$ so **2 < x < 4**.

If $2 < x < 4$, then $L = |x-3| < 1$ so $\sum_{n=1}^{\infty} \dfrac{(x-3)^n}{n}$ is absolutely convergent (and convergent).

If $x < 2$ or $x > 4$ then $L > 1$ so the series diverges. (What happens at the "endpoints," x=2 and x=4, where L=1?)

Practice 3: For which values of x is the series $\sum_{n=1}^{\infty} \dfrac{(x-5)^n}{n^2}$ absolutely convergent?

Note: If the terms of a series contain **factorials** or things raised to the **nth power**, it is usually a good idea to use the Ratio Test as the first test you try.

Rearrangements

Absolutely convergent series share an important property with finite sums — no matter what order we add the numbers, the sum is always the same. Stated another way, the sum of an absolutely convergent series is always the same value, even if the terms are rearranged.

Conditionally convergent series do not have this property — the order in which we add the terms does matter. If the terms of a conditionally convergent series are rearranged or reordered, the sum after the rearrangement may be different than the sum before the rearrangement. A rather amazing fact is that the terms of a conditionally convergent series can be rearranged to obtain any sum we want.

We illustrate this strange result by showing that we can rearrange the alternating harmonic series, a series conditionally convergent to approximately 0.69, so that the sum of the rearranged series is 2 rather than 0.69..

$$\sum_{n=1}^{\infty} (-1)^{n+1} \frac{1}{n} = 1 - \frac{1}{2} + \frac{1}{3} - \frac{1}{4} + \frac{1}{5} - \frac{1}{6} + \dots \text{ is conditionally convergent to approximately } 0.69.$$

First we note that the sum of the positive terms alone is a divergent series:

$$1 + \frac{1}{3} + \frac{1}{5} + \frac{1}{7} + \dots = \sum_{n=1}^{\infty} \frac{1}{2n-1} \text{ which diverges by the Limit Comparison Test,}$$

so the partial sums of the positive terms eventually exceed any number we pick.

Similarly, the sum of the negative terms alone is also a divergent series:

$$-\frac{1}{2} - \frac{1}{4} - \frac{1}{6} - \frac{1}{8} + \dots = -\frac{1}{2} \sum_{n=1}^{\infty} \frac{1}{n} \text{ which diverges,}$$

so the partial sums of the negative terms eventually become as large negatively as we want.

Finally, we pick a target number we want for the sum (in this illustration, we picked a target of 2).

Then the following clever strategy tells us how to chose the order of the terms, the rearrangement, so the sum of the rearranged series is the target number, 2 :

(1) select the positive terms, in the order they appear in the original series, until the partial sum exceeds our target number, then

(2) select the negative terms, in the order they appear in the original series, until the partial sum falls below our target number, and

(3) keep repeating steps (1) and (2) with the previously unused terms of the original series.

In order to rearrange the terms of the alternating harmonic series so the sum is 2, we pick positive terms, in order, until the partial sum **is larger than** 2. This requires the first 8 positive terms:

$s_1 = 1,$

$s_2 = 1 + \frac{1}{3} \approx 1.3333, \ldots$

$s_7 = 1 + \frac{1}{3} + \frac{1}{5} + \frac{1}{7} + \frac{1}{9} + \frac{1}{11} + \frac{1}{13} \approx 1.955133755$

$s_8 = 1 + \frac{1}{3} + \frac{1}{5} + \frac{1}{7} + \frac{1}{9} + \frac{1}{11} + \frac{1}{13} + \frac{1}{15} \approx 2.021800422$.

Then we pick negative terms, in order, until the partial sum **is less than** two. This only requires 1 negative term:

$s_9 = 1 + \frac{1}{3} + \frac{1}{5} + \frac{1}{7} + \frac{1}{9} + \frac{1}{11} + \frac{1}{13} + \frac{1}{15} - \frac{1}{2} \approx 1.521800422$.

Then we pick more unused positive terms until the partial sum exceeds 2. This requires many more positive terms:

$s_{10} = 1 + \frac{1}{3} + \frac{1}{5} + \frac{1}{7} + \frac{1}{9} + \frac{1}{11} + \frac{1}{13} + \frac{1}{15} - \frac{1}{2} + \frac{1}{17} \approx 1.580623951$

$s_{11} = 1 + \frac{1}{3} + \frac{1}{5} + \frac{1}{7} + \frac{1}{9} + \frac{1}{11} + \frac{1}{13} + \frac{1}{15} - \frac{1}{2} + \frac{1}{17} + \frac{1}{19} \approx 1.63325553$

$s_{12} = s_{11} + \frac{1}{21} \approx 1.680874578$, $s_{13} = s_{12} + \frac{1}{23} \approx 1.724352839$

$s_{14} \approx 1.764352839$, $s_{15} \approx 1.801389876$, $s_{16} \approx 1.835872634$, $s_{17} \approx 1.868130699$

$s_{18} \approx 1.898433729$, $s_{19} \approx 1.927005158$, $s_{20} \approx 1.954032185$, $s_{21} \approx 1.97967321$,

$s_{22} \approx s_{21} + \frac{1}{41} \approx 2.004063454$.

Then we pick more previously unused negative terms, in order, until the partial sum is less than two. Again only 1 negative term is required:

$s_{23} = s_{22} - \frac{1}{4} \approx 1.754063454$.

As we continue to repeat this process, we "eventually" use all of the terms of the original conditionally convergent series and the partial sums of the new "rearranged" series get, and stay, arbitrarily close to the target number, 2. The same method can be used to rearrange the terms of the alternating harmonic series (or any conditionally convergent series) to sum to 0.3, 3, 30 or any positive target number we want. How do you think the strategy needs to be changed to rearrange a conditionally convergent series to sum to a **negative** target number?

PROBLEMS

In problems 1 – 30 determine whether the given series Converge Absolutely, Converge Conditionally, or Diverge and give reasons for your conclusions.

1. $\sum_{n=1}^{\infty} (-1)^n \frac{1}{n+2}$

2. $\sum_{n=1}^{\infty} (-1)^{n+1} \frac{1}{\sqrt{n}}$

3. $\sum_{n=1}^{\infty} (-1)^{n+1} \frac{5}{n^3}$

4. $\sum_{n=1}^{\infty} (-1)^n \frac{1}{2 + \ln(n)}$

5. $\sum_{n=1}^{\infty} (-0.5)^n$

6. $\sum_{n=1}^{\infty} (-0.5)^{-n}$

10.7 Absolute Convergence and the Ratio Test

7. $\sum_{n=1}^{\infty} (-1)^n \frac{1}{n^2}$

8. $\sum_{n=1}^{\infty} (-1)^{n+1} \frac{1}{3+n^2}$

9. $\sum_{n=1}^{\infty} (-1)^{n+1} \frac{\ln(n)}{n}$

10. $\sum_{n=1}^{\infty} (-1)^{n+1} \frac{\ln(n)}{n^2}$

11. $\sum_{n=1}^{\infty} (-1)^n \frac{1}{n + \ln(n)}$

12. $\sum_{n=1}^{\infty} (-1)^{n+1} \frac{5}{\sqrt{n+7}}$

13. $\sum_{n=1}^{\infty} (-1)^n \sin(\frac{1}{n})$ (recall that if $0 < x < 1$, then $0 < \sin(x) < x$)

14. $\sum_{n=1}^{\infty} (-1)^n \sin(\frac{1}{n^2})$

15. $\sum_{n=1}^{\infty} (-1)^n \sqrt{n} \sin(\frac{1}{n^2})$

16. $\sum_{n=1}^{\infty} \frac{\cos(\pi n)}{n}$

17. $\sum_{n=1}^{\infty} (-1)^{n+1} \frac{\ln(n)}{\ln(n^3)}$

18. $\sum_{n=1}^{\infty} (-1)^{n+1} \frac{n^2+7}{n^2+10}$

19. $\sum_{n=1}^{\infty} (-1)^{n+1} \frac{n^2+7}{n^3+10}$

20. $\sum_{n=1}^{\infty} (-1)^{n+1} \frac{n^2+7}{n^4+10}$

21. $\sum_{n=1}^{\infty} (-1)^{n+1} \frac{(n^2+7)^2}{n^2+10}$

22. $\sum_{n=1}^{\infty} \frac{\sin(n)}{n^2}$

23. $\sum_{n=1}^{\infty} \frac{\sin(\pi n)}{n}$

24. $\sum_{n=1}^{\infty} (-n)^{-n}$

25. $\sum_{n=1}^{\infty} (-1)^{n+1} \frac{1+\sqrt{3n}}{n+2}$

26. $\sum_{n=1}^{\infty} \frac{(-2)^n}{n^2}$

27. $\sum_{n=1}^{\infty} (-1)^{n+1} \frac{(-3)^n}{n^3}$

28. $\sum_{n=2}^{\infty} (-1)^{n+1} \left(\frac{\ln(n)}{\ln(n^5)} \right)^2$

29. $\sum_{n=1}^{\infty} \frac{(-2)^n}{n \cdot 3^n}$

30. $\sum_{n=1}^{\infty} \frac{3^n}{n^3}$

The Ratio Test is commonly used with series that contain factorials, and factorials are also going to become more common in the next few sections. Problems 31 – 40 ask you to simplify factorial expressions in order to get ready for that usage.

(Definitions: $0! = 1$, $1! = 1$, $2! = 1 \cdot 2 = 2$, $3! = 1 \cdot 2 \cdot 3 = 6$, $4! = 24$, and, in general, $n! = 1 \cdot 2 \cdot 3 \cdot \ldots \cdot (n-1) \cdot n$)

31. Show that $\frac{n!}{(n+1)!} = \frac{1}{n+1}$

32. Show that $\frac{n!}{(n+2)!} = \frac{1}{(n+1)(n+2)}$

33. Show that $\frac{n!}{(n+3)!} = \frac{1}{(n+1)(n+2)(n+3)}$

34. Show that $\frac{(n+1)!}{(n+2)!} = \frac{1}{n+2}$

35. Show that $\frac{(n-1)!}{(n+1)!} = \frac{1}{(n)(n+1)}$

36. Show that $\frac{2(n!)}{(2n)!} = \frac{2}{(n+1) \cdot (n+2) \cdot \ldots \cdot (2n)}$

37. Show that $\frac{(2n)!}{(2n+1)!} = \frac{1}{2n+1}$

38. Show that $\frac{(2n)!}{(2(n+1))!} = \frac{1}{(2n+1)(2n+2)}$

39. Show that $\dfrac{n^n}{n!} = \dfrac{n}{1} \cdot \dfrac{n}{2} \cdot \dfrac{n}{3} \cdot \ldots \cdot \dfrac{n}{n-1} \cdot \dfrac{n}{n}$

40. For $n > 0$, which is larger, $7!$ or $\dfrac{(n+7)!}{n!}$?

In problems 41 – 56, (a) determine the value of $L = \lim\limits_{n \to \infty} \left| \dfrac{a_{n+1}}{a_n} \right|$ for the given series, and (b) state the conclusion of the Ratio Test as it applies to the series. (c) If the Ratio Test is inconclusive, use some other method to determine if the given series converges or diverges.

41. $\displaystyle\sum_{n=1}^{\infty} \dfrac{1}{n}$

42. $\displaystyle\sum_{n=1}^{\infty} \dfrac{1}{n^2}$

43. $\displaystyle\sum_{n=2}^{\infty} \dfrac{1}{n^3}$

44. $\displaystyle\sum_{n=2}^{\infty} \dfrac{1}{\sqrt{n}}$

45. $\displaystyle\sum_{n=1}^{\infty} \left(\dfrac{1}{2}\right)^n$

46. $\displaystyle\sum_{n=1}^{\infty} \left(\dfrac{1}{3}\right)^n$

47. $\displaystyle\sum_{n=5}^{\infty} 1^n$

48. $\displaystyle\sum_{n=1}^{\infty} (-2)^n$

49. $\displaystyle\sum_{n=1}^{\infty} \dfrac{1}{n!}$

50. $\displaystyle\sum_{n=1}^{\infty} \dfrac{5}{n!}$

51. $\displaystyle\sum_{n=1}^{\infty} \dfrac{2^n}{n!}$

52. $\displaystyle\sum_{n=1}^{\infty} \dfrac{5^n}{n!}$

53. $\displaystyle\sum_{n=1}^{\infty} \left(\dfrac{1}{2}\right)^{3n}$

54. $\displaystyle\sum_{n=1}^{\infty} \left(\dfrac{1}{3}\right)^{2n}$

55. $\displaystyle\sum_{n=5}^{\infty} (0.9)^{2n+1}$

56. $\displaystyle\sum_{n=5}^{\infty} (-0.8)^{2n+1}$

For each series in problems 57 – 74 find the values of x for which the value of $L = \lim\limits_{n \to \infty} \left| \dfrac{a_{n+1}}{a_n} \right| < 1$. From the Ratio Test we can conclude that each series converges absolutely (and thus converges) for those values of x.

57. $\displaystyle\sum_{n=5}^{\infty} (x-5)^n$

58. $\displaystyle\sum_{n=1}^{\infty} \dfrac{(x-5)^n}{n}$

59. $\displaystyle\sum_{n=1}^{\infty} \dfrac{(x-5)^n}{n^2}$

60. $\displaystyle\sum_{n=1}^{\infty} \dfrac{(x-2)^n}{n^2}$

61. $\displaystyle\sum_{n=1}^{\infty} \dfrac{(x-2)^n}{n!}$

62. $\displaystyle\sum_{n=1}^{\infty} \dfrac{(x-10)^n}{n!}$

63. $\displaystyle\sum_{n=1}^{\infty} \dfrac{(2x-12)^n}{n^2}$

64. $\displaystyle\sum_{n=1}^{\infty} \dfrac{(4x-12)^n}{n^2}$

65. $\displaystyle\sum_{n=1}^{\infty} \dfrac{(6x-12)^n}{n!}$

66. $\displaystyle\sum_{n=1}^{\infty} (x-3)^{2n}$

67. $\displaystyle\sum_{n=2}^{\infty} \dfrac{(x+1)^{2n}}{n}$

68. $\displaystyle\sum_{n=2}^{\infty} \dfrac{(x+2)^{2n+1}}{n^2}$

69. $\displaystyle\sum_{n=1}^{\infty} \frac{(x-5)^{3n+1}}{n^2}$

70. $\displaystyle\sum_{n=1}^{\infty} \frac{(x+4)^{2n+1}}{n!}$

71. $\displaystyle\sum_{n=1}^{\infty} \frac{(x+3)^{2n-1}}{(n+1)!}$

72. $S(x) = \displaystyle\sum_{n=0}^{\infty} (-1)^n \frac{x^{2n+1}}{(2n+1)!}$

73. $C(x) = \displaystyle\sum_{n=0}^{\infty} (-1)^n \frac{x^{2n}}{(2n)!}$

74. $E(x) = \displaystyle\sum_{n=0}^{\infty} \frac{x^n}{n!}$

Rearrangements

In problems 75 – 80 use the strategy in the illustrative example to find the first 15 terms of a rearrangement of the given conditionally convergent series so that the rearranged series converges to the given target number.

75. $\displaystyle\sum_{n=1}^{\infty} (-1)^n \frac{1}{n}$, target number = 0.3 .

76. $\displaystyle\sum_{n=1}^{\infty} (-1)^{n+1} \frac{1}{n}$, target number = 0.7 .

77. $\displaystyle\sum_{n=1}^{\infty} (-1)^{n+1} \frac{1}{n}$, target number = 1 .

78. $\displaystyle\sum_{n=1}^{\infty} (-1)^{n+1} \frac{1}{\sqrt{n}}$, target number = 0.4 .

79. $\displaystyle\sum_{n=1}^{\infty} (-1)^{n+1} \frac{1}{\sqrt{n}}$, target number = 1 .

80. $\displaystyle\sum_{n=1}^{\infty} (-1)^{n+1} \frac{1}{n}$, target number = –1 .

Practice Answers

Practice 1: (a) $\displaystyle\sum_{n=2}^{\infty} (-1)^n \frac{5}{\ln(n)}$ converges by the Alternating Series Test

$\displaystyle\sum_{n=2}^{\infty} \left|(-1)^n \frac{5}{\ln(n)}\right| = \displaystyle\sum_{n=2}^{\infty} \frac{5}{\ln(n)}$ which diverges by comparison with the divergent series $\displaystyle\sum_{n=2}^{\infty} \frac{5}{n}$.

Therefore, $\displaystyle\sum_{n=2}^{\infty} (-1)^n \frac{5}{\ln(n)}$ is **conditionally convergent** .

(b) $\displaystyle\sum_{k=1}^{\infty} \frac{\cos(\pi k)}{k^2} = \frac{-1}{1^2} + \frac{1}{2^2} + \frac{-1}{3^2} + \ldots$

$\displaystyle\sum_{k=1}^{\infty} \left|\frac{\cos(\pi k)}{k^2}\right| = \displaystyle\sum_{k=1}^{\infty} \frac{1}{k^2}$ which is convergent (P–test, p = 2) so

$\displaystyle\sum_{k=1}^{\infty} \frac{\cos(\pi k)}{k^2}$ is **absolutely convergent** (and convergent).

Practice 2: (a) $a_n = (-1)^{n+1} \dfrac{e^n}{n!}$ so $a_{n+1} = (-1)^{n+2} \dfrac{e^{n+1}}{(n+1)!}$. Then

$$\left| \frac{a_{n+1}}{a_n} \right| = \left| \frac{(-1)^{n+2} \frac{e^{n+1}}{(n+1)!}}{(-1)^{n+1} \frac{e^n}{n!}} \right| = \left| \frac{e^{n+1}}{e^n} \frac{n!}{(n+1)!} \right| = \left| \frac{e}{n+1} \right| \longrightarrow 0 < 1$$

so $\sum_{n=1}^{\infty} (-1)^{n+1} \dfrac{e^n}{n!}$ is absolutely convergent.

(b) $a_n = \dfrac{n^5}{3^n}$ so $a_{n+1} = \dfrac{(n+1)^5}{3^{n+1}}$. Then

$$\left| \frac{a_{n+1}}{a_n} \right| = \left| \frac{\frac{(n+1)^5}{3^{n+1}}}{\frac{n^5}{3^n}} \right| = \left| \frac{3^n}{3^{n+1}} \frac{(n+1)^5}{n^5} \right| = \left| \frac{1}{3} \left(\frac{n+1}{n} \right)^5 \right| \longrightarrow \frac{1}{3} < 1$$

so $\sum_{n=1}^{\infty} \dfrac{n^5}{3^n}$ is absolutely convergent.

Practice 3: $a_n = \dfrac{(x-5)^n}{n^2}$ so $a_{n+1} = \dfrac{(x-5)^{n+1}}{(n+1)^2}$. Then

$$\left| \frac{a_{n+1}}{a_n} \right| = \left| \frac{\frac{(x-5)^{n+1}}{(n+1)^2}}{\frac{(x-5)^n}{n^2}} \right| = \left| \frac{(x-5)^{n+1}}{(x-5)^n} \frac{n^2}{(n+1)^2} \right| \to |x-5| = L.$$

Now we simply need to solve the inequality $|x-5| < 1$ ($L < 1$) for x.

If $|x-5| < 1$, then $-1 < x - 5 < 1$ so $\mathbf{4 < x < 6}$.

If $4 < x < 6$, then $L = |x-5| < 1$ so $\sum_{n=1}^{\infty} \dfrac{(x-5)^n}{n^2}$ is absolutely convergent (and convergent).

Also, if $x < 4$ or $x > 6$ then $L > 1$ so $\sum_{n=1}^{\infty} \dfrac{(x-5)^n}{n^2}$ diverges.

"Endpoints": If $x = 4$, then $\sum_{n=1}^{\infty} \dfrac{(x-5)^n}{n^2} = \sum_{n=1}^{\infty} \dfrac{(-1)^n}{n^2}$ which converges.

If $x = 6$, then $\sum_{n=1}^{\infty} \dfrac{(x-5)^n}{n^2} = \sum_{n=1}^{\infty} \dfrac{1}{n^2}$ which converges.

Appendix: A Proof of the Ratio Test

The Ratio Test has three parts, (a), (b), and (c), and each part requires a separate proof.

(a) L<1 $\Rightarrow$ the series is absolutely convergent. The basic pattern of the proof for this part is to show that the given series is, term–by–term, less than a convergent geometric series. Then we conclude by the Comparison Test that the given series converges.

Suppose $\lim_{n \to \infty} \left| \frac{a_{n+1}}{a_n} \right| = L < 1$. Then there is a number r between L and 1 so that the ratios $\left| \frac{a_{n+1}}{a_n} \right|$ are eventually (for all n > some N) less than r:

for all n > N, $\left| \frac{a_{n+1}}{a_n} \right| < r < 1$.

Then $|a_{N+1}| < r |a_N|$, $|a_{N+2}| < r |a_{N+1}| < r^2 |a_N|$, $|a_{N+3}| < r |a_{N+2}| < r^3 |a_N|$, and, in general, $|a_{N+k}| < r^k |a_N|$.

So $|a_N| + |a_{N+1}| + |a_{N+2}| + |a_{N+3}| + |a_{N+4}| + \ldots$

$$< |a_N| + r|a_N| + r^2|a_N| + r^3|a_N| + r^4|a_N| + \ldots$$

$$= |a_N| \cdot \{ 1 + r + r^2 + r^3 + r^4 + \ldots \}$$

$$= |a_N| \cdot \frac{1}{1-r}, \text{ since the powers of r form a convergent geometric series,}$$

and the series $\sum_{n=N}^{\infty} |a_n|$ is convergent by the Comparison Test.

Finally, we can conclude that the series $\sum_{n=1}^{\infty} |a_n| = \sum_{n=1}^{N-1} |a_n| + \sum_{n=N}^{\infty} |a_n|$ is convergent, since it is the sum of two convergent series. $\sum_{n=1}^{\infty} a_n$ is absolutely convergent.

(b) L>1 $\Rightarrow$ the series is divergent. The basic idea in this part is to show that the terms of the given series do not approach 0. Then we can conclude by the Nth Term Test that the given series diverges.

Suppose $\lim_{n \to \infty} \left| \frac{a_{n+1}}{a_n} \right| = L > 1$. Then the ratios $\left| \frac{a_{n+1}}{a_n} \right|$ are eventually (for all n > some N) larger than 1 so $|a_{N+1}| > |a_N|$, $|a_{N+2}| > |a_{N+1}| > |a_N|$, $|a_{N+3}| > |a_{N+2}| > |a_N|$, and, for all k > N, $|a_k| > |a_N|$.

Thus $\lim_{n \to \infty} |a_n| \geq |a_N| \neq 0$ and $\lim_{n \to \infty} a_n \neq 0$, so by the Nth Term Test for Divergence (Section 10.2) we can conclude that the series $\sum_{n=1}^{\infty} a_n$ is divergent.

(c) $L=1 \Rightarrow$ nothing. Part (c) can be verified by giving two series, one convergent and one divergent, for which $L = 1$.

If $a_n = \dfrac{1}{n^2}$, then $\sum_{n=1}^{\infty} a_n = \sum_{n=1}^{\infty} \dfrac{1}{n^2}$ is convergent by the P–Test with p=2, and

$$\lim_{n \to \infty} \left| \frac{a_{n+1}}{a_n} \right| = \lim_{n \to \infty} \left| \frac{1/(n+1)^2}{1/n^2} \right| = \lim_{n \to \infty} \left(\frac{n}{n+1} \right)^2 = 1.$$

If $a_n = \dfrac{1}{n}$, then $\sum_{n=1}^{\infty} a_n = \sum_{n=1}^{\infty} \dfrac{1}{n}$ is the divergent harmonic series, and

$$\lim_{n \to \infty} \left| \frac{a_{n+1}}{a_n} \right| = \lim_{n \to \infty} \left| \frac{1/(n+1)}{1/n} \right| = \lim_{n \to \infty} \frac{n}{n+1} = 1.$$

Since $L =1$ for each of these series, one convergent and one divergent, knowing that $L = 1$ for a series does not let us conclude that the series converges or that it diverges.

10.8 POWER SERIES: $\sum_{n=0}^{\infty} a_n x^n$ and $\sum_{n=0}^{\infty} a_n(x-c)^n$

So far most of the series we have examined have consisted of numbers (numerical series), but the most important series contain powers of a variable, and they define functions of that variable.

Definition of Power Series

A **power series** is an expression of the form $\sum_{n=0}^{\infty} a_n x^n = a_0 + a_1 x + a_2 x^2 + a_3 x^3 + \ldots + a_n x^n + \ldots$

where $a_0, a_1, a_2, a_3, \ldots$ are constants, called the coefficients of the series, and x is a variable.

(Note: For n = 0 we use the convention for power series that $x^0 = 1$ even when x = 0. This convention simply makes it easier for us to represent the series using the summation notation.)

For each value of the variable, the power series is simply a numerical series that may converge or diverge. If the power series does converge, the value of the function is the sum of the series, and the domain of the function is the set of x values for which the series converges. Power series are particularly important in mathematics and applications because many important functions such as $\sin(x)$, $\cos(x)$, e^x, and $\ln(x)$ can be represented and approximated by power series.

The following are examples of power series:

$$f(x) = 1 + x + x^2 + x^3 + x^4 + \ldots = \sum_{n=0}^{\infty} x^n \quad (a_n = 1 \text{ for all n})$$

$$g(x) = 1 + x + \frac{x^2}{2!} + \frac{x^3}{3!} + \frac{x^4}{4!} + \ldots = \sum_{n=0}^{\infty} \frac{x^n}{n!} \quad (a_n = \frac{1}{n!} \text{ for all n and with the definition that } 0! = 1)$$

$$h(x) = x - \frac{x^3}{3!} + \frac{x^5}{5!} - \frac{x^7}{7!} + \ldots = \sum_{n=0}^{\infty} (-1)^n \cdot \frac{x^{2n+1}}{(2n+1)!} \quad (a_n = \frac{(-1)^n}{(2n+1)!} \text{ for all n.})$$

Power series look like long (very long) polynomials, and in many ways they behave like polynomials.

This section focuses on what a power series is and on determining where a given power series converges. Section 10.9 looks at the arithmetic (sums, differences, products) and calculus (derivative and integrals) of power series. Section 10.10 examines how to represent particular functions such as $\sin(x)$ and e^x and others as power series.

Finding Where a Power Series Converges

The power series $f(x) = \sum_{n=0}^{\infty} a_n x^n$ always converges at $x = 0$: $f(0) = \sum_{n=0}^{\infty} a_n (0)^n = a_0$. To find which other values of x make a power series converge, we could try x values one–by–one, but that is very inefficient and time consuming. Instead, the Ratio Test allows us to get answers for lots of x values all at once. (Since we are using a_n to represent the coefficient of the nth term $a_n x^n$, we let $c_n = a_n x^n$ represent the nth term and we use the ratio $\dfrac{c_{n+1}}{c_n}$.)

Example 1: Find all of the values of x for which the power series $\sum_{n=0}^{\infty} (2n+1) \cdot x^n$ converges.

Solution: $c_n = (2n+1) \cdot x^n$ so $c_{n+1} = (2(n+1)+1) \cdot x^{n+1} = (2n+3) \cdot x^{n+1}$. Then, using the Ratio Test,

$$\left| \frac{c_{n+1}}{c_n} \right| = \left| \frac{(2n+3) \cdot x^{n+1}}{(2n+1) \cdot x^n} \right| = \left| \frac{2n+3}{2n+1} \cdot \frac{x^{n+1}}{x^n} \right| = \left| \frac{2n+3}{2n+1} \cdot x \right| \to |x| = L.$$

From the Ratio Test we know the series converges if $L < 1$: if $|x| < 1$ or, in other words, $-1 < x < 1$. We also know the series diverges if $L > 1$ so the series diverges if $|x| > 1$: if $x > 1$ or $x < -1$.

Finally, we need to check the two remaining values of x: the **endpoints** $x = -1$ and $x = 1$.

When $x = 1$, $\sum_{n=0}^{\infty} (2n+1) \cdot x^n = \sum_{n=0}^{\infty} (2n+1) \cdot 1^n = \sum_{n=0}^{\infty} (2n+1)$ which diverges since the terms do not approach 0. When $x = -1$, $\sum_{n=0}^{\infty} (2n+1) \cdot x^n = \sum_{n=0}^{\infty} (2n+1) \cdot (-1)^n$ which also diverges because the terms do not approach 0.

The power series $\sum_{n=0}^{\infty} (2n+1) \cdot x^n$ converges if and only if $-1 < x < 1$. In other words, the series converges when x is in the interval $(-1, 1)$ and it diverges when x is outside the interval $(-1, 1)$.

Example 2: Find all of the values of x for which the power series $\sum_{n=1}^{\infty} \dfrac{x^n}{n \cdot 3^n}$ converges.

Solution: $c_n = \dfrac{x^n}{n \cdot 3^n}$ so $c_{n+1} = \dfrac{x^{n+1}}{(n+1) \cdot 3^{n+1}}$. Using the Ratio Test,

$$\left| \frac{c_{n+1}}{c_n} \right| = \left| \frac{\frac{x^{n+1}}{(n+1) \cdot 3^{n+1}}}{\frac{x^n}{n \cdot 3^n}} \right| = \left| \frac{n}{n+1} \cdot \frac{3^n}{3^{n+1}} \cdot \frac{x^{n+1}}{x^n} \right| = \left| \frac{n}{n+1} \cdot \frac{1}{3} \cdot x \right| \to \left| \frac{x}{3} \right| = L.$$

Solving $|\frac{x}{3}| < 1$, we have $-1 < \frac{x}{3} < 1$ or $-3 < x < 3$. The series converges for $-3 < x < 3$ and it diverges for $x < -3$ and for $x > 3$.

Finally, we need to check the two remaining values of x: the **endpoints** $x = -3$ and $x = 3$.

When $x = -3$, $\sum_{n=1}^{\infty} \frac{x^n}{n \cdot 3^n} = \sum_{n=1}^{\infty} \frac{(-3)^n}{n \cdot 3^n} = \sum_{n=1}^{\infty} \frac{(-1)^n}{n}$ which converges by the Alternating Series Test.

When $x = 3$, $\sum_{n=1}^{\infty} \frac{x^n}{n \cdot 3^n} = \sum_{n=1}^{\infty} \frac{(3)^n}{n \cdot 3^n} = \sum_{n=1}^{\infty} \frac{1}{n}$, the harmonic series, which diverges.

In summary, the power series $\sum_{n=1}^{\infty} \frac{x^n}{n \cdot 3^n}$ converges if $-3 \leq x < 3$, if x is in the interval $[-3, 3)$.

Note: The Ratio Test is very powerful for determining where a power series converges: put $c_n = a_n x^n$, calculate the limit of the ratio $\left| \frac{c_{n+1}}{c_n} \right|$, and then solve the resulting absolute value inequality for x.

Typically, we also need to check the endpoints of the interval by replacing x with the two endpoint values and then determining if the resulting numerical series converge or diverge at these endpoints. The Ratio Test does not help with the endpoints.

Practice 1: Find all of the values of x for which the series $\sum_{n=1}^{\infty} \frac{5^n \cdot x^n}{n}$ converges.

Interval of Convergence, Radius of Convergence

In each of the previous examples, the values of x for which the power series converge form an interval. The next theorem says that always happens.

Interval of Convergence Theorem for Power Series

The values of x for which the power series $\sum_{n=0}^{\infty} a_n x^n$ converges form an interval.

(i) If this power series converges for $x = c$, then the series converges for all satisfying $|x| < |c|$.

(ii) If this power series diverges for $x = d$, then the series diverges for all satisfying $|x| > |d|$.

A proof of the Interval of Convergence Theorem is given after the Practice Answers.

Meaning of the Interval of Convergence Theorem: If a power series $\sum_{n=0}^{\infty} a_n x^n$ converges for a value $x = c$, then the series also converges for all values of x closer to the origin than c. If the power series diverges for a value $x = d$, then the power series diverges for all values of x farther from the origin than d.

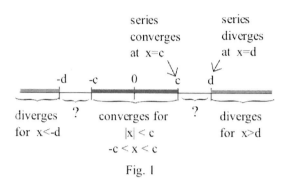

Fig. 1

This guarantees that the values where the power series converges form an interval, from $-|c|$ to $|c|$. This Theorem does **not** tell us about the convergence of the power series at the endpoints of the interval — we need to check those two points individually. This Theorem also does **not** tell us about the convergence of the power series for values of x with $|c| < |x| < |d|$. See Fig. 1.

Example 3: Suppose we know that a power series $\sum_{n=0}^{\infty} a_n x^n$ converges at $x = 4$ and diverges at $x = 9$.

What can we conclude (converge or diverge or not enough information) about the series when $x = 2, -3, -4, 5, -6, 8, -9, 10, -11$?

Solution: We know the power series converges at $x = 4$ ($c = 4$) so we can conclude that the series converges for $x = 2$ and $x = -3$ since $|2|<|4|$ and $|-3|<|4|$.

We know the power series diverges at $x = 9$ ($d = 9$) so we can conclude that the series diverges for $x = 10$ and $x = -11$ since $|10|>|9|$ and $|-11|>|9|$.

The remaining values of x ($-4, 5, -6, 8,$ and -9) do not satisfy $|x| < 4$ or $|x| > 9$ so the series may converge or may diverge — we don't have enough information.

Fig. 2 shows the regions where convergence of this power series is guaranteed, where divergence is guaranteed, and where we don't have enough information.

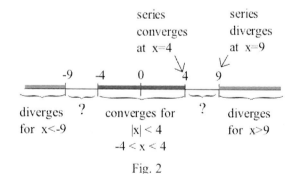

Fig. 2

Practice 2: Suppose we know that a power series $\sum_{n=0}^{\infty} a_n x^n$ converges at $x = 3$ and diverges at $x = -7$.

What can we say about the convergence of the series for $x = -1, 2, -3, 4, -6, 7, -8,$ and 17?
Sketch the regions of known convergence and known divergence.

Definition: The **interval of convergence** of a power series $\sum_{n=0}^{\infty} a_n x^n$ is the interval of values of x for which the series converges.

From Example 1 we know the interval of convergence of $\sum_{n=0}^{\infty} (2n+1) \cdot x^n$ is $(-1, 1)$.

From Example 2 we know the interval of convergence of $\sum_{n=1}^{\infty} \dfrac{x^n}{n \cdot 3^n}$ is $[-3, 3)$.

Definition:

For each power series $\sum_{n=0}^{\infty} a_n x^n$ there is a number R, called the **radius of convergence**, so that the series converges for $|x| < R$ and diverges when $|x| > R$.
(The series may converge or may diverge at $|x| = R$.)
(Fig. 3)

Fig. 3

The radius of convergence is half of the length of the interval of convergence.

Example 4: What is the radius of convergence of each series in Examples 1 and 2?

Solution: The power series $\sum_{n=0}^{\infty} (2n+1) \cdot x^n$ converges if $-1 < x < 1$ so $R = 1$.

The power series $\sum_{n=1}^{\infty} \dfrac{x^n}{n \cdot 3^n}$ converges if $-3 \leq x < 3$, so $R = 3$.

The convergence or divergence of a power series at the endpoints of the interval of convergence does not affect the value of the radius of convergence R, and the value of R does not tell us about the convergence of the power series at the endpoints of the interval of convergence, at $x = R$ and $x = -R$.

Practice 3: What is the radius of convergence of the series in Practice 1?

> **Summary**
>
> For a power series $\sum_{n=0}^{\infty} a_n x^n$ exactly one of these three situations occurs:
>
> (i) the series converges only for $x = 0$. (Then we say the radius of convergence is 0.)
>
> (ii) the series converges for all x with $|x| < R$ and diverges for all x with $|x| > R$. (Then we say the radius of convergence is R.)
>
> (iii) the series converges for all values of x. (Then we say the radius of convergence is infinite.)

The following list shows the intervals and radii of convergence for several power series. Four of the series in the list have the same radius of convergence, $R = 1$, but slightly different intervals of convergence. (The $\sum$ below simply means a series whose starting index is some finite value of n and whose upper index is ∞.)

Series	Radius of Convergence	Interval of Convergence
$\sum n! \cdot x^n$	$R = 0$	$\{0\}$, a single point
$\sum x^n$	$R = 1$	$(-1, 1)$
$\sum \dfrac{x^n}{n}$	$R = 1$	$[-1, 1)$
$\sum (-1)^n \dfrac{x^n}{n}$	$R = 1$	$(-1, 1]$
$\sum \dfrac{x^n}{n^2}$	$R = 1$	$[-1, 1]$
$\sum \dfrac{x^n}{2^n}$	$R = 2$	$(-2, 2)$
$\sum \dfrac{x^n}{n!}$	$R = \infty$	$(-\infty, \infty)$

Power Series Centered at c

Sometimes it is useful to "shift" a power series. These shifted power series contain powers of "x – c" instead of powers of "x," but many of the properties we have examined still hold.

Definition: A power series centered at c is a series of the form

$$\sum_{n=0}^{\infty} a_n(x-c)^n = a_0 + a_1(x-c) + a_2(x-c)^2 + a_3(x-c)^3 + \ldots + a_n(x-c)^n + \ldots$$

where $a_0, a_1, a_2, a_3, \ldots$ are constants, called the coefficients of the series, and x is a variable.

Note: As usual for power series, for n = 0 we use the convention that $(x-c)^0 = 1$, even when x = c.

A power series centered at c always converges for x = c, and the interval of convergence is an interval **centered at c**. The radius of convergence is half the length of the interval of convergence (Fig. 4).

If a power series centered at c converges for a value of x, then the series converges for all values closer to c. If a power series centered at c diverges for a value of x, then the series diverges for all values farther from c.

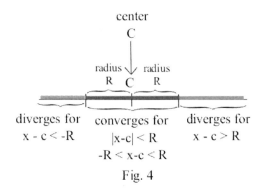
Fig. 4

Example 5: Suppose we know that a power series $\sum_{n=0}^{\infty} a_n(x-4)^n$ converges at x = 6 and diverges at x = 0. What can we conclude (converge or diverge or not enough information) about the series when x = 3, 9, –1, 2, and 7?

Solution: We know the power series converges at x = 6 so we can conclude that the series converges for values of x **closer to 4** than |6 – 4| = 2 units: the series converges at x = 3.

We know the power series diverges at x = 0 so we can conclude that the series diverges for values of x **farther from 4** than |0 – 4| = 4 units: the series diverges at x = 9.

The remaining values of x (–1, 2 and 7) do not satisfy |x – 4| < 2 or |x – 4| > 4 so the series may converge or may diverge.

Fig. 5 shows the regions where convergence of this power series is guaranteed, where divergence is guaranteed, and where we don't have enough information.

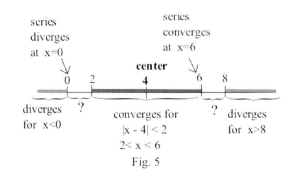
Fig. 5

Practice 4: Suppose we know that a power series $\sum_{n=0}^{\infty} a_n(x+5)^n$ converges at $x = -1$ and diverges at $x = 1$. What can we conclude about the series when $x = -2, -9, 0, -11,$ and 3?

The Ratio Test is still our primary tool for finding an interval of convergence of a power series, even if the power series is centered at c rather than at 0.

Example 6: Find the interval and radius of convergence of $\sum_{n=1}^{\infty} \dfrac{(x-5)^n}{n \cdot 2^n}$.

Solution: $c_n = \dfrac{(x-5)^n}{n \cdot 2^n}$ so $c_{n+1} = \dfrac{(x-5)^{n+1}}{(n+1) \cdot 2^{n+1}}$. The ratio $\left| \dfrac{c_{n+1}}{c_n} \right|$ for the Ratio Test appears to be messy, but if we group the similar pieces algebraically, the ratio simplifies nicely:

$$\left| \dfrac{c_{n+1}}{c_n} \right| = \left| \dfrac{\dfrac{(x-5)^{n+1}}{(n+1) \cdot 2^{n+1}}}{\dfrac{(x-5)^n}{n \cdot 2^n}} \right| = \left| \dfrac{n}{n+1} \cdot \dfrac{2^n}{2^{n+1}} \cdot \dfrac{(x-5)^{n+1}}{(x-5)^n} \right| = \left| \dfrac{n}{n+1} \cdot \dfrac{1}{2} \cdot (x-5) \right| \to \left| \dfrac{(x-5)}{2} \right| = L.$$

Solving $\left| \dfrac{(x-5)}{2} \right| < 1$, we have $-1 < \dfrac{(x-5)}{2} < 1$ so $-2 < x-5 < 2$ and $3 < x < 7$. The series converges for $3 < x < 7$, and it diverges for $x < 3$ and for $x > 7$.

Finally, we need to check the two remaining values of x: the **endpoints** $x = 3$ and $x = 7$.

When $x = 3$, $\sum_{n=1}^{\infty} \dfrac{(x-5)^n}{n \cdot 2^n} = \sum_{n=1}^{\infty} \dfrac{(-2)^n}{n \cdot 2^n} = \sum_{n=1}^{\infty} \dfrac{(-1)^n}{n}$ which converges by the Alternating Series Test.

When $x = 7$, $\sum_{n=1}^{\infty} \dfrac{(x-5)^n}{n \cdot 2^n} = \sum_{n=1}^{\infty} \dfrac{(2)^n}{n \cdot 2^n} = \sum_{n=1}^{\infty} \dfrac{1}{n}$, the harmonic series, which diverges.

The power series $\sum_{n=1}^{\infty} \dfrac{(x-5)^n}{n \cdot 2^n}$ converges if $3 \leq x < 7$. The interval of convergence is $[3, 7)$, and the radius of convergence is $R = \dfrac{1}{2}$ (length of the interval of convergence) $= \dfrac{1}{2}(7-3) = 2$.

Practice 5: Find the interval and radius of convergence of $\sum_{n=0}^{\infty} \dfrac{n \cdot (x-3)^n}{5^n}$.

10.8 Power Series   Contemporary Calculus

A power series looks like a very long polynomial. However, a regular polynomial with a finite number of terms is defined at every value of x, but a power series may diverge for many values of the variable x. As we continue to work with power series we need to be alert to where the power series converges (and behaves like a finite polynomial) and where the power series diverges. We need to know the interval of convergence of the power series, and, typically, we use the Ratio Test to find that interval.

PROBLEMS

In problems 1 – 24, (a) find all values of x for which each given power series converges, and (b) graph the interval of convergence for the series on a number line.

1. $\sum_{n=1}^{\infty} x^n$

2. $\sum_{n=1}^{\infty} (x-3)^n$

3. $\sum_{n=1}^{\infty} (x+2)^n$

4. $\sum_{n=1}^{\infty} (x+5)^n$

5. $\sum_{n=3}^{\infty} \frac{x^n}{n}$

6. $\sum_{n=3}^{\infty} \frac{(x-2)^n}{n}$

7. $\sum_{n=1}^{\infty} \frac{(x+3)^n}{n}$

8. $\sum_{n=1}^{\infty} \frac{(x-5)^n}{n^2}$

9. $\sum_{n=1}^{\infty} \frac{(x-7)^{2n+1}}{n^2}$

10. $\sum_{n=1}^{\infty} \frac{(x+1)^{2n}}{n^3}$

11. $\sum_{n=2}^{\infty} (2x)^n$

12. $\sum_{n=2}^{\infty} (5x)^n$

13. $\sum_{n=1}^{\infty} (\frac{x}{3})^{2n+1}$

14. $\sum_{n=1}^{\infty} n(\frac{x}{4})^{2n+1}$

15. $\sum_{n=1}^{\infty} (2x-6)^n$

16. $\sum_{n=1}^{\infty} (3x+1)^n$

17. $\sum_{n=0}^{\infty} \frac{x^n}{n!}$

18. $\sum_{n=0}^{\infty} \frac{(x-5)^n}{n!}$

19. $\sum_{n=1}^{\infty} \frac{n^2 \cdot x^n}{3^n}$

20. $\sum_{n=1}^{\infty} \frac{n^5 \cdot x^n}{3^n}$

21. $\sum_{n=1}^{\infty} n! \cdot x^n$

22. $\sum_{n=1}^{\infty} n! \cdot (x+2)^n$

23. $\sum_{n=3}^{\infty} n! \cdot (x-7)^n$

24. $\sum_{n=0}^{\infty} \frac{3^n \cdot x^n}{n!}$

In problems 25 – 34, the letters "a" and "b" represent positive constants. Find all values of x for which each given power series converges.

25. $\sum_{n=1}^{\infty} (x-a)^n$

26. $\sum_{n=1}^{\infty} (x+b)^n$

27. $\sum_{n=1}^{\infty} \frac{(x-a)^n}{n}$

28. $\sum_{n=1}^{\infty} \frac{(x-a)^n}{n^2}$

29. $\sum_{n=1}^{\infty} (ax)^n$

30. $\sum_{n=1}^{\infty} (\frac{x}{a})^n$

31. $\sum_{n=1}^{\infty} (ax-b)^n$

32. $\sum_{n=1}^{\infty} (ax+b)^n$

33. A friend claimed that the interval of convergence for a power series of the form $\sum_{n=1}^{\infty} a_n \cdot (x-4)^n$ is the interval $(1, 9)$. Without checking your friend's work, how can you be certain that your friend is wrong?

34. Which of the following intervals are possible intervals of convergence for the power series in problem 33?

    $(2, 6), (0, 4), x = 0, [1, 7], (-1, 9], x = 4, [3, 5), [-4, 4), x = 3$.

35. Which of the following intervals are possible intervals of convergence for $\sum_{n=1}^{\infty} a_n \cdot (x-7)^n$?

    $(3, 10), (5, 9), x = 0, [1, 13], (-1, 15], x = 4, [3, 11), [0, 14), x = 7$.

36. Fill in each blank with a number so the resulting interval could be the interval of convergence for the power series $\sum_{n=1}^{\infty} a_n \cdot (x-3)^n$: $(0, \underline{\quad}), (\underline{\quad}, 7), [1, \underline{\quad}], (\underline{\quad}, 15], [\underline{\quad}, 11), [0, \underline{\quad}), x = \underline{\quad}$.

37. Fill in each blank with a number so the resulting interval could be the interval of convergence for the power series $\sum_{n=1}^{\infty} a_n \cdot (x-1)^n$: $(0, \underline{\quad}), (\underline{\quad}, 7), [1, \underline{\quad}], (\underline{\quad}, 5], [\underline{\quad}, 11), [0, \underline{\quad}), x = \underline{\quad}$.

In problems 38 – 45, use the patterns you noticed in the earlier problems and examples to build a power series with the given intervals of convergence. (There are many possible correct answers — find one.)

38. $(-5, 5)$ 39. $[-3, 3)$ 40. $[-2, 2]$ 41. $(0, 6)$

42. $[0, 8)$ 43. $[2, 8)$ 44. $[3, 7]$ 45. $x = 3$

In problems 46 – 59, find the interval of convergence for each series. For x in the interval of convergence, find the sum of the series as a function of x. (Hint: You know how to find the sum of a geometric series.)

46. $\sum_{n=0}^{\infty} x^n$ 47. $\sum_{n=0}^{\infty} (x-3)^n$ 48. $\sum_{n=0}^{\infty} (2x)^n$ 49. $\sum_{n=0}^{\infty} (3x)^n$

50. $\sum_{n=0}^{\infty} x^{2n}$ 51. $\sum_{n=0}^{\infty} x^{3n}$ 52. $\sum_{n=0}^{\infty} \left(\frac{x-6}{2}\right)^n$ 53. $\sum_{n=0}^{\infty} \left(\frac{x-6}{5}\right)^n$

54. $\sum_{n=0}^{\infty} \left(\frac{x}{2}\right)^n$ 55. $\sum_{n=0}^{\infty} \left(\frac{x}{5}\right)^n$ 56. $\sum_{n=0}^{\infty} \left(\frac{x}{3}\right)^{2n}$ 57. $\sum_{n=0}^{\infty} \left(\frac{x}{2}\right)^{3n}$

58. $\sum_{n=0}^{\infty} \left(\frac{1}{2}\sin(x)\right)^n$ 59. $\sum_{n=0}^{\infty} \left(\frac{1}{3}\cos(x)\right)^n$

Practice Answers

Practice 1: $c_n = \dfrac{5^n \cdot x^n}{n}$ so $c_{n+1} = \dfrac{5^{n+1} \cdot x^{n+1}}{n+1}$. Then, using the Ratio Test,

$$\left| \frac{c_{n+1}}{c_n} \right| = \left| \frac{\frac{5^{n+1} x^{n+1}}{n+1}}{\frac{5^n x^n}{n}} \right| = \left| \frac{n}{n+1} \cdot \frac{5^{n+1}}{5^n} \cdot \frac{x^{n+1}}{x^n} \right| = \left| \frac{n}{n+1} \cdot 5 \cdot x \right| \to |5x| = L.$$

Solving $|5x| < 1$, we have $-1 < 5x < 1$ or $-1/5 < x < 1/5$. The series converges for $-1/5 < x < 1/5$ and it diverges for $x < -1/5$ and for $x > 1/5$.

Finally, we need to check the two remaining values of x: the **endpoints** $x = -1/5$ and $x = 1/5$.

When $x = -1/5$, $\displaystyle\sum_{n=1}^{\infty} \frac{5^n x^n}{n} = \sum_{n=1}^{\infty} \frac{5^n(-1/5)^n}{n} = \sum_{k=1}^{\infty} \frac{(-1)^n}{n}$ which converges by the Alternating Series Test.

When $x = 1/5$, $\displaystyle\sum_{n=1}^{\infty} \frac{5^n x^n}{n} = \sum_{n=1}^{\infty} \frac{5^n(1/5)^n}{n} = \sum_{k=1}^{\infty} \frac{1}{n}$, the harmonic series, which diverges.

In summary, the power series $\displaystyle\sum_{n=1}^{\infty} \frac{5^n x^n}{n}$ converges if $-1/5 \leq x < 1/5$, if x is in the interval $[-1/5, 1/5)$.

Practice 2: The series converges at $x = -1$ and $x = 2$.

The convergence is unknown at

$x = -3$ (endpoint?), 4, -6, and 7 (endpoint?)

The series diverges at $x = -8$ and $x = 17$.

The regions of known convergence and known divergence are shown in Fig. 6.

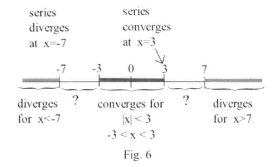

Fig. 6

Practice 3: The radius of convergence is **1/5**.

Practice 4: The series converges at $x = -2$.

The convergence is unknown at

$x = -9$ (endpoint?), 0, and -11 (endpoint?)

The series diverges at $x = 3$.

The regions of known convergence and known divergence are shown in Fig. 7.

Fig. 7

Practice 5: $c_n = \dfrac{n \cdot (x-3)^n}{5^n}$ so $c_{n+1} = \dfrac{(n+1) \cdot (x-3)^{n+1}}{5^{n+1}}$. Then, using the Ratio Test,

$$\left| \frac{c_{n+1}}{c_n} \right| = \left| \frac{\frac{(n+1) \cdot (x-3)^{n+1}}{5^{n+1}}}{\frac{n \cdot (x-3)^n}{5^n}} \right| = \left| \frac{n+1}{n} \cdot \frac{5^n}{5^{n+1}} \cdot \frac{(x-3)^{n+1}}{(x-3)^n} \right| = \left| \frac{n+1}{n} \cdot \frac{1}{5} \cdot (x-3) \right| \to \left| \frac{x-3}{5} \right| = L.$$

Solving $\left| \dfrac{x-3}{5} \right| < 1$, we have $-1 < \dfrac{x-3}{5} < 1$ so $-5 < x-3 < 8$. The series converges for $-2 < x < 8$

and it diverges for $x < -2$ and for $x > 8$. The radius of convergence is 5.

To find the interval of convergence we still need to check the endpoints $x = -2$ and $x = 8$:

When $x = -2$, $\displaystyle\sum_{n=0}^{\infty} \frac{n \cdot (x-3)^n}{5^n} = \sum_{n=1}^{\infty} \frac{n \cdot (-5)^n}{5^n} = \sum_{n=1}^{\infty} n \cdot (-1)^n$ which diverges by the nth Term Test.

When $x = 8$, $\displaystyle\sum_{n=0}^{\infty} \frac{n \cdot (x-3)^n}{5^n} = \sum_{n=1}^{\infty} \frac{n \cdot (5)^n}{5^n} = \sum_{n=1}^{\infty} n$ which diverges by the nth Term Test.

The interval of convergence is $-2 < x < 8$ or $(-2, 8)$.

Appendix: Proof of the Interval of Convergence Theorem

(i) Suppose the power series $\displaystyle\sum_{n=0}^{\infty} a_n x^n$ converges at $x = c$: $\displaystyle\sum_{n=0}^{\infty} a_n c^n$ converges.

Then the terms of the series $a_n c^n$ must approach 0, $\displaystyle\lim_{n \to \infty} a_n c^n = 0$, so there is a number N so that

if $n \geq N$, then $|a_n c^n| < 1$ and $|a_n| < \dfrac{1}{|c^n|}$ for all $n > N$.

If $|x| < |c|$, then $\displaystyle\sum_{n=0}^{\infty} |a_n x^n| = \{|a_0| + |a_1 x| + \ldots + |a_{N-1} x^{N-1}|\} + \{|a_N x^N| + |a_{N+1} x^{N+1}| + \ldots\}$.

The first piece, $|a_0| + |a_1 x| + \ldots + |a_{N-1} x^{N-1}|$, consists of a finite number of terms so it is a finite number.

The second piece, $|a_N x^N| + |a_{N+1} x^{N+1}| + \ldots$ is less than a convergent geometric series:

$$|a_N x^N| + |a_{N+1} x^{N+1}| + |a_{N+2} x^{N+2}| + |a_{N+3} x^{N+3}| + \ldots$$

$$< \frac{1}{|c^N|} |x^N| + \frac{1}{|c^{N+1}|} |x^{N+1}| + \frac{1}{|c^{N+2}|} |x^{N+2}| + \frac{1}{|c^{N+3}|} |x^{N+3}| + \ldots$$

$$= \left|\frac{x}{c}\right|^N + \left|\frac{x}{c}\right|^{N+1} + \left|\frac{x}{c}\right|^{N+2} + \left|\frac{x}{c}\right|^{N+3} + \ldots \text{ which converges since } |x| < |c| \text{ and } \left|\frac{x}{c}\right| < 1.$$

If $|x| < |c|$, then $\displaystyle\sum_{n=0}^{\infty} |a_n x^n|$ converges so $\displaystyle\sum_{n=0}^{\infty} a_n x^n$ converges.

(ii) This part follows from part (i) of the Theorem. Suppose that the power series $\sum_{n=0}^{\infty} a_n x^n$ diverges at $x = d$: $\sum_{n=0}^{\infty} a_n d^n$ diverges. If the series converges for some x_0 with $|x_0| > |d|$, we can put $c = x_0$ and conclude from part (i) that the series must converge at $x = d$ because $|c| = |x_0| > |d|$. This contradicts the fact that the series diverges at $x = d$, so the series cannot converge for any x_0 with $|x_0| > |d|$.

If $\sum_{n=0}^{\infty} a_n d^n$ diverges and $|x| > |d|$, then the power series $\sum_{n=0}^{\infty} a_n x^n$ diverges.

10.9 REPRESENTING FUNCTIONS AS POWER SERIES

Power series define functions, but how are these power series functions related to functions we know about such as $\sin(x)$, $\cos(x)$, e^x, and $\ln(x)$? How can we represent common functions as power series, and why would we want to do so? The next two sections provide partial answers to these questions. In this section we start with a function defined by a geometric series and show how we can obtain power series representations for several related functions. And we look at a few ways in which power series representations of functions are used. The next section examines a more general method for obtaining power series representations for functions.

The foundation for the examples in this section is a power series whose sum we know. The power series $\sum_{n=0}^{\infty} x^n$ is also a geometric series, with the common ratio $r = x$, and, for $|x| < 1$, we know the sum of the series is $\frac{1}{1-x}$.

Geometric Series Formula

For $|x| < 1$, $\sum_{n=0}^{\infty} x^n = 1 + x + x^2 + x^3 + x^4 + \ldots = \frac{1}{1-x}$.

One simple but powerful method of obtaining power series for related functions is to replace each "x" with a function of x.

Substitution in Power Series

Suppose $f(x)$ is defined by a power series

$$f(x) = \sum_{n=0}^{\infty} a_n x^n = a_0 + a_1 x + a_2 x^2 + a_3 x^3 + \ldots + a_n x^n + \ldots$$

that converges for $-R < x < R$.

Then $f(x^p) = \sum_{n=0}^{\infty} a_n \{x^p\}^n = a_0 + a_1 x^p + a_2 \{x^p\}^2 + a_3 \{x^p\}^3 + \ldots + a_n \{x^p\}^n + \ldots$

$$= a_0 + a_1 x^p + a_2 x^{2p} + a_3 x^{3p} + \ldots + a_n x^{np} + \ldots$$

converges for $-R < x^p < R$, and

$$f(x-c) = \sum_{n=0}^{\infty} a_n (x-c)^n = a_0 + a_1(x-c) + a_2(x-c)^2 + a_3(x-c)^3 + \ldots + a_n(x-c)^n + \ldots$$

converges for $-R < x - c < R$.

We can use this substitution method to obtain power series for some functions related to the Geometric Series Formula $\frac{1}{1-x}$.

Example 1: Find power series for (a) $\frac{1}{1-x^2}$, (b) $\frac{1}{1+x}$, and (c) $\frac{x}{1-x}$.

Solution:
(a) Substituting "x^2" for "x" in the Geometric Series Formula, we get

$$\frac{1}{1-x^2} = 1 + \{x^2\} + \{x^2\}^2 + \{x^2\}^3 + \{x^2\}^4 + \ldots = \sum_{n=0}^{\infty} (x^2)^n$$

$$= 1 + x^2 + x^4 + x^6 + x^8 + \ldots = \sum_{n=0}^{\infty} x^{2n} \quad \text{for } -1 < x < 1.$$

(b) Substituting "$-x$" for "x" in the Geometric Series Formula,

$$\frac{1}{1+x} = \frac{1}{1-(-x)} = 1 + \{-x\} + \{-x\}^2 + \{-x\}^3 + \{-x\}^4 + \ldots = \sum_{n=0}^{\infty} (-x)^n$$

$$= 1 - x + x^2 - x^3 + x^4 + \ldots = \sum_{n=0}^{\infty} (-1)^n x^n \quad \text{for } -1 < x < 1.$$

(c) We need to recognize that $\frac{x}{1-x}$ is a product, $\frac{x}{1-x} = x \cdot \frac{1}{1-x}$. Then

$$x \cdot \frac{1}{1-x} = x \{ 1 + x + x^2 + x^3 + x^4 + \ldots \}$$

$$= x + x^2 + x^3 + x^4 + x^5 + \ldots = \sum_{n=0}^{\infty} x^{n+1} \quad \text{or, equivalently,} \quad \sum_{n=1}^{\infty} x^n \quad \text{for } -1 < x < 1.$$

Practice 1: Find power series for (a) $\frac{1}{1-x^3}$, (b) $\frac{1}{1+x^2}$, and (c) $\frac{5x}{1+x}$.

One of the features of polynomials that makes them very easy to differentiate and integrate is that we can differentiate and integrate them term–by–term. The same result is true for power series.

Term-by-Term Differentiation and Integration of Power Series

Suppose $f(x)$ is defined by a power series

$$f(x) = \sum_{n=0}^{\infty} a_n x^n = a_0 + a_1 x + a_2 x^2 + a_3 x^3 + \ldots + a_n x^n + \ldots$$

that converges for $-R < x < R$.

Then,

(a) the derivative of f is given by the power series obtained by term–by–term differentiation of f:

$$f'(x) = \sum_{n=1}^{\infty} n \cdot a_n x^{n-1} = a_1 + 2a_2 x + 3a_3 x^2 + 4a_4 x^3 + \ldots + n \cdot a_n x^{n-1} + \ldots$$

(b) an antiderivative of f is given by the power series obtained by term–by–term integration of f:

$$\int f(x)\, dx = C + \sum_{n=0}^{\infty} a_n \frac{x^{n+1}}{n+1} = C + a_0 x + a_1 \frac{x^2}{2} + a_2 \frac{x^3}{3} + a_3 \frac{x^4}{4} + \ldots + a_n \frac{x^{n+1}}{n+1} + \ldots$$

The power series for the derivative and antiderivative of f converge for $-R < x < R$. (The power series for f, f' and the antiderivative of f may differ in whether or not they converge at the **endpoints** of the interval of convergence, but they all converge for $-R < x < R$.)

The proof of this result is rather long and technical and is omitted.

Like the previous substitution method, term–by–term differentiation and integration can be used to obtain power series for some functions related to the Geometric Series Formula $\frac{1}{1-x}$.

Example 2: Find power series for (a) $\ln(1-x)$, and (b) $\arctan(x)$.

Solution: These two are more challenging than the previous examples because we need to recognize that these two functions are integrals of functions whose power series we already know.

(a) $\ln(1-x) = \int \frac{-1}{1-x}\, dx = -\int \{1 + x + x^2 + x^3 + x^4 + \ldots\}\, dx$

$$= -\left\{ x + \frac{x^2}{2} + \frac{x^3}{3} + \frac{x^4}{4} + \ldots \right\} + C = C - \sum_{n=1}^{\infty} \frac{x^n}{n}.$$

We can find the value of C by using the fact that $\ln(1) = 0$:

for $x = 0$, $0 = \ln(1-0) = C - \sum_{n=1}^{\infty} \frac{0^n}{n} = C$ so $C = 0$ and

$$\ln(1-x) = -\left\{ x + \frac{x^2}{2} + \frac{x^3}{3} + \frac{x^4}{4} + \ldots \right\} = -\sum_{n=1}^{\infty} \frac{x^n}{n} \quad \text{for } -1 \le x < 1.$$

(b) $\arctan(x) = \int \frac{1}{1+x^2} dx = \int \left\{ 1 - x^2 + x^4 - x^6 + x^8 - \ldots \right\} dx$

$$= C + \left\{ x - \frac{x^3}{3} + \frac{x^5}{5} - \frac{x^7}{7} + \frac{x^9}{9} - \ldots \right\} = C + \sum_{n=0}^{\infty} (-1)^n \frac{x^{2n+1}}{2n+1}.$$

We can find the value of C by using the fact that $\arctan(0) = 0$:

for $x = 0$, $0 = \arctan(0) = C + \sum_{n=0}^{\infty} (-1)^n \frac{0^{2n+1}}{2n+1} = C$ so $C = 0$ and

$$\arctan(x) = x - \frac{x^3}{3} + \frac{x^5}{5} - \frac{x^7}{7} + \frac{x^9}{9} - \ldots = \sum_{n=0}^{\infty} (-1)^n \frac{x^{2n+1}}{2n+1} \quad \text{for } -1 \le x \le 1.$$

Practice 2: Find a power series for $\ln(1 + x)$.

Power series can also be used to help us evaluate definite integrals.

Example 3: Use the power series for $\arctan(x)$ to represent the definite integral $\int_0^{0.5} \arctan(x) \, dx$ as a numerical series. Then approximate the value of the integral by calculating the sum of the first four terms of the numerical series.

Solution: $\int_0^{0.5} \arctan(x) \, dx = \int_0^{0.5} \left\{ x - \frac{x^3}{3} + \frac{x^5}{5} - \frac{x^7}{7} + \frac{x^9}{9} - \ldots \right\} dx$

$$= \left. \frac{x^2}{2} - \frac{x^4}{4 \cdot 3} + \frac{x^6}{6 \cdot 5} - \frac{x^8}{8 \cdot 7} + \frac{x^{10}}{10 \cdot 9} - \ldots \right|_0^{0.5}$$

$$= \left\{ \frac{1}{2}(0.5)^2 - \frac{1}{12}(0.5)^4 + \frac{1}{30}(0.5)^6 - \frac{1}{56}(0.5)^8 + \frac{1}{90}(0.5)^{10} - \ldots \right\} - \{0\}.$$

The sum of the first four terms is approximately 0.120243. Since the numerical series is an alternating series, we know that the fourth partial sum, 0.120243, is within the value of the next term, $\frac{1}{90}(0.5)^{10} \approx 0.000011$, of the exact value of the sum. The exact value of the definite integral is between $0.120243 - 0.000011 = 0.120232$ and $0.120243 + 0.000011 = 0.120254$.

Practice 3: Use the power series for $x^2 \cdot \ln(1+x)$ to represent the definite integral $\int_0^{0.2} x^2 \cdot \ln(1+x) \, dx$ as a numerical series. Then approximate the value of the integral by calculating the sum of the first three terms of the numerical series.

All of the power series used in this section have followed from the Geometric Series Formula, and their main purpose here was to illustrate some uses of substitution and term–by–term differentiation and integration to obtain power series for related functions. Many functions, however, are not related to a geometric series, and the next section discusses a method for representing them using power series. Once we can represent these new functions using power series, we can then use substitution and term–by–term differentiation and integration to obtain power series for functions related to them.

The following table collects some of the power series representations we have obtained in this section.

Table of Series Based on $\dfrac{1}{1-x} = \sum\limits_{n=0}^{\infty} x^n$

$$\frac{1}{1-x} = 1 + x + x^2 + x^3 + x^4 + \ldots = \sum_{n=0}^{\infty} x^n \quad \text{with interval of convergence } (-1, 1).$$

$$\frac{1}{1+x} = 1 - x + x^2 - x^3 + x^4 + \ldots = \sum_{n=0}^{\infty} (-1)^n x^n = \frac{1}{1-(-x)}$$

$$\frac{1}{1-x^2} = 1 + x^2 + x^4 + x^6 + x^8 + \ldots = \sum_{n=0}^{\infty} x^{2n} = \frac{1}{1-(x^2)}$$

$$\frac{1}{1+x^2} = 1 - x^2 + x^4 - x^6 + x^8 - \ldots = \sum_{n=0}^{\infty} (-1)^n x^{2n} = \frac{1}{1-(-x^2)}$$

$$\frac{1}{1-x^3} = 1 + x^3 + x^6 + x^9 + x^{12} + \ldots = \sum_{n=0}^{\infty} x^{3n} = \frac{1}{1-(x^3)}$$

$$\ln(1-x) = -\left\{ x + \frac{x^2}{2} + \frac{x^3}{3} + \frac{x^4}{4} + \ldots \right\} = -\sum_{n=1}^{\infty} \frac{x^n}{n} = \int \frac{-1}{1-x} \, dx$$

$$\ln(1+x) = x - \frac{x^2}{2} + \frac{x^3}{3} - \frac{x^4}{4} + \ldots = \sum_{n=1}^{\infty} (-1)^{n+1} \frac{x^n}{n} = \int \frac{1}{1+x} \, dx$$

$$\arctan(x) = x - \frac{x^3}{3} + \frac{x^5}{5} - \frac{x^7}{7} + \frac{x^9}{9} - \ldots = \sum_{n=0}^{\infty} (-1)^n \frac{x^{2n+1}}{2n+1} = \int \frac{1}{1+x^2}\,dx$$

$$\frac{1}{(1-x)^2} = 1 + 2x + 3x^2 + 4x^3 + 5x^4 + \ldots = \sum_{n=1}^{\infty} n \cdot x^{n-1} = D\left(\frac{1}{1-x}\right)$$

$$\frac{1}{(1+x)^2} = 1 - 2x + 3x^2 - 4x^3 + 5x^4 - \ldots = \sum_{n=1}^{\infty} (-1)^n n \cdot x^{n-1} = D\left(\frac{-1}{1+x}\right)$$

Fig. 1 shows the graphs of arctan(x) and the first few polynomials x, $x - \frac{x^3}{3}$, $x - \frac{x^3}{3} + \frac{x^5}{5}$ that approximate arctan(x). This type of approximation will be discussed a little in Section 10.10 and a lot in Section 10.11.

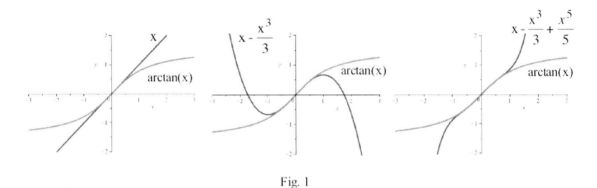

Fig. 1

PROBLEMS

In problems 1 – 14, use the substitution method and a known power series to find power series for the given functions.

1. $\dfrac{1}{1-x^4}$

2. $\dfrac{1}{1-x^5}$

3. $\dfrac{1}{1+x^4}$

4. $\dfrac{1}{1+x^5}$

5. $\dfrac{1}{5+x} = \dfrac{1}{5} \cdot \dfrac{1}{1+(x/5)}$

6. $\dfrac{1}{3-x} = \dfrac{1}{3} \cdot \dfrac{1}{1-(x/3)}$

7. $\dfrac{x^2}{1+x^3}$

8. $\dfrac{x}{1+x^4}$

9. $\ln(1+x^2)$

10. $\ln(1+x^3)$

11. $\arctan(x^2)$

12. $\arctan(x^3)$

13. $\dfrac{1}{(1-x^2)^2}$

14. $\dfrac{1}{(1+x^2)^2}$

10.9   Representing Functions as Power Series   Contemporary Calculus   7

In problems 15–21, represent each definite integral as a numerical series. Calculate the sum of the first three terms for each series.

15. $\int_0^{0.5} \dfrac{1}{1-x^3}\,dx$

16. $\int_0^{0.5} \dfrac{1}{1+x^3}\,dx$

17. $\int_0^{0.6} \ln(1+x)\,dx$

18. $\int_0^{0.5} x^2 \cdot \arctan(x)\,dx$

19. $\int_0^{0.3} \dfrac{1}{(1-x)^2}\,dx$

20. $\int_0^{0.7} \dfrac{x^3}{(1-x)^2}\,dx$

In problems 21 – 27, use the Table of Series to help represent each function as a power series. Then calculate each limit.

21. $\lim_{x \to 0} \dfrac{\arctan(x)}{x}$

22. $\lim_{x \to 0} \dfrac{\ln(1-x)}{2x}$

23. $\lim_{x \to 0} \dfrac{\ln(1+x)}{2x}$

24. $\lim_{x \to 0} \dfrac{\arctan(x^2)}{x}$

25. $\lim_{x \to 0} \dfrac{\ln(1-x^2)}{3x}$

26. $\lim_{x \to 0} \dfrac{\ln(1+x^2)}{3x}$

In problems 27 – 32, use the Table of Series or the substitution method to determine a power series for each function and then determine the interval of convergence of each power series.

27. $\dfrac{1}{1+x}$

28. $\dfrac{1}{1-x^2}$

29. $\ln(1-x)$

30. $\ln(1+x)$

31. $\arctan(x)$

32. $\arctan(x^2)$

The series given below for $\sin(x)$ and e^x are derived in Section 10.10. Use these given series and the methods of this section to answer problems 33 – 42.

$$\sin(x) = x - \dfrac{x^3}{3!} + \dfrac{x^5}{5!} - \dfrac{x^7}{7!} + \ldots = \sum_{k=0}^{\infty} (-1)^k \dfrac{x^{2k+1}}{(2k+1)!}, \quad e^x = 1 + x + \dfrac{x^2}{2!} + \dfrac{x^3}{3!} + \dfrac{x^4}{4!} + \ldots = \sum_{k=0}^{\infty} \dfrac{x^k}{k!}$$

33. Find a power series for $\sin(x^2)$.

34. Find a power series for $\sin(2x)$.

35. Find a power series for $e^{(-x^2)}$.

36. Find a power series for $e^{(2x)}$.

37. Find a power series for $\cos(x)$.

38. Find a power series for $\cos(x^2)$.

39. Represent the integral as a numerical series: $\int_0^1 \sin(x^2)\,dx$

40. Represent the integral as a numerical series: $\int_0^1 e^{(-x^2)}\,dx$

41. $\lim_{x \to 0} \dfrac{\sin(x)}{x}$

42. $\lim_{x \to 0} \dfrac{\sin(x) - x}{x^3}$

Practice Answers

Practice 1: Geometric Series Formula: $\dfrac{1}{1-x} = \sum_{n=0}^{\infty} x^n$ for $|x| < 1$.

(a) Replacing "x" with "x^3" we have $\dfrac{1}{1-x^3} = \sum_{n=0}^{\infty} x^{3n}$ for $|x^3| < 1$ or $|x| < 1$.

(b) Replacing "x" with "$-x^2$" we have $\dfrac{1}{1-(-x^2)} = \dfrac{1}{1+x^2} = \sum_{n=0}^{\infty}(-x^2)^n = \sum_{n=0}^{\infty}(-1)^n x^{2n}$

for $|-x| < 1$ or $|x| < 1$.

(c) Using the result of part (b), $\dfrac{5x}{1+x} = 5x \dfrac{1}{1+x} = 5x \cdot \sum_{n=0}^{\infty}(-1)^n x^n = 5 \cdot \sum_{n=0}^{\infty}(-1)^n x^{n+1}$

for $|-x| < 1$ or $|x| < 1$.

Practice 2: $\ln(1+x) = \int \dfrac{1}{1+x}\,dx = \int \sum_{n=0}^{\infty}(-1)^n x^n\, dx = \int 1 - x + x^2 - x^3 + x^4 - \ldots\, dx$

$= x - \dfrac{x^2}{2} + \dfrac{x^3}{3} - \dfrac{x^4}{4} + \dfrac{x^5}{5} - \ldots + C$. Putting $x=0$, we get $C=0$. Then

$\ln(1+x) = \sum_{n=0}^{\infty}(-1)^n \dfrac{x^{n+1}}{n+1}$ or, equivalently, $\sum_{n=1}^{\infty}(-1)^{n+1} \dfrac{x^n}{n}$

Practice 3: Using the result of Practice 2,

$x^2 \cdot \ln(1+x) = x^2 \cdot \sum_{n=1}^{\infty}(-1)^{n+1}\dfrac{x^n}{n} = \sum_{n=1}^{\infty}(-1)^{n+1}\dfrac{x^{n+2}}{n}$. Then

$\int x^2 \cdot \ln(1+x)\,dx = \int \sum_{n=1}^{\infty}(-1)^{n+1}\dfrac{x^{n+2}}{n}\,dx = \sum_{n=1}^{\infty}\dfrac{(-1)^{n+1}}{n}\dfrac{x^{n+3}}{n+3}\Big|_0^{0.2}$

$= \left\{ \dfrac{1}{4}(0.2)^4 - \dfrac{1}{10}(0.2)^5 + \dfrac{1}{18}(0.2)^6 - \dfrac{1}{28}(0.2)^7 + \ldots \right\} - \{0\}$.

$s_3 = \dfrac{1}{4}(0.2)^4 - \dfrac{1}{10}(0.2)^5 + \dfrac{1}{18}(0.2)^6 \approx 0.0003716$ with an error less than $|a_4| = \dfrac{1}{28}(0.2)^7 \approx 4.57 \cdot 10^{-7}$

Appendix: Partial Sums of Power Series using MAPLE

MAPLE commands for $\sum_{n=1}^{\infty}\dfrac{100(0.7)^n}{n}$, $\sum_{n=1}^{\infty}\dfrac{100(0.7)^n}{n^2}$, $\sum_{n=0}^{\infty}\dfrac{100(0.7)^n}{n!}$, $\sum_{n=0}^{\infty}(-1)^n \dfrac{100(0.7)^n}{1+\sqrt{n}}$

```
> sum((.7)^n/n , n=1..100) ;   (then press ENTER key)
> sum((.7)^n/n^2 , n=1..100) ;
> sum((.7)^n/n! , n=0..100) ;
> sum((-1)^n*(.7)^n/(1+sqrt(n)) , n=0..100) ;
```

10.10 TAYLOR AND MACLAURIN SERIES

This section discusses a method for representing a variety of functions as power series, and power series representations are derived for $\sin(x)$, $\cos(x)$, e^x, and several functions related to them. These power series are used to evaluate the functions and limits and to approximate definite integrals.

We start with an examination of how to determine the formula for a polynomial from information about the polynomial when $x = 0$, and then this process is extended to determine a series representation for a function from information about the function when $x = 0$.

Polynomials

Polynomials are among the easiest functions to work with, and they have a variety of "nice" properties including the following:

> The values of $P(x)$ and its derivatives at $x = 0$ completely determine the formula for $P(x)$.

If the values of $P(x)$ and all of its derivatives at $x = 0$ are known, then we can use those values to find a formula for $P(x)$.

Example 1: Suppose $P(x)$ is a cubic polynomial with $P(0) = 7$, $P\,'(0) = 5$, $P\,''(0) = 16$, and $P\,'''(0) = 18$. (Since $P(x)$ is a cubic, its higher derivatives are all 0.) Find a formula for $P(x)$.

Solution: Since $P(x)$ is a cubic polynomial, then $P(x) = a_0 + a_1 x + a_2 x^2 + a_3 x^3$ for some numbers a_0, a_1, a_2, and a_3. We want to find the values of those numbers, and we can do so by substituting 0 for x in the expressions for $P, P\,', P\,''$, and $P\,'''$ and using the given information.

$$7 = P(0) = a_0 + a_1 \cdot 0 + a_2 \cdot 0^2 + a_3 \cdot 0^3 = a_0 \text{ so } a_0 = 7.$$

$$P\,'(x) = a_1 + 2a_2 x + 3a_3 x^2. \quad 5 = P\,'(0) = a_1 + 2a_2 \cdot 0 + 3a_3 \cdot 0^2 = a_1 \text{ so } a_1 = 5.$$

$$P\,''(x) = 2a_2 + 6a_3 x. \quad 16 = P\,''(0) = 2a_2 + 6a_3 \cdot 0 = 2a_2 \text{ so } a_2 = 16/2 = 8.$$

$$P\,'''(x) = 6a_3. \quad 18 = P\,''(0) = 6a_3 \text{ so } a_3 = 18/6 = 3.$$

$P(x) = 7 + 5x + 8x^2 + 3x^3$. You should verify that this cubic polynomial and its derivatives have the values specified in the problem.

Practice 1: Suppose $P(x)$ is a 4th degree polynomial with $P(0) = -3$, $P\,'(0) = 4$, $P\,''(0) = 10$, $P\,'''(0) = 12$, and $P^{(4)}(0) = 24$. (Since $P(x)$ is a 4th degree polynomial, the higher derivatives are all 0.) Find a formula for $P(x)$.

For polynomials, the n_{th} derivative evaluated at $x = 0$ is $P^{(n)}(0) = (n)(n-1)(n-2)\ldots(2)(1)\, a_n = n! \cdot a_n$, so the coefficient a_n of the nth term of the polynomial is $a_n = P^{(n)}(0)/n!$.

Series

In many important ways power series behave like polynomials, very big polynomials, and this is one of those ways. The next result says that if a function can be represented by a power series, then the coefficients of the power series just depend on the values of the derivatives of the function evaluated at 0.

Maclaurin Series for f(x)

If a function $f(x)$ has a power series representation $f(x) = \sum_{n=0}^{\infty} a_n x^n$ for $|x| < R$

then the coefficients are given by $a_n = \dfrac{f^{(n)}(0)}{n!}$.

The **Maclaurin Series** for $f(x)$ is

$$f(x) = \sum_{n=0}^{\infty} \frac{f^{(n)}(0)}{n!} x^n = f(0) + f'(0)\cdot x + \frac{f''(0)}{2!}\cdot x^2 + \frac{f'''(0)}{3!}\cdot x^3 + \ldots + \frac{f^{(n)}(0)}{n!}\cdot x^n + \ldots$$

Proof: Suppose $f(x) = \sum_{n=0}^{\infty} a_n x^n = a_0 + a_1 x + a_2 x^2 + a_3 x^3 + \ldots + a_n x^n + \ldots$ for $|x| < R$.

Then $f(0) = a_0 + a_1 \cdot 0 + a_2 \cdot 0^2 + a_3 \cdot 0^3 + \ldots + a_n \cdot 0^n + \ldots = a_0$ so $a_0 = f(0) = \dfrac{f^{(0)}(0)}{0!}$.

(We are using the conventions that $f^{(0)}(x) = f(x)$ and that $0! = 1$.)

$f'(x) = a_1 + 2a_2 x + 3a_3 x^2 + \ldots + n a_n x^{n-1} + \ldots$

so $f'(0) = a_1 + 2a_2 \cdot 0 + 3a_3 \cdot 0^2 + \ldots + n a_n \cdot 0^{n-1} + \ldots = a_1$ and $a_1 = \dfrac{f'(0)}{1!}$.

$f''(x) = 2a_2 + 2\cdot 3 a_3 x + \ldots + (n-1)\cdot n \cdot a_n x^{n-2} + \ldots$

so $f''(0) = 2a_2 + 2\cdot 3 a_3 \cdot 0 + \ldots + (n-1)\cdot n \cdot a_n \cdot 0^{n-2} + \ldots = 2a_2$ and $a_2 = \dfrac{f''(0)}{2} = \dfrac{f''(0)}{2!}$.

$f'''(x) = 2\cdot 3 a_3 + \ldots + (n-2)\cdot(n-1)\cdot n \cdot a_n x^{n-3} + \ldots$

so $f'''(0) = 2\cdot 3 a_3 + \ldots + (n-2)\cdot(n-1)\cdot n \cdot a_n \cdot 0^{n-3} + \ldots = 2\cdot 3 a_3$ and $a_3 = \dfrac{f'''(0)}{2\cdot 3} = \dfrac{f'''(0)}{3!}$.

In general, $f^{(n)}(x) = 1\cdot 2 \cdot 3 \cdot \ldots \cdot (n-1)\cdot n \, a_n + \{\text{terms still containing powers of } x\}$

so $f^{(n)}(0) = 1\cdot 2 \cdot 3 \cdot \ldots \cdot (n-1)\cdot n \, a_n + \{0\} = n! \, a_n$ and $a_n = \dfrac{f^{(n)}(0)}{n!}$.

A similar result, and proof, is also true for a "shifted" power series, a power series centered at some value c. Such shifted series are called Taylor series.

Taylor Series for f(x) centered at c

If a function $f(x)$ has a power series representation $f(x) = \sum_{n=0}^{\infty} a_n(x-c)^n$ for $|x-c| < R$

then the coefficients are given by $a_n = \dfrac{f^{(n)}(c)}{n!}$.

The **Taylor Series** for $f(x)$ at c is

$$f(x) = \sum_{n=0}^{\infty} \frac{f^{(n)}(c)}{n!}(x-c)^n = f(c) + f'(c)\cdot(x-c) + \frac{f''(c)}{2!}\cdot(x-c)^2 + \frac{f'''(c)}{3!}\cdot(x-c)^3 + \ldots + \frac{f^{(n)}(c)}{n!}\cdot(x-c)^n + \ldots$$

The proof is very similar to the proof for Maclaurin series and is not included here.

A Maclaurin series is a Taylor series centered at $c = 0$, and Maclaurin series are a special case of Taylor series.

Note: These statements for Maclaurin series and Taylor series do not say that every function is or can be written as a power series. However, if a function is a power series, then its coefficients must follow the given pattern. Fortunately, most of the important functions such as $\sin(x)$, $\cos(x)$, e^x, and $\ln(x)$ can be written as power series.

You should notice that the first term of the Taylor series is simply the value of the function f at the point $x = c$: it provides the best constant function approximation of f near $x = c$. The sum of the first two terms of the Taylor series pattern for a function, $f(c) + f'(c)\cdot(x-c)$, is the formula for the tangent line to f at $x = c$ and is the linear approximation of $f(x)$ near $x = c$ that we first examined in Chapter 2. The Taylor series formula extends these approximations to higher degree polynomials, and the partial sums of the Taylor series provide higher degree polynomial approximations of f near $x = c$.

Taylor series and Maclaurin series were first discovered by the Scottish mathematician/astronomer James Gregory (1638–1675), but the results were not published until after his death. The English mathematician Brook Taylor (1685–1731) independently rediscovered these results and included them in a book in 1715. The Scottish mathematician/engineer Colin Maclaurin (1698–1746) quoted Taylor's work in his *Treatise on Fluxions* published in 1742. Maclaurin's book was widely read, and the Taylor series centered at $c = 0$ became known as Maclaurin series.

Example 2: Find the Maclaurin series for $f(x) = \sin(x)$ and the radius of convergence of the series.

Solution: $f(x) = \sin(x)$ so $f(0) = \sin(0)$ and $a_0 = f(0) = 0$.

$f'(x) = \cos(x)$ so $f'(0) = \cos(0) = 1$ and $a_1 = f'(0) = 1$.

$f''(x) = -\sin(x)$ so $f''(0) = -\sin(0) = 0$ and $a_2 = \dfrac{f''(0)}{2!} = 0$.

$f'''(x) = -\cos(x)$ so $f'''(0) = -\cos(0) = -1$ and $a_3 = \dfrac{f'''(0)}{3!} = \dfrac{-1}{3!}$.

$f^{(4)}(x) = \sin(x)$ and the pattern repeats:

$a_4 = 0, a_5 = \dfrac{1}{5!}, a_6 = 0, a_7 = \dfrac{-1}{7!}, a_8 = 0, a_9 = \dfrac{1}{9!}, \ldots$.

$$\boxed{\sin(x) = x - \frac{x^3}{3!} + \frac{x^5}{5!} - \frac{x^7}{7!} + \frac{x^9}{9!} - \frac{x^{11}}{11!} + \ldots = \sum_{n=0}^{\infty} (-1)^n \frac{x^{2n+1}}{(2n+1)!}}$$

Notice that the Maclaurin series for $\sin(x)$ alternates and contains only odd powers of x.

We use the Ratio Test to find the radius of convergence. Let $c_n = (-1)^n \dfrac{x^{2n+1}}{(2n+1)!}$. Then

$$c_{n+1} = (-1)^{n+1} \frac{x^{2(n+1)+1}}{(2(n+1)+1)!} = (-1)^{n+1} \frac{x^{2n+3}}{(2n+3)!} \quad \text{so}$$

$$\left| \frac{c_{n+1}}{c_n} \right| = \left| \frac{(-1)^{n+1} \dfrac{x^{2n+3}}{(2n+3)!}}{(-1)^n \dfrac{x^{2n+1}}{(2n+1)!}} \right| = \left| \frac{x^{2n+3}}{x^{2n+1}} \frac{(2n+1)!}{(2n+3)!} \right| = \left| x^2 \frac{1}{(2n+2)(2n+3)} \right| \to 0 < 1$$

for every value of x.

The radius of convergence is $R = \infty$, and the interval of convergence is $(-\infty, \infty)$.

The Maclaurin series for $\sin(x)$ converges for every value of x.

Fig. 1 shows the graphs of $\sin(x)$ and the first few approximating polynomials x, $x - \dfrac{x^3}{3!}$, and $x - \dfrac{x^3}{3!} + \dfrac{x^5}{5!}$ for $-\pi \leq x \leq \pi$.

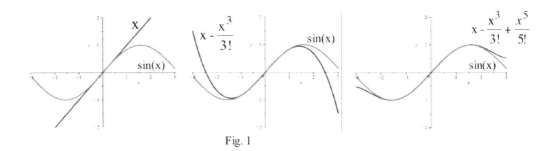

Fig. 1

By focusing our attention near $x = 0$, Fig. 1 shows the "goodness" of the Taylor polynomial fit to the function $f(x) = \sin(x)$. However, Fig. 2 shows that if x is not close to 0 then the values of the Taylor polynomials are far from the values of $f(x) = \sin(x)$. Typically the Taylor polynomials of a function are closest to the function when x is close to the number at which the series was centered, the value of c.

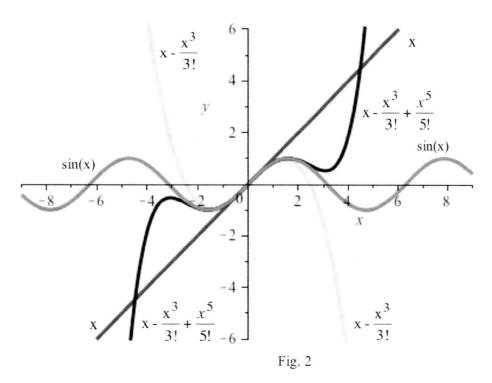

Fig. 2

Practice 2: Find the Maclaurin series for $f(x) = \cos(x)$ and the radius of convergence of the series. (Suggestion: Use the Term–by–Term Differentiation result of Section 10.9 .)

Once we have power series representations for $\sin(x)$ and $\cos(x)$, we can use the methods of Section 10.9 and the known series to approximate values of sine and cosine, determine power series representations of related functions, calculate limits, and approximate definite integrals.

Example 3: Use the series $\sin(x) = x - \frac{x^3}{3!} + \frac{x^5}{5!} - \frac{x^7}{7!} + \frac{x^9}{9!} - \frac{x^{11}}{11!} + \ldots$ to represent $\sin(0.5)$ as a numerical series. Approximate the value of $\sin(0.5)$ by calculating the partial sum of the first three non–zero terms and give a bound on the "error" between this approximation and the exact value of $\sin(0.5)$.

Solution: $\sin(0.5) = (0.5) - \frac{(0.5)^3}{3!} + \frac{(0.5)^5}{5!} - \frac{(0.5)^7}{7!} + \frac{(0.5)^9}{9!} - \frac{(0.5)^{11}}{11!} + \ldots$.

$\sin(0.5) \approx (0.5) - \frac{(0.5)^3}{3!} + \frac{(0.5)^5}{5!} = \frac{1}{2} - \frac{1}{48} + \frac{1}{3840} \approx 0.479427083333$.

Since this is an alternating series, the difference between the approximation and the exact value is less than the next term in the alternating series: "error" $< \dfrac{(0.5)^7}{7!} = \dfrac{1}{645120} \approx 0.00000155$.

If we use the sum of the first four nonzero terms to approximate the value of sin(0.5), then the "error" of the approximation is less than $\dfrac{(0.5)^9}{9!} = \dfrac{1}{185794560} \approx 5.4 \times 10^{-9}$.

We were able to obtain a bound for the error in the approximation of sin(0.5) because we were dealing with an alternating series, a type of series for which we have an error bound. However, many power series are not alternating series. In Section 10.11 we discuss a general error bound for Taylor series.

Practice 3: Use the sum of the first two nonzero terms of the Maclaurin series for cos(x) to approximate the value of cos(0.2). Give a bound on the "error" between this approximation and the exact value of cos(0.2).

Calculator Note: When you press the buttons on a calculator to evaluate sin(0.5) or cos(0.2), the calculator does not look up the answer in a table. Instead, the calculator is programmed with series representations for sine and cosine and other functions, and it calculates a partial sum of the appropriate series to obtain a numerical answer. It adds enough terms so that the 8 or 9 digits shown on the display are (usually) correct. In Section 10.11 we examine these methods in more detail and consider how to determine the number of terms needed in the partial sum to achieve the desired number of accurate digits in the answer.

Example 4: Represent $\sin(x^3)$ and $\int \sin(x^3)\, dx$ as power series. Then use the first three nonzero terms to approximate the value of $\int_0^1 \sin(x^3)\, dx$ and obtain a bound on the "error" of this approximation.

Solution: $\sin(x) = x - \dfrac{x^3}{3!} + \dfrac{x^5}{5!} - \dfrac{x^7}{7!} + \dfrac{x^9}{9!} - \dfrac{x^{11}}{11!} + \ldots$ so

$$\sin(x^3) = (x^3) - \dfrac{(x^3)^3}{3!} + \dfrac{(x^3)^5}{5!} - \dfrac{(x^3)^7}{7!} \ldots = x^3 - \dfrac{x^9}{3!} + \dfrac{x^{15}}{5!} - \dfrac{x^{21}}{7!} \ldots \, .$$

$$\int_0^1 \sin(x^3)\, dx = \int_0^1 \left\{ x^3 - \dfrac{x^9}{3!} + \dfrac{x^{15}}{5!} - \dfrac{x^{21}}{7!} \ldots \right\} dx = \left. \dfrac{x^4}{4} - \dfrac{x^{10}}{10 \cdot 3!} + \dfrac{x^{16}}{16 \cdot 5!} - \dfrac{x^{22}}{22 \cdot 7!} + \ldots \right|_0^1$$

$$= \left\{ \dfrac{1}{4} - \dfrac{1}{10 \cdot 3!} + \dfrac{1}{16 \cdot 5!} - \dfrac{1}{22 \cdot 7!} + \ldots \right\} - \{ 0 \}.$$

$$\frac{1}{4} - \frac{1}{10 \cdot 3!} + \frac{1}{16 \cdot 5!} \approx 0.2338542 \text{ and } \frac{1}{22 \cdot 7!} = \frac{1}{110880} \approx 0.0000090 \text{ so}$$

$$\int_0^1 \sin(x^3)\, dx \approx 0.2338542$$ and this approximation is within 0.0000090 of the exact value.

If we took just one more term, $\int_0^1 \sin(x^3)\, dx \approx \frac{1}{4} - \frac{1}{10 \cdot 3!} + \frac{1}{16 \cdot 5!} - \frac{1}{22 \cdot 7!} \approx 0.233845515$

is within $\frac{1}{28 \cdot 9!} \approx 0.000000098$ of the exact value of the integral.

Practice 4: Represent $x \cdot \cos(x^3)$ and $\int x \cdot \cos(x^3)\, dx$ as power series. Then use the first two nonzero terms to approximate the value of $\int_0^{1/2} x \cdot \cos(x^3)\, dx$ and obtain a bound on the "error" of this approximation.

Graphically

Each partial sum of the series $\sin(x) = x - \frac{x^3}{3!} + \frac{x^5}{5!} - \frac{x^7}{7!} + \frac{x^9}{9!} - \frac{x^{11}}{11!} + \ldots$ contains a finite number of terms and is simply a polynomial:

$$P_1(x) = x$$

$$P_3(x) = x - \frac{x^3}{3!} = x - \frac{1}{6} x^3$$

$$P_5(x) = x - \frac{x^3}{3!} + \frac{x^5}{5!} = x - \frac{1}{6} x^3 + \frac{1}{120} x^5, \ldots$$

Fig. 1 showed the graphs of $\sin(x)$ and $P_1(x), P_3(x)$, and $P_5(x)$. As you saw, all of these polynomials are "good" approximations of $\sin(x)$ when x is very close to 0. The higher degree polynomials $P_n(x)$ provide "good" approximations of $\sin(x)$ over larger intervals.

Power Series for e^x

Example 5: Find the Maclaurin series for $f(x) = e^x$ and the radius of convergence of the series.

Solution: This is a very important series.

$f(x) = e^x$ so $f(0) = e^0 = 1$ and $a_0 = f(0) = 1$.

$f'(x) = e^x$ so $f'(0) = e^0 = 1$ and $a_1 = f'(0) = 1$.

$f''(x) = e^x$ so $f''(0) = e^0 = 1$ and $a_2 = \dfrac{f''(0)}{2!} = \dfrac{1}{2!}$.

For every value of n, $f^{(n)}(x) = e^x$ so $f^{(n)}(0) = e^0 = 1$ and $a_n = \dfrac{f''(0)}{n!} = \dfrac{1}{n!}$. Then

$$e^x = 1 + x + \frac{x^2}{2!} + \frac{x^3}{3!} + \frac{x^4}{4!} + \frac{x^5}{5!} + \ldots = \sum_{n=0}^{\infty} \frac{x^n}{n!} .$$

We can use the Ratio Test to find the radius of convergence. $c_n = \dfrac{x^n}{n!}$ so $c_{n+1} = \dfrac{x^{n+1}}{(n+1)!}$.

$\left| \dfrac{c_{n+1}}{c_n} \right| = \left| \dfrac{\frac{x^{n+1}}{(n+1)!}}{\frac{x^n}{n!}} \right| = \left| \dfrac{x^{n+1}}{x^n} \dfrac{n!}{(n+1)!} \right| = \left| x \cdot \dfrac{1}{n+1} \right| \to 0 < 1$ for every value of x.

The radius of convergence is $R = \infty$, and the interval of convergence is $(-\infty, \infty)$. The Maclaurin series for e^x converges for every value of x.

Practice 5: Evaluate the partial sums of the first six terms of the numerical series for $e = e^1$ and $\dfrac{1}{\sqrt{e}} = e^{-1/2}$ and compare these partial sums with the values your calculator gives.

(Note: The numerical series for e^1 is not an alternating series so we do not have a bound for the approximation yet. We will in the next section.)

Fig. 3 shows the graphs of e^x and the approximating polynomials $1 + x$, $1 + x + \dfrac{x^2}{2!}$, and $1 + x + \dfrac{x^2}{2!} + \dfrac{x^3}{3!}$ for values of near 0.

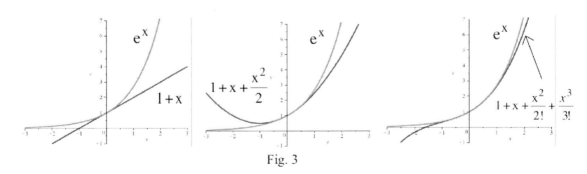

Fig. 3

The following series converge for all values of x in the interval I:

$$\sin(x) = x - \frac{x^3}{3!} + \frac{x^5}{5!} - \frac{x^7}{7!} + \frac{x^9}{9!} - \frac{x^{11}}{11!} + \ldots = \sum_{n=0}^{\infty} (-1)^n \frac{x^{2n+1}}{(2n+1)!} \qquad I = (-\infty, \infty).$$

$$\cos(x) = 1 - \frac{x^2}{2!} + \frac{x^4}{4!} - \frac{x^6}{6!} + \frac{x^8}{8!} - \frac{x^{10}}{10!} + \ldots = \sum_{n=0}^{\infty} (-1)^n \frac{x^{2n}}{(2n)!} \qquad I = (-\infty, \infty).$$

$$e^x = 1 + x + \frac{x^2}{2!} + \frac{x^3}{3!} + \frac{x^4}{4!} + \frac{x^5}{5!} + \ldots = \sum_{n=0}^{\infty} \frac{x^n}{n!} \qquad I = (-\infty, \infty).$$

$$\ln(x) = (x-1) - \frac{1}{2}(x-1)^2 + \frac{1}{3}(x-1)^3 - \frac{1}{4}(x-1)^4 + \ldots = \sum_{n=1}^{\infty} (-1)^{n+1} \frac{(x-1)^n}{n} \qquad I = (0, 2].$$

Typically, these series converge very quickly to the value of the functions when x is close to 0 (or when x is close to 1 for ln(x)), but the convergence can be rather slow when x is far from 0. For example, the first 2 terms of the Taylor series for sine approximate sin(0.1) correctly to 6 decimal places, but 11 terms are needed to approximate sin(5) with the same accuracy.

Multiplying Power Series

We can add and subtract power series term–by–term, and we have already multiplied power series by single terms such as x and x^2, but occasionally it is useful to multiply a power series by another power series. The method for multiplying series is the same method we use to multiply a polynomial by another polynomial, but it becomes very tedious to get more than the first few terms of the resulting product.

Example 6: Find the first 5 nonzero terms of

$$\frac{1}{1-x} \cdot \sin(x) = (1 + x + x^2 + x^3 + \ldots) \cdot \left(x - \frac{x^3}{6} + \frac{x^5}{120} - \ldots\right).$$

10.10   Taylor and Maclaurin Series   Contemporary Calculus   10

Solution: 1   + x   + x^2 + x^3 + x^4 + x^5 + ...

times   x $-\dfrac{x^3}{6}$ $+\dfrac{x^5}{120}$ – ...

──

                x   + x^2 + x^3 + x^4 + x^5 + ...   (from multiplying by x)

                            $-\dfrac{1}{6}x^3$ $-\dfrac{1}{6}x^4$ $-\dfrac{1}{6}x^5$ + ...   (from multiplying by $-x^3/6$)

                                                        $+\dfrac{1}{120}x^5$ + ...   (from multiplying by $x^5/120$)

──

=   x   + x^2 + $\dfrac{5}{6}x^3$ + $\dfrac{5}{6}x^4$ + $\dfrac{101}{120}x^5$ + ...   (from adding previous terms)

Practice 6:   Find the first 3 nonzero terms of

$$e^x \cdot \sin(x) = \left(1 + x + \frac{x^2}{2} + \frac{x^3}{6} + ...\right) \cdot \left(x - \frac{x^3}{6} + \frac{x^5}{120} - ...\right).$$

It is also possible to divide one power series by another power series using a procedure similar to "long division" of a polynomial by a polynomial, but we will not discuss that algorithm.

PROBLEMS

1. Find a formula for a polynomial P of degree 2 such that P(0) = 7, P'(0) = –5, and P''(0) = 8.

2. Find a formula for a polynomial P of degree 3 such that P(0) = –1, P'(0) = 2, P''(0) = –5, and P'''(0) = 12.

3. Find a formula for a polynomial P of degree 2 such that P(3) = –2, P'(3) = 5, and P''(3) = 4.

4. Find a formula for a polynomial P of degree 2 such that P(1) = –2, P'(1) = 5, and P''(1) = 4.

In problems 5 – 8, calculate the first several terms of the Maclaurin series for the given functions and compare with the series representations we found in Section 10.9 . (The series should be the same.)

5. ln(1 + x) to the x^4 term   6. ln(1 – x) to the x^4 term

7. arctan(x) to the x^3 term   8. 1/(1 – x) to the x^4 term

In problems 9 – 12, calculate the first several terms of the Maclaurin series for the given functions.

9. cos(x) to the x^6 term   10. tan(x) to the x^5 term

11. sec(x) to the x^4 term   12. e^{3x} to the x^4 term

10.10   Taylor and Maclaurin Series   Contemporary Calculus

In problems 13 - 18, calculate the first several terms of the Taylor series for the given functions at the given point c.

13. $\ln(x)$ for $c = 1$

14. $\sin(x)$ for $c = \pi$

15. $\sin(x)$ for $c = \pi/2$

16. $\sqrt{x}$ for $c = 1$

17. $\sqrt{x}$ for $c = 9$

In problems 18 – 21, use the first three nonzero terms of the Maclaurin series for each function to approximate the numerical values. Then compare the Maclaurin series approximation with the value your calculator gives.

18. $\sin(0.1)$, $\sin(0.2)$, $\sin(0.5)$, $\sin(1)$, and $\sin(2)$

19. $\cos(0.1)$, $\cos(0.2)$, $\cos(0.5)$, $\cos(1)$, and $\cos(2)$

20. $\ln(1.1)$, $\ln(1.2)$, $\ln(1.3)$, $\ln(2)$, and $\ln(3)$

21. $\arctan(0.1)$, $\arctan(0.2)$, $\arctan(0.5)$, $\arctan(1)$, and $\arctan(2)$

In problems 22 – 27, calculate the first three nonzero terms of the power series for each of the integrals.

22. $\int \cos(x^2)\,dx$ and $\int \cos(x^3)\,dx$

23. $\int \sin(x^2)\,dx$ and $\int \sin(x^3)\,dx$

24. $\int e^{(x^2)}\,dx$ and $\int e^{(x^3)}\,dx$

25. $\int e^{(-x^2)}\,dx$ and $\int e^{(-x^3)}\,dx$

26. $\int \ln(x)\,dx$ and $\int x\ln(x)\,dx$

27. $\int x\sin(x)\,dx$ and $\int x^2\sin(x)\,dx$

In problems 28 – 35, use the series representation of these functions to calculate the limits.

28. $\lim_{x \to 0} \dfrac{1 - \cos(x)}{x}$

29. $\lim_{x \to 0} \dfrac{1 - \cos(x)}{x^2}$

30. $\lim_{x \to 0} \dfrac{\ln(x)}{x - 1}$

31. $\lim_{x \to 0} \dfrac{1 - e^x}{x}$

32. $\lim_{x \to 0} \dfrac{1 + x - e^x}{x^2}$

33. $\lim_{x \to 0} \dfrac{\sin(x)}{x}$

34. $\lim_{x \to 0} \dfrac{x - \sin(x)}{x^3}$

35. $\lim_{x \to 0} \dfrac{x - \dfrac{x^3}{6} - \sin(x)}{x^5}$

36. Use the series for e^x and e^{-x} to write a series representation for $\cosh(x) = \tfrac{1}{2}(e^x + e^{-x})$.

(The function "cosh" is called the hyperbolic cosine function.)

37. Use the series for e^x and e^{-x} to write a series representation for $\sinh(x) = \tfrac{1}{2}(e^x - e^{-x})$.

(The function "sinh" is called the hyperbolic sine function.)

38. Show that **D**(series for cosh(x) in problem 36) is the series for sinh(x) in problem 37.

39. Show that **D**(series for sinh(x) in problem 37) is the series for cosh(x) in problem 36.

Euler's Formula

So far we have only discussed series with real numbers, but sometimes it is useful to replace the variable with complex numbers. The next problems ask you to make such a substitution and then to derive and use one of the most famous formulas in mathematics, Euler's formula. (Recall that $i = \sqrt{-1}$ is called the complex unit and that its powers follow the pattern $i^2 = -1$, $i^3 = (i^2)(i) = -i$, $i^4 = (i^2)(i^2) = 1$, $i^5 = (i^4)(i) = i, \ldots$)

40. Start with the series $e^x = 1 + x + \frac{x^2}{2!} + \frac{x^3}{3!} + \frac{x^4}{4!} + \frac{x^5}{5!} + \frac{x^6}{6!} + \frac{x^7}{7!} + \frac{x^8}{8!} + \ldots$

    (a) Substitute "ix" for "x" and write a series for e^{ix}.

    (b) In part (a) simplify each power of i and write a simplified series for e^{ix}. (e.g., $(ix)^3/3!$ simplifies to $i^3 x^3/3! = -i \cdot x^3/3!$)

    (c) Sort the terms in the series in part (b) into those terms that do not contain i and those terms that do contain i. Then rewrite the series for e^{ix} in the form
    $e^{ix} = \{$ terms that did not contain i $\} + i \cdot \{$ terms that did contain i $\}$.

    (d) You should recognize the sum in each bracket in part (c) as the series for an elementary function (hint: think trigonometry). Rewrite the pattern in part (c) as
    $e^{ix} = \{$ function $\} + i \cdot \{$ another function $\}$.

41. The answer you should have gotten in problem 40d, $e^{ix} = \cos(x) + i \cdot \sin(x)$, is called Euler's formula. Use Euler's formula to calculate the values of $e^{i(\pi/2)}$ and $e^{\pi i}$.

42. Use Euler's formula to show that $e^{\pi i} + 1 = 0$. This is one of the most remarkable formulas in mathematics because it connects five of the most fundamental constants (the additive identity 0, the multiplicative identity 1, the complex unit i, and the two most commonly used irrational numbers π and e in a simple but non-obvious way.

Binomial Series

You have probably seen the pattern for expanding $(1 + x)^n$ where n is a nonnegative integer:

$(1 + x)^0 = 1$

$(1 + x)^1 = 1 + x$

$(1 + x)^2 = 1 + 2x + x^2$

$(1 + x)^3 = 1 + 3x + 3x^2 + x^3$

$(1 + x)^4 = 1 + 4x + 6x^2 + 4x^3 + x^4$

$(1 + x)^5 = 1 + 5x + 10x^2 + 10x^3 + 5x^4 + x^5$

```
Row         Pascal's Triangle
 0 ············· 1
 1 ··········  1   1
 2 ········  1   2   1
 3 ······· 1   3   3   1
 4 ······ 1   4   6   4   1
 5 ····· 1   5  10  10   5   1
 6 ···· 1   6  15  20  15   6   1
```

Each number in Pascal's Triangle is the sum of the two numbers closest to it in the row immediately above it.

Fig. 4

either using Pascal's triangle (Fig. 4) or using the binomial coefficients, written $\binom{n}{k}$ and defined as

$$\binom{n}{0} = 1 \quad \text{and} \quad \binom{n}{k} = \frac{n(n-1)(n-2)\cdots(n-k+1)}{k!} = \frac{n!}{k!\,(n-k)!} \;.$$

43. Calculate the binomial coefficients $\binom{3}{0}$, $\binom{3}{1}$, $\binom{3}{2}$, and $\binom{3}{3}$ and verify that

   (i) they agree with the entries in the 3rd row of Pascal's triangle

   (ii) they agree with the coefficients of the terms of $(1 + x)^3$.

44. Calculate the binomial coefficients $\binom{4}{0}$, $\binom{4}{1}$, $\binom{4}{2}$, $\binom{4}{3}$, and $\binom{4}{4}$ and verify that

   (i) they agree with the entries in the 4th row of Pascal's triangle

   (ii) they agree with the coefficients of the terms of $(1 + x)^4$.

Using binomial coefficients, the pattern for nonnegative integer powers of $(1 + x)$ can be described in a very compact way:

$$(1 + x)^n = \sum_{k=0}^{n} \binom{n}{k} x^k \;.$$

When n is a positive integer, $(1 + x)^n$ expands to be a polynomial of degree n.
But what happens when n is a negative integer or perhaps not even an integer? This was a question that Newton himself investigated, and it led him to a general pattern, called the Binomial Series Theorem, for $(1 + x)^m$ when m is any real number. And now you can do it, too.

45. Let $f(x) = (1 + x)^{5/2}$ and determine the first 5 terms of the Maclaurin series for f(x).

46. Let $f(x) = (1 + x)^{-3/2}$ and determine the first 5 terms of the Maclaurin series for f(x).

47. Let $f(x) = (1 + x)^m$ and determine the first 4 terms of the Maclaurin series for $f(x)$. This is the start of the derivation of the Binomial Series Theorem given below.

Binomial Series Theorem

If m is any real number and $|x| < 1$

then $(1 + x)^m = 1 + mx + \dfrac{m(m-1)}{2} x^2 + \dfrac{m(m-1)(m-2)}{3!} x^3 + \ldots = \sum\limits_{k=0}^{\infty} \binom{m}{k} x^k$

where $\binom{m}{k} = \dfrac{m(m-1)(m-2) \cdots (m-k+1)}{k!}$ (for $k \geq 1$)   and $\binom{m}{0} = 1$.

---

48. Use the Ratio Test to show that $\sum\limits_{k=0}^{\infty} \binom{m}{k} x^k$ converges for $|x| < 1$.

Practice Answers

Practice 1: $P(x) = a_0 + a_1 x + a_2 x^2 + a_3 x^3 + a_4 x^4$ with $P(0) = -3$, $P'(0) = 4$, $P''(0) = 10$,
$P'''(0) = 12$, and $P^{(4)}(0) = 24$.

$-3 = P(0) = a_0 + a_1 \cdot 0 + a_2 \cdot 0 + a_3 \cdot 0 + a_4 \cdot 0 = a_0$ so $a_0 = -3$

$P'(x) = a_1 + 2a_2 x + 3a_3 x^2 + 4a_4 x^3$

$4 = P'(0) = a_1 + 2a_2 \cdot 0 + 3a_3 \cdot 0 + 4a_4 \cdot 0 = a_1$ so $a_1 = 4$

$P''(x) = 2a_2 + 6a_3 x + 12a_4 x^2$

$10 = P''(0) = 2a_2 + 6a_3 \cdot 0 + 12a_4 \cdot 0 = 2a_2$ so $a_2 = 10/2 = 5$

$P'''(x) = 6a_3 + 24a_4 x$

$12 = P'''(0) = 6a_3 + 24a_4 \cdot 0 = 6a_3$ so $a_3 = 12/6 = 2$

$P^{(4)}(x) = 24a_4$

$24 = P^{(4)}(0) = 24a_4$ so $a_4 = 24/24 = 1$.

Then $P(x) = -3 + 4x + 5x^2 + 2x^3 + 1x^4$.

Practice 2: $\cos(x) = D(\sin(x)) = D\left(x - \dfrac{x^3}{3!} + \dfrac{x^5}{5!} - \dfrac{x^7}{7!} + \dfrac{x^9}{9!} - \dfrac{x^{11}}{11!} + \ldots\right)$

$$= 1 - 3 \cdot \dfrac{x^2}{3!} + 5 \cdot \dfrac{x^4}{5!} - 7 \cdot \dfrac{x^6}{7!} + 9 \cdot \dfrac{x^8}{9!} - 11 \cdot \dfrac{x^{10}}{11!} + \ldots$$

$$= 1 - \dfrac{x^2}{2!} + \dfrac{x^4}{4!} - \dfrac{x^6}{6!} + \dfrac{x^8}{8!} - \dfrac{x^{10}}{10!} + \ldots = \sum_{n=0}^{\infty} (-1)^n \dfrac{x^{2n}}{(2n)!}$$

Practice 3: $\cos(x) = 1 - \dfrac{x^2}{2!} + \dfrac{x^4}{4!} - \dfrac{x^6}{6!} + \dfrac{x^8}{8!} - \dfrac{x^{10}}{10!} + \ldots$

Using the first two nonzero terms, $\cos(0.2) \approx 1 - \dfrac{(0.2)^2}{2!} = 1 - \dfrac{0.04}{2} = 0.98$.

Since $\cos(0.2) = 1 - \dfrac{(0.2)^2}{2!} + \dfrac{(0.2)^4}{4!} - \dfrac{(0.2)^6}{6!} + \ldots$ is a convergent alternating series, the error is less than the absolute value of the next term.

Then $\cos(0.2) \approx 1 - \dfrac{(0.2)^2}{2!} = 0.98$ with an error less than $\left| \dfrac{(0.2)^4}{4!} \right| = \dfrac{0.0016}{24} \approx 0.000067$:

$|\cos(0.2) - 0.98| < 0.000067$. (In fact, $\cos(0.2) \approx 0.9800665778$.)

Practice 4: $\cos(x) = 1 - \dfrac{x^2}{2!} + \dfrac{x^4}{4!} - \dfrac{x^6}{6!} + \dfrac{x^8}{8!} - \dfrac{x^{10}}{10!} + \ldots$

$\cos(x^3) = 1 - \dfrac{(x^3)^2}{2!} + \dfrac{(x^3)^4}{4!} - \dfrac{(x^3)^6}{6!} + \dfrac{(x^3)^8}{8!} - \ldots = 1 - \dfrac{x^6}{2!} + \dfrac{x^{12}}{4!} - \dfrac{x^{18}}{6!} + \dfrac{x^{24}}{8!} - \dfrac{x^{30}}{10!} + \ldots$

$x \cdot \cos(x^3) = x - \dfrac{x^7}{2!} + \dfrac{x^{13}}{4!} - \dfrac{x^{19}}{6!} + \dfrac{x^{25}}{8!} - \dfrac{x^{31}}{10!} + \ldots$

$\displaystyle\int x \cdot \cos(x^3)\, dx = \dfrac{x^2}{2} - \dfrac{1}{8} \cdot \dfrac{x^8}{2!} + \dfrac{1}{14} \cdot \dfrac{x^{14}}{4!} - \dfrac{1}{20} \cdot \dfrac{x^{20}}{6!} + \dfrac{1}{26} \cdot \dfrac{x^{26}}{8!} - \dfrac{1}{32} \cdot \dfrac{x^{32}}{10!} + \ldots + C$

$\displaystyle\int_0^{1/2} x \cdot \cos(x^3)\, dx \approx \left. \dfrac{x^2}{2} - \dfrac{1}{8} \cdot \dfrac{x^8}{2!} \right|_0^{1/2} = \left(\dfrac{(0.5)^2}{2} - \dfrac{(0.5)^8}{2!\,8} \right) - (0) \approx 0.124755859$

with $|\text{error}| \leq \dfrac{(0.5)^{14}}{4!\,14} \approx 1.82 \cdot 10^{-7} = 0.000000182$.

Practice 5: $e^x = 1 + x + \dfrac{x^2}{2!} + \dfrac{x^3}{3!} + \dfrac{x^4}{4!} + \dfrac{x^5}{5!} + \ldots$. Using the first six terms,

$e^1 \approx 1 + 1 + \dfrac{1}{2!} + \dfrac{1}{3!} + \dfrac{1}{4!} + \dfrac{1}{5!} \approx 2.71666666666$ (My calculator gives $e^1 \approx 2.718281828$)

$e^{-1/2} \approx 1 + (-1/2) + \dfrac{(-1/2)^2}{2!} + \dfrac{(-1/2)^3}{3!} + \dfrac{(-1/2)^4}{4!} + \dfrac{(-1/2)^5}{5!} \approx 0.6065104167$

(My calculator gives $e^{-1/2} \approx 0.6065306597$).

Practice 6:

$$1 + x + \frac{x^2}{2} + \frac{x^3}{6} + \ldots \qquad (= e^x)$$

times

$$x - \frac{x^3}{6} + \frac{x^5}{120} - \ldots \qquad (= \sin(x))$$

$$x + x^2 + \frac{x^3}{2} + \frac{x^4}{6} + \ldots \qquad \text{(from multiplying by } x\text{)}$$

$$-\frac{x^3}{6} - \frac{x^4}{6} - \frac{x^5}{12} - \ldots \qquad \text{(from multiplying by } -x^3/6\text{)}$$

$$\frac{x^5}{120} + \ldots \qquad \text{(from multiplying by } x^5/120\text{)}$$

---

product is

$$x + x^2 + \frac{x^3}{3} + 0 - \frac{-9x^5}{120} + \ldots \qquad \text{(from adding the previous terms)}$$

The sum of the first three nonzero terms is $e^x \cdot \sin(x) = x + x^2 + \frac{x^3}{3} + \ldots$.

MAPLE command to plot Fig. 2

plot({x, x-x^3/6, x-x^3/6+x^5/120, sin(x)}, x=-9..9, y=-6..6, color=[blue, green, black, red], thickness=3);

10.11 APPROXIMATION USING TAYLOR POLYNOMIALS

The previous two sections focused on obtaining power series representations for functions, finding their intervals of convergence, and using those power series to approximate values of functions, limits, and integrals. In the cases where the power series resulted in an alternating numerical series, we were also able to use the Estimation Bound for Alternating Series (Section 10.6) to get a bound on the "error:"

"error" = | {exact value} – {partial sum approximation} | < | next term in the series | .

If the power series did not result in an alternating numerical series, we did not have a bound on the size of the error of the approximation.

In this section we introduce Taylor Polynomials (partial sums of the Taylor Series) and obtain a bound on the approximation error, the value |{ exact value of f(x) } – { Taylor Polynomial approximation of f(x) }| . The bound we get is valid even if the Taylor series is not an alternating series, and the pattern for the error bound looks very much like **the next term in the series**, the first unused term in the partial sum of the Taylor series. In mathematics, this error bound is important for determining which functions are approximated by their Taylor series. In computer and calculator applications, the error bound is important to designers to ensure that their machines calculate enough digits of functions such as e^x and sin(x) for various values of x. In general, knowing this error bound can help us work efficiently by allowing us to use only the number of terms we really need.

We also examine graphically how well the Taylor Polynomials of f(x) approximate f(x)

Taylor Polynomials

If we add a finite number of terms of a power series, the result is a polynomial.

Definition

For a function f, the nth **degree Taylor Polynomial** (centered at c), written $P_n(x)$, is the partial sum of the terms up to the nth degree of the Taylor Series for f:

$$P_n(x) = \sum_{k=0}^{n} \frac{f^{(k)}(c)}{k!} (x-c)^k$$

$$= f(c) + f'(c)(x-c) + \frac{f''(c)}{2!}(x-c)^2 + \frac{f'''(c)}{3!}(x-c)^3 + \frac{f^{(4)}(c)}{4!}(x-c)^4 + \ldots + \frac{f^{(n)}(c)}{n!}(x-c)^n$$

Example 1: Write the first four Taylor Polynomials, $P_0(x)$ to $P_3(x)$, centered at 0 for e^x, and then graph them for $-1 < x < 1$.

Solution: The Maclaurin series for e^x is $e^x = 1 + x + \frac{x^2}{2!} + \frac{x^3}{3!} + \frac{x^4}{4!} + \frac{x^5}{5!} + \ldots = \sum_{n=0}^{\infty} \frac{x^n}{n!}$ so

$$P_0(x) = 1, \quad P_1(x) = 1 + x, \quad P_2(x) = 1 + x + \frac{x^2}{2}, \quad \text{and} \quad P_3(x) = 1 + x + \frac{x^2}{2} + \frac{x^3}{6}.$$

The graphs of e^x and $P_1(x), P_2(x),$ and $P_3(x)$ are shown in Fig. 1.

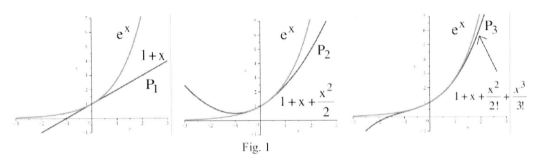

Fig. 1

Notice that $P_0(x)$ and e^x agree in value when $x = 0$,

$P_1(x)$, e^x, and their first derivatives agree in value when $x = 0$,

$P_2(x)$, e^x, their first derivatives, and their second derivatives agree in value when $x = 0$.

Practice 1: Write the Taylor Polynomials $P_0(x), P_2(x),$ and $P_4(x)$ centered at 0 for $\cos(x)$, and then graph them for $-\pi < x < \pi$. Write the Taylor Polynomials $P_1(x)$ and $P_3(x)$.

When we center the Taylor Polynomial at $x = c \neq 0$, the Taylor Polynomials approximate the function and its derivatives well for x close to c.

Example 2: Write the Taylor Polynomials $P_0(x), P_2(x),$ and $P_4(x)$ **centered at $3\pi/2$** for $\sin(x)$, and then graph them for $2 < x < 8$.

Solution: The Taylor series, centered at $3\pi/2$, for $\sin(x)$ is

$$\sin(x) = -1 + \frac{1}{2!}(x - 3\pi/2)^2 - \frac{1}{4!}(x - 3\pi/2)^4 + \frac{1}{6!}(x - 3\pi/2)^6 + \ldots = \sum_{n=0}^{\infty} (-1)^{n+1} \frac{1}{(2n)!}(x - 3\pi/2)^{2n}.$$

Then $P_0(x) = -1$, $P_2(x) = -1 + \frac{1}{2}(x - 3\pi/2)^2$, and $P_4(x) = -1 + \frac{1}{2}(x - 3\pi/2)^2 - \frac{1}{24}(x - 3\pi/2)^4$.

The graphs of $\sin(x), P_0(x), P_2(x),$ and $P_4(x)$ are shown in Fig. 2.

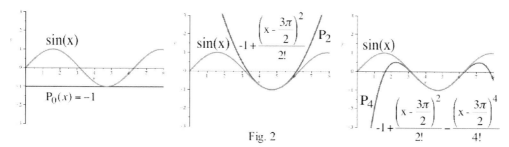

Fig. 2

Practice 2: Write the Taylor Polynomials $P_0(x), P_1(x)$, and $P_3(x)$ **centered at $\pi/2$** for $\cos(x)$, and then graph them for $-1 < x < 4$.

The Remainder

Approximation formulas such as the Taylor Polynomials are useful by themselves, but in many applied situations we want to know how good the approximation is or how many terms of a series are required to obtain a needed level of accuracy. If 2 terms of a series give you the needed level of accuracy for your application, it is a waste of time and money to use 100 terms. On the other hand, sometimes even 100 terms may not give the accuracy you need. Fortunately, it is possible to obtain a guarantee on how close a particular Taylor Polynomial approximation is to the exact value. Then we can work efficiently and use the number of terms that we need. The next theorem gives a pattern for the amount of "error" in our Taylor Polynomial approximation and can be used to obtain a bound on the size of the "error."

Taylor's Formula with Remainder

If f has n+1 derivatives in an interval I containing c, and x is in I,

then there is a number z, strictly <u>between</u> c and x, so that

$$f(x) = P_n(x) + R_n(x) \qquad \text{where} \quad R_n(x) = \frac{f^{(n+1)}(z)}{(n+1)!}(x-c)^{n+1}.$$

This says that $f(x)$ is equal to the nth degree Taylor Polynomial plus a Remainder, and the Remainder $R_n(x)$ has the form given in the theorem. Notice that the pattern for R_n looks like the pattern for the $(n+1)^{st}$ term of the Taylor series for $f(x)$ except that it contains $f^{(n+1)}(z)$ instead of $f^{(n+1)}(c)$. This particular pattern for $R_n(x)$ is called the Lagrange form of the remainder, and is named for the French–Italian mathematician and astronomer Joseph Lagrange (1736–1813).

The main idea of the proof of the Taylor's Formula with Remainder is straightforward, but the technical details are rather complicated. The main idea and the technical details are given in the Appendix.

10.11 Approximation Using Taylor Polynomials   Contemporary Calculus   4

The pattern for the remainder, $\dfrac{f^{(n+1)}(z)}{(n+1)!}(x-c)^{n+1}$, contains three pieces, $(n+1)!$, $(x-c)^{n+1}$, and $f^{(n+1)}(z)$ for some z between x and c. The Taylor Remainder Formula is typically used in two ways:

In one type of use, the Taylor Polynomial is given so x, c, and n are known, and we can evaluate $(n+1)!$ and $(x-c)^{n+1}$ exactly. That leaves the piece $f^{(n+1)}(z)$ for some z between x and c. If we can find a bound for the value of $|f^{(n+1)}(z)|$ for all z between x and c, then we can put it together with the values of $(n+1)!$ and $(x-c)^{n+1}$ to obtain a bound for the remainder term $R_n(x)$.

In the other common usage, the amount of acceptable "error" is given, so x, c, and $R_n(x)$ are known, and we need to find a value of n that guarantees the required accuracy.

Corollary: A Bound for the Remainder $R_n(x)$

If   f has n+1 derivatives in an interval I containing c, and x is in I, and
$|f^{(n+1)}(z)| \leq M$ for **all** z between x and c,

then   "error" $= |f(x) - P_n(x)| = |R_n(x)| \leq M \cdot \dfrac{|x-c|^{n+1}}{(n+1)!}$.

Example 3: We plan to approximate the values of e^x with $P_3(x) = 1 + x + \dfrac{x^2}{2} + \dfrac{x^3}{6}$. Find a bound for the "error" of the approximation, $R_3(x)$, if x is in the interval
(a) $[-1, 1]$, (b) $[-3, 2]$ and (c) $[-0.2, 0.3]$.

Solution: $f(x) = e^x$, c = 0 (a Maclaurin series), n = 3, and $f^{(n+1)}(x) = f^{(4)}(x) = e^x$.

(a) For x in the interval $[-1, 1]$:
$|(x-c)^{n+1}| = |x^4| \leq |1^4| = 1$. $(n+1)! = 4! = 24$.
For x in $[-1, 1]$, $|f^{(n+1)}(x)| = |e^x| \leq e^1$. A "crude" but "easy to use" bound for e^1 is $e^1 < (3)^1 = 3 = M$. (A more precise bound is $e^1 < (2.72)^1 < 2.72$.)

Then $|R_3(x)| < M \cdot \dfrac{|x-c|^{n+1}}{(n+1)!} < 3 \cdot \dfrac{1}{24} = 0.125$.

For all $-1 < x < 1$, $P_3(x) = 1 + x + \dfrac{x^2}{2} + \dfrac{x^3}{6}$ is within 0.125 of e^x.

(b) For x in the interval $[-3, 2]$: $|(x-c)^{n+1}| = |x^4| \leq |(-3)^4| = 81$ and $(n+1)! = 4! = 24$.
For x in $[-3, 2]$, $|f^{(n+1)}(x)| = |e^x| \leq e^2$. A "crude" but "easy to use" bound for e^2 is $e^2 < (3)^2 = 9 = M$. (A more precise bound is $e^2 < (2.72)^2 < 7.4$.)

Then $|R_3(x)| < M \cdot \frac{|x-c|^{n+1}}{(n+1)!} < 9 \cdot \frac{81}{24} = 30.375$. Obviously we cannot have much confidence in our use of $P_3(x)$ to approximate e^x on the interval $[-3, 2]$.

(c) For x in the interval $[-0.2, 0.3]$: $|(x-c)^{n+1}| = |x^4| \leq |0.3^4| = 0.0081$.

$(n+1)! = 4! = 24$.

For x in $[-0.2, 0.3]$, $|f^{(n+1)}(x)| = |e^x| \leq e^{0.3}$. A bound for $e^{0.3}$ is

$e^{0.3} < (2.72)^{0.3} < 1.4 = M$ — obtained using a calculator.

Then $|R_3(x)| < M \cdot \frac{|x-c|^{n+1}}{(n+1)!} < 1.4 \cdot \frac{0.0081}{24} = 0.0004725$.

For all $-0.2 < x < 0.3$, $P_3(x) = 1 + x + \frac{x^2}{2} + \frac{x^3}{6}$ is within 0.0004725 of e^x.

When the interval is small, we can be confident that $P_3(x)$ provides a good approximation of e^x, but as the interval grows, so does our bound on the remainder. To guarantee a good approximation on a larger interval, we typically need $(n+1)!$ to be larger so we need to use a higher degree Taylor Polynomial $P_n(x)$.

Practice 3: Find a value of n to guarantee that $P_n(x)$ is within 0.001 of e^x for x in the interval $[-3, 2]$.

Example 4: We want to approximate the values of $f(x) = \sin(x)$ on the interval $[-\pi/2, \pi/2]$ with an error less that 10^{-10}. How many terms of the Maclaurin series for $\sin(x)$ are needed?

Solution: For every value of n, $|f^{(n+1)}(x)|$ is $|\sin(x)|$ or $|\cos(x)|$ so $M = 1$ in the Bound for the Remainder. Then "error" $= |R_n(x)| < 1 \cdot \frac{|x-0|^{n+1}}{(n+1)!} \leq \frac{(\pi/2)^{n+1}}{(n+1)!}$, and we need to find a value of n so that $\frac{(\pi/2)^{n+1}}{(n+1)!}$ is less than 10^{-10}. A bit of numerical experimentation on a calculator shows that

$\frac{(\pi/2)^{14}}{14!} \approx 6.39 \times 10^{-9}$, $\frac{(\pi/2)^{15}}{15!} \approx 6.69 \times 10^{-10}$, and $\frac{(\pi/2)^{16}}{16!} \approx 6.57 \times 10^{-11}$

so we can take $n = 15$: $P_{15}(x) = x - \frac{x^3}{3!} + \frac{x^5}{5!} - \frac{x^7}{7!} + \frac{x^9}{9!} - \frac{x^{11}}{11!} + \frac{x^{13}}{13!} - \frac{x^{15}}{15!}$.

If $-\pi/2 \leq x \leq \pi/2$, then $|P_{15}(x) - \sin(x)| < 10^{-10}$.

Practice 4: How many terms of the Maclaurin series for e^x are needed to approximate e^x to within 10^{-10} for $0 \leq x \leq 1$?

Calculator Notes

Imagine that you are in charge of designing or selecting an algorithm for a calculator to use when the SIN button is pushed. (Smartest move: find a mathematician who knows about "numerical analysis" and the design and implementation of algorithms.) You know that if the value of x is relatively close to 0, then SIN(x) can be quickly approximated to 10 digits (the size of the display of the calculator) by using a "few" terms of the Taylor series for sin(x): if $-1.57 \le x \le 1.57$, then

$$x - \frac{x^3}{3!} + \frac{x^5}{5!} - \frac{x^7}{7!} + \frac{x^9}{9!} - \frac{x^{11}}{11!} + \frac{x^{13}}{13!} - \frac{x^{15}}{15!}$$

$$= x\left(1 - \frac{x^2}{2 \cdot 3}\left(1 - \frac{x^2}{4 \cdot 5}\left(1 - \frac{x^2}{6 \cdot 7}\left(1 - \frac{x^2}{8 \cdot 9}\left(1 - \frac{x^2}{10 \cdot 11}\left(1 - \frac{x^2}{12 \cdot 13}\left(1 - \frac{x^2}{14 \cdot 15}\right)\right)\right)\right)\right)\right)\right)$$

gives the value of sin(x) with 10 digits of accuracy.

(The second pattern looks more complicated, but is usually preferred because it uses fewer multiplications and avoids very large values such as x^{15} and 15!) But you also want your algorithm to give 10 digits of accuracy even when x is larger, say 10 or 101.7. Rather than computing <u>many</u> more terms of the Maclaurin series for sine, some algorithms simply shift the problem closer to 0. First they use the fact that sin(x) = sin(x – 2π) to keep shifting the problem until the argument is in the interval [0, 2π]:

sin(10) = sin(10 – 2π) = sin(3.71681469)

sin(101.7) = sin(101.7 – 2π) = sin(101.7 – 4π) = ... = sin(101.7 – 32π) = sin(1.169035085).

Once the argument is between 0 and 2π, additional trigonometric facts are used:

if the new value of x is larger than π, use sin(x) = –sin(x – π) to replace "x" with "x – π" (and keep track of the change in sign of the answer). The new x value is in the interval [0, π].

Finally, we can shift the problem into the interval [0, π/2]:

if the new value of x is larger than π/2, use sin(x) = sin(π – x) to replace "x" with "π – x." This new x value is in the interval [0, π/2] ≈ [0, 1.57] and the 7 terms of the sine series shown above are sufficient to approximate sin(x) with 10 digits of accuracy.

There are, however, major problems when calculators encounter the sine or exponential of a very large number. Since calculators only store the leading finite number of digits of a number (usually 10 or 12 digits), the calculator can not distinguish large numbers that differ past that leading number of stored digits: one calculator correctly says that (10^12+1) – 10^12 = 1, but it incorrectly reports that (10^13+1) – 10^13 = 0. Since it calculates "10^13+1 = 10^13", it also would falsely report the same values for sin(10^13+1) and sin(10^13). In fact, the people who programmed this particular type of calculator recognized the problem, and the calculator gives an error message if it is asked to calculate sin(10^11). This particular calculator reports e^230 ≈ 7.7 x 10^{99} . It reports an error for e^231 since the largest number it can display is 9.9 x 10^{99} and e^231 exceeds that value. What happens on your calculator?

PROBLEMS

In problems 1 – 10, calculate the Taylor polynomials P_0, P_1, P_2, P_3, and P_4 for the given function centered at the given value of c. Then graph the function and the Taylor polynomials on the given interval.

1. $f(x) = \sin(x), c = 0, [-2, 4]$
2. $f(x) = \cos(x), c = 0, [-2, 4]$
3. $f(x) = \ln(x), c = 1, [0.1, 3]$
4. $f(x) = \arctan(x), c = 0, [-3, 3]$
5. $f(x) = \sqrt{x}, c = 1, [0, 3]$
6. $f(x) = \sqrt{x}, c = 9, [0, 20]$
7. $f(x) = (1 + x)^{-1/2}, c = 0, [-2, 3]$
8. $f(x) = e^{2x}, c = 0, [-2, 4]$
9. $f(x) = \sin(x), c = \pi/2, [-1, 5]$
10. $f(x) = \sin(x), c = \pi, [-1, 5]$

In problems 11 – 18, a function $f(x)$ and a value of n are given. Determine a formula for $R_n(x)$ and find a bound for $|R_n(x)|$ on the given interval. This bound for $|R_n(x)|$ is our "guaranteed accuracy" for P_n to approximate $f(x)$ on the given interval. (Use $c = 0$.)

11. $f(x) = \sin(x), n = 5, [-\pi/2, \pi/2]$
12. $f(x) = \sin(x), n = 9, [-\pi/2, \pi/2]$
13. $f(x) = \sin(x), n = 5, [-\pi, \pi]$
14. $f(x) = \sin(x), n = 9, [-\pi, \pi]$
15. $f(x) = \cos(x), n = 10, [-1, 2]$
16. $f(x) = \cos(x), n = 10, [-1, 5]$
17. $f(x) = e^x, n = 6, [-1, 2]$
18. $f(x) = e^x, n = 10, [-1, 3]$

In problems 19 – 24, determine how many terms of the Taylor series for $f(x)$ are needed to approximate f to within the specified error on the given interval. (For each function use the center $c = 0$.)

19. $f(x) = \sin(x)$ within 0.001 on $[-1, 1]$
20. $f(x) = \sin(x)$ within 0.001 on $[-3, 3]$
21. $f(x) = \sin(x)$ within 0.00001 on $[-1.6, 1.6]$
22. $f(x) = \cos(x)$ within 0.001 on $[-2, 2]$
23. $f(x) = e^x$ within 0.001 on $[0, 2]$
24. $f(x) = e^x$ within 0.001 on $[-1, 4]$

Series Approximations of π

The following problems illustrate some of the ways series have been used to obtain very precise approximations of π. Several of these methods use the series for $\arctan(x)$,

$$\arctan(x) = x - \frac{x^3}{3} + \frac{x^5}{5} - \frac{x^7}{7} + \frac{x^9}{9} - \ldots = \sum_{n=0}^{\infty} (-1)^n \frac{x^{2n+1}}{2n+1},$$

which converges rapidly if $|x|$ is close to zero.

Method I: $\tan(\frac{\pi}{4}) = 1$ so $\frac{\pi}{4} = \arctan(1) = 1 - \frac{1}{3} + \frac{1}{5} - \frac{1}{7} + \frac{1}{9} - \ldots = \sum_{n=0}^{\infty} (-1)^n \frac{1}{2n+1}$ and

$$\pi = 4\left\{ 1 - \frac{1}{3} + \frac{1}{5} - \frac{1}{7} + \frac{1}{9} - \ldots \right\}.$$

25. (a) Approximate π as $4\left\{ 1 - \frac{1}{3} + \frac{1}{5} - \frac{1}{7} + \frac{1}{9} \right\}$ and compare this value with the value your calculator gives for π.

   (b) The series for arctan(1) is an alternating series so we have an "easy" error bound. Use the error bound for an alternating series to find a bound for the error if 50 terms of the arctan(1) series are used.

   (c) Using the error bound for an alternating series, how many terms of the arctan(1) series are needed to guarantee that the series approximation of π is within 0.0001 of the exact value of π?
   (The arctan(1) series converges so slowly that it is not used to approximate π.)

Method II: $\tan(a + b) = \frac{\tan(a) + \tan(b)}{1 - \tan(a)\tan(b)}$ so $\tan(\arctan(\frac{1}{2}) + \arctan(\frac{1}{3})) = \frac{\frac{1}{2} + \frac{1}{3}}{1 - \frac{1}{2} \cdot \frac{1}{3}} = 1$. Then

$\frac{\pi}{4} = \arctan(1) = \arctan(\frac{1}{2}) + \arctan(\frac{1}{3})$, and the series for $\arctan(\frac{1}{2})$ and $\arctan(\frac{1}{3})$ converge much more rapidly than the series for arctan(1).

26. (a) Approximate π as
   $4\left\{ \text{(sum of the first 4 terms of the arctan}(\frac{1}{2})\text{ series)} + \text{(sum of the first 4 terms of the arctan}(\frac{1}{3})\text{ series)} \right\}$.
   Then compare this value with the value your calculator gives for π.

   (b) The series for $\arctan(\frac{1}{2})$ and $\arctan(\frac{1}{3})$ are each alternating series. Use the error bound for an alternating series to find a bound for the error if 10 terms of each series are used.

   (c) How many terms of each series are needed to guarantee that the series approximation of π is within 0.0001 of the exact value of π?

Other Methods: We will not justify these methods, but they converge to π more rapidly than the first two methods.

   A: $\frac{\pi}{4} = 4 \cdot \arctan(\frac{1}{5}) - \arctan(\frac{1}{239})$ (due to Machin in 1706)

   B: $\pi = 48 \cdot \arctan(\frac{1}{18}) + 32 \cdot \arctan(\frac{1}{57}) - 20 \cdot \arctan(\frac{1}{239})$

27. (a) Use the first 3 terms of each series in formula A to approximate π. How much does it differ from the value your calculator gives you?

   (b) Why does formula A converge more rapidly (using fewer terms) than methods I and II?

28. (a) Use the first 3 terms of each series in formula B to approximate π. How much does it differ from the value your calculator gives you?

   (b) Why does formula B converge more rapidly (using fewer terms) than Methods I and II and formula A?

Practice Answers

Practice 1: $\cos(x) = 1 - \dfrac{x^2}{2!} + \dfrac{x^4}{4!} - \dfrac{x^6}{6!} + \dfrac{x^8}{8!} - \dfrac{x^{10}}{10!} + \ldots = \sum_{n=0}^{\infty} (-1)^n \dfrac{x^{2n}}{(2n)!}$ so

$P_0(x) = 1$, $P_2(x) = 1 - \dfrac{x^2}{2}$, and $P_4(x) = 1 - \dfrac{x^2}{2} + \dfrac{x^4}{24}$. Their graphs are shown in Fig. 3.

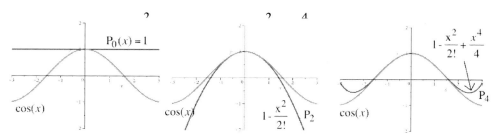

Fig. 3

Practice 2:

$\cos(x) = -(x - \pi/2) + \dfrac{1}{3!}(x - \pi/2)^3 - \dfrac{1}{5!}(x - \pi/2)^5 + \dfrac{1}{7!}(x - \pi/2)^7 - \ldots$

$= \sum_{n=0}^{\infty} (-1)^{n+1} \dfrac{1}{(2n+1)!}(x - \pi/2)^{2n+1}$.

Then $P_0(x) = 0$, $P_1(x) = -(x - \pi/2)$, and $P_3(x) = -(x - \pi/2) + \dfrac{1}{6}(x - \pi/2)^3$. The graphs of $\cos(x)$, $P_1(x)$, and $P_3(x)$ are shown in Fig. 4.

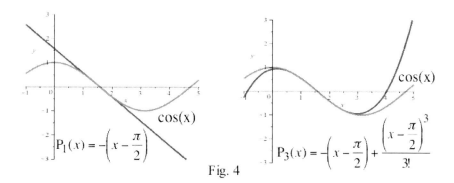

Fig. 4

Practice 3: For x in the interval $[-3, 2]$, $|(x-c)^{n+1}| = |x^3| \leq |(-3)^3| = 27$.

For x in $[-3, 2]$, $|f^{(n+1)}(x)| = |e^x| \leq e^2$. A "crude" bound for e^2 is $e^2 < (3)^2 = 9 = M$.

Then $|R_n(x)| < M \cdot \frac{(x-c)^{n+1}}{(n+1)!} < 9 \cdot \frac{27}{n!}$, and we want a value of n so $9 \cdot \frac{27}{n!} \leq 0.001$:

we want $n! \geq \frac{(9)(27)}{0.001} = 243{,}000$. Using a calculator, we see that $8! = 40{,}320$ is not large enough, but $9! = 362{,}880 > 243{,}000$ so we can use $n = 9$.

For x in the interval $[-3, 2]$, $P_9(x) = 1 + x + \frac{x^2}{2!} + \frac{x^3}{3!} + \frac{x^4}{4!} + \frac{x^5}{5!} + \frac{x^6}{6!} + \frac{x^7}{7!} + \frac{x^8}{8!} + \frac{x^9}{9!}$ is within 0.001 of e^x.

Practice 4: $R_n(x) \leq 10^{-10}$. $f(x) = e^x$, $c = 0$, and for every n, $f^{(n+1)}(x) = e^x$. For $0 \leq x \leq 1$,

$|f^{(n+1)}(x)| = |e^x| \leq e < 2.72 = M$. We want to find a value for n so

$M \cdot \frac{(x-c)^{n+1}}{(n+1)!} = 2.72 \cdot \frac{(1-0)^{n+1}}{(n+1)!} < 10^{-10}$. Some numerical experimentation on a calculator

shows that $2.72 \cdot \frac{1}{15!} \approx 1.58 \cdot 10^{-9}$ and $2.72 \cdot \frac{1}{16!} \approx 9.9 \cdot 10^{-11}$ so we can take $n = 15$.

For $0 \leq x \leq 1$, $P_{15}(x) = 1 + x + \frac{x^2}{2!} + \frac{x^3}{3!} + \frac{x^4}{4!} + \ldots + \frac{x^{15}}{15!}$ is within 10^{-10} of e^x.

Appendix: Idea and details of a Proof of Taylor's Formula with Remainder

Main idea of the proof:

We define a new differentiable function $g(t)$ and show that $g(x) = 0$ and $g(c) = 0$.

Then, by Rolle's Theorem, we can conclude that there is a number z, between x and c, so that $g'(z) = 0$. Finally, we set $g'(z) = 0$ and algebraically obtain the given formula for $R_n(x)$.

Let $R_n(x) = f(x) - P_n(x)$ be the difference between $f(x)$ and the nth Taylor polynomial for $P_n(x)$.

Define a differentiable function $g(t)$ to be

$$g(t) = f(x) - \left\{ f(t) + f'(t)(x-t) + \frac{f''(t)}{2!}(x-t)^2 + \frac{f'''(t)}{3!}(x-t)^3 + \ldots + \frac{f^{(n)}(t)}{n!}(x-t)^n \right\} - R_n(x)\frac{(x-t)^{n+1}}{(x-c)^{n+1}}.$$

This may seem to be a strange way to define a function, but it turns out to have the properties we need:

$$g(x) = f(x) - \{ f(x) + 0 + 0 + 0 + \ldots + 0 \} - R_n(x)\frac{0}{(x-c)^{n+1}} = f(x) - f(x) = 0, \text{ and}$$

$$g(c) = f(x) - \left\{ f(c) + f'(c)(x-c) + \frac{f''(c)}{2!}(x-c)^2 + \frac{f'''(c)}{3!}(x-c)^3 + \frac{f^{(4)}(c)}{4!}(x-c)^4 + \frac{f^{(n)}(c)}{n!}(x-c)^n \right\}$$
$$- R_n(x)\frac{(x-c)^{n+1}}{(x-c)^{n+1}}$$
$$= f(x) - P_n(x) - R_n(x) = 0 \text{ since } R_n(x) = f(x) - P_n(x).$$

Then, by Rolle's Theorem, there is a number z, strictly between x and c, so $g'(z) = 0$.

Notice that g is defined to be a function of t so we treat x and c as constants and differentiate with respect to t. The key pattern is that when we differentiate a term such as $\frac{f'''(t)}{3!} \cdot (x-t)^3$ with respect to t, we need to use the product rule. The resulting derivative has two terms:

$$\frac{d}{dt}\left\{\frac{f'''(t)}{3!}(x-t)^3\right\} = \frac{f'''(t)}{3!}\frac{d}{dt}(x-t)^3 + (x-t)^3 \cdot \frac{d}{dt}\frac{f'''(t)}{3!}$$

$$= \frac{f'''(t)}{3!}(3)(x-t)^2(-1) + \frac{f^{(4)}(t)}{3!}(x-t)^3 = -\frac{f'''(t)}{2!}(x-t)^2 + \frac{f^{(4)}(t)}{3!}(x-t)^3.$$

When we differentiate $g(t)$ with respect to t, we get a complicated pattern, but most of the terms cancel:

$$g'(t) = \frac{d}{dt} g(t) = 0 - \Big\{ \ f'(t)$$

$$- f'(t) + f''(t)(x-t)$$

$$- f''(t)(x-t) + \frac{f'''(t)}{2!}(x-t)^2$$

$$- \frac{f'''(t)}{2!}(x-t)^2 + \frac{f^{(4)}(t)}{3!}(x-t)^3$$

$$- \ldots - \frac{f^{(n)}(t)}{(n-1)!}(x-t)^{n-1} + \frac{f^{(n+1)}(t)}{n!}(x-t)^n \Big\} - R_n(x)\cdot(n+1)\cdot\frac{(x-t)^n(-1)}{(x-c)^{n+1}}$$

$$= -\frac{f^{(n+1)}(t)}{n!}(x-t)^n + R_n(x)\cdot(n+1)\cdot\frac{(x-t)^n}{(x-c)^{n+1}}$$

$$= (x-t)^n \left\{ R_n(x)\cdot(n+1)\cdot\frac{1}{(x-c)^{n+1}} - \frac{f^{(n+1)}(t)}{n!} \right\}.$$

By Rolle's Theorem, there is a value z, between x and c, for the variable t so $g'(z) = 0$. Then

$$(x-z)^n \left\{ R_n(x)\cdot(n+1)\cdot\frac{1}{(x-c)^{n+1}} - \frac{f^{(n+1)}(z)}{n!} \right\} = 0.$$

z is strictly between x and c so $z \neq x$ and we can divide each side by $(x-z)^n$ to get

$$R_n(x)\cdot(n+1)\cdot\frac{1}{(x-c)^{n+1}} - \frac{f^{(n+1)}(z)}{n!} = 0.$$

Finally, $R_n(x)\cdot(n+1)\cdot\frac{1}{(x-c)^{n+1}} = \frac{f^{(n+1)}(z)}{n!}$ so $R_n(x) = \frac{f^{(n+1)}(z)}{n!(n+1)}\cdot(x-c)^{n+1} = \frac{f^{(n+1)}(z)}{(n+1)!}(x-c)^{n+1}$,

the result we wanted to prove.

MAPLE command to plot $\cos(x)$ and $P_3(x)$.

plot({1-x^2/2+x^4/24,cos(x)},x=-3..3,y=-2..2,color=[blue,red],thickness=3);

10.12 INTRODUCTION TO FOURIER SERIES

When we discussed Maclaurin series in earlier sections we used information about the derivatives of a function f(x) to create an infinite series of the form

$$\sum_{n=0}^{\infty} a_n \cdot x^n = a_0 + a_1 \cdot x^1 + a_2 \cdot x^2 + a_3 \cdot x^3 + a_4 \cdot x^4 + \ldots$$

In this case the "building blocks" of the series were powers of x ($x^0, x^1, x^2, x^3,\ldots$). and this is why the series is called a "power series." The coefficients $a_n = \dfrac{f^{(n)}(0)}{n!}$ of the Maclaurin series told us how much of each power to include in our series, and we found the formula involving derivatives that enabled us to calculate the values of the coefficients. For general Taylor series the "building blocks" were powers of (x-c) for some fixed center c, and we had a similar formula to calculate the values of the coefficients for those series. We then used the Taylor and Maclaurin series to approximate functions "near c" and sometimes even for "every value of x."

Fourier series have a number of similarities with power series:
    we will approximate functions using "building blocks"
    we will need to calculate the values of the coefficients of the building blocks, and
    we will need to be concerned about where the approximations are "good."
But our building blocks for the Fourier series will be the trigonometric functions sin(x), sin(2x), sin(3x), ... and cos(x), cos(2x), cos(3x), ... and the result will be a "trigonometric series." Our formula for calculating the values of the coefficients will involve integrals rather than derivatives. Finally, since each building block repeats its values every 2π units, we will only (at first) use Fourier series to approximate 2π-periodic functions. (This is not as serious a restriction as it might seem.)

First goal: Finding the coefficients

Our first goal is to find a relationship between the function f(x) and the coefficients a_n and b_n in the series

$$\frac{a_0}{2} + \sum_{n=1}^{\infty}\{a_n \cdot \cos(nx) + b_n \cdot \sin(nx)\}$$

$$= \frac{a_0}{2} + \{a_1 \cdot \cos(x) + b_1 \cdot \sin(x)\} + \{a_2 \cdot \cos(2x) + b_2 \cdot \sin(2x)\} + \{a_3 \cdot \cos(3x) + b_3 \cdot \sin(3x)\} + \ldots$$

The key to finding the values of the coefficients depends on the following results about the integrals of the products of any two of our building blocks, sin(mx) and cos(nx), for positive integer values of m and n.

$$\int_{x=0}^{2\pi} \sin(nx)\cdot\sin(mx)\,dx = \begin{cases} \pi & \text{if } m=n \quad \text{(using integral formula \#13)} \\ 0 & \text{if } m\neq n \quad \text{(using integral formula \#25)} \end{cases}$$

$$\int_{x=0}^{2\pi} \cos(nx)\cdot\cos(mx)\,dx = \begin{cases} \pi & \text{if } m=n \quad \text{(using integral formula \#14)} \\ 0 & \text{if } m\neq n \quad \text{(using integral formula \#26)} \end{cases}$$

$$\int_{x=0}^{2\pi} \sin(nx)\cdot\cos(mx)\,dx = 0 \quad \text{for all integer values of m and n} \quad \text{(using integral formula \#27)}$$

The technical term is that the set of functions { sin(x), cos(x), sin(2x), cos(2x), sin(3x), cos(3x), ...} forms an "orthogonal" family on the interval $[0, 2\pi]$: for any two functions from this set

$$\int_{x=0}^{2\pi} f(x)\cdot g(x)\,dx = \begin{cases} \pi & \text{if f and g are the same member of the set} \\ 0 & \text{if f and g are different members of the set} \end{cases}$$

Example 1: Suppose we have the function $f(x) = 3 + 2\cos(3x) - 7\sin(4x)$ that is already a finite trigonometric series with $a_0 = 6$, $a_3 = 2$, $b_4 = -7$, and all of the other coefficients are 0. Evaluate the integral of the product of f(x) with a general building block, sin(nx) (for every value of n).

Solution:
$$\int_{x=0}^{2\pi} \sin(nx)\cdot f(x)\,dx = \int_{x=0}^{2\pi} \sin(nx)\cdot(3 + 2\cos(3x) - 7\sin(4x))\,dx$$

$$= \int_{x=0}^{2\pi} \sin(nx)\cdot 3\,dx + \int_{x=0}^{2\pi} \sin(nx)\cdot 2\cos(3x) + \int_{x=0}^{2\pi} \sin(nx)\cdot(-7\sin(4x))\,dx$$

$$= 0 + 0 + \begin{cases} -7\pi & \text{if } n=4 \\ 0 & \text{if } n\neq 4 \end{cases}.$$

It appears that we can find the value of b_n by dividing this last value by π:

$$b_n = \frac{1}{\pi}\int_{x=0}^{2\pi} \sin(nx)\cdot f(x)\,dx$$

Practice 1: Using the same function $f(x) = 3 + 2\cos(3x) - 7\sin(4x)$, evaluate the integral of the product with the cosine blocks, cos(nx), and show that

$$a_3 = \frac{1}{\pi}\int_{x=0}^{2p} \cos(3x)\cdot f(x)\,dx \quad \text{and} \quad a_n = \frac{1}{\pi}\int_{x=0}^{2p} \cos(nx)\cdot f(x)\,dx \quad \text{for } n = 1, 2, 3, \ldots$$

The general cases for the Example and Practice problems say that if f(x) is already a trigonometric polynomial with

$$f(x) = \frac{a_0}{2} + \sum_{n=1}^{\infty} \{a_n \cdot \cos(nx) + b_n \cdot \sin(nx)\}$$

$$= \frac{a_0}{2} + \{a_1 \cdot \cos(x) + b_1 \cdot \sin(x)\} + \{a_2 \cdot \cos(2x) + b_2 \cdot \sin(2x)\} + \{a_3 \cdot \cos(3x) + b_3 \cdot \sin(3x)\} + \ldots$$

then we can find the coefficients of the terms of f(x) using

$$a_n = \frac{1}{\pi} \int_{x=0}^{2\pi} \cos(nx) \cdot f(x) \, dx \quad \text{and} \quad b_n = \frac{1}{\pi} \int_{x=0}^{2\pi} \sin(nx) \cdot f(x) \, dx \, .$$

What we have just done is similar to our beginning work with Maclaurin series in Section 10.10. There we started with a polynomial P(x) and found that the coefficients were given by the formula $a_n = \frac{f^{(n)}(0)}{n!}$ using derivatives of P(x). Here we started with a trigonometric polynomial f(x) and found that the coefficients a_n and b_n were given by formulas using integrals of products with f(x). In Section 10.10 we then extended the Maclaurin series to functions that were not polynomials. Here we will make a similar extension of trigonometric series to functions that are not trigonometric polynomials.

Definition: If f(x) is integrable on the interval $[0, 2\pi]$, then the

Fourier Series of f(x) is $\dfrac{a_0}{2} + \sum_{n=1}^{\infty} \{a_n \cdot \cos(nx) + b_n \cdot \sin(nx)\}$ with

Fourier coefficients $\quad a_n = \dfrac{1}{\pi} \int_{x=0}^{2\pi} \cos(nx) \cdot f(x) \, dx \quad$ and

$$b_n = \frac{1}{\pi} \int_{x=0}^{2\pi} \sin(nx) \cdot f(x) \, dx \quad \text{for n=0, 1, 2, 3, ...}$$

Before going further with the development and discussion, let's take a look at how this actually works with some different types of functions – a differentiable function, a function that is continuous but not differentiable, and a function that is not even continuous. At the end of this section is a MAPLE program that automatically calculates the Fourier coefficients and builds the Fourier series.

Fourier Series approximation of a differentiable function $f(x) = x^2 \cdot (2\pi - x)$

The series of graphs below show how the higher degree Fourier series of f become better and better approximations of the graph of f on the interval $[0, 2\pi]$.

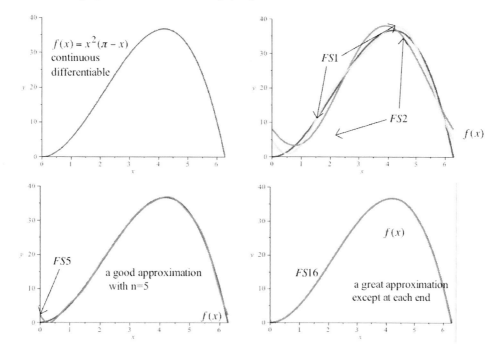

FS5(x) = 20.67085112-12.56637062*cos(x)-12.*sin(x)-3.141592654*cos(2*x)-1.5*sin(2*x)
       -1.396263402*cos(3*x)-.4444444444*sin(3*x)-.7853981635*cos(4*x)-.1875*sin(4*x)
       -.5026548246*cos(5*x)-0.096*sin(5*x)

Taylor and Maclaurin series require that we have a differentiable function of f or we could not calculate the coefficients for the series. For Fourier series, however, we only need that the function of f be integrable, a much less demanding condition. The next example illustrates the convergence of the Fourier series of a function that has a "corner" so it is not differentiable (at that point).

Note: We only need f to be an integrable function in order to be able to calculate the coefficients of the Fourier series, but that is not enough to guarantee that the Fourier series we get converges to f(x) for every value of x. In fact, there are continuous functions for which the Fourier series does not converge to f(x) for an infinite number of vales of x. The whole study of conditions that do and do not guarantee the convergence of Fourier series led to some very interesting, very beautiful and very deep results in mathematics.

Fourier Series approximation of a continuous function with a corner: $f(x) = 4 - |\pi - x|$

These figures illustrate that the Fourier series can converge to a function that is not differentiable at a point.

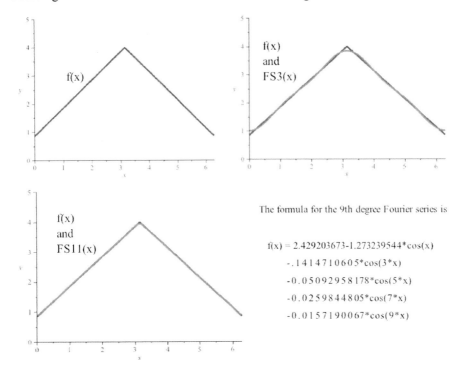

The formula for the 9th degree Fourier series is

$f(x) = 2.429203673 - 1.273239544 * \cos(x)$
$- .1414710605 * \cos(3*x)$
$- 0.05092958178 * \cos(5*x)$
$- 0.0259844805 * \cos(7*x)$
$- 0.0157190067 * \cos(9*x)$

Because of the symmetry of $f(x)$ around π, all of the sine terms, the b_n, are 0.

The next example illustrates that the Fourier coefficients can even be found for functions which have some discontinuities (but they can still be integrated), and that the resulting Fourier series can still do a good job of approximating the function between the breaks.

Fourier series approximation of a discontinuous function:

$f(x) = |1.3 - \text{Int}(x/2.3)|$

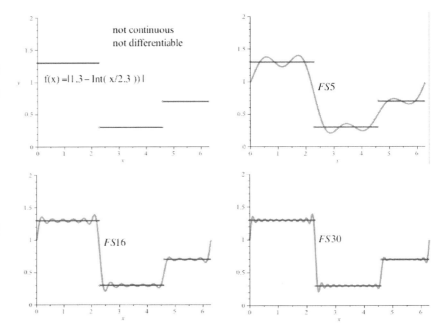

What good are Fourier Series?

Historically Fourier series were important because they provided a method of analyzing data that arose from the interaction of various periodic influences such as the orbits of the planets (influenced by the gravitational attractions of the sun and other planets whose orbits are almost periodic) or the tides (influenced by the attraction of the moon and also by local conditions). More recently, Fourier series provide a way to efficiently store and regenerate the musical tones of various instruments. Each tone for an instrument can be efficiently stored by saving only the coefficients, and we only need to save the first "several" terms of the series since the higher order coefficients correspond to high frequency sounds that are beyond the human hearing range.

Fourier series, and variations on that idea, have also been used extensively in signal processing and to clean up noisy signals. Since "random noise" is usually high frequency, the Fourier series of each piece of the signal can be calculated (automatically) and only the lower degree terms kept in order to reproduce a "clean" result. The following figures illustrate a noisy signal that has been cleaned up in this way. This might represent an attempt to reclaim voice information from a recording that has been damaged or originally contained a lot of background noise.

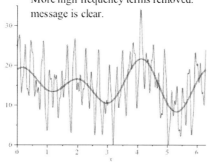

And Fourier series still enable us to solve problems of the type that led Fourier to develop them in the first place: if we know the temperature at each point on the boundary of a region (such as a solid circular disk) what will the temperature become at each point on the interior of the disk? And they are very useful for solving certain types of differential equations.

What if the function is not 2π-periodic?

If the function f is periodic with period P, we can "squeeze" f to create a new function g that does repeat every 2π units. Then after calculating the Fourier series for g, we can "unsqueeze" g to get a series for f.

Problems

The point of this section was only to use the Taylor series approach to create a new kind of infinite series, one whose building blocks were trigonometric functions, and the to show that this approach actually worked to approximate functions that were not even differentiable or continuous. There are still other infinite series that use different building blocks, but the point here was to illustrate that not all useful infinite series are power series.

Main Reference

Fourier Analysis, T.W. Korner, Cambridge University Press, 1988 (available in paperback)

This is a beautifully written book that is willing to forego some of the completeness and generalities of the results in order to present an understandable development of the main ideas and their applications and the personalities involved in this development. The level is aimed at a university student in their 3rd or 4th year with a strong background in mathematics (physics helps too), but the stories and descriptions of the applications and the flow of ideas are mostly accessible to very good and motivated students with a year of calculus.

MAPLE

You don't need a computer to calculate and graph the Fourier series of a function (your calculator can do the work), but Maple does a really nice job. The following program will automatically calculate the coefficients, build the Fourier series and graph both the original function and its Fourier series. One variation will even animate the approximation degree by degree. To use the program you need to enter the formula for the function (f:=x-> ...) and the degree of the approximation you want (N:= ...). The comments in italics are not part of the program.

with(plots):
f:=x->abs(1.3-floor(x/2.3));   *the original function – pick your own*
a0:=evalf((1/Pi)*int(f(x),x=0..2*Pi)):
PF:=plot(f(x), x=0..2*Pi, y=0..2, color=blue, thickness=3, discont=true):
a0:=evalf((1/Pi)*int(f(x),x=0..2*Pi)):

The next commands automatically construct the Fourier series
N:=15:   *degree of the approximating Fourier series – pick your own*
fs[0]:=a0/2;
FSplot[0]:=plot(fs[0], x=0..2*Pi, color=red, thickness=2, title="degree = "||i):
R[0]:=display(PF,FSplot[0], title="degree = 0"):
for i from 1 to N do
a:=evalf((1/Pi)*int(cos(i*x)*f(x), x=0..2*Pi)):
b:=evalf((1/Pi)*int(sin(i*x)*f(x), x=0..2*Pi)):
fs[i]:=fs[i-1]+a*cos(i*x)+b*sin(i*x);od:
fs[N];   *prints the approximating formula of the Fourier series of degree N*
plot({f(x),fs[N]}, x=0..2*Pi, color=[red,blue], thickness=2, title="degree = "||N);   *plots f and Nth degree Fourier series*

This set of commands will animate the approximation degree by degree
for i from 1 to N do
FSplot[i]:=plot(fs[i], x=0..2*Pi, color=red, thickness=2, title="degree = "||i):
R[i]:=display(PF, FSplot[i]):
od:
M:=[seq(R[i], i=0..N)]:
display(M, axes=normal, insequence=true);

Chapter 10: Odd Answers

Section 10.0

1. (a) 32, 64 (b) 2^5 (c) 2^n 3. (a) $-1, +1$ (b) $-1 = (-1)^5$ (c) $(-1)^n$

5. (a) 120, 720 (b) 5! or 5·24 (c) n! or $n \cdot a_{n-1}$ 7. 1, 3/2, 11/6, 25/12, 137/60, 147/60

9. 1, 1/2, 3/4, 5/8, 11/16, 21/32   11. 1, 0, 1, 0, 1, 0

13. (a) $g(5) = -1$, $g(6) = +1$ (b) see the figure for $g(x)$.

15. (a) $t(5) = 1 - 1/2 + 1/4 - 1/8 + 1/16 - 1/32 = 21/32$,
    $t(6) = 43/64$. The graph of t(x) is shown.

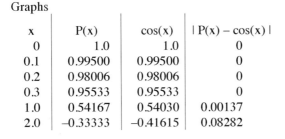

17. (a) $P(x) = 1 - \frac{x^2}{2}$ (b) Graphs

x	P(x)	cos(x)	| P(x) − cos(x) |
0	1.0	1.0	0
0.1	0.995	0.99500	0
0.2	0.98	0.98006	0.00006
0.3	0.955	0.95533	0.00033
1.0	0.5	0.54030	0.04030
2.0	−1.0	−0.41615	0.58385

(c) $P(x) = 1 - \frac{x^2}{2} + \frac{x^4}{24}$

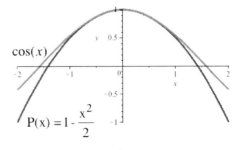

Graphs

x	P(x)	cos(x)	| P(x) − cos(x) |
0	1.0	1.0	0
0.1	0.99500	0.99500	0
0.2	0.98006	0.98006	0
0.3	0.95533	0.95533	0
1.0	0.54167	0.54030	0.00137
2.0	−0.33333	−0.41615	0.08282

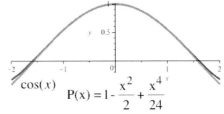

19. $P(x) = Ax + B$. $5 = P(0) = A \cdot 0 + B = B$ so $B = 5$. $3 = P'(0) = A$. $P(x) = 3x + 5$.

21. $P(x) = Ax + B$. $4 = P(0) = A \cdot 0 + B = B$ so $B = 4$. $-1 = P'(0) = A$. $P(x) = -1x + 4$.

23. $P(x) = 0x + 4 = 4$.   25. $P(x) = Ax + B$. $P(0) = B$. $P'(0) = A$.

27. $P(x) = Ax^2 + Bx + C$. $-2 = P(0) = A \cdot 0 + B \cdot 0 + C = C$. $7 = P'(0) = 2A \cdot 0 + B = B$.
    $6 = P''(0) = 2A$ so $A = 6/2 = 3$. $P(x) = 3x^2 + 7x - 2$.

29. $P(x) = Ax^2 + Bx + C$. $8 = P(0) = A \cdot 0 + B \cdot 0 + C = C$. $5 = P'(0) = 2A \cdot 0 + B = B$.
    $10 = P''(0) = 2A$ so $A = 10/2 = 5$. $P(x) = 5x^2 + 5x + 8$.

31. $P(x) = Ax^2 + Bx + C$. $-3 = P(0) = A \cdot 0 + B \cdot 0 + C = C$. $-2 = P'(0) = 2A \cdot 0 + B = B$.
    $4 = P''(0) = 2A$ so $A = 4/2 = 2$. $P(x) = 2x^2 - 2x - 3$.

33. $P(x) = Ax^3 + Bx^2 + Cx + D$. $5 = P(0) = A \cdot 0 + B \cdot 0 + C \cdot 0 + D = D$. $3 = P'(0) = 3A \cdot 0 + 2B \cdot 0 + C = C$.
    $4 = 6A0 + 2B = 2B$ so $B = 4/2 = 2$. $6 = P'''(0) = 6A$ so $A = 6/6 = 1$.
    $P(x) = 1x^3 + 2x^2 + 3x + 5$.

35. $P(x) = Ax^3 + Bx^2 + Cx + D$. $4 = P(0) = A \cdot 0 + B \cdot 0 + C \cdot 0 + D = D$. $-1 = P'(0) = 3A \cdot 0 + 2B \cdot 0 + C = C$.
    $-2 = 6A0 + 2B = 2B$ so $B = -2/2 = -1$. $-12 = P'''(0) = 6A$ so $A = -12/6 = -2$.
    $P(x) = -2x^3 - 1x^2 - 1x + 4$.

37. $P(x) = Ax^3 + Bx^2 + Cx + D$. $4 = P(0) = A \cdot 0 + B \cdot 0 + C \cdot 0 + D = D$. $0 = P'(0) = 3A \cdot 0 + 2B \cdot 0 + C = C$.
    $-4 = 6A0 + 2B = 2B$ so $B = -4/2 = -2$. $36 = P'''(0) = 6A$ so $A = 36/6 = 6$.
    $P(x) = 6x^3 - 2x^2 + 0x + 4 = 6x^3 - 2x^2 + 4$.

39. $A = P'''(0)/6$, $B = P''(0)/2$, $C = P'(0)$, and $D = P(0)$.

Section 10.1

1. $\dfrac{1}{n^2}$ 3. $\dfrac{n-1}{n} = 1 - \dfrac{1}{n}$ 5. $\dfrac{n}{2^n}$

7. $\{-1, 0, 1/3, 1/2, 3/5, 2/3, ...\}$ Graph is shown.   9. $\{1, 2/3, 3/5, 4/7, 5/9, 6/11, ...\}$ Graph is shown.

11. $\{2, 3\tfrac{1}{2}, 2\tfrac{2}{3}, 3\tfrac{1}{4}, 2\tfrac{4}{5}, 3\tfrac{1}{6}, ...\}$ Graph is shown.   13. $\{0, \tfrac{1}{2}, -\tfrac{2}{3}, \tfrac{3}{4}, -\tfrac{4}{5}, \tfrac{5}{6}, ...\}$ Graph is shown.

Prob. 7

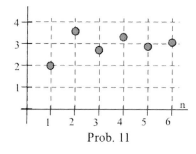
Prob. 9

Prob. 11

15. $\{1, \tfrac{1}{2}, \tfrac{1}{3!}, \tfrac{1}{4!}, \tfrac{1}{5!}, \tfrac{1}{6!}, ...\} = \{1, \tfrac{1}{2}, \tfrac{1}{6}, \tfrac{1}{24}, \tfrac{1}{120}, \tfrac{1}{720}, ...\}$ The graph is shown below.

Prob. 13

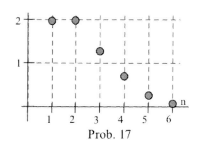
Prob. 15

Prob. 17

17. $\{\frac{2^1}{1!}, \frac{2^2}{2!}, \frac{2^3}{3!}, \frac{2^4}{4!}, \frac{2^5}{5!}, \frac{2^6}{6!}, ...\}$ The graph is shown.

19. $a_1 = 2, a_2 = -2, a_3 = 2, a_4 = -2, a_5 = 2, a_6 = -2, a_7 = 2, a_8 = -2, a_9 = 2, a_{10} = -2$

21. $\{\sin(2\pi/3), \sin(4\pi/3), \sin(6\pi/3), \sin(8\pi/3), \sin(10\pi/3), \sin(12\pi/3), \sin(14\pi/3), \sin(16\pi/3),$
    $\sin(18\pi/3), \sin(20\pi/3), ...\}$

23. $c_1 = 1, c_2 = 3, c_3 = 6, c_4 = 10, c_5 = 15, c_6 = 21, c_7 = 28, c_8 = 36, c_9 = 45, c_{10} = 55$

25. $\{a_n\}$ appears to converge. $\{b_n\}$ does not appear to converge.

27. $\{e_n\}$ does not appear to converge. $\{f_n\}$ appears to converge.

29. $\{1 - \frac{2}{n}\}$ converges to 1. 31. $\{\frac{n^2}{n+1}\}$ grows arbitrarily large and diverges.

33. $\{\frac{n}{2n-1}\}$ converges to $\frac{1}{2}$. 35. $\{\ln(3 + \frac{7}{n})\}$ converges to $\ln(3) \approx 1.099$.

37. $\{4 + (-1)^n\}$ alternates in value between 3 and 5 and does not appraoch a single number.
    The sequence diverges.

39. $\{\frac{1}{n!}\}$ converges to 0.

41. $\{(1 - \frac{1}{n})^n\}$ converges to $e^{-1} = \frac{1}{e}$. (See Section 3.7, Example 7.)

43. $\{\frac{(n+2)(n-5)}{n^2}\} = \{\frac{n^2 - 3n - 10}{n^2}\} = \{1 - \frac{3}{n} - \frac{10}{n^2}\}$ converges to 1.

45. Take $N = \sqrt{\frac{3}{\varepsilon}}$. If $n > N = \sqrt{\frac{3}{\varepsilon}}$ then $n^2 > \frac{3}{\varepsilon}$ and $\varepsilon > \frac{3}{n^2} = \left|\frac{3}{n^2} - 0\right|$.

47. Take $N = \frac{1}{\varepsilon}$. If $n > N = \frac{1}{\varepsilon}$ then $\varepsilon > \frac{1}{n} = |(3 - \frac{1}{n}) - 3| = |\frac{3n-1}{n} - 3|$.

49. $\{\frac{1}{n^{th} \text{ prime}}\}$ is a subsequence of $\{\frac{1}{n^{th} \text{ integer}}\} = \{\frac{1}{n}\}$ which converges to 0, so we can
    conclude that $\{\frac{1}{n^{th} \text{ prime}}\}$ converges to 0.

51. $\{(-2)^n(\frac{1}{3})^n\} = \{(-1)^n(\frac{2}{3})^n\}$.
    If n is even, $\{(-1)^n(\frac{2}{3})^n\} = \{(\frac{2}{3})^n\}$ which converges to 0. If n is odd,
    $\{(-1)^n(\frac{2}{3})^n\} = \{-(\frac{2}{3})^n\}$ which also converges to 0. Since "n even" and "n odd" account
    for all of the positive integers, we can conclude that $\{(-2)^n(\frac{1}{3})^n\}$ converges to 0.

53. $\left\{(1+\frac{5}{n^2})^{(n^2)}\right\}$ is a subsequence of $\left\{(1+\frac{5}{n})^n\right\}$ which converges to e^5 (Section 3.7, Example 7) so $\left\{(1+\frac{5}{n^2})^{(n^2)}\right\}$ also converges to e^5.

55. $a_n = 7 - \frac{2}{n}$ so $a_{n+1} = 7 - \frac{2}{n+1}$. $a_{n+1} - a_n = (7 - \frac{2}{n+1}) - (7 - \frac{2}{n}) = \frac{2}{n} - \frac{2}{n+1} = \frac{2}{n(n+1)} > 0$ for all $n \geq 1$.
Therefore, $a_{n+1} > a_n =$ and $\{a_n\}$ is monotonically increasing.

57. $a_n = 2^n$ so $a_{n+1} = 2^{n+1}$. $a_{n+1} - a_n = 2^{n+1} - 2^n = 2^n \cdot 2 - 2^n = 2^n(2-1) = 2^n > 0$ for all $n \geq 1$.
Therefore, $a_{n+1} > a_n =$ and $\{a_n\}$ is monotonically increasing.

59. $a_n = \frac{n+1}{n!}$ so $a_{n+1} = \frac{(n+1)+1}{(n+1)!} = \frac{n+2}{(n+1)!}$. Then

$$\frac{a_{n+1}}{a_n} = \frac{\frac{n+2}{(n+1)!}}{\frac{n+1}{n!}} = \frac{n+2}{n+1} \cdot \frac{n!}{(n+1)!} = \frac{n+2}{n+1} \cdot \frac{1 \cdot 2 \cdot 3 \cdots n}{1 \cdot 2 \cdot 3 \cdots n \cdot (n+1)} = \frac{n+2}{n+1} \cdot \frac{1}{n+1} < 1 \text{ for all } n \geq 1$$

so $a_{n+1} < a_n$ for all $n \geq 1$ and $\{a_n\}$ is monotonically decreasing.

61. $a_n = (\frac{5}{4})^n$ so $a_{n+1} = (\frac{5}{4})^{n+1}$. Then

$$\frac{a_{n+1}}{a_n} = \frac{(\frac{5}{4})^{n+1}}{(\frac{5}{4})^n} = \frac{5}{4} > 1 \text{ for all } n \text{ so } a_{n+1} > a_n \text{ for all } n > 0 \text{ and } \{a_n\} \text{ is montonically increasing.}$$

63. $a_n = \frac{n}{e^n}$ so $a_{n+1} = \frac{n+1}{e^{n+1}}$. Then

$$\frac{a_{n+1}}{a_n} = \frac{\frac{n+1}{e^{n+1}}}{\frac{n}{e^n}} = \frac{n+1}{n} \cdot \frac{e^n}{e^{n+1}} = \frac{n+1}{n} \cdot \frac{1}{e} < 1 \text{ for } n > 1 \text{ (reason: } e > 2 \text{ so } n \cdot e > 2n > n+1 \text{ so } \frac{n+1}{n \cdot e} < 1).$$

So $a_{n+1} < a_n$ for all $n > 0$ and $\{a_n\}$ is monotonically decreasing.

65. Let $f(x) = 5 - \frac{3}{x}$. Then $f'(x) = \frac{3}{x^2} > 0$ for all x so $f(x)$ is increasing. From that we can conclude that $a_n = f(n)$ is monotonically increasing.

67. Let $f(x) = \cos(\frac{1}{x})$. Then $f'(x) = -\sin(\frac{1}{x}) \cdot (\frac{-1}{x^2}) = \frac{1}{x^2} \cdot \sin(\frac{1}{x}) > 0$ for all $x \geq 1$. From that we can conclude that $a_n = f(n)$ is monotonically increasing.

69. This is similar to problem 59. The ratio method works nicely.

71. One method is to examine $a_{n+1} - a_n = (1 - \frac{1}{2^{n+1}}) - (1 - \frac{1}{2^n}) = \frac{1}{2^n} - \frac{1}{2^{n+1}} = \frac{1}{2^n} - \frac{1}{2 \cdot 2^n} = \frac{1}{2 \cdot 2^n} > 0$

   for all n so $a_{n+1} > a_n$ for all n and $\{a_n\}$ is monotonically increasing.

   The ratio and derivative methods also work.

   $(D(1 - \frac{1}{2^x}) = D(1 - 2^{-x}) = 0 - 2^{-x} \cdot \ln(2) \cdot D(-x) = 2^{-x} \ln(2) = \frac{\ln(2)}{2^x} > 0$ for $x > 0$.)

73. This is similar to problem 63. The ratio method works nicely.

75. N = 4: $a_1 = 4$, $a_2 = \frac{1}{2}(4 + \frac{4}{4}) = \frac{5}{2} = 2.5$, $a_3 = \frac{1}{2}(2.5 + \frac{4}{2.5}) = 2.05$, $a_n = \frac{1}{2}(2.05 + \frac{4}{2.05}) \approx 2.00061$.

   N = 9: $a_1 = 9$, $a_2 = \frac{1}{2}(9 + \frac{9}{9}) = \frac{10}{2} = 5$, $a_3 = \frac{1}{2}(5 + \frac{9}{5}) = 3.2$, $a_n = \frac{1}{2}(3.2 + \frac{9}{3.2}) = 3.00625$.

   N = 5: $a_1 = 5$, $a_2 = \frac{1}{2}(5 + \frac{5}{5}) = \frac{6}{2} = 3$. $a_3 = \frac{1}{2}(3 + \frac{5}{3}) \approx 2.333$, $a_n = \frac{1}{2}(2.333 + \frac{5}{2.333}) \approx 2.238$.

77. (a) $p = 0.02$, and we want to solve $0.01 = \frac{0.02}{0.02k + 1}$ for k. Then $0.02k + 1 = \frac{0.02}{0.01} = 2$ so

   $0.02k = 1$ and $k = \frac{1}{0.02} = 50$ generations.

   (b) We want to solve $\frac{1}{2} p = \frac{p}{kp + 1}$ for k in terms of p. $kp + 1 = \frac{p}{0.5p} = 2$ so $kp = 1$ and

   $k = \frac{1}{p}$ generations.

79. (a) The first "few" grains can be anywhere on the x–axis.

   (b) After a "lot of grains" have been placed, there will be a large pile of sand close to 3 on the x–axis.

81. $-1 \leq \sin(n) \leq 1$ for all integers n.

   (a) The first few grains will be scattered between –1 and +1 on the x–axis.

   (b) After a "lot of grains" have been placed, the sand will be scattered "uniformly" along the interval from –1 to +1. (See part (c).)

   (c) This argument is rather sophisticated, but the result is interesting: no two grains ever end up on the same point.

   We assume that two grains do end up on the same point, and then derive a contradiction. From this we conclude that our original assumption (two grains on one point) was false.

   Assume that two grains do end up on the same point so $a_m = a_n$ for distinct integers m and n. Then $\sin(m) = \sin(n)$ so $0 = \sin(m) - \sin(n) = 2 \cdot \sin(\frac{m-n}{2}) \cdot \cos(\frac{m+n}{2})$ and either $\sin(\frac{m-n}{2}) = 0$ or $\cos(\frac{m+n}{2}) = 0$. If $\sin(\frac{m-n}{2}) = 0$, then $\frac{m-n}{2} = \pi K$ for some integer K and $\pi = \frac{m-n}{2K}$ where m, n, and K are integers. Then π is a rational number, a contradiction of the fact that π is irrational.

   If $\cos(\frac{m+n}{2}) = 0$, then $\frac{m+n}{2} = \frac{\pi}{2} + K\pi = \pi(\frac{1}{2} + K)$ for some integer K so $\pi = \frac{m+n}{1 + 2K}$, a rational number. This again contradicts the irrationality of π, so out original assumption (two grains on the same point) was false.

Section 10.2

1. $\sum_{k=1}^{\infty} \frac{1}{k}$

3. $\sum_{k=1}^{\infty} \frac{2}{3k}$

5. $\sum_{k=1}^{\infty} \left(-\frac{1}{2}\right)^k$ or $\sum_{k=1}^{\infty} (-1)^k \cdot \frac{1}{2^k}$

7. The graph is given.

9. The graph is given.

11. The graph is given.

Problem 7

Problem 9

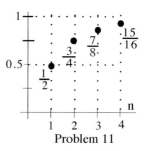
Problem 11

13. $a_1 = 3$, $a_2 = -1$, $a_3 = 2$, $a_4 = 1$

15. $a_1 = 4$, $a_2 = 0.5$, $a_3 = -0.2$, $a_4 = 0.5$

17. $a_1 = 1$, $a_2 = 0.1$, $a_3 = 0.01$, $a_4 = 0.001$

19. $\sum_{k=1}^{\infty} \frac{8}{10^k}$

21. $\sum_{k=1}^{\infty} \frac{5}{10^k}$

23. $\sum_{k=1}^{\infty} \frac{a}{10^k}$

25. $\sum_{k=1}^{\infty} \frac{17}{100^k}$

27. $\sum_{k=1}^{\infty} \frac{7}{100^k}$

29. $\sum_{k=1}^{\infty} \frac{abc}{1000^k}$

31. $\sum_{k=0}^{\infty} 30 \cdot (0.8)^k$

33. $80, 64, 51.2, 100 \cdot (0.8)^n$

35. $(1/4)^n \to 0$ so the series may converge or may diverge. (Later we will see that it converges.)

37. $(4/3)^n \to \infty \neq 0$ so the series diverges.

39. $\frac{\sin(n)}{n} \to 0$ so the series may converge or may diverge.

41. $\cos(1/n) \to \cos(0) = 1 \neq 0$ so the series diverges.

43. $\frac{n^2 - 20}{n^5 + 4} \to 0$ so the series may converge or may diverge. (Later we will see that it converges.)

Section 10.3

1. $\sum_{k=0}^{\infty} \left(\frac{1}{3}\right)^k = \frac{1}{1-\left(\frac{1}{3}\right)} = \frac{3}{2}$

2. $\sum_{k=0}^{\infty} \left(\frac{2}{3}\right)^k = \frac{1}{1-\left(\frac{2}{3}\right)} = 3$

3. $\frac{1}{8} \cdot \sum_{k=0}^{\infty} \left(\frac{1}{2}\right)^k = \frac{1}{8} \cdot \frac{1}{1-\left(\frac{1}{2}\right)} = \frac{1}{4}$

5. $-\frac{2}{3} \cdot \sum_{k=0}^{\infty} \left(-\frac{2}{3}\right)^k = -\frac{2}{3} \cdot \frac{1}{1-\left(-\frac{2}{3}\right)} = -\frac{2}{5}$

7. (a) $\frac{1}{2} \cdot \sum_{k=0}^{\infty} \left(\frac{1}{2}\right)^k = \frac{1}{2} \cdot \frac{1}{1-\left(\frac{1}{2}\right)} = \frac{1}{2} \cdot \frac{2}{1} = 1$, $\quad \frac{1}{3} \cdot \sum_{k=0}^{\infty} \left(\frac{1}{3}\right)^k = \frac{1}{3} \cdot \frac{1}{1-\left(\frac{1}{3}\right)} = \frac{1}{3} \cdot \frac{3}{2} = \frac{1}{2}$

   (b) $\frac{1}{a} \cdot \sum_{k=0}^{\infty} \left(\frac{1}{a}\right)^k = \frac{1}{a} \cdot \frac{1}{1-\left(\frac{1}{a}\right)} = \frac{1}{a} \cdot \frac{a}{a-1} = \frac{1}{a-1}$

9. (a) $40 \cdot (0.4)^{n-1}$ (b) $40 \cdot \sum_{k=0}^{\infty} (0.4)^k$ (c) $40 \cdot \frac{1}{1-0.4} = \frac{40}{0.6} = 66\frac{2}{3}$ ft.

11. (a) $\sum_{k=1}^{\infty} \left(\frac{1}{2}\right)^k$ (b) $\frac{1}{2}, \frac{1}{4}, \left(\frac{1}{2}\right)^n$ (c) All of the cake.

13. $1 + \frac{1}{4} + \left(\frac{1}{4}\right)^2 + \left(\frac{1}{4}\right)^3 + \ldots = \sum_{k=0}^{\infty} \left(\frac{1}{4}\right)^k = \frac{4}{3}$.

15. (a) Area $= 1 + \frac{3}{9} + \frac{3}{9} \cdot \frac{4}{9} + \frac{3}{9}\left(\frac{4}{9}\right)^2 + \frac{3}{9}\left(\frac{4}{9}\right)^3 + \ldots = 1 + \frac{3}{9}\left\{1 + \frac{4}{9} + \left(\frac{4}{9}\right)^2 + \left(\frac{4}{9}\right)^3 + \ldots \right\}$

    $= 1 + \frac{3}{9} \left\{ \frac{1}{1-(4/9)} \right\} = 1 + \frac{3}{5} = \frac{8}{5} = 1.6$.

    (b) Let L be the length of the original triangle ($L = 3\sqrt{\frac{4}{\sqrt{3}}}$) and P_n be the perimeter at the nth step. Then $P_0 = 3L$. $P_1 = 3 \cdot 4 \cdot \left(\frac{L}{3}\right) = 4L$,

    $P_2 = 3 \cdot 4^2 \cdot \left(\frac{L}{3^2}\right) = 3L\left(\frac{4}{3}\right)^2$

    $P_3 = 3 \cdot 4^3 \cdot \left(\frac{L}{3^3}\right) = 3L\left(\frac{4}{3}\right)^3$

    $P_4 = 3 \cdot 4^4 \cdot \left(\frac{L}{3^4}\right) = 3L\left(\frac{4}{3}\right)^4$, and, in general,

    $P_n = 3 \cdot 4^n \cdot \left(\frac{L}{3^n}\right) = 3L\left(\frac{4}{3}\right)^n$.

    Since $\frac{4}{3} > 1$, the sequence of terms $3L\left(\frac{4}{3}\right)^n$ grows without bound, and the perimeter "approaches infinity."

17. (a) Height $= 2 + 2(\frac{1}{2}) + 2(\frac{1}{4}) + 2(\frac{1}{8}) + ... = 2\{ 1 + \frac{1}{2} + (\frac{1}{2})^2 + (\frac{1}{2})^3 + ... \} = 2 \cdot \frac{1}{1-\frac{1}{2}} = 4$.

(b) Surface area $= 4\pi(1)^2 + 4\pi(\frac{1}{2})^2 + 4\pi(\frac{1}{4})^2 + 4\pi(\frac{1}{8})^2 + ...$

$= 4\pi\{ 1 + \frac{1}{4} + (\frac{1}{4})^2 + (\frac{1}{4})^3 + ... \} = 4\pi \cdot \frac{1}{1-\frac{1}{4}} = \frac{16\pi}{3} \approx 16.755$.

(c) Volume $= \frac{4\pi}{3}(1)^3 + \frac{4\pi}{3}(\frac{1}{2})^3 + \frac{4\pi}{3}(\frac{1}{4})^3 + \frac{4\pi}{3}(\frac{1}{8})^3 + ...$

$= \frac{4\pi}{3}\{ 1 + \frac{1}{8} + (\frac{1}{8})^2 + (\frac{1}{8})^3 + ... \} = \frac{4\pi}{3} \cdot \frac{1}{1-\frac{1}{8}} = \frac{32\pi}{21} \approx 4.787$.

19. $0.8888... = \frac{8}{10} + \frac{8}{10^2} + \frac{8}{10^3} + ... = \frac{8}{10}\{ 1 + \frac{1}{10} + (\frac{1}{10})^2 + (\frac{1}{10})^3 + ...\} = \frac{8}{10}\{\frac{10}{9}\} = \frac{8}{9}$.

$0.9999... = \frac{9}{10} + \frac{9}{10^2} + \frac{9}{10^3} + ... = \frac{9}{10}\{ 1 + \frac{1}{10} + (\frac{1}{10})^2 + (\frac{1}{10})^3 + ...\} = \frac{9}{10}\{\frac{10}{9}\} = 1$.

$0.285714... = \frac{285714}{1000000} + \frac{285714}{1000000^2} + \frac{285714}{1000000^3} + ...$

$= \frac{285714}{1000000}\{ 1 + \frac{1}{1000000} + (\frac{1}{1000000})^2 + (\frac{1}{1000000})^3 + ...\}$

$= \frac{285714}{1000000}\{\frac{1000000}{999999}\} = \frac{285714}{999999}$.

21. Series converges for $|2x+1| < 1$: $-1 < x < 0$.

23. Series converges for $|1-2x| < 1$: $0 < x < 1$.

25. Series converges for $|7x| < 1$: $-\frac{1}{7} < x < \frac{1}{7}$.

27. Series converges for $|\frac{x}{2}| < 1$: $-2 < x < 2$.

29. Series converges for $|2x| < 1$: $-\frac{1}{2} < x < \frac{1}{2}$.

31. Series converges for $|\sin(x)| < 1$: for all $x \neq \frac{\pi}{2} \pm N\pi$ for integer values of N.

33. The formula is correct if $|x| < 1$. The value $x = 2$ does not satisfy the condition $|x| < 1$, so the formula does not apply.

35. $s_4 = (\frac{1}{3} - \frac{1}{4}) + (\frac{1}{4} - \frac{1}{5}) = \frac{1}{3} - \frac{1}{5}$, $s_5 = \frac{1}{3} - \frac{1}{6}$, $s_n = \frac{1}{3} - \frac{1}{n+1} \to \frac{1}{3}$

37. $s_4 = (1^3 - 2^3) + (2^3 - 3^3) + (3^3 - 4^3) = 1 - 4^3$, $s_5 = 1 - 5^3$, $s_n = 1 - (n+1)^3 \to -\infty$.

39. $s_4 = (f(3) - f(4)) + (f(4) - f(5)) = f(3) - f(5)$, $s_5 = f(3) - f(6)$, $s_n = f(3) - f(n+1)$

41. $s_4 = \sin(1) - \sin(\frac{1}{5}) \approx 0.643$, $s_5 = \sin(1) - \sin(\frac{1}{6}) \approx 0.676$, $s_n = \sin(1) - \sin(\frac{1}{n+1}) \to \sin(1) \approx 0.841$.

43. $s_4 = (\frac{1}{2^2} - \frac{1}{3^2}) + (\frac{1}{3^2} - \frac{1}{4^2}) + (\frac{1}{4^2} - \frac{1}{5^2}) = \frac{1}{4} - \frac{1}{25}$, $s_5 = \frac{1}{4} - \frac{1}{36}$, $s_n = \frac{1}{4} - \frac{1}{(n+1)^2} \to \frac{1}{4}$

45. & 47. On your own.

Section 10.3.5

Integrals and sums

1. The sum.
2. The integral.
3. $\sum_{k=1}^{\infty} f(k)$
4. $\sum_{k=1}^{\infty} f(k)$
5. $\sum_{k=2}^{\infty} f(k)$
6. (b) $f(1) + f(2)$
7. (b) $f(1) + f(2)$
8. (d) $f(3) + f(4)$
9. (c) $f(2) + f(3)$
10. (b), (d), (a), (c) : $\int_{2}^{4} f(x)\,dx < f(2) + f(3) < \int_{1}^{3} f(x)\,dx < f(1) + f(2)$
11. (c), (a), (d), (b) : $f(1) + f(2) + f(3) < \int_{1}^{4} f(x)\,dx < f(2) + f(3) + f(4) < \int_{2}^{5} f(x)\,dx$

Comparisons

12. (a) No. You are definitely too tall. (b) Apply. You **may** meet the requirements.
    (c) No. Definitely too short. (d) Apply. You **may** meet the requirements.
    (e) You do not meet the requirements if you are {shorter than Sam} or {taller than Tom}.
    (f) You do not have enough information if you are {shorter than Tom} or {taller than Sam}.

13. (a) You did well (better than Wendy). (b) You may have done well or poorly.
    (c) You may have done well or poorly. (d) You did poorly (worse than Paula).

14. (a) Baker is too easy (easier than Index). (b) Baker may be right for you.
    (c) Baker may be right for you. (d) Baker is too hard for you (harder than Liberty Bell).
    (e) Baker may be a good climb for you if it is harder than Index and easier than Liberty Bell.
    (f) Baker is too easy if Baker is easier than Index. Baker is too hard if Baker is harder than Liberty Bell.

15. (a) Expect Unknown to be (very) good. (b) Unknown is still unknown.
    (c) Unknown is still unknown. (d) Unknown is bad.

16. $\sum_{k=1}^{\infty} \dfrac{1}{k^2 + 1} < \sum_{k=1}^{\infty} \dfrac{1}{k^2}$

17. $\sum_{k=2}^{\infty} \dfrac{1}{k^3 - 5} > \sum_{k=2}^{\infty} \dfrac{1}{k^3}$

18. $\sum_{k=1}^{\infty} \dfrac{1}{k^2 + 3k - 1} < \sum_{k=1}^{\infty} \dfrac{1}{k^2}$

19. $\sum_{k=3}^{\infty} \dfrac{1}{k^2 + 5k} > \sum_{k=3}^{\infty} \dfrac{1}{k^3 + k - 1}$

Ratios of successive terms

20. $a_k = 3k$, $a_{k+1} = 3(k+1)$, $\dfrac{a_{k+1}}{a_k} = \dfrac{k+1}{k}$.

21. $a_k = k + 3$, $a_{k+1} = (k+1) + 3$, $\dfrac{a_{k+1}}{a_k} = \dfrac{k+4}{k+3}$.

22. $a_k = 2k + 5$, $a_{k+1} = 2(k+1) + 5$, $\dfrac{a_{k+1}}{a_k} = \dfrac{2k+7}{2k+5}$.

23. $a_k = 3/k$, $a_{k+1} = \dfrac{3}{k+1}$, $\dfrac{a_{k+1}}{a_k} = \dfrac{\frac{3}{k+1}}{\frac{3}{k}} = \dfrac{k}{k+1}$.

24. $a_k = k^2$, $a_{k+1} = (k+1)^2$, $\dfrac{a_{k+1}}{a_k} = \dfrac{(k+1)^2}{k^2}$.   25. $a_k = 2^k$, $a_{k+1} = 2^{k+1}$, $\dfrac{a_{k+1}}{a_k} = \dfrac{2^{k+1}}{2^k} = 2$.

26. $a_k = (1/2)^k$, $a_{k+1} = (1/2)^{k+1}$, $\dfrac{a_{k+1}}{a_k} = \dfrac{(1/2)^{k+1}}{(1/2)^k} = \dfrac{1}{2}$.

27. $a_k = x^k$, $a_{k+1} = x^{k+1}$, $\dfrac{a_{k+1}}{a_k} = \dfrac{x^{k+1}}{x^k} = x$.

28. $a_k = (x-1)^k$, $a_{k+1} = (x-1)^{k+1}$, $\dfrac{a_{k+1}}{a_k} = \dfrac{(x-1)^{k+1}}{(x-1)^k} = x - 1$.

29. $\sum\limits_{k=1}^{\infty} (\dfrac{1}{2})^k$ is a geometric series with $r = 1/2$ so the series converges. $\dfrac{a_{k+1}}{a_k} = \dfrac{(1/2)^{k+1}}{(1/2)^k} = \dfrac{1}{2}$.

30. $\sum\limits_{k=1}^{\infty} (\dfrac{1}{5})^k$ is a geometric series with $r = 1/5$ so the series converges. $\dfrac{a_{k+1}}{a_k} = \dfrac{(1/5)^{k+1}}{(1/5)^k} = \dfrac{1}{5}$.

31. $\sum\limits_{k=1}^{\infty} 2^k$ is a geometric series with $r = 2$ so the series diverges. $\dfrac{a_{k+1}}{a_k} = \dfrac{2^{k+1}}{2^k} = 2$.

32. $\sum\limits_{k=1}^{\infty} (-3)^k$ is a geometric series with $r = -3$ so the series diverges. $\dfrac{a_{k+1}}{a_k} = \dfrac{(-3)^{k+1}}{(-3)^k} = -3$.

33. $\sum\limits_{k=1}^{\infty} 4 = 4 + 4 + 4 + \ldots$ diverges by the Nth Term Test for Divergence since $a_n = 4$ for all n, and

$a_n = 4$ does not approach 0. $\dfrac{a_{k+1}}{a_k} = \dfrac{4}{4} = 1$.

34. $\sum\limits_{k=1}^{\infty} (-1)^k$ diverges by the Nth Term Test for Divergence since a_n does not approach 0. (It also is a

geometric series with $r = -1$ and $|r| = 1$.) $\dfrac{a_{k+1}}{a_k} = \dfrac{(-1)^{k+1}}{(-1)^k} = -1$.

35. $\sum\limits_{k=1}^{\infty} \dfrac{1}{k}$ is the harmonic series which diverges. $\dfrac{a_{k+1}}{a_k} = \dfrac{\frac{1}{k+1}}{\frac{1}{k}} = \dfrac{k}{k+1}$.

36. $\sum\limits_{k=1}^{\infty} \dfrac{7}{k} = 7 \cdot \sum\limits_{k=1}^{\infty} \dfrac{1}{k}$ is the divergent harmonic series. $\dfrac{a_{k+1}}{a_k} = \dfrac{\frac{7}{k+1}}{\frac{7}{k}} = \dfrac{k}{k+1}$.

Alternating terms

37. If $a_5 > 0$, then $s_4 < s_5$.

38. If $a_5 = 0$, then $s_4 = s_5$.

39. If $a_5 < 0$, then $s_4 > s_5$.

40. If $a_{n+1} > 0$ for all n, then $s_n < s_{n+1}$ for all n.

41. If $a_{n+1} < 0$ for all n, then $s_n > s_{n+1}$ for all n.

42. If $a_4 > 0$ and $a_5 < 0$, then $s_3 < s_4$ and $s_4 > s_5$.

43. If $a_4 = 0.2$ and $a_5 = -0.1$ and $a_6 = 0.2$, then $s_3 < s_5 < s_4$.

44. If $a_4 = -0.3$ and $a_5 = 0.2$ and $a_6 = -0.1$, then $s_3 > s_5 > s_4$.

45. If $a_4 = -0.3$ and $a_5 = -0.2$ and $a_6 = 0.1$, then $s_3 > s_4 > s_5$.

46. $s_1 = 2, s_2 = 1, s_3 = 3, s_4 = 2, s_5 = 4, s_6 = 3, s_7 = 5, s_8 = 4$.

47. $s_1 = 2, s_2 = 1, s_3 = 1.9, s_4 = 1.1, s_5 = 1.8, s_6 = 1.2$, $s_7 = 1.7, s_8 = 1.3$. The graph is given.

48. $s_1 = 2, s_2 = 1, s_3 = 2, s_4 = 1, s_5 = 2, s_6 = 1, s_7 = 2, s_8 = 1$. The graph is given.

49. $s_1 = -2, s_2 = -0.5, s_3 = -1.3, s_4 = -0.7, s_5 = -1.1, s_6 = -0.9$, $s_7 = 1.1, s_8 = 1.0$. The graph is given.

50. $s_1 = 5, s_2 = 6, s_3 = 5.4, s_4 = 5.0, s_5 = 5.2, s_6 = 5.3$, $s_7 = 5.4, s_8 = 5.2$. The graph is given.

51. If the a_k alternate in sign, then the graph of the partial sums s_n follows an "up–down–up–down" pattern?

52. If the a_k alternate in sign and decrease in magnitude (the $|a_k|$ is decreasing), then the graph of the partial sums s_n forms a "narrowing funnel" pattern.

53. (a) The terms a_k alternate in sign for the graphs D, E, and F.
    (b) The $|a_k|$ decrease for the graphs A and D.
    (c) The terms a_k alternate in sign and decrease in absolute value for the graph D.

54. (a) The terms a_k alternate in sign for the graphs C, D, E, and F in Fig. 14.
    (b) The $|a_k|$ decrease for the graphs B and C.
    (c) The terms a_k alternate in sign and decrease in absolute value for the graph C.

Prob. 46

Prob. 47

Prob. 48

Prob. 49

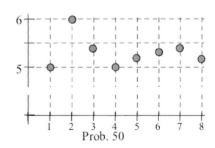
Prob. 50

55. The graph of the first eight partial sums of

$$\sum_{k=0}^{\infty} \left(-\frac{1}{2}\right)^k = 1 - \frac{1}{2} + \frac{1}{4} - \ldots = \frac{2}{3}$$ is given.

Notice the "narrowing funnel" shape of the graph.

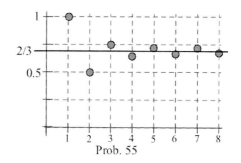
Prob. 55

56. The graph of the first eight partial sums of

$$\sum_{k=0}^{\infty} (-0.6)^k = 1 - 0.6 + 0.36 - \ldots = 0.625$$

is given.

Notice the "narrowing funnel" shape of the graph.

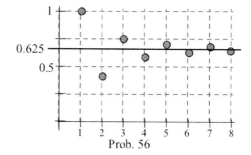
Prob. 56

57. The graph is given of the first eight partial sums of the divergent series

$$\sum_{k=0}^{\infty} (-2)^k = 1 - 2 + 4 - \ldots$$

This is a divergent series (N^{th} Term Test for Divergence).

Notice the "widening funnel" shape of the graph.

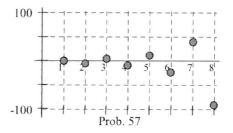
Prob. 57

Section 10.4 (Odd numbered problem solutions followed by even numbered problem answers.)

1. $\int_{1}^{\infty} \frac{1}{2x+5} \, dx = \frac{1}{2} \ln|2x+5| \Big|_{1}^{A} = \frac{1}{2} \ln|2A+5| - \frac{1}{2} \ln|7| \to \infty$ (as $A \to \infty$) so $\sum_{k=1}^{\infty} \frac{1}{2k+5}$ diverges.

3. $\int_{1}^{\infty} (2x+5)^{-3/2} \, dx = -(2x+5)^{-1/2} \Big|_{1}^{A} = \frac{-1}{\sqrt{2A+5}} - \frac{-1}{\sqrt{7}} \to \frac{1}{\sqrt{7}}$ (as $A \to \infty$) so $\sum_{k=1}^{\infty} \frac{1}{(2k+5)^{3/2}}$
converges.

5. $\int \frac{1}{x \cdot (\ln(x))^2} \, dx = \frac{-1}{\ln(x)} + C$ (using a u–substitution with $u = \ln(x)$ and $du = \frac{1}{x} dx$) so

$\int_{2}^{\infty} \frac{1}{x \cdot (\ln(x))^2} \, dx = \frac{-1}{\ln(x)} \Big|_{2}^{A} = \frac{-1}{\ln(A)} - \frac{-1}{\ln(2)} \to \frac{1}{\ln(2)}$ (as $A \to \infty$) so $\sum_{k=2}^{\infty} \frac{1}{k \cdot (\ln(k))^2}$ converges.

7. $\int_{1}^{\infty} \frac{1}{x^2+1} \, dx = \arctan(x) \Big|_{1}^{A} = \arctan(A) - \arctan(1) \to \frac{\pi}{2} - \frac{\pi}{4}$ (as $A \to \infty$) so $\sum_{k=1}^{\infty} \frac{1}{k^2+1}$ converges.

9. This is a telescoping series:

$$\sum_{k=1}^{\infty} \left\{ \frac{1}{k} - \frac{1}{k+3} \right\} = \left\{ 1 - \frac{1}{4} \right\} + \left\{ \frac{1}{2} - \frac{1}{5} \right\} + \left\{ \frac{1}{3} - \frac{1}{6} \right\} + \left\{ \frac{1}{4} - \frac{1}{7} \right\} + \left\{ \frac{1}{5} - \frac{1}{8} \right\} + \ldots \to 1 + \frac{1}{2} + \frac{1}{3}$$

The Integral Test also works:

$$\int_{1}^{\infty} \frac{1}{x} - \frac{1}{x+3} \, dx = \ln|x| - \ln|x+3| \Big|_{1}^{A} = \{\ln|A| - \ln|A+3|\} - \{\ln(1) - \ln(4)\}$$

$$= \ln\left|\frac{4A}{A+3}\right| \to \ln(4) \text{ (as } A \to \infty) \text{ so } \sum_{k=1}^{\infty} \left\{ \frac{1}{k} - \frac{1}{k+3} \right\} \text{ converges.}$$

(Notice that the "telescoping series" method gives the value of the series, but the Integral Test only tells us that the series converges. For this series, the "telescoping series" method is both easier and more precise.)

11. $\int_{1}^{\infty} \frac{1}{x(x+5)} \, dx = \int_{1}^{\infty} \frac{1}{5} \left\{ \frac{1}{x} - \frac{1}{x+5} \right\} dx$ (using the method of Partial Fraction Decomposition)

$$= \frac{1}{5} \{ \ln|x| - \ln|x+5| \} = \frac{1}{5} \left\{ \ln\left|\frac{x}{x+5}\right| \right\} \Big|_{1}^{A} = \frac{1}{5} \left\{ \ln\left|\frac{A}{A+5}\right| - \ln\left|\frac{1}{6}\right| \right\} \to \frac{1}{5} \left\{ \ln(1) - \ln\left(\frac{1}{6}\right) \right\}$$

(as $A \to \infty$) so $\sum_{k=1}^{\infty} \frac{1}{k \cdot (k+5)}$ converges.

13. $\int_{1}^{\infty} x \cdot e^{-(x^2)} \, dx = \frac{-1}{2} e^{-(x^2)} \Big|_{1}^{A} = \left(\frac{-1}{2} e^{-(A^2)}\right) - \left(\frac{-1}{2} e^{-1}\right) = \frac{1}{2e} - \frac{1}{2e^{(A^2)}} \to \frac{1}{2e}$ (as $A \to \infty$) so

$\sum_{k=1}^{\infty} k \cdot e^{-(k^2)}$ converges.

15. $\int \frac{1}{\sqrt{6x+10}} \, dx = \frac{1}{3} \sqrt{6x+10} + C$ (using a u–substitution with $u = 6x+10$ and $du = 6 \, dx$). Then

$$\int_{1}^{\infty} \frac{1}{\sqrt{6x+10}} \, dx = \frac{1}{3} \sqrt{6x+10} \Big|_{1}^{A} = \frac{1}{3}\sqrt{6A+10} - \frac{1}{3}\sqrt{16} \to \infty \text{ (as } A \to \infty)$$

so $\sum_{k=1}^{\infty} \frac{1}{\sqrt{6k+10}}$ diverges.

17. $p = 3 > 1$ so $\sum_{k=1}^{\infty} \frac{1}{k^3}$ converges.

19. $p = 1/2 < 1$ so $\sum_{k=2}^{\infty} \frac{1}{\sqrt{k}}$ diverges.

21. $p = 3/2 > 1$ so $\sum_{k=3}^{\infty} \frac{1}{k^{3/2}}$ converges.

23. $\sum_{k=1}^{\infty} \frac{1}{k^3}$: $\int_{1}^{11} \frac{1}{x^3} dx = 0.4958677$, $1 + \int_{1}^{10} \frac{1}{x^3} dx = 1.495$ so $0.4958677 < s_{10} < 1.495$.

$\int_{1}^{101} \frac{1}{x^3} dx = 0.499951$, $1 + \int_{1}^{100} \frac{1}{x^3} dx = 1.49995$ so $0.499951 < s_{100} < 1.49995$.

$\int_{1}^{1000001} \frac{1}{x^3} dx = 0.5000000$, $1 + \int_{1}^{1000000} \frac{1}{x^3} dx = 1.5000000$ so $0.5000000 < s_{1000000} < 1.5000000$.

25. $\sum_{k=1}^{\infty} \frac{1}{k+1000}$: $\int_{1}^{11} \frac{1}{x+1000} dx = 0.0099404$, $\frac{1}{1001} + \int_{1}^{10} \frac{1}{x+1000} dx = 0.0099498$

so $\mathbf{0.0099}404 < s_{10} < \mathbf{0.0099}498$. (This is a very precise estimate of s_{10}.)

$\int_{1}^{101} \frac{1}{x+1000} dx = 0.09522$, $\frac{1}{1001} + \int_{1}^{100} \frac{1}{x+1000} dx = 0.0953$ so $\mathbf{0.0952}2 < s_{100} < \mathbf{0.095}3$.

$\int_{1}^{1000001} \frac{1}{x+1000} dx = 6.90776$, $\frac{1}{1001} + \int_{1}^{1000000} \frac{1}{x+1000} dx = 6.90875$ so $\mathbf{6.907}76 < s_{1000000} < \mathbf{6.908}75$.

27. $\sum_{k=1}^{\infty} \frac{1}{k^2+100}$: $\int_{1}^{11} \frac{1}{x^2+100} dx = \frac{1}{10} \arctan(\frac{x}{10})\Big|_{1}^{11} = 0.0733$, $\frac{1}{101} + \int_{1}^{10} \frac{1}{x^2+100} dx = 0.0783$

so $\mathbf{0.073} < s_{10} < \mathbf{0.078}$. Also, $\mathbf{0.137} < s_{100} < \mathbf{0.147}$ and $\mathbf{0.1471} < s_{1000000} < \mathbf{0.157}$.

29. For $\mathbf{q \neq 1}$, let $u = \ln(x)$ and $du = \frac{1}{x} dx$.

Then $\int \frac{1}{x \cdot (\ln(x))^q} dx = \int \frac{1}{(u)^q} du = \frac{1}{1-q} u^{-q+1} = \frac{1}{1-q} (\ln(x))^{1-q} + C$.

Then $\int_{2}^{\infty} \frac{1}{x \cdot (\ln(x))^q} dx = \frac{1}{1-q} (\ln(x))^{1-q} \Big|_{2}^{A} = \frac{1}{1-q} (\ln(A))^{1-q} - \frac{1}{1-q} (\ln(2))^{1-q}$.

If $q < 1$, then $\frac{1}{1-q} (\ln(A))^{1-q} - \frac{1}{1-q} (\ln(2))^{1-q} \to \infty$ (as $A \to \infty$) so $\sum_{k=2}^{\infty} \frac{1}{k \cdot (\ln k)^q}$ diverges.

If $q > 1$, then $\frac{1}{1-q} (\ln(A))^{1-q} - \frac{1}{1-q} (\ln(2))^{1-q} \to -\frac{1}{1-q} (\ln(2))^{1-q}$ (as $A \to \infty$)

so $\sum_{k=2}^{\infty} \frac{1}{k \cdot (\ln k)^q}$ converges.

If $\mathbf{q = 1}$, then

$$\int_2^\infty \frac{1}{x \cdot (\ln(x))^q}\, dx = \int_2^\infty \frac{1}{x \cdot \ln(x)}\, dx = \ln|\ln(x)|\Big|_2^A = \ln|\ln(A)| - \ln|\ln(2)| \to \infty \text{ (as } A \to \infty)$$

so $\sum_{k=2}^\infty \frac{1}{k \cdot (\ln k)}$ diverges.

"Q–Test:" $\sum_{k=2}^\infty \frac{1}{k \cdot (\ln k)^q} \begin{cases} \text{diverges} & \text{if } q \le 1 \\ \text{converges} & \text{if } q > 1 \end{cases}$

31. $q = 3 > 1$ so $\sum_{k=2}^\infty \frac{1}{k \cdot (\ln k)^3}$ converges.

33. $\sum_{k=2}^\infty \frac{1}{k \cdot \ln(k^3)} = \sum_{k=2}^\infty \frac{1}{3k \cdot \ln(k)} = \frac{1}{3} \sum_{k=2}^\infty \frac{1}{k \cdot \ln(k)}$ which diverges ($q = 1$).

Section 10.4 Some Even Answers

2. Converge   4. Diverge   6. Converge   8. Converge   10. Converge

12. Converge   14. Converge   16. Converge   18. Diverge   20. Diverge

30. Diverge   32. Diverge

Section 10.5 (Odd numbered problem solutions followed by even numbered problem answers.)

1. $\sum_{k=1}^\infty \frac{\cos^2(k)}{k^2} \le \sum_{k=1}^\infty \frac{1}{k^2}$ which converges by the P–Test (p=2) so $\sum_{k=1}^\infty \frac{\cos^2(k)}{k^2}$ converges.

3. $\sum_{n=3}^\infty \frac{5}{n-1} > 5 \sum_{n=3}^\infty \frac{1}{n}$ which is the harmonic series and is divergent, so $\sum_{n=3}^\infty \frac{5}{n-1}$ diverges.

5. $-1 \le \cos(x) \le 1$ so $2 \le 3 + \cos(x) \le 4$. Then $\sum_{j=1}^\infty \frac{3 + \cos(j)}{j} > 2 \sum_{j=1}^\infty \frac{1}{j}$ which is the harmonic series and is divergent, so $\sum_{j=1}^\infty \frac{3 + \cos(j)}{j}$ diverges.

7. $\sum_{k=1}^\infty \frac{\ln(k)}{k} > \sum_{k=1}^\infty \frac{1}{k}$ which is the harmonic series and is divergent, so $\sum_{k=1}^\infty \frac{\ln(k)}{k}$ diverges.

9. $\sum_{k=1}^\infty \frac{k+9}{k \cdot 2^k} = \sum_{k=1}^\infty \frac{k+9}{k} \cdot \frac{1}{2^k} < 10 \sum_{k=1}^\infty \frac{1}{2^k}$ which is a convergent geometric series ($r = \frac{1}{2}$)

so $\sum_{k=1}^\infty \frac{k+9}{k \cdot 2^k}$ converges.

11. $\sum_{n=1}^{\infty} \frac{1}{1+2+3+\ldots+(n-1)+n} = \sum_{n=1}^{\infty} \frac{1}{\frac{n(n+1)}{2}} = \sum_{n=1}^{\infty} \frac{2}{n(n+1)} < 2 \sum_{n=1}^{\infty} \frac{1}{n^2}$ which converges by

the P–Test (p = 2) so $\sum_{n=1}^{\infty} \frac{1}{1+2+3+\ldots+(n-1)+n}$ converges.

13. Let $a_k = \frac{k+1}{k^2+4}$ and $b_k = \frac{1}{k}$. Then $\frac{a_k}{b_k} = \frac{k^2+k}{k^2+4} \to 1$ and $\sum_{k=3}^{\infty} \frac{1}{k}$ diverges so $\sum_{k=3}^{\infty} \frac{k+1}{k^2+4}$ diverges.

15. Let $a_w = \frac{5}{w+1}$ and $b_w = \frac{5}{w}$. Then $\frac{a_w}{b_w} = \frac{w}{w+1} \to 1$ and $\sum_{w=1}^{\infty} \frac{1}{w}$ diverges so $\sum_{w=1}^{\infty} \frac{5}{w+1}$ diverges.

17. $\sum_{k=1}^{\infty} \frac{k^3}{(1+k^2)^3} = \sum_{k=1}^{\infty} \left(\frac{k}{1+k^2}\right)^3$. Let $a_k = \left(\frac{k}{1+k^2}\right)^3$ and $b_k = \frac{1}{k^3}$.

Then $\frac{a_k}{b_k} = \left(\frac{k}{1+k^2}\right)^3 \cdot \frac{k^3}{1} = \left(\frac{k^2}{1+k^2}\right)^3 \to (1)^3 = 1$ and $\sum_{k=1}^{\infty} \frac{1}{k^3}$ converges by the

P–Test so $\sum_{k=1}^{\infty} \frac{k^3}{(1+k^2)^3}$ converges.

19. $\sum_{n=1}^{\infty} \left(\frac{5-\frac{1}{n}}{n}\right)^3 = \sum_{n=1}^{\infty} \left(\frac{5}{n} - \frac{1}{n^2}\right)^3 = \sum_{n=1}^{\infty} \left(\frac{5n-1}{n^2}\right)^3$. Let $a_n = \left(\frac{5n-1}{n^2}\right)^3$ and $b_n = \frac{1}{n^3}$.

Then $\frac{a_n}{b_n} = \left(\frac{5n-1}{n^2}\right)^3 \cdot \frac{n^3}{1} = \left(\frac{5n-1}{n^2} \cdot \frac{n}{1}\right)^3 = \left(\frac{5n-1}{n}\right)^3 \to 5^3 = 125$ (positive and finite).

$\sum_{k=1}^{\infty} \frac{1}{k^3}$ converges by the P–Test so $\sum_{n=1}^{\infty} \left(\frac{5-\frac{1}{n}}{n}\right)^3$ converges.

21. $\sum_{j=1}^{\infty} \left(1 - \frac{1}{j}\right)^j$ diverges by the Nth Term Test for Divergence since $a_j = \left(1-\frac{1}{j}\right)^j \to e^{-1} \neq 0$ as $j \to \infty$.

We could use the Limit Comparison Test by taking $b_j = e^{-1}$ and showing that $\frac{a_j}{b_j} \to 1$, but the Nth Term Test for Divergence is more direct for this series.

23. $\sum_{k=1}^{\infty} \frac{7k}{\sqrt{k^3+5}}$: The dominant term series is $\sum_{k=1}^{\infty} \frac{k}{k^{3/2}} = \sum_{k=1}^{\infty} \frac{1}{k^{1/2}}$ which diverges by the P–Test (p=1/2).

25. $\sum_{j=1}^{\infty} \frac{j^3 - 4j + 3}{2j^4 + 7j^6 + 9}$: The dominant term series is $\sum_{j=1}^{\infty} \frac{j^3}{j^6} = \sum_{j=1}^{\infty} \frac{1}{j^3}$ which converges by the P–Test (p=3).

27. $\sum_{n=1}^{\infty} \left(\frac{\arctan(3n)}{2n} \right)^2$: The dominant term series is $\sum_{n=1}^{\infty} \left(\frac{\pi/2}{2n} \right)^2 = \frac{\pi^2}{16} \sum_{n=1}^{\infty} \frac{1}{n^2}$ which converges by the P–Test (p=2).

29. $\sum_{j=1}^{\infty} \frac{\sqrt{j^3 + 4j^2}}{j^2 + 3j - 2}$: The dominant term series is $\sum_{j=1}^{\infty} \frac{j^{3/2}}{j^2} = \sum_{j=1}^{\infty} \frac{1}{j^{1/2}}$ which diverges by the P–Test.

31. $\sum_{n=2}^{\infty} \frac{n^2 + 10}{n^3 - 2}$ diverges using dominant terms and the P–Test (p=1).

33. $\sum_{k=1}^{\infty} \frac{3}{2k + 1}$ diverges using dominant terms and the P–Test (p=1).

35. $\sum_{n=1}^{\infty} \frac{2n^3 + n^2 + 5}{(3 + n^2)^2}$ diverges using dominant terms and the P–Test (p=1).

37. $\sum_{k=1}^{\infty} \left(\frac{1 - \frac{2}{k}}{k} \right)^3 = \sum_{k=1}^{\infty} \left(\frac{k - 2}{k^2} \right)^3$ converges using dominant terms $\left(\frac{k}{k^2} \right)^3 = \left(\frac{1}{k} \right)^3$ and the P–Test (p=3).

39. $\sum_{k=1}^{\infty} \frac{k + 5}{k \cdot 3^k}$ converges by using dominant terms $\frac{k}{k \cdot 3^k} = \frac{1}{3^k} = \left(\frac{1}{3} \right)^k$ and the Geometric Series Test (r = 1/3).

41. $\sum_{k=1}^{\infty} \frac{k + 2}{\sqrt{k^2 + 1}}$ diverges using dominant terms and the Nth Term Test for Divergence.

43. $\sum_{j=1}^{\infty} \frac{3}{e^j + j}$ converges using dominant terms $\frac{1}{e^j} = \left(\frac{1}{e} \right)^j$ and the Geometric Series Test (r = 1/e).

45. $\sum_{n=1}^{\infty} \left(\frac{\tan(3)}{2 + n} \right)^2$ converges by using dominant terms $\frac{1}{n^2}$ and the P–Test (p=2).

47. $\sum_{k=1}^{\infty} \sin^3\left(\frac{1}{n} \right)$ converges by comparison with the convergent series $\sum_{n=1}^{\infty} \frac{1}{n^3}$

49. $\sum_{j=1}^{\infty} \cos^3(\frac{1}{n})$ diverges using the Nth Term Test for Divergence: the terms approach $1 \neq 0$.

51. $\sum_{n=1}^{\infty} (1 - \frac{2}{n})^n$ diverges using the Nth Term Test for Divergence: the terms approach $\frac{1}{e^2} \neq 0$.

Section 10.5 Some Even Answers

2. Converges	4. Converges	6. Converges	8. Converges	10. Diverges
12. Converges	14. Converges	16. Diverges	18. Converges	20. Diverges
22. Diverges	24. Diverges	26. Converges	28. Converges	30. Converges
32. Converges	34. Converges	36. Converges	38. Converges	40. Converges
42. Converges	44. Converges	46. Converges	48. Diverges	50. Converges

You still need to supply reasons for each answer given below.

R1. Converge	R2. Converge	R3. Diverge	R4. Diverge	R5. Converge
R6. Converge	R7. Converge	R8. Diverge	R9. Converge	R10. Diverge
R11. Converge	R12. Diverge	R13. Diverge	R14. Converge	R15. Converge
R16. Converge	R17. Diverge	R18. Diverge	R19. Diverge	R20. Converge

R21. Diverge

Section 10.6 (Odd numbered problem solutions followed by some even numbered problem answers.)

1. $1, 0.2, 0.8, 0.4$ Alternating (so far). The graph of s_n is shown.

Prob. 1

3. $-1, 1, -2, 2$ Alternating (so far). The graph of s_n is shown.

5. $-1, -1.6, -1.2, -1$ Not alternating. The graph of s_n is shown.

Prob. 3

7. Alternating: $a_1 = 2, a_2 = -1, a_3 = 2, a_4 = -1, a_5 = 2$

9. Not alternating: $a_1 = 2, a_2 = 1, a_3 = -0.9, a_4 = 0.8, a_5 = -0.1$

11. Not alternating: $a_1 = -1, a_2 = 2, a_3 = -1.2, a_4 = 0.2, a_5 = 0.2$

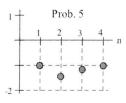
Prob. 5

13. Graphs A and C are not the graphs of partial sums of alternating series.

15. Graph B is not the graph of an alternating series.

17. Converges.   19. Converges.   21. Diverges.   23. Converges.

25. Converges.   27. Diverges.   29. Converges.   31. Converges.

33. $s_4 = -\frac{1}{\ln(2)} + \frac{1}{\ln(3)} - \frac{1}{\ln(4)} + \frac{1}{\ln(5)} \approx -0.63247$.

   $|s_4 - S| < \frac{1}{\ln(6)} \approx 0.55811$. $-1.19058 < S < -0.07436$

35. $s_4 = (-0.8)^2 + (-0.8)^3 + (-0.8)^4 + (-0.8)^5 \approx 0.20992$. $|s_4 - S| < (0.8)^6 \approx 0.26214$.

   $-0.05222 < S < 0.47206$. (For your information: $s_{10} \approx 0.317378$, $s_{50} \approx 0.355550$, $s_{100} \approx 0.355556$)

37. $s_4 = \sin(1) - \sin(\frac{1}{2}) + \sin(\frac{1}{3}) - \sin(\frac{1}{4}) \approx 0.441836$. $|s_4 - S| < \sin(\frac{1}{5}) \approx 0.198669$.

   $0.243167 < S < 0.640505$. ($s_{10} \approx 0.503356$, $s_{50} \approx 0.0.540897$, $s_{100} \approx 0.5458219$)

39. $s_4 = -1 + \frac{1}{8} - \frac{1}{27} + \frac{1}{64} \approx -0.896412$. $|s_4 - S| < \frac{1}{125} = 0.008$. $-0.904412 < S < -0.888412$.

   ($s_{10} \approx -0.901116$, $s_{50} \approx -0.901539$, $s_{100} \approx -0.901542$)

41. $|\frac{1}{(n+1)+6}| \leq 0.01$ so $n = 93$ works. Use s_{93}.

43. $|\frac{1}{\sqrt{n+1}}| \leq \frac{1}{100}$ so $\sqrt{n+1} \geq 100$ and $n = 10{,}000 - 1$ works. Use s_{9999}.

45. $|\frac{1}{3^{n+1}}| \leq \frac{2}{1000}$ so $3^{n+1} \geq 500$ and $n = 5$ works. Use s_5.

47. $|\frac{1}{(n+1)^2}| \leq \frac{1}{1000}$ so $(n+1)^2 \geq 1000$ and $n = 31$ works. Use s_{31}.

49. $|\frac{1}{(n+1) + \ln(n+1)}| \leq \frac{4}{100}$ so $(n+1) + \ln(n+1) \geq 25$. Some "calculator experimentation" shows that $n = 21$ works. $(20+1) + \ln(20+1) \approx 24.04$ so $n = 20$ is too small. $(21+1) + \ln(21+1) \approx 25.09$ so $n = 21$ works. Use s_{21}.

51. (a) $S(0.3) = x - \frac{(0.3)^3}{2 \cdot 3} + \frac{(0.3)^5}{2 \cdot 3 \cdot 4 \cdot 5} - \frac{(0.3)^7}{2 \cdot 3 \cdot 4 \cdot 5 \cdot 6 \cdot 7} + \ldots + (-1)^n \frac{(0.3)^{2n+1}}{(2n+1)!} + \ldots$

   (b) $s_3 = (0.3) - \frac{(0.3)^3}{2 \cdot 3} + \frac{(0.3)^5}{2 \cdot 3 \cdot 4 \cdot 5} \approx 0.29552025$.

   (c) $|S - s_3| \leq \frac{(0.3)^7}{2 \cdot 3 \cdot 4 \cdot 5 \cdot 6 \cdot 7} \approx 0.000000043$. ($\sin(0.3) \approx 0.295520206661$)

53. (a) $S(0.1) = x - \frac{(0.1)^3}{2 \cdot 3} + \frac{(0.1)^5}{2 \cdot 3 \cdot 4 \cdot 5} - \frac{(0.1)^7}{2 \cdot 3 \cdot 4 \cdot 5 \cdot 6 \cdot 7} + \ldots + (-1)^n \frac{(0.1)^{2n+1}}{(2n+1)!} + \ldots$

   (b) $s_3 = (0.1) - \frac{(0.1)^3}{2 \cdot 3} + \frac{(0.1)^5}{2 \cdot 3 \cdot 4 \cdot 5} \approx 0.099833416667$.

   (c) $|S - s_3| \leq \frac{(0.1)^7}{2 \cdot 3 \cdot 4 \cdot 5 \cdot 6 \cdot 7} \approx 1.98 \cdot 10^{-11}$ .. ($\sin(0.1) \approx 0.099833416647$)

55. (a) $C(1) = 1 - \frac{1^2}{2} + \frac{1^4}{2 \cdot 3 \cdot 4} - \frac{1^6}{2 \cdot 3 \cdot 4 \cdot 5 \cdot 6} + \ldots + (-1)^n \frac{1^{2n}}{(2n)!} + \ldots = 1 - \frac{1}{2} + \frac{1}{24} - \frac{1}{720} + \ldots + (-1)^n \frac{1^{2n}}{(2n)!} + \ldots$

(b) $s_3 = 1 - \frac{1^2}{2} + \frac{1^4}{2 \cdot 3 \cdot 4} \approx 0.5416667$.

(c) $|S - s_3| \le \frac{(1)^7}{2 \cdot 3 \cdot 4 \cdot 5 \cdot 6 \cdot 7} \approx 0.0013889\ldots$ ($\cos(1) \approx 0.5403023$)

57. (a) $C(-0.2) = 1 - \frac{(-0.2)^2}{2} + \frac{(-0.2)^4}{2 \cdot 3 \cdot 4} - \frac{(-0.2)^6}{2 \cdot 3 \cdot 4 \cdot 5 \cdot 6} + \ldots + (-1)^n \frac{1^{2n}}{(2n)!} + \ldots$

(b) $s_3 = 1 - \frac{(-0.2)^2}{2} + \frac{(-0.2)^4}{2 \cdot 3 \cdot 4} \approx 0.98006666667$.

(c) $|S - s_3| \le \frac{(-0.2)^6}{2 \cdot 3 \cdot 4 \cdot 5 \cdot 6} \approx 8.9 \cdot 10^{-8} \ldots$ ($\cos(-0.2) \approx 0.980066577841$)

59. (a) $E(-1) = 1 + (-1) + \frac{(-1)^2}{2} + \frac{(-1)^3}{2 \cdot 3} + \frac{(-1)^4}{2 \cdot 3 \cdot 4} + \ldots + \frac{(-1)^n}{n!} + \ldots = 1 - 1 + \frac{1}{2} - \frac{1}{6} + \frac{1}{24} - \frac{1}{120} + \ldots$

(b) $s_3 = 1 - 1 + \frac{1}{2} = 0.5$.

(c) $|S - s_3| \le \frac{1}{6} \approx 0.16667\ldots$ ($e^{-1} \approx 0.36787944$)

61. (a) $E(-0.2) = 1 + (-0.2) + \frac{(-0.2)^2}{2} + \frac{(-0.2)^3}{2 \cdot 3} + \frac{(-0.2)^4}{2 \cdot 3 \cdot 4} + \ldots + \frac{(-1)^n}{n!} + \ldots$

(b) $s_3 = 1 + (-0.2) + \frac{(-0.2)^2}{2} = 0.82$ (c) $|S - s_3| \le \frac{(0.2)^3}{6} \approx 0.0013333\ldots$ ($e^{-0.2} \approx 0.8187307$)

Section 10.6 Some Even Answers

2. Alternating (so far) 4. Not alternating 6. Alternating (so far)

8. Alternating (so far) 10. Alternating (so far) 12. Not alternating

14. B and C. 16. A. 18. Converges. 20. Converges.

22. Converges. 24. Converges (to 0). 26. Diverges. 28. Converges.

30. Converges. 42. $n \approx 2.7 \cdot 10^{43}$ 44. $n = 26$ works. 46. $n = 16$ works.

48. $n = 21$ works.

Section 10.7 (Odd numbered problem solutions followed by some even numbered problem answers.)

1. Conditionally convergent 3. Absolutely convergent 5. Absolutely convergent

7. Absolutely convergent 9. Conditionally convergent 11. Conditionally convergent

13. Conditionally convergent 15. Absolutely convergent 17. Divergent

19. Conditionally convergent 21. Divergent 23. Absolutely convergent

25. Conditionally convergent 27. Divergent 29. Absolutely convergent

31. $\dfrac{n!}{(n+1)!} = \dfrac{1\cdot 2\cdot 3 \ldots \cdot n}{1\cdot 2\cdot 3 \ldots \cdot n\cdot (n+1)} = \dfrac{1}{n+1}$ 33. $\dfrac{n!}{(n+3)!} = \dfrac{1\cdot 2\cdot 3 \ldots \cdot n}{1\cdot 2\cdot 3 \ldots \cdot n\cdot (n+1)\cdot (n+2)\cdot (n+3)} = \dfrac{1}{(n+1)(n+2)(n+3)}$

35. $\dfrac{(n-1)!}{(n+1)!} = \dfrac{1\cdot 2\cdot 3 \ldots \cdot (n-1)}{1\cdot 2\cdot 3 \ldots \cdot (n-1)\cdot (n)\cdot (n+1)} = \dfrac{1}{(n)(n+1)}$

37. $\dfrac{(2n)!}{(2n+1)!} = \dfrac{1\cdot 2\cdot 3 \ldots \cdot n\cdot (n+1)\cdot \ldots \cdot (2n)}{1\cdot 2\cdot 3 \ldots \cdot n\cdot (n+1)\cdot \ldots \cdot (2n)\cdot (2n+1)} = \dfrac{1}{2n+1}$ 39. $\dfrac{n^n}{n!} = \dfrac{n\cdot n\cdot n\cdot n\cdot \ldots \cdot n\cdot n}{1\cdot 2\cdot 3\cdot 4\cdot \ldots \cdot (n-1)\cdot n}$

41. Ratio = $\left| \dfrac{n}{n+1} \right| \to 1 = L$. Diverges (Harmonic series)

43. Ratio = $\left| \left(\dfrac{n}{n+1}\right)^3 \right| \to 1 = L$. Converges by the P–Test (p = 3).

45. Ratio = $\left| \dfrac{1}{2} \right| \to \dfrac{1}{2} = L$. Converges (Geometric series with r = 1/2).

47. Ratio = $|1| \to 1 = L$. Diverges by the Nth Term Test for Divergence.

49. Ratio = $\left| \dfrac{n!}{(n+1)!} \right| = \left| \dfrac{1}{n+1} \right| \to 0 = L$. Converges by the Ratio Test.

51. Ratio = $\left| \dfrac{2^{n+1}}{(n+1)!} \dfrac{n!}{2^n} \right| = \left| \dfrac{2}{n+1} \right| \to 0 = L$. Converges by the Ratio Test.

53. Ratio = $\left| \dfrac{(1/2)^{3(n+1)}}{(1/2)^{3n}} \right| = \left| \left(\dfrac{1}{2}\right)^3 \right| = \dfrac{1}{8} \to \dfrac{1}{8} = L$. Converges by the Ratio Test.

55. Ratio = $\left| \dfrac{(0.9)^{2(n+1)+1}}{(0.9)^{2n+1}} \right| = |(0.9)^2| = 0.81 \to 0.81 = L$. Converges by the Ratio Test.

57. Ratio = $\left| \dfrac{(x-5)^{n+1}}{(x-5)^n} \right| = |x-5| \to |x-5| = L$. Series converges absolutely if and only if $|x-5| < 1$: $4 < x < 6$.

59. Ratio = $\left| \dfrac{(x-5)^{n+1}}{(n+1)^2} \dfrac{n^2}{(x-5)^n} \right| = \left| (x-5)\cdot \left(\dfrac{n}{n+1}\right)^2 \right| \to |x-5| = L$. Series converges absolutely if and only if $|x-5| < 1$: $4 < x < 6$.

61. Ratio = $\left| \dfrac{(x-2)^{n+1}}{(n+1)!} \dfrac{n!}{(x-2)^n} \right| = \left| (x-2)\cdot \dfrac{1}{n+1} \right| \to 0 = L$ for all values of x so the series converges absolutely for all values of x.

63. Ratio = $\left| \dfrac{(2x-12)^{n+1}}{(n+1)^2} \dfrac{n^2}{(2x-12)^n} \right| = \left| (2x-12)\cdot \left(\dfrac{n}{n+1}\right)^2 \right| \to |2x-12| = L$. Series converges absolutely

if and only if $|2x - 12| < 1$: $\frac{11}{2} < x < \frac{13}{2}$.

65. Ratio = $\left| \frac{(6x-12)^{n+1}}{(n+1)!} \frac{n!}{(6x-12)^n} \right| = \left| (6x-12) \cdot \frac{1}{n+1} \right| \to 0 = L$ for all values of x so the series converges absolutely for all values of x.

67. Ratio = $\left| \frac{(x+1)^{2(n+1)}}{n+1} \frac{n}{(x+1)^{2n}} \right| = \left| (x+1)^2 \cdot \frac{n}{n+1} \right| \to (x+1)^2 = L$ for all values of x. Series converges absolutely if and only if $(x+1)^2 < 1$: $-2 < x < 0$.

69. Ratio = $\left| \frac{(x-5)^{3(n+1)+1}}{(n+1)^2} \frac{n^2}{(x-5)^{3n+1}} \right| = \left| (x-5)^3 \cdot \left(\frac{n}{n+1}\right)^2 \right| \to |(x-5)^3| = L$ for all values of x. Series converges absolutely if and only if $|(x-5)^3| < 1$: $4 < x < 6$.

71. Ratio = $\left| \frac{(x+3)^{2(n+1)-1}}{((n+1)+1)!} \frac{(n+1)!}{(x+3)^{2n-1}} \right| = \left| (x+3)^2 \cdot \frac{1}{n+2} \right| \to 0 = L$ for all values of x so the series converges absolutely for all values of x.

73. Ratio = $\left| \frac{x^{2(n+1)}}{(2(n+1))!} \frac{(2n)!}{x^{2n}} \right| = \left| x^2 \cdot \frac{1}{(2n+1)(2n+2)} \right| \to 0 = L$ for all values of x so the series converges absolutely for all values of x.

Section 10.7 Some Even Answers

2. Conditionally convergent
4. Conditionally convergent
6. Divergent
8. Absolutely convergent
10. Absolutely convergent
12. Conditionally convergent
14. Absolutely convergent
16. Conditionally convergent
18. Divergent
20. Absolutely convergent
22. Absolutely convergent
24. Absolutely convergent
26. Divergent
28. Divergent
30. Divergent
42. L = 1. Convergent by P–Test.
44. L = 1. Divergent by P–Test.
46. L = 1/3. Convergent Geo. series.
48. Divergent by N^{th} Term Test.
50. L=0. Convergent by Ratio Test.
52. L = 0. Convergent by Ratio Test.
54. L = $(1/3)^2$. Convergent by Ratio Test.
56. L = 0.16. Convergent by Ratio Test.
58. Absolutely convergent for $4 < x < 6$.
60. Absolutely convergent for $1 < x < 3$.
62. Absolutely convergent for all x.
64. Absolutely convergent for $11/4 < x < 13/4$.
66. Absolutely convergent for $2 < x < 4$.
68. Absolutely convergent for $-3 < x < -1$.
70. Absolutely convergent for all x.
72. Absolutely convergent for all x.
74. Absolutely convergent for all x.

Section 10.8 (Odd numbered problem solutions)

1. Ratio test: $\left|\dfrac{a_{n+1}}{a_n}\right| = \left|\dfrac{x^{n+1}}{x^n}\right| = |x| \to |x| = L.$ $|x| < 1$ if and only if $-1 < x < 1$.

   Endpoints: if $x = -1$ or $x = 1$, then the terms do not approach 0 so the series diverges.
   Interval of convergence: $-1 < x < 1$. (You can provide the graph of this interval.)

3. Ratio test: $\left|\dfrac{a_{n+1}}{a_n}\right| = \left|\dfrac{(x+2)^{n+1}}{(x+2)^n}\right| = |x+2| \to |x+2| = L.$ $|x+2| < 1$ if and only if

   $-1 < x+2 < 1$ so $-3 < x < -1$.

   Endpoints: if $x = -3$ or $x = -1$, then the terms do not approach 0 so the series diverges.
   Interval of convergence: $-3 < x < -1$. (You can provide the graph of this interval.)

5. Ratio test: $\left|\dfrac{a_{n+1}}{a_n}\right| = \left|\dfrac{x^{n+1}/(n+1)}{x^n/n}\right| = \left|x \cdot \dfrac{n}{n+1}\right| \to |x| = L.$ $|x| < 1$ if and only if $-1 < x < 1$.

   Endpoints: if $x = -1$, then $\sum\limits_{n=1}^{\infty} \dfrac{x^n}{n} = \sum\limits_{n=1}^{\infty} \dfrac{(-1)^n}{n}$ which converges by the Alternating Series Test

   if $x = 1$, then $\sum\limits_{n=1}^{\infty} \dfrac{x^n}{n} = \sum\limits_{n=1}^{\infty} \dfrac{(1)^n}{n}$ which diverges (harmonic series)

   Interval of convergence: $-1 \leq x < 1$. (You can provide the graph of this interval.)

7. Ratio test: $\left|\dfrac{a_{n+1}}{a_n}\right| = \left|\dfrac{(x+3)^{n+1}/(n+1)}{(x+3)^n/n}\right| = \left|(x+3) \cdot \dfrac{n}{n+1}\right| \to |x+3| = L.$ $|x+3| < 1$ if and only if

   $-1 < x+3 < 1$ or $-4 < x < -2$.

   Endpoints: if $x = -4$, then $\sum\limits_{n=1}^{\infty} \dfrac{(x+3)^n}{n} = \sum\limits_{n=1}^{\infty} \dfrac{(-1)^n}{n}$ which converges by the Alternating Series Test

   if $x = -2$, then $\sum\limits_{n=1}^{\infty} \dfrac{(x+3)^n}{n} = \sum\limits_{n=1}^{\infty} \dfrac{(1)^n}{n}$ which diverges (harmonic series)

   Interval of convergence: $-4 \leq x < -2$. (You can provide the graph of this interval.)

9. Ratio test: $\left|\dfrac{a_{n+1}}{a_n}\right| = \left|\dfrac{(x-7)^{2(n+1)+1}/(n+1)^2}{(x-7)^{2n+1}/n^2}\right| = \left|(x-7)^2 \cdot \left(\dfrac{n}{n+1}\right)^2\right| \to (x-7)^2 = L.$ $(x-7)^2 < 1$ if

   and only if $-1 < x-7 < 1$ or $6 < x < 8$.

   Endpoints: if $x = 6$, then $\sum\limits_{n=1}^{\infty} \dfrac{(x-7)^{2n+1}}{n^2} = \sum\limits_{n=1}^{\infty} \dfrac{(-1)^{2n+1}}{n^2} = \sum\limits_{n=1}^{\infty} \dfrac{-1}{n^2}$ which converges by the P–Test

   if $x = 8$, then $\sum\limits_{n=1}^{\infty} \dfrac{(x-7)^{2n+1}}{n^2} = \sum\limits_{n=1}^{\infty} \dfrac{(1)^{2n+1}}{n^2}$ which converges by the P–Test (p=2).

   Interval of convergence: $6 \leq x \leq 8$. (You can provide the graph of this interval.)

11. Ratio $= |2x| \to |2x| = L$. $|2x| < 1$ if and only if $-1 < 2x < 1$ or $-1/2 < x < 1/2$.

   Endpoints: if $x = -1/2$, then the series $= \sum_{n=1}^{\infty} (2 \cdot (\frac{-1}{2}))^n = \sum_{n=1}^{\infty} (-1)^n$ which diverges

   if $x = 1/2$, then the series $= \sum_{n=1}^{\infty} (2 \cdot (\frac{1}{2}))^n = \sum_{n=1}^{\infty} (1)^n$ which diverges

   Interval of convergence: $-1/2 < x < 1/2$. (You can provide the graph of this interval.)

13. Ratio $= |(\frac{x}{3})^2| \to |\frac{x^2}{9}| = L$. $|\frac{x^2}{9}| < 1$ if and only if $-1 < \frac{x^2}{9} < 1$ or $-3 < x < 3$.

    The series diverges at both endpoints, $x = -3$ and $x = 3$, so the interval of convergence is $-3 < x < 3$.

15. Ratio $= |2x - 6| \to |2x - 6| = L$. $|2x - 6| < 1$ if and only if $-1 < 2x - 6 < 1$ or $5/2 < x < 7/2$.

    The series diverges at both endpoints, $x = 5/2$ and $x = 7/2$, so the interval of convergence is $5/2 < x < 7/2$.

17. Ratio $= |\frac{n!}{(n+1)!} \frac{x^{n+1}}{x^n}| = |\frac{1}{n+1} \cdot x| \to 0 = L$, and $L < 1$ for all x so the interval of convergence is the entire real number line.

19. Ratio $= |\frac{(n+1)^2}{n^2} \frac{3^n}{3^{n+1}} \frac{x^{n+1}}{x^n}| = |(\frac{n+1}{n})^2 \cdot \frac{x}{3}| \to |\frac{x}{3}| = L$. $|\frac{x}{3}| < 1$ if and only if $-1 < \frac{x}{3} < 1$.

    The series diverges at both endpoints, $x = -3$ and $x = 3$, so the interval of convergence is $-3 < x < 3$.

21. Ratio $= |\frac{(n+1)!}{n!} \frac{x^{n+1}}{x^n}| = |(n+1) \cdot x| \to \infty > 1$ if $x \neq 0$ and $|(n+1) \cdot x| \to 0 < 1$ if $x = 0$.

    The series diverges for $x \neq 0$, and the series converges (and is boring) when $x = 0$. The "interval" of convergence is a single point: $\{0\}$.

23. Ratio $= |\frac{(n+1)!}{n!} \frac{(x-7)^{n+1}}{(x-7)^n}| = |(n+1) \cdot (x-7)| \to \infty > 1$ if $x \neq 7$ and $|(n+1) \cdot (x-7)| \to 0 < 1$ if $x = 7$.

    The series diverges for $x \neq 7$, and the series converges (and is boring) when $x = 7$. The "interval" of convergence is a single point: $\{7\}$.

25. Ratio $= |\frac{(x-a)^{n+1}}{(x-a)^n}| = |x - a| \to |x - a| = L$. $|x - a| < 1$ if and only if $a - 1 < x < a + 1$.

    The series diverges at both endpoints, $x = a-1$ and $x = a+1$, so the interval of convergence is $a-1 < x < a+1$.

27. Ratio $= |\frac{(x-a)^{n+1}/(n+1)}{(x-a)^n/n}| = |\frac{n}{n+1}(x-a)| \to |x - a| = L$. $|x - a| < 1$ if and only if $a - 1 < x < a + 1$.

    Endpoints: if $x = a-1$, then $\sum_{n=1}^{\infty} \frac{(x-a)^n}{n} = \sum_{n=1}^{\infty} \frac{(-1)^n}{n}$ which converges by the Alternating Series Test

    if $x = a+1$, then $\sum_{n=1}^{\infty} \frac{(x-a)^n}{n} = \sum_{n=1}^{\infty} \frac{(1)^n}{n}$ which diverges (harmonic series)

    Interval of convergence: $a-1 \leq x < a+1$.

29. Ratio = $\left|\dfrac{(ax)^{n+1}}{(ax)^n}\right| = |ax| \to |ax| = L$. $|ax| < 1$ if and only if $\dfrac{-1}{a} < x < \dfrac{1}{a}$.

   The series diverges at both endpoints, $x = -1/a$ and $x = 1/a$, so the interval of convergence is $\dfrac{-1}{a} < x < \dfrac{1}{a}$.

31. Ratio = $\left|\dfrac{(ax-b)^{n+1}}{(ax-b)^n}\right| = |ax - b| \to |ax - b| = L$. $|ax - b| < 1$ if and only if $-1 < ax - b \le 1$ or $\dfrac{b-1}{a} < x < \dfrac{b+1}{a}$.

   The series diverges at both endpoints so the interval of convergence is $\dfrac{b-1}{a} < x < \dfrac{b+1}{a}$.

33. We can be certain the friend is wrong because the interval of convergence must be symmetric about the point $x = 4$, and the friend's interval, $1 < x < 9$, is not symmetric about $x = 4$.

35. $(5, 9), [1, 13], (-1, 15], [3, 11), [0, 14), x = 7$ are all possible intervals of convegence for the series.

37. $(0, 2), (-5, 7), [1, 1], (-3, 5], [-9, 11], [0, 2), x = 1$.

Note: There are many possible correct answers for problems 38 – 45.

39. $\displaystyle\sum_{n=1}^{\infty} \dfrac{1}{n}\left(\dfrac{x}{3}\right)^n$

41. $\displaystyle\sum_{n=1}^{\infty} \dfrac{(x-3)^n}{3^n} = \sum_{n=1}^{\infty} \left(\dfrac{x-3}{3}\right)^n$

43. $\displaystyle\sum_{n=1}^{\infty} \dfrac{1}{n}\left(\dfrac{x-5}{3}\right)^n$

45. $\displaystyle\sum_{n=1}^{\infty} n! \cdot (x-3)^n$

47. Interval of convergence: $2 < x < 4$. $\sum = \dfrac{1}{1-(x-3)} = \dfrac{1}{4-x}$.

49. Interval of convergence: $\dfrac{-1}{3} < x < \dfrac{1}{3}$. $\sum = \dfrac{1}{1-3x}$.

51. Interval of convergence: $-1 < x < 1$. $\sum = \dfrac{1}{1-x^3}$.

53. Interval of convergence: $1 < x < 11$. $\sum = \dfrac{1}{1-\dfrac{x-6}{5}} = \dfrac{5}{11-x}$.

55. Interval of convergence: $-5 < x < 5$. $\sum = \dfrac{1}{1-\dfrac{x}{5}} = \dfrac{5}{5-x}$.

57. Interval of convergence: $-2 < x < 2$. $\sum = \dfrac{1}{1-(x/2)^3} = \dfrac{8}{8-x^3}$.

59. $\left|\dfrac{1}{3}\cos(x)\right| < 1$ **for all x**, so for all x the sum $\sum = \dfrac{1}{1-\dfrac{1}{3}\cos(x)} = \dfrac{3}{3-\cos(x)}$.

Section 10.9 (Odd numbered problem solutions)

1. $\dfrac{1}{1-x^4} = 1 + x^4 + x^8 + x^{12} + x^{16} + \ldots = \sum\limits_{n=0}^{\infty} x^{4n}$

3. $\dfrac{1}{1+x^4} = 1 - x^4 + x^8 - x^{12} + x^{16} + \ldots = \sum\limits_{n=0}^{\infty} (-1)^n x^{4n}$

5. $\dfrac{1}{5+x} = \dfrac{1}{5} \cdot \dfrac{1}{1+(x/5)} = \dfrac{1}{5}\left\{ 1 - \dfrac{x}{5} + \left(\dfrac{x}{5}\right)^2 - \left(\dfrac{x}{5}\right)^3 + \left(\dfrac{x}{5}\right)^4 + \ldots \right\} = \dfrac{1}{5}\sum\limits_{n=0}^{\infty} (-1)^n \left(\dfrac{x}{5}\right)^n$

7. $\dfrac{x^2}{1+x^3} = x^2\left\{\dfrac{1}{1+x^3}\right\} = x^2\left\{ 1 - x^3 + x^6 - x^9 + x^{12} + \ldots \right\} = x^2 \sum\limits_{n=0}^{\infty} (-1)^n x^{3n} = \sum\limits_{n=0}^{\infty} (-1)^n x^{3n+2}$

9. $\ln(1+x^2) = x^2 - \dfrac{x^4}{2} + \dfrac{x^6}{3} - \dfrac{x^8}{4} + \ldots = \sum\limits_{n=1}^{\infty} (-1)^{n+1} \dfrac{x^{2n}}{n}$

11. $\arctan(x^2) = x^2 - \dfrac{x^6}{3} + \dfrac{x^{10}}{5} - \dfrac{x^{14}}{7} + \dfrac{x^{18}}{9} - \ldots = \sum\limits_{n=0}^{\infty} (-1)^n \dfrac{x^{2(2n+1)}}{2n+1} = \sum\limits_{n=0}^{\infty} (-1)^n \dfrac{x^{4n+2}}{2n+1}$

13. $\dfrac{1}{(1-x^2)^2} = 1 + 2x^2 + 3x^4 + 4x^6 + 5x^8 + \ldots = \sum\limits_{n=1}^{\infty} n \cdot x^{2(n-1)} = \sum\limits_{n=1}^{\infty} n \cdot x^{2n-2}$

15. $\int\limits_0^{0.5} \dfrac{1}{1-x^3}\,dx \approx \int\limits_0^{0.5} 1 + x^3 + x^6 + x^9 + \ldots\,dx = x + \dfrac{x^4}{4} + \dfrac{x^7}{7} + \ldots \Big|_0^{0.5} \approx 0.516741$

17. $\int\limits_0^{0.6} \ln(1+x)\,dx \approx \int\limits_0^{0.6} x - \dfrac{x^2}{2} + \dfrac{x^3}{3} - \ldots\,dx = \dfrac{x^2}{2} - \dfrac{x^3}{2 \cdot 3} + \dfrac{x^4}{3 \cdot 4} - \ldots \Big|_0^{0.6} = 0.1548$

19. $\int\limits_0^{0.3} \dfrac{1}{(1-x)^2}\,dx \approx \int\limits_0^{0.3} 1 + 2x + 3x^2 + \ldots\,dx = x + x^2 + x^3 + \ldots \Big|_0^{0.3} = 0.417$

21. $\lim\limits_{x \to 0} \dfrac{\arctan(x)}{x} = \lim\limits_{x \to 0} \dfrac{1}{x}\left\{ x - \dfrac{x^3}{3} + \dfrac{x^5}{5} - \dfrac{x^7}{7} + \dfrac{x^9}{9} - \ldots \right\} = \lim\limits_{x \to 0} 1 - \dfrac{x^2}{3} + \dfrac{x^4}{5} - \ldots = 1$

23. $\lim\limits_{x \to 0} \dfrac{\ln(1+x)}{2x} = \lim\limits_{x \to 0} \dfrac{1}{2x}\left\{ x - \dfrac{x^2}{2} + \dfrac{x^3}{3} - \dfrac{x^4}{4} + \ldots \right\} = \lim\limits_{x \to 0} \dfrac{1}{2} - \dfrac{x}{4} + \dfrac{x^2}{6} - \dfrac{x^3}{8} + \ldots = \dfrac{1}{2}$

25. $\lim\limits_{x \to 0} \dfrac{\ln(1-x^2)}{3x} = \lim\limits_{x \to 0} \dfrac{1}{3x}\left\{ -x^2 - \dfrac{x^4}{2} - \dfrac{x^6}{3} - \dfrac{x^8}{4} - \ldots \right\} = \lim\limits_{x \to 0} -\dfrac{x}{3} - \dfrac{x^3}{6} - \dfrac{x^5}{9} - \ldots = 0$

27. $\dfrac{1}{1+x} = \sum\limits_{n=0}^{\infty}(-1)^n x^n$. Using the Ratio Test, the ratio $= \left|\dfrac{x^{n+1}}{x^n}\right| = |x| \to |x| = L$. $|x| < 1$ if and only if $-1 < x < 1$.

The series diverges at the endpoints $x = -1$ and $x = 1$ so the interval of convergence is $-1 < x < 1$.

29. $\ln(1-x) = -\sum\limits_{n=1}^{\infty}\dfrac{x^n}{n}$. Using the Ratio Test, the ratio $= \left|\dfrac{x^{n+1}}{x^n}\dfrac{n}{n+1}\right| = \left|x \cdot \dfrac{n}{n+1}\right| \to |x| = L$.

$|x| < 1$ if and only if $-1 < x < 1$. The series converges when $x = -1$ and diverges when $x = 1$ so the interval of convergence is $-1 \leq x < 1$.

31. $\arctan(x) = \sum\limits_{n=0}^{\infty}(-1)^n \dfrac{x^{2n+1}}{2n+1}$.

Using the Ratio Test, the ratio $= \left|\dfrac{x^{2(n+1)+1}}{x^{2n+1}}\dfrac{2n+1}{2(n+1)+1}\right| = \left|x^2 \cdot \dfrac{2n+1}{2n+3}\right| \to |x^2| = L$. $|x^2| < 1$

if and only if $-1 < x^2 < 1$ so $-1 < x < 1$. The series converges when $x = -1$ and when $x = 1$ so the interval of convergence is $-1 \leq x \leq 1$.

33. $\sin(x^2) = (x^2) - \dfrac{(x^2)^3}{3!} + \dfrac{(x^2)^5}{5!} - \dfrac{(x^2)^7}{7!} + \ldots = x^2 - \dfrac{x^6}{3!} + \dfrac{x^{10}}{5!} - \dfrac{x^{14}}{7!} + \ldots$

$= \sum\limits_{k=0}^{\infty}(-1)^k \dfrac{(x^2)^{2k+1}}{(2k+1)!} = \sum\limits_{k=0}^{\infty}(-1)^k \dfrac{x^{4k+2}}{(2k+1)!}$

35. $e^{(-x^2)} = 1 + (-x^2) + \dfrac{(-x^2)^2}{2!} + \dfrac{(-x^2)^3}{3!} + \dfrac{(-x^2)^4}{4!} + \ldots = 1 - x^2 + \dfrac{x^4}{2!} - \dfrac{x^6}{3!} + \dfrac{x^8}{4!} + \ldots = \sum\limits_{k=0}^{\infty}(-1)^k \dfrac{x^{2k}}{k!}$

37. $\cos(x) = D(\sin(x)) = D\left(x - \dfrac{x^3}{3!} + \dfrac{x^5}{5!} - \dfrac{x^7}{7!} + \ldots\right) = 1 - \dfrac{x^2}{2!} + \dfrac{x^4}{4!} - \dfrac{x^6}{6!} + \ldots = \sum\limits_{k=0}^{\infty}(-1)^k \dfrac{x^{2k}}{(2k)!}$

39. Using the result of Problem 33,

$\displaystyle\int_0^1 \sin(x^2)\, dx = \int_0^1 x^2 - \dfrac{x^6}{3!} + \dfrac{x^{10}}{5!} - \dfrac{x^{14}}{7!} + \ldots\, dx = \dfrac{x^3}{3} - \dfrac{x^7}{3! \cdot 7} + \dfrac{x^{11}}{5! \cdot 11} - \dfrac{x^{15}}{7! \cdot 15} + \ldots \Big|_0^1$

$= \left\{\dfrac{1}{3} - \dfrac{1}{3! \cdot 7} + \dfrac{1}{5! \cdot 11} - \dfrac{1}{7! \cdot 15} + \ldots\right\} - \{0\}$.

41. $\lim\limits_{x \to 0}\dfrac{\sin(x)}{x} = \lim\limits_{x \to 0}\dfrac{x - \dfrac{x^3}{3!} + \dfrac{x^5}{5!} - \dfrac{x^7}{7!} + \ldots}{x} = \lim\limits_{x \to 0} 1 - \dfrac{x^2}{3!} + \dfrac{x^4}{5!} - \dfrac{x^6}{7!} + \ldots = 1 + (\text{all 0s}) = 1$.

Section 10.10 (Odd numbered problem solutions)

1. $P(x) = 4x^2 - 5x + 7$ 2. $P(x) = 2x^3 - \frac{5}{2}x^2 + 2x - 1$ 3. $P(x) = 2(x-3)^2 + 5(x-3) - 2$

5. $\ln(1 + x) = x - \frac{x^2}{2} + \frac{x^3}{3} - \frac{x^4}{4} + \ldots$ 7. $\arctan(x) = x - \frac{x^3}{3} + \ldots$

9. $\cos(x) = 1 - \frac{x^2}{2!} + \frac{x^4}{4!} - \frac{x^6}{6!} + \ldots$

11. $\sec(x) = 1 + \frac{x^2}{2!} + \frac{5x^4}{4!} + \ldots$ (The higher derivatives of $\sec(x)$ get "messy.")

13. Around $c = 1$, $\ln(x) = (x-1) - \frac{(x-1)^2}{2} + \frac{(x-1)^3}{3} - \frac{(x-1)^4}{4} + \ldots$

15. Around $c = \pi/2$, $\sin(x) = 1 - \frac{(x - \pi/2)^2}{2!} + \frac{(x - \pi/2)^4}{4!} - \frac{(x - \pi/2)^6}{6!} + \ldots$

17. Around $c = 9$, $\sqrt{x} = 3 + \frac{1}{2 \cdot 3}(x-9) - \frac{1}{4 \cdot 3^3}\frac{(x-9)^2}{2!} + \frac{3}{8 \cdot 3^5}\frac{(x-9)^3}{3!} - \frac{15}{16 \cdot 3^7}\frac{(x-9)^4}{4!} + \ldots$

19. Using the first three nonzero terms for $\cos(x)$,

   $P(x) = 1 - \frac{x^2}{2!} + \frac{x^4}{4!}$. See the Cosine Table.

21. Using the first three nonzero terms for $\arctan(x)$,

   $P(x) = x - \frac{x^3}{3} + \frac{x^5}{5}$. See the Arctan Table.

23. $\int \sin(x^2)\,dx = \int x^2 - \frac{x^6}{6} + \frac{x^{10}}{120}\,dx$

    $= \frac{x^3}{3} - \frac{x^7}{42} + \frac{x^{11}}{1320} + C$

   $\int \sin(x^3)\,dx = \int x^3 - \frac{x^9}{6} + \frac{x^{15}}{120}\,dx$

    $= \frac{x^4}{4} - \frac{x^{10}}{60} + \frac{x^{16}}{1920} + C$

x	cos(x)	P(x)
0.1	0.995004165	0.995004167
0.2	0.98006657	0.98006666
0.5	0.87758	0.87604
1	0.54030	0.54167
2	–0.4161	–0.3333

x	arctan(x)	P(x)
0.1	0.09966865	0.09966867
0.2	0.197396	0.197397
0.5	0.4636	0.4646
1	0.7854	0.8667
2	1.1071	5.7333

25. $\int e^{(-x^2)}\,dx = \int 1 + (-x^2) + \frac{(-x^2)^2}{2}\,dx = \int 1 - x^2 + \frac{x^4}{2}\,dx = x - \frac{x^3}{3} + \frac{x^5}{10} + C$

   $\int e^{(-x^3)}\,dx = \int 1 + (-x^3) + \frac{(-x^3)^2}{2}\,dx = \int 1 - x^3 + \frac{x^6}{2}\,dx = x - \frac{x^4}{4} + \frac{x^7}{14} + C$

27. $\int x \sin(x) \, dx = \int x \left\{ x - \frac{x^3}{6} + \frac{x^5}{120} \right\} dx = \int x^2 - \frac{x^4}{6} + \frac{x^6}{120} \, dx = \frac{x^3}{3} - \frac{x^5}{30} + \frac{x^7}{840} + C$

$\int x^2 \sin(x) \, dx = \int x^2 \left\{ x - \frac{x^3}{6} + \frac{x^5}{120} \right\} dx = \int x^3 - \frac{x^5}{6} + \frac{x^7}{120} \, dx = \frac{x^4}{4} - \frac{x^6}{36} + \frac{x^8}{960} + C$

29. $\lim_{x \to 0} \frac{1 - \cos(x)}{x^2} = \lim_{x \to 0} \frac{1 - \left\{ 1 - \frac{x^2}{2!} + \frac{x^4}{4!} - \frac{x^6}{6!} + \ldots \right\}}{x^2}$

$= \lim_{x \to 0} \frac{\frac{x^2}{2!} - \frac{x^4}{4!} + \frac{x^6}{6!} - \ldots}{x^2} = \lim_{x \to 0} \frac{1}{2!} - \frac{x^2}{4!} + \frac{x^4}{6!} - \ldots = \frac{1}{2}$.

31. $\lim_{x \to 0} \frac{1 - e^x}{x} = \lim_{x \to 0} \frac{1 - \left\{ 1 + x + \frac{x^2}{2!} + \frac{x^3}{3!} + \ldots \right\}}{x}$

$= \lim_{x \to 0} \frac{-x - \frac{x^2}{2!} - \frac{x^3}{3!} - \ldots}{x} = \lim_{x \to 0} -1 - \frac{x}{2!} - \frac{x^2}{3!} - \ldots = -1$

33. $\lim_{x \to 0} \frac{\sin(x)}{x} = \lim_{x \to 0} \frac{x - \frac{x^3}{3!} + \frac{x^5}{5!} - \ldots}{x} = \lim_{x \to 0} 1 - \frac{x^2}{3!} + \frac{x^4}{5!} - \ldots = 1$

35. $\lim_{x \to 0} \frac{x - \frac{x^3}{6} - \sin(x)}{x^5} = \lim_{x \to 0} \frac{x - \frac{x^3}{6} - \left\{ x - \frac{x^3}{3!} + \frac{x^5}{5!} - \frac{x^7}{7!} \ldots \right\}}{x^5}$

$= \lim_{x \to 0} \frac{-\frac{x^5}{5!} + \frac{x^7}{7!} \ldots}{x^5} = \lim_{x \to 0} -\frac{1}{5!} + \frac{x^2}{7!} \ldots = -\frac{1}{120}$

37. $\sinh(x) = \frac{1}{2}(e^x - e^{-x}) = \frac{1}{2}\left(\left\{ 1 + x + \frac{x^2}{2!} + \frac{x^3}{3!} + \frac{x^4}{4!} + \ldots \right\} - \left\{ 1 - x + \frac{x^2}{2!} - \frac{x^3}{3!} + \frac{x^4}{4!} + \ldots \right\} \right)$

$= \frac{1}{2}\left(2x + 2\frac{x^3}{3!} + 2\frac{x^5}{5!} + 2\frac{x^7}{7!} + \ldots \right) = x + \frac{x^3}{3!} + \frac{x^5}{5!} + \frac{x^7}{7!} + \ldots$

39. $\mathbf{D}\left(x + \frac{x^3}{3!} + \frac{x^5}{5!} + \frac{x^7}{7!} + \ldots \right) = 1 + 3\frac{x^2}{3!} + 5\frac{x^4}{5!} + 7\frac{x^6}{7!} + \ldots = 1 + \frac{x^2}{2!} + \frac{x^4}{4!} + \frac{x^6}{6!} + \ldots$

41. $e^{ix} = \cos(x) + i \cdot \sin(x)$. When $x = \pi/2$, then $e^{ix} = e^{i(\pi/2)} = \cos(\pi/2) + i \cdot \sin(\pi/2) = i$.

If $x = \pi$, then $e^{ix} = e^{\pi i} = \cos(\pi) + i \cdot \sin(\pi) = -1$. This result is often restated in the form

$e^{\pi i} + 1 = 0$, a formula that relates the 5 most common constants in all of mathematics, $e, \pi, i, 1$, and 0.

43. $\binom{3}{0} = 1$ (by the definition), $\binom{3}{1} = \dfrac{3!}{1! \cdot 2!} = \dfrac{3 \cdot 2 \cdot 1}{(1) \cdot (2 \cdot 1)} = 3$,

$\binom{3}{2} = \dfrac{3!}{2! \cdot 1!} = \dfrac{3 \cdot 2 \cdot 1}{(2 \cdot 1) \cdot (1)} = 3$, and $\binom{3}{3} = \dfrac{3!}{0! \cdot 3!} = \dfrac{3 \cdot 2 \cdot 1}{(1) \cdot (3 \cdot 2 \cdot 1)} = 1$.

45. The Maclaurin series for $(1+x)^{5/2}$ is

$$1 + \tfrac{5}{2}x + \left(\tfrac{5}{2}\right)\left(\tfrac{3}{2}\right)\tfrac{x^2}{2!} + \left(\tfrac{5}{2}\right)\left(\tfrac{3}{2}\right)\left(\tfrac{1}{2}\right)\tfrac{x^3}{3!} + \left(\tfrac{5}{2}\right)\left(\tfrac{3}{2}\right)\left(\tfrac{1}{2}\right)\left(\tfrac{-1}{2}\right)\tfrac{x^4}{4!} + \left(\tfrac{5}{2}\right)\left(\tfrac{3}{2}\right)\left(\tfrac{1}{2}\right)\left(\tfrac{-1}{2}\right)\left(\tfrac{-3}{2}\right)\tfrac{x^5}{5!} + \ldots$$

47. If $f(x) = (1+x)^m$, then $f(0) = 1$. $f'(x) = m(1+x)^{m-1}$ so $f'(0) = m$.

$f''(x) = m(m-1)(1+x)^{m-2}$ so $f''(0) = m(m-1)$. $f'''(x) = m(m-1)(m-2)(1+x)^{m-3}$

so $f'''(0) = m(m-1)(m-2)$. $f^{(4)}(x) = m(m-1)(m-2)(m-3)(1+x)^{m-4}$ so $f'''(0) = m(m-1)(m-2)(m-3)$.

And so on. Then the Maclaurin series for $(1+x)^m$ is

$$1 + mx + m(m-1)\tfrac{x^2}{2!} + m(m-1)(m-2)\tfrac{x^3}{3!} + m(m-1)(m-2)(m-3)\tfrac{x^4}{4!} + \ldots$$

Section 10.11 (Odd numbered problem solutions)

1. $f(x) = \sin(x), c = 0, [-2, 4]$: $f'(x) = \cos(x), f''(x) = -\sin(x), f'''(x) = -\cos(x), f^{(iv)}(x) = \sin(x)$ so

    $a_0 = 0, a_1 = 1, a_2 = 0, a_3 = -1/6, a_4 = 0$. Then $P_0(x) = 0$, $P_1(x) = 0 + x = x$,

    $P_2(x) = 0 + x + 0 = x$, $P_3(x) = 0 + x + 0 - x^3/6 = x - x^3/6$,

    and $P_4(x) = 0 + x + 0 - x^3/6 + 0 = x - x^3/6$.

3. $f(x) = \ln(x), c = 1, [0.1, 3]$: $f'(x) = 1/x, f''(x) = -1/x^2, f'''(x) = 2/x^3, f^{(iv)}(x) = -6/x^4$ so

    (using $c = 1$) $a_0 = 0, a_1 = 1, a_2 = -1/2, a_3 = 1/3, a_4 = -1/4$. Then $P_0(x) = 0$, $P_1(x) = (x-1)$,

    $P_2(x) = (x-1) - \tfrac{1}{2}(x-1)^2$, $P_3(x) = (x-1) - \tfrac{1}{2}(x-1)^2 + \tfrac{1}{3}(x-1)^3$, and

    $P_4(x) = (x-1) - \tfrac{1}{2}(x-1)^2 + \tfrac{1}{3}(x-1)^3 - \tfrac{1}{4}(x-1)^4$.

5. $f(x) = \sqrt{x} = x^{1/2}, c = 1, [1, 3]$: $f'(x) = \tfrac{1}{2}x^{-1/2}, f''(x) = \tfrac{-1}{4}x^{-3/2}, f'''(x) = \tfrac{3}{8}x^{-5/2}$, and

    $f^{(iv)}(x) = \tfrac{-15}{16}x^{-7/2}$ so $a_0 = 1, a_1 = \tfrac{1}{2}, a_2 = -\tfrac{1}{8}, a_3 = \tfrac{1}{16}, a_4 = \tfrac{-5}{128}$. Then $P_0(x) = 1$,

    $P_1(x) = 1 + \tfrac{1}{2}(x-1)$, $P_2(x) = 1 + \tfrac{1}{2}(x-1) - \tfrac{1}{8}(x-1)^2$,

    $P_3(x) = 1 + \tfrac{1}{2}(x-1) - \tfrac{1}{8}(x-1)^2 + \tfrac{1}{16}(x-1)^3$, and

    $P_4(x) = 1 + \tfrac{1}{2}(x-1) - \tfrac{1}{8}(x-1)^2 + \tfrac{1}{16}(x-1)^3 - \tfrac{5}{128}(x-1)^4$.

7. $f(x) = (1+x)^{-1/2}$, $c = 0$, $[-2, 3]$: $f'(x) = \frac{-1}{2}(1+x)^{-3/2}$, $f''(x) = \frac{3}{4}(1+x)^{-5/2}$,

   $f'''(x) = \frac{-15}{8}(1+x)^{-7/2}$, $f^{(iv)}(x) = \frac{105}{16}(1+x)^{-9/2}$ so $a_0 = 1$, $a_1 = \frac{-1}{2}$, $a_2 = \frac{3}{8}$, $a_3 = \frac{-5}{16}$,

   and $a_4 = \frac{35}{128}$. Then $P_0(x) = 1$, $P_1(x) = 1 - \frac{1}{2}x$, $P_2(x) = 1 - \frac{1}{2}x + \frac{3}{8}x^2$,

   $P_3(x) = 1 - \frac{1}{2}x + \frac{3}{8}x^2 - \frac{5}{16}x^3$, and $P_4(x) = 1 - \frac{1}{2}x + \frac{3}{8}x^2 - \frac{5}{16}x^3 + \frac{35}{128}x^4$.

9. $f(x) = \sin(x)$, $c = \pi/2$, $[-1, 5]$: $f'(x) = \cos(x)$, $f''(x) = -\sin(x)$, $f'''(x) = -\cos(x)$, $f^{(iv)}(x) = \sin(x)$ so

   (using $c = \pi/2$) $a_0 = 1$, $a_1 = 0$, $a_2 = -1/2$, $a_3 = 0$, $a_4 = 1/4!$. Then $P_0(x) = 1$, $P_1(x) = 1$,

   $P_2(x) = 1 - \frac{1}{2}(x - \frac{\pi}{2})^2$, $P_3(x) = 1 - \frac{1}{2}(x - \frac{\pi}{2})^2$, and $P_4(x) = 1 - \frac{1}{2}(x - \frac{\pi}{2})^2 + \frac{1}{4!}(x - \frac{\pi}{2})^4$.

11. $f(x) = \sin(x)$, $c = 0$, $n = 5$, $-\pi/2 \leq x \leq \pi/2$: $R_5(x) = \frac{f^{(6)}(z)}{6!}(x - c)^6 = \frac{f^{(6)}(z)}{720}x^6$ for some z between

    x and 0.

    $|R_5(x)| \leq \frac{|-\sin(z)|}{720}|x|^6 \leq \frac{1}{720}(\frac{\pi}{2})^6 \approx 0.02086$.

13. same as problem 11 except $-\pi \leq x \leq \pi$: $R_5(x) = \frac{f^{(6)}(z)}{6!}(x-c)^6 = \frac{f^{(6)}(z)}{720}x^6$ for some

    z between x and 0. $|R_5(x)| \leq \frac{|-\sin(z)|}{720}|x|^6 \leq \frac{1}{720}(\pi)^6 \approx 1.335$.

15. $f(x) = \cos(x)$, $c = 0$, $n = 10$, $-1 \leq x \leq 2$: $R_{10}(x) = \frac{f^{(11)}(z)}{11!}(x-c)^{11} = \frac{\sin(z)}{11!}x^{11}$ for some z

    between x and 0. $|R_{10}(x)| = \frac{|\sin(z)|}{11!}x^{11} \leq \frac{1}{11!}(2)^{11} = \frac{2048}{39916800} \approx 0.000051$.

    Since the only nonzero terms of the power series for $f(x) = \cos(x)$ (about $c = 0$) are the even powers of x, P_{10} is the same as P_{11} so we could use the error term for P_{11} instead of the one for P_{10}. The advantage of using the P_{11} error term is that we have a larger factorial in the denominator of R_{11} and get a smaller bound on the error of the approximation.

    Taking $n = 11$, $-1 \leq x \leq 2$: $R_{11}(x) = \frac{f^{(12)}(z)}{12!}(x-c)^{12} = \frac{|\cos(z)|}{12!}x^{12}$ for some z between x

    and 0. $|R_{11}(x)| = \frac{|\cos(z)|}{12!}x^{12} \leq \frac{1}{12!}(2)^{12} = \frac{4096}{479001600} \approx 0.00000855$.

17. $f(x) = e^x$, $c = 0$, $n = 6$, $-1 \leq x \leq 2$: $R_6(x) = \frac{f^{(7)}(z)}{7!}(x-c)^7 = \frac{f^{(7)}(z)}{5040}x^7$ for some z between x and

    0. Using the estimate $e < 3$, $|R_6(x)| = \frac{|e^z|}{7!}|x|^7 < \frac{3^2}{7!}(2)^7 = \frac{1152}{5040} \approx 0.2286$.

19. $f(x) = \sin(x), c = 0, [-1, 1], E = $ "error" $ = 0.001$. The derivatives of $\sin(x)$ are $\pm\sin(x)$ or $\pm\cos(x)$ and all of them have maximum absolute value less than or equal to 1.

$|R_n(x)| = \dfrac{|f^{(n+1)}(z)|}{(n+1)!} |x-c|^{n+1} \leq \dfrac{1}{(n+1)!} |1|^{n+1} = \dfrac{1}{(n+1)!}$ so we want to find a value of n that makes $\dfrac{1}{(n+1)!} \leq 0.001$. It is difficult to solve factorial equations algebraically, but a "calculator investigation" shows that $\dfrac{1}{(5+1)!} = \dfrac{1}{720} \approx 0.00139 > 0.001$, and $\dfrac{1}{(6+1)!} = \dfrac{1}{5040} \approx 0.000198 < 0.001$ so we should **use n = 6**. That means we need to use the 3 terms involving x, x^3 and x^5.

21. $f(x) = \sin(x), c = 0, [-1.6, 1.6], E = $ "error" $ = 0.00001$. The derivatives of $\sin(x)$ are $\pm\sin(x)$ or $\pm\cos(x)$ and all of them have maximum absolute value less than or equal to 1.

$|R_n(x)| = \dfrac{|f^{(n+1)}(z)|}{(n+1)!} |x-c|^{n+1} \leq \dfrac{1}{(n+1)!} |1.6|^{n+1} = \dfrac{1}{(n+1)!}(1.6)^{n+1}$ so we want to find a value of n that makes $\dfrac{1}{(n+1)!}(1.6)^{n+1} \leq 0.00001$. Some calculator investigation shows that $\dfrac{1}{(9+1)!}(1.6)^{9+1} \approx 0.00003 > 0.00001$ and $\dfrac{1}{(10+1)!}(1.6)^{10+1} \approx 0.0000044 < 0.00001$ so we should **use n = 10**. That means we need to use the 5 terms involving x, x^3, x^5, x^7 and x^9.

23. $f(x) = e^x, c = 0, [0, 2], E = $ "error" $ = 0.001$. The derivatives of e^x are all e^x.

$|R_n(x)| = \dfrac{|f^{(n+1)}(z)|}{(n+1)!} |x-c|^{n+1} \leq \dfrac{|e^z|}{(n+1)!} |x|^{n+1} \leq \dfrac{3^2}{(n+1)!}(2)^{n+1}$ (using $e < 3$). Some calulator investigation shows $\dfrac{3^2}{(9+1)!}(2)^{9+1} \approx 0.0025 > 0.001$ and $\dfrac{3^2}{(10+1)!}(2)^{10+1} \approx 0.00046 < 0.001$ so we should **use n = 10**. (Using a better upper bound for the value of e such as 2.75 or 2.72 does not change the conclusion: use n = 10.)

25. (a) $4\{1 - \dfrac{1}{3} + \dfrac{1}{5} - \dfrac{1}{7} + \dfrac{1}{9}\} \approx 4\{0.83492063\} = 3.33968252$ compared with $\pi \approx 3.14159265$ from a calculator.

(b) Let $A = 4\{1 - \dfrac{1}{3} + \dfrac{1}{5} - \dfrac{1}{7} + ... - \dfrac{1}{99}\}$. Then $|A - \pi| < |51st $ term $| = \dfrac{4}{101} \approx 0.0396$.

(c) Let $B = 4\{1 - \dfrac{1}{3} + \dfrac{1}{5} - \dfrac{1}{7} + ... \pm \dfrac{1}{2n-1}\}$.

Then $|B - \pi| < |$ next term $| = \dfrac{4}{2(n+1) - 1} = \dfrac{4}{2n+1}$. We want $\dfrac{4}{2n+1} \leq 0.0001$ so $n \geq 1999.5$. Take **n = 2000 terms** to get the precision we want.

27. (a) A: Put $C = 16 \cdot \arctan(\frac{1}{5}) - 4 \cdot \arctan(\frac{1}{239})$

$= 16\{ \frac{1}{5} - (\frac{1}{3})(\frac{1}{5})^3 + (\frac{1}{5})(\frac{1}{5})^5 \} - 4\{ \frac{1}{239} - (\frac{1}{3})(\frac{1}{239})^3 + (\frac{1}{5})(\frac{1}{239})^5 \}$

$\approx 16\{ 0.197397333333 \} - 4\{ 0.004184076002 \} = 3.14162102879$.

($C - \pi \approx 0.0000284$.)

(b) Formula A converges more rapidly than Methods I and II because we are using smaller values of x, x = 1/5 and x = 1/239, and the powers of these smaller values of x approach 0 more quickly than the values of x, x = 1 and x = 1/2 and x = 1/3, used in Methods I and II.

11.0 MOVING BEYOND TWO DIMENSIONS

So far our study of calculus has taken place almost exclusively in the xy–plane, a 2–dimensional space. The functions we worked with typically had the form $y = f(x)$ so the graphs of these functions could be drawn in the xy–plane. And we have considered limits, derivatives, integrals, and their applications in two dimensions. However, we live in a three (or more) dimensional space, and some ideas and applications require that we move beyond two dimensions.

This chapter marks the start of our move into three dimensions and the mathematics of higher dimensions. The next several chapters extend the ideas and techniques of limits, derivatives, rates of change, maximums and minimums, and integrals beyond two dimensions. The work you have already done in two dimensions is an absolutely vital foundation for these extensions. As we work beyond two dimensions you should be alert for the the parts of the ideas and techniques that extend very easily (many of them) and those that require more extensive changes.

> Section 11.1 introduces vectors and some of the vocabulary, techniques and applications of vectors in the plane. This section still takes place in two dimensions, but the ideas are important for our move into higher dimensional spaces.

> Section 11.2 introduces the three–dimensional rectangular coordinate system, visualization in three dimensions, and measuring distances between points in three dimensions.

> Section 11.3 extends the basic vector ideas, techniques and applications to three dimensions.

> Sections 11.4 and 11.5 introduce two important types of multiplication, the dot product and the cross product, for vectors in 3–dimensional space and examines what they measure and some of their applications.

> Section 11.6 considers the simplest objects, lines and planes, in 3–dimensional space.

> Section 11.7 introduces surfaces described by second–degree equations and catalogs the possible shapes they can have.

Chapter 11 is the first step in our move beyond two dimensions. It contains the fundamental geometry of points and vectors in three dimensions. The concepts and techniques of this chapter are important and useful by themselves, and they are a necessary foundation for the study of calculus in three and more dimensions in Chapter 12 and beyond.

11.1 VECTORS IN THE PLANE

Measurements of some quantities such as mass, speed, temperature, and height can be given by a single number, but a single number is not enough to describe measurements of some quantities in the plane such as displacement or velocity. Displacement or velocity not only tell us how much or how fast something has moved but also tell the direction of that movement. For quantities that have both length (magnitude) and direction, we use vectors.

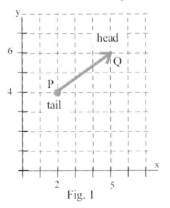

A **vector** is a quantity that has both a magnitude and a direction, and vectors are represented geometrically as directed line segments (arrows). The vector **V** given by the directed line segment from the starting point $P = (2,4)$ to the point $Q = (5,6)$ is shown in Fig. 1. The starting point is called the **tail** of the vector and the ending point is called the **head** of the vector. Geometrically, two vectors are equal if they have the same length and point in the same direction. Fig. 2 shows a number of vectors that are equal to vector **V** in Fig. 1. The equality of vectors in the plane depends only on their lengths and directions. Equality of vectors does not depend on their locations in the plane.

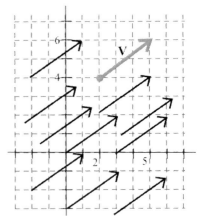

A vector in the plane can be represented algebraically as an ordered pair of numbers measuring the horizontal and vertical displacement of the endpoint of the vector from the beginning point of the vector. The numbers in the ordered pair are called the **components** of the vector. Vector **V** in Fig. 1 can be represented as $\mathbf{V} = \langle 5-2, 6-4 \rangle = \langle 3, 2 \rangle$, an ordered pair of numbers enclosed by "bent" brackets. All of the vectors in Fig. 2 are also represented algebraically by $\langle 3, 2 \rangle$.

All of these directed line segments represent the vector V
Fig. 2

Notation: In our work with vectors, it is important to recognize when we are describing a number or a point or a vector. To help keep those distinctions clear, we use different notations for numbers, points and vectors:

a number: regular lower case letter: $a, b, x, y, x_1, y_1, ...$
A number is called a scalar quantity or simply a **scalar**.

a point: regular upper case letter: $A, B, ...$
ordered pair of numbers enclosed by ( ): $(2, 3), (a, b), (x_1, y_1), ...$

a vector: **bold** upper case letter: **A, B, U, V**, ...
ordered pair of numbers enclosed by $\langle \ \rangle$: $\langle 2, 3 \rangle, \langle a, b \rangle, \langle x_1, y_1 \rangle, ...$
a letter with an arrow over it: $\vec{A}, \vec{B}, \vec{U}, \vec{V}, ...$

Definition: Equality of Vectors

Geometrically, two vectors are equal if their lengths are equal and their directions are the same.

Algebraically, two vectors are equal if their respective components are equal:
 if $U = \langle a, b \rangle$ and $V = \langle x, y \rangle$, then $U = V$ if and only if $a = x$ and $b = y$.

Example 1: Vectors **U** and **V** are given in Fig. 3.

(a) Represent **U** and **V** using the $\langle \ \rangle$ notation.

(b) Sketch **U** and **V** as line segments starting at the point (0,0).

(c) Sketch **U** and **V** as line segments starting at the point (–1,5).

(d) If (x,y) is the starting point, what is the ending point of the line segment representing the vector **U**?

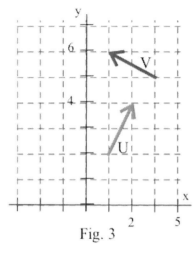

Fig. 3

Solution:

(a) The components of a vector are the displacements from the starting to the ending points so $U = \langle 2-1, 4-2 \rangle = \langle 1, 2 \rangle$ and $V = \langle 1-3, 6-5 \rangle = \langle -2, 1 \rangle$.

(b) If **U** starts at (0,0), then the ending point of the line segment is (0+1, 0+2) = (1,2).

The ending point of **V** is (0–2, 0+1) = (–2, 1). See Fig. 4.

(c) The ending point of the line segment for **U** is (–1+1, 5+2) = (0,7). For **V**, the ending point is (–1–2, 5+1) = (–3, 6). See Fig. 4.

(d) If (x,y) is the starting point for $U = \langle 1, 2 \rangle$ then the ending point is (x+1, y+2).

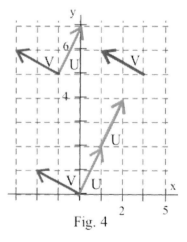

Fig. 4

Practice 1: $A = \langle 3, 4 \rangle$ and $W = \langle -2, 3 \rangle$.

(a) Represent **A** and **W** as line segments beginning at the point (0, 0).

(b) Represent **A** and **W** as line segments beginning at the point (2, –4).

(c) If **A** and **W** begin at the point (p, q), at which points do they end?

(d) How long is a line segment representing vector **A**? **W**?

(e) What is the slope of a line segment representing vector **A**? **W**?

(f) Find a vector whose line segment representation is perpendicular to **A**. To **W**.

The magnitude of a vector **V**, written |**V**|, is the length of the line segment representing the vector. That length is the distance between the starting point and the ending point of the line segment. The magnitude can be calculated by using the distance formula.

The **magnitude** or **length** of a vector $\mathbf{V} = \langle a, b \rangle$ is $|\mathbf{V}| = \sqrt{a^2 + b^2}$.

The only vector in the plane with magnitude 0 is $\langle 0, 0 \rangle$, called the **zero vector** and written **0** or $\vec{0}$. The zero vector is a line segment of length 0 (a point), and it has no specific direction or slope.

Adding Vectors

If two people are pushing a box in the same direction along a line, one with a force of 30 pounds and the other with a force of 40 pounds (Fig. 5), then the result of their efforts is equivalent to a single force of 70 pounds along the same line. However, if the people are pushing in different directions (Fig. 6), the problem of finding the result of their combined effort is slightly more difficult. Vector addition provides a simple solution.

Fig. 5

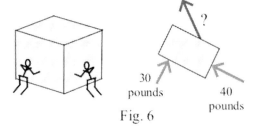

Fig. 6

Definition: Vector Addition

If $\mathbf{A} = \langle a_1, a_2 \rangle$ and $\mathbf{B} = \langle b_1, b_2 \rangle$, then $\mathbf{A} + \mathbf{B} = \langle a_1 + b_1, a_2 + b_2 \rangle$.

The result of applying two forces, represented by the vectors **A** and **B**, is equivalent to the single force represented by the vector **A** + **B**. In Fig. 6, the effort of person A can be represented by the vector $\mathbf{A} = \langle 30, 0 \rangle$ and the effort of person B by the vector $\mathbf{B} = \langle 0, 40 \rangle$. Their combined effort is equivalent to a single force vector $\mathbf{C} = \mathbf{A} + \mathbf{B} = \langle 30, 40 \rangle$. (Since |**C**| = 50 pounds, if the two people cooperated and pushed in the direction of **C**, they could achieve the same result by each exerting 10 pounds less force.)

Example 2: Let $A = \langle 3, 5 \rangle$ and $B = \langle -1, 4 \rangle$. (a) Graph **A** and **B** each starting at the origin.

(b) Calculate $C = A + B$ and graph it, starting at the origin.

(c) Calculate the magnitudes of **A**, **B**, and **C**.

(d) Find a vector **V** so $A + V = \langle 4, 2 \rangle$.

Solution: (a) The graphs of **A** and **B** are shown in Fig. 7.

(b) $C = \langle 3, 5 \rangle + \langle -1, 4 \rangle = \langle 2, 9 \rangle$. The graph of **C** is shown in Fig. 7.

(c) $|A| = \sqrt{3^2 + 5^2} = \sqrt{34} \approx 5.8$, $|B| = \sqrt{17} \approx 4.1$, and $|C| = \sqrt{85} \approx 9.2$.

(d) Let $V = \langle x, y \rangle$. Then $A + V = \langle 3+x, 5+y \rangle = \langle 4, 2 \rangle$ so $3+x = 4$ and $x = 1$. Also, $5+y = 2$ so $y = -3$ and $V = \langle 1, -3 \rangle$

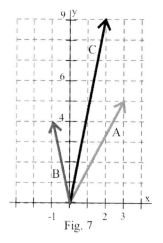
Fig. 7

Practice 2: Let $A = \langle -2, 5 \rangle$ and $B = \langle 7, -4 \rangle$. (a) Graph **A** and **B** each starting at the origin.

(b) Calculate $C = A + B$ and graph it, starting at the origin.

(c) Find and graph a vector **V** so $V + C = 0$.

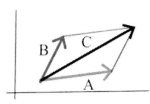
Fig. 8

The parallelogram method and the head–to–tail method are two commonly used methods for adding vectors graphically.

The parallelogram method (Fig. 8):

i) arrange the vectors **A** and **B** to have a common starting point

ii) use the two given vectors to complete a parallelogram

iii) draw a vector **C** from the common starting point of the two original vectors to the opposite corner of the parallelogram: $C = A + B$

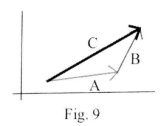
Fig. 9

The head–to–tail method (Fig. 9):

i) position the tail of vector **B** at the head of the vector **A**

ii) draw a vector **C** from the tail of **A** to the head of **B**: $C = A + B$

The head–to–tail method is particularly useful when we need to add several vectors together. We can simply string them along head–to–tail, head–to–tail, ... and finally draw their sum as a directed line segment from the tail of the first vector to the head of the last vector (Fig. 10).

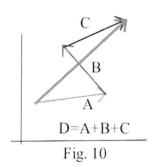
Fig. 10

Practice 3: Draw the vectors $U = A + C$ and $V = A + B + C$ for A, B, and C given in Fig. 11.

Fig. 11

Scalar Multiplication

We can multiply a vector by a number (a scalar) by multiplying each component by that number.

Fig. 12

Definition: Scalar Multiplication

If k is a scalar and $A = \langle a_1, a_2 \rangle$ is a vector,
then $kA = \langle ka_1, ka_2 \rangle$, a vector.

Multiplying by a scalar k gives a vector that is $|k|$ times as long as the original vector. If k is positive, then A and kA have the same direction. If k is negative, then A and kA point in opposite directions (Fig. 12).

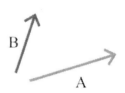

Fig. 13

Example 3: Vectors A and B are shown in Fig. 13.
Graph and label $C = 2A$, $D = \frac{1}{2} B$, $E = -2B$, $F = B + 2A$, and $G = A + (-1)A$.

Solution: The vectors are shown in Fig. 14.

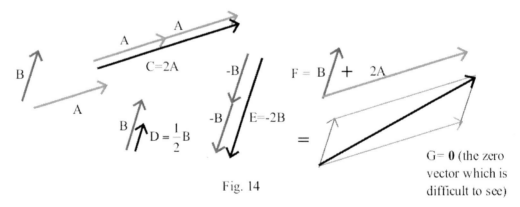

Fig. 14

G = **0** (the zero vector which is difficult to see)

Practice 4: Vectors U and V are shown in Fig. 15.
Graph and label $A = 2U$, $B = -\frac{1}{2} U$, $C = (-1)V$, and $D = U + (-1)V$.

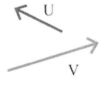

Fig. 15

Subtracting Vectors

We can also subtract vectors algebraically and graphically.

Definition: Vector Subtraction

If $\mathbf{A} = \langle a_1, a_2 \rangle$ and $\mathbf{B} = \langle b_1, b_2 \rangle$, then $\mathbf{A} - \mathbf{B} = \mathbf{A} + (-1)\mathbf{B} = \langle a_1 - b_1, a_2 - b_2 \rangle$, a vector.

Graphically, we can construct the line segment representing the vector

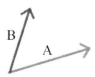

$\mathbf{A} - \mathbf{B}$ either using the head–to–tail method (Fig. 16) to add $\mathbf{A}$ and $-\mathbf{B}$, or by moving $\mathbf{A}$ and $\mathbf{B}$ so they have a common starting point (Fig. 17) and then drawing the line segment from the head of $\mathbf{B}$ to the head of $\mathbf{A}$.

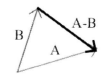

Practice 5: Vectors $\mathbf{A}, \mathbf{B}$ and $\mathbf{C}$ are shown in Fig. 18. Graph $\mathbf{U} = \mathbf{A} - \mathbf{B}$ and $\mathbf{V} = \mathbf{C} - \mathbf{A}$.

Fig. 16

Fig. 17

Fig. 18

Algebraic Properties of Vector Operations

Some of the properties of vectors are given below.

If $\mathbf{A}, \mathbf{B}$, and $\mathbf{C}$ are vectors in the plane and x and y are scalars, then

1. $\mathbf{A} + \mathbf{B} = \mathbf{B} + \mathbf{A}$

2. $(\mathbf{A} + \mathbf{B}) + \mathbf{C} = \mathbf{A} + (\mathbf{B} + \mathbf{C})$

3. $\mathbf{A} + \mathbf{0} = \mathbf{A}$ ($\mathbf{0} = \langle 0,0 \rangle$ is called the additive identity vector)

4. $\mathbf{A} + (-1)\mathbf{A} = \mathbf{0}$ ($-\mathbf{A} = (-1)\mathbf{A}$ is called the additive inverse vector of A)

5. $x(\mathbf{A} + \mathbf{B}) = x\mathbf{A} + x\mathbf{B}$

6. $(x + y)\mathbf{A} = x\mathbf{A} + y\mathbf{A}$

These and additional properties of vectors are easily verified using the definitions of vector equality, vector addition and scalar multiplication.

Unit Vector, Direction of a Vector, Standard Basis Vectors

Definitions:

A **unit vector** is a vector whose length is 1.

The **direction** of a nonzero vector $\mathbf{A}$ is the unit vector $\frac{1}{|\mathbf{A}|}\mathbf{A} = \frac{\mathbf{A}}{|\mathbf{A}|}$.

The **standard basis vectors** in the plane are $\mathbf{i} = \langle 1, 0 \rangle$ and $\mathbf{j} = \langle 0, 1 \rangle$. (Fig. 19)

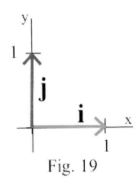

Fig. 19

Every nonzero vector $\mathbf{A}$ is the product of its magnitude and its direction: $\mathbf{A} = |\mathbf{A}|\frac{\mathbf{A}}{|\mathbf{A}|}$.

The standard basis vectors are unit vectors.

Every vector in the plane can be written as a sum of scalar multiples of these two basis vectors:
if $\mathbf{A} = \langle a_1, a_2 \rangle$, then $\mathbf{A} = \langle a_1, 0 \rangle + \langle 0, a_2 \rangle = a_1\mathbf{i} + a_2\mathbf{j}$.

Example 4: Let $\mathbf{A} = 5\mathbf{i} + 12\mathbf{j}$ and $\mathbf{B} = 3\mathbf{i} - 4\mathbf{j}$.

(a) Determine the directions of $\mathbf{A}, \mathbf{B}$, and $\mathbf{C} = \mathbf{A} - 3\mathbf{j}$.

(b) Write $3\mathbf{A} + 2\mathbf{B}$ and $4\mathbf{A} - 5\mathbf{B}$ in terms of the standard basis vectors.

Solution: (a) $|\mathbf{A}| = \sqrt{25 + 144} = \sqrt{169} = 13$ so the direction of $\mathbf{A}$ is

$\frac{1}{13}\langle 5, 12 \rangle = \langle \frac{5}{13}, \frac{12}{13} \rangle = \frac{5}{13}\mathbf{i} + \frac{12}{13}\mathbf{j}$. The direction of $\mathbf{B}$ is $\frac{3}{5}\mathbf{i} - \frac{4}{5}\mathbf{j}$.

$|\mathbf{C}| = |5\mathbf{i} + 9\mathbf{j}| = \sqrt{106}$ so the direction of $\mathbf{C}$ is $\frac{5}{\sqrt{106}}\mathbf{i} + \frac{9}{\sqrt{106}}\mathbf{j}$.

(b) $3\mathbf{A} + 2\mathbf{B} = 3(5\mathbf{i} + 12\mathbf{j}) + 2(3\mathbf{i} - 4\mathbf{j}) = 15\mathbf{i} + 36\mathbf{j} + 6\mathbf{i} - 8\mathbf{j} = 21\mathbf{i} + 28\mathbf{j}$.

$4\mathbf{A} - 5\mathbf{B} = 4(5\mathbf{i} + 12\mathbf{j}) - 5(3\mathbf{i} - 4\mathbf{j}) = 20\mathbf{i} + 48\mathbf{j} - 15\mathbf{i} + 20\mathbf{j} = 5\mathbf{i} + 68\mathbf{j}$.

Practice 6: Let $\mathbf{U} = 7\mathbf{i} + 24\mathbf{j}$ and $\mathbf{V} = 15\mathbf{i} - 8\mathbf{j}$.

Determine the directions of $\mathbf{U}, \mathbf{V}$, and $\mathbf{W} = \mathbf{U} + 3\mathbf{i}$.

Often in applications a vector is described in terms of a magnitude at an angle to some line. In those situations we typically need to use trigonometry to determine the components of the vector.

Example 5: Suppose you are pulling on the rope with a force of 50 pounds at an angle of 25° to the horizontal ground (Fig. 20). What are the components of this force vector parallel and perpendicular to the ground?

Fig. 20

Solution: The horizontal component (parallel to the ground) is $50 \cos(25°) \approx 45.3$ pounds.

The vertical component (perpendicular to the ground) is $50 \sin(25°) \approx 21.1$ pounds.

A force of approximately 45.3 pounds operates to pull the box along the ground (Fig. 21), and a force of approximately 21.1 pounds is operating to lift the box.

The following result from trigonometry is used to find the components of vectors in the plane.

If a vector **V** with magnitude |**V**| makes an angle of θ with a horizontal line,

then $\mathbf{V} = |\mathbf{V}|\cos(\theta)\,\mathbf{i} + |\mathbf{V}|\sin(\theta)\,\mathbf{j} = \langle |\mathbf{V}|\cos(\theta), |\mathbf{V}|\sin(\theta) \rangle$.

Practice 7: A horizontal force of 50 pounds is required to move the box in Fig. 22. If you can pull on the rope with a total force of 70 pounds, what is the largest angle that the rope can make with the ground and still move the box?

Additional Applications of Vectors in the Plane

The following applications are more complicated than the previous ones, but they begin to illustrate the range and power of vector methods for solving applied problems. In general, vector methods allow us to work separately with the horizontal and vertical components of a problem, and then put the results together into a complete answer.

Example 6: In water with no current, your boat can travel at 20 knots (nautical miles per hour). Suppose your boat is on the ocean and you want to follow a course to travel due north, but the water current is $\mathbf{W} = -6\mathbf{i} - 8\mathbf{j}$ (Fig. 23). At what angle θ, east of due north, should you steer your boat so the resulting course **R** is due north?

Solution: First, we should notice that since **R** points due north, the **i** component **R** is 0: $\mathbf{R} = \langle 0, s \rangle$. We also need to recognize that **V** makes an angle of $90° - \theta$ with the horizontal so $\mathbf{V} = \langle 20\cos(90° - \theta), 20\sin(90° - \theta) \rangle$. Finally $\mathbf{V} + \mathbf{W} = \mathbf{R}$ so $\langle 20\cos(90° - \theta) - 6, 20\sin(90° - \theta) - 8 \rangle = \langle 0, s \rangle$. Equating the first components of this vector equation, we have $20\cos(90° - \theta) - 6 = 0$ so $\cos(90° - \theta) = 6/20 = 0.3$, $90° - \theta \approx 72.5°$, and $\theta \approx 17.5°$. You should steer your boat approximately 17.5° east of due north in order to maintain a course taking you due north. Your speed along this course is $|\mathbf{R}| = s = 20\sin(90° - \theta) - 8 \approx 20\sin(72.5°) - 8 \approx 11.1$ knots.

Practice 8: With the same boat and water current as in Example 6, at what angle θ, east of due north, should you steer your boat so the resulting course **R** is due east? What is your resulting speed due east?

Example 7: A video camera weighing 15 pounds is going to be suspended by two wires from the ceiling of a room as shown in Fig. 24. What is the resulting tension in each wire? (The tension in a wire is the magnitude of the force vector.)

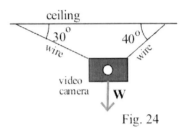

Fig. 24

Solution: The force vector of the camera is straight down so
$\mathbf{W} = \langle 0, -15 \rangle$. Let vector **A** be the force vector for the left (30°) wire, and vector **B** be the force vector for the right (40°) vector. Vector **A** has magnitude |**A**| and can be represented as $\langle -|\mathbf{A}|\cos(30°), |\mathbf{A}|\sin(30°) \rangle$. Similarly, $\mathbf{B} = \langle |\mathbf{B}|\cos(40°), |\mathbf{B}|\sin(40°) \rangle$. Since the system is in equilibrium, the sum of the force vectors is 0 so

$\mathbf{0} = \mathbf{A} + \mathbf{B} + \mathbf{W} = \langle -|\mathbf{A}|\cos(30°) + |\mathbf{B}|\cos(40°) + 0, |\mathbf{A}|\sin(30°) + |\mathbf{B}|\sin(40°) - 15 \rangle$.

From the components of the vector equation we have two equations,

$0 = -|\mathbf{A}|\cos(30°) + |\mathbf{B}|\cos(40°) + 0$ and $0 = |\mathbf{A}|\sin(30°) + |\mathbf{B}|\sin(40°) - 15$,

that we want to solve for the tensions |**A**| and |**B**|.

From the first, we get $|\mathbf{A}|\cos(30°) = |\mathbf{B}|\cos(40°)$ so $|\mathbf{B}| = |\mathbf{A}| \frac{\cos(30°)}{\cos(40°)}$.

Substituting this value for |**B**| into the second equation we have

$0 = |\mathbf{A}|\sin(30°) + |\mathbf{A}|\frac{\cos(30°)}{\cos(40°)}\sin(40°) - 15 = |\mathbf{A}|\{\sin(30°) + \cos(30°)\tan(40°)\} - 15$

so $|\mathbf{A}| = \frac{15}{\sin(30°) + \cos(30°)\tan(40°)} \approx 12.2$ pounds. Putting this value back into

$|\mathbf{B}| = |\mathbf{A}|\frac{\cos(30°)}{\cos(40°)}$, we get $|\mathbf{B}| = (12.2)\frac{\cos(30°)}{\cos(40°)} \approx 13.9$ pounds.

Practice 9: What are the tensions in the wires if the angles are changed to 35° and 50°?

PROBLEMS

In problems 1 – 4, vectors **U** and **V** are given graphically. Sketch the vectors $3\mathbf{U}$, $-2\mathbf{V}$, $\mathbf{U}+\mathbf{V}$, and $\mathbf{U}-\mathbf{V}$.

1. **U** and **V** are given in Fig. 25.
2. **U** and **V** are given in Fig. 26.
3. **U** and **V** are given in Fig. 27.
4. **U** and **V** are given in Fig. 28.

Fig. 25

Fig. 26

Fig. 27

Fig. 28

In problems 5 – 10, vectors **U** and **V** are given.

(a) Sketch the vectors $\mathbf{U}, \mathbf{V}, 3\mathbf{U}, -2\mathbf{V}, \mathbf{U}+\mathbf{V}$, and $\mathbf{U}-\mathbf{V}$.

(b) Calculate |**U**| and |**V**| and find the directions of **U** and **V**.

(c) Find the slopes of the line segments representing **U** and **V** and their angles with the x–axis.

5. $\mathbf{U} = \langle 1, 4 \rangle$ and $\mathbf{V} = \langle 3, 2 \rangle$
6. $\mathbf{U} = \langle 2, 5 \rangle$ and $\mathbf{V} = \langle 6, 1 \rangle$
7. $\mathbf{U} = \langle -2, 5 \rangle$ and $\mathbf{V} = \langle 3, -7 \rangle$
8. $\mathbf{U} = \langle -3, 4 \rangle$ and $\mathbf{V} = \langle 1, -5 \rangle$
9. $\mathbf{U} = \langle -4, -3 \rangle$ and $\mathbf{V} = \langle 3, -4 \rangle$
10. $\mathbf{U} = \langle -5, 2 \rangle$ and $\mathbf{V} = \langle -2, -5 \rangle$

In problems 11 – 14, vectors **A**, **B**, and **C** are given. Calculate $\mathbf{U} = \mathbf{A} + \mathbf{B} - \mathbf{C}$ and $\mathbf{V} = \mathbf{A} - \mathbf{B} + \mathbf{C}$.

11. **A**, **B**, and **C** in Fig. 29.
12. **A**, **B**, and **C** in Fig. 30.
13. $\mathbf{A} = \langle 1, 4 \rangle, \mathbf{B} = \langle 3, 1 \rangle, \mathbf{C} = \langle 5, 2 \rangle$
14. $\mathbf{A} = \langle -1, 5 \rangle, \mathbf{B} = \langle 2, 0 \rangle, \mathbf{C} = \langle 6, -2 \rangle$

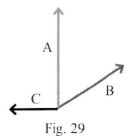
Fig. 29

In problems 15 – 20, find a vector **V** with the given properties.

15. |**V**| = 3 and direction $0.6\mathbf{i} + 0.8\mathbf{j}$

16. |**V**| = 2 and direction $0.6\mathbf{i} - 0.8\mathbf{j}$

17. |**V**| = 5 and **V** makes an angle of $35°$ with the positive x–axis.

18. |**V**| = 2 and **V** makes an angle of $150°$ with the positive x–axis.

19. |**V**| = 7 and **V** has slope 3.

20. |**V**| = 7 and **V** has slope –2.

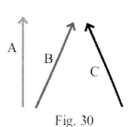
Fig. 30

In problems 21 – 26, find the direction of each function at the given point. That is, find a unit vector, there are two, parallel to the tangent line to the curve at the given point).

21. $f(x) = x^2 + 3x - 2$ at $(1, 2)$

22. $f(x) = \sin(3x) + e^x$ at $(0, 1)$

23. $f(x) = \ln(x^2 + 1)$ at $(0, 0)$

24. $f(x) = \dfrac{2 + \sin(x)}{1 + x}$ at $(0, 2)$

25. $f(x) = \cos^2(3x)$ at $(\pi, 1)$

26. $f(x) = \arctan(x)$ at $(0, 0)$

In problems 27 – 34, a vector **U** is shown or given as $\mathbf{U} = \langle a, b \rangle$.

(a) Sketch the "shadow vector" (Fig. 31) of **U** on the x–axis. (This is the "projection of **U**" onto the x–axis.)

(b) Sketch the "shadow vector" of **U** on the y–axis. (This is the "projection of **U**" onto the y–axis.)

(c) Represent each of these "shadow vectors" in the form $a\mathbf{i} + b\mathbf{j}$.

"shadow vector" of U on the x-axis
Fig. 31

27. **U** is given in Fig. 32.

28. **U** is given in Fig. 33.

29. **U** is given in Fig. 34.

30. **U** is given in Fig. 35.

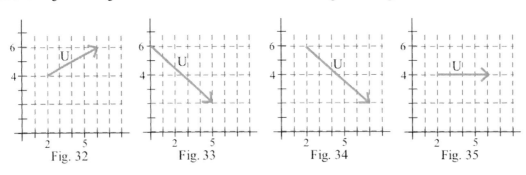

Fig. 32   Fig. 33   Fig. 34   Fig. 35

31. $\mathbf{U} = \langle 1, 4 \rangle$

32. $\mathbf{U} = \langle -2, 3 \rangle$

33. $\mathbf{U} = \langle 5, -2 \rangle$

34. $\mathbf{U} = \langle -1, -3 \rangle$

In problems 35 – 38, vectors **A** and **B** are given. Find a vector **C** so that $\mathbf{A} + \mathbf{B} + \mathbf{C} = \mathbf{0}$.

35. **A** and **B** are shown in Fig. 36.

36. **A** and **B** are shown in Fig. 37.

37. $\mathbf{A} = \langle 7, 4 \rangle$ and $\mathbf{B} = \langle -3, 2 \rangle$

38. $\mathbf{A} = \langle -5, -3 \rangle$ and $\mathbf{B} = \langle 2, -4 \rangle$

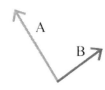

Fig. 36

39. Suppose you are pulling on the rope with a force of 60 pounds at an angle of 65° to the horizontal ground. What are the components of this force vector parallel and perpendicular to the ground?

Fig. 37

40. Suppose you are pulling on the rope with a force of 100 pounds at an angle of 15° to the horizontal ground. What are the components of this force vector parallel and perpendicular to the ground?

41. Two ropes are attached to the bumper of a car. Rope A is pulled with a force of 50 pounds at an angle of 45° to the horizontal ground, and rope B is pulled with a force of 70 pounds at an angle of 35° to the horizontal ground. The same effect can be produced by a single rope pulling with what force and at what angle to the ground?

42. Two ropes are attached to the bumper of a car. Rope A is pulled with a force of 60 pounds at an angle of 30° to the horizontal ground, and rope B is pulled with a force of 80 pounds at an angle of 15° to the horizontal ground. The same effect can be produced by a single rope pulling with what force and at what angle to the ground?

43. Rope A is pulled with a force of 100 pounds at an angle of 30° to the horizontal ground, rope B is pulled with a force of 90 pounds at an angle of 25° to the horizontal, and rope C is pulled with a force of 80 pounds at an angle of 15° to the horizontal. The same effect can be produced pulling on a single rope with what force and at what angle to the ground?

44. A plane is flying due east at 200 miles per hour when it encounters a wind $\mathbf{W} = 30\mathbf{i} + 40\mathbf{j}$.
    (a) What is the path of the plane in this wind if the pilot keeps it pointed due east?
    (b) What direction should the pilot point the plane in order to fly due east?

45. A boat is moving due north at 18 miles per hour when it encounters a current $\mathbf{C} = -3\mathbf{i} + 4\mathbf{j}$.
    (a) What is the path of the boat in this current if the boater keeps it pointed due north?
    (b) What direction should the boater steer in order to go due north?

46. Suppose you leave home and hike 10 miles due north, then 8 miles in the direction 40° east of north, and then 6 miles due east. (a) How far are you from home? (b) What direction should you hike in order to return home?

47. A 60 foot rope is attached to the tops of two poles that are 50 feet apart, and a 100 pound person is going hand–over–hand from one end of the rope to the other (Fig. 38).
    (a) What is the tension in each part of the rope when the person is half way?
    (b) What is the tension in the rope when the person is 10 feet (horizontally) from the start?

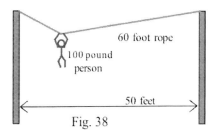

Fig. 38

Practice Answers

Practice 1: (a) and (b) See Fig. 39.

(c) **A** ends at the point $(p+3, q+4)$. **W** ends at the point $(p-2, q+3)$.

(d) We can use the Pythagorean distance formula to determine the length of the hypotenuse.
For **A**, length $= \sqrt{3^2 + 4^2} = \sqrt{25} = 5$.
For **W**, length $= \sqrt{(-2)^2 + 3^2} = \sqrt{13} \approx 3.6$.

Fig. 39

(e) Slope = rise/run. For **A**, slope = 4/3. For **W**, slope = 3/(–2).

(f) Two lines are perpendicular if one slope is the negative reciprocal of the other. If **B** is perpendicular to **A**, then the slope of **B** is –1/(slope of **A**) = –3/4. The vector $\mathbf{B} = \langle 4, -3 \rangle$ is one vector that has the slope we want. $\mathbf{B} = \langle -4, 3 \rangle$, and $\mathbf{B} = \langle 2, -3/2 \rangle$ are two other vectors with the same slope, and there are lots of others. $\mathbf{U} = \langle 3, 2 \rangle$ has slope 2/3 and is perpendicular to **W**.

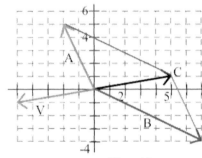

Practice 2: (a) **A** and **B** are shown in Fig. 40.

(b) $\mathbf{C} = \langle -2, 5 \rangle + \langle 7, -4 \rangle = \langle 5, 1 \rangle$. The graph of **C** is shown in Fig. 40.

(c) $\mathbf{V} = \langle -5, -1 \rangle$. The graph of **V** is shown in Fig. 40.

Fig. 40

Practice 3: See Fig. 41.

Practice 4: See Fig. 42.

Fig. 41

Fig. 42

Practice 5: See Fig. 43.

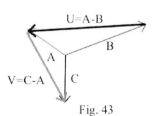

Fig. 43

Practice 6: $|U| = \sqrt{(7)^2 + (24)^2} = \sqrt{625} = 25$, so the direction of **U** is

$$\frac{\mathbf{U}}{|\mathbf{U}|} = \frac{7\mathbf{i} + 24\mathbf{j}}{25} = \frac{7}{25}\mathbf{i} + \frac{24}{25}\mathbf{j}.$$

$|V| = \sqrt{(15)^2 + (-8)^2} = \sqrt{289} = 17$, so the direction of **V** is $\frac{\mathbf{V}}{|\mathbf{V}|} = \frac{15\mathbf{i} - 8\mathbf{j}}{17} = \frac{15}{17}\mathbf{i} - \frac{8}{17}\mathbf{j}$.

$\mathbf{W} = \mathbf{U} + 3\mathbf{i} = (7\mathbf{i} + 24\mathbf{j}) + 3\mathbf{i} = 10\mathbf{i} + 24\mathbf{j}$, so $|W| \sqrt{(10)^2 + (24)^2} = \sqrt{676} = 26$.

The direction of **W** is $\frac{10\mathbf{i} + 24\mathbf{j}}{26} = \frac{5}{13}\mathbf{i} + \frac{12}{13}\mathbf{j}$.

Practice 7: $|V| = 70$ pounds, and you want the horizontal component, $|V|\cos(\theta)$, to be 50 pounds, so $70\cos(\theta) = 50$ and $\theta = \arccos(5/7) \approx 44.4°$.

Practice 8: $\mathbf{R} = \langle s, 0 \rangle$. **V** makes an angle of $90° - \theta$ with the horizontal so
$\mathbf{V} = \langle 20\cos(90° - \theta), 20\sin(90° - \theta) \rangle$.
Also, $\mathbf{V} + \mathbf{W} = \mathbf{R}$ so $\langle 20\cos(90° - \theta) - 6, 20\sin(90° - \theta) - 8 \rangle = \langle s, 0 \rangle$.

Equating the second components of this vector equation, we have
$20\sin(90° - \theta) - 8 = 0$ so $\sin(90° - \theta) = 8/20 = 0.8$, $90° - \theta \approx 23.6°$, and $\theta \approx 66.4°$.

You should steer your boat approximately 66.4° east of due north in order to maintain a course taking you due north. Your speed due east is

$|R| = s = 20\cos(90° - \theta) - 6 \approx 20\cos(90° - 66.4°) - 6 = 12.3$ knots.

Practice 9: The method of solution is the same as Example 7.

$\mathbf{W} = \langle 0, -15 \rangle$, $\mathbf{A} = \langle -|A|\cos(35°), |A|\sin(35°) \rangle$, $\mathbf{B} = \langle |B|\cos(50°), |B|\sin(50°) \rangle$, and

$\mathbf{0} = \mathbf{A} + \mathbf{B} + \mathbf{W} = \langle -|A|\cos(35°) + |B|\cos(50°) + 0, |A|\sin(35°) + |B|\sin(50°) - 15 \rangle$.

Imitating the algebraic steps of Example 7, we get

$|A| = \dfrac{15}{\sin(35°) + \cos(35°)\tan(50°)} \approx 9.68$ pounds and

$|B| = |A|\dfrac{\cos(35°)}{\cos(50°)} \approx 12.33$ pounds.

11.2 RECTANGULAR COORDINATES IN THREE DIMENSIONS

In this section we move into 3–dimensional space. First we examine the 3–dimensional rectangular coordinate system, how to locate points in three dimensions, distance between points in three dimensions, and the graphs of some simple 3–dimensional objects. Then, as we did in two dimensions, we discuss vectors in three dimensions, the basic properties and techniques with 3–dimensional vectors, and some of their applications. The extension of the algebraic representations and techniques from 2 to three dimensions is straightforward, but it usually takes practice to visualize 3–dimensional objects and to sketch them on a 2–dimensional piece of paper.

3–Dimensional Rectangular Coordinate System

In the 2–dimensional rectangular coordinate system we have two coordinate axes that meet at right angles at the origin (Fig. 1), and it takes two numbers, an ordered pair (x, y), to specify the rectangular coordinate location of a point in the plane (2 dimensions). Each ordered pair (x, y) specifies the location of exactly one point, and the location of each point is given by exactly one ordered pair (x, y). The x and y values are the coordinates of the point (x, y).

The situation in three dimensions is very similar. In the 3–dimensional rectangular coordinate system we have three coordinate axes that meet at right angles (Fig. 2), and three numbers, an ordered triple (x, y, z), are needed to specify the location of a point. Each ordered triple (x, y, z) specifies the location of exactly one point, and the location of each point is given by exactly one ordered triple (x, y, z). The x, y and z values are the coordinates of the point (x, y, z). Fig. 3 shows the location of the point $(4, 2, 3)$.

Right–hand orientation of the coordinate axes (Fig. 4): Imagine your right hand in front hand in front of you with the palm toward your face, your thumb pointing up, you index finger straight out, and your next finger toward your face (and the two bottom fingers bent into the palm (Fig. 4). Then, in the right hand coordinate system, your thumb points along the positive z-axis, your index finger along the positive x-axis, and the other finger along the positive y-axis. Other orientations of the axes are possible and valid (with appropriate labeling), but the right–hand system is the most common orientation and is the one we will generally use.

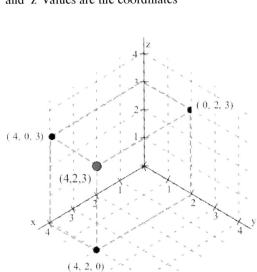

Fig. 3: Locating the point $(4, 2, 3)$

The three coordinate axes determine three planes (Fig.5): the xy–plane consisting of all points with z–coordinate 0, the xz–plane consisting of all points with y–coordinate 0, and the yz–plane with x–coordinate 0. These three planes then divide the 3–dimensional space into 8 pieces called **octants**. The only octant we shall refer to by name is the **first octant** which is the octant determined by the positive x, y, and z–axes (Fig. 6).

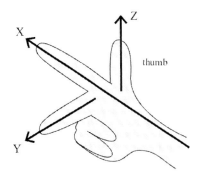

Fig. 4: Right-hand coordinate system

Fig. 5: Coordinate Planes

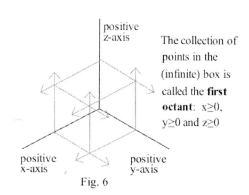

The collection of points in the (infinite) box is called the **first octant**: $x \geq 0$, $y \geq 0$ and $z \geq 0$

Fig. 6

Visualization in three dimensions: Some people have difficulty visualizing points and other objects in three dimensions, and it may be useful for you to spend a few minutes to create a small model of the 3–dimensional axis system for your desk. One model consists of a corner of a box (or room) as in Fig. 7: the floor is the xy–plane; the wall with the window is the xz–plane; and the wall with the door is the yz–plane. Another simple model uses a small Styrofoam ball and three pencils (Fig. 8): just stick the pencils into the ball as in Fig. 8, label each pencil as the appropriate axis, and mark a few units along each axis (pencil). By referring to such a model for your early work in three dimensions, it becomes easier to visualize the locations of points and the shapes of other objects later.

This visualization can be very helpful.

Fig. 7

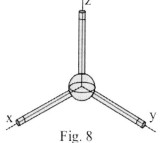

Fig. 8

Each ordered triple (x, y, z) specifies the location of a single point, and this location point can be plotted by locating the point $(x, y, 0)$ on the xy–plane and then going up z units (Fig. 9). (We could also get to the same (x, y, z) point by finding the point $(x, 0, z)$ on the xz–plane and then going y units parallel to the y–axis, or by finding $(0, y, z)$ on the yz–plane and then going x units parallel to the x–axis.)

Example 1: Plot the locations of the points $P = (0, 3, 4), Q = (2, 0, 4),$

$R = (1, 4, 0), S = (3, 2, 1),$ and $T(-1, 2, 1)$.

Solution: The points are shown in Fig. 10.

Practice 1: Plot and label the locations of the points
$A = (0, -2, 3), B = (1, 0, -5), C = (-1, 3, 0),$ and
$D = (1, -2, 3)$ on the coordinate system in Fig. 11.

Fig. 9

Fig. 10

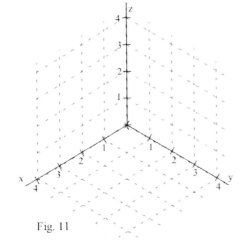

Fig. 11

Practice 2: The opposite corners of a rectangular box are at $(0, 1, 2)$ and $(2, 4, 3)$. Sketch the box and find its volume.

Once we can locate points, we can begin to consider the graphs of various collections of points. By the graph of "z = 2" we mean the collection of all points (x, y, z) which have the form "$(x, y, 2)$". Since no condition is imposed on the x and y variables, they take all possible values. The graph of $z = 2$ (Fig. 12) is a plane parallel to the xy–plane and 2 units above the xy–plane. Similarly, the graph of $y = 3$ is a plane parallel to the xz–plane (Fig. 13a), and $x = 4$ is a plane parallel to the yz–plane (Fig. 13b). (Note: The planes have been drawn as rectangles, but they actually extend infinitely far.)

Fig. 12: Plane z=2

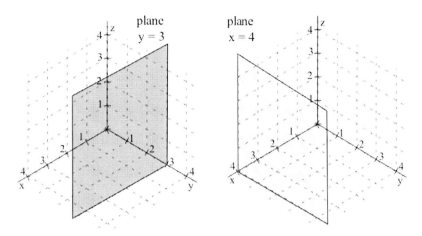

Fig. 13: Planes y = 3 and x = 4

Practice 3: Graph the planes (a) x = 2, (b) y = –1, and (c) z = 3 in Fig. 14. Give the coordinates of the point that lies on all three planes.

Example 2: Graph the set of points (x, y, z) such that x = 2 and y = 3.

Solution: The points that satisfy the conditions all have the form (2, 3, z), and, since no restriction has been placed on the z–variable, z takes all values. The result is the line (Fig. 15) through the point (2, 3, 0) and parallel to the z–axis.

Fig. 14

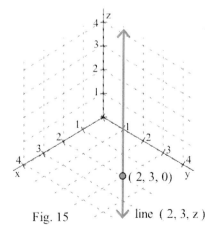

Fig. 15

Practice 4: On Fig. 15, graph the points that have the form (a) (x, 1, 4) and (b) (2, y, –1).

In Section 11.5 we will examine planes and lines that are not parallel to any of the coordinate planes or axes.

Example 3: Graph the set of points (x, y, z) such that $x^2 + z^2 = 1$.

Solution: In the xz–plane (y = 0), the graph of $x^2 + z^2 = 1$ is a circle centered at the origin and with radius 1 (Fig. 16a). Since no restriction has been placed on the y–variable, y takes all values. The result is the cylinder in Figs. 16b and 16c, a circle moved parallel to the y–axis.

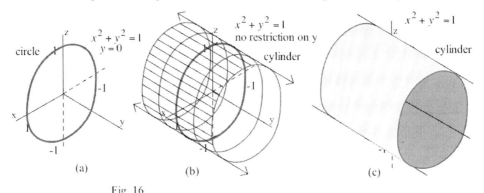

Fig. 16

Practice 5: Graph the set of points (x, y, z) such that $y^2 + z^2 = 4$. (Suggestion: First graph $y^2 + z^2 = 4$ in the yz–plane (x = 0) and then extend the result as x takes on all values.)

Distance Between Points

In two dimensions we can think of the distance between points as the length of the hypotenuse of a right triangle (Fig. 17), and that leads to the Pythagorean formula: distance $= \sqrt{\Delta x^2 + \Delta y^2}$. In three dimensions we can also think of the distance between points as the length of the hypotenuse of a right triangle (Fig. 18), but in this situation the calculations appear more complicated. Fortunately, they are straightforward:

Fig. 17

$$\text{distance}^2 = \text{base}^2 + \text{height}^2 = \left(\sqrt{\Delta x^2 + \Delta y^2}\right)^2 + \Delta z^2$$
$$= \Delta x^2 + \Delta y^2 + \Delta z^2 \quad \text{so distance} = \sqrt{\Delta x^2 + \Delta y^2 + \Delta z^2} \quad .$$

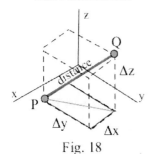

Fig. 18

If $P = (x_1, y_1, z_1)$ and $Q = (x_2, y_2, z_2)$ are points in space, then the distance between P and Q is

$$\text{distance} = \sqrt{\Delta x^2 + \Delta y^2 + \Delta z^2}$$
$$= \sqrt{(x_2-x_1)^2 + (y_2-y_1)^2 + (z_2-z_1)^2} \quad .$$

The 3–dimensional pattern is very similar to the 2–dimensional pattern with the additional piece Δz^2.

Example 4: Find the distances between all of the pairs of the given points. Do any three of these points form a right triangle? Do any three of these points lie on a straight line?

Points: $A = (1, 2, 3), B = (7, 5, -3), C = (8, 7, -1), D = (11, 13, 5)$.

Solution: $\text{Dist}(A, B) = \sqrt{6^2 + 3^2 + (-6)^2} = \sqrt{36 + 9 + 36} = \sqrt{81} = 9$. Similarly,

$\text{Dist}(A,C) = \sqrt{90}$, $\text{Dist}(A, D) = 15$, $\text{Dist}(B, C) = 3$, $\text{Dist}(B, D) = 12$, and $\text{Dist}(C, D) = 9$.

$\{\text{Dist}(A, B)\}^2 + \{\text{Dist}(B, D)\}^2 = \{\text{Dist}(A, D)\}^2$ so the points A, B, and D form a right triangle with the right angle at point B. Also, the points A, B, and C form a right triangle with the right angle at point B since $9^2 + 3^2 = (\sqrt{90})^2$

$\text{Dist}(B, C) + \text{Dist}(C, D) = \text{Dist}(B, D)$ so the points B, C, and D line on a straight line. The points are shown in Fig. 19. In three dimensions it is often difficult to determine the size of an angle from a graph or to determine whether points are collinear.

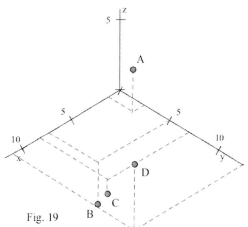

Fig. 19

Practice 6: Find the distances between all of the pairs of the points $A = (3, 1, 2), B = (9, 7, 5), C = (9, 7, 9)$. Which two of these points are closest together? Which two are farthest apart? Do these three points form a right triangle?

In two dimensions, the set of points at a fixed distance from a given point is a circle, and we used the distance formula to determine equations describing circles: the circle with center $(2, 3)$ and radius 5 (Fig. 20) is given by $(x-2)^2 + (y-3)^2 = 5^2$ or $x^2 + y^2 - 4x - 6y = 12$. The same ideas work for spheres in three dimensions.

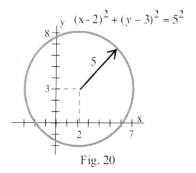

Fig. 20

Spheres: The set of points (x, y, z) at a fixed distance r from a point (a, b, c) is a sphere (Fig. 21) with center (a, b, c) and radius r.

The sphere is given by the equation $(x-a)^2 + (y-b)^2 + (z-c)^2 = r^2$.

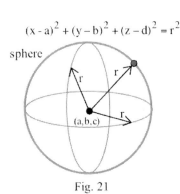

Fig. 21

Example 5: Write the equations of the following two spheres: (A) center $(2, -3, 4)$ and radius 3, and (B) center $(4, 3, -5)$ and radius 4. What is the minimum distance between a point on A and a point on B? What is the maximum distance between a point on A and a point on B?

Solution: (A) $(x-2)^2 + (y+3)^2 + (z-4)^2 = 3^2$.
(B) $(x-4)^2 + (y-3)^2 + (z+5)^2 = 4^2$.

The distance between the centers is
$\sqrt{(4-2)^2 + (3+3)^2 + (-5-4)^2} = \sqrt{121} = 11$, so

the minimum distance between points on the spheres (Fig. 22) is

11 – (one radius) – (other radius) = 11 – 3 – 4 = 4.

The maximum distance between points on the spheres is 11 + 3 + 4 = 18.

Practice 7: Write the equations of the following two spheres:
(A) center $(1, -5, 3)$ and radius 10, and (B) center $(7, -7, 0)$ and radius 2.
What is the minimum distance between a point on A and a point on B?
What is the maximum distance between a point on A and a point on B?

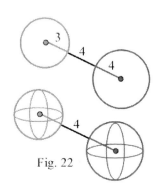

Fig. 22

Beyond Three Dimensions

At first it may seem strange that there is anything beyond three dimensions, but fields as different as physics, statistics, psychology, economics and genetics routinely work in higher dimensional spaces. In three dimensions we use an ordered 3–tuple (x, y, z) to represent and locate a point, but there is no logical or mathematical reason to stop at three. Physicists talk about "space–time space," a 4–dimensional space where a point is represented by a 4–tuple (x, y, z, t) with x, y, and z representing a location and t represents time. This is very handy for describing complex motions, and the "distance" between two "space–time" points tells how far apart they are in (3–dimensional) distance and time. "String theorists," trying to model the early behavior and development of the universe, work in 10–dimensional space and use 10–tuples to represent points in that space.

On a more down to earth scale, any object described by 5 separate measures (numbers) can be thought of as a point in 5–dimensional space. If a pollster asks students 5 questions, then one student's responses can be represented as an ordered 5–tuple (a, b, c, d, e) and can be thought of as a point in five dimensional space. The collection of responses from an entire class of students is a cloud of points in 5–space, and the center of mass of that cloud (the point formed as the mean of all of the individual points) is often used as a group response. Psychologists and counselors sometimes use a personality profile that rates people on four independent scales (IE, SN, TF, JP). The "personality type" of each person can be represented as an ordered 4-tuple, a point in 4-dimensional "personality-type space." If the distance between two people is small in "personality-type space," then they have similar "personality types." Some matchmaking services ask clients a number of questions (each question is a dimension in this "matching space") and then try to find a match a small distance away.

Many biologists must deal with huge amounts of data, and often this data is represented as ordered n-tuples, points in n-dimensional space. In the book <u>The History and Geography of Human Genes</u> (1994), the authors summarize more than 75,000 allele frequencies in nearly 7,000 human populations in the form of maps. "To construct one of the maps, eighty-two genes were examined in many populations throughout the world. Each population was represented on a computer grid as a point in eighty-two dimensional space, with its position along each dimensional axis representing the frequency of one of the alleles in question." (Natural History, 6/94, p. 84)

Geometrically, it is difficult to work in more than three dimensions, but length/distance calculations are still easy.

Definitions for n dimensions:

A point in n-dimensional space is an ordered n-tuple $(a_1, a_2, a_3, \ldots, a_n)$.

If $A = (a_1, a_2, a_3, \ldots, a_n)$ and $B = (b_1, b_2, b_3, \ldots, b_n)$ are points in n-dimensional space, then the distance between A and B is

$$\text{distance} = \sqrt{(b_1-a_1)^2 + (b_2-a_2)^2 + (b_3-a_3)^2 + \ldots + (b_n-a_n)^2} \ .$$

Example 6: Find the distance between the points $P = (1, 2, -3, 5, 6)$ and $Q = (5, -1, 4, 0, 7)$.

Solution: Distance $= \sqrt{(5-1)^2 + (-1-2)^2 + (4--3)^2 + (0-5)^2 + (7-6)^2} = \sqrt{16+9+49+25+1} = \sqrt{100} = 10$.

Practice 8: Write an equation for the 5-dimensional sphere with radius 8 and center $(3, 5, 0, -2, 4)$.

PROBLEMS

In problems 1 – 4, plot the given points.

1. $A = (0,3,4)$, $B = (1,4,0)$, $C = (1,3,4)$, $D = (1,4,2)$
2. $E = (4,3,0)$, $F = (3,0,1)$, $G = (0,4,1)$, $H = (3,3,1)$
3. $P = (2,3,-4)$, $Q = (1,-2,3)$, $R = (4,-1,-2)$, $S = (-2,1,3)$
4. $T = (-2,3,-4)$, $U = (2,0,-3)$, $V = (-2,0,0)$, $W = (-3,-1,-2)$

In problems 5 – 8, plot the lines.

5. $(3, y, 2)$ and $(1, 4, z)$
6. $(x, 3, 1)$ and $(2, 4, z)$
7. $(x, -2, 3)$ and $(-1, y, 4)$
8. $(3, y, -2)$ and $(-2, 4, z)$

In problems 9 – 12, three collinear points are given. Plot the points and the draw a line through them.

9. $(4,0,0)$, $(5,2,1)$, and $(6,4,2)$
10. $(1,2,3)$, $(3,4,4)$, and $(5,6,5)$
11. $(3,0,2)$, $(3,2,3)$, and $(3,6,5)$
12. $(-1,3,4)$, $(2,3,2)$, and $(5,3,0)$

In problems 13 – 16, calculate the distances between the given points and determine if any three of them are collinear. (Note: P, Q, R are collinear if $dist(P,Q) + dist(Q,R) = dist(P,R)$)

13. $A = (5,3,4)$, $B = (3,4,4)$, $C = (2,2,3)$, $D = (1,6,4)$
14. $A = (6,2,1)$, $B = (3,2,1)$, $C = (3,2,5)$, $D = (1,-4,2)$
15. $A = (3,4,2)$, $B = (-1,6,-2)$, $C = (5,3,4)$, $D = (2,2,3)$
16. $A = (-1,5,0)$, $B = (1,3,2)$, $C = (5,-1,3)$, $D = (3,1,2)$

In problems 17 – 20 you are given three corners of a box whose sides are parallel to the xy, xz, and yz planes. Find the other five corners and calculate the volume of the box.

17. $(1,2,1)$, $(4,2,1)$, and $(1,4,3)$
18. $(5,0,2)$, $(1,0,5)$, and $(1,5,2)$
19. $(4,5,0)$, $(1,4,3)$, and $(1,5,3)$
20. $(4,0,1)$, $(0,3,1)$, and $(0,0,5)$

In problems 21 – 24, graph the given planes.

21. $y = 1$ and $z = 2$
22. $x = 4$ and $y = 2$
23. $x = 1$ and $y = 0$
24. $x = 2$ and $z = 0$

In problems 25 – 28, the center and radius of a sphere are given. Find an equation for the sphere.

25. Center $= (4, 3, 5)$, radius $= 3$
26. Center $= (0, 3, 6)$, radius $= 2$
27. Center $= (5, 1, 0)$, radius $= 5$
28. Center $= (1, 2, 3)$, radius $= 4$

11.2 Rectangular Coordinates in Three Dimensions Contemporary Calculus

In problems 29 – 32, the equation of a sphere is given. Find the center and radius of the sphere.

29. $(x-3)^2 + (y+4)^2 + (z-1)^2 = 16$

30. $(x+2)^2 + y^2 + (z-4)^2 = 25$

31. $x^2 + y^2 + z^2 - 4x - 6y - 8z = 71$

32. $x^2 + y^2 + z^2 + 6x - 4y = 12$

Problems 33 – 36 name all of the shapes that are possible for the intersection of the two given shapes in three dimensions.

33. A line and a plane

34. Two planes

35. A plane and a sphere

36. Two spheres

In problems 37 – 44, sketch the graphs of each collection of points. Name the shape of each graph.

37. All (x, y, z) such that (a) $x^2 + y^2 = 4$ and $z = 0$, (b) $x^2 + y^2 = 4$ and $z = 2$.

38. All (x, y, z) such that (a) $x^2 + z^2 = 4$ and $y = 0$, (b) $x^2 + z^2 = 4$ and $y = 1$.

39. All (x, y, z) such that $x^2 + y^2 = 4$ and no restriction on z.

40. All (x, y, z) such that $x^2 + z^2 = 4$ and no restriction on y.

41. All (x,y,z) such that (a) $y = \sin(x)$ and $z = 0$, (b) $y = \sin(x)$ and $z = 1$,
    (c) $y = \sin(x)$ and no restriction on z.

42. All (x,y,z) such that (a) $z = x^2$ and $y = 0$, (b) $z = x^2$ and $y = 2$,
    (c) $z = x^2$ and no restriction on y.

43. All (x,y,z) such that (a) $z = 3 - y$ and $x = 0$, (b) $z = 3 - y$ and $x = 2$,
    (c) $z = 3 - y$ and no restriction on x.

44. All (x,y,z) such that (a) $z = 3 - x$ and $y = 0$, (b) $z = 3 - x$ and $y = 2$,
    (c) $z = 3 - x$ and no restriction on y.

The volume of a sphere with radius r is $\frac{4}{3}\pi r^3$. Use that formula to help determine the volumes of the following parts of spheres in problems 45 and 46.

45. All (x,y,z) such that (a) $x^2 + y^2 + z^2 \leq 4$ and $z \geq 0$, (b) $x^2 + y^2 + z^2 \leq 4$, $z \geq 0$, and $y \geq 0$,
    (c) $x^2 + y^2 + z^2 \leq 4$, $z \geq 0$, $y \geq 0$, and $x \geq 0$.

46. All (x,y,z) such that (a) $x^2 + y^2 + z^2 \leq 9$ and $x \geq 0$, (b) $x^2 + y^2 + z^2 \leq 9$, $x \geq 0$, and $z \geq 0$,
    (c) $x^2 + y^2 + z^2 \leq 9$, $x \geq 0$, $z \geq 0$, and $y \geq 0$.

"Shadow" Problems

The following "shadow" problems assume that we have an object in the first octant. Then light rays parallel to the x–axis cast a shadow of the object on the yz–plane (Fig. 23). Similarly, light rays parallel to the y–axis cast a shadow of the object on the xz–plane, and rays parallel to the z–axis cast a shadow on the xy–plane. (The point of these and many of the previous problems is to get you thinking and visualizing in three dimensions.)

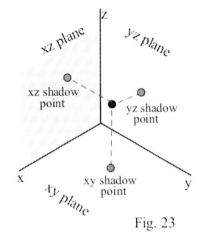

Fig. 23

S1. Give the coordinates of the shadow points of the point (1,2,3) on each of the coordinate planes.

S2. Give the coordinates of the shadow points of the point (4,1,2) on each of the coordinate planes.

S3. Give the coordinates of the shadow points of the point (a,b,c) on each of the coordinate planes.

S4. A line segment in the first octant begins at the point (4,2,1) and ends at (1,3,3). Where do the shadows of the line segment begin and end on each of the coordinate planes? Are the shadows of the line segment also line segments?

S5. A line segment begins at the point (1,2,4) and ends at (1,4,3). Where do the shadows of the line segment begin and end on each of the coordinate planes? Are the shadows of the line segment also line segments?

S6. A line segment begins at the point (a,b,c) and ends at (p,q,r). Where do the shadows of the line segment begin and end on each of the coordinate planes? Are the shadows of the line segment also line segments?

S7. The three points (0,0,0), (4,0,3), and (4,0,2) are the vertices of a triangle in the first octant. Describe the shadow of this triangle on each of the coordinate planes. Are the shadows always triangles?

S8. The three points (1,2,3), (4,3,1), and (2,3,4) are the vertices of a triangle in the first octant. Describe the shadow of this triangle on each of the coordinate planes. Are the shadows always triangles?

S9. The three points (a,b,c), (p,q,r), and (x,y,z) are the vertices of a triangle in the first octant. Describe the shadow of this triangle on each of the coordinate planes. Are the shadows always triangles?

S10. A line segment in the first octant is 10 inches long. (a) What is the shortest shadow it can have on a coordinate plane? (b) What is the longest shadow it can have on a coordinate plane?

S11. A triangle in the first octant has an area of 12 square inches. (a) What is the smallest area its shadow can have on a coordinate plane? (b) What is the largest area?

S12. Design a solid 3–dimensional object whose shadow on one coordinate plane is a square, on another coordinate plane a circle, and on the third coordinate plane a triangle.

Practice Answers

Practice 1: The points are plotted in Fig. 24.

Practice 2: The box is shown in Fig. 25.

$\Delta x = 2$ = width, $\Delta y = 3$ = length, and $\Delta z = 1$ = height, so

volume = (2)(3)(1) = 6 cubic units.

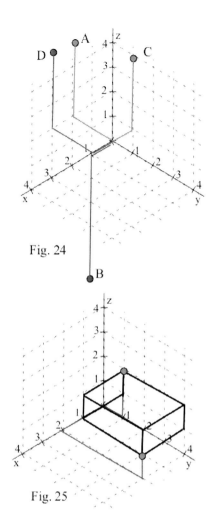

Fig. 24

Fig. 25

Practice 3: The planes are shown in Fig. 26(a).

Each pair of planes intersects along a line, shown as a dark lines in Fig. 26(b), and the three lines intersect at the point $(2, -1, 3)$. This is the only point that lies on all three of the planes.

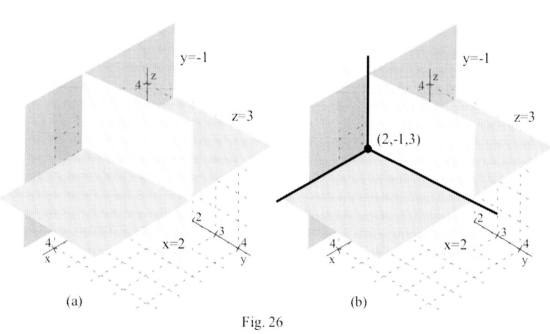

Fig. 26

Practice 4: The points that satisfy $(x, 1, 4)$ are shown in Fig. 27. The collection of these points form a line. One way to sketch the graph of the line is to first plot the point where the line crosses one of the coordinate planes, $(0, 1, 4)$ in this case, and then sketch a line through that point and parallel to the appropriate axis.

The line of points that satisfy $(2, y, -1)$ are also shown in Fig. 27, as well as the point $(2, 0, -1)$ where the line intersects the xz–plane.

Fig. 27

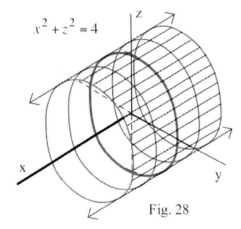

Fig. 28

Practice 5: The graph, a cylinder with radius 2 around the x–axis, is shown in Fig. 28. The dark circle is the graph of points satisfying $y^2 + z^2 = 4$ **and** $x = 0$.

Practice 6:

$$\text{Dist}(A,B) = \sqrt{6^2 + 6^2 + 3^2} = 9,$$
$$\text{Dist}(A,C) = \sqrt{6^2 + 6^2 + 7^2} = 11, \text{ and}$$
$$\text{Dist}(B,C) = \sqrt{0^2 + 0^2 + 4^2} = 4.$$

B and C are closest. A and C are farthest apart.

$4^2 + 9^2 \neq 11^2$ so the points do not form a right triangle.

Practice 7: (A) $(x-1)^2 + (y+5)^2 + (z-3)^2 = 10^2$. (B) $(x-7)^2 + (y+7)^2 + (z-0)^2 = 2^2$.

The distance between the centers is

$$\sqrt{(7-1)^2 + (-7+5)^2 + (0-3)^2} = \sqrt{49} = 7.$$

The radius of sphere A is larger than the distance between the centers plus the radius of sphere B so sphere B is inside sphere A (Fig. 29). The minimum distance between a point on A and a point on B is $10 - (5 + 2 + 2) = 1$. The maximum distance is $10 + (5 + 2 + 2) = 19$.

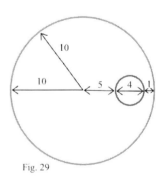

Fig. 29

Practice 8: A point $P = (v, w, x, y, z)$ is on the sphere if and only if the distance from P to the center $(3, 5, 0, -2, 4)$ is 8. Using the distance formula, and squaring each side, we have

$$(v-3)^2 + (w-5)^2 + (x-0)^2 + (y+2)^2 + (z-4)^2 = 8^2.$$

11.3 VECTORS IN THREE DIMENSIONS

Once you understand the 3–dimensional coordinate system, 3–dimensional vectors are a straightforward extension of vectors in two dimensions. Vectors in three dimensions are more difficult to visualize and sketch, but all of the 2–dimensional algebraic techniques extend very naturally, with just one more component.

A vector in any setting is a **quantity that has both a direction and a magnitude**, and in three dimensions vectors can be represented geometrically as directed line segments, (arrows). The vector **V** given by the line segment from the starting point (tail) $P = (1, 2, 3)$ to the ending point (head) $Q = (4, 1, 4)$ is shown in Fig. 1. The vector **V** from P to Q is represented algebraically by the ordered triple enclosed in "bent" brackets: $\mathbf{V} = \langle 3, -1, 1 \rangle$ with each component representing the displacement from P to Q. (We continue to reserve the "round brackets" ( ) to represent points.) Fig. 1 also shows several other geometric representations of vector **V**.

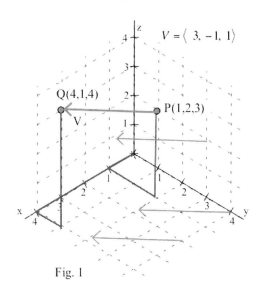

Fig. 1

Definitions and Properties

The following definitions, arithmetic operations, and properties of vectors in 3–dimensional space are straightforward generalizations from two dimensions.

Definition: Equality of Vectors

Geometrically, two vectors are equal if their lengths are equal and their directions are the same.

Algebraically, two vectors are equal if their respective components are equal:

if $\mathbf{U} = \langle a, b, c \rangle$ and $\mathbf{V} = \langle x, y, z \rangle$,

then $\mathbf{U} = \mathbf{V}$ if and only if $a = x$, $b = y$, and $c = z$.

The definitions of scalar multiplication, vector addition and vector subtraction in three dimensions are similar to the definitions in two dimensions, but each vector has one more component.

Definitions: Vector Arithmetic

If $\mathbf{A} = \langle a_1, a_2, a_3 \rangle$ and $\mathbf{B} = \langle b_1, b_2, b_3 \rangle$ are vectors and k is a scalar, then

then $\quad k\mathbf{A} = \langle ka_1, ka_2, ka_3 \rangle$

$\mathbf{A} + \mathbf{B} = \langle a_1 + b_1, a_2 + b_2, a_3 + b_3 \rangle$

$\mathbf{A} - \mathbf{B} = \mathbf{A} + (-1)\mathbf{B} = \langle a_1 - b_1, a_2 - b_2, a_3 - b_3 \rangle$.

Example 1: For $A = \langle 3, -4, 2 \rangle$ and $B = \langle 5, 1, -3 \rangle$, calculate $C = 3B$, $D = 2A + 3B$, and $E = 5A - 2B$.

Solution: $C = 3B = 3\langle 5, 1, -3 \rangle = \langle 15, 3, -9 \rangle$.

$D = 2A + 3B = 2\langle 3, -4, 2 \rangle + 3\langle 5, 1, -3 \rangle = \langle 6+15, -8+3, 4-9 \rangle = \langle 21, -5, -5 \rangle$.

$E = 5A - 2B = 5\langle 3, -4, 2 \rangle - 2\langle 5, 1, -3 \rangle = \langle 5, -22, 16 \rangle$.

Practice 1: For $A = \langle 5, -4, 1 \rangle$ and $B = \langle 2, -3, 4 \rangle$, calculate $C = 5A$, $D = 3A + 4B$, and $E = 2B - 3A$.

Each of the given vector arithmetic operations also has a geometric interpretation:

Fig. 2

Multiplying by a scalar k results in a vector that is $|k|$ times as long as the original vector, $|kA| = |k| |A|$. If k is positive, then A and kA have the same direction. If k is negative, then A and kA point in opposite directions (Fig. 2)

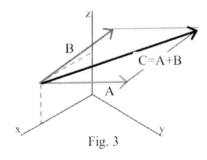

Fig. 3

The sum $C = A + B$ vector can be found geometrically by using the parallelogram or head–to–tail methods described in Section 11.1. (Fig. 3)

The difference $D = A - B$ vector can be sketched by adding A and $-B$ or by drawing A and B with a common starting point and then drawing the line segment from the head of B to the head of A. (Fig. 4)

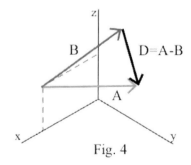

Fig. 4

Because it is more difficult to make precise drawings and measurements in three dimensions, the geometric methods are seldom used to perform vector arithmetic in three dimensions. These geometric interpretations are still very powerful and are important for understanding the meaning of various arithmetic operations and for understanding how certain algorithms are developed.

Visualizing vector arithmetic in three dimensions: If you took the time in Section 11.2 to build a small model of a 3–dimensional coordinate system, you can use it now to see and handle some 3–dimensional vectors. Sharpened pencils or skewer sticks make good physical "vectors."

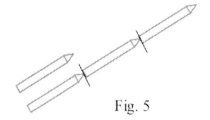
Fig. 5

Visualizing the vectors **A** and 3**A** is easy — just tape together a short pencil and one three times as long (Fig. 5). How could you modify this arrangement to illustrate **A** and –3**A**?

Addition and subtraction are more difficult, but the following vectors fit together nicely:
C = **A** + **B** with **A** = $\langle 2, 3, 6 \rangle$ and
B = $\langle 4, 0, 0 \rangle$ (Fig. 6), and **D** = **A** – **B** with
A = $\langle 4, 7, 4 \rangle$ and **B** = $\langle 4, 2, 4 \rangle$.

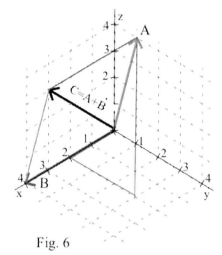
Fig. 6

The length of a vector in three dimensions follows directly from the formula for the distance between points in 3–dimensional space.

> The **magnitude** or **length** of a vector **V** = $\langle a, b, c \rangle$ is $|\mathbf{V}| = \sqrt{a^2 + b^2 + c^2}$.

Since the components a, b, and c of the vector **V** = $\langle a, b, c \rangle$ represent the displacements of the ending point from the starting point in the x, y, and z directions, we can represent **V** as a line segment from the point (0,0,0) to the point (a,b,c). Then the length of **V** is the distance from the point (0,0,0) to the point (a,b,c): length = { distance from (0,0,0) to (a,b,c) } = $\sqrt{a^2 + b^2 + c^2}$.
The only vector in 3–dimensional space with magnitude 0 is the zero vector **0** = $\langle 0, 0, 0 \rangle$. The zero vector has no specific direction.

Example 2: Determine the lengths of **A** = $\langle 2, 8, 16 \rangle$, **B** = $\langle -4, 8, 8 \rangle$, **C** = {vector represented by the line segment from (1,2,3) to (7,–1,9) }, **D** = **A** – **B**, and **E** = **B** + **C**.

Solution: $|\mathbf{A}| = \sqrt{2^2 + 8^2 + 16^2} = \sqrt{324} = 18$. $|\mathbf{B}| = \sqrt{(-4)^2 + 8^2 + 8^2} = \sqrt{144} = 12$.
C = $\langle 7-1, -1-2, 9-3 \rangle = \langle 6, -3, 6 \rangle$ so $|\mathbf{C}| = \sqrt{81} = 9$.
D = **A** – **B** = $\langle 2-(-4), 8-8, 16-8 \rangle = \langle 6, 0, 8 \rangle$ so $|\mathbf{D}| = \sqrt{100} = 10$.
E = **B** + **C** = $\langle -4+6, 8+(-3), 8+6 \rangle = \langle 2, 5, 14 \rangle$ so $|\mathbf{E}| = \sqrt{225} = 15$.

Practice 2: Determine the lengths of $A = \langle 2, 3, 6 \rangle$, $B = \langle 2, 1, 2 \rangle$, and $C = A - 2B$.

Definitions:

The **direction** of a nonzero vector A is the unit vector
$$U = \frac{1}{|A|} A = \frac{A}{|A|}.$$

The **standard basis vectors** in the plane are
$$i = \langle 1, 0, 0 \rangle, j = \langle 0, 1, 0 \rangle, \text{ and } k = \langle 0, 0, 1 \rangle. \text{ (Fig. 7)}$$

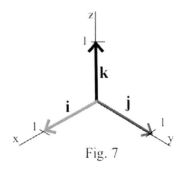
Fig. 7

Example 3: Determine the lengths and directions of $A = 6i + 2j + 9k$, $B = 6i + 3j - 6k$, $C = 3A + 2B$, and $D = B - 2A$.

Solution: $|A| = \sqrt{6^2 + 2^2 + 9^2} = \sqrt{121} = 11$. Direction of A is $\frac{A}{|A|} = \frac{6}{11}i + \frac{2}{11}j + \frac{9}{11}k$.

$|B| = \sqrt{6^2 + 3^2 + (-6)^2} = \sqrt{81} = 9$. Direction of B is $\frac{B}{|B|} = \frac{2}{3}i + \frac{1}{3}j - \frac{2}{3}k$.

$C = 3A + 2B = 30i + 12j + 15k$. $|C| = \sqrt{1269} \approx 35.6$.

The direction of C is $\frac{C}{|C|} = \frac{30}{\sqrt{1269}}i + \frac{12}{\sqrt{1269}}j + \frac{15}{\sqrt{1269}}k \approx 0.84i + 0.34j + 0.42k$.

$D = B - 2A = -6i - 1j - 24k$. $|D| = \sqrt{613} \approx 24.8$.

The direction of D is $\frac{D}{|D|} = \frac{-6}{\sqrt{613}}i - \frac{1}{\sqrt{613}}j - \frac{24}{\sqrt{613}}k \approx 0.24i - 0.04j - 0.97k$.

Practice 3: Determine the lengths and directions of $A = 3i + 2j - 6k$, $B = 6j - 8k$, $C = A + 3B$, and $D = 2B - 3A$.

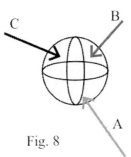
Fig. 8

Example 4: Three players are pushing on a ball, but the ball is not moving (Fig. 8). Player A is pushing with a force of 45 pounds in the direction $\frac{1}{9}i - \frac{4}{9}j + \frac{8}{9}k$, and player B is pushing with a force of 60 pounds in the direction $\frac{4}{6}i + \frac{4}{6}j + \frac{2}{6}k$. How hard and in what direction is player C pushing?

Solution: Since we know the magnitude and direction of the force vectors for players A and B, we can determine the force vector for each player:

$A = \{ \text{magnitude} \} \{ \text{direction} \} = 45 \{ \frac{1}{9}i - \frac{4}{9}j + \frac{8}{9}k \} = 5i - 20j + 40k$, and

$B = \{ \text{magnitude} \} \{ \text{direction} \} = 60 \{ \frac{4}{6}i + \frac{4}{6}j + \frac{2}{6}k \} = 40i + 40j + 20k$.

Pushing together, their force vector is $A + B = 45i + 20j + 60k$. Since the ball is not moving, the force vectors of A, B, and C equal the zero vector, and we can solve for C's force vector:

$$\mathbf{C} = -(\mathbf{A} + \mathbf{B}) = -45\mathbf{i} - 20\mathbf{j} - 60\mathbf{k}.$$

C's force is $|\mathbf{C}| = \sqrt{(-45)^2 + (-20)^2 + (-60)^2} = \sqrt{6025} \approx 77.6$ pounds. C is pushing in

the direction $\dfrac{\mathbf{C}}{|\mathbf{C}|} = \dfrac{-45}{\sqrt{6025}}\mathbf{i} - \dfrac{20}{\sqrt{6025}}\mathbf{j} - \dfrac{60}{\sqrt{6025}}\mathbf{k} \approx -0.60\mathbf{i} - 0.26\mathbf{j} - 0.77\mathbf{k}.$

At this point, you should find the arithmetic of vectors in three dimensions is not much different or harder than in two dimensions. Angles, however, are another story, one we consider in Section 11.4. Fortunately, there is a straightforward process for determining the angle between two 3–dimensional vectors and it is useful in a variety of applications.

Beyond Three Dimensions

Just as we can represent points in 4, 5, or n–dimensional space, we can also work with n–dimensional vectors, $\langle a_1, a_2, a_3, \ldots a_n \rangle$. Even though it is no longer easy (or possible?) to work geometrically with these vectors, the arithmetic operations of scalar multiplication, vector addition, vector subtraction, and length are still defined component–by–component and are still easy.

Example 5: Write the vector **V** for the directed line segment from $P = (1,2,-3,5,6)$ to $Q = (5,-1,4,0,7)$, and find the length and direction of **V**.

Solution: $\mathbf{V} = \langle 5-1, -1-2, 4--3, 0-5, 7-6 \rangle = \langle 4, -3, 7, -5, 1 \rangle.$
$|\mathbf{V}| = \sqrt{4^2 + (-3)^2 + 7^2 + (-5)^2 + 1^2} = \sqrt{100} = 10.$
Direction of **V** is $\dfrac{\mathbf{V}}{|\mathbf{V}|} = \langle 0.4, -0.3, 0.7, -0.5, 0.1 \rangle.$

Practice 4: Calculate the lengths of $\mathbf{A} = \langle 4, 2, -5, 1, 0 \rangle$, $\mathbf{B} = \langle 6, 0, 2, -3, 6 \rangle$, and $\mathbf{C} = 2\mathbf{A} - 3\mathbf{B}$.

We can even determine formulas for some collections of points in higher dimensions.

Example 6: Find a formula for the set of points (w,x,y,z) in 4–dimensional space that are at a distance of 5 units from the point $(5,3,-2,1)$. (This set is "4–sphere" with radius 5 and center $(5,3,-2,1)$.)

Solution: We want the distance from (w,x,y,z) to $(5,3,-2,1)$, $\sqrt{(w-5)^2 + (x-3)^2 + (y+2)^2 + (z-1)^2}$, to be 5 so

$$\sqrt{(w-5)^2 + (x-3)^2 + (y+2)^2 + (z-1)^2} = 5 \text{ and}$$

$$(w-5)^2 + (x-3)^2 + (y+2)^2 + (z-1)^2 = 25.$$

PROBLEMS

In problems 1 – 4 the vectors **A** and **B** are shown. Sketch and label **C** = 2**A**, **D** = –**B**, and **E** = **A** – **B**.

1. See Fig. 9. 2. See Fig. 10. 3. See Fig. 11. 4. See Fig. 12.

Fig. 9

Fig. 10

Fig. 11

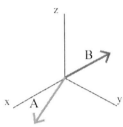
Fig. 12

In problems 5 – 12, vectors **U** and **V** are given. Calculate **W** = 2**U** + **V**, |**U**|, |**V**|, and |**W**|, and the directions of **U**, **V**, and **W**.

5. $U = \langle 2, 3, 6 \rangle$, $V = \langle 2, -9, 6 \rangle$

6. $U = \langle 6, 3, 6 \rangle$, $V = \langle 2, 4, 4 \rangle$

7. $U = \langle 5, 2, 14 \rangle$, $V = \langle 4, -7, 4 \rangle$

8. $U = \langle 8, 4, 1 \rangle$, $V = \langle 4, 4, -2 \rangle$

9. $U = 9i + 6j + 2k$, $V = 3i + 6j - 6k$

10. $U = 24i + 2j + 24k$, $V = 10i - 25j + 2k$

11. $U = 10i + 11j + 2k$, $V = 6i + 3j - 6k$

12. $U = 8i + 1j + 4k$, $V = 3i + 12j + 4k$

13. $A = \langle 3, 6, -2 \rangle$, $B = \langle 5, 0, -4 \rangle$. Find **C** so **A** + **B** + **C** = **0**.

14. $A = \langle 1, -3, 7 \rangle$, $B = \langle -5, 2, -3 \rangle$. Find **C** so **A** + **B** + **C** = **0**.

15. $A = \langle 9, \pi, -3 \rangle$, $B = \langle e, 7, 4 \rangle$, and $C = \langle -6, 2, 0 \rangle$. Find **D** so **A** + **B** + **C** + **D** = **0**.

16. $A = \langle -4, 3, 1 \rangle$, $B = \langle 5, 5, -\pi \rangle$, and $C = \langle 0, -2, 1 \rangle$. Find **D** so **A** + **B** + **C** + **D** = **0**.

17. Which of the following vectors has the smallest magnitude and which has the largest:
$A = \langle 6, 9, 2, 3 \rangle$, $B = \langle -8, 0, 6, 0 \rangle$, $C = \langle -6, 3, 3, 6 \rangle$, and $D = \langle 9, 1, 8, -5 \rangle$?

18. Which of the following vectors has the smallest magnitude and which has the largest:
$A = \langle 11, 2, -10, 1 \rangle$, $B = \langle -5, 14, 2, 6 \rangle$, $C = \langle 2, 8, 16, -5 \rangle$, and $D = \langle 12, 3, 7, 3 \rangle$?

19. $A = \langle 2, 4, 3 \rangle$. Sketch **A** and find the "shadows" of **A** on the coordinate planes (e.g., on the xy, xz, and yz planes).

19. $A = \langle 2, 4, 3 \rangle$. Sketch **A** and find the "shadows" of **A** on the coordinate planes (e.g., on the xy, xz, and yz planes).

20. $B = \langle 4, 1, 2 \rangle$. Sketch **B** and find the "shadows" of **B** on the coordinate planes (e.g., on the xy, xz, and yz planes).

21. $\mathbf{C} = \langle 5, 2, 3 \rangle$. Sketch **C** and find the "shadows" of **C** on the coordinate planes.

22. $\mathbf{D} = \langle 3, 4, 0 \rangle$. Sketch **D** and find the "shadows" of **D** on the coordinate planes.

23. $\mathbf{A} = \langle 1, 0, 0 \rangle$. Sketch **A** and find three nonparallel vectors that are perpendicular to **A**. How many vectors are perpendicular to **A**?

24. $\mathbf{B} = \langle 0, 0, 1 \rangle$. Sketch **B** and find three nonparallel vectors that are perpendicular to **B**. How many vectors are perpendicular to **B**?

25. $\mathbf{C} = \langle 1, 2, 0 \rangle$. Sketch **C** and find two nonparallel vectors that are perpendicular to **C**.

26. $\mathbf{C} = \langle 0, 2, 3 \rangle$. Sketch **C** and find two nonparallel vectors that are perpendicular to **C**.

In problems 27 – 30, you are asked to sketch smooth curves that go through given points with given directions. Later, in Section 12.1, we will discuss how to find parametric equations for curves that satisfy conditions of this type.

27. Sketch a smooth curve that goes through the point (0,0,1) with direction $\langle 1, 0, 0 \rangle$ and then bends and goes through the point (0,1,0) with direction $\langle 0, 1, 0 \rangle$.

28. Sketch a smooth curve that goes through the point (0,0,1) with direction $\langle 0.8, 0, 0.6 \rangle$ and then bends and goes through the point (0,2,0) with direction $\langle 0, 0, 1 \rangle$.

29. Sketch a smooth curve that goes through the point (2,0,0) with direction $\langle 0, 0, 1 \rangle$ and then bends and goes through the point (0,1,2) with direction $\langle -1, 0, 0 \rangle$.

30. Sketch a smooth curve that goes through the point (4, 1, 2) with direction $\langle 0, 0, -1 \rangle$ and then bends and goes through the point (0,0,0) with direction $\langle 0, -1, 0 \rangle$.

31. Find a linear equation for $x(t)$ so $x(0) = 3$ and $x(1) = 7$, for $y(t)$ so $y(0) = 5$ and $y(1) = 4$, and for $z(t)$ so $z(0) = 1$ and $z(1) = 1$.

32. Find a linear equation for $x(t)$ so $x(0) = 1$ and $x(1) = 5$, for $y(t)$ so $y(0) = 2$ and $y(1) = 0$, and for $z(t)$ so $z(0) = 3$ and $z(1) = 5$.

33. Find a linear equation for $x(t)$ so $x(0) = 2$ and $x(1) = 5$, for $y(t)$ so $y(0) = 3$ and $y(1) = 3$, and for $z(t)$ so $z(0) = 6$ and $z(1) = 1$.

34. Find a linear equation for $x(t)$ so $x(0) = 0$ and $x(1) = -3$, for $y(t)$ so $y(0) = -2$ and $y(1) = 1$, and for $z(t)$ so $z(0) = 4$ and $z(1) = 1$.

Practice Answers

Practice 1: $C = 5A = 5\langle 5, -4, 1 \rangle = \langle 25, -20, 5 \rangle$.

$D = 3A + 4B = 3\langle 5, -4, 1 \rangle + 4\langle 2, -3, 4 \rangle = \langle 15+8, -12-12, 3+16 \rangle = \langle 23, -24, 19 \rangle$.

$E = 2B - 3A = 2\langle 2, -3, 4 \rangle - 3\langle 5, -4, 1 \rangle = \langle 4-15, -6+12, 8-3 \rangle = \langle -11, 6, 5 \rangle$.

Practice 2: $|A| = \sqrt{2^2 + 3^2 + 6^2} = \sqrt{49} = 7$. $|B| = \sqrt{2^2 + 1^2 + 2^2} = \sqrt{9} = 3$.

$C = A - 2B = \langle 2, 3, 6 \rangle - 2\langle 2, 1, 2 \rangle = \langle -2, 1, 2 \rangle$ so $|C| = \sqrt{9} = 3$.

Practice 3: $|A| = \sqrt{3^2 + 2^2 + (-6)^2} = \sqrt{49} = 7$. Direction of A is $\frac{A}{|A|} = \frac{3}{7}\mathbf{i} + \frac{2}{7}\mathbf{j} - \frac{6}{7}\mathbf{k}$.

$|B| = \sqrt{0^2 + 6^2 + (-8)^2} = \sqrt{100} = 10$. Direction of B is $\frac{B}{|B|} = \frac{6}{10}\mathbf{j} - \frac{8}{10}\mathbf{k}$.

$C = A + 3B = 3\mathbf{i} + 20\mathbf{j} - 30\mathbf{k}$. $|C| = \sqrt{1309} \approx 36.18$.

Direction of C is $\frac{C}{|C|} = \frac{3}{\sqrt{1309}}\mathbf{i} + \frac{20}{\sqrt{1309}}\mathbf{j} - \frac{30}{\sqrt{1309}}\mathbf{k} \approx 0.08\mathbf{i} + 0.55\mathbf{j} - 0.83\mathbf{k}$.

$D = 2B - 3A = -9\mathbf{i} + 6\mathbf{j} + 2\mathbf{k}$. $|D| = \sqrt{121} = 11$.

Direction of D is $\frac{D}{|D|} = \frac{-9}{11}\mathbf{i} + \frac{6}{11}\mathbf{j} + \frac{2}{11}\mathbf{k} \approx -0.82\mathbf{i} + 0.55\mathbf{j} + 0.18\mathbf{k}$.

Practice 4: $|A| = \sqrt{4^2 + 2^2 + (-5)^2 + 1^2 + 0} = \sqrt{46} \approx 6.8$.

$|B| = \sqrt{6^2 + 0^2 + 2^2 + (-3)^2 + 6^2} = \sqrt{85} \approx 9.2$.

$C = 2A - 3B = 2\langle 4, 2, -5, 1, 0 \rangle - 3\langle 6, 0, 2, -3, 6 \rangle = \langle -10, 4, -16, 11, -18 \rangle$.

$|C| = \sqrt{(-10)^2 + 4^2 + (-16)^2 + 11^2 + (-18)^2} = \sqrt{817} \approx 28.6$.

11.4 DOT PRODUCT

In the previous sections we looked at the meaning of vectors in two and three dimensions, but the only operations we used were addition and subtraction of vectors and multiplication by a scalar. Some of the applications of 2–dimensional vectors used the angles that the vectors made with the coordinate axes and with each other, but, so far, in three dimensions we have not used angles. This section addresses both of those situations. It introduces a way to multiply two vectors, in two and three dimensions, called the dot product, and this dot product provides us with a relatively easy way to determine angles between vectors. Section 11.5 introduces a different method of multiplying two vectors, the cross product, in three dimensions that has other useful applications.

Since we will soon have three different types of multiplications for a vector (scalar, dot, and cross), it is important that you distinguish among them and call each multiplication operation by its full name.

Definition: Dot Product

Two dimensions: The **dot product** of $\mathbf{A} = \langle a_1, a_2 \rangle$ and $\mathbf{B} = \langle b_1, b_2 \rangle$

is $\mathbf{A} \bullet \mathbf{B} = a_1 b_1 + a_2 b_2$.

Three dimensions: The **dot product** of $\mathbf{A} = \langle a_1, a_2, a_3 \rangle$ and $\mathbf{B} = \langle b_1, b_2, b_3 \rangle$

is $\mathbf{A} \bullet \mathbf{B} = a_1 b_1 + a_2 b_2 + a_3 b_3$.

Both vectors in the dot product must have the same number of components, and the result of the dot product $\mathbf{U} \bullet \mathbf{V}$ is a scalar.

Example 1: For $\mathbf{A} = \langle 4, 1, 8 \rangle$ and $\mathbf{B} = \langle 2, -4, 4 \rangle$, calculate $\mathbf{A} \bullet \mathbf{B}$, $\mathbf{A} \bullet \mathbf{A}$, $\mathbf{B} \bullet \mathbf{B}$, and $(\mathbf{A} - \mathbf{B}) \bullet (\mathbf{A} + 2\mathbf{B})$.

Solution: $\mathbf{A} \bullet \mathbf{B} = \langle 4, 1, 8 \rangle \bullet \langle 2, -4, 4 \rangle = (4)(2) + (1)(-4) + (8)(4) = 8 - 4 + 32 = 36$.
$\mathbf{A} \bullet \mathbf{A} = \langle 4, 1, 8 \rangle \bullet \langle 4, 1, 8 \rangle = (4)(4) + (1)(1) + (8)(8) = 81$.
$\mathbf{B} \bullet \mathbf{B} = \langle 2, -4, 4 \rangle \bullet \langle 2, -4, 4 \rangle = (2)(2) + (-4)(-4) + (4)(4) = 36$.
You should notice that $\mathbf{A} \bullet \mathbf{A} = |\mathbf{A}|^2$ and $\mathbf{B} \bullet \mathbf{B} = |\mathbf{B}|^2$.
Finally, $\mathbf{A} - \mathbf{B} = \langle 2, 5, 4 \rangle$ and $\mathbf{A} + 2\mathbf{B} = \langle 8, -7, 16 \rangle$
so $(\mathbf{A} - \mathbf{B}) \bullet (\mathbf{A} + 2\mathbf{B}) = \langle 2, 5, 4 \rangle \bullet \langle 8, -7, 16 \rangle = (2)(8) + (5)(-7) + (4)(16) = 45$.

Practice 1: For $\mathbf{U} = \langle 2, 6, -3 \rangle$ and $\mathbf{V} = \langle -1, 2, 2 \rangle$, calculate $\mathbf{U} \bullet \mathbf{V}$, $\mathbf{U} \bullet \mathbf{U}$, $\mathbf{V} \bullet \mathbf{V}$, $\mathbf{U} \bullet (\mathbf{U} + \mathbf{V})$, and $\mathbf{U} \bullet \mathbf{U} + \mathbf{U} \bullet \mathbf{V}$. Does $\mathbf{U} \bullet \mathbf{U} = |\mathbf{U}|^2$? Does $\mathbf{U} \bullet \mathbf{V} = \mathbf{V} \bullet \mathbf{U}$?

11.4 Dot Product   Contemporary Calculus

As you might have noticed in Example 1 and Practice 1, the dot product seems to have some of the properties of ordinary multiplication of numbers.

Properties of the Dot Product:
(1) $\mathbf{A} \cdot \mathbf{A} = |\mathbf{A}|^2$
(2) $\mathbf{A} \cdot \mathbf{B} = \mathbf{B} \cdot \mathbf{A}$
(3) $k(\mathbf{A} \cdot \mathbf{B}) = (k\mathbf{A}) \cdot \mathbf{B} = \mathbf{A} \cdot (k\mathbf{B})$
(4) $\mathbf{A} \cdot (\mathbf{B} + \mathbf{C}) = \mathbf{A} \cdot \mathbf{B} + \mathbf{A} \cdot \mathbf{C}$

All of these properties can be proved using the definition of the dot product.

Proof of (1): If $\mathbf{A} = \langle a_1, a_2, a_3 \rangle$ then $\mathbf{A} \cdot \mathbf{A} = (a_1)^2 + (a_2)^2 + (a_3)^2$ and

$$|\mathbf{A}|^2 = \left(\sqrt{(a_1)^2 + (a_2)^2 + (a_3)^2}\right)^2 = (a_1)^2 + (a_2)^2 + (a_3)^2 \text{ so } \mathbf{A} \cdot \mathbf{A} = |\mathbf{A}|^2.$$

Proof of (3): $k(\mathbf{A} \cdot \mathbf{B}) = k(a_1 b_1 + a_2 b_2 + a_3 b_3) = k a_1 b_1 + k a_2 b_2 + k a_3 b_3$.

$(k\mathbf{A}) \cdot \mathbf{B} = \langle k a_1, k a_2, k a_3 \rangle \cdot \langle b_1, b_2, b_3 \rangle = k a_1 b_1 + k a_2 b_2 + k a_3 b_3$. And

$\mathbf{A} \cdot (k\mathbf{B}) = \langle a_1, a_2, a_3 \rangle \cdot \langle k b_1, k b_2, k b_3 \rangle = a_1(k b_1) + a_2(k b_2) + a_3(k b_3)$

$= k a_1 b_1 + k a_2 b_2 + k a_3 b_3$ so $k(\mathbf{A} \cdot \mathbf{B}) = (k\mathbf{A}) \cdot \mathbf{B} = \mathbf{A} \cdot (k\mathbf{B})$

Practice 2: Prove Property (2) for 3–dimensional vectors.

The next result about dot products is very important, and much of the usefulness of dot products follows from it. It enables us to easily determine the angle between two vectors in two or three (or more) dimensions.

Angle Property of Dot Products

$\mathbf{A} \cdot \mathbf{B} = |\mathbf{A}| |\mathbf{B}| \cos(\theta)$ where θ is the angle between $\mathbf{A}$ and $\mathbf{B}$. Equivalently,

if $\mathbf{A}$ and $\mathbf{B}$ are nonzero vectors, then the angle θ between $\mathbf{A}$ and $\mathbf{B}$ satisfies $\cos(\theta) = \dfrac{\mathbf{A} \cdot \mathbf{B}}{|\mathbf{A}| |\mathbf{B}|}$.

Proof of the Angle Property: The proof uses the Law of Cosines and several of the properties of the dot product.

The vectors $\mathbf{A}$, $\mathbf{B}$ and $\mathbf{A} - \mathbf{B}$ can be arranged to form a triangle (Fig. 1) with the angle θ between $\mathbf{A}$ and $\mathbf{B}$. Applying the Law of Cosines to this triangle, we have

$$|\mathbf{A} - \mathbf{B}|^2 = |\mathbf{A}|^2 + |\mathbf{B}|^2 - 2|\mathbf{A}||\mathbf{B}| \cos(\theta).$$

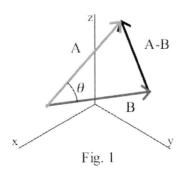

Fig. 1

We can also use the properties of the dot product to expand $|\mathbf{A} - \mathbf{B}|^2$
in a different way: $|\mathbf{A} - \mathbf{B}|^2 = (\mathbf{A} - \mathbf{B}) \cdot (\mathbf{A} - \mathbf{B})$

$= \mathbf{A} \cdot \mathbf{A} - \mathbf{A} \cdot \mathbf{B} - \mathbf{B} \cdot \mathbf{A} + \mathbf{B} \cdot \mathbf{B} = |\mathbf{A}|^2 - 2\mathbf{A} \cdot \mathbf{B} + |\mathbf{B}|^2$.

From these two representations for $|\mathbf{A} - \mathbf{B}|^2$ we have that

$|\mathbf{A}|^2 - 2\mathbf{A} \cdot \mathbf{B} + |\mathbf{B}|^2 = |\mathbf{A}|^2 + |\mathbf{B}|^2 - 2|\mathbf{A}||\mathbf{B}|\cos(\theta)$ so

$-2\mathbf{A} \cdot \mathbf{B} = -2|\mathbf{A}||\mathbf{B}|\cos(\theta)$ and $\mathbf{A} \cdot \mathbf{B} = |\mathbf{A}||\mathbf{B}|\cos(\theta)$.

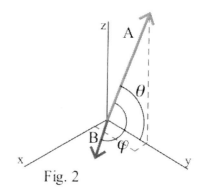
Fig. 2

Example 2: Let $\mathbf{A} = \langle 2, 5, 14 \rangle$ and $\mathbf{B} = \langle 2, 1, -2 \rangle$. Find the angles (a) between $\mathbf{A}$ and $\mathbf{B}$ and (b) between $\mathbf{A}$ and the positive y–axis (Fig. 2).

Solution: (a) $|\mathbf{A}| = \sqrt{4+25+196} = 15$, $|\mathbf{B}| = \sqrt{4+1+4} = 3$, $\mathbf{A} \cdot \mathbf{B} = 4+5-28 = -19$, and

$\cos(\varphi) = \dfrac{\mathbf{A} \cdot \mathbf{B}}{|\mathbf{A}||\mathbf{B}|} = \dfrac{-19}{(15)(3)} \approx -0.4222$ so $\varphi \approx 2.01$ or about $115.0°$.

(b) The basis vector $\mathbf{j} = \langle 0, 1, 0 \rangle$ points along the positive y–axis so the angle between $\mathbf{A}$ and the positive y–axis is the same as the angle between $\mathbf{A}$ and $\mathbf{j}$.

$|\mathbf{A}| = 15$, $|\mathbf{j}| = 1$, and $\mathbf{A} \cdot \mathbf{j} = (2)(0) + (5)(1) + (14)(0) = 5$ so

$\cos(\theta) = \dfrac{\mathbf{A} \cdot \mathbf{j}}{|\mathbf{A}||\mathbf{j}|} = \dfrac{5}{(15)(1)} \approx 0.333$ so $\theta \approx 1.23$ or about $70.5°$.

Practice 3: Let $\mathbf{A} = \langle 2, -6, 3 \rangle$, $\mathbf{B} = \langle 4, 8, -1 \rangle$ and $\mathbf{C} = \langle 3, 0, -4 \rangle$ and determine the angles between the vectors (a) $\mathbf{A}$ and $\mathbf{B}$, (b) $\mathbf{A}$ and $\mathbf{C}$, (c) $\mathbf{B}$ and the negative x–axis, and (d) $\mathbf{C}$ and the positive y–axis.

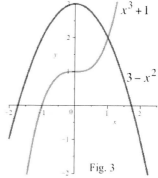
Fig. 3

Example 3: Find the angle of intersection of the graphs of $f(x) = x^3 + 1$ and $g(x) = 3 - x^2$ at the point $(1, 2)$. (The angle of intersection is the angle between tangent vectors to the graphs at the point.) Fig. 3.

Fig. 4

Solution: $f'(x) = 3x^2$, so the slope of f at $(1,2)$ is $f'(1) = 3(1)^2 = 3$: $\dfrac{\text{rise}}{\text{run}} = \dfrac{3}{1}$ and a vector, $\mathbf{A} = 1\mathbf{i} + 3\mathbf{j}$, with this slope is shown in Fig. 4. Similarly, $g'(x) = -2x$, so the slope of g at $(1,2)$ is $g'(1) = -2(1) = -2$: $\dfrac{\text{rise}}{\text{run}} = \dfrac{-2}{1}$ and vector $\mathbf{B} = 1\mathbf{i} - 2\mathbf{j}$ has the same slope. Then $|\mathbf{A}| = \sqrt{10}$, $|\mathbf{B}| = \sqrt{5}$, and $\mathbf{A} \cdot \mathbf{B} = -5$, so

$\cos(\theta) = \dfrac{-5}{\sqrt{10}\sqrt{5}} \approx -0.707$. Then $\theta = \arccos(-0.707) \approx 2.356$ (or $135°$).

Note: If $y = f(x)$, then a tangent vector to the graph of f at the point $(x_0, f(x_0))$ is $\mathbf{T} = \langle 1, f'(x_0) \rangle$.

If a curve is given parametrically by $x(t)$ and $y(t)$,

then a tangent vector to the curve when $t = t_0$ is $\mathbf{T} = x'(t_0)\mathbf{i} + y'(t_0)\mathbf{j} = \langle x'(t_0), y'(t_0) \rangle$.

Some books define the dot product $\mathbf{A} \cdot \mathbf{B}$ as $\mathbf{A} \cdot \mathbf{B} = |\mathbf{A}| |\mathbf{B}| \cos(\theta)$ and then derive the definition we gave, $\mathbf{A} \cdot \mathbf{B} = a_1 b_1 + a_2 b_2 + a_3 b_3$, as a property. Either way, the pattern $\mathbf{A} \cdot \mathbf{B} = a_1 b_1 + a_2 b_2 + a_3 b_3$ is typically used to compute the dot product, and the angle property $\mathbf{A} \cdot \mathbf{B} = |\mathbf{A}| |\mathbf{B}| \cos(\theta)$ is typically used to help us see what the dot product measures and to help us derive and simplify some vector algorithms.

Criteria for A and B to be Perpendicular

Let $\mathbf{A}$ and $\mathbf{B}$ be nonzero vectors. $\mathbf{A}$ and $\mathbf{B}$ are perpendicular if and only if $\mathbf{A} \cdot \mathbf{B} = 0$.

Proof: If $\mathbf{A}$ and $\mathbf{B}$ are perpendicular, then $\theta = \pm \pi/2$ so $\mathbf{A} \cdot \mathbf{B} = |\mathbf{A}| |\mathbf{B}| \cos(\theta) = |\mathbf{A}| |\mathbf{B}| (0) = 0$.

If $0 = \mathbf{A} \cdot \mathbf{B} = |\mathbf{A}| |\mathbf{B}| \cos(\theta)$, then $\cos(\theta) = 0$ so $\theta = \pm \pi/2 \ (\pm 2\pi n)$ and $\mathbf{A}$ and $\mathbf{B}$ are perpendicular.

Example 4: (a) Find a vector perpendicular to $\mathbf{V} = \langle 1, 2, 3 \rangle$.

(b) Find a vector perpendicular to the line $4x + 3y = 24$.

Solution: (a) We need a nonzero vector $\mathbf{N}$ so that $\mathbf{N} \cdot \mathbf{V} = 0$. If $\mathbf{N} = \langle a, b, c \rangle$, then we want to find values for a, b, and c so that $a + 2b + 3c = 0$, and there are lots of values for a, b, and c that work: $\mathbf{N} = \langle 0, -3, 2 \rangle, \langle 3, 0, -1 \rangle, \langle 2, -1, 0 \rangle, \langle 1, 1, -1 \rangle, \langle 1, -2, 1 \rangle$ and lots of others all give $\mathbf{N} \cdot \mathbf{V} = 0$. Fig. 5 illustrates why a single vector in three dimensions can have perpendicular vectors that point in an infinite number of different directions.

(b) The points $P = (6, 0)$ and $Q = (0, 8)$ both lie on the line, so the vector $\mathbf{V}$ from P to Q is parallel to the line, and $\mathbf{V} = \langle 0-6, 8-0 \rangle = \langle -6, 8 \rangle$.

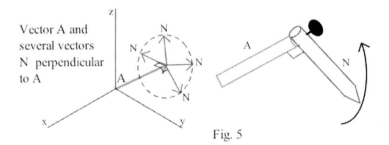

Fig. 5

If $\mathbf{N}$ is perpendicular to $\mathbf{V}$, then $\mathbf{N}$ is perpendicular to the line, and $\mathbf{N} = \langle 4, 3 \rangle$ is perpendicular to $\mathbf{V}$ since $\mathbf{N} \cdot \mathbf{V} = 0$. The vector $\mathbf{N} = \langle 4, 3 \rangle$ is perpendicular to the line $4x + 3y = 24$. Every scalar multiple $k\mathbf{N}$ with $k \neq 0$ is also perpendicular to the line.

Practice 4: Find a vector $\mathbf{N}$ perpendicular to the line $-5x + 2y = 30$. Is $\mathbf{N} = \langle -5, 2 \rangle$ perpendicular to $-5x + 2y = 30$?

You might have noticed a pattern in the vectors perpendicular to the lines in Example 4 and Practice 4. The vector $\langle 4, 3 \rangle$ is perpendicular to the line $4x + 3y = 24$, and the vector $\langle -5, 2 \rangle$ is perpendicular to the line $-5x + 2y = 30$. The next result says this pattern is not an accident.

> **Finding a Vector Perpendicular to a Line**
>
> The vector $\mathbf{N} = a\mathbf{i} + b\mathbf{j}$ is perpendicular to the line $ax + by = c$.

Problem 66 asks you to prove this result.

Projection of a Vector onto a Vector

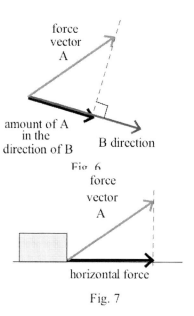

Fig. 6

Fig. 7

The length of a force vector tells us the amount of force in the direction of the vector, but sometimes we want to know the size of the force in another direction (Fig. 6). One of the examples in two dimensions (Fig. 7) involved finding the amount of "horizontal force" obtained when we pulled on a box at an angle to the horizontal. Similar questions can also be asked if one of the directions is not horizontal (Fig. 8) and in three or more dimensions (Fig. 9). Since we now have a method for determining the angle between two vectors in three dimensions, the solutions are relatively straightforward. The vector representing the amount of a vector $\mathbf{A}$ in the direction of a vector $\mathbf{B}$ is called the "projection of $\mathbf{A}$ onto $\mathbf{B}$" and is denoted as $\mathbf{Proj_B\ A}$.

Fig. 9

Visualizing the projection of A onto B : Fig. 10 shows several geometric examples of the projection of a vector $\mathbf{A}$ onto a vector $\mathbf{B}$. We arrange $\mathbf{A}$ and $\mathbf{B}$ to have the same starting point, draw a (dotted) line through the head of $\mathbf{A}$ and perpendicular to $\mathbf{B}$, and form the projection of $\mathbf{A}$ onto $\mathbf{B}$ as the vector from the starting point of $\mathbf{B}$ to the point where the dotted line intersects $\mathbf{B}$ (or an extension of $\mathbf{B}$). The projection of $\mathbf{A}$ onto $\mathbf{B}$ is a vector along the line of $\mathbf{B}$ — the direction of the projection of $\mathbf{A}$ onto $\mathbf{B}$ is either the same direction as $\mathbf{B}$, $\mathbf{B}/|\mathbf{B}|$, or opposite the direction of $\mathbf{B}$, $-\mathbf{B}/|\mathbf{B}|$.

Fig. 8

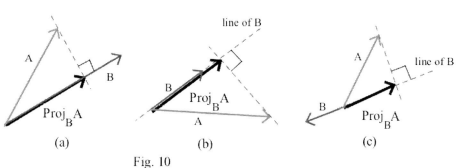

Fig. 10

Fig. 11 shows some examples of the projection of **B** onto **A**, $\text{Proj}_A \mathbf{B}$. The resulting projection vector is always along the line of **A**.

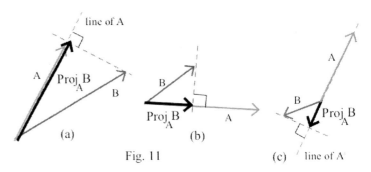

Fig. 11

Once we understand the geometric meaning of "the projection of **A** onto **B**," trigonometry enables us to determine the vector projection of **A** onto **B**: $\text{Proj}_B \mathbf{A}$ (Fig. 12), and its magnitude, $|\text{Proj}_B \mathbf{A}|$, called the scalar projection.

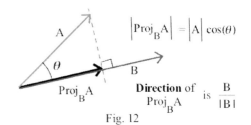

$\left|\text{Proj}_B \mathbf{A}\right| = |\mathbf{A}|\cos(\theta)$

Direction of $\text{Proj}_B \mathbf{A}$ is $\dfrac{\mathbf{B}}{|\mathbf{B}|}$

Fig. 12

Definitions: Vector Projection, Scalar Projection

The **vector projection of A onto B** is the

(magnitude of the projection) times (the direction of **B**): $\text{Proj}_B \mathbf{A} = (|\mathbf{A}|\cos(\theta))\left(\dfrac{\mathbf{B}}{|\mathbf{B}|}\right)$

The **scalar projection of A onto B** is $|\mathbf{A}|\cos(\theta)$ where θ is the angle between **A** and **B**.

Note: "Projection of **A** onto **B**" usually means Vector Projection.

We can use properties of the dot product to simplify the calculation of projections.

Since θ is the angle between **A** and B, then $\cos(\theta) = \dfrac{\mathbf{A} \cdot \mathbf{B}}{|\mathbf{A}||\mathbf{B}|}$ so the scalar projection of **A** onto **B** is $|\mathbf{A}|\cos(\theta) = |\mathbf{A}|\dfrac{\mathbf{A} \cdot \mathbf{B}}{|\mathbf{A}||\mathbf{B}|} = \dfrac{\mathbf{A} \cdot \mathbf{B}}{|\mathbf{B}|}$. Putting this result into the definition of the vector projection of **A** onto **B**, we get

$$(|\mathbf{A}|\cos(\theta))\left(\dfrac{\mathbf{B}}{|\mathbf{B}|}\right) = \dfrac{\mathbf{A} \cdot \mathbf{B}}{|\mathbf{B}|}\left(\dfrac{\mathbf{B}}{|\mathbf{B}|}\right) = \dfrac{\mathbf{A} \cdot \mathbf{B}}{|\mathbf{B}|^2}\mathbf{B}.$$

Calculating Scalar and Vector Projections

Vector projection of **A** onto **B** is $\text{Proj}_B \mathbf{A} = \left(\dfrac{\mathbf{A} \cdot \mathbf{B}}{|\mathbf{B}|^2}\right)\mathbf{B}$ (a vector).

Scalar projection of **A** onto **B** = $\dfrac{\mathbf{A} \cdot \mathbf{B}}{|\mathbf{B}|}$ (a scalar) = magnitude of $\text{Proj}_B \mathbf{A}$.

Example 5: For $\mathbf{A} = \langle 6, -2, 3 \rangle$ and $\mathbf{B} = \langle 4, 8, -1 \rangle$, calculate scalar and vector projections of

(a) **A** onto **B**, (b) **B** onto **A**, (c) **A** onto the positive x–axis,

(d) **A** onto the positive y–axis, and (e) **A** onto the positive z–axis.

Solution: $|\mathbf{A}| = 7$, $|\mathbf{B}| = 9$, and $\mathbf{A} \cdot \mathbf{B} = 24 - 16 - 3 = 5$.

(a) The scalar projection of **A** onto **B** is $\frac{\mathbf{A} \cdot \mathbf{B}}{|\mathbf{B}|} = \frac{5}{9}$.

The vector projection of **A** onto **B** is $\mathbf{Proj_B\, A} = \left(\frac{\mathbf{A} \cdot \mathbf{B}}{|\mathbf{B}|^2}\right) \mathbf{B} = \left(\frac{5}{81}\right) \langle 4, 8, -1 \rangle = \langle \frac{20}{81}, \frac{40}{81}, \frac{-5}{81} \rangle$.

(b) Scalar projection of **B** onto **A** is $\frac{\mathbf{A} \cdot \mathbf{B}}{|\mathbf{A}|} = \frac{5}{7}$. Vector projection is $\left(\frac{\mathbf{A} \cdot \mathbf{B}}{|\mathbf{A}|^2}\right) \mathbf{A} = \langle \frac{30}{49}, \frac{-10}{49}, \frac{15}{49} \rangle$.

(c) **i** has the same direction as the positive x–axis. Scalar projection of **A** onto **i** is $\frac{\mathbf{A} \cdot \mathbf{i}}{|\mathbf{i}|} = 6$.

Vector projection of **A** onto **i** is $\mathbf{Proj_i\, A} = \left(\frac{\mathbf{A} \cdot \mathbf{i}}{|\mathbf{i}|^2}\right) \mathbf{i} = \langle 6, 0, 0 \rangle$.

(d) and (e) The scalar projections of **A** onto **j** and **k** are -2 and 3, respectively.

The vector projections of **A** onto **j** and **k** are $\langle 0, -2, 0 \rangle$ and $\langle 0, 0, 3 \rangle$, respectively.

Practice 5: For $\mathbf{U} = \langle 9, -2, 6 \rangle$ and $\mathbf{V} = \langle 1, 2, -2 \rangle$, calculate the scalar and vector projections of

(a) **U** onto **V**, (b) **V** onto **U + V**, and (c) **V** onto the positive y–axis.

Applications

Projections are useful in a number of situations. The two examples given here illustrate only two of a variety of those uses. In the first example below, we use the geometric meaning of projection to derive a formula for the distance from a point to a line. In the second example, we illustrate how projections can be used to calculate work.

Example 6: Find the distance from the point $P = (p, q)$ to a line

$ax + by = c$. (Fig. 13)

Solution: Using vectors and projections, finding this distance can be broken into several simple steps (Fig. 14). The algorithm:

(1) Find a vector **N** perpendicular to the line: $\mathbf{N} = \langle a, b \rangle$.(Fig. 14a)

(2) Find a point **Q** on the line and call it (x_0, y_0). (Fig. 14b)

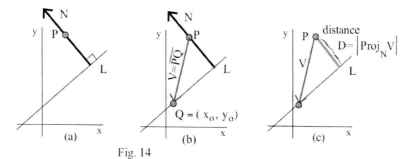

Fig. 14

(3) Form the vector **V** from P to Q: $\mathbf{V} = \langle p - x_0, q - y_0 \rangle$.

(4) Find the absolute value of the scalar projection of **V** onto **N**: $\left| \frac{\mathbf{V} \cdot \mathbf{N}}{|\mathbf{N}|} \right|$ (Fig. 14c)

The formula: The distance from P to the line is this absolute value of the scalar projection:

$$\text{distance} = \left| \frac{\mathbf{V} \cdot \mathbf{N}}{|\mathbf{N}|} \right| = \left| \frac{a(p - x_0) + b(q - y_0)}{\sqrt{a^2 + b^2}} \right|$$

$$= \frac{|ap + bq - (ax_0 + by_0)|}{\sqrt{a^2 + b^2}} = \frac{|ap + bq - c|}{\sqrt{a^2 + b^2}} \quad \text{since } ax_0 + by_0 = c.$$

Practice 6: Step through the algorithm in Example 6 to find the distance from the point $P = (2, 7)$ to the line $3x - 4y = 20$.

The projection of a force vector onto a vector with a different direction tells us the amount of the force in that other direction, a useful result to know for solving work problems.

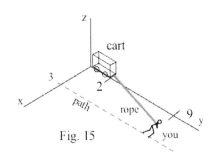

Fig. 15

Example 7: A cart moves on a track located on the y–axis, and you are pulling on a rope with a force of 70 pounds. Find the amount of work that you do in moving the cart from the point $P = (0, 2, 0)$ to the point $Q = (0, 9, 0)$ if you have the rope over your shoulder 4 feet above the ground and walk 12 feet in front of the cart along a path 3 feet to the side of the y–axis (Fig. 15).

Solution: Work = (distance moved)(force in the direction of the movement)

First, we can convert the given information into a vector form: the force vector has a magnitude of 70 pounds in the direction $\langle \frac{3}{13}, \frac{12}{13}, \frac{4}{13} \rangle$ so the force vector is $\mathbf{F} = \langle \frac{210}{13}, \frac{840}{13}, \frac{280}{13} \rangle$. The movement of the cart is in the direction of the vector from P to Q, $\mathbf{D} = Q - P = \langle 0, 7, 0 \rangle$, so the amount of work is

work = (distance moved)(magnitude of the force in the direction of the movement)

= (length of PQ)(scalar projection of F onto direction of PQ)

$= (|\mathbf{D}|)(\frac{\mathbf{F} \cdot \mathbf{V}}{|\mathbf{V}|}) = \mathbf{F} \cdot \mathbf{V} = \langle \frac{210}{13}, \frac{840}{13}, \frac{280}{13} \rangle \cdot \langle 0, 7, 0 \rangle = \frac{5880}{13} \approx 452.3$ foot–pounds.

Work

If a constant force vector **F** moves an object from a point P to a point Q,

then the amount of work done is Work = **F**•**D** where **D** is the displacement vector from P to Q.

Practice 7: In Example 7, determine the amount of work done if you walk 6 feet to the side of the y–axis. (All of the other distances are the same as in Example 7.)

In Chapter 13, we discuss how to determine the amount of work done if the force is variable or if the object moves along a curved path.

Beyond Three Dimensions

If **A** and **B** have the same number of components, then we can define their dot product, the angle between them, and the projection of one onto the other with the same patterns as for two and three dimensions.

Definitions:

If $\mathbf{A} = \langle a_1, a_2, \ldots, a_n \rangle$ and $\mathbf{B} = \langle b_1, b_2, \ldots, b_n \rangle$ are nonzero vectors in n–dimensional space,

then $\mathbf{A} \cdot \mathbf{B} = a_1 b_1 + a_2 b_2 + \ldots + a_n b_n$,

the angle θ between **A** and **B** satisfies $\cos(\theta) = \frac{\mathbf{A} \cdot \mathbf{B}}{|\mathbf{A}||\mathbf{B}|}$, and

the vector projection of A onto B is $\mathrm{Proj}_\mathbf{B} \mathbf{A} = \left(\frac{\mathbf{A} \cdot \mathbf{B}}{|\mathbf{B}|^2} \right) \mathbf{B}$.

Now, even though we may not visualize 4 or 5–dimensional vectors, we can calculate the dot product and the angle between two vectors.

Practice 8: The psychological profiles for you and a friend were $\mathbf{Y} = \langle 5, 1, -7, 5 \rangle$ and $\mathbf{F} = \langle 6, 10, 8, 5 \rangle$ for the four personality categories measured by the profile. Should you say you and your friend are "very alike" ($\theta < 30°$), "somewhat alike" ($30° \leq \theta < 60°$), "different" ($60° \leq \theta \leq 120°$), "somewhat opposite" ($120° < \theta \leq 150°$), or "very opposite" ($150° < \theta \leq 180°$)? What about you and and another friend with the profile $\mathbf{A} = \langle 10, -4, -10, 3 \rangle$?

This section has involved very little "calculus," but the ideas of dot products and projections of vectors are very powerful and useful, and they will be used often as we develop "vector calculus" in later chapters.

PROBLEMS

1. $\mathbf{A} = \langle 1, 2, 3 \rangle$, $\mathbf{B} = \langle -2, 4, -1 \rangle$. Calculate $\mathbf{A} \cdot \mathbf{B}$, $\mathbf{B} \cdot \mathbf{A}$, $\mathbf{A} \cdot \mathbf{A}$, $\mathbf{A} \cdot (\mathbf{B}+\mathbf{A})$, and $(2\mathbf{A}+3\mathbf{B}) \cdot (\mathbf{A} - 2\mathbf{B})$.

2. $\mathbf{A} = \langle 6, -1, 2 \rangle$, $\mathbf{B} = \langle 2, 4, -3 \rangle$. Calculate $\mathbf{A} \cdot \mathbf{B}$, $\mathbf{B} \cdot \mathbf{A}$, $\mathbf{A} \cdot \mathbf{A}$, $\mathbf{A} \cdot (\mathbf{B}+\mathbf{A})$, and $(2\mathbf{A}+3\mathbf{B}) \cdot (\mathbf{A}-2\mathbf{B})$.

3. $\mathbf{U} = \langle 6, -1, 2 \rangle$, $\mathbf{V} = \langle 2, 4, -3 \rangle$. Calculate $\mathbf{U} \cdot \mathbf{V}$, $\mathbf{U} \cdot \mathbf{U}$, $\mathbf{U} \cdot \mathbf{i}$, $\mathbf{U} \cdot \mathbf{j}$, $\mathbf{U} \cdot \mathbf{k}$, and $(\mathbf{V} + \mathbf{i}) \cdot \mathbf{U}$.

11.4 Dot Product

4. $U = \langle -3, 3, 2 \rangle$, $V = \langle 2, 4, -3 \rangle$. Calculate $U \cdot V$, $U \cdot U$, $V \cdot i$, $V \cdot j$, $V \cdot k$, $(V + k) \cdot U$.

5. $S = 2i - 4j + k$, $T = 3i + j - 5k$, $U = i + 3j + 2k$. Calculate $S \cdot T$, $T \cdot U$, $T \cdot T$, $(S + T) \cdot (S - T)$, and $(S \cdot T) U$.

6. $S = i - 3j + 2k$, $T = 5i + 3j - 2k$, $U = 2i + 4j + 2k$. Calculate $S \cdot T$, $S \cdot U$, $S \cdot S$, $(T + U) \cdot (T - U)$, and $S(T \cdot U)$.

In problems 7 – 18, calculate the angle between the given vectors. Also calculate the angles between the first vector and each of the coordinate axes.

7. $A = \langle 1, 2, 3 \rangle$, $B = \langle -2, 4, -1 \rangle$.

8. $A = \langle 6, -1, 2 \rangle$, $B = \langle 2, 4, -3 \rangle$.

9. $U = \langle 6, -1, 2 \rangle$, $V = \langle 2, 4, -3 \rangle$.

10. $U = \langle -3, 3, 2 \rangle$, $V = \langle 2, 4, -3 \rangle$.

11. $S = 2i - 4j + k$, $T = 3i + j - 5k$.

12. $S = i - 3j + 2k$, $T = 5i + 3j - 2k$.

13. $A = 2i - 3j + 5k$, $B = -5i + 0j + 2k$.

14. $A = 4i - 3j + 2k$, $B = 3i + 2j - 3k$.

15. $A = \langle 5, -2, 0 \rangle$, $B = \langle -3, 4, 0 \rangle$.

16. $A = \langle 5, 0, 0 \rangle$, $B = \langle 0, 4, -3 \rangle$.

17. $U = \langle 1, 0, 3 \rangle$, $V = \langle -2, 0, 1 \rangle$.

18. $U = \langle 0, 1, 2 \rangle$, $V = \langle 2, 4, 0 \rangle$.

In problems 19 – 28, determine the angle of intersection of the graphs of the given functions at the given point (i.e., determine the angle between the vectors tangent to the functions at the given point).

19. $f(x) = x^2 + 3x - 2$, $g(x) = 3x - 1$ at $(1, 2)$

20. $f(x) = x^2 + 3x - 2$, $g(x) = 3 - x^2$ at $(1, 2)$

21. $f(x) = e^x$, $g(x) = \cos(x)$ at $(0, 1)$

22. $f(x) = \sin(x)$, $g(x) = \cos(x)$ at $(\pi/4, \frac{\sqrt{2}}{2})$

23. $f(x) = 1 + \arctan(3x)$, $g(x) = \ln(e + x)$ at $(0, 1)$

24. $f(x) = \sin(x^2)$, $g(x) = 1 - \cos(x^2)$ at $(0, 0)$

25. $f: x = 3t, y = t^2 + t - 1$; $g: x = 2t + 1, y = 2t - 1$ at the point when $t = 1$

26. $f: x = \sin(t), y = \cos(t)$; $g: x = t^3, y = t^2 + 1$ at the point when $t = 0$

27. $f: x = e^t + 3, y = 2 + \cos(5t)$; $g: x = t^2 + 3t + 4, y = 3 + \ln(1 - t)$ at the point when $t = 0$

28. $f: x = 2 + \cos(5t), y = e^t + 3$; $g: x = 3 + \ln(1 - t), y = t^2 + 3t + 4$ at the point when $t = 0$

In problems 29 – 48, find a vector N that is perpendicular to the given vector or line. (Typically there are several correct answers.)

29. $A = \langle 1, -2, 0 \rangle$

30. $B = \langle -5, 0, 3 \rangle$

31. $C = \langle 7, 3 \rangle$

32. $D = \langle 7, -3 \rangle$

33. $E = \langle 2, -1, 3 \rangle$

34. $S = \langle 1, 2, 5 \rangle$

35. $T = 3i + j - 5k$

36. $U = i + 3j + 2k$

37. $V = 2i - 4j + k$

38. **W** = –6**i** – 4**j** + **k**   39. **A** = 2**i** – 3**j**   40. **B** = 3**i** + 2**j**

41. **C** = 3**i** – 2**j**   42. $x + y = 6$ 43. $3x + 2y = 6$

44. $5x – 3y = 30$ 45. $x – 4y = 8$ 46. $5x + y = 10$

47. $y = 3$ 48. $x = 2$

In problems 49 – 52 sketch **Proj$_B$ A** .

49. **A** and **B** in Fig. 16.   50. **A** and **B** in Fig. 17.   51. **A** and **B** in Fig. 18.   52. **A** and **B** in Fig. 19.

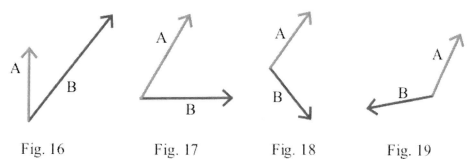

Fig. 16   Fig. 17   Fig. 18   Fig. 19

In problems 53 – 56 sketch **Proj$_A$ B** .

53. **A** and **B** in Fig. 16.   54. **A** and **B** in Fig. 17.   55. **A** and **B** in Fig. 18.   56. **A** and **B** in Fig. 19.

In problems 57 – 63, calculate **Proj$_B$ A** and **Proj$_A$ B** .

57. **A** = $\langle 1, –2, 0 \rangle$, **B** = $\langle –5, 0, 3 \rangle$ 58. **A** = $\langle 1, 2, 3 \rangle$, **B** = $\langle –2, 4, –1 \rangle$

59. **A** = 2**i** – 3**j** + 5**k**, **B** = –5**i** + 0**j** + 2**k**   60. **A** = 4**i** – 3**j** + 2**k**, **B** = 3**i** + 2**j** – 3**k**

61. **A** = $\langle 5, 0, 0 \rangle$, **B** = $\langle 0, 4, –3 \rangle$ 62. **A** = $\langle 2, –1, 3 \rangle$, **B** = $\langle 1, 2, 5 \rangle$

63. **A** = $\langle 1, –2, 3 \rangle$, **B** = **j**

64. Suppose **A** and **B** have the same length. Which has the larger magnitude: **Proj$_B$ A** or **Proj$_A$ B**? Justify your answer.

65. Suppose |**A**| = 3 |**B**| . Which has the larger magnitude: **Proj$_B$ A** or **Proj$_A$ B**? Justify your answer.

66. Prove that the vector **N** = a**i** + b**j** is perpendicular to the line $ax + by = c$.
    (Suggestion: Pick any two points $P = (x_0, y_0)$ and $Q = (x_1, y_1)$ on the line. Then the vector **V** with starting point P and ending point Q has the same direction as the line, and **V** = $\langle x_1–x_0, y_1–y_0 \rangle$. Now show that **N** is perpendicular to **V** .)

In problems 67 – 72, calculate the distance from the given point to the given line using (a) the algorithm of Example 6, and (b) the formula found in Example 6.

67. $(1, 3), y = 7 - x$
68. $(-2, 1), 3x - 2y = 6$
69. $(5, 3), 3y = 3x + 7$
70. $(-3, -4), y = 3x + 2$
71. $(0, 0), 4x + 3y = 7$
72. $(0, 0), ax + by = c$

73. Fig. 20 shows the position of a road and a house. How close is the road to the house (minimum distance)?

74. In Fig. 21, how close is the wire to the magnet?

Fig. 21

75. A person is standing directly below the electrical transmission wires in Fig. 22. Assuming the wires are so taut that they follow a straight line, how close do they come to the person's head?

Fig. 20

76. The **direction cosines** of a vector $\mathbf{A} = a_1\mathbf{i} + a_2\mathbf{j} + a_3\mathbf{k}$ are the cosines of the angles $\mathbf{A}$ makes with each of the coordinate vectors $\mathbf{i}, \mathbf{j},$ and $\mathbf{k}$: if $\mathbf{A}$ makes angles $\theta_x, \theta_y,$ and θ_z with the x, y, and z axes, respectively, then the direction cosines of $\mathbf{A}$ are $\cos(\theta_x), \cos(\theta_y),$ and $\cos(\theta_z)$.

Show that $\cos(\theta_x) = \dfrac{a_1}{|\mathbf{A}|}, \cos(\theta_y) = \dfrac{a_2}{|\mathbf{A}|}, \cos(\theta_z) = \dfrac{a_3}{|\mathbf{A}|}$,
and that $\cos^2(\theta_x) + \cos^2(\theta_y) + \cos^2(\theta_z) = 1$ for every nonzero vector $\mathbf{A}$.

Fig. 22

77. A car moves on a track located on the y–axis, and you are pulling on a rope with a force of 50 pounds. Find the amount of work that you do in moving the cart from the origin to the point $Q = (0, 10, 0)$ if you have the rope over your shoulder 4 feet above the ground and walk 10 feet in front of the cart along a path 5 feet to the side of the y–axis.

78. Redo Problem 77 assuming that you are now pulling on the rope with a force of 100 pounds.

79. A wind blowing parallel to the y–axis exerts a force of 8 pounds on a kite. How much work does the wind do in moving the kite in a straight line from the point $(20, 30, 40)$ to the point $(50, 90, 150)$.

80. Redo problem 79 assuming that the wind is blowing parallel to the x–axis.

81. How much work does the person in Fig. 23 do moving the box 20 feet along the ground?

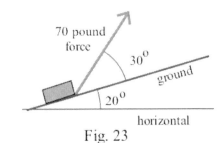

Fig. 23

Beyond Three Dimensions

83. $\mathbf{A} = \langle 1, 2, 3, 4 \rangle$, $\mathbf{B} = \langle -2, 4, -1, 3 \rangle$. Calculate $\mathbf{A} \cdot \mathbf{B}$, $\mathbf{B} \cdot \mathbf{A}$, and the angle between $\mathbf{A}$ and $\mathbf{B}$.

84. $\mathbf{A} = \langle -3, 4, 5, -1 \rangle$, $\mathbf{B} = \langle -2, 4, -2, -4 \rangle$. Calculate $\mathbf{A} \cdot \mathbf{B}$, $\mathbf{B} \cdot \mathbf{A}$, and the angle between $\mathbf{A}$ and $\mathbf{B}$.

In problems 85 – 88, a particular personality profile assigns a number between –1 and + 1 to each person on each of five personality characteristics. Using the categories ("very alike," "somewhat alike," , etc.) of Practice 8, determine the correct category for the pair of personality profiles given in each problem.

85. $\mathbf{A} = \langle 1, -0.2, 0.3, -0.6, 0.4 \rangle$, $\mathbf{B} = \langle -0.5, 0.3, 0.3, -0.1, 0.2 \rangle$

86. $\mathbf{A} = \langle 0.2, -0.3, -0.3, -0.7, 0.6 \rangle$, $\mathbf{B} = \langle 0.4, -0.2, -0.4, -0.5, 0.8 \rangle$

87. $\mathbf{A} = \langle 0.1, 0.2, 0.3, 0.4, 0.5 \rangle$, $\mathbf{B} = \langle 0.3, 0.4, 0.5, 0.6, 0.7 \rangle$

88. $\mathbf{A} = \langle 0.8, 0.3, -0.5, 0.2, 0.6 \rangle$, $\mathbf{B} = \langle -0.2, -0.4, -0.6, -0.4, 0.1 \rangle$

Practice Answers

Practice 1: $\mathbf{U} \cdot \mathbf{V} = (2)(-1) + (6)(2) + (-3)(2) = 4$. $\mathbf{U} \cdot \mathbf{U} = (2)(2) + (6)(6) + (-3)(-3) = 49$.
$\mathbf{V} \cdot \mathbf{V} = (-1)(-1) + (2)(2) + (2)(2) = 9$.
$\mathbf{U} \cdot (\mathbf{U}+\mathbf{V}) = \langle 2, 6, -3 \rangle \langle 1, 8, -1 \rangle = 53$. $\mathbf{U} \cdot \mathbf{U} + \mathbf{U} \cdot \mathbf{V} = 49 + 4 = 53$.
$|\mathbf{U}|^2 = (\sqrt{2^2 + 6^2 + (-3)^2})2 = 2^2 + 6^2 + (-3)^2 = 49 = \mathbf{U} \cdot \mathbf{U}$.
$\mathbf{V} \cdot \mathbf{U} = (-1)(2) + (2)(6) + (2)(-3) = 4$ so $\mathbf{U} \cdot \mathbf{V} = \mathbf{V} \cdot \mathbf{U}$.

Practice 2: $\mathbf{A} \cdot \mathbf{B} = a_1 b_1 + a_2 b_2 + a_3 b_3 = b_1 a_1 + b_2 a_2 + b_3 a_3 = \mathbf{B} \cdot \mathbf{A}$.

Practice 3: $|\mathbf{A}| = \sqrt{4+36+9} = 7$, $|\mathbf{B}| = \sqrt{16+64+1} = 9$, and $|\mathbf{C}| = \sqrt{9+0+16} = 5$.

(a) $\cos(\theta) = \dfrac{\mathbf{A} \cdot \mathbf{B}}{|\mathbf{A}||\mathbf{B}|} = \dfrac{8-48-3}{(7)(9)} = \dfrac{-43}{63} \approx -0.683$ so $\theta \approx 2.32$ (radians) or $133.04°$.

(b) $\cos(\theta) = \dfrac{\mathbf{A} \cdot \mathbf{C}}{|\mathbf{A}||\mathbf{C}|} = \dfrac{6+0-12}{(7)(5)} = \dfrac{-6}{35} \approx -0.171$ so $\theta \approx 1.74$ or $99.87°$.

(c) $\cos(\theta) = \dfrac{\mathbf{B} \cdot (-\mathbf{i})}{|\mathbf{B}||-\mathbf{i}|} = \dfrac{-4+0+0}{(9)(1)} = \dfrac{-4}{9} \approx -0.444$ so $\theta \approx 2.03$ or $116.36°$.

(d) $\cos(\theta) = \dfrac{\mathbf{C} \cdot \mathbf{j}}{|\mathbf{C}||\mathbf{j}|} = \dfrac{0+0+0}{(5)(1)} = 0$ so $\theta = \pi/2$ or $90°$. $\mathbf{C}$ and $\mathbf{j}$ are perpendicular.

Practice 4: First we need to find two points on the line and then use those two points to form a vector parallel to the line: $P = (-6, 0)$ and $Q = (0, 15)$ are on the line, and $\mathbf{V} = \langle 0-(-6), 15-0 \rangle = \langle 6, 15 \rangle$ is parallel to the line. $\mathbf{N} \cdot \mathbf{V} = \langle -5, 2 \rangle \cdot \langle 6, 15 \rangle = -30 + 30 = 0$ so $\mathbf{N} = \langle -5, 2 \rangle$ is perpendicular to $-5x + 2y = 30$. Every scalar multiple $k\mathbf{N}$ with $k \neq 0$ is also perpendicular to the line.

Practice 5: (a) $|\mathbf{U}| = 11$, $|\mathbf{V}| = 3$, $\mathbf{U} \cdot \mathbf{V} = -7$. scalar projection of $\mathbf{U}$ onto $\mathbf{V}$ is $\frac{\mathbf{U} \cdot \mathbf{V}}{|\mathbf{V}|} = \frac{-7}{3}$.

Vector projection of $\mathbf{U}$ onto $\mathbf{V}$ is $\left(\frac{\mathbf{U} \cdot \mathbf{V}}{|\mathbf{V}|^2} \right) \mathbf{V} = \langle \frac{-7}{9}, \frac{-14}{9}, \frac{14}{9} \rangle$.

(b) $\mathbf{U} + \mathbf{V} = \langle 10, 0, 4 \rangle$, $|\mathbf{U} + \mathbf{V}| = \sqrt{116}$, $\mathbf{V} \cdot (\mathbf{U} + \mathbf{V}) = 10 + 0 - 8 = 2$.

Scalar projection of $\mathbf{V}$ onto $\mathbf{U} + \mathbf{V}$ is $\frac{\mathbf{V} \cdot (\mathbf{U} + \mathbf{V})}{|\mathbf{U} + \mathbf{V}|} = \frac{2}{\sqrt{116}} \approx 0.19$.

Vector projection of $\mathbf{V}$ onto $\mathbf{U} + \mathbf{V}$ is $\left(\frac{\mathbf{V} \cdot (\mathbf{U} + \mathbf{V})}{|\mathbf{U} + \mathbf{V}|^2} \right) (\mathbf{U} + \mathbf{V}) = \langle \frac{5}{29}, 0, \frac{2}{29} \rangle$.

(c) Scalar projection of $\mathbf{V}$ onto the positive y–axis is $\frac{\mathbf{V} \cdot \mathbf{j}}{|\mathbf{j}|} = 2$.

Vector projection of $\mathbf{V}$ onto $\mathbf{j}$ is $\left(\frac{\mathbf{V} \cdot \mathbf{j}}{|\mathbf{j}|^2} \right) \mathbf{j} = \langle 0, 2, 0 \rangle$.

Practice 6: (1) $\mathbf{N} = \langle 3, -4 \rangle$. Take $Q = (0, -5)$ (any other point on the line also works -- try one).

(3) $\mathbf{V}$ is the vector from P to Q: $\mathbf{V} = \langle -2, -12 \rangle$.

(4) scalar projection of $\mathbf{V}$ onto $\mathbf{N}$ is $\frac{\mathbf{V} \cdot \mathbf{N}}{|\mathbf{N}|} = \frac{-6 + 48}{\sqrt{9 + 16}} = \frac{42}{5} = 8.4$, the distance from the point to the line.

We get the same answer, but perhaps less understanding, using the formula:

$$\frac{|ap + bq - c|}{\sqrt{a^2 + b^2}} = \frac{|(3)(2) + (-4)(7) - 20|}{\sqrt{9 + 16}} = \frac{|6 - 28 - 20|}{5} = \frac{42}{5}.$$

Practice 7: The direction of the force vector is $\langle 6, 12, 4 \rangle / |\langle 6, 12, 4 \rangle| = \langle \frac{6}{14}, \frac{12}{14}, \frac{4}{14} \rangle$ so $\mathbf{F} = 70 \langle \frac{6}{14}, \frac{12}{14}, \frac{4}{14} \rangle = \langle 30, 60, 20 \rangle$. Then the work done is

Work $= \mathbf{F} \cdot \mathbf{D} = \langle 30, 60, 20 \rangle \cdot \langle 0, 7, 0 \rangle = 0 + (60 \text{ pounds})(7 \text{ feet}) + 0 = 420$ foot–pounds.

Practice 8: $|\mathbf{Y}| = \sqrt{5^2 + 1^2 + (-7)^2 + 5^2} = \sqrt{100} = 10$, $|\mathbf{F}| = 15$, and $|\mathbf{A}| = 15$.

For $\mathbf{Y}$ and $\mathbf{F}$, $\cos(\theta) = \frac{\mathbf{Y} \cdot \mathbf{F}}{|\mathbf{Y}||\mathbf{F}|} = \frac{30 + 10 - 56 + 25}{(10)(15)} = \frac{9}{150}$ so $\theta \approx 86.6°$: "different."

For $\mathbf{Y}$ and $\mathbf{A}$, $\cos(\theta) = \frac{\mathbf{Y} \cdot \mathbf{A}}{|\mathbf{Y}||\mathbf{A}|} = \frac{50 - 4 + 70 + 15}{(10)(15)} = \frac{131}{150}$ so $\theta \approx 29.2°$: "very alike."

11.5 CROSS PRODUCT

This section is the final one about the arithmetic of vectors, and it introduces a second type of vector–vector multiplication called the cross product. The material in this section and the previous sections is the foundation for the next several chapters on the calculus of vector–valued functions and functions of several variables, and all of the vector arithmetic is used extensively.

The dot product of two vectors results in a scalar, a number related to the magnitudes of the two original vectors and to the angle between them, and the dot product is defined for two vectors in 2–dimensional, 3–dimension, and higher dimensional spaces. The cross product of a vector and a vector differs from the dot product in several significant ways: the cross product is only defined for two vectors in 3–dimensional space, and the cross product of two vectors is a vector. At first, the definition of the cross product given below may seem strange, but the resulting vector has some very useful properties as well as some unusual ones. The torque wrench described next illustrates some of the properties we get with the cross product.

Torque wrench: As you pull down on the torque wrench in Fig. 1, a force is applied to the bolt that twists it into the wall. This "twisting" force is the result of two vectors, the length and a direction of the wrench **A** and the magnitude and direction of the pulling force **B**. To model this "twisting into the wall" result of **A** and **B**, we want a vector **C** that points into the wall and depends on the magnitudes of **A** and **B** as well as on the angle between the wrench and the direction of the pull.

Fig. 1

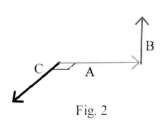
Fig. 2

If the pull is downward (Fig. 1), we want **C** to point into the page.

If the pull is upward (Fig. 2), we want **C** to point out of the page.

If the angle between **A** and **B** is close to $\pm 90^\circ$ (Fig. 3), we want the magnitude of **C** to be large.

If the angle between **A** and **B** is small (Fig. 4), we want the magnitude of **C** to be small.

Fig. 3

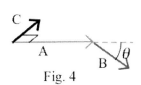
Fig. 4

There is a way to combine the vectors **A** and **B** to produce a vector **C** with the properties that model the torque wrench. This vector **C**, called the cross product of **A** and **B**, also turns out to be very useful when we discuss planes through given points and tangent planes to surfaces. It is not at all obvious from the definition given below for the cross product that the cross product has a relationship to torque wrenches, planes, or anything else of interest or use to us, but it does and we will investigate those applied and geometric properties. Try not to be repelled by the unusual definition — it leads to some lovely results.

> **Definition of the Cross Product (Vector Product):**
>
> For $\mathbf{A} = \langle a_1, a_2, a_3 \rangle$ and $\mathbf{B} = \langle b_1, b_2, b_3 \rangle$, the **cross product** of $\mathbf{A}$ and $\mathbf{B}$ is
>
> $\mathbf{A} \times \mathbf{B} = (a_2 b_3 - a_3 b_2)\mathbf{i} + (a_3 b_1 - a_1 b_3)\mathbf{j} + (a_1 b_2 - a_2 b_1)\mathbf{k}$, a vector.

The symbols "$\mathbf{A} \times \mathbf{B}$" are read "$\mathbf{A}$ cross $\mathbf{B}$."

Many people find it difficult to remember a complicated formula like the definition of the cross product. Fortunately, there is an easy way to do so, but it requires a digression into the calculation of determinants.

Determinants

Determinants appear in a number of areas of mathematics, and you may have already seen them as part of Cramer's Rule for solving systems of equations. Here we only need them as a device for making it easier to remember and calculate and use the cross product.

Definition of the 2x2 ("two by two") Determinant: The determinant $\begin{vmatrix} a & b \\ c & d \end{vmatrix} = ad - bc$.

Some people prefer to remember the visual pattern in Fig. 5.

Example 1: Evaluate the determinants: $\begin{vmatrix} 1 & 4 \\ 3 & 5 \end{vmatrix}$, $\begin{vmatrix} x & y \\ -2 & 3 \end{vmatrix}$, and $\begin{vmatrix} \mathbf{i} & \mathbf{j} \\ 0 & 4 \end{vmatrix}$.

Solution:
$\begin{vmatrix} 1 & 4 \\ 3 & 5 \end{vmatrix} = (1)(5) - (4)(3) = 5 - 12 = -7.$

$\begin{vmatrix} x & y \\ -2 & 3 \end{vmatrix} = (x)(3) - (y)(-2) = 3x + 2y.$

$\begin{vmatrix} \mathbf{i} & \mathbf{j} \\ 0 & 4 \end{vmatrix} = (\mathbf{i})(4) - (\mathbf{j})(0) = 4\mathbf{i}.$

Fig. 5: Pattern for a 2x2 determinant

Practice 1: Evaluate the determinants: $\begin{vmatrix} -3 & 4 \\ 5 & 6 \end{vmatrix}$, $\begin{vmatrix} x & y \\ 0 & -3 \end{vmatrix}$, and $\begin{vmatrix} \mathbf{i} & \mathbf{j} \\ -4 & 3 \end{vmatrix}$.

A 3x3 determinant can be defined in terms of several 2x2 determinants.

Definition of the 3x3 Determinant: $\begin{vmatrix} a_1 & a_2 & a_3 \\ b_1 & b_2 & b_3 \\ c_1 & c_2 & c_3 \end{vmatrix} = a_1 \begin{vmatrix} b_2 & b_3 \\ c_2 & c_3 \end{vmatrix} - a_2 \begin{vmatrix} b_1 & b_3 \\ c_1 & c_3 \end{vmatrix} + a_3 \begin{vmatrix} b_1 & b_2 \\ c_1 & c_2 \end{vmatrix}.$

Many people prefer to remember the visual pattern in Fig. 6.

$$\begin{vmatrix} a_1 & a_2 & a_3 \\ b_1 & b_2 & b_3 \\ c_1 & c_2 & c_3 \end{vmatrix} = \begin{vmatrix} \boxed{a_1} & a_2 & a_3 \\ b_1 & b_2 & b_3 \\ c_1 & c_2 & c_3 \end{vmatrix}^{+\ -\ +} - \begin{vmatrix} a_1 & \boxed{a_2} & a_3 \\ b_1 & b_2 & b_3 \\ c_1 & c_2 & c_3 \end{vmatrix}^{+\ -\ +} + \begin{vmatrix} a_1 & a_2 & \boxed{a_3} \\ b_1 & b_2 & b_3 \\ c_1 & c_2 & c_3 \end{vmatrix}^{+\ -\ +}$$

$$= +a_1 \begin{vmatrix} b_2 & b_3 \\ c_2 & c_3 \end{vmatrix} - a_2 \begin{vmatrix} b_1 & b_3 \\ c_1 & c_3 \end{vmatrix} + a_3 \begin{vmatrix} b_1 & b_2 \\ c_1 & c_2 \end{vmatrix}$$

Fig. 6: Pattern for a 3x3 determinant

In the 3x3 definition, the first 2x2 determinant, $\begin{vmatrix} b_2 & b_3 \\ c_2 & c_3 \end{vmatrix}$, is the part of the original 3x3 table after the first row and the first column have been removed, the row and column containing a_1. The second 2x2 determinant $\begin{vmatrix} b_1 & b_3 \\ c_1 & c_3 \end{vmatrix}$ is what remains of the original table after the first row and the second column have been removed, the row and column containing a_2. The third 2x2 determinant $\begin{vmatrix} b_1 & b_2 \\ c_1 & c_2 \end{vmatrix}$ is what remains of the original table after the first row and the third column have been removed, the row and column containing a_3. (Note: The leading signs attached to the three terms alternate: **+ − +**.)

Example 2: Evaluate the determinants $\begin{vmatrix} 2 & 3 & 5 \\ 0 & -4 & 1 \\ -3 & 4 & 0 \end{vmatrix}$ and $\begin{vmatrix} \mathbf{i} & \mathbf{j} & \mathbf{k} \\ 3 & 4 & 1 \\ 0 & -2 & 5 \end{vmatrix}$.

Solution: $\begin{vmatrix} 2 & 3 & 5 \\ 0 & -4 & 1 \\ -3 & 4 & 0 \end{vmatrix} = (2)\begin{vmatrix} -4 & 1 \\ 4 & 0 \end{vmatrix} - (3)\begin{vmatrix} 0 & 1 \\ -3 & 0 \end{vmatrix} + (5)\begin{vmatrix} 0 & -4 \\ -3 & 4 \end{vmatrix} = (2)(-4) - (3)(3) + (5)(-12) = -77.$

$\begin{vmatrix} \mathbf{i} & \mathbf{j} & \mathbf{k} \\ 3 & 4 & 1 \\ 0 & -2 & 5 \end{vmatrix} = \mathbf{i} \begin{vmatrix} 4 & 1 \\ -2 & 5 \end{vmatrix} - \mathbf{j} \begin{vmatrix} 3 & 1 \\ 0 & 5 \end{vmatrix} + \mathbf{k} \begin{vmatrix} 3 & 4 \\ 0 & -2 \end{vmatrix} = +22\mathbf{i} - 15\mathbf{j} + (-6)\mathbf{k}.$

Practice 2: Evaluate the determinants $\begin{vmatrix} 3 & 5 & 0 \\ 1 & 4 & -1 \\ -2 & 0 & 6 \end{vmatrix}$ and $\begin{vmatrix} \mathbf{i} & \mathbf{j} & \mathbf{k} \\ 2 & -1 & 3 \\ 4 & 0 & 5 \end{vmatrix}$.

The original definition of the cross product can now be rewritten using the determinant notation.

Determinant Form of the Cross Product Definition:

For $\mathbf{A} = \langle a_1, a_2, a_3 \rangle$ and $\mathbf{B} = \langle b_1, b_2, b_3 \rangle$, $\mathbf{A} \times \mathbf{B} = \begin{vmatrix} \mathbf{i} & \mathbf{j} & \mathbf{k} \\ a_1 & a_2 & a_3 \\ b_1 & b_2 & b_3 \end{vmatrix}$.

The second determinant in Example 2 represents the cross product $\mathbf{A} \times \mathbf{B}$ for $\mathbf{A} = \langle 3, 4, 1 \rangle$ and $\mathbf{B} = \langle 0, -2, 5 \rangle$, and the second determinant in Practice 2 is the cross product $\mathbf{A} \times \mathbf{B}$ for $\mathbf{A} = \langle 2, -1, 3 \rangle$ and $\mathbf{B} = \langle 4, 0, 5 \rangle$.

The cross products of various pairs of the basis vectors $\mathbf{i}, \mathbf{j}$, and $\mathbf{k}$ are relatively easy to evaluate, and they begin to illustrate some of the properties of cross products.

Example 3: Use the determinant form of the definition of the cross product to evaluate

(a) $\mathbf{i} \times \mathbf{j}$, (b) $\mathbf{j} \times \mathbf{i}$, and (c) $\mathbf{i} \times \mathbf{i}$.

Solution: $\mathbf{i} \times \mathbf{j} = \begin{vmatrix} \mathbf{i} & \mathbf{j} & \mathbf{k} \\ 1 & 0 & 0 \\ 0 & 1 & 0 \end{vmatrix} = \mathbf{i}\begin{vmatrix} 0 & 0 \\ 1 & 0 \end{vmatrix} - \mathbf{j}\begin{vmatrix} 1 & 0 \\ 0 & 0 \end{vmatrix} + \mathbf{k}\begin{vmatrix} 1 & 0 \\ 0 & 1 \end{vmatrix} = 0\mathbf{i} + 0\mathbf{j} + 1\mathbf{k} = \mathbf{k}$.

$\mathbf{j} \times \mathbf{i} = \begin{vmatrix} \mathbf{i} & \mathbf{j} & \mathbf{k} \\ 0 & 1 & 0 \\ 1 & 0 & 0 \end{vmatrix} = \mathbf{i}\begin{vmatrix} 1 & 0 \\ 0 & 0 \end{vmatrix} - \mathbf{j}\begin{vmatrix} 0 & 0 \\ 1 & 0 \end{vmatrix} + \mathbf{k}\begin{vmatrix} 0 & 1 \\ 1 & 0 \end{vmatrix} = 0\mathbf{i} + 0\mathbf{j} + (-1)\mathbf{k} = -\mathbf{k}$.

$\mathbf{i} \times \mathbf{i} = \begin{vmatrix} \mathbf{i} & \mathbf{j} & \mathbf{k} \\ 1 & 0 & 0 \\ 1 & 0 & 0 \end{vmatrix} = \mathbf{i}\begin{vmatrix} 0 & 0 \\ 0 & 0 \end{vmatrix} - \mathbf{j}\begin{vmatrix} 1 & 0 \\ 1 & 0 \end{vmatrix} + \mathbf{k}\begin{vmatrix} 1 & 0 \\ 1 & 0 \end{vmatrix} = 0\mathbf{i} + 0\mathbf{j} + 0\mathbf{k} = \mathbf{0}$.

You should note that $\mathbf{i} \times \mathbf{j} = \mathbf{k}$ is perpendicular to the vectors $\mathbf{i}$ and $\mathbf{j}$ and the xy–plane. Similarly, $\mathbf{j} \times \mathbf{i} = -\mathbf{k}$ is also perpendicular to $\mathbf{i}$ and $\mathbf{j}$ and the xy–plane.

Practice 3: Use the determinant form of the definition of the cross product to evaluate

(a) $\mathbf{j} \times \mathbf{k}$, (b) $\mathbf{k} \times \mathbf{j}$, and (c) $\mathbf{j} \times \mathbf{j}$.

The cross products of pairs of basis vectors follow a simple pattern given below and in Fig. 7.

$\mathbf{i} \times \mathbf{j} = \mathbf{k}$ $\mathbf{j} \times \mathbf{i} = -\mathbf{k}$ $\mathbf{i} \times \mathbf{i} = \mathbf{0}$

$\mathbf{j} \times \mathbf{k} = \mathbf{i}$ $\mathbf{k} \times \mathbf{j} = -\mathbf{i}$ $\mathbf{j} \times \mathbf{j} = \mathbf{0}$

$\mathbf{k} \times \mathbf{i} = \mathbf{j}$ $\mathbf{i} \times \mathbf{k} = -\mathbf{j}$ $\mathbf{k} \times \mathbf{k} = \mathbf{0}$

Pattern for the Cross Product of the basis vectors

clockwise is +

counterclockwise is −

Fig. 7

Example 4: Evaluate $\mathbf{A} \times \mathbf{B}$ for $\mathbf{A} = \langle 2, -3, 0 \rangle$ and $\mathbf{B} = \langle 3, 1, -4 \rangle$.

Solution: $\mathbf{A} \times \mathbf{B} = \begin{vmatrix} \mathbf{i} & \mathbf{j} & \mathbf{k} \\ 2 & -3 & 0 \\ 3 & 1 & -4 \end{vmatrix} = \mathbf{i} \begin{vmatrix} -3 & 0 \\ 1 & -4 \end{vmatrix} - \mathbf{j} \begin{vmatrix} 2 & 0 \\ 3 & -4 \end{vmatrix} + \mathbf{k} \begin{vmatrix} 2 & -3 \\ 3 & 1 \end{vmatrix} = 12\mathbf{i} + 8\mathbf{j} + 11\mathbf{k}$.

Practice 4: Evaluate $\mathbf{A} \times \mathbf{B}$ for $\mathbf{A} = \langle 3, 0, -5 \rangle$ and $\mathbf{B} = \langle -2, 4, 1 \rangle$.

Properties of the Cross Product:

(a) $\mathbf{0} \times \mathbf{A} = \mathbf{A} \times \mathbf{0} = \mathbf{0}$

(b) $\mathbf{A} \times \mathbf{A} = \mathbf{0}$

(c) $\mathbf{A} \times \mathbf{B} = -\mathbf{B} \times \mathbf{A}$

(d) $k(\mathbf{A} \times \mathbf{B}) = k\mathbf{A} \times \mathbf{B} = \mathbf{A} \times k\mathbf{B}$

(e) $\mathbf{A} \times (\mathbf{B} + \mathbf{C}) = (\mathbf{A} \times \mathbf{B}) + (\mathbf{A} \times \mathbf{C})$

The proofs of all of these properties are straightforward applications of the definition of the cross product as is illustrated below for part (c). Proofs of (a) and (b) are given in the Appendix after the Practice Answers, and the proofs of (d) and (e) are left as exercises.

Proof of (c): If $\mathbf{A} = \langle a_1, a_2, a_3 \rangle$ and $\mathbf{B} = \langle b_1, b_2, b_3 \rangle$, then

$$\mathbf{B} \times \mathbf{A} = \begin{vmatrix} \mathbf{i} & \mathbf{j} & \mathbf{k} \\ b_1 & b_2 & b_3 \\ a_1 & a_2 & a_3 \end{vmatrix} = \mathbf{i} \begin{vmatrix} b_2 & b_3 \\ a_2 & a_3 \end{vmatrix} - \mathbf{j} \begin{vmatrix} b_1 & b_3 \\ a_1 & a_3 \end{vmatrix} + \mathbf{k} \begin{vmatrix} b_1 & b_2 \\ a_1 & a_2 \end{vmatrix}$$

$$= \mathbf{i}(a_3 b_2 - a_2 b_3) - \mathbf{j}(a_3 b_1 - a_1 b_3) + \mathbf{k}(a_2 b_1 - a_1 b_2).$$

$$\mathbf{A} \times \mathbf{B} = \begin{vmatrix} \mathbf{i} & \mathbf{j} & \mathbf{k} \\ a_1 & a_2 & a_3 \\ b_1 & b_2 & b_3 \end{vmatrix} = \mathbf{i} \begin{vmatrix} a_2 & a_3 \\ b_2 & b_3 \end{vmatrix} - \mathbf{j} \begin{vmatrix} a_1 & a_3 \\ b_1 & b_3 \end{vmatrix} + \mathbf{k} \begin{vmatrix} a_1 & a_2 \\ b_1 & b_2 \end{vmatrix}$$

$$= \mathbf{i}(a_2 b_3 - a_3 b_2) - \mathbf{j}(a_1 b_3 - a_3 b_1) + \mathbf{k}(a_1 b_2 - a_2 b_1) = -\mathbf{B} \times \mathbf{A}.$$

A vector has both a direction and a magnitude, and the direction and magnitude of the vector $\mathbf{A} \times \mathbf{B}$ each give us useful information: the direction of $\mathbf{A} \times \mathbf{B}$ is perpendicular to $\mathbf{A}$ and $\mathbf{B}$, and the magnitude of $\mathbf{A} \times \mathbf{B}$ is the area of the parallelogram with sides $\mathbf{A}$ and $\mathbf{B}$. These are the two properties of the cross product that get used most often in the later chapters, and they enable us to visualize $\mathbf{A} \times \mathbf{B}$.

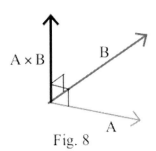

Fig. 8

The **direction** property of **A** x **B**:

$\mathbf{A} \cdot (\mathbf{A} \times \mathbf{B}) = 0$ and $\mathbf{B} \cdot (\mathbf{A} \times \mathbf{B}) = 0$

so **A** x **B** is perpendicular to **A** and to **B**. (Fig. 8)

Proof: $\mathbf{A} \cdot (\mathbf{A} \times \mathbf{B}) = \langle a_1, a_2, a_3 \rangle \cdot \langle a_2 b_3 - a_3 b_2, a_1 b_3 - a_3 b_1, a_1 b_2 - a_2 b_1 \rangle$

$= a_1 a_2 b_3 - a_1 a_3 b_2 + a_2 a_1 b_3 - a_2 a_3 b_1 + a_3 a_1 b_2 - a_3 a_2 b_1 = 0$.

The proof that $\mathbf{B} \cdot (\mathbf{A} \times \mathbf{B}) = 0$ is similar.

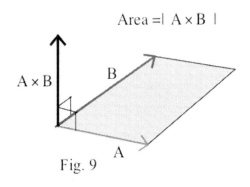

Fig. 9

The **magnitude** property of **A** x **B**:

If **A** and **B** are nonzero vectors with angle θ between them $(0 \leq \theta \leq \pi)$,

then $|\mathbf{A} \times \mathbf{B}| = |\mathbf{A}||\mathbf{B}||\sin(\theta)|$

= **area of the parallelogram** formed by the vectors **A** and **B**. (Fig. 9)

The proof that $|\mathbf{A} \times \mathbf{B}| = |\mathbf{A}||\mathbf{B}||\sin(\theta)|$ is algebraically complicated and is given in the Appendix after the Practice Answers. These properties of the direction and magnitude are sometimes used to define the cross product, and then the algebraic definition is derived from them.

Corollary to the magnitude property of **A** x **B**:

The **area of the triangle** formed by the vectors **A** and **B** is $\frac{1}{2} |\mathbf{A} \times \mathbf{B}|$.

Visualizing the cross product: The cross product **A** x **B** is perpendicular to both **A** and **B** and satisfies a "right hand rule" so we can visualize the direction of **A** x **B** using, of course, your right hand.

If **A** and **B** are the indicated fingers (Fig. 10 and Fig. 11)) then your extended right thumb points in the direction of **A** x **B**.

The relative length of **A** x **B** can be estimated from the magnitude property of

A x **B**: $|\mathbf{A} \times \mathbf{B}|$ = parallelogram area.

Fig. 10

Fig. 11

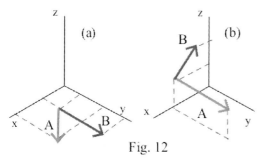

Fig. 12

Example 5: Fig. 12 shows two pairs of vectors **A** and **B**. For each pair sketch the direction of **A** x **B**. For which pair is | **A** x **B** | larger?

Solution: See Fig. 13. | **A** x **B** | is larger for (b) since the area of their parallelogram is larger in (b).

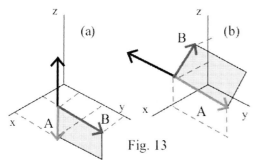

Fig. 13

Practice 5: Fig. 14 shows two pairs of vectors **A** and **B**. For each pair sketch the direction of **A** x **B**. For which pair is | **A** x **B** | larger?

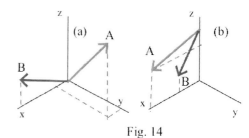

Fig. 14

Torque Wrench Revisited

Now we can use the ideas and properties of the cross product to analyze the original torque wrench problem.

> **Definition**: The **torque vector** produced by a lever arm vector **A** and a force vector **B** is **A** x **B**.

The direction of the torque vector tells us whether the wrench is driving the bolt into the wall or pulling it out of the wall. The magnitude of the torque vector describes the strength of the tendency of the wrench to drive the bolt in or pull it out.

Example 6: Fig. 15 shows two force vectors acting at the end of a 10 inch wrench. Which vector produces the larger torque?

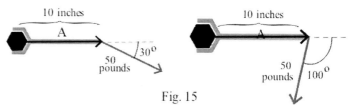

Fig. 15

Solution: |**B**| = 50 pounds with $\theta = 30°$ so

| **A** x **B** | = |**A**||**B**| |sin(θ)|

= (10 inches)(50 pounds) |sin(30°)| $\approx$ 250 pound–inches of force.

|**C**| = 30 pounds with $\theta = 100°$ so

| **A** x **C** | = |**A**||**C**| |sin(θ)| = (10 inches)(30 pounds)| sin(100°) | $\approx$ 295.4 pound–inches of force.

Vector **C** produces the larger torque: the smaller force, used intelligently, produced the larger result.

Practice 6: In Fig. 16 which force vector produces the larger torque?

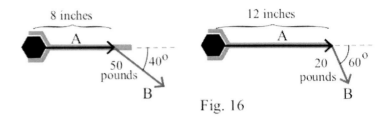

Fig. 16

The Triple Scalar Product A•(B x C)

The combination of the dot and cross products, **A•(B x C)**, for the three vectors **A**, **B**, and **C** in 3–dimensional space is called the triple scalar product because the result of these operations is a scalar: **A•(B x C)** = **A•**(vector) = scalar. And the magnitude of this scalar has a nice geometric meaning.

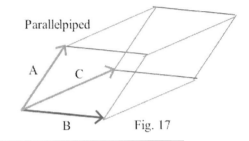

Fig. 17

> Geometric meaning of | **A•(B x C)** |
>
> For the vectors **A**, **B**, and **C** in 3–dimensional space (Fig.17)
>
> | **A•(B x C)** | = volume of the parallelpiped (box) with sides **A**, **B**, and **C** .

Proof: From the definition of the dot product,

$$\mathbf{A} \cdot (\mathbf{B} \times \mathbf{C}) = |\mathbf{B} \times \mathbf{C}||\mathbf{A}|\cos(\theta) \text{ so}$$

$$|\mathbf{A} \cdot (\mathbf{B} \times \mathbf{C})| = |\mathbf{B} \times \mathbf{C}||\mathbf{A}||\cos(\theta)|.$$

Volume = (area of the base)(height),
and the area of the base of the box is | **B x C** |.

Since **B x C** is perpendicular to the base, the height h is the projection of **A** onto **B x C** (Fig. 18): h = |**A**| | cos(θ) |.

Then Volume = | **B x C** | |**A**| | cos(θ) | which we showed was equal to | **A•(B x C)** | .

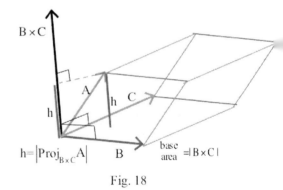

Fig. 18

Problem 46 asks you to show that the triple scalar product can be calculated as a 3x3 determinant.

Beyond Three Dimensions

The objects we examined in previous sections (points, distances, vectors, dot products, angles between vectors, projections) all had rather nice extensions to more than three dimensions. The cross product is different: the cross product **A x B** we have defined requires that **A** and **B** be 3–dimensional vectors, and there is no easy extension to vectors in more than three dimensions that preserves the properties of the cross product.

PROBLEMS

In problems 1 – 12, evaluate the determinants.

1. $\begin{vmatrix} 3 & 4 \\ 2 & 5 \end{vmatrix}$
2. $\begin{vmatrix} 4 & -1 \\ 3 & 1 \end{vmatrix}$
3. $\begin{vmatrix} x & 5 \\ y & 2 \end{vmatrix}$
4. $\begin{vmatrix} 5 & a \\ b & 3 \end{vmatrix}$

5. $\begin{vmatrix} 1 & 0 \\ 0 & 1 \end{vmatrix}$
6. $\begin{vmatrix} 0 & 1 \\ 1 & 0 \end{vmatrix}$
7. $\begin{vmatrix} 1 & 3 & 2 \\ 0 & 5 & 2 \\ 1 & 1 & 0 \end{vmatrix}$
8. $\begin{vmatrix} 2 & 3 & 0 \\ 1 & -3 & 2 \\ -1 & 0 & 4 \end{vmatrix}$

9. $\begin{vmatrix} x & y & z \\ 1 & 2 & 3 \\ 3 & 1 & 2 \end{vmatrix}$
10. $\begin{vmatrix} a & b & c \\ 0 & 3 & 5 \\ 2 & 1 & 3 \end{vmatrix}$
11. $\begin{vmatrix} 2 & 3 & 5 \\ 0 & -4 & 1 \\ -3 & 4 & 0 \end{vmatrix}$
12. $\begin{vmatrix} x & 0 & 0 \\ 0 & 3 & 0 \\ 0 & 0 & 1-x \end{vmatrix}$

In problems 13 – 18, vectors **A** and **B** are given. Calculate (a) **A** x **B**, (b) (**A** x **B**)·**A**, (c) (**A** x **B**)·**B**, and (d) |**A** x **B**|.

13. $\mathbf{A} = \langle 3, 4, 5 \rangle$, $\mathbf{B} = \langle -1, 2, 0 \rangle$
14. $\mathbf{A} = \langle -2, 2, 2 \rangle$, $\mathbf{B} = \langle 3, 1, 2 \rangle$
15. $\mathbf{A} = \langle 1, -3, 2 \rangle$, $\mathbf{B} = \langle -2, 6, 4 \rangle$
16. $\mathbf{A} = \langle 6, 8, -2 \rangle$, $\mathbf{B} = \langle 3, 4, -1 \rangle$
17. $\mathbf{A} = 3\mathbf{i} - 1\mathbf{j} + 4\mathbf{k}$, $\mathbf{B} = 1\mathbf{i} - 2\mathbf{j} + 5\mathbf{k}$
18. $\mathbf{A} = 4\mathbf{i} - 1\mathbf{j} + 0\mathbf{k}$, $\mathbf{B} = 3\mathbf{i} - 2\mathbf{j} + 0\mathbf{k}$

In problems 19 – 22, state whether the result of the given calculation is a vector, a scalar, or is not defined.

19. **A**·(**B** x **C**)
20. **A** x (**B**·**C**)
21. (**A**·**B**) x (**A**·**C**)
22. **A**(**B** x **C**)

23. Prove property (d) of the Properties of the Cross Product: $k(\mathbf{A} \times \mathbf{B}) = k\mathbf{A} \times \mathbf{B} = \mathbf{A} \times k\mathbf{B}$.

24. Prove property (e) of the Properties of the Cross Product: $\mathbf{A} \times (\mathbf{B} + \mathbf{C}) = (\mathbf{A} \times \mathbf{B}) + (\mathbf{A} \times \mathbf{C})$.

25. Explain geometrically why $\mathbf{A} \times \mathbf{A} = \mathbf{0}$.

26. If |**A**| and |**B**| are fixed, what angle(s) between **A** and **B** maximizes |**A** x **B**|? Why?

In problems 27 – 30, vectors **A** and **B** are given graphically. Sketch **A** x **B**.

27. See Fig. 19.
28. See Fig. 20.
29. See Fig. 21.
30. See Fig. 22.

Fig. 19

Fig. 20

Fig. 21

Fig. 22

Fig. 23

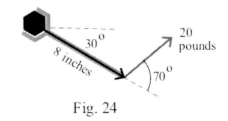

Fig. 24

31. (a) Calculate the torque produced by the wrench and force shown in Fig. 23.

   (b) Calculate the torque produced by the wrench and force shown in Fig. 24.

32. When a tire nut is "frozen" (stuck), a pipe is sometimes put over the handle of the tire wrench (Fig. 25). Using the vocabulary and ideas of vectors, explain why this is effective.

Fig. 25

33. Does the torque on wrench **A** produced by **B** plus the torque produced by **C** equal the torque produced by **B + C** ? Why or why not?

Areas

34. Sketch the parallelogram with sides $\mathbf{A} = \langle 5, 1, 0 \rangle$ and $\mathbf{B} = \langle 2, 4, 0 \rangle$ and find its area. Sketch and find the area of the triangle with sides **A** and **B**.

35. Sketch the parallelogram with sides $\mathbf{A} = \langle 1, 2, 0 \rangle$ and $\mathbf{B} = \langle 0, 4, 2 \rangle$ and find its area. Sketch and find the area of the triangle with sides **A** and **B**.

36. Sketch the triangle with vertices $P = (4, 0, 1)$, $Q = (1, 3, 1)$, and $R = (2, 0, 5)$ and find its area.

37. Sketch the triangle with vertices $P = (1, 4, -2)$, $Q = (3, 5, 1)$, and $R = (5, 2, 2)$ and find its area.

38. Sketch the triangle with vertices $P = (a, 0, 0)$, $Q = (0, b, 0)$, and $R = (0, 0, c)$ and find its area.

Triple Scalar Products

39. Sketch a parallelpiped with edges $\mathbf{A} = \langle 2, 1, 0 \rangle$, $\mathbf{B} = \langle -1, 4, 1 \rangle$, $\mathbf{C} = \langle 1, 1, 2 \rangle$ and find its volume.

40. Sketch a parallelpiped with edges $\mathbf{A} = \langle 2, 0, 3 \rangle$, $\mathbf{B} = \langle 0, 4, 5 \rangle$, $\mathbf{C} = \langle 4, 3, 0 \rangle$ and find its volume.

41. Sketch a parallelpiped with edges $\mathbf{A} = \langle a, 0, 0 \rangle$, $\mathbf{B} = \langle 0, b, 0 \rangle$, $\mathbf{C} = \langle 0, 0, c \rangle$ and find its volume.

Use the result that "the volume of the tetrahedron with edges **A**, **B**, **C** (Fig. 26) is 1/6 the volume of the parallelpiped with the same edges" to find the areas of the tetrahedrons in problems 42 – 45.

42. Sketch the tetrahedron with vertices $P = (0,0,0)$, $Q = (3,1,0)$, $R = (0,4,0)$, and $S = (0,0,3)$ and find its volume.

43. Sketch the tetrahedron with vertices $P = (1,0,2)$, $Q = (3,1,2)$, $R = (0,4,3)$, and $S = (0,1,4)$ and find its volume.

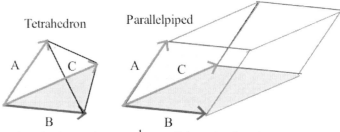

Tetrahedron volume = $\frac{1}{6}$ (Parallelpiped volume)

Fig. 26

44. Sketch the tetrahedron with vertices $P = (0,0,0)$, $Q = (2,0,0)$, $R = (0,4,0)$, and $S = (0,0,6)$ and find its volume.

45. Sketch the tetrahedron with vertices $P = (0,0,0)$, $Q = (a,0,0)$, $R = (0,b,0)$, and $S = (0,0,c)$ and find its volume.

46. Show that if $\mathbf{A} = \langle a_1, a_2, a_3 \rangle$, $\mathbf{B} = \langle b_1, b_2, b_3 \rangle$, and $\mathbf{C} = \langle c_1, c_2, c_3 \rangle$,

    then $\mathbf{A} \cdot (\mathbf{B} \times \mathbf{C}) = \begin{vmatrix} a_1 & a_2 & a_3 \\ b_1 & b_2 & b_3 \\ c_1 & c_2 & c_3 \end{vmatrix}$.

Right Tetrahedrons

47. The four points $(0,0,0), (2,0,0), (0,4,0),$ and $(0,0,4)$ form a tetrahedron (Fig. 27) with four triangular faces. Find the areas A_{xy}, A_{xz}, A_{yz}, and A_{xyz} of the four triangular faces.

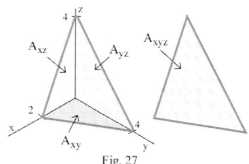
Fig. 27

48. The four points $(0,0,0), (2,0,0), (0,4,0),$ and $(0,0,6)$ form a tetrahedron (Fig. 28) with four triangular faces. Find the areas A_{xy}, A_{xz}, A_{yz}, and A_{xyz} of the four triangular faces.

Fig. 28

49. Verify that the answers to problems 47 and 48 satisfy the relationship $(A_{xy})^2 + (A_{xz})^2 + (A_{yz})^2 = (A_{xyz})^2$.

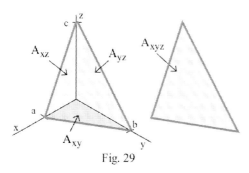
Fig. 29

50. For the right tetrahedron with vertices $(0,0,0), (a,0,0), (0,b,0),$ and $(0,0,c)$, determine the areas of the four triangular faces (Fig. 29) and prove the Pythagorean type result for areas of triangles in a right tetrahedron:

$$(A_{xy})^2 + (A_{xz})^2 + (A_{yz})^2 = (A_{xyz})^2 .$$

51. The Pythagorean pattern $a^2 + b^2 = c^2$ can be thought of as relating a line segment C in two dimensions and its "shadows" a and b on the coordinate axes. Show that this "shadow" interpretation also holds for the area of a triangle in three dimensions and the areas of its "shadows" on the three coordinate planes (Fig. 30):

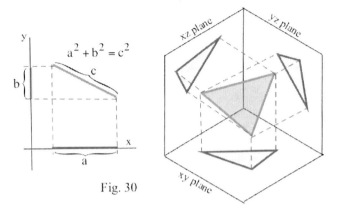

Fig. 30

$$(\text{area of dark triangle})^2 = (\text{xy shadow area})^2 + (\text{xz shadow area})^2 + (\text{yz shadow area})^2 .$$

Areas of Regions in the Plane

Among its several uses, the cross product also leads to a simple, easily programmed algorithm for finding the area of a "simple" (no edges cross) polygon in the plane, and this algorithm is used to approximate the areas of other regions as well.

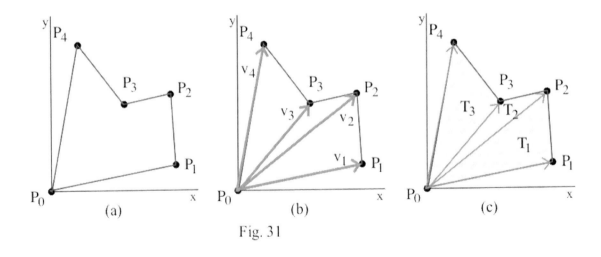

Fig. 31

Suppose $P_0 = (0, 0)$, $P_1 = (x_1, y_1)$, ..., $P_4 = (x_4, y_4)$ are 5 vertices of a simple polygon (Fig. 31a), with one vertex at the origin and then labeling the others as we travel counterclockwise around the polygon. Let $\mathbf{V}_1$ be the vector from P_0 to P_1, $\mathbf{V}_2$ from P_0 to P_2, ... (Fig. 31b). Then the area of the polygon in Fig. 31c is the sum of the 3 triangular areas $T_1, T_2,$ and T_3 and each triangular area can be found using a cross product: $T_1 = \frac{1}{2} |\mathbf{V}_1 \times \mathbf{V}_2| = \frac{1}{2}(x_1 y_2 - x_2 y_1)$,

$T_2 = \frac{1}{2} |\mathbf{V}_2 \times \mathbf{V}_3| = \frac{1}{2}(x_2 y_3 - x_3 y_2)$, and $T_3 = \frac{1}{2} |\mathbf{V}_3 \times \mathbf{V}_4| = \frac{1}{2}(x_3 y_4 - x_4 y_4)$.

Finally, the total area is the sum

$$\text{Area} = T_1 + T_2 + T_3$$

$$= \frac{1}{2} \{ (x_1 y_2 - x_2 y_1) + (x_2 y_3 - x_3 y_2) + (x_3 y_4 - x_4 y_3) \}$$

$$= \frac{1}{2} \sum_{k=1}^{n-1} (x_k y_{k+1} - x_{k+1} y_k) \quad \text{with } n = 4.$$

The last summation formula works for polygons with at least three vertices. In fact, this algorithm is used by computers to report the area of a region traced by a cursor or stylus: the computer reads the (x,y) location of the cursor several times per second and uses the data and this algorithm to calculate the area of the region (as approximated by a many–sided polygon).

52. Use the given pattern to find the area of the rectangle with vertices $(0,0), (2,0), (2,3),$ and $(0,3)$. Does the pattern give the area of the rectangle?

53. Use the given pattern to find the area of the pentagon with vertices $(0,0), (4,1), (5,3), (4,4), (2,4),$ and $(1,3)$.

54. How can we modify the algorithm to handle the situation in which none of the vertices are at the origin? Show that your modification works for the rectangle with vertices $(1,3), (3,3), (3,6),$ and $(1,6)$.

Note: The cross product satisfies a "right hand rule" so if we go counterclockwise from **U** to **V** (Fig. 32a) then **U** x **V** is positive, and if we go clockwise from **U** to **V** (Fig. 32b) then **U** x **V** is negative.

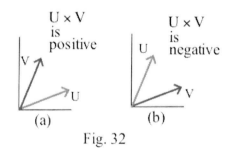

Fig. 32

55. In Fig. 33a, $\frac{1}{2}$ **V**$_1$ x **V**$_2$ gives the area of T_1 as a positive number; $\frac{1}{2}$ **V**$_2$ x **V**$_3$ gives the area of T_2 as a negative number; and $\frac{1}{2}$ **V**$_3$ x **V**$_4$ gives the area of T_3 as a positive number.

Explain geometrically how these positive and negative numbers "fit together" to give the correct area for the region in Fig. 33b.

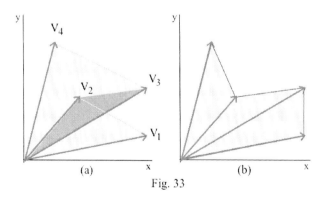

Fig. 33

Practice Answers

Practice 1: $\begin{vmatrix} -3 & 4 \\ 5 & 6 \end{vmatrix} = (-3)(6) - (4)(5) = -38.$ $\begin{vmatrix} x & y \\ 0 & -3 \end{vmatrix} = (x)(-3) - (y)(0) = -3x.$

$\begin{vmatrix} \mathbf{i} & \mathbf{j} \\ -4 & 3 \end{vmatrix} = (\mathbf{i})(3) - (\mathbf{j})(-4) = 3\mathbf{i} + 4\mathbf{j}.$

Practice 2: $\begin{vmatrix} 3 & 5 & 0 \\ 1 & 4 & -1 \\ -2 & 0 & 6 \end{vmatrix} = (3)\begin{vmatrix} 4 & -1 \\ 0 & 6 \end{vmatrix} - (5)\begin{vmatrix} 1 & -1 \\ -2 & 6 \end{vmatrix} + (0)\begin{vmatrix} 1 & 4 \\ -2 & 0 \end{vmatrix} = (3)(24) - (5)(4) + (0)(8) = 52.$

$\begin{vmatrix} \mathbf{i} & \mathbf{j} & \mathbf{k} \\ 2 & -1 & 3 \\ 4 & 0 & 5 \end{vmatrix} = \mathbf{i}\begin{vmatrix} -1 & 3 \\ 0 & 5 \end{vmatrix} - \mathbf{j}\begin{vmatrix} 2 & 3 \\ 4 & 5 \end{vmatrix} + \mathbf{k}\begin{vmatrix} 2 & -1 \\ 4 & 0 \end{vmatrix} = -5\mathbf{i} + 2\mathbf{j} + 4\mathbf{k}.$

Practice 3: $\mathbf{j} \times \mathbf{k} = \begin{vmatrix} \mathbf{i} & \mathbf{j} & \mathbf{k} \\ 0 & 1 & 0 \\ 0 & 0 & 1 \end{vmatrix} = \mathbf{i}\begin{vmatrix} 1 & 0 \\ 0 & 1 \end{vmatrix} - \mathbf{j}\begin{vmatrix} 0 & 0 \\ 0 & 1 \end{vmatrix} + \mathbf{k}\begin{vmatrix} 0 & 1 \\ 0 & 0 \end{vmatrix} = 1\mathbf{i} - 0\mathbf{j} + 0\mathbf{k} = \mathbf{i}.$

$\mathbf{k} \times \mathbf{j} = \begin{vmatrix} \mathbf{i} & \mathbf{j} & \mathbf{k} \\ 0 & 0 & 1 \\ 0 & 1 & 0 \end{vmatrix} = -\mathbf{i}.$ $\mathbf{j} \times \mathbf{j} = \begin{vmatrix} \mathbf{i} & \mathbf{j} & \mathbf{k} \\ 0 & 1 & 0 \\ 0 & 1 & 0 \end{vmatrix} = \mathbf{0}.$

Practice 4: $\mathbf{A} \times \mathbf{B} = \begin{vmatrix} \mathbf{i} & \mathbf{j} & \mathbf{k} \\ 3 & 0 & -5 \\ -2 & 4 & 1 \end{vmatrix} = \mathbf{i}\begin{vmatrix} 0 & -5 \\ 4 & 1 \end{vmatrix} - \mathbf{j}\begin{vmatrix} 3 & -5 \\ -2 & 1 \end{vmatrix} + \mathbf{k}\begin{vmatrix} 3 & 0 \\ -2 & 4 \end{vmatrix} = 20\mathbf{i} + 7\mathbf{j} + 12\mathbf{k}.$

Practice 5: See Fig. 34. The pair in (a) produces the larger torque.

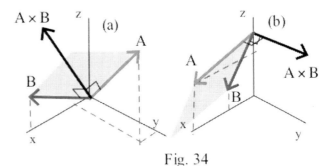

Fig. 34

Practice 6: For **B**,

| torque | = (8 inches)(50 pounds) sin(40°)

≈ 257.1 inch–pounds.

For **C**, | torque | = (12 inches)(20 pounds) sin(60°) ≈ 207.8 inch–pounds.

Force **B** produces the larger torque: sometimes strength is enough.

Appendix: Some Proofs

Proof of (a): $\mathbf{0} \times \mathbf{A} = \mathbf{A} \times \mathbf{0} = \mathbf{0}$. If $\mathbf{A} = \langle a_1, a_2, a_3 \rangle$, then

$$\mathbf{0} \times \mathbf{A} = \begin{vmatrix} \mathbf{i} & \mathbf{j} & \mathbf{k} \\ 0 & 0 & 0 \\ a_1 & a_2 & a_3 \end{vmatrix} = \mathbf{i} \begin{vmatrix} 0 & 0 \\ a_2 & a_3 \end{vmatrix} - \mathbf{j} \begin{vmatrix} 0 & 0 \\ a_1 & a_3 \end{vmatrix} + \mathbf{k} \begin{vmatrix} 0 & 0 \\ a_1 & a_2 \end{vmatrix} = 0\mathbf{i} - 0\mathbf{j} + 0\mathbf{k} \; .$$

The proof that $\mathbf{A} \times \mathbf{0} = \mathbf{0}$ is similar.

Proof of (b): $\mathbf{A} \times \mathbf{A} = \mathbf{0}$. If $\mathbf{A} = \langle a_1, a_2, a_3 \rangle$, then

$$\mathbf{A} \times \mathbf{A} = \begin{vmatrix} \mathbf{i} & \mathbf{j} & \mathbf{k} \\ a_1 & a_2 & a_3 \\ a_1 & a_2 & a_3 \end{vmatrix} = \mathbf{i} \begin{vmatrix} a_2 & a_3 \\ a_2 & a_3 \end{vmatrix} - \mathbf{j} \begin{vmatrix} a_1 & a_3 \\ a_1 & a_3 \end{vmatrix} + \mathbf{k} \begin{vmatrix} a_1 & a_2 \\ a_1 & a_2 \end{vmatrix} = 0\mathbf{i} - 0\mathbf{j} + 0\mathbf{k} = \mathbf{0} \; .$$

Proof that $|\mathbf{A} \times \mathbf{B}| = |\mathbf{A}||\mathbf{B}| \, |\sin(\theta)|$:

$\mathbf{A} \times \mathbf{B} = (a_2 b_3 - a_3 b_2)\mathbf{i} + (a_3 b_1 - a_1 b_3)\mathbf{j} + (a_1 b_2 - a_2 b_1)\mathbf{k}$ so

$$\begin{aligned}
|\mathbf{A} \times \mathbf{B}|^2 &= (\mathbf{A} \times \mathbf{B}) \cdot (\mathbf{A} \times \mathbf{B}) \\
&= (a_2 b_3 - a_3 b_2)^2 + (a_3 b_1 - a_1 b_3)^2 + (a_1 b_2 - a_2 b_1)^2 \\
&= a_2^2 b_3^2 - 2a_2 b_3 a_3 b_2 + a_3^2 b_2^2 + a_3^2 b_1^2 - 2a_3 b_1 a_1 b_3 + a_1^2 b_3^2 + a_1^2 b_2^2 - 2a_1 b_2 a_2 b_1 + a_2^2 b_1^2 \\
&= (a_1^2 + a_2^2 + a_3^2)(b_1^2 + b_2^2 + b_3^2) - (a_1 b_1 + a_2 b_2 + a_3 b_3)^2 \quad \text{(expand \& check)} \\
&= |\mathbf{A}|^2 |\mathbf{B}|^2 - (\mathbf{A} \cdot \mathbf{B})^2 \\
&= |\mathbf{A}|^2 |\mathbf{B}|^2 - (|\mathbf{A}||\mathbf{B}|\cos(\theta))^2 \quad \text{since } \mathbf{A} \cdot \mathbf{B} = |\mathbf{A}||\mathbf{B}|\cos(\theta) \\
&= |\mathbf{A}|^2 |\mathbf{B}|^2 - |\mathbf{A}|^2 |\mathbf{B}|^2 \cos^2(\theta) \\
&= |\mathbf{A}|^2 |\mathbf{B}|^2 \{ 1 - \cos^2(\theta) \} \\
&= |\mathbf{A}|^2 |\mathbf{B}|^2 \sin^2(\theta) \; .
\end{aligned}$$

Then, taking the square root of each side of $|\mathbf{A} \times \mathbf{B}|^2 = |\mathbf{A}|^2 |\mathbf{B}|^2 \sin^2(\theta)$, we have

$|\mathbf{A} \times \mathbf{B}| = |\mathbf{A}||\mathbf{B}| \, |\sin(\theta)| \; .$

11.6 LINES AND PLANES IN THREE DIMENSIONS

In two dimensions the graph of a linear equation, either y=ax+b or parametric (x(t),y(t)), is always a straight line, and a point and slope or two points completely determine the line. In three dimensions the graph of a linear equation, either z=ax+by+c or parametric (x(t), y(t), z(t)), has more freedom, and it can be a line or a plane. In this section we examine the equations of lines and planes and their graphs in 3–dimensional space, discuss how to determine their equations from information known about them, and look at ways to determine intersections, distances, and angles in three dimensions. Lines and planes are the simplest graphs in three dimensions, and they are useful for a variety of geometric and algebraic applications. They are also the building blocks we need to find tangent lines to curves and tangent planes to surfaces (Fig. 1) in three dimensions.

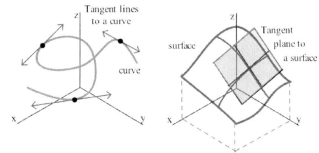

Fig. 1: Tangent lines and planes in three dimensions

Lines in Three Dimensions

Early in calculus we often used the point–slope formula to write the equation of the line through a given point $P = (x_0, y_0)$ with a given slope m: $y - y_0 = m(x - x_0)$. If the point $P = (x_0, y_0)$ is given and the direction of the line is parallel to a given vector $\mathbf{A} = \langle a, b \rangle$, then it is easier to use parametric equations to specify an equation for the line:

a point $Q = (x, y) \neq P$ is on the line if and only if $\dfrac{y - y_0}{x - x_0} = \dfrac{\text{rise}}{\text{run}} = \dfrac{b}{a} = \dfrac{b \cdot t}{a \cdot t}$ for some $t \neq 0$

so the equations $y - y_0 = b \cdot t$, and $x - x_0 = a \cdot t$ describe points on the line and

$x = x_0 + a \cdot t, y = y_0 + b \cdot t$.

Parametric Equation of a Line in Two Dimensions

Parametric equations for a line through the point $P = (x_0, y_0)$ and parallel to the vector $\mathbf{A} = \langle a, b \rangle$ are

$x = x(t) = x_0 + a \cdot t$ and $y = y(t) = y_0 + b \cdot t$. (Fig. 2)

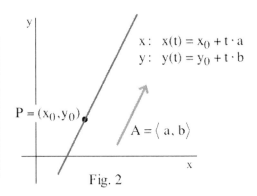

Fig. 2

Notice that the coordinates of the point (x_0, y_0) become the constant terms for x(t) and y(t), and the components of the vector $\langle a, b \rangle$ become the coefficients of the variable terms in the parametric equations. This same pattern is true for lines in three (and more) dimensions.

Example 1: Find parametric equations for the lines through the point $P = (1,2)$ that are
(a) parallel to the vector $\mathbf{A} = \langle 3, 5 \rangle$, and (b) parallel to the vector $\mathbf{B} = \langle 6, 10 \rangle$.
Then graph the two lines.

Solution: (a) $x(t) = 1 + 3t, y(t) = 2 + 5t$. (b) $x(t) = 1 + 6t, y(t) = 2 + 10t$.

The graphs of the lines are shown in Fig. 3. In this example, both sets of parametric equations have the same line when graphed. If we interpret t as time, and $(x(t), y(t))$ as the location of an object at time t, then the graph is a picture of all of the points on the path of the object (for all times). The objects in (a) and (b) have the same path, but they are at different points on the path at time t (except when $t = 0$).

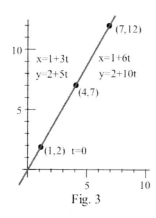

Fig. 3

Practice 1: Find parametric equations for the lines through the point $P = (3,-1)$ that are (a) parallel to the vector $\mathbf{A} = \langle 2, -4 \rangle$, and (b) parallel to the vector $\mathbf{B} = \langle 1, 5 \rangle$. Then graph the two lines.

The parametric pattern works for lines in three dimensions.

Parametric Equation of a Line in Three Dimensions

An equation of a line through the point $P = (x_0, y_0, z_0)$ and parallel to the vector $\mathbf{A} = \langle a, b, c \rangle$ is given by the parametric equations
$x = x(t) = x_0 + at$,
$y = y(t) = y_0 + bt$,
$z = z(t) = z_0 + ct$. (Fig. 4)

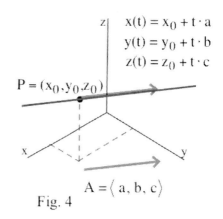

Fig. 4

Proof: To show that $P = (x_0, y_0, z_0)$ is on the line, put $t = 0$ and evaluate the three parametric equations:
$x = x(0) = x_0 + 0, y = y(0) = y_0 + 0$, and $z = z(0) = z_0 + 0$.

To show that the line described by the parametric equations has the same direction as $\mathbf{A}$, we pick another point Q on the line and show that the vector from P to Q is parallel to $\mathbf{A}$.

Put $t = 1$, and let $Q = (x(1), y(1), z(1)) = (x_0 + a, y_0 + b, z_0 + c)$. Then the vector from P to Q is $\mathbf{V} = \langle (x_0 + a) - x_0, (y_0 + b) - y_0, (z_0 + c) - z_0 \rangle = \langle a, b, c \rangle = \mathbf{A}$ so the line described by the parametric equations is parallel to $\mathbf{A}$.

Example 2: Find parametric equations for the line (a) through the point $P = (3, 0, 2)$ and parallel to the vector $\mathbf{A} = \langle 1, 2, 0 \rangle$, and (b) through the two points $P = (3, 0, 2)$ and $Q = (5, -1, 1)$.

Solution: (a) $x(t) = 3 + 1t, y(t) = 0 + 2t, z(t) = 2 + 0t$.

(b) We can use the two points to get a direction for the line. The direction of the line is parallel to the vector from P to Q, $\langle 2, -1, -1 \rangle$, so
$x(t) = 3 + 2t, y(t) = 0 - 1t, z(t) = 2 - 1t$.
The graphs of these two lines are shown in Fig. 5.

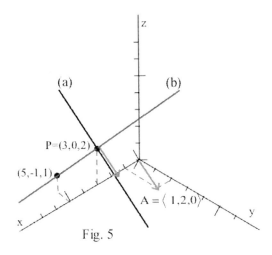

Fig. 5

Practice 2: Find parametric equations for the line
(a) through the point $P = (2, -1, 0)$ and parallel to the vector $\mathbf{A} = \langle 3, -4, 1 \rangle$, and (b) through the two points $P = (3, 0, 2)$ and $Q = (2, 5, 4)$.

Given a point $P = (x_0, y_0, z_0)$ and a vector $\mathbf{A} = \langle a, b, c \rangle$, the point Q is on the line through P in the direction of $\mathbf{A}$ if and only if $Q = (x_0 + at, y_0 + bt, z_0 + ct)$ for some value of t.

Once we are able to write the equations of lines in three dimensions, it is natural to ask about the points and angles of intersection of these lines.

Example 3: (a) Find the point of intersection of the lines K: $x_K = 2 + t, y_K = 3 + 2t, z_K = 0 + t$ and L: $x_L = 5 - t, y_L = 1 + 2t, z_L = -1 + t$.

(b) Find the angle of intersection of the lines K and L.

(c) Where does line L intersect the xy–plane?

Solution: (a) If we could find a value of t so that $x_K = x_L$, $y_K = y_L$, and $z_K = z_L$, that would say that the lines not only intersect at the point (x_K, y_K, z_K), but that the two objects were at that point at the same time. For these parametric equations, there is no value of t such that $x_K = x_L$, $y_K = y_L$, and $z_K = z_L$, but it is still possible for the lines to intersect, just not at the same "time."

To see if the lines go through a common point, but at different "times," we can change the parameter for the line L to "s" instead of "t," and represent L as $x_L = 5 - s, y_L = 1 + 2s, z_L = -1 + s$. Then the equations $x_K = x_L$, $y_K = y_L$, and $z_K = z_L$ become

x: $2 + t = 5 - s$, y: $3 + 2t = 1 + 2s$, and z: $0 + t = -1 + s$.

Solving the first two equations for s and t, we get $s = 2$ and $t = 1$. These values also satisfy the equation for the z–coordinate, $0 + t = -1 + s$, so $x = 2 + t = 3, y = 3 + 2t = 5$, and $z = 0 + t = 1$. The point $(3, 5, 1)$ lies on both lines. (If the values of s and t from the x–component and y–component equations do not satisfy the z–component equation, the lines do not intersect.)

(b) Since the lines intersect, we can find their angle of intersection. Line K is parallel to
A = $\langle 1, 2, 1 \rangle$, the coefficients of the t terms, and L is parallel to **B** = $\langle -1, 2, 1 \rangle$, and the angle between the lines equals the angle between **A** and **B**:

$$\cos(\theta) = \frac{\mathbf{A} \cdot \mathbf{B}}{|\mathbf{A}||\mathbf{B}|} = \frac{4}{\sqrt{6}\sqrt{6}} = \frac{2}{3} \text{ so } \theta \approx 0.84 \text{ (about } 48.2°\text{).}$$

(c) Every point on the xy–plane has z–coordinate equal to 0, so we can set $-1 + t = 0$ and solve for $t = 1$. When $t = 1$, then $x = 5 - (1) = 4$ and $y = 1 + 2(1) = 3$ so line L intersects the xy–plane at the point $(4, 3, 0)$.

Practice 3: If the pairs of lines in (a) or (b) intersect, find the point and angle of intersection.

(a) K: $x = 1 + t, y = 1 - 2t, z = -3 + 2t$ and L: $x = 8 + 4t, y = -4 + t, z = -5 - 8t$.

(b) K: $x = 1 + t, y = 1 - 2t, z = 2 + 2t$ and L: $x = 8 + 4t, y = -4 + t, z = 3 + t$.

(c) Where does L: $x = 8 + 4t, y = -4 + t, z = 3 + t$ intersect the yz–plane?

Practice 4: An arrow is shot from the point (1,2,3) and travels in a straight line in the direction $\langle 4, 5, 1 \rangle$. Will the arrow go over a 10 foot high wall built on the xy–plane along the line $y = 20$? (Fig. 6)

Planes in Three Dimensions

The vectors in a plane point in infinitely many directions (Fig. 7) so, at first thought, you might think it would be more difficult to find an equation for a plane than for a line.

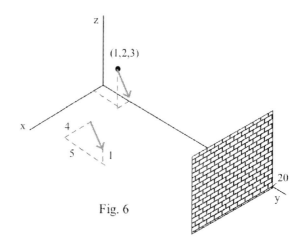

Fig. 6

Fortunately, however, there is only one vector (and its scalar multiples) that is perpendicular to the plane (Fig. 8), and this "normal" vector makes the task easy.

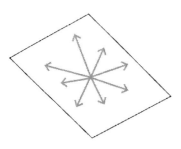

Fig. 7: Vectors in a plane

Suppose $P = (x_0, y_0, z_0)$ is a point on the plane that has normal vector **N** = $\langle a, b, c \rangle$. Let $Q = (x, y, z)$ be another point. Since **N** is perpendicular to every vector on the plane, the point Q is on the plane if and only if **N** is perpendicular to the vector from P to Q.

That is the idea that leads to an easy equation for the plane.

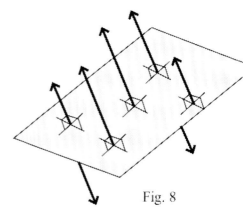

Fig. 8

Let **V** = vector from P to Q = $\langle x - x_0, y - y_0, z - z_0 \rangle$. Then Q is on the plane if and only if **V** is perpendicular to **N**: **V**•**N** = 0. But **V**•**N** = $a(x - x_0) + b(y - y_0) + c(z - z_0)$, so the point Q is on the plane if and only if $a(x - x_0) + b(y - y_0) + c(z - z_0) = 0$.

Equation for a Plane in Three Dimensions:
(Point–Normal Form)

An equation for a plane through the point $P = (x_0, y_0, z_0)$ with normal vector $\mathbf{N} = \langle a, b, c \rangle$ is $a(x - x_0) + b(y - y_0) + c(z - z_0) = 0$. (Fig. 9)

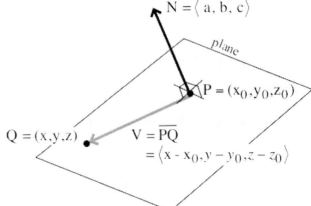

Equation of the plane
$a(x - x_0) + b(y - y_0) + c(z - z_0) = 0$

Fig. 9

The Point–Normal form is the fundamental pattern for the equation of a plane, and other information can usually be translated so the Point–Normal form can be used. If we have point P and two vectors **U** and **V** in the plane, then we can use the result that the cross product of two vectors is perpendicular to each of them to find a vector perpendicular to the plane: **N** = **U** x **V**. Once we have **N**, we can use the Point–Normal form for the equation of the plane. If we have three points P, Q, and R, we can form the vectors **U** from P to Q and **V** from P to R, calculate the normal vector **N** = **U** x **V** and then use the Point–Normal form for the equation for the plane.

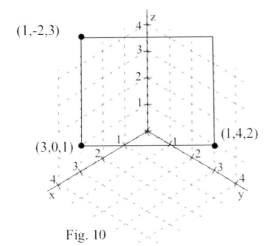

Fig. 10

Example 4: Find the equation of the plane:

(a) through the point $(1, -2, 3)$ and with normal vector $\mathbf{N} = \langle 5, 3, -4 \rangle$,

(b) through the points $P = (1, -2, 3)$, $Q = (3, 0, 1)$ and $R = (1, 4, 2)$. (Fig. 10)

Solution: (a) The point (x,y,z) is on the plane if and only if
$5(x-1) + 3(y+2) - 4(z-3) = 0$, or, equivalently,
$5x + 3y - 4z = -13$.

(b) Let **U** = vector from P to Q = $\langle 2, 2, -2 \rangle$ and **V** = vector from P to R = $\langle 0, 6, -1 \rangle$.

Then $\mathbf{N} = \mathbf{U} \times \mathbf{V} = \begin{vmatrix} \mathbf{i} & \mathbf{j} & \mathbf{k} \\ 2 & 2 & -2 \\ 0 & 6 & -1 \end{vmatrix} = \mathbf{i}\begin{vmatrix} 2 & -2 \\ 6 & -1 \end{vmatrix} - \mathbf{j}\begin{vmatrix} 2 & -2 \\ 0 & -1 \end{vmatrix} + \mathbf{k}\begin{vmatrix} 2 & 2 \\ 0 & 6 \end{vmatrix} = 10\mathbf{i} + 2\mathbf{j} + 12\mathbf{k}$.

The equation of the plane is $10(x-1) + 2(y+2) + 12(z-3) = 0$ or $10x + 2y + 12z = 42$ (or $5x+y+6z=21$).

Practice 5: Find the equation of the plane:

(a) through the point (4, 1, 0) and with normal vector
$\mathbf{N} = \langle 3, -2, 6 \rangle$,

(b) determined by the lines K: $x = 2 + t, y = 2 + 2t, z = 4 - t$ and
L: $x = 2 - 3t, y = 2 + t, z = 4 + 4t$. (Fig. 11)
(The lines intersect at (2,2,4).)

Fig. 11

Example 5: (a) Find a normal vector to the plane $3x - 2y + 4z = 12$.

(b) Where does the plane $3x - 2y + 4z = 12$ intersect each coordinate axis?

(c) Where does the line $x = 3 + 5t, y = -4 + 2t, z = 1 - 2t$ intersect the plane $3x - 2y + 4z = 12$?

Solution: (a) We can get one normal vector to the plane simply by using the coefficients of the variables of the equation of the plane: $\mathbf{N} = \langle 3, -2, 4 \rangle$. Any other nonzero vector is normal to the plane if and only if it is a nonzero scalar multiple of $\mathbf{N}$.

(b) Every point on the x–axis has y=0 and z=0, so we can find where the plane intersects the x–axis by setting y and z equal to zero in the plane equation and solving for x:
$3x - 2(0) + 4(0) = 12$ so $x = 4$. The plane intersects the x–axis at (4,0,0). Similarly, the plane intersects the y–axis at (0,–6,0) and the z–axis at (0,0,3).

(c) Substitute the parametric patterns for x, y, and z from the line into the equation for the plane and then solve for t: $3(3 + 5t) - 2(-4 + 2t) + 4(1 - 2t) = 12$ so
$9 + 15t + 8 - 4t + 4 - 8t = 12$
$21 + 3t = 12$ and $t = -3$.
Then $x = 3 + 5(-3) = -12$, $y = -10$, and $z = 7$. The point $(-12, -10, 7)$ is on the line and on the plane.

Practice 6: (a) Find a normal vector to the plane $3x + 10y - 4z = 30$.

(b) Where does the plane $3x + 10y - 4z = 30$ intersect each coordinate axis?

(c) Where does the line $x = 4 + t, y = -2 + 2t, z = 4 - t$ intersect the plane $3x + 10y + 4z = 30$?

Normal vectors also provide us with a way to determine the angle between a line and a plane and the angle between two planes.

Angles of Intersection

The angle between a line and a plane (Fig. 12) is

$\pi/2$ – (angle between the line and the normal vector of the plane) .

The angle between two planes (Fig. 13) is the angle between the normal vectors of the planes.

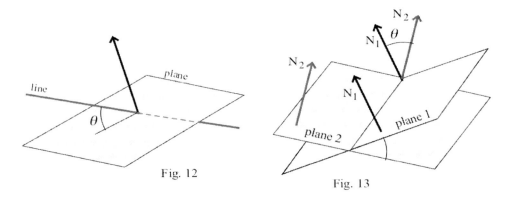

Fig. 12

Fig. 13

If the normal vectors of two planes have different directions, then the planes intersect in a line (the set of points common to both planes is a line), and we can determine parametric equations for that line. One method is to eliminate the y variable from the equations of the planes and write x in terms of z: $x = x(z)$. Then we eliminate the x variable and write y in terms of z: $y = y(z)$. Finally, we treat the variable z as the parameter "t" in the parametric equations for the line, and we have $x = x(t), y = y(t), z = t$.

Example 6: Let P be the plane $12x + 7y - 3z = 43$ and Q be the plane $4x + 7y + 13z = 19$.

(a) Find a parametric equation representation of the line of intersection of the two planes.

(b) Find the angle between the planes.

Solution: (a) This is basically an algebra problem to use the equations of the two planes to solve for two of the variables in terms of the third variable. Then we can treat that third variable as the parameter t and write the equation of the line of intersection in parametric form. We can eliminate y and solve for x in terms of z: (equation for P) – (equation for Q) is $8x - 16z = 24$ so $x = 3 + 2z$. Then we can eliminate x and solve for y in terms of z: (equation for P) – 3(equation for Q) is $-14y - 42z = -14$ so $y = 1 - 3z$. Treating the variable z as our parameter "t" we have the line **$x = 3 + 2t, y = 1 - 3t,$ and $z = t$**.

As a check, when $t = 0$ then $x = 3, y = 1,$ and $z = 0$, and the point $(3,1,0)$ lies on both planes. When $t = 1$, then $x = 5, y = -2,$ and $z = 1$, and the point $(5,-2,1)$ also lies on both planes.

(b) The angle between the planes is the angle between the normal vectors of the planes. $\mathbf{N}_P = \langle 12, 7, -3 \rangle, \mathbf{N}_Q = \langle 4, 7, 13 \rangle$ so

$$\cos(\theta) = \frac{\mathbf{N}_P \cdot \mathbf{N}_Q}{|\mathbf{N}_P||\mathbf{N}_Q|} = \frac{58}{\sqrt{202}\sqrt{234}} \approx 0.267 \text{ so } \theta \approx 1.30 \text{ (about } 74.5°).$$

Practice 7: Let R be the plane $2x + 3y - z = 13$ and S be the plane $2x - y + 3z = 1$.

(a) Find the line of intersection of the two planes. (b) Find the angle between the planes.

Sometimes an alternate method is easier: find two points that lie on the intersection and then write the parametric equations for the line through those two points.

Example 7: Let P be the plane $7x - y - 11z = 10$ and Q be the plane $9x + y - 5z = 22$.

Find a parametric equation representation of the line of intersection of the two planes.

Solution: Set one variable equal to 0, say z=0, so we then have $7x - y = 10$ and $9x + y = 22$. Adding these two equations together gives $16x = 32$ so x=2 and then y=4 so one point on the intersection of the planes is A = (2, 4, 0). Setting x=0, we have $-y - 11z = 10$ and $y - 5z = 22$. Adding these together gives $-16z = 32$ so z=–2 and then y=12 so another point on the intersection is B = (0, 12, -2). A parametric equation representation of the line through A and B is $x(t) = 2 - 2t$, $y(t) = 4 + 8t$, $z(t) = -2t$. (We could have put y=0 and then found the point C = (3, 0, 1). Check that point C satisfies the equations we just found.)

Distance Algorithms

Distances between objects are needed in a variety of applications in three dimensions:

- How close does the power line come to the school (Fig. 14)?

- How close can airplanes on two different linear flight paths come to each other (Fig. 15)?

- How far is the charged particle from the planar plate (Fig. 16)?

Below we give a collection of distance algorithms, geometric constructions, and formulas for the distances between different types of objects. At first this may seem to be a large task, but most of the patterns use the idea of vector projection and follow from thinking about the geometry of the situations.

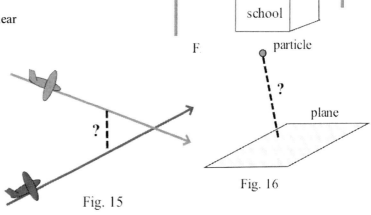

Fig. 15

Fig. 16

The distance from a point to a line in two dimensions was discussed in Section 11.3 and is presented again here because it uses the type of reasoning we need for three dimensions and because the resulting formula for two dimensions reappears for some distances in three dimensions.

Two dimensions: Distance from a **point** $P = (x_0, y_0)$ to a **line** $ax + by = c$ (Fig.17).

(1) Find **N** perpendicular to the line: $\mathbf{N} = \langle a, b \rangle$ works.

(2) Find a point Q on the line and form the vector **V** from P to Q.

(3) Distance = | Projection of **V** onto **N** |

$$= \frac{|\mathbf{V} \cdot \mathbf{N}|}{|\mathbf{N}|} = \frac{|ax_0 + by_0 - c|}{\sqrt{a^2 + b^2}}.$$

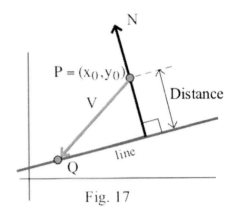

Fig. 17

Three dimensions: Distance from a **point** P to a **plane** with normal vector **N** (Fig. 18).

(1) Find a point Q on the plane and form the vector **V** from P to Q.

(2) Distance = | Projection of **V** onto **N** |

$$= \frac{|\mathbf{V} \cdot \mathbf{N}|}{|\mathbf{N}|}.$$

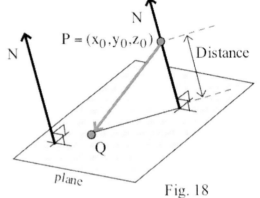

Fig. 18

Three dimensions: Distance from a **line** parallel to **U** to a **line** parallel to **V** (**U** not parallel to **V**) (Fig. 19).

(1) Find a point P on one line and a point Q on the other line.

(2) Form the vector **W** from P to Q.

(3) Calculate $\mathbf{N} = \mathbf{U} \times \mathbf{V}$.

(4) Distance = | projection of **W** onto **N** | = $\frac{|\mathbf{W} \cdot \mathbf{N}|}{|\mathbf{N}|}$.

Fig. 19

(If **U** and **V** are parallel, pick a point on one line and then use the "point to line" formula.

In each of the previous situations, the distances were the lengths of suitable projections and the distance patterns involved dot products. In the next case, we also need the length of a projection, but then we use the Pythagorean formula to solve for the distance we want. The simplified result looks similar to the previous patterns, but has a cross product instead of a dot product.

Three dimensions: Distance from a **point** P to a **line** parallel to **U** (Fig. 20).

(1) Find a point Q on the line and form the vector **V** from P to Q.

(2) Put $\mathbf{W} = |\text{ projection of } \mathbf{V} \text{ onto } \mathbf{U}| = \dfrac{|\mathbf{V} \cdot \mathbf{U}|}{|\mathbf{U}|} = \dfrac{|\mathbf{V}||\mathbf{U}||\cos(\theta)|}{|\mathbf{U}|} = |\mathbf{V}||\cos(\theta)|$.

(3) Then $(\text{distance})^2 = |\mathbf{V}|^2 - |\mathbf{W}|^2$
$$= |\mathbf{V}|^2 - |\mathbf{V}|^2 \cos^2(\theta)$$
$$= |\mathbf{V}|^2 (1 - \cos^2(\theta))$$
$$= |\mathbf{V}|^2 \sin^2(\theta)$$
$$= \dfrac{|\mathbf{V}|^2 |\mathbf{U}|^2 \sin^2(\theta)}{|\mathbf{U}|^2} = \left(\dfrac{|\mathbf{V} \times \mathbf{U}|}{|\mathbf{U}|} \right)^2.$$

(4) Distance $= \dfrac{|\mathbf{V} \times \mathbf{U}|}{|\mathbf{U}|}$.

Fig. 20

Example 7: A power line runs in a straight line from the point A = (200, 0, 100) to the point B = (100, 700, 200). How close does the line come to the corner of a school at P = (300, 400, 0)?

Solution: This problem uses the pattern for the distance from a point to a line in three dimensions.

P = (300, 400, 0) and **U** = the vector from A to B = $\langle -100, 700, 100 \rangle = 100 \langle -1, 7, 1 \rangle$:

$|\mathbf{U}| = 100\sqrt{51}$.

Since A is on the line, let **V** = vector from P to A = $\langle -100, -400, 100 \rangle = 100 \langle -1, -4, 1 \rangle$.

$$\mathbf{V} \times \mathbf{U} = (100)(100) \begin{vmatrix} \mathbf{i} & \mathbf{j} & \mathbf{k} \\ -1 & -4 & 1 \\ -1 & 7 & 1 \end{vmatrix} = (100)^2(-11\mathbf{i} - 0\mathbf{j} - 11\mathbf{k}). \quad |\mathbf{V} \times \mathbf{U}| = 100^2 \sqrt{242}.$$

Finally, distance from power line to school $= \dfrac{|\mathbf{V} \times \mathbf{U}|}{|\mathbf{U}|} = \dfrac{100^2 \sqrt{242}}{100\sqrt{51}} \approx 217.8$ feet.

PROBLEMS

In problems 1 – 8, find parametric equations for the lines.

1. The line through the point (2, –3, 1) and parallel to the vector $\langle 3, 4, 2 \rangle$.

2. The line through the point (0, 5, –2) and parallel to the vector $\langle -3, 1, -4 \rangle$.

3. The line through the point (–2, 1, 4) and parallel to the vector $\langle 5, 0, -3 \rangle$.

4. The line through the origin and parallel to the vector $\langle 1, 2, 3 \rangle$.

5. The line through the points (2, –1, 3) and (3, 4, –2).

6. The line through the points (7, 3, –4) and (5, 0, –2).

7. The line through the points (3, –2, 1) and (3, 4, –1).

8. The line through the origin and (3, 4, –2).

In problems 9 – 12, the equations for a pair of lines are given. Determine whether the lines intersect, and if they do intersect, find the point and angle of intersection.

9. Line L: $x = 2 + t, y = -1 + t, z = 3 + 2t$. Line K: $x = 2 - t, y = -1 + 2t, z = 3 + 4t$.

10. Line L: $x = 6 + 2t, y = 3 - 2t, z = -2 + 3t$. Line K: $x = 6 + t, y = 3 + 5t, z = -2 - 3t$.

11. Line L: $x = 1 + 3t, y = 5 - t, z = -2 + 2t$. Line K: $x = 9 + 4t, y = 5, z = 4 + 3t$.

12. Line L: $x = 1 + 2t, y = 1 + 3t, z = 3 + 5t$. Line K: $x = 2 + t, y = 3 + t, z = 1 + t$.

In problems 13 – 26, find equations for the planes.

13. The plane through the point $(2, 3, 1)$ and perpendicular to the vector $\langle 5, -2, 4 \rangle$.

14. The plane through the point $(4, 0, -2)$ and perpendicular to the vector $\langle 3, 1, -5 \rangle$.

15. The plane through the point $(-3, 5, 6)$ and perpendicular to the vector $\langle 0, 3, 0 \rangle$.

16. The plane through the origin and perpendicular to the vector $\langle 2, -2, 1 \rangle$.

17. The plane through the points $(1, 2, 3), (5, 2, 1)$, and $(4, -1, 3)$.

18. The plane through the points $(3, 5, 3), (-2, 5, 4)$, and $(1, 5, 6)$.

19. The plane through the points $(-4, 2, 5), (1, 2, 1)$, and $(3, -3, 5)$.

20. The plane through the origin, $(1, 2, 3)$, and $(4, 5, 6)$.

21. The plane through the point $(2, -5, 7)$ and parallel to the xy–plane.

22. The plane through the point $(2, 4, 1)$ and parallel to the yz–plane.

23. The plane through the point $(4, 2, 3)$ and parallel to the plane $3x - 2y + 5z = 15$.

24. The plane through the origin and parallel to the plane $2x + 3y - z = 12$.

25. The plane through the point $(4, 1, 3)$ and perpendicular to the line $x = 2 + 5t, y = 1 - 3t, z = 2t$.

26. The plane through the point $(2, 7, 4)$ and perpendicular to the y–axis.

Try to answer problems 27 – 32 without doing any algebra –– just think visually.

27. Where does the plane $x = 0$ intersect the plane $z = 0$?

28. Where does the plane $y = 2$ intersect the plane $z = 3$?

29. Where does the plane $3x + 2y + z = 30$ intersect the x–axis?

30. Where does the plane $3x + 2y + z = 30$ intersect the y–axis?

31. Where do the three planes $x = 4, y = 2$, and $z = 1$ intersect?

32. Where does the y–axis intersect the plane $z = 3$?

In problems 33 – 36, two planes are given. Represent their line of intersection using parametric equations and find the angle between the planes.

33. $4x – 2y + 2z = 10$ and $3x – 2y + 3z = 36$.
34. $x + y + 3z = 9$ and $2x + y – 3z = 18$.
35. $5y – z = 10$ and $x + 2y + 4z = 16$.
36. $x = 4$ and $3x – 5y + z = 20$.

In problems 37 – 40, find where the given line intersects the plane and find the angle the line makes with the plane.

37. Line L: $x = 7 + 2t, y = 5 + t, z = 2 + 4t$ and the plane $5x + y – 2z = 20$.
38. Line L: $x = –2 + t, y = 12 – 3t, z = –5 – t$ and the plane $5x + y – 2z = 20$.
39. Line L: $x = 4 + 2t, y = 2 – 3t, z = 7 + t$, and the plane $z = 5$.
40. The x–axis and the plane $4x – 2y + 5z = 12$.
41. Is it possible for three distinct planes to intersect at a single point?
42. Is it possible for three distinct planes to intersect along a line?
43. A bird is flying in a straight line from the feeder (Fig. 21) to the corner of the house. Write an equation for its line of flight.

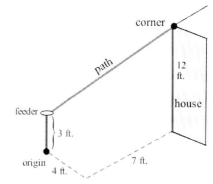

Fig. 21

44. What angle does the plane $3x + 2y + z = 10$ make with
    (a) the xy–plane? (b) the xz–plane? (c) the yz–plane?

45. What angle does the plane $ax + by + cz = d$ make with each coordinate plane?

46. The four corners of a mirror are located at A(2,2,0), B(2,6,0), C(0,2,3), and D(0,6,3) (Fig. 22). A laser at L(5,0,0) directs a beam of light along the line $x = 5 – t, y = t, z = 0.5t$.
    (a) Write an equation for the plane of the mirror.
    (b) Where does the light beam hit the mirror?
    (c) What is the angle of incidence of the light with the mirror?

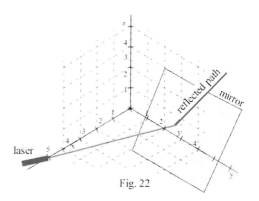

Fig. 22

Many of the following applications can be solved in several ways including the methods of vectors and dot products from section 11.4.

47. When it was built, the Great Pyramid at Giza, Egypt was 481 feet tall and had a square base with length 756 feet on each side.
    (a) Find the angle each side of the pyramid makes with the base.
    (b) Find the angle each side makes with an adjacent side.
    (c) Find the angle each edge makes with the base.

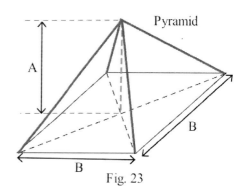

Fig. 23

48. In order to write a program to analyze a general pyramid (Fig. 23) with square base of length B and height A you need to determine the following:

    (a) the angle each side makes with the base,
    (b) the area of each side,
    (c) the angle each edge makes with the base,
    (d) the angle each side makes with an adjacent side, and
    (e) the volume of the pyramid.

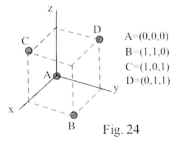
Fig. 24

49. Four molecules are located at the corners of a cube as shown in Fig. 24. The center of the cube is the point O = (0.5, 0.5, 0.5) Show that the angles AOB, AOC, and BOC are equal.

50. The four points (1,0,0), (–0.5,0.866,0), (–0.5,–0.866,0), and (0,0,1.414) are the vertices of an equilateral tetrahedron with center O = (0, 0, 0.354) (Fig. 25), and a molecule is located at each vertex.

    (a) Show that the tetrahedron is really equilateral.
    (b) Show that the angles AOB, AOC, and BOC are equal.
    (c) Find the angle between the plane determined by AOB and the plane determined by AOC.

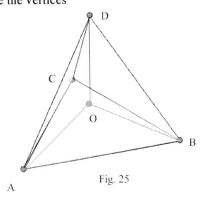
Fig. 25

Distances in Three Dimensions

51. Find the distance from the point $(4,-1,2)$ to the line $x = 2 + t, y = 3 + 2t, z = 4t$.

52. Find the distance from the point $(4,-1,2)$ to the line $x = 1 - 3t, y = 2 + t, z = 3$.

53. Find the distance from the point $(2, 3, 1)$ to the plane $4x + 3y - z = 10$.

54. Find the distance from the point $(4,-3,0)$ to the plane $-2x + 5y + 3z = 15$.

55. Find the distance (shortest distance) between the line $x = 1 + 3t, y = 2 + 5t, z = 1 - t$ and the line $x = 3 - 2t, y = 5 + t, z = 2 + 2t$.

56. Find the distance (shortest distance) between the line $x = 5 + 2t, y = 2 + t, z = 2 - 3t$ and the line $x = 3 - 2t, y = 1 - 3t, z = 1$.

In problems 57 – 62, the parameterized straight–line paths of two objects are given.

(a) Do the objects "crash" (so they are at the same location at the same time)? If so, at what time?

(b) Do the paths of the objects intersect (so the objects are at the same point but at different times)? If so, how close do the objects get to each other?

(c) Do the objects and their paths miss each other? If so, how close do the objects get to each other and how close do their paths get to each other?

57. Object A is at $x = 9 + t, y = 18 + t, z = 25 - 2t$ and object B is at $x = 3 + 2t, y = 30 - t$, and $z = 7 + t$.

58. Object A is at $x = -1 + t, y = -3 + 2t, z = 1 + t$ and object B is at $x = 2, y = t$, and $z = -2 + 2t$.

59. Object A is at $x = 5 - 5t, y = t, z = 5t$ and object B is at $x = 6 - 3t, y = 5 - 2t$, and $z = -3 + 4t$.

60. Object A is at $x = -4 + 5t, y = 3 + 2t, z = 16 - 3t$ and object B is at $x = 12 - t, y = 6 + 3t$, and $z = 3 + 4t$.

61. Object A is at $x = 5 - 2t, y = 0, z = 1$ and object B is at $x = 0, y = -1 + t$, and $z = 0$.

62. Object A is at $x = 1 + 3t, y = 2 + 2t, z = 3 + t$ and object B is at $x = 7 - t, y = 5 + 2t$, and $z = 3 + 3t$.

63. The bearing of an airplane is due north, and it passes directly above the origin at an altitude of 30,000 feet. How close does the airplane come to a balloon 5,000 feet directly above the point $x = 2,000$ and $y = 4,000$? (Assume the earth is "almost flat" in this region.)

64. At time t, airplane A is at $(-3 + t, 0, 1)$ and car B is at $(0, -5 + 2t, 0)$.

    (a) How close do they come to each other?
    (b) How close do their paths come to each other?

65. At time t, car A is at $(-3 + t, 2 + 2t, 0)$ and airplane B is at $(t, -5 + 2t, t)$.

    (a) How close do they come to each other?
    (b) How close do their come to each other?

66. Create your own problem, like problems 59 – 64, so the objects on different paths crash at the point $(3, 4, 5)$ at $t = 2$.

67. Create your own problem, like problems 59 – 64, with two objects on different paths so object A goes through the point $(3, 4, 5)$ at $t = 2$ and object B goes through the point $(3, 4, 5)$ at $t = 3$. (Then the paths intersect, but the objects do not crash.)

Practice Answers

Practice 1: (a) $x(t) = 3 + 2t, y(t) = -1 - 4t$.

(b) $x(t) = 3 + t, y(t) = -1 + 5t$.

The graphs are shown in Fig. 26.

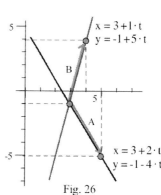

Fig. 26

Practice 2: (a) $x(t) = 2 + 3t, y(t) = -1 - 4t, z(t) = 0 + t$.

(b) The line is parallel to the vector $\mathbf{B} = \langle -1, 5, 2 \rangle$ from P to Q. Using P as the starting point, a parametric equation of the line is $x(t) = 3 - 1t$, $y(t) = 0 + 5t, z(t) = 2 + 2t$. (Using Q as the starting point, $x(t) = 2 - t$, $y(t) = 5 + 5t$, $z(t) = 4 + 2t$.)

Practice 3: Replacing the t parameter with s for line L and then setting the components equal to each other, we get: x: $1 + t = 8 + 4s$, y: $1 - 2t = -4 + s$, and z: $-3 + 2t = -5 - 8s$. Solving the first two equations for t and s, $t = 3$ and $s = -1$. These values for t and s also satisfy the third equation so $x = 1 + (3) = 4, y = 1 - 2(3) = -5$, and $z = -3 + 2(3) = 3$. The point $(4, -5, 3)$ lies on both lines.

The lines are parallel to $\mathbf{A} = \langle 1, -2, 2 \rangle$ and $\mathbf{B} = \langle 4, 1, -8 \rangle$ so

$$\cos(\theta) = \frac{\mathbf{A} \cdot \mathbf{B}}{|\mathbf{A}||\mathbf{B}|} = \frac{-14}{(3)(9)} \text{ and } \theta \approx 2.12 \text{ (about } 121.2°).$$

(b) Replacing the t parameter with s for line L and then setting the components equal to each other, we get: x: $1 + t = 8 + 4s$, y: $1 - 2t = -4 + s$, and z: $2 + 2t = 3 + s$. Solving the first two equations (they are the same as in part (a)) for t and s, $t = 3$ and $s = -1$. But these values do not satisfy the third equation, $2 + 2(3) \neq 3 + (-1)$, so the lines do not intersect.

(c) Every point in the yz–plane has x coordinate 0, so set $8 + 4t = 0$ to get $t = -2$. Then $y = -4 + (-2) = -6$ and $z = 3 + (-2) = 1$ so the line intersects the yz–plane at $(0, -6, 1)$.

Practice 4: The parametric equations for the line of travel of the arrow are $x = 1 + 4t, y = 2 + 5t, z = 3 + t$. The arrow reaches the wall when $y = 20$ so $2 + 5t = 20$ and $t = 18/5$. At that time, $t = 18/5$, the height of the arrow is $z = 3 + t = 3 + (18/5) = 33/5 = 6.6$ feet so the arrow does not go over the wall.

Practice 5: (a) The point (x,y,z) is on the plane if and only if $3(x-4) - 2(y-1) + 6(z-0) = 0$, or, equivalently, $3x - 2y + 6z = 10$.

(b) Taking the directions of the lines K and L from their parametric equations, we know line K is parallel to $\mathbf{U} = \langle 1, 2, -1 \rangle$ and line L is parallel to $\mathbf{V} = \langle -3, 1, 4 \rangle$. Then

$$\mathbf{N} = \mathbf{U} \times \mathbf{V} = \begin{vmatrix} \mathbf{i} & \mathbf{j} & \mathbf{k} \\ 1 & 2 & -1 \\ -3 & 1 & 4 \end{vmatrix} = \mathbf{i} \begin{vmatrix} 2 & -1 \\ 1 & 4 \end{vmatrix} - \mathbf{j} \begin{vmatrix} 1 & -1 \\ -3 & 4 \end{vmatrix} + \mathbf{k} \begin{vmatrix} 1 & 2 \\ -3 & 1 \end{vmatrix} = 9\mathbf{i} - 1\mathbf{j} + 7\mathbf{k}.$$

The point $(2,2,4)$ is on both lines so it is on the plane. Using the point $(2,2,4)$ and the normal vector $\mathbf{N} = \langle 9, -1, 7 \rangle$, the equation of the plane is

$9(x-2) - 1(y-2) + 7(z-4) = 0$ or $9x - y + 7z = 44$.

Practice 6: (a) $\mathbf{N} = \langle 3, 10, -4 \rangle$ and all nonzero scalar multiples of **N** are normal to the plane.

(b) The plane crosses the x–axis at $(10,0,0)$, the y–axis at $(0,3,0)$, and the z–axis at $(0,0,-7.5)$.

(c) Solving $3(4 + t) + 10(-2 + 2t) - 4(4 - t) = 30$ for t, we get
$12 + 3t - 20 + 20t - 16 + 4t = 30$ so $-24 + 27t = 30$ and $t = 2$. Then $x = 6, y = 2$, and $z = 2$. The point $(6,2,2)$ is on the line and on the plane.

Practice 7: (a) We can eliminate y and solve for x in terms of z: (equation for R) + 3(equation for S) is $8x + 8z = 16$ so $x = 2 - z$. Then we can eliminate x and solve for y in terms of z: (equation for R) – (equation for S) is $4y - 4z = 12$ so $y = 3 + z$. Treating the variable z as our parameter "t" we have the line $x = 2 - t, y = 3 + t,$ and $z = t$.

As a check, when $t = 0$ then $x = 2, y = 3$, and $z = 0$, and the point $(2,3,0)$ lies on both planes. When $t = 1$, then $x = 1, y = 4$, and $z = 1$, and the point $(1,4,1)$ also lies on both planes.

(b) The angle between the planes is the angle between the normal vectors of the planes. $\mathbf{N_R} = \langle 2, 3, -1 \rangle, \mathbf{N_S} = \langle 2, -1, 3 \rangle$ so

$$\cos(\theta) = \frac{\mathbf{N_R} \cdot \mathbf{N_S}}{|\mathbf{N_R}||\mathbf{N_S}|} = \frac{-2}{\sqrt{14}\sqrt{14}} = \frac{-1}{7} \approx -0.143 \text{ so } \theta \approx 1.71 \text{ (about } 98.2°).$$

11.7 Vector Reflections

Vectors were originally used in physics and engineering (forces, work, ...), but a very common use now is in computer graphics, and a single frame in an animated movie such as "Cars" may require working with hundreds of millions of vectors. Realistic lighting and surface texture require calculating what happens when a ray is reflected off of a mirror or shiny surface. We will start examining that situation in 2D (Fig. 1), a ray reflected off of a line or curve, and later extend it to 3D, a ray reflecting off of a surface. The theorem illustrates a modern use of the projection vector.

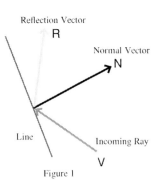

Figure 1

Reflection Theorem:

If a incident vector ray **V** is reflected off of a line L that has normal vector **N**,

then the reflection vector is $\mathbf{R} = \mathbf{V} - 2 \cdot \text{Proj}_\mathbf{N} \mathbf{V}$. (Fig. 1)

Proof: The basis of the proof is very visual and geometric (Fig. 2). (i) $\mathbf{A} = \text{Proj}_\mathbf{N} \mathbf{V}$. (ii) $\mathbf{B} = -2 \cdot \text{Proj}_\mathbf{N} \mathbf{V}$ on the vector. (iii) $\mathbf{C} = \mathbf{V} - 2 \cdot \text{Proj}_\mathbf{N} \mathbf{V}$. Finally, we can use geometry to justify that the vector **C** in (iii) is the reflection vector we want.

Example 1: Find the reflection vector R when an incoming vector $\mathbf{V} = \langle -3, 1 \rangle$ is reflected by the line $3x + 2y = 12$ (Fig. 3). Then give parametric equations for the reflected line when the reflection occurs at the point (2, 6).

Solution: The line has normal vector $\mathbf{N} = \langle 3, 2 \rangle$ so

$$\text{Proj}_\mathbf{N} \mathbf{V} = \frac{\mathbf{V} \cdot \mathbf{N}}{\mathbf{N} \cdot \mathbf{N}} \mathbf{N} = \frac{-7}{13} \langle 3, 2 \rangle = \left\langle \frac{-21}{13}, \frac{-14}{13} \right\rangle$$

and the reflection vector is

$$\mathbf{R} = \mathbf{V} - 2 \cdot \text{Proj}_\mathbf{N} \mathbf{V} = \langle -3, 1 \rangle - 2 \left\langle \frac{-21}{13}, \frac{-14}{13} \right\rangle$$

$$= \left\langle -3 + \frac{42}{13}, 1 + \frac{28}{13} \right\rangle = \left\langle \frac{3}{13}, \frac{41}{13} \right\rangle$$

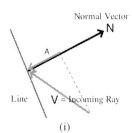

Fig. 3

One representation of the reflected line is $x(t) = 2 + \frac{3}{13}t$, $y(t) = 6 + \frac{41}{13}t$.

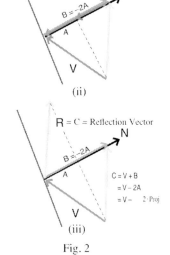

Fig. 2

Since this operation is done millions of times for each frame, it is important that the operation is simple and quick.

Practice 1: Find the reflection vector R when an incoming vector $\mathbf{V} = \langle -1, -2 \rangle$ is reflected by the line $-x + 2y = 2$ (Fig. 4). Give parametric equations for the reflected line when the reflection occurs at the point (1.5, 1.75).

Fig. 4

We can also reflect off a curve at a point – just reflect off the tangent line to the curve at the point.

Example 2: Find the reflection vector R when an incoming vector $V = \langle 3, -1 \rangle$ is reflected by the ellipse ($2\cos(t), \sin(t)$) at the point where $t = 1.2$ on the ellipse (Fig. 5).

Solution: $x'(t) = -2\sin(t)$ and $y'(t) = \cos(t)$ so a tangent vector to the ellipse when $t = 1.2$ is $T = \langle -2\sin(1.2), \cos(1.2) \rangle \approx \langle -1.864, 0.362 \rangle$ and then a normal vector is $N \approx \langle 0.362, 1.864 \rangle$. Finally,

$$\text{Proj}_N V = \frac{V \cdot N}{N \cdot N} N \approx \frac{-0.778}{3.606} \langle 0.362, 1.864 \rangle = \langle -0.078, -0.402 \rangle$$

so $R = V - 2 \cdot \text{Proj}_N V = \langle 3, -1 \rangle - 2 \langle -0.078, -0.402 \rangle = \langle 3.156, -0.197 \rangle$

Practice 2: Find the reflection vector R when an incoming vector $V = \langle -1, 2 \rangle$ is reflected by the parabola (t, t^2) at the point where $t = 1.2$ on the parabola.

These ideas and computations extend very nicely to reflection vectors in 3D, and those reflections use the same formula: $R = V - 2 \cdot \text{Proj}_N V$. In the case of the reflection of a vector by a plane, we already know how to quickly find a normal vector to the plane so the reflection calculation is straightforward. To reflect off some other surface we will need a normal vector, and we will see how to find such a normal vector in Section 13.4.

Practice 3: Find the reflection vector R when an incoming vector $V = \langle 2, -3, -1 \rangle$ is reflected by the plane $2x - 3y + z = 10$ at the point where (5, 1 3) on the plane.

Reflection Problems

For Problems 1 – 6, (a) determine the reflection vector R when an incoming vector V is reflected by the given line, and (b) determine parametric equations for the reflected line when the reflection occurs at the given point.

1. The incoming vector $V = \langle 2, -1 \rangle$ is reflected by the line $3x + y = 6$ at the point (1, 3).

2. The incoming vector $V = \langle -1, 1 \rangle$ is reflected by the line $3x + y = 6$ at the point (1, 3).

3. The incoming vector $V = \langle 2, 3 \rangle$ is reflected by the line $5x - 2y = 7$ at the point (3, 4).

4. The incoming vector $V = \langle 0, -2 \rangle$ is reflected by the line $5x - 2y = 7$ at the point (3, 4).

Problems 5 and 6 can be easily done without the Reflection Theorem, but, of course, the theorem works.

5. The incoming vector $V = \langle -3, 2 \rangle$ is reflected by the y-axis at the point (0, 3).

6. The incoming vector $V = \langle 3, -1 \rangle$ is reflected by the x-axis at the point (2, 0).

11.7 Vector Reflections   Contemporary Calculus

For Problems 7 – 12, (a) determine the reflection vector R when an incoming vector V is reflected by the given curve, and (b) determine parametric equations for the reflected line when the reflection occurs at the given point.

7. The incoming vector $V = \langle -3, 1 \rangle$ is reflected by the ellipse ($2\cos(t)$, $\sin(t)$) at the point where $t = 0.9$ on the ellipse.

8. The incoming vector $V = $ is reflected by the ellipse ($2\cos(t)$, $\sin(t)$) at the point where $t = 0.9$ on the ellipse.

9. The incoming vector $V = \langle 2, 1 \rangle$ is reflected by the curve $\left(t^2, t^3 \right)$ at the point where $t = 2$.

10. The incoming vector $V = \langle -1, 1 \rangle$ is reflected by the curve $\left(t^2, t^3 \right)$ at the point where $t = 2$.

11. The incoming vector $V = \langle -1, 1 \rangle$ is reflected by the curve $y = x^2$ at the point (2, 4).

12. The incoming vector $V = \langle 2, 1 \rangle$ is reflected by the curve $y = x^2$ at the point (2, 4).

For Problems 13 – 16, (a) determine the reflection vector R when an incoming vector V is reflected by the given plane, and (b) determine parametric equations for the reflected line when the reflection occurs at the given point.

13. The incoming vector $V = \langle 2, 6, 3 \rangle$ is reflected by the plane $x + 2y + 3z = 13$ at the point (2, 4, 1).

14. The incoming vector $V = \langle 4, 1, 3 \rangle$ is reflected by the plane $3x - 2y + 4z = 5$ at the point (1, 3, 2).

15. The incoming vector $V = \langle 3, 2, 1 \rangle$ is reflected by the plane $x = 0$ at the point (0, 4, 2).

16. The incoming vector $V = \langle 2, -3, -1 \rangle$ is reflected by the plane $z = 0$ at the point (3, 4, 0).

Practice Answers

Practice 1: The line has normal vector $N = \langle -1, 2 \rangle$ so $\text{Proj}_N V = \dfrac{V \cdot N}{N \cdot N} N \approx \dfrac{-3}{5} \langle -1, 2 \rangle = \left\langle \dfrac{3}{5}, \dfrac{-6}{5} \right\rangle$

and the reflection vector is $R = V - 2 \cdot \text{Proj}_N V = \langle -1, -2 \rangle - 2\left\langle \dfrac{3}{5}, \dfrac{-6}{5} \right\rangle = \left\langle \dfrac{-11}{5}, \dfrac{2}{5} \right\rangle$.

The reflected line is $x(t) = 1.5 - \dfrac{11}{5}t$, $y(t) = 1.75 + \dfrac{2}{5}t$.

Practice 2: x'(t) = 1 and y'(t) = 2t so a tangent vector to the parabola when t = 1.2 is T = $\langle 1, 2.4 \rangle$ and then a normal vector is N $\approx \langle -2.4, 1 \rangle$. Finally, $\text{Proj}_N V = \frac{V \cdot N}{N \cdot N} N \approx \frac{4.4}{6.76} \langle -2.4, 1 \rangle = \langle -1.56, 0.65 \rangle$ so **R** = V − 2·Proj_NV = $\langle -1, 2 \rangle - 2\langle -1.56, 0.65 \rangle = \langle 2.12, 0.7 \rangle$

y(t) = 0.783 − 2.099t.

Related web sites:

Ray tracing in Wikipedia – a nice overview

http://en.wikipedia.org/wiki/Ray_tracing_(graphics)

Just look at the pictures in this one (about movie "Cars" from Pixar)

http://graphics.pixar.com/library/RayTracingCars/paper.pdf

"Rendering this image used **111 million diffuse rays, 37 million specular rays, and 26 million shadow rays**. The rays cause **1.2 billion ray-triangle intersection tests**. With multiresolution geometry caching, the render time is 106 minutes."

Appendix: Sketching Planes and Conics in the XYZ Coordinate System

Some mathematicians draw horrible sketches of 3–dimensional objects and they still lead productive, happy lives. Some mathematics students are terrible 3D artists and still get A grades. But it really takes very little time and practice to do decent sketches of planes and conic sections in 3D, and it can be satisfying to have the curve you know is an ellipse actually look like an ellipse. This Appendix illustrates some step–by–step ways to draw the basic building blocks for many 3D shapes: the axis system, planes and conic sections.

First Step: Invest in a pencil and a small, inexpensive, clear plastic $30-60-90^o$ triangle with a centimeter scale (Fig. 1). They make it much easier to create good 3D sketches. Many of the directions in this Appendix suggest drawing "help lines" to assist you in putting the various objects in the appropriate positions and orientations. The final drawings often look better if these "help lines" are removed when the sketch is finished, so a pencil is better than a pen. Many of the directions require you to draw lines parallel to the axes and to draw parallelograms, and a clear plastic straightedge (or a triangle) is very useful for this. Finally, the centimeter scale produces small sketches appropriate for personal work.

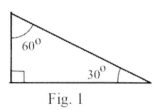
Fig. 1

The following directions are for "by hand" sketches, but they can also help you when using CAD (computer–aided design) and Draw computer programs.

A. The XYZ axis system — everything starts here!

Fig. 2

Including an axis system in a 3D sketch gives the viewer an orientation and a perspective for the location of an object.

(1) Draw a vertical line segment.
(2) Sketch 2 other line segments making 120° angles with the vertical segment. The 30–60–90° triangle is useful here (Fig. 2).
(3) If any of the variables take negative values, you can extend the appropriate axis to the negative values using dashed lines.
(4) If a scale is needed, put "tick" marks along the axes at uniform intervals. (Fig. 3)

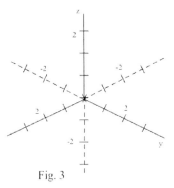
Fig. 3

Since the xyz–coordinate system is needed in so many sketches, you should eventually get used to sketching it without the aid of a ruler. ("Trick:" To get the y-axis, start at the origin, go right 2 units and down one unit, plot a point, and draw the line through this point and the origin. This line is the y-axis. The x-axis is similar: go left two and down one.)

Appendix: 3D Sketches

B . The XY, XZ, and YZ coordinate planes. (Actually, rectangular pieces of the coordinate planes.)

The following rectangular pieces of the coordinate planes are useful by themselves, and they are very important aids for drawing curves and conics later.

Keys: Start with an xyz–axis system. Use lines parallel to each axis. The result should be a parallelogram.

Piece of the XY coordinate plane: (Fig. 4)
(1) Pick a point on the x–axis and draw a line segment to the
    left of and parallel to the y–axis.
(2) From the end of the segment in step (1), draw a line to
    the y–axis that is parallel to the x–axis.

Piece of the XZ coordinate plane: (Fig. 5)
(1) Pick a point on the x–axis and draw a vertical line segment (up and parallel to the z–axis).
(2) From the end of the segment in step (1), draw a line to
    the z–axis that is parallel to the x–axis.

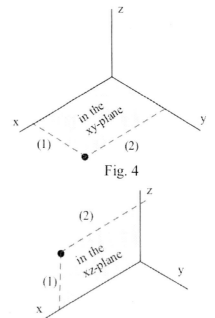
Fig. 4

Fig. 5

Plane (piece) parallel to the xy–plane: (Fig. 6)
(1) Locate and label the appropriate point on the z–axis, for example, z = 2.
(2) From the point in step (1), draw line segments parallel to the
    x–axis and the y–axis.
(3) From the ends of the segments in step (2), draw additional lines parallel
    to the y–axis and the x–axis to complete the parallelogram.

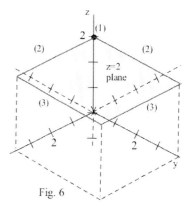
Fig. 6

Plane (piece) parallel to the xz–plane: (Fig. 7)
(1) Locate and label the appropriate point on the y–axis, for example, y = 2.
(2) From the point in step (1), draw line segments parallel to the x–axis
    and the z–axis.
(3) From the ends of the segments in step (2), draw additional lines
    parallel to the z–axis and the x–axis to complete the parallelogram.

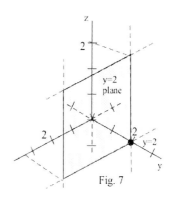
Fig. 7

Appendix: 3D Sketches

Practice 1: Sketch the planes z = 1 and x = 2 in Fig. 8.

Practice 2: Sketch the planes z = –1 and y = 1 on an XYZ system.

Practice 3: Sketch the rectangular box with opposite corners at
(0, 0, 0) and (4, 3, 2).

Challenge 1: Sketch the plane that contains the points
(0, 0, 3), (4, 0, 3), and (0, 2, 3).

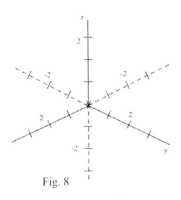

Fig. 8

C. Ellipses

Keys: Plot the vertices and make a parallelogram "frame" for the ellipse. Sketch short tangent segments at the midpoints of the sides of the parallelogram.

Example 1: An ellipse in the xy–plane with vertices at (3,0,0), (–3,0,0), (0,2,0), and (0,–2,0). (Fig. 9)
(1) Plot the vertices in the xy–plane (z=0).
(2) Sketch a parallelogram "frame" by drawing lines through (3,0) and (–3,0) that are parallel to the y–axis, and lines through (0,2) and (0,–2) that are parallel to the x–axis.
(3) At each vertex sketch a short "tangent segment" that lies on the side of the parallelogram frame.
(4) Finish the sketch by smoothly connecting the "tangent segments."

If your sketch requires several conics, it is useful to erase all or most of the parallelogram frame.

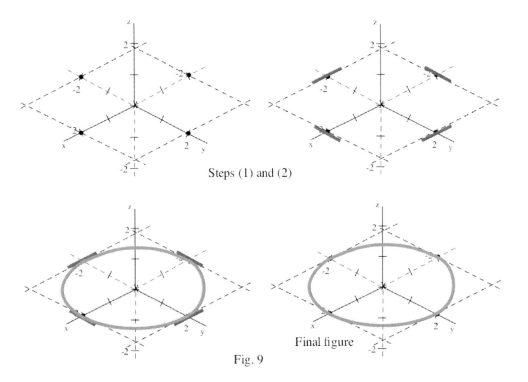

Fig. 9

Appendix: 3D Sketches

Example 2: An ellipse in the xz–plane with vertices at (3,0,0), (–3,0,0), (0,0,2), and (0,0,–2). Fig. 10 shows the intermediate steps to construct this ellipse as well as the final result.

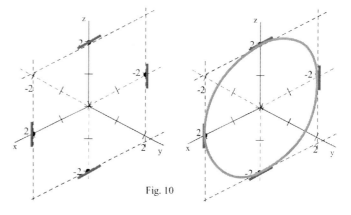

Fig. 10

Practice 4: Sketch the ellipse with vertices at (1, 0, 0), (0, 0, 0), (0, 0, 3), and (0, 0, –3) on the XYZ system in Fig. 11.

Practice 5: Sketch the ellipse with vertices at (3, 0, 2), (–3, 0, 2), (0, 1, 2), and (0, –1, 2).

Practice 6: Sketch the elliptical cylinder $\dfrac{y^2}{9} + z^2 = 1$.

Challenge 2: Sketch the ellipse with vertices at (4,2,0), (2,0,3), (0,2,6), and (2,4,3).

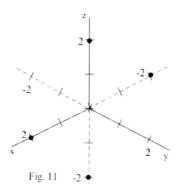

Fig. 11

D. Parabolas

Keys: Plot the vertex and one other point on the parabola. Make a parallelogram "frame" for the parabola and plot a symmetric point. Sketch short "tangent segments" at the plotted points.

Example 3: Sketch the parabola lying in the xy-plane that satisfies $y = x^2 - 4x + 6$. (Fig. 12)

(1) Plot the vertex (2,1,0). When x = 1, then y = (1)2 – 4(1) + 6 = 3. Plot (1,3,0).

(2) Sketch a parallelogram "frame" by drawing lines through (2,1,0) parallel to the x–axis and the y–axis, and through (1,3,0) parallel to the x–axis and the y–axis.

(3) Plot the "symmetric point" (3,3,0) and draw a line through it parallel to the x–axis and the y–axis.

(4) Sketch a short "tangent segment" at the vertex (2,1,0) (this "tangent segment" lies on the side of the parallelogram). Add "tangent segments" at the other two plotted points (1,3,0) and (3,3,0) (these "tangent segments are **not** parallel to the sides of the parallelogram).

(5) Finish the sketch by smoothly connecting the "tangent segments."

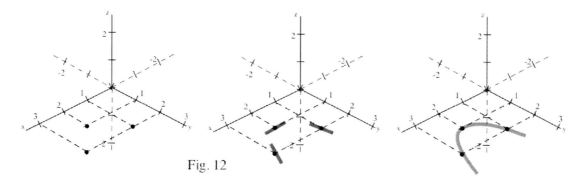

Fig. 12

Appendix: 3D Sketches

Example 4: Sketch the parabola lying in the xz-plane that satisfies $z = x^2 + 1$.

Fig. 13 shows a beginning step and the final result.

Practice 7: Sketch the parabola with vertex at (0,2,0) that contains the point (0,1,2) on the XYZ system in Fig. 14.

Fig. 13

Practice 8: Sketch the parabola with vertex at (2,0,2) that contains the point (0,0,0).

Practice 9: Sketch the parabola $x = (y - 1)^2$ on the plane $z = 1$.

Challenge 3: Sketch the parabola with vertex (4,2,0) that contains the symmetric points (0,1,3) and (0,3,3).

Fig. 14

E . General curves in coordinate planes

Keys: Start with a regular rectangular coordinate graph of the function and a few "tangent segments." Plot a domain–range parallelogram in 3D along with the points and the "tangent segments."

Example 5: Sketch the curve $y = \sin(x)$, $0 \le x \le 3\pi$, in the xy–plane. (Fig. 15)

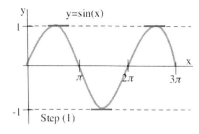

(1) Graph $y = \sin(x)$, $0 \le x \le 3\pi$, in the 2D rectangular coordinate system, label a few points and add "tangent segments" at those points.
(2) Sketch the domain–range parallelogram, $0 \le x \le 3\pi$ and $-1 \le y \le 1$.
(3) Sketch the points and "tangent segments" in the parallelogram in step (2).
(4) Finish the sketch by smoothly connecting the "tangent segments."

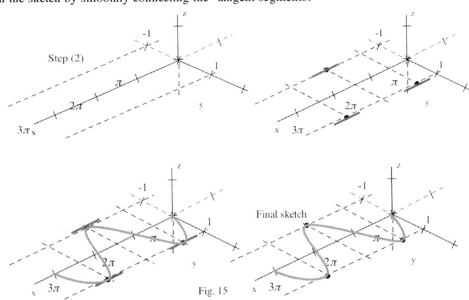

Fig. 15

Practice 10: On the XYZ system in Fig. 16 sketch a curve

(a) in the xz-plane (y=0) that satisfies $z = 1 + \cos(x), -\pi \le x \le 3\pi$,

(b) in the y = 2 plane that satisfies $z = 1 + \cos(x), -\pi \le x \le 3\pi$,.

Practice 11: On an XYZ system sketch the curve (a) in the yz-plane (x=0) that satisfies $z = y$ for $0 \le y \le 4$, (b) in the x = 2 plane that satisfies $z = y$ for $0 \le y \le 4$.

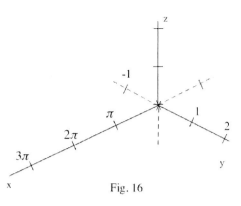

Fig. 16

Practice 12: Sketch the curve $y = 4 - x^2$, $-2 \le x \le 3$ (a) in the xy–plane and (b) in the z = 3 plane.

Challenge 4: Sketch the graph of $z = |x| + |y|$ on the plane $\{y = -x$, no restrictions on $z\}$.

Final Note

Sketching 3D curves on a 2D piece of paper presents challenges for most of us, but with a bit of practice (and a systematic approach) most of us can learn to do decent sketches of a some simple 3D curves. It certainly helps if the curve lies in a plane.

11.1 Selected Answers

5. (b) $|U| = \sqrt{17}$, $|V| = \sqrt{13}$

   direction of U is $\langle 1/\sqrt{17}, 4/\sqrt{17} \rangle$, direction of V is $\langle 3/\sqrt{13}, 2/\sqrt{13} \rangle$

   (c) slope of U is $4/1 = 4$, slope of V is $2/3$

   angle of U with x-axis is $\theta = \arctan(4) = 1.326$ ($\approx 76°$)

   angle of V with x-axis is $\theta = \arctan(2/3) = 0.588$ ($\approx 33.7°$)

7. (b) $|U| = \sqrt{29}$, $|V| = \sqrt{58}$

   direction of U is $\langle -2/\sqrt{29}, 5/\sqrt{29} \rangle$, direction of V is $\langle 3/\sqrt{58}, -7/\sqrt{58} \rangle$

   (c) slope of U is $-5/2$, slope of V is $-7/3$

   angle of U with x-axis is $\theta = \arctan(-5/2) = -1.190$ ($\approx -68.8°$)

   angle of V with x-axis is $\theta = \arctan(-7/3) = -1.166$ ($\approx -66.8°$)

9. (b) $|U| = \sqrt{25} = 5$, $|V| = \sqrt{25} = 5$

   direction of U is $\langle -4/5, -3/5 \rangle$, direction of V is $\langle 3/5, -4/5 \rangle$

   (c) slope of U is $3/4$, slope of V is $-4/3$

   angle of U with x-axis is $\theta = \arctan(3/4) = 0.643$ ($\approx 36.9°$)

   angle of V with x-axis is $\theta = \arctan(-4/) = -0.927$ ($\approx -53.1°$)

13. $U = A + B - C = \langle -1, 3 \rangle$, $V = A - B + C = \langle 3, 5 \rangle$

15. $V = 3\langle 0.6, 0.8 \rangle = \langle 1.8, 2.4 \rangle$ 17. $V = \langle 4.10, 2.87 \rangle$

19. $V = \langle 7/\sqrt{10}, 21/\sqrt{10} \rangle$ or $\langle -7/\sqrt{10}, -21/\sqrt{10} \rangle$ 21. $V = \langle 1/\sqrt{26}, 5/\sqrt{26} \rangle$ or $\langle -1/\sqrt{26}, -5/\sqrt{26} \rangle$

23. $V = \langle 1, 0 \rangle$ or $\langle -1, 0 \rangle$ 25. $V = \langle 1, 0 \rangle$ or $\langle -1, 0 \rangle$

31. shadow on x-axis $1i + 0j$, on y-axis is $0i + 4j$

33. shadow on x-axis $5i + 0j$, on y-axis is $0i - 2j$

37. $C = \langle -4, -6 \rangle$ 38. $C = \langle 3, 7 \rangle$

39. $\langle 25.36, 0 \rangle$ and $\langle 0, 54.37 \rangle$ 40. $\langle 96.59, 0 \rangle$ and $\langle 0, 25.88 \rangle$

41. magnitude = 119.5 pounds, angle $\approx 39.2°$ 42. magnitude = 139 pounds, angle $\approx 21.4°$

43. magnitude = 268.45 pounds, angle $\approx 23.9°$ 44. (a) path = $\langle 230, 40 \rangle$ (b) aim $11.5°$ south of east

46. (a) You are 19.6 miles from home   (b) You should hike in the direction $34.6°$ west of south

47. (a) The tension in each rope is 90.45 pounds.

    (b) The tension in the short rope is 97.1 pounds, The tension in the long rope is 59.2 pounds.

11.2 Selected Answers

13. dist(A,B)= $\sqrt{5}$, dist(A,C)= $\sqrt{11}$, dist(A,d)= 5, dist(B,C)= $\sqrt{6}$, dist(B,D)= $\sqrt{8}$, dist(C,D)= $\sqrt{18}$
    No three of these points are colinear.

15. dist(A,B)= 6, dist(A,C)= 3, dist(A,d)= $\sqrt{6}$, dist(B,C)= 9, dist(B,D)= $\sqrt{50}$, dist(C,D)= $\sqrt{11}$
    The points A, B, and C are colinear.

17. corners: (1,2,3), (4,2,3), (4,4,3), (4,4,1), (1,4,1). volume = (3)(2)(2) = 12

19. corners: (1,4,0), (1,5,0), (4,4,0), (4,4,3), (4,5,3). volume = (3)(1)(3) = 9

25. $(x-4)^2 + (y-3)^2 + (z-5)^2 = 9$ 26. $x^2 + (y-3)^2 + (z-6)^2 = 4$

27. $(x-5)^2 + (y-1)^2 + z^2 = 25$ 29. center (3, -4, 1), radius = 4

30. center (-2, 0, 4), radius = 5   31. center (2, 3, 4), radius = 10

33. empty set (no intersection), a point, a line   34. empty set (no intersection), a line, a plane

35. empty set (no intersection), a point, a circle   36. empty set (no intersection), a point, a circle, a sphere

45. (a) $\dfrac{16\pi}{3}$ (for half sphere)   (b) $\dfrac{8\pi}{3}$ (for quarter sphere)   (c) $\dfrac{4\pi}{3}$ (for 1/8 sphere)

46. (a) 18π (b) 9π (c) $\dfrac{9\pi}{2}$

S1. (1, 2, 0) on xy-plane, (1, 0, 3) on xz-plane, (0, 2, 3) on yz-plane

S2. (4, 1, 0) on xy-plane, (4, 0, 2) on xz-plane, (0, 1, 2) on yz-plane

S3. (a, b, 0) on xy-plane, (a, 0, c) on xz-plane, (0, b, c) on yz-plane

S4. (4, 2, 0) to (1, 3, 0) on xy-plane, (4, 0, 1) to (1, 0, 3) on xz-plane, (0, 2, 1) to (0, 3, 3) on yz-plane

S7. xy-plane: line segment from (0,0,0) to (4,0,0). yz-plane: line segment from (0,0,0) to (0,0,3).
    xz-plane: triangle with vertices (0,0,0), (4,0,3), and (4,0,2)

S8. xy-plane: triangle with vertices (1,2,0), (4,3,0), and (2,3,0)
    xz-plane: triangle with vertices (1,0,3), (4,0,1), and (2,0,4)
    yz-plane: triangle with vertices (0,2,3), (0,3,1), and (0,3,4)

S10. (a) 0   (b) 10   S11. (a) 0   (b) 12

11.3 Selected Answers

5. $\mathbf{W} = \langle 6, -3, 18 \rangle$, $|\mathbf{U}| = 7$, $|\mathbf{V}| = 11$, $|\mathbf{W}| = \sqrt{369} \approx 19.21$

    { dir. of $\mathbf{U}$} = $\mathbf{U}/|\mathbf{U}|$ = $\langle 2/7, 3/7, 6/7 \rangle$, { dir. of $\mathbf{V}$} = $\mathbf{V}/|\mathbf{V}|$ = $\langle 2/11, -9/11, 6/11 \rangle$

    { dir. of $\mathbf{W}$} = $\mathbf{W}/|\mathbf{W}|$ = $\langle 6/\sqrt{369}, -3/\sqrt{369}, 18/\sqrt{369} \rangle \approx \langle 0.31, -0.16, 0.94 \rangle$

7. $\mathbf{W} = \langle 14, -3, 32 \rangle$, $|\mathbf{U}| = 15$, $|\mathbf{V}| = 9$, $|\mathbf{W}| = \sqrt{1229} \approx 35.06$

    { dir. of $\mathbf{U}$} = $\mathbf{U}/|\mathbf{U}|$ = $\langle 5/15, 2/15, 14/15 \rangle$, { dir. of $\mathbf{V}$} = $\mathbf{V}/|\mathbf{V}|$ = $\langle 4/9, -7/9, 4/9 \rangle$

    { dir. of $\mathbf{W}$} = $\mathbf{W}/|\mathbf{W}|$ = $\langle 14/\sqrt{1229}, -3/\sqrt{1229}, 32/\sqrt{1229} \rangle \approx \langle 0.40, -0.09, 0.91 \rangle$

9. $\mathbf{W} = \langle 21, 18, -2 \rangle$, $|\mathbf{U}| = 11$, $|\mathbf{V}| = 9$, $|\mathbf{W}| = \sqrt{769} \approx 27.73$

    { dir. of $\mathbf{U}$} = $\mathbf{U}/|\mathbf{U}|$ = $\langle 9/11, 6/11, 2/11 \rangle$, { dir. of $\mathbf{V}$} = $\mathbf{V}/|\mathbf{V}|$ = $\langle 1/3, 2/3, -2/3 \rangle$

    { dir. of $\mathbf{W}$} = $\mathbf{W}/|\mathbf{W}|$ = $\langle 21/\sqrt{769}, 18/\sqrt{769}, -2/\sqrt{769} \rangle \approx \langle 0.76, 0.65, -0.07 \rangle$

11. $\mathbf{W} = \langle 26, 25, -2 \rangle$, $|\mathbf{U}| = 15$, $|\mathbf{V}| = 9$, $|\mathbf{W}| = \sqrt{1305} \approx 36.12$

    { dir. of $\mathbf{U}$} = $\mathbf{U}/|\mathbf{U}|$ = $\langle 10/15, 11/15, 2/15 \rangle$, { dir. of $\mathbf{V}$} = $\mathbf{V}/|\mathbf{V}|$ = $\langle 2/3, 1/3, -2/3 \rangle$

    { dir. of $\mathbf{W}$} = $\mathbf{W}/|\mathbf{W}|$ = $\langle 26/\sqrt{1305}, 25/\sqrt{1305}, -2/\sqrt{1305} \rangle \approx \langle 0.72, 0.69, -0.06 \rangle$

13. $\mathbf{C} = \langle -8, -6, 6 \rangle$ 14. $\mathbf{C} = \langle 4, 1, -4 \rangle$ 15. $\mathbf{C} = \langle -3-e, -9-\pi, -1 \rangle$

17. smallest magnitude is $\mathbf{C}$, largest magnitude is $\mathbf{D}$
18. smallest magnitude is $\mathbf{D}$, largest magnitude is $\mathbf{C}$

23. $\langle 0, 1, 0 \rangle$, $\langle 0, 0, 1 \rangle$, $\langle 0, 3, -4 \rangle$ are all perpendicular to $\mathbf{A}$ as is ever non-zero vector with x-coordinate equal to 0 (= vectors that lie in the yz-plane). There are an infinite number of nonparallel vectors that are perpendicular to $\mathbf{A}$.

24. $\langle 1, 0, 0 \rangle$, $\langle 0, 3, 0 \rangle$, $\langle 5, -4, 0 \rangle$ are all perpendicular to $\mathbf{B}$ as is ever non-zero vector with z-coordinate equal to 0 (= vectors that lie in the xy-plane). There are an infinite number of nonparallel vectors that are perpendicular to $\mathbf{B}$.

25. $\langle 0, 0, 2 \rangle$, $\langle -2, 1, 0 \rangle$, $\langle 2, -1, 7 \rangle$ are all perpendicular to $\mathbf{C}$. There are an infinite number of nonparallel vectors that are perpendicular to $\mathbf{C}$.

31. $x(t) = 3 + 4t$, $y(t) = 5 - t$, $z(t) = 1$
32. $x(t) = 1 + 4t$, $y(t) = 2 - 2t$, $z(t) = 3 + 2t$
33. $x(t) = 2 + 3t$, $y(t) = 3$, $z(t) = 6 - 5t$

11.4 Selected Answers

1. $A \cdot B = 3$, $B \cdot A = 3$, $A \cdot A = 14$, $A \cdot (B+A) = 17$, and $(2A+3B) \cdot (A - 2B) = -101$

2. $A \cdot B = 2$, $B \cdot A = 2$, $A \cdot A = 41$, $A \cdot (B+A) = 43$, and $(2A+3B) \cdot (A - 2B) = -94$

3. $U \cdot V = 2$, $U \cdot U = 41$, $U \cdot i = 6$, $U \cdot j = -1$, $U \cdot k = 2$, and $(V + k) \cdot U = 8$

4. $U \cdot V = 0$, $U \cdot U = 22$, $V \cdot i = 2$, $V \cdot j = 4$, $V \cdot k = -3$, and $(V + k) \cdot U = 2$

5. $S \cdot T = -3$, $T \cdot U = -4$, $T \cdot T = 35$, $(S + T) \cdot (S - T) = -14$, and $(S \cdot T)U = \langle -3, -9, -6 \rangle$

7. angle between **A** and **B** is 1.39 ($\approx 79.9^o$), angle between **A** and x-axis is 1.30 ($\approx 74.5^o$)
    angle between **A** and y-axis is 1.01 ($\approx 57.7^o$), angle between **A** and z-axis is 0.641 ($\approx 36.7^o$)

9. angle between **U** and **V** is 1.51 ($\approx 86.7^o$), angle between **U** and x-axis is 0.36 ($\approx 20.4^o$)
    angle between **U** and y-axis is 1.73 ($\approx 98.98^o$), angle between **U** and z-axis is 1.25 ($\approx 71.8^o$)

11. angle between **S** and **T** is 1.68 ($\approx 96.3^o$), angle between **S** and x-axis is 1.12 ($\approx 64.1^o$)
    angle between **S** and y-axis is 2.63 ($\approx 150.5^o$), angle between **S** and z-axis is 1.35 ($\approx 77.4^o$)

13. angle between **A** and **B** is 1.57 ($\approx 90^o$), angle between **A** and x-axis is 1.24 ($\approx 71.1^o$)
    angle between **A** and y-axis is 2.08 ($\approx 119.1^o$), angle between **A** and z-axis is 0.624 ($\approx 35.8^o$)

15. angle between **A** and **B** is 2.59 ($\approx 148.7^o$), angle between **A** and x-axis is 0.38 ($\approx 21.8^o$)
    angle between **A** and y-axis is 1.95 ($\approx 111.8^o$), angle between **A** and z-axis is 1.57 ($\approx 90^o$)

17. angle between **U** and **V** is 1.43 ($\approx 81.9^o$), angle between **U** and x-axis is 1.25 ($\approx 71.6^o$)
    angle between **U** and y-axis is 1.57 ($\approx 90^o$), angle between **U** and z-axis is 0.322 ($\approx 18.4^o$)

19. 0.124 ($\approx 7.13^o$)   20. 2.48 ($\approx 142.1^o$)   21. 0.785 ($\approx 45^o$)

22. 1.23 ($\approx 70.5^o$)   23. 0.897 ($\approx 51.4^o$)   24. 0 ($= 0^o$)

25. 0 ($= 0^o$)   26. 1.57 ($\approx 90^o$)   27. 0.32 ($\approx 18.4^o$)

29. $N = \langle -2, -1, 0 \rangle$ is one correct answer.   30. $N = \langle 3, 0, 5 \rangle$ is one correct answer.

31. $N = \langle 3, -7 \rangle$ is one correct answer.   32. $N = \langle 3, 7 \rangle$ is one correct answer.

33. $N = \langle -1, 1, 1 \rangle$ is one correct answer.   34. $N = \langle -5, 0, 1 \rangle$ is one correct answer.

36. $N = \langle 0, 2, -3 \rangle$ is one correct answer.   37. $N = \langle 1, 1, 2 \rangle$ is one correct answer.

38. $N = \langle 1, 0, 6 \rangle$ is one correct answer.   39. $N = \langle 3, 2 \rangle$ is one correct answer.

40. $N = \langle -2, 3 \rangle$ is one correct answer.   41. $N = \langle 2, 3 \rangle$ is one correct answer.

43. $\mathbf{N} = \langle 3, 2 \rangle$ is one correct answer.   45. $\mathbf{N} = \langle 1, -4 \rangle$ is one correct answer.

46. $\mathbf{N} = \langle 5, 1 \rangle$ is one correct answer.   47. $\mathbf{N} = \langle 0, 3 \rangle$ is one correct answer.

57. $\text{Proj}_\mathbf{B} \mathbf{A} = \langle 25/34, 0, -15/34 \rangle$, $\text{Proj}_\mathbf{A} \mathbf{B} = \langle -1, 2, 0 \rangle$

59. $\text{Proj}_\mathbf{B} \mathbf{A} = \langle 0,0,0 \rangle$, $\text{Proj}_\mathbf{A} \mathbf{B} = \langle 0,0,0 \rangle$. **A** and **B** are perpendicular.

61. $\text{Proj}_\mathbf{B} \mathbf{A} = \langle 0,0,0 \rangle$, $\text{Proj}_\mathbf{A} \mathbf{B} = \langle 0,0,0 \rangle$. **A** and **B** are perpendicular.

63. $\text{Proj}_\mathbf{B} \mathbf{A} = \langle 0,-2,0 \rangle$, $\text{Proj}_\mathbf{A} \mathbf{B} = \langle -1/7, 2/7, -3/7 \rangle$

65. $|\text{Proj}_\mathbf{B} \mathbf{A}| = \left| \dfrac{\mathbf{A} \cdot \mathbf{B}}{|\mathbf{B}|} \right|$, $\text{Proj}_\mathbf{A} \mathbf{B} = \left| \dfrac{\mathbf{A} \cdot \mathbf{B}}{|\mathbf{A}|} \right| = \left| \dfrac{\mathbf{A} \cdot \mathbf{B}}{3|\mathbf{B}|} \right| = \dfrac{1}{3} \left| \dfrac{\mathbf{A} \cdot \mathbf{B}}{|\mathbf{B}|} \right|$. $|\text{Proj}_\mathbf{B} \mathbf{A}|$ is larger.

67. distance is $3/\sqrt{2} \approx 2.12$ 68. distance is 3.88   69. distance is 3.06

70. distance is 0.95   71. distance is 1.40

73. distance is 15.4 feet   74. distance is 27.76 inches   75. 9.18 m

77. work $= \dfrac{5000}{\sqrt{141}} \approx 421$ foot-pounds   78. work = 842 foot-pounds

79. work = 480 foot-pounds   80. work = 240 foot-pounds

81. work = 1212.1 foot-pounds   82. A work = 2349 ft-lbs, B work = 2441 ft-lbs

83. $\mathbf{A} \bullet \mathbf{B} = 15$, angle ≈ 1.05 ($= 60^\circ$)   84. $\mathbf{A} \bullet \mathbf{B} = 16$, angle ≈ 1.21 ($\approx 69.3^\circ$)

85. angle $\approx 112^\circ$, "different"   86. angle $\approx 19.9^\circ$, "very alike"

87. angle $\approx 9.45^\circ$, "very alike"   88. angle $= 90^\circ$, "different"

11.5 Selected Answers

1. 7
2. 7
3. $2x - 5y$
4. $15 - ab$
5. 1
6. -1
7. -6
8. -42
9. $x + 7y - 5z$
10. $4a + 10b - 6c$
11. -77
12. $3x - 3x^2$

13. (a) $\langle -10, -5, 10 \rangle$ (b) 0 (c) 0 (d) 15

15. (a) $\langle -24, -8, 0 \rangle$ (b) 0 (c) 0 (d) $\sqrt{640}$

17. (a) $\langle 3, -11, -5 \rangle$ (b) 0 (c) 0 (d) ≈ 12.45

19. scalar
20. not defined
21. not defined
22. not defined

25. The angle between a vector **A** and itself is 0 so **AxA** = |**A**| |**A**| sin(0) = 0. Alternately, | **AxA** | = the area of the parallelogram determined by **A** and **A**, and that area is 0.

26. | **AxB** | = |**A**| |**B**| | sin(θ) | which is maximum when | sin(θ) | = 1, and | sin(θ) | = 1 when $\theta = \pm\pi/2$.

31. (a) torque = **AxB** = $\langle 12\cos(-30^o), 12\sin(-30^o), 0 \rangle \times \langle 0, 70, 0 \rangle$

   = $\{840\cos(-30^o)\}\mathbf{k} \approx 727.46\mathbf{k}$ inch-pounds

   (b) torque = **AxB** = $\langle 8\cos(-30^o), 8\sin(-30^o), 0 \rangle \times \langle 20\cos(40^o), 20\sin(40^o), 0 \rangle$

   = $\{160\cos(-30^o)\sin(40^o) - 160\sin(-30^o)\cos(40^o)\}\mathbf{k} \approx 150.35\mathbf{k}$ inch-pounds

33. Yes. {torque on **A** by **B**} + {torque on **A** by **C**} = **AxB** + **AxC** = **Ax**(**B**+**C**) = {torque on **A** by (**B**+**C**)}

34. parallelogram area = | **AxB** | = 18 , triangle area = 9

35. parallelogram area = | **AxB** | = 6 , triangle area = 3

37. triangle area = $\dfrac{\sqrt{180}}{2} \approx 6.71$

38. triangle area = $\dfrac{\sqrt{(bc)^2 + (ac)^2 + (ab)^2}}{2}$

39. parallelpiped volume = | (**AxB**)•**C** | = 17
40. parallelpiped volume = | (**AxB**)•**C** | = 78

41. parallelpiped volume = | (**AxB**)•**C** | = |a|·|b|·|c| = | abc | cubic units

42. tetrahedron volume = $\dfrac{1}{6}$| 36**k** | = 6 cubic units
43. tetrahedron volume = $\dfrac{15}{6}$ cubic units

44. tetrahedron volume = 8 cubic units
45. tetrahedron volume = $\dfrac{|\ abc\ |}{6}$ cubic units

47. $A_{xy} = 4$, $A_{xz} = 4$, $A_{yz} = 8$, and $A_{xyz} = \sqrt{96}$
48. $A_{xy} = 4$, $A_{xz} = 6$, $A_{yz} = 12$, and $A_{xyz} = \sqrt{196} = 14$

11.6 Selected Answers

1. $x(t) = 2 + 3t$, $y(t) = -3 + 4t$, $z(t) = 1 + 2t$

3. $x(t) = -2 + 5t$, $y(t) = 1$, $z(t) = 4 - 3t$

5. $x(t) = 2 + t$, $y(t) = -1 + 5t$, $z(t) = 3 - 5t$

7. $x(t) = 3$, $y(t) = -2 + 6t$, $z(t) = 1 - 2t$

9. Lines intersect at the point $(2, -1, 3)$ when $t = 0$, $\theta = \arccos\left(\dfrac{9}{\sqrt{6}\sqrt{21}}\right) \approx \arccos(0.802) \approx 0.604\ (\approx 36.7°)$

11. $L(0) = (1, 5, -2) = K(-2\_)$. The lines intersect at the point $(1, 5, -2)$.
    $\theta = \arccos\left(\dfrac{18}{5\sqrt{14}}\right) \approx \arccos(0.962) \approx 0.277\ (\approx 15.8°)$

13. $5(x-2) + (-2)(y-3) + 4(z-1) = 0$ or $5x - 2y + 4z = 8$

14. $3x + y - 5z = 22$

15. $0(x+3) + 3(y-5) + 0(z-6) = 0$ or $3y = 15$

16. $2x - 2y + z = 0$

17. $(-6)(x-1) + (-6)(y-2) + (-12)(z-3) = 0$ or $x + y + 2z = 9$

18. $y = 5$

19. $20x + 28y + 25z = 101$

20. $-x + 2y - z = 0$

21. $z = 7$

22. $x = 2$

23. $3x - 2y + 5z = 23$

24. $2x + 3y - z = 0$

25. $5x - 3y + 2z = 23$

26. $y = 7$

27. They intersect along the y-axis

29. Plane intersects the x-axis at $x=10$

31. They intersect at the point $(4, 2, 1)$

32. y-axis never intersects the plane $z = 3$

33. $x(t) = -26 + t$, $y(t) -57 + 3t$, $z(t) = t$. $\mathbf{N_1} = \langle 4, -2, 2\rangle$, $\mathbf{N_2} = \langle 3, -2, 3\rangle$
    $\theta = \arccos\left(\dfrac{22}{\sqrt{24}\sqrt{22}}\right) \approx \arccos(0.957) \approx 0.294\ (\approx 16.8°)$

34. $x(t) = 9 + 6t$, $y^*(t) = -9t$, $z(t) = t$. $\theta \approx 1.066\ (\approx 61.1°)$

35. $x(t) = 12 - \dfrac{22}{5}t$, $y(t) = 2 + \dfrac{1}{5}t$, $z(t) = t$. $\mathbf{N_1} = \langle 0, 5, -1\rangle$, $\mathbf{N_2} = \langle 1, 2, 4\rangle$
    $\theta = \arccos\left(\dfrac{6}{\sqrt{26}\sqrt{21}}\right) \approx 1.311\ (\approx 75.1°)$

37. They intersect at the point $(-11/3, -1/3, -58/3)$. $\arccos\left(\dfrac{3}{\sqrt{30}\sqrt{21}}\right) \approx 1.451\ (\approx 83.1°)$ so the angle of intersection is $\theta = \pi/2 - 1.451 \approx 0.120\ (\approx 6.9°)$

38. They intersect at the point $(0, 6, -7)$. Angle of intersection is approximately $0.222\ (\approx 12.7°)$

39. They intersect at the point $(0, 8, 5)$. Angle of intersection is approximately $0.271\ (\approx 15.5°)$

41. Yes

42. Yes

43. $x(t) = -7t$, $y(t) = 4t$, $z(t) = 3 + 9t$

44. (a) $\approx 1.30\ (\approx 74.5°)$ (b) $\approx 1.01\ (\approx 57.7°)$ (c) $\approx 0.64\ (\approx 36.7°)$

45. $\theta = \arccos\left(\dfrac{a}{\sqrt{a^2+b^2+c^2}}\right)$ with the xy-plane. $\theta = \arccos\left(\dfrac{b}{\sqrt{a^2+b^2+c^2}}\right)$ with the xz-plane.

$\theta = \arccos\left(\dfrac{c}{\sqrt{a^2+b^2+c^2}}\right)$ with the yz-plane.

47. (a) $\theta = \arctan(481/378) \approx 0.905$ ($\approx 51.8°$) (b) $\cos(\varphi) \approx 0.382$ so $\varphi \approx 1.179$ ($\approx 84.8°$)

(c) $\alpha = \arctan(481/534.6) \approx 0.733$ ($\approx 42.0°$)

51. distance ≈ 4.879 52. distance ≈ 2.145 53. distance ≈ 1.18 54. distance ≈ 6.164

55. distance ≈ 1.32 56. distance ≈ 1.35

57. (a) The objects "crash" at the point (15, 24, 13) when t=6. (b) Paths intersect fo {min. dist.} = 0

(c) No, the objects crash, and their paths intersect.

58. (a) The objects "crash" at the point (2, 3, 4) when t=3.

59. (a) The objects do not crash. They are never at the same point at the same time.

(b) The paths of the objects intersect: object A is at (0,1,5) when t=1 and B is at (0,1,5) when t=2.

(c) {minimum distance between objects} ≈ 0.85 , {min. distance between paths} = 0 since paths intersect.

61. (a) The objects do not crash. They are never at the same point at the same time.

(b) The paths of the objects do not intersect.

(c) {minimum distance between objects} ≈ 2.79 , {min. distance between paths} = 1

63. (a) Shortest distance between the airplane and the car is $\sqrt{58} \approx 7.62$.

(b) Shortest distance between paths is $13/\sqrt{5} \approx 5.81$.

11.7 Selected Answers

1. $\mathbf{V} = \langle 2, -1 \rangle$, $\mathbf{N} = \langle 3, 1 \rangle$, $\text{Proj}_\mathbf{N}\mathbf{V} = \left\langle \dfrac{3}{2}, \dfrac{1}{2} \right\rangle$, $\mathbf{R} = \mathbf{V} - 2\cdot\text{Proj}_\mathbf{N}\mathbf{V} = \langle -1, -2 \rangle$.

Point is (1, 3) and the line is $x(t) = 1 - t$, $y(t) = 3 - 2t$.

2. $\mathbf{V} = \langle -1, 1 \rangle$, $\mathbf{N} = \langle 3, 1 \rangle$, $\text{Proj}_\mathbf{N}\mathbf{V} = \left\langle -\dfrac{3}{5}, -\dfrac{1}{5} \right\rangle$, $\mathbf{R} = \left\langle \dfrac{1}{5}, \dfrac{7}{5} \right\rangle$.

Point is (1, 3) and the line is $x(t) = 1 + \dfrac{1}{5}t$, $y(t) = 3 + \dfrac{7}{5}t$.

Prob. 1

3. $\mathbf{V} = \langle 2, 3 \rangle$, $\mathbf{N} = \langle 5, -2 \rangle$, $\text{Proj}_{\mathbf{N}}\mathbf{V} = \langle \frac{20}{29}, -\frac{8}{29} \rangle$, $\mathbf{R} = \mathbf{V} - 2\cdot\text{Proj}_{\mathbf{N}}\mathbf{V} = \langle \frac{18}{29}, \frac{103}{29} \rangle$.

    Point is $(3, 4)$ and the line is $x(t) = 3 + \frac{18}{29}t$, $y(t) = 4 + \frac{103}{29}t$.

4. $\mathbf{V} = \langle 0, -2 \rangle$, $\mathbf{N} = \langle 5, -2 \rangle$, $\text{Proj}_{\mathbf{N}}\mathbf{V} = \langle \frac{20}{29}, -\frac{8}{29} \rangle$, $\mathbf{R} = \langle -\frac{40}{29}, -\frac{42}{29} \rangle$.

    Point is $(3, 4)$ and the line is $x(t) = 3 - \frac{40}{29}t$, $y(t) = 4 - \frac{42}{29}t$.

Prob. 3

5. $\mathbf{V} = \langle -3, 2 \rangle$, $\mathbf{N} = \langle 1, 0 \rangle$, $\text{Proj}_{\mathbf{N}}\mathbf{V} = \langle -3, 0 \rangle$, $\mathbf{R} = \mathbf{V} - 2\cdot\text{Proj}_{\mathbf{N}}\mathbf{V} = \langle 3, 2 \rangle$.

    Point is $(0, 3)$ and the line is $x(t) = 3t$, $y(t) = 3 + 2t$.

6. $\mathbf{V} = \langle 3, -1 \rangle$, $\mathbf{N} = \langle 0, 1 \rangle$, $\text{Proj}_{\mathbf{N}}\mathbf{V} = \langle 0, -1 \rangle$, $\mathbf{R} = \langle 3, 2 \rangle$.

    Point is $(2, 0)$ and the line is $x(t) = 2 + 3t$, $y(t) = 2t$.

Prob. 7

7. $\mathbf{V} = \langle -3, 1 \rangle$, $\mathbf{N} = \langle -0.622, -1.567 \rangle$, $\text{Proj}_{\mathbf{N}}\mathbf{V} = \langle -0.065, -0.164 \rangle$,

    $\mathbf{R} = \mathbf{V} - 2\cdot\text{Proj}_{\mathbf{N}}\mathbf{V} = \langle -2.869, 1.329 \rangle$. Point is $(1.243, 0.783)$ and the

    line is $x(t) = 1.243 - 2.869t$, $y(t) = 0.783 + 1.329t$.

8. $\mathbf{V} = \langle 2, 1 \rangle$, $\mathbf{N} = $, $\text{Proj}_{\mathbf{N}}\mathbf{V} = \langle 0.165, 1.550 \rangle$, $\mathbf{R} = \langle 0.770, -2.099 \rangle$.

    Point is $(1.243, 0.783)$ and the line is $x(t) = 1.243 + 0.770t$,

    $y(t) = 0.783 - 2.099t$.

Prob. 9

9. $\mathbf{V} = \langle 2, 1 \rangle$, $\mathbf{N} = \langle -12, 4 \rangle$, $\text{Proj}_{\mathbf{N}}\mathbf{V} = \langle 1.5, -0.5 \rangle$,

    $\mathbf{R} = \mathbf{V} - 2\cdot\text{Proj}_{\mathbf{N}}\mathbf{V} = \langle -1, 2 \rangle$. Point is $(4, 8)$ and the line is $x(t) = 4 - t$, $y(t) = 8 + 2t$.

10. $\mathbf{V} = \langle -1, 1 \rangle$, $\mathbf{N} = \langle -12, 4 \rangle$, $\text{Proj}_{\mathbf{N}}\mathbf{V} = \langle -1.2, 0.4 \rangle$, $\mathbf{R} = \langle 1.4, 0.2 \rangle$.

    Point is $(4, 8)$ and the line is $x(t) = 4 + 1.4t$, $y(t) = 8 + 0.2t$.

11. $\mathbf{V} = \langle -1, 1 \rangle$, $\mathbf{N} = \langle -4, 1 \rangle$, $\text{Proj}_{\mathbf{N}}\mathbf{V} = \langle -1.176, 0.294 \rangle$, $\mathbf{R} = \mathbf{V} - 2\cdot\text{Proj}_{\mathbf{N}}\mathbf{V} = \langle 1.353, 0.412 \rangle$.

    Point is $(2, 4)$ and the line is $x(t) = 2 + 1.353t$, $y(t) = 4 + 0.412t$.

12. $\mathbf{V} = \langle 2, 1 \rangle$, $\mathbf{N} = \langle -4, 1 \rangle$, $\text{Proj}_{\mathbf{N}}\mathbf{V} = \langle 1.647, -0.412 \rangle$, $\mathbf{R} = \langle -1.294, 1.824 \rangle$.

    Point is $(2, 4)$ and the line is $x(t) = 2 - 1.294t$, $y(t) = 4 + 1.824t$.

Prob. 11

13. $\mathbf{V} = \langle 2, 6, 3 \rangle$, $\mathbf{N} = \langle 1, 2, 3 \rangle$, $\text{Proj}_\mathbf{N}\mathbf{V} = \left\langle \frac{23}{14}, \frac{23}{7}, \frac{69}{14} \right\rangle$,

    $\mathbf{R} = \mathbf{V} - 2\cdot\text{Proj}_\mathbf{N}\mathbf{V} = \left\langle -\frac{9}{7}, -\frac{4}{7}, -\frac{48}{7} \right\rangle$. Point is $(2, 4, 1)$ and the

    line is $x(t) = 2 - \frac{9}{7}t$, $y(t) = 4 - \frac{4}{7}t$, $z(t) = 1 - \frac{48}{7}t$.

Prob. 13

14. $\mathbf{V} = \langle 4, 1, 3 \rangle$, $\mathbf{N} = \langle 3, -2, 4 \rangle$, $\text{Proj}_\mathbf{N}\mathbf{V} = \left\langle \frac{66}{29}, -\frac{44}{29}, \frac{88}{29} \right\rangle$,

    $\mathbf{R} = \left\langle -\frac{16}{29}, \frac{117}{29}, -\frac{89}{29} \right\rangle$.

    Point is $(1, 3, 2)$ and the line is $x(t) = 1 - \frac{16}{29}t$, $y(t) = 3 + \frac{117}{29}t$, $z(t) = 2 - \frac{89}{29}t$.

15. $\mathbf{V} = \langle 3, 2, 1 \rangle$, $\mathbf{N} = \langle 1, 0, 0 \rangle$, $\text{Proj}_\mathbf{N}\mathbf{V} = \langle 3, 0, 0 \rangle$,

    $\mathbf{R} = \mathbf{V} - 2\cdot\text{Proj}_\mathbf{N}\mathbf{V} = \langle -3, 2, 1 \rangle$.

    Point is $(0, 4, 2)$ and line is $x(t) = -3t$, $y(t) = 4 + 2t$, $z(t) = 2 + t$

Prob. 14

16. $\mathbf{V} = \langle 2, -3, -1 \rangle$, $\mathbf{N} = \langle 0, 0, 1 \rangle$, $\text{Proj}_\mathbf{N}\mathbf{V} = \langle 0, 0, -1 \rangle$, $\mathbf{R} = \langle 2, -3, 1 \rangle$.

    Point is $(2, -3, -1)$ and line is $x(t) = 2 + 2t$, $y(t) = -3 - 3t$, $z(t) = -1 + t$.

TRIGONOMETRY FACTS

Right Angle Trigonometry

$$\sin(\theta) = \frac{\text{opp}}{\text{hyp}} \qquad \cos(\theta) = \frac{\text{adj}}{\text{hyp}}$$

$$\tan(\theta) = \frac{\text{opp}}{\text{adj}} \qquad \cot(\theta) = \frac{\text{adj}}{\text{opp}} \qquad \sec(\theta) = \frac{\text{hyp}}{\text{adj}} \qquad \csc(\theta) = \frac{\text{hyp}}{\text{opp}}$$

Trigonometric Functions

$$\sin(\theta) = \frac{y}{r} \qquad \cos(\theta) = \frac{x}{r}$$

$$\tan(\theta) = \frac{y}{x} \qquad \cot(\theta) = \frac{x}{y} \qquad \sec(\theta) = \frac{r}{x} \qquad \csc(\theta) = \frac{r}{y}$$

Fundamental Identities

$$\tan(\theta) = \frac{\sin(\theta)}{\cos(\theta)} \qquad \cot(\theta) = \frac{\cos(\theta)}{\sin(\theta)} \qquad \sec(\theta) = \frac{1}{\cos(\theta)} \qquad \csc(\theta) = \frac{1}{\sin(\theta)}$$

$$\sin^2(\theta) + \cos^2(\theta) = 1 \qquad \tan^2(\theta) + 1 = \sec^2(\theta) \qquad 1 + \cot^2(\theta) = \csc^2(\theta)$$

$$\sin(-\theta) = -\sin(\theta) \qquad \cos(-\theta) = \cos(\theta) \qquad \tan(-\theta) = -\tan(\theta)$$

$$\sin(\tfrac{\pi}{2} - \theta) = \cos(\theta) \qquad \cos(\tfrac{\pi}{2} - \theta) = \sin(\theta) \qquad \tan(\tfrac{\pi}{2} - \theta) = \cot(\theta)$$

Law of Sines: $\dfrac{\sin(A)}{a} = \dfrac{\sin(B)}{b} = \dfrac{\sin(C)}{c}$

Law of Cosines: $a^2 = b^2 + c^2 - 2bc\cdot\cos(A)$
$b^2 = a^2 + c^2 - 2ac\cdot\cos(B)$
$c^2 = a^2 + b^2 - 2ab\cdot\cos(C)$

Angle Addition and Subtraction Formulas

$\sin(x+y) = \sin(x)\cdot\cos(y) + \cos(x)\cdot\sin(y)$ $\qquad \sin(x-y) = \sin(x)\cdot\cos(y) - \cos(x)\cdot\sin(y)$

$\cos(x+y) = \cos(x)\cdot\cos(y) - \sin(x)\cdot\sin(y)$ $\qquad \cos(x-y) = \cos(x)\cdot\cos(y) + \sin(x)\cdot\sin(y)$

$\tan(x+y) = \dfrac{\tan(x) + \tan(y)}{1 - \tan(x)\cdot\tan(y)}$ $\qquad \tan(x-y) = \dfrac{\tan(x) - \tan(y)}{1 + \tan(x)\cdot\tan(y)}$

Function Product Formulas

$\sin(x)\cdot\sin(y) = \tfrac{1}{2}\cos(x-y) - \tfrac{1}{2}\cos(x+y)$

$\cos(x)\cdot\cos(y) = \tfrac{1}{2}\cos(x-y) + \tfrac{1}{2}\cos(x+y)$

$\sin(x)\cdot\cos(y) = \tfrac{1}{2}\sin(x+y) + \tfrac{1}{2}\sin(x-y)$

Function Sum Formulas

$\sin(x) + \sin(y) = 2\sin(\tfrac{x+y}{2})\cdot\cos(\tfrac{x-y}{2})$

$\cos(x) + \cos(y) = 2\cos(\tfrac{x+y}{2})\cdot\cos(\tfrac{x-y}{2})$

$\tan(x) + \tan(y) = \dfrac{\sin(x+y)}{\cos(x)\cdot\cos(y)}$

Double Angle Formulas

$\sin(2x) = 2\sin(x)\cdot\cos(x)$

$\cos(2x) = \cos^2(x) - \sin^2(x) = 2\cos^2(x) - 1$

$\tan(2x) = \dfrac{2\tan(x)}{1 - \tan^2(x)}$

Half Angle Formulas

$\sin(\tfrac{x}{2}) = \pm\sqrt{\tfrac{1}{2}(1 - \cos(x))}$ $\qquad \pm$ depends on

$\cos(\tfrac{x}{2}) = \pm\sqrt{\tfrac{1}{2}(1 + \cos(x))}$ $\qquad$ quadrant of x/2

$\tan(\tfrac{x}{2}) = \dfrac{1 - \cos(x)}{\sin(x)}$

Calculus Reference Facts

Derivatives

Notation: $D(f) = Df$ represents the derivative with respect to x of the function $f(x)$

$$D(f) = Df = \frac{d}{dx} f(x) = f'(x)$$

$D(k) = 0$ k a constant $D(f+g) = Df + Dg$ $D(f \cdot g) = f \cdot Dg + g \cdot Df$

$D(k \cdot f) = k \cdot Df$ k a constant $D(f-g) = Df - Dg$ $D(f/g) = \dfrac{g \cdot Df - f \cdot Dg}{g^2}$

$D(f^n) = n f^{n-1} \cdot Df$

$D(f(g(x))) = f'(g(x)) \cdot Dg$ (Chain Rule)

$D(\sin(f)) = \cos(f) \cdot Df$ $D(\tan(f)) = \sec^2(f) \cdot Df$ $D(\sec(f)) = \sec(f) \tan(f) \cdot Df$

$D(\cos(f)) = -\sin(f) \cdot Df$ $D(\cot(f)) = -\csc^2(f) \cdot Df$ $D(\csc(f)) = -\csc(f) \cot(f) \cdot Df$

$D(e^f) = e^f \cdot Df$ $D(a^f) = a^f \ln(a) \cdot Df$

$D(\ln|f|) = \dfrac{1}{f} \cdot Df$ Logarithmic Differentiation: $Df = f \cdot D(\ln|f|)$

$D(\log_a |f|) = \dfrac{1}{f \cdot \ln(a)} \cdot Df$

$D(\arcsin(f)) = \dfrac{1}{\sqrt{1-f^2}} \cdot Df$ $D(\arctan(f)) = \dfrac{1}{1+f^2} \cdot Df$ $D(\text{arcsec}(f)) = \dfrac{1}{|f|\sqrt{f^2-1}} \cdot Df$

$D(\arccos(f)) = \dfrac{-1}{\sqrt{1-f^2}} \cdot Df$ $D(\text{arccot}(f)) = \dfrac{-1}{1+f^2} \cdot Df$ $D(\text{arccsc}(f)) = \dfrac{-1}{|f|\sqrt{f^2-1}} \cdot Df$

Integrals — General Properties

$\displaystyle\int k \cdot f \, dx = k \cdot \int f \, dx$ $\displaystyle\int (f-g) \, dx = \int f \, dx - \int g \, dx$

$\displaystyle\int (f+g) \, dx = \int f \, dx + \int g \, dx$ $\displaystyle\int f \cdot (g') \, dx = f \cdot g - \int g \cdot (f') \, dx$

Calculus Reference Facts

Integrals — Particular Functions

1. $\int k\, dx = k\cdot x + C$

2. $\int x^n\, dx = \frac{1}{n+1}\cdot x^{n+1} + C \quad \text{if } n \neq -1 \qquad \int x^{-1}\, dx = \int \frac{1}{x}\, dx = \ln|x| + C$

3. $\int (ax+b)^n\, dx = \frac{1}{n+1}\cdot\frac{1}{a}\cdot(ax+b)^{n+1} + C \quad n \neq -1$

    (a) $\int (ax+b)^{-1}\, dx = \int \frac{1}{ax+b}\, dx = \frac{1}{a}\cdot\ln|ax+b| + C$

    (b) $\int \sqrt{ax+b}\, dx = \frac{2}{3a}\cdot(ax+b)^{3/2} + C$

    (c) $\int \frac{1}{\sqrt{ax+b}}\, dx = \frac{2}{a}\cdot(ax+b)^{1/2} + C$

4. $\int \frac{1}{x(ax+b)}\, dx = \frac{1}{b}\cdot\ln\left|\frac{x}{ax+b}\right| + C$

5. $\int \frac{1}{(x+a)(x+b)}\, dx = \frac{1}{b-a}\{\ln|x+a| - \ln|x+b|\} + C = \frac{1}{b-a}\ln\left|\frac{x+a}{x+b}\right| + C \quad a \neq b$

    (a) $\int \frac{1}{(x+a)(x+a)}\, dx = \int \frac{1}{(x+a)^2}\, dx = -\frac{1}{x+a} + C$

6. $\int x(ax+b)^n\, dx = \frac{(ax+b)^{n+1}}{a}\cdot\left\{\frac{ax+b}{n+2} - \frac{b}{n+1}\right\} + C \quad n \neq -1, -2$

    (a) $\int x(ax+b)^{-1}\, dx = \int \frac{x}{ax+b}\, dx = \frac{x}{a} - \frac{b}{a^2}\cdot\ln|ax+b| + C$

    (b) $\int x(ax+b)^{-2}\, dx = \int \frac{x}{(ax+b)^2}\, dx = \frac{1}{a^2}\cdot\left\{\ln|ax+b| + \frac{b}{ax+b}\right\} + C$

7. $\int \sin(ax)\, dx = -\frac{1}{a}\cos(ax) + C \qquad\qquad 8.\ \int \cos(ax)\, dx = \frac{1}{a}\sin(ax) + C$

9. $\int \tan(ax)\, dx = \int \frac{\sin(ax)}{\cos(ax)}\, dx = -\frac{1}{a}\ln|\cos(ax)| + C = \ln|\sec(ax)| + C$

10. $\int \cot(ax)\, dx = \int \frac{\cos(ax)}{\sin(ax)}\, dx = \frac{1}{a}\ln|\sin(x)| + C$

11. $\int \sec(ax)\, dx = \frac{1}{a}\ln|\sec(ax) + \tan(ax)| + C \qquad 12.\ \int \csc(ax)\, dx = \frac{1}{a}\ln|\csc(ax) - \cot(ax)| + C$

13. $\int \sin^2(ax)\, dx = \frac{x}{2} - \frac{\sin(2ax)}{4a} + C = \frac{x}{2} - \frac{\sin(ax)\cos(ax)}{2a} + C$

14. $\int \cos^2(ax)\,dx = \frac{x}{2} + \frac{\sin(2ax)}{4a} + C = \frac{x}{2} + \frac{\sin(ax)\cos(ax)}{2a} + C$

15. $\int \tan^2(ax)\,dx = \frac{1}{a}\tan(ax) - x + C$

16. $\int \cot^2(ax)\,dx = -\frac{1}{a}\cot(ax) - x + C$

17. $\int \sec^2(ax)\,dx = \frac{1}{a}\tan(ax) + C$

18. $\int \csc^2(ax)\,dx = -\frac{1}{a}\cot(ax) + C$

19. $\int \sin^n(ax)\,dx = \frac{-\sin^{n-1}(ax)\cos(ax)}{na} + \frac{n-1}{n}\int \sin^{n-2}(ax)\,dx$

  (a) $\int \sin^3(ax)\,dx = \frac{-\sin^2(ax)\cos(ax)}{3a} - \frac{2}{3a}\cos(ax) + C$

  (b) $\int \sin^4(ax)\,dx = \frac{-\sin^3(ax)\cos(ax)}{4a} + \frac{3x}{8} - \frac{3\sin(ax)\cos(ax)}{8a} + C$

20. $\int \cos^n(ax)\,dx = \frac{\cos^{n-1}(ax)\sin(ax)}{na} + \frac{n-1}{n}\int \cos^{n-2}(ax)\,dx$

21. $\int \tan^n(ax)\,dx = \frac{\tan^{n-1}(ax)}{(n-1)a} - \int \tan^{n-2}(ax)\,dx \qquad n \neq 1$

  (a) $\int \tan^3(ax)\,dx = \frac{1}{2a}\tan^2(ax) + \frac{1}{a}\ln|\cos(ax)| + C$

  (b) $\int \tan^4(ax)\,dx = \frac{1}{3a}\tan^3(ax) - \frac{1}{a}\tan(ax) + C$

22. $\int \cot^n(ax)\,dx = -\frac{\cot^{n-1}(ax)}{n-1} - \int \cot^{n-2}(ax)\,dx \qquad n \neq 1$

23. $\int \sec^n(ax)\,dx = \frac{\sec^{n-2}(ax)\tan(ax)}{(n-1)a} + \frac{n-2}{n-1}\int \sec^{n-2}(ax)\,dx \quad n \neq 1$

  (a) $\int \sec^3(ax)\,dx = \frac{1}{2a}\sec(ax)\tan(ax) + \frac{1}{2a}\ln|\sec(ax) + \tan(ax)| + C$

  (b) $\int \sec^4(ax)\,dx = \frac{1}{3a}\sec^2(ax)\tan(ax) + \frac{2}{3a}\tan(ax) + C$

24. $\int \csc^n(ax)\,dx = -\frac{\csc^{n-2}(ax)\cot(ax)}{(n-1)a} + \frac{n-2}{n-1}\int \csc^{n-2}(ax)\,dx \quad n \neq 1$

25. $\int \sin(ax)\sin(bx)\,dx = \frac{\sin((a-b)x)}{2(a-b)} - \frac{\sin((a+b)x)}{2(a+b)} + C \qquad a^2 \neq b^2$

26. $\int \cos(ax)\cos(bx)\,dx = \frac{\sin((a-b)x)}{2(a-b)} + \frac{\sin((a+b)x)}{2(a+b)} + C \qquad a^2 \neq b^2$

27. $\int \sin(ax)\cos(bx)\,dx = \frac{-\cos((a+b)x)}{2(a+b)} - \frac{\cos((a-b)x)}{2(a-b)} + C \qquad a^2 \neq b^2$

Calculus Reference Facts

28. $\int x^n \sin(ax)\, dx = -\frac{1}{a} x^n \cos(ax) + \frac{n}{a^2} \int x^{n-1} \cos(ax)\, dx$

29. $\int x^n \cos(ax)\, dx = \frac{1}{a} x^n \sin(ax) - \frac{n}{a^2} \int x^{n-1} \sin(ax)\, dx$

30. $\int e^{ax}\, dx = \frac{1}{a} e^{ax} + C$

31. $\int b^{ax}\, dx = \frac{b^{ax}}{a \cdot \ln(b)} + C$

32. $\int x^n e^{ax}\, dx = \frac{1}{a} x^n e^{ax} - \frac{n}{a} \int x^{n-1} e^{ax}\, dx + C$

(a) $\int x e^{ax}\, dx = \frac{1}{a} x e^{ax} - \frac{1}{a^2} e^{ax} = \frac{e^{ax}}{a^2} (ax - 1) + C$

(b) $\int x^2 e^{ax}\, dx = \frac{1}{a} x^2 e^{ax} - \frac{2}{a^2} x e^{ax} + \frac{2}{a^3} e^{ax} = \frac{e^{ax}}{a^3} (a^2 x^2 - 2ax + 2) + C$

33. $\int x^n b^{ax}\, dx = \frac{1}{\ln(b)} \left\{ \frac{1}{a} x^n b^{ax} - \frac{n}{a} \int x^{n-1} b^{ax}\, dx \right\} + C$

34. $\int \frac{1}{\sqrt{a^2 - x^2}}\, dx = \arcsin\left(\frac{x}{a}\right) + C$

35. $\int \frac{1}{a^2 + x^2}\, dx = \frac{1}{a} \arctan\left(\frac{x}{a}\right) + C$

36. $\int \frac{1}{|x| \sqrt{x^2 - a^2}}\, dx = \frac{1}{a} \operatorname{arcsec}\left(\frac{x}{a}\right) + C$

37. $\int \frac{1}{a^2 - x^2}\, dx = \frac{1}{2a} \ln\left|\frac{x+a}{x-a}\right| + C$

38. $\int \ln(x)\, dx = x \cdot \ln(x) - x + C$

39. $\int x^n \ln(x)\, dx = \frac{x^{n+1}}{(n+1)^2} \left\{ (n+1) \cdot \ln(x) - 1 \right\} + C$

40. $\int \frac{1}{x \cdot \ln(x)}\, dx = \ln|\ln(x)| + C$

41. $\int e^{ax} \sin(nx)\, dx = \frac{e^{ax}}{a^2 + n^2} \left\{ a \cdot \sin(nx) - n \cdot \cos(nx) \right\} + C$

42. $\int e^{ax} \cos(nx)\, dx = \frac{e^{ax}}{a^2 + n^2} \left\{ a \cdot \cos(nx) + n \cdot \sin(nx) \right\} + C$

43. $\int \frac{1}{\sqrt{x^2 \pm a^2}}\, dx = \ln\left| x + \sqrt{x^2 \pm a^2} \right| + C$

44. $\int \sqrt{x^2 \pm a^2}\, dx = \frac{x}{2} \sqrt{x^2 \pm a^2} + \frac{1}{2} a^2 \ln\left| x + \sqrt{x^2 \pm a^2} \right| + C$

45. $\int x^2 \sqrt{x^2 \pm a^2}\, dx = \frac{1}{8} x (2x^2 \pm a^2) \sqrt{x^2 \pm a^2} - \frac{1}{8} a^4 \ln\left| x + \sqrt{x^2 \pm a^2} \right| + C$